VOLUME

12

J—Kyoto
pages 1-312

Compton's
Encyclopedia

and Fact-Index

Compton's Learning Company, a division of
Encyclopædia Britannica, Inc.
Chicago · Auckland · Geneva · London · Madrid · Manila
Paris · Rome · Seoul · Sydney · Tokyo · Toronto

1990 EDITION COMPTON'S ENCYCLOPEDIA

COPYRIGHT © 1990 by COMPTON'S LEARNING COMPANY
DIVISION OF ENCYCLOPÆDIA BRITANNICA, INC.

COPYRIGHT ©   1922, 1923, 1924, 1925, 1926, 1927, 1928, 1929, 1930, 1931, 1932, 1933,
1934, 1935, 1936, 1937, 1938, 1939, 1940, 1941, 1942, 1943, 1944, 1945, 1946, 1947, 1948,
1949, 1950, 1951, 1952, 1953, 1954, 1955, 1956, 1957, 1958, 1959, 1960, 1961, 1962, 1963,
1964, 1965, 1966, 1967, 1968, 1969, 1970, 1971, 1972, 1973, 1974, 1975, 1976, 1977, 1978,
1979, 1980, 1981, 1982, 1983, 1984, 1985, 1986, 1987, 1988, 1989, 1990
BY COMPTON'S LEARNING COMPANY, DIVISION OF ENCYCLOPÆDIA BRITANNICA, INC.

Library of Congress Catalog Card Number: 88-63360
International Standard Book Number: 0-85229-512-X
Printed in U.S.A.

THE UNIVERSITY OF CHICAGO
COMPTON'S ENCYCLOPEDIA IS PUBLISHED WITH THE EDITORIAL ADVICE
OF THE FACULTIES OF THE UNIVERSITY OF CHICAGO

"Let knowledge grow from more to more and thus be human life enriched"

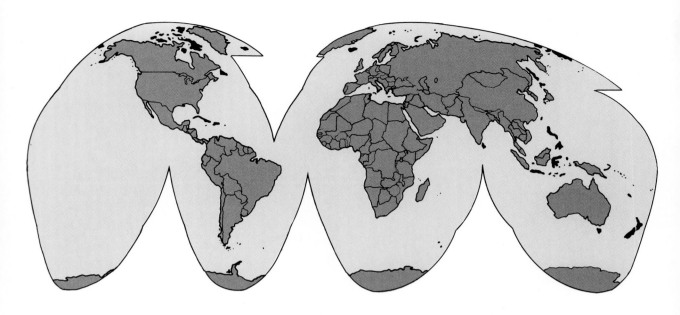

HERE AND THERE IN VOLUME 12

From the A-1 satellite to the zygote cell, thousands of subjects are gathered together in Compton's Encyclopedia and Fact-Index. Organized alphabetically, they are drawn from every field of knowledge. Readers who want to explore their favorite fields in this volume can use this subject-area outline. While it may serve as a study guide, a specialized learning experience, or simply a key for browsing, it is not a complete table of contents.

EXPLORING VOLUME 12

What is the environment of the greatest number of species of land reptiles on Earth?   156.

What does the feast of Hanuka commemorate?   150.

Why did King Herod order the death of all children up to two years of age?   103–4.

Which is the largest member of the cat family to be found on the American continents?   12.

Name the disputed territory that has three administrative capitals.   22.

How does the entire Soviet Union tell time by a clock in the Moscow Kremlin?   304.

How do bird-watchers identify the female belted kingfisher?   246.

Detail, 'Kublai Khan Hunting', hanging scroll, attributed to Liu Kuan-tao, 13–14th Century, collection of the National Palace Museum, Taipei; photograph, Wan-go H.C. Weng, Lyme, N.H.

Who was the founder of the foreign dynasty that unified China?   308.

How did a trip to Tunisia affect Paul Klee's art?   254.

Why did Moslems build a dome over a rock?   100–1.

What was the theme of the Korean mask plays in the late 14th century? 281, 292 illustration.

Who was the only ex-president to be elected to the United States Senate? 128.

What woman was burned at the stake for witchcraft and made a saint five centuries later? 120.

What large animal is only an inch long at birth? 172.

Who learned to "hear" through her fingertips? 196.

How did the reign of a wicked king prove to be a blessing to England? 124.

What common objects helped Franklin find electricity in the lightning? 254.

How do Muslims believe the Koran originated? 268.

What city is held sacred by three faiths? 99.

Who was the first Congressman to enter active duty in World War II? 131.

What country had the first jury system? 158.

Where was America's chief slave market during the 18th century? 17.

How long have forks been used in England? 256.

Which sovereign received a pair of the first machine-knit silk stockings? 260.

What was Tokyo's name before 1868? 65.

What American hero served for a brief time as an admiral in the Russian navy? 139.

What birds are hatched out on a bed of fishbones? 245.

What animal resembles an umbrella? 97.

What lawyer wrote a famous national song? 229.

Who was the only president of the United States to be impeached? 127.

What Roman governor washed his hands to signify his innocence in the death of a prisoner? 104.

Why was a Confederate leader given the nickname Stonewall? 10.

What state is noted for its thoroughbred horses? 208 illustration.

Whose teachings on nonviolent resistance impressed young Martin Luther King, Jr.? 244.

In Japan, which is placed first—a person's given name or his family name? 48.

Who coined the term "beat generation"? 229.

What do a squid and a rocket have in common? 106 illustrations.

What president was a tailor in his youth? 126.

Which president of the United States was the first to be elected in a two-party campaign? 93.

Who built the West Point fortifications? 301.

What was the only jet plane used in combat during World War II? 111, 110 illustration.

Why does a kite fly? 253.

What were the "turtle ships"? 284, 288 illustration.

What reformer made Scotland Protestant? 265.

One of the early United States presidents was also an architect, agriculturalist, inventor, linguist, and scientist. Who was he? 94–5.

What is the most common Korean surname? 271.

What is a sheepshank? 264.

Why was Kyoto the only major Japanese city to escape Allied bombing raids during World War II? 312.

What was the controversial Sister Kenny method for the treatment of infantile paralysis? 207.

Why are the small islands off the coast of Florida called "keys"? 230.

Who claimed he "invented" jazz? 84 illustration.

Where is a sampot worn by both sexes? 169.

What sort of habitat has more than 40,000 species of plant life? 155.

How did the outlaws Frank and Jesse James die? 21.

What was the Invisible Empire of the South? 309.

Which African nation has 100 different ethnic groups? 225.

Name the woman who became a labor organizer when she was more than 50 years old. 139.

What are the so-called "Florida lobsters"? 230.

Where is the largest continuous, intact rain forest? The largest tract of jungle? 153.

How did the novelist Jerzy Kosinski teach himself to write in English? 301.

Why did Stone Age men wear jewelry? 112.

Who was the "king of ragtime"? 141.

What is the "Pittsburgh of Russia"? 231.

People employed in certain kinds of work are usually excused from jury duty. Which professions may be exempted? 160.

How did a royal court astrologer discover the laws of planetary motion? 228.

What is slash-and-burn farming? 157.

Who was the gypsy violinist who became a jazz guitarist after a caravan fire mutilated his left hand? 87 list.

What was the Mau Mau rebellion? 227.

Which African capital city had its beginnings as an Egyptian army camp? 231.

Which psychologist first classified personalities as introverts and extroverts? 152.

What popular gem did superstitious people believe could relieve insanity? 112.

When did the first black indentured servants arrive in America? 22.

Which plants are protected by ant patrols? 156.

According to critics, what was the first major novel written in any language? 80.

Who was Mexico's first president of Indian descent? 145.

Which writer became internationally famous after his death because a friend ignored the provisions of his will? 167.

The letter J

The history of the letter J is linked with the history of I. The Romans and their European successors used I both for the vocalic "i" and for the consonantal "y" (as in the English word "yet"). The English letter J did not come into existence until the end of medieval times, when scribes began to use a tailed form of "i," with or without the dot, next to the short form of "i" (1).

When printing was invented, the tailed form of "i" (2) was often used for an initial "i," which is usually consonantal. Not until the 17th century, however, was the distinction between J or j as a consonant and I or i as a vowel fully established.

i   j

1

𝕁 ℐ

2

ANDREW JACKSON—
7th President of
the United States

JACKSON, Andrew (1767–1845; president 1829–37). Fiery, iron-willed General Andrew Jackson, seventh president of the United States, was the best-loved and the most-hated president the young nation had known. Old Hickory, as his troops called him, was the first poor boy to become president. He was the first president to be elected from the frontier, the first to be called the "people's president," the first to found a modern political party, and the first to make the presidency a powerful office.

The frontiersmen, the farmers, the workers, and the small businessmen loved him. His foes in politics and in finance accused him of being a tyrant and angrily called him King Andrew.

Jackson's Astonishing Personality

Through his long stormy life Jackson acted in many opposite ways. He grew up in the rough life of the Tennessee frontier, yet he charmed Washington society with his fine manners. He hanged two men as spies, ordered six soldiers shot for mutiny, killed one man in a duel and wounded others, yet spoiled his little adopted son. He swore, gambled, owned fighting cocks, and raced horses, yet built a church for his wife and he deeply revered God. He was not a great soldier but he won every battle he led. He insisted that others obey, yet broke the law whenever he pleased. He flew into rages when anger suited his purpose, yet showed the greatest patience with his slaves, his family, and his friends.

This was the man who led a new era in American life —the "Jackson era." In war, in politics, and in his own daily life he always lived according to the rugged, straightforward code of the American frontier.

Youngest Son of Scotch-Irish Immigrants

His parents were Andrew Jackson, for whom he was named, and Elizabeth Hutchinson Jackson. They

Andrew Jackson

lived in northern Ireland near the little coast town of Carrickfergus (Crag of Fergus), about nine miles from Belfast. They were Scotch-Irish and poor. Andrew, senior, was probably a tenant farmer; Elizabeth, a linen weaver. Their first two sons, Hugh and Robert, were born in Ireland.

In 1765 the family sailed for "better days in America," landing at Charleston, S. C. They journeyed in a wagon train to join earlier Scotch-Irish immigrants at the Waxhaw settlements near the North Carolina boundary. Andrew, senior, hewed out a small tract of

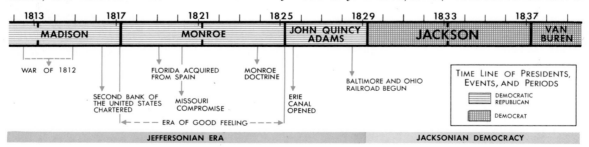

Time line: 1813 — 1817 — 1821 — 1825 — 1829 — 1833 — 1837

MADISON — MONROE — JOHN QUINCY ADAMS — JACKSON — VAN BUREN

WAR OF 1812 — SECOND BANK OF THE UNITED STATES CHARTERED — FLORIDA ACQUIRED FROM SPAIN — MISSOURI COMPROMISE — MONROE DOCTRINE — ERIE CANAL OPENED — BALTIMORE AND OHIO RAILROAD BEGUN

‹- - - ERA OF GOOD FEELING - - - ›

TIME LINE OF PRESIDENTS, EVENTS, AND PERIODS
▭ DEMOCRATIC REPUBLICAN
▦ DEMOCRAT

JEFFERSONIAN ERA — JACKSONIAN DEMOCRACY

forest on Twelve Mile Creek; but the hard pioneer life exhausted him, and he died early in March 1767. Just a few days later, on March 15, 1767, his third son was born—and named Andrew.

Andrew's birthplace has been disputed. Some historians believe he was born at the home of Elizabeth Jackson's sister, Mrs. George McKemy, across the border in North Carolina. Others say he was born a few miles farther south, in South Carolina, at the home of another of Elizabeth's sisters, Mrs. James Crawford. In 1824 Andrew Jackson wrote: "I was born in South Carolina, as I have been told, at the plantation whereon James Crawford lived, about one mile from the Carolina Road and of the Waxhaw Creek."

The state of South Carolina, in 1953, established the Andrew Jackson Historical State Park, 11 miles north of Lancaster, S. C. The state said that the park includes the area of Jackson's birthplace.

Mischievous Boyhood on the Frontier

After Andrew's birth, Elizabeth Jackson and her three sons made their home with the Crawfords, who were fairly well to do according to frontier standards. Mrs. Jackson worked as housekeeper for her invalid sister to support the boys.

Andrew grew to be a spindly, long-legged, rather homely and somewhat sickly boy. Lank, sandy-reddish hair spilled over his high forehead. His beaky nose and jutting jaw warned of his fierce determination. Sensitive to ridicule, he fought anyone who dared tease him and frequently even picked fights. When his quick temper flared, his deeply set bright blue eyes seemed almost to blaze.

Neighbors called him the most mischievous youngster in the whole region. They also said that he always defended the smaller boys and helped them learn how to shoot, fish, race, run, and wrestle. He especially loved to wrestle. One schoolmate remembered: "I could throw him three times out of four; but he would never stay throwed. He was dead game, even then, and never would give up."

His mother hoped that schooling would tame him, and her ambition was to have him become a Presbyterian minister. She sent Andrew and his brothers to an "old-field school," a log shanty. There he learned some arithmetic and how to read and write. He may have gone to other schools, but he learned little more than the necessities demanded by frontier living. He had no use for books, but neighbors already noted his determined "git up and go" spirit.

Boy Soldier in the American Revolution

Andrew was only 13 years old when the American Revolution swept the Waxhaw region. In May 1780 Colonel Tarleton's British raiders slashed out a savage victory over Waxhaw militiamen. Andrew and his brother Robert helped their mother bind up the wounded in the log church. Their elder brother Hugh, a volunteer in a light-horse company, had died a few months earlier. Shortly after the Waxhaw slaughter, Robert and 13-year-old Andrew snatched up their

muskets and rode their half-wild "Carolina ponies" to join the volunteers in the battle of Hanging Rock, S. C., Aug. 1, 1780.

The next year the two boys served with the Waxhaw fighters, battling the British in backwood skirmishes. In the spring, British soldiers captured the lads but failed to break their spirit. When a red-coated officer pointed to his muddied jackboots and commanded Andrew to clean them, the boy refused. The officer slashed his saber at Andrew's head. Flinging up his arm, he partly blocked the blow but carried scars of the cuts on his scalp and hands the rest of his life. Robert too refused and was cut severely.

Imprisoned, Suffers Smallpox, Left Alone

The soldiers marched the wounded lads 40 miles over wilderness roads to prison in Camden, S. C. Their wounds were not treated, they had no bedding, little clothing, and almost no food or water. Smallpox broke out in the filthy prison, striking both Robert and Andrew. Their courageous mother managed to get their release in exchange for British prisoners at Waxhaw and took the sick, half-starved boys home— Andrew, fighting delirium, stumbling behind the

Refusing to clean the British officer's boots, 14-year-old Andrew Jackson tries to ward off a saber blow. His older brother, Robert, right, watches in horror but also refuses.

Astride his white charger, General Jackson and an aide study the attack of veteran British redcoats in the battle of New Orleans. The mixture of uniforms in Jackson's army show frontiersmen, regulars, militia, and coatless freebooters. They smashed the British.

horses that carried his mother and dying brother.

Elizabeth's nursing saved Andrew. As soon as he began to recover she made her way 160 miles to Charleston to help nurse American troops held in British prison ships. Soon after, she died of ship fever—and Andrew never could learn where she was buried. Throughout his life the memory of her courage and devotion led him to champion and idealize women.

Adrift and Then New Purpose

The last of the family, Andrew, not yet 15 years old, was left to make his own way. He spent the next few months with relatives at Waxhaw. He briefly tried to learn the saddler's trade, then taught school for a short time. Turning 16, the restless lad picked up his few belongings, tied them behind his saddle, and spurred his horse to Charleston—the most elegant American city of its time.

There the rawboned youngster, standing over six feet tall and rail thin, somehow made enough money to live the merry life of a Charleston blade. It was there too that he probably learned the simple, good manners of the Southern aristocracy. After a year of "chancy" living he had little left except a fine horse. He must have looked into his heart and mind and realized that he was wasting his life.

Suddenly he determined to leave Charleston and study to become a lawyer "back in the settlements." He realized his lack of education but also knew that frontiersmen did not ask that a lawyer have great "book learning." It was enough for them that a lawyer be honest, fair, straightforward, and not afraid to stand up for what he thought right. Andrew felt that he could satisfy the frontiersmen.

Studies Law and Starts His Career

For two years he read law at Salisbury, N. C. At the age of 19, in 1786, he began practice in Martins-

ville, N. C., but the community was too well established for his liking. In 1788 he packed his pistols into his saddlebags and rode the Wilderness Road west to Nashville, Tenn. There was the true frontier of the United States in 1788—a dark, strong land of mountains, white-water rivers, and tiny stockaded settlements in the wilderness.

Standing on the wooded bank of the Cumberland River, Nashville was a village of log cabins. Jackson took lodging at the home of Mrs. John Donelson, widow of Colonel Donelson, one of the founders of Nashville. There he met their daughter, the slim, black-haired Rachel Donelson Robards—his own age, 21. Rachel was living at home, having separated from her husband, Lewis Robards of Kentucky. She had married Lewis when she was only 16 years old.

Marriage and Devoted Home Life

Early in 1789 Jackson became prosecuting attorney for the Nashville region. He quickly showed himself to be a rugged, hard-hitting prosecutor. His skimpy knowledge of law in other parts of the nation, however, led him into the most grievous situation of his life. In 1791 he heard the report that Rachel's husband, Robards, had got a divorce in Virginia. Without looking into its legality, Jackson married the lively, handsome Rachel. In his ignorance he did not realize that the divorce was not final. Years later, when he was a candidate for president, his enemies were to accuse him of "running off with another man's wife." The unfounded scandal hastened Rachel's death.

Even Jackson's foes, however, were quick to admit that there was never a more devoted couple. Like Andrew, Rachel had grown up on the frontier. Like

Holding his beaver hat, Jackson greets supporters in a little town on his way to his inauguration. One of the older men, right, wearing a tricorn hat, still dresses in Revolutionary War style.

In 1829 happy crowds stormed the White House to celebrate Jackson's first inauguration day. Pistol-packing frontiersmen joined soldiers and shouting men and women at tubs of punch.

him, she knew very little about spelling or grammar or other book learning; but, also like him, she had courage, generosity, and fine simple manners. (*See also* White House, section "Hostesses of the White House.")

For the frontier, Jackson and Rachel lived very well. His marriage into the Donelson family gave him added prestige. He was fortunate in buying land and in holding lands given to him as legal fees—at one time he is said to have owned 50,000 acres. For their home, he established a plantation, Hunter's Hill, where he built a frame house—one of the first in that region of log cabins. Hunter's Hill was considered quite elegant in Nashville. While Jackson rode the wilderness on his law circuit, Rachel managed the plantation and developed it into one of the most prosperous in all Tennessee.

Best of all, as Jackson never tired of saying, she made a comfortable warm-hearted home for him. They had no children, and so adopted a nephew of Rachel's —naming him Andrew Jackson, Jr. They also took another of her nephews, Andrew Jackson Donelson, into their home, later sending him to West Point.

A friend recalled: "I arrived at his house one wet, chilly evening in February, and came upon him in the twilight, sitting alone before the fire, a lamb and a child between his knees. He started a little, called a servant to remove the two innocents to another room, and explained to me how it was. The child had cried because the lamb was out in the cold and begged him to bring it in, which he had done to please the child, his adopted son, not then two years old."

Builds the Hermitage

About 1804 Jackson suffered heavy financial loss. He could not collect money he had lent to an eastern

man. To meet the demands of his own creditors, Jackson sold most of his slaves and property, including the fine Hunter's Hill plantation. He took his family to a much smaller property 12 miles from Nashville. He called it the Hermitage.

Within a few years Rachel and he developed the Hermitage into one of the most famous plantations in the country. Even in their handsome brick home they delighted to sit at the hearth in the evening, each puff-

Jackson assumed so much power as president, especially with the veto, that political enemies called him King Andrew.

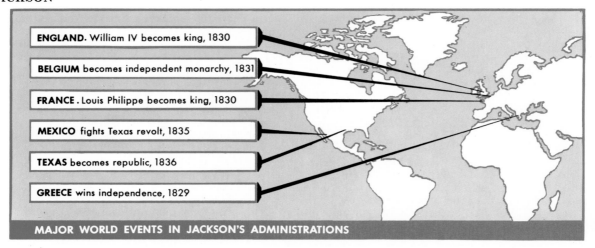

ENGLAND. William IV becomes king, 1830

BELGIUM becomes independent monarchy, 1831

FRANCE. Louis Philippe becomes king, 1830

MEXICO fights Texas revolt, 1835

TEXAS becomes republic, 1836

GREECE wins independence, 1829

MAJOR WORLD EVENTS IN JACKSON'S ADMINISTRATIONS

ing a friendly clay pipe—usually surrounded by the children of their adopted son and nephews. Rachel and Andrew Jackson were bountiful hosts.

On days of worship they gathered their family into the little chapel Jackson built for Rachel at the Hermitage. Rachel was of the Presbyterian faith, as his mother had been. Jackson did not formally enter the faith until after Rachel's death. When he became president, he attended what is now the National Presbyterian Church in Washington.

Jackson was a progressive farmer. He was one of the first to use a cotton gin, which greatly increased his output of the valuable crop. He raised and sold the finest horses in the region. Under Rachel's direction, the slaves carefully cultivated the wide fields of cotton, corn, and wheat.

Jackson Begins His Political Career

Jackson's work as prosecuting attorney made him known throughout the Tennessee region. In that rough frontier country he won respect for his blunt fairness and his willingness to fight or duel at the drop of a hat. Men obeyed him through both respect and fear.

In 1795 they selected him as a delegate to help draw up a constitution for Tennessee, preparatory to statehood in 1796. When Tennessee was admitted as the 16th state in 1796, it was entitled to only one representative in Congress. Jackson was elected.

The nation's capital was still Philadelphia, an old city of some 65,000 people, proud of its culture and refinement. The national government was in the hands of the eastern aristocracy. Into this staid city and into the Congress of bewigged and beribboned gentlemen strode Andrew Jackson in December 1796. He was "the man from the West," and Philadelphia had rarely seen anything like this bold spirit. The elegant Albert Gallatin, later secretary of the treasury, described Congressman Jackson as a "tall, lank backwoodsman with his queue done up in an eel skin."

The Honorable Andrew Jackson at once showed the 4th Congress of the United States his fiery, hard-hitting personality. His speeches were few but meaning-

ful. He was not a ready speaker. Jefferson, in fact, said that Jackson's "violent passions choked his utterance." Yet when principle was involved, Jackson could not be moved. He ardently believed in Jefferson's ideals of democracy as opposed to the Federalist program, which favored the well to do of the nation. When Congress proposed a resolution to approve completely the Federalist administration of George Washington, Jackson firmly voted, "No."

It was in that 4th Congress too that Jackson first showed he could control his temper when to his advantage. As a "freshman congressman," he patiently worked his way through debates and committees to get legislation helping the people of Tennessee.

The next year, 1797, when he was only 30 years old, they elected him senator. Congress now recognized him as "spokesman for the West," representing the liberalism characteristic of life in the newer regions of America—the rugged lands west of the Alleghenies. The restrictions of city life and the intricacies of politics, however, irked Jackson, the man of action. He was, moreover, involved in business troubles back home. In the spring of 1798 he resigned from the Senate and became a judge of the Supreme Court of Tennessee—at only 31.

War of 1812 Brings Renown

In 1802 Jackson was elected major general of the militia. In 1804 he resigned from the Supreme Court and gave up political life. He devoted himself to paying off his debts, developing the Hermitage, and training the militia. It seemed that he would spend the rest of his days as just another well-to-do planter.

Not far ahead, however, lay the turning point in his life—his spectacular service in the War of 1812. His first victories were over the Creek Indians. Encouraged by the British attacks on the Americans, the Creeks raided frontier settlements in Georgia and Alabama. After several slashing skirmishes, Jackson and his Tennessee militia crushed the Creeks at the battle of Horseshoe Bend, Ala., March 27, 1814.

The Creek campaign was typical of Jackson as a man

and as a general. Not a great military strategist, he simply bulled ahead, determined to win. Without taking time to set up an adequate supply line, he relentlessly led his men through the winter wilderness in attack after attack. Sometimes he and his men had only roasted acorns for food. He himself was sick throughout the six-month campaign and his shoulder was still shattered from a recent duel, but he never faltered. His eyes blazing and his voice shrieking in anger, he put down two mutinies that arose from lack of supplies. To prevent a third, he had a rebellious soldier shot.

The triumph over the Creeks forced them to give up most of their rich lands in Georgia and Alabama and released the American forces to fight the British in the North. The victorious campaign also won acclaim for Jackson as a fighting, winning soldier, and he was commissioned a major general in the regular army.

Wins Battle of New Orleans

Jackson was then ordered to defend New Orleans. Finding the city ignoring its danger, he put it under martial law and rallied the citizens to prepare for attack. To build up his small regular army, he recruited frontier riflemen from Tennessee and Kentucky and organized a force of raw volunteers—free Negroes, planters, and pirates headed by the freebooter, Jean Lafitte (*see* Lafitte). This was the awkward force of some 5,500 that Jackson fused together by his driving, fighting spirit.

Beyond the crude American ramparts of cotton bales lay 10,000 British regulars. These were veteran troops who had fought in Europe's Napoleonic Wars. Beginning late in December 1814 they bombarded the American defenses, setting the cotton bale ramparts afire. Between skirmishes and shellings, Jackson's men doggedly threw up earthen breastworks.

On Jan. 8, 1815, with only contempt for Jackson's amateur army, the British troops charged. It was a slaughter. Wave after wave of the charging redcoats fell before the grapeshot and rifle bullets of the grim American defenders. Shattered, the British withdrew, having suffered 2,237 casualties, including three generals. Jackson's casualties that day were only 71. (*See also* War of 1812.)

The tragic mistake of the battle was that it was fought after the peace had been signed days earlier, Dec. 24, 1814, ending the war. In that era of slow communication, news of the peace did not reach Jackson in time to prevent the conflict.

Jackson's victory, of course, in no way affected the outcome of the War of 1812, but it did make him a national hero. With the exception of Gen. William Henry Harrison, no other American general had achieved anything like a military triumph. Jackson's resounding defeat of the British restored the people's enthusiastic faith in themselves.

Takes Florida Problem into Own Hands

In 1817 Jackson was again ordered to the Alabama-Georgia region to defend settlers against attacks by Seminole Indians from Florida. In 1818, without awaiting further orders, he pushed over the frontier into Spanish-held Florida. There he captured Pensacola and hanged two British subjects as spies. These high-handed acts threatened to involve the United States in war with both Britain and Spain. President James Monroe felt that Jackson had exceeded his authority; but John Quincy Adams, secretary of state, smoothed matters with both nations. Jackson's daring made him even more popular in the West.

When Spain ceded Florida to the United States in 1821, President Monroe appointed Jackson the first governor. Soon tiring of politics he resigned late in 1821. He planned to retire to private life, but in 1823 was once more elected to the Senate. He again resigned in 1825.

Marches to Presidency

Meanwhile, however, his friends in the West were already promoting him as the man who could break the power of the East in the national government. From Washington through Monroe, the presidency of the United States had gone to men from Virginia and New England—all statesmen and aristocrats. It had become routine, moreover, for the secretary of state to be nominated for the presidency and get it.

Now, however, the nation was entering a new age of development. Foreign af-

One of the most beautiful of pre-Civil War homes, the Hermitage was built in 1819 and enlarged in 1831. It is about 12 miles east of Nashville. Some cedars on the grounds were planted by Jackson. The tomb where he and Rachel are buried is in the formal garden.

fairs were now of less concern than the building of America. With the opening of the West and the increase of small business and industry in the East—especially in New York and Pennsylvania—the changes in the nation seemed to call for a new voice to express the will of the "common people." The western frontiersmen and farmers and the eastern workers wanted a voice of vigor that could be heard beyond the bounds of tradition.

Jackson had never been bound by tradition. In 1824 the Tennessee legislature nominated him for the presidency of the United States. He received more votes than any of the other four candidates in the election but not a majority. This lack of majority meant, of course, that the House of Representatives must choose the president (see President; Voting). One of the candidates, Henry Clay, gave his votes to John Quincy Adams, who thus became the sixth president of the United States (see Adams, John Quincy). Adams then made Clay his secretary of state. This led Jackson's supporters to claim "bargain and corruption."

Becomes the Seventh President

Though that charge is now generally considered groundless, it whipped up even more enthusiasm for Jackson. As a Democrat he swept the election of 1828 by an electoral vote of 178 to 83 cast for Adams as a National Republican (Whig). John C. Calhoun was re-elected vice-president (see Calhoun).

Jackson's election was a tragic victory for him. Throughout the campaign, political foes not only slandered his character but also slandered Mrs. Jackson. The old, twisted stories about their marriage tortured her. On Dec. 22, 1828, she died of a heart attack.

On March 4, 1829, Andrew Jackson was inaugurated the seventh president of the United States, a grief-stricken, embittered old warrior. The celebration of his inauguration riotously heralded a new era in American politics. Hordes of the "common people" swarmed through the White House to cheer their hero, Old Hickory. The crush was so great that friends had to help him escape by a side door.

When Jackson took office many in the East actually feared him. Jefferson earlier wrote: "I feel very much alarmed at the prospect of seeing General Jackson president. He is one of the most unfit men I know of for the place . . . He is a dangerous man." Actually Jackson's political beliefs were near those of Jefferson. Jackson had such complete faith in the common people that he declared: "The duties of all public officers are so plain and simple that men of intelligence may readily qualify themselves for their performance."

The Spoils System

Jackson's belief in the people and his loyalty to his supporters led him to extend what is called the "spoils system." This is the practice of discharging from public office men of the defeated political party and replacing them by men of the winning party. The system had long been practiced in state governments, and even Jefferson had removed Federalists for men in

This photograph of Jackson, tired, sick, but still unbeatable, was made just a few weeks before his death, June 8, 1845.

his own party. As the next three presidents were of the same party, they, of course, made few changes.

Jackson represented the first real break in that traditional alliance, and he had pledged to sweep the "corrupt" opposition out of office. He quickly removed 919 federal employees in favor of his own party appointments. This, however, was only about one eleventh of the federal total. In his eight years as president, he removed only about one fifth—about the same proportion as Jefferson did.

In answer to criticism of Jackson's policy, Senator William L. Marcy of New York replied, "To the victor belong the spoils." This use of political patronage, or rewarding political service with public office, helped to build our modern major parties (see Political Parties). In an effort to curb the excesses of the spoils system, the Civil Service was established in 1883 (see Civil Service).

Bank of the United States and Re-election

As the "spokesman of the West," Jackson distrusted the powerful financiers of the East. He especially detested the monopoly held by the Bank of the United States and vetoed a new charter for the bank. He declared that its control of the nation's money was a menace to both business and democratic government.

The election of 1832 was fought on the issue of "Jackson or the bank." Jackson won by 219 electoral votes to only 49 for Henry Clay. Martin Van Buren, a close adviser to Jackson, became vice-president.

Though the bank's old charter still had three years to run, Jackson removed the government funds from it and deposited them in state banks. They began to issue enormous quantities of paper money, leading to wild speculation. A panic was in the making, but it did not strike until after Jackson's successor, Martin Van Buren, took office in 1837.

Enlarges Power of the President

In all that he did, Jackson departed from the tradition that held that the president of the United States was little more than a dignified supervisor of the government. Jackson believed that the president was directly responsible for the nation's good, and so he set a strong new idea of the presidency. When he did not agree with Congress, he freely used the right of veto. His six predecessors, between them, had vetoed only nine bills. Jackson vetoed 12, besides frequently using the pocket veto (*see* Veto).

Jackson usually ignored his Cabinet officers, with the exception of Van Buren. When he sought advice, which was seldom, he conferred with a little group of friends, the "kitchen cabinet"—then usually did what he had planned to do in the first place.

He further strengthened the presidency by his firm stand in a conflict between South Carolina and the federal government. The conflict had been brewing since January 1830, when Daniel Webster, in a famed debate with Senator Robert Y. Hayne of South Carolina, upheld the authority of the federal government over the individual states (*see* Webster, Daniel). In 1832, however, South Carolina became defiant. Objecting to a high tariff, it invoked "states' rights" to nullify it—that is, to issue an ordinance forbidding the law in the state.

Jackson had already declared his opposition to nullification and secession. At a Jefferson anniversary dinner in 1830, attended by leading South Carolinians, he had made a ringing toast: "Our Federal Union—it must be preserved!" Now at the declaration of the nullification act of 1832 he issued a proclamation to South Carolina that he would enforce the law—by bayonets, if necessary. He got from Congress a Force Act empowering the Army and Navy to collect tariff duties in South Carolina. Meanwhile, he recommended that the tariff be revised. Henry Clay wrote a tariff bill satisfactory to South Carolina, which then repealed its nullification act.

As an expansionist—one who believed in pushing back the frontiers—Jackson took a different stand on states' rights. Georgia passed a law to force Indians from lands granted to them by treaty. The United States Supreme Court ruled that the law should not be enforced. When Georgia defied the ruling, Jackson refused to use his power to uphold the Court. Instead, he remarked, "John Marshall has made the decision—now let him enforce it." It suited Jackson to see the rich lands taken over by settlers.

Picks Own Successor and Retires

Through his aggressive leadership and patronage, Jackson had welded together a vigorous new party— the Democratic party (*see* Political Parties). He, moreover, so controlled it that he chose the candidate to succeed him as president, Martin Van Buren.

When Jackson left office in 1837, he retired to his Tennessee home, the Hermitage. The financial panic of 1837 took most of his money, and his health worsened. He continued, however, to advise his party leaders and to receive visitors. He died on June 8, 1845, and was buried in the Hermitage garden.

BIBLIOGRAPHY FOR ANDREW JACKSON

Beard, C.A. The Presidents in American History, rev. ed. (Messner, 1981).

Csinski, Alice. Andrew Jackson (Children's, 1987).

DeGregorio, W.A. The Complete Book of U.S. Presidents (Dembner, 1984).

Remini, R.V. Andrew Jackson, 3 vols. (Harper, 1984).

Schlesinger, A.M., Jr. The Age of Jackson (Little, 1945).

Van Deusen, G.G. The Jacksonian Era, 1828–1848 (Harper, 1987).

JACKSON, Jesse (born 1941). Although he did not win the Democratic presidential nomination in 1988, Jesse Jackson's second national campaign established him as the best-known black leader in the United States. During the long campaign he won more Democratic primary votes than any contender other than the party nominee.

Jackson was born in Greenville, S.C., on Oct. 8, 1941. After one year at the University of Illinois on a football scholarship, he transferred to North Carolina Agricultural and Technical State College, where he became an outstanding quarterback. While in school he became active in the civil rights movement. After graduation in 1964, Jackson attended the Chicago Theological Seminary. Before graduating he joined Martin Luther King, Jr.'s Southern Christian Leadership Conference (SCLC). King appointed him head of SCLC's Operation Breadbasket in Chicago. Its goals were to gain jobs and services for blacks through the use of business picketing and boycotts.

Jackson remained with SCLC for three years after King's death. Then, in 1971 he formed Operation PUSH (People United to Save Humanity) in Chicago to continue Operation Breadbasket's work. He also traveled throughout the United States in a campaign for education and against drug abuse and gangs. In 1979 he became active in foreign affairs, visiting South Africa to speak out against apartheid and touring Israel to promote a Palestinian state. His 1984 presidential campaign culminated in a rousing speech at the Democratic convention. In 1986 Jackson launched the National Rainbow Coalition as a base from which to begin his 1988 campaign.

JACKSON, Stonewall (1824–63). No leader in the American Civil War was more skilled or gallant than Stonewall Jackson. His earnestness of purpose, determination to do right as he saw it, and military genius made him admired by friend and foe alike.

Thomas Jonathan Jackson was born on Jan. 21, 1824, in Clarksburg, Va. (now West Virginia). When Thomas was 3 years old his parents died penniless, and he went to live with his uncle.

Library of Congress

Stonewall Jackson in 1863

After attending a small country school in Virginia, he decided to go to West Point. He set out for Washington, D.C., traveling part of the way on foot. When he arrived he presented himself before the secretary of war and asked for an appointment to the Military Academy. The secretary, impressed by the boy's determination, immediately gave him the appointment.

After his graduation, in 1846, he served in the Mexican War. In seven months he rose from second lieutenant to major. In 1852 he resigned from the army to teach at Virginia Military Institute.

He continued teaching until 1861, when the crisis arose between the North and the South. Jackson wanted to see the Union preserved, but he believed that the South had a just cause. He therefore supported it. His record won him a commission as colonel and rapid promotion to brigadier general.

General Barnard S. Bee is credited with giving Jackson his nickname. At the first battle of Bull Run, Jackson's troops held firm when others wavered. Bee rallied his disorganized men with: "There is Jackson standing like a stone wall." Thereafter Jackson was known as Stonewall.

Stonewall Jackson marched his men swiftly and over long distances into battle. His troops became known as "Jackson's foot cavalry." His strict discipline and long marches tested his men to the limits of their endurance, but they admired and loved their commander. They called him Old Jack and cheered whenever he appeared.

In May 1863 at Chancellorsville, Jackson half-circled the Union Army and surprised it from behind. This attack contributed largely to the Confederate victory. But at dusk on May 2, as Jackson and his escort returned from an observation point, one of his own outposts mistook them for a detachment of Federal cavalry and fired. Jackson fell, mortally wounded, and died eight days later.

Jackson is remembered as a great general and as an earnest and religious man. On the march he carried two books: Napoleon's 'Maxims of War' and the Bible.

JACKSON, Miss. A surrounding area rich in farmlands, timber, and oil and natural gas deposits has helped Jackson, Mississippi's capital, become the state's largest city. It is an important railroad, shipping, manufacturing, and educational center.

Jackson is located on the Pearl River, with New Orleans 171 miles (275 kilometers) to the south and Vicksburg 41 miles (66 kilometers) to the west. The governor's mansion and its grounds occupy a full block in the city's center. Nearby is the State Capitol, completed in 1903. Clustered about the mansion and the Capitol are the completely restored Old Capitol—which houses the State Historical Museum—the War Memorial Building, and the State Fairgrounds.

A French Canadian, Louis Le Fleur, built a trading post here in 1792 called Le Fleur's Bluff. Soon after Mississippi was admitted to the Union in 1817, the legislature decided to establish the capital at Le Fleur's Bluff. It was renamed Jackson, for Andrew Jackson, seventh president of the United States. The legislature met there for the first time in 1822. Jackson grew rapidly after 1900. Oil and gas fields were discovered nearby in the 1930s. The city has a commission form of government. (*See also* Mississippi.) Population (1980 census), 202,895.

JACKSONVILLE, Fla. The city of Jacksonville has grown prosperous as a shipping, commercial, banking, and industrial center. Jacksonville, in northeastern Florida, is located on a bend of the Saint Johns River, 22 miles (36 kilometers) from the Atlantic Ocean. A dredged channel

in the river is 38 feet (12 meters) deep. The city's banks finance developments in the state and on islands in the Caribbean Sea. Its industries draw raw materials from the area's farms and orchards, pine forests, and minerals. The business district lies close to the Saint Johns north bank.

Jacksonville is a gateway for visitors to the winter playgrounds along the east coast of Florida. Its 8 miles (13 kilometers) of docks receive and ship some 15 million tons a year. The tonnage includes petroleum products, logs and lumber, fruits and vegetables, naval stores, and fertilizers. The city manufactures chemicals, pulp and paper products, fabricated metal products, paints, plastics, and heavy machinery parts. Other industries include printing and publishing, shipbuilding, and ship repair.

Fort Caroline National Memorial marks the site of Florida's first European settlement, founded in 1564. The Indian name for the river ford once located at this point was *Wacca Pilatka* (cows crossing over). Early English settlers translated this to Cowford. The town, founded in 1822, was named Jacksonville in honor of the military hero Andrew Jackson. It became a city in 1832. At that time the St. Johns River was the chief artery of traffic to the interior. During the Civil War, Southern seamen attempted to run the Union blockade of the port. Union forces briefly occupied the city four times. In the 1880s the river channel was deepened to accommodate large vessels.

Jacksonville's economy is boosted by the United States Naval Station at nearby Mayport. Educational and cultural institutions incude Jacksonville University, founded in 1934; Florida Junior College (1966); the University of North Florida (1972); Edward Waters College; Cummer Gallery of Art; Jacksonville Art Museum; and Haydon Burns Library. Tourist and convention facilities focus on the adjacent beach communities of Atlantic Beach, Neptune Beach, Jacksonville Beach, and Ponte Vedra Beach. The city hosts the Gator Bowl football game each year on the Saturday before January 1.

A new charter consolidated the governments of Jacksonville and most of Duval County in October 1968, making the city one of the nation's largest in area—827 square miles (2,142 square kilometers). The area is administered by a mayor-council form of government. (*See also* Florida.) Population (1980 census), 540,898.

JACK THE RIPPER. From Aug. 7 to Nov. 10, 1888, an unknown murderer killed at least seven women, all prostitutes, in the East End of London, England. These murders constitute one of the most notorious unsolved criminal cases of modern times. The name Jack the Ripper was signed to a series of taunting notes sent to police authorities, presumably by the murderer.

That the murders were all committed by the same person is likely. Each victim's throat was slashed, and each body was mutilated in a manner suggesting that the killer had a considerable knowledge of anatomy. There was a great public outcry over the crimes, and the police made strenuous efforts to capture the murderer. The failure to catch the murderer was a factor that led to the resignation of London's police commissioner.

A sizable literature has grown up about Jack the Ripper. Novels as well as serious investigations into his identity have been popular for many decades. One of the most successful novels was 'The Lodger', published in 1913, by Mrs. Belloc Lowndes, from which three motion pictures have been made. A list of the literature about the crimes can be found in 'Jack the Ripper: a Bibliography and Review of the Literature' (1979), by Alexander Kelly.

JACOBINS. The most powerful influence of the French Revolution was exercised by the Jacobins. Jacobin clubs were formed throughout France to preserve the advances made by the Revolution. Max-

imilien Robespierre, a Jacobin leader, and Georges-Jacques Danton, who participated in Jacobin club debates, helped inaugurate the Reign of Terror that disgraced the revolutionary movement. It ended only after their executions.

The Jacobins were formed as the Breton Club in 1789. Its members were Brittany delegates to the National Assembly, then meeting in Versailles, near Paris. Early members—some nobles, many professionals, and a few peasants—were conservatives. This was to change drastically, however, when the membership was opened to others and the club, later known as the Friends of the Constitution, was joined by many extremists. Many conservative members withdrew or were expelled.

In October 1789, after the king and the Assembly had moved to Paris, the club occupied a monastery that had been formerly used by Dominican monks. Because the monastery was on the Rue Saint Jacques, the monks had been known as Jacobins. The name was soon adopted officially by the club. When the radical Robespierre became a Jacobin leader, the word Jacobin was used as a tag for the most fiery revolutionists.

In the fall of 1792 the Jacobins demanded that King Louis XVI and his queen, Marie Antoinette, be tried for conspiring with foreign rulers against the Revolution. Over the opposition of moderates in the National Assembly, they were tried and executed. Until Robespierre was beheaded, in July 1794, the Jacobins influenced French action more strongly than the Assembly. The Jacobin Club was outlawed in November 1794. (*See also* French Revolution; Danton; Louis; Marie Antoinette; Robespierre.)

JACOBSEN, Jens Peter (1847–85). The novelist and poet who inaugurated the naturalist movement in Danish literature was Jens Peter Jacobsen. An ardent student of the natural sciences, he also translated Charles Darwin's 'On the Origin of Species' and 'The Descent of Man' into Danish (*see* Darwin).

Jacobsen's life was short and made difficult by persistent ill health. He was born in Thisted, Denmark, on April 7, 1847. He went to school in Copenhagen, where he divided his attention between literature and the sciences. He fought against tuberculosis the last 12 years of his life, yet he produced two novels, a number of short stories, and poetry. His short story "Mogens," published in 1872, is considered the first piece of naturalist writing in Danish literature. It traces the life of a young man as he progresses from daydreams to reality. His first novel, 'Fru Marie Grubbe' (1876), is the story of a woman who begins life in wealth and ends in poverty. His second novel, 'Niels Lyhne' (1880), develops the theme of "Mogens": the dreamer who through disillusionment becomes a realist. In these works, Jacobsen shows how individuals are captive to their biological and psychological needs irrespective of society's standards.

Jacobsen died in Thisted on April 30, 1885. His poems were published the following year.

JACQUARD, Joseph-Marie (1752–1834). The inventor of the loom that served as the incentive for the technological revolution of the textile industry was Joseph-Marie Jacquard. The loom, which could perform all weaving motions, bore Jacquard's name. It could produce complex patterns as easily as earlier machines had produced plain cloth, and it served as the basis of the modern automatic loom.

Jacquard was born on July 7, 1752, in Lyon, France. He developed the idea for his loom in 1790 but, because of the French Revolution, did not show it until 1801. In 1803 he was summoned to Paris to demonstrate the machine. He was given a patent for the loom and was also awarded a medal. In 1806 the loom was declared public property, and Jacquard was given a pension and a royalty payment for each machine. Silk weavers, fearing that the loom might eliminate their jobs, became bitterly hostile and physically attacked both Jacquard and the machines. The loom eventually gained acceptance because of its advantages, and by 1812 there were 11,000 in use in France. The loom soon spread to England and throughout the world.

The weaving of cloth on the Jacquard loom was controlled by punch cards that enabled the loom to weave any pattern automatically. The punch cards were soon adopted in many other fields. For example, the American statistician Herman Hollerith in 1890 used them as a way of feeding data to his census machine. The English inventor Charles Babbage adapted the cards as a control mechanism for his calculator. Punch cards are now one of the means by which programming is fed into computers (for illustration, *see* Computers). Jacquard died on Aug. 7, 1834, in Oullins, near Lyon.

Punched cards at the top of the Jacquard loom controlled the weaving of different patterns.

The Bettmann Archive

Areas controlled by the Jagiellon dynasty

JAGIELLON DYNASTY. The monarchs that ruled over Poland-Lithuania, Bohemia, and Hungary in the 15th and 16th centuries were members of the Jagiellon family. They took their name from Jagiello, the grand duke of Lithuania, who became king of Poland in 1386 with the name Wladyslaw II Jagiello. His son Wladyslaw III Warnenczyk succeeded him as king in 1434 and assumed the throne of Hungary as well in 1440.

Following the death of Wladyslaw III in 1444, his brother Casimir IV became king and later put his own son Wladyslaw on the thrones of both Hungary and Bohemia. John I Albert, another son of Casimir, succeeded his father as king of Poland from 1492 to 1501, and he was succeeded by his brother Alexander I from 1501 to 1506. A fourth brother, Sigismund I, ruled Poland from 1506 to 1548. Jagiellon rule in Hungary and Bohemia ended in 1526, when the Turks defeated Sigismund's nephew Louis II at the Battle of Mohacs.

Sigismund II Augustus, the only son of Sigismund I, ruled Poland-Lithuania from 1548 to 1572, a reign troubled by the growing power of the nobles and landed gentry. During his reign he managed to play off the various factions against each other. In 1569 he engineered a union of Poland and Lithuania, but when he died in 1572 there was no male heir—and the dynasty came to an end.

JAGUAR. The largest member of the cat family found on the American continents is the jaguar. Its average length is between 6 and 7 feet (1.8 and 2.1 meters). It has a large head and massive legs. Jaguars vary in color, but usually they are yellowish brown, with black spots like those of the leopard. Its spots, however, are larger and more angular.

The jaguar was once found from the southern United States to Uruguay, but now it is a species in danger of extinction and survives mainly in undeveloped rainforests in Central and South America.

Although jaguars usually stalk or ambush their prey, which consists mostly of peccaries, they are excellent swimmers and sometimes take capybaras, crocodiles, and fish. The scientific name of the jaguar is *Leo onca*.

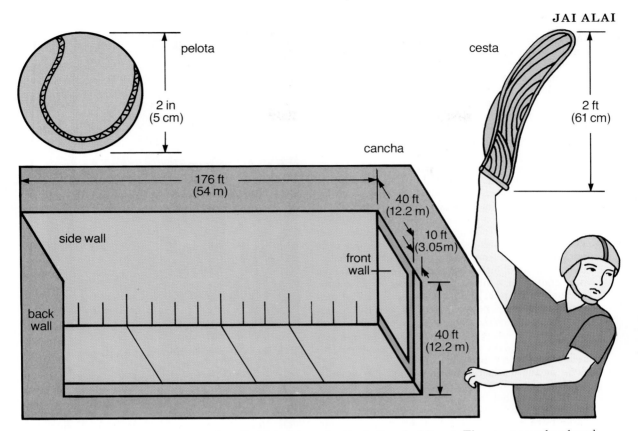

pelota

cesta

cancha

side wall

front wall

back wall

176 ft (54 m)

40 ft (12.2 m)

10 ft (3.05 m)

40 ft (12.2 m)

2 in (5 cm)

2 ft (61 cm)

JAI ALAI. The game now commonly called jai alai was first played by the Spanish Basques who called the sport *pelota vasca*. Jai alai (pronounced high lie) means "merry festival" in the Basque language. The game was imported by Cuba in 1900, and there it got its new name. The origin of the sport is unknown, but it probably evolved in the 17th century.

The pelota, Spanish for "ball," used in today's game is about three fourths the size of a baseball but much harder and livelier. It is handmade of virgin rubber covered with one layer of linen thread and two coats of specially treated goatskin.

The game is played with a long, curved, wicker basket called a cesta with which players throw the ball at speeds of more than 150 miles (240 kilometers) per hour. The frame of the cesta is made from chestnut wood. A special Spanish reed is handwoven over the frame and ribs. The cesta is fitted with a glove and is strapped to the player's hand. It is handmade for each player. The front court player's cesta is slightly smaller than that of a back court player.

The game is played on a three-walled cancha, or court, that is about 176 feet (54 meters) in length, although the length varies. The walls and floor are constructed of high-impact materials that can withstand the constant hammering of the pelota. The rules of the game are simple. The ball is always put into play by a server, who must throw it to the front wall first. Afterward it may rebound off the side or back wall. The object is to make the opposing player miss the ball or foul it out. The game may be played as singles or doubles.

Jai alai is fast, exciting, and dangerous, requiring much skill and coordination. There have been many serious injuries and even deaths. In 1966 fiberglass helmets were introduced in the United States as a safety measure. Jai alai is played mostly in Spain, France, Italy, Mexico, the United States, the Philippines, and Indonesia.

Jai alai is played in two formats, partidos and quinielas. The partido is a match game played by two teams for 10 to 40 points. It is most popular in Spain, France, and Mexico. Quiniela games have from six to eight teams competing in round-robin fashion and are usually played for 5 to 10 points. This system is popular in the United States, Mexico, and the Philippines.

Jai alai became popular in the United States after the state of Florida passed a law in 1935 permitting pari-mutuel wagering on the sport. The first fronton, or jai alai arena, was located in Miami, Fla. Today there are several in Florida, and frontons have been built in Connecticut, Rhode Island, and Nevada. The predominant organization governing jai alai is the International Federation of Pelota Vasca, which has headquarters in San Sebastian and Madrid, Spain. In 1966 the United States Amateur Jai Alai Players Association was formed in Miami, Fla. The international federation conducts world championships every four years. Annual championship tournaments are held in the United States and other countries.

JAINISM. Along with Hinduism and Buddhism, Jainism is one of the major religions that developed within the ancient civilization of India. The name of the religion derives from the term Jina, meaning "victor" or "conqueror." The goal of Jainism explains this term. It is the spiritual progress of the individual through a succession of stages until he is able to conquer and renounce dependence on the world and the self. Thereby the individual is freed from all contamination by the material world.

Followers of Jainism believe that the world, space, and time are eternal and uncreated. There is a center containing a region of souls in which all living things—people, animals, gods, and devils—exist. Below this region is a series of hells—places of punishment and torture, and above the region are levels of heavens and celestial areas in which souls live once they are liberated from bodies. All reality in the universe is divided into two parts: living substances called souls and nonliving substances, or nonsouls. The soul, in its pure state, possesses unlimited perception, knowledge, happiness, and power. But once a soul is entrapped in matter—such as the human body—these faculties are limited by location in space, contaminated by the senses, and subject to the chain of cause and effect, birth and death.

The means of liberation for the soul is yoga, a discipline of self-control and meditation. Yoga consists of right belief, right knowledge, and right action. It aims at these goals through knowledge of reality, faith in the teachings of religious leaders who are called Tirthankaras, and doing no evil.

The chief concept that guides behavior in Jainism is ahimsa, or reverence for life, the principle of nonviolence and noninjury toward all living things. This principle has led to a belief in the equality of all souls and to the freedom to associate with anyone. Because of ahimsa, the social distinctions prevalent in the Hindu caste system never became firmly established in Jainism (*see* Hinduism).

Believers are of two types, monks and lay followers. The monks lead a far more austere life than do lay members because they devote their whole lives to the stages of spiritual perfection. Monks must adhere scrupulously to the principle of ahimsa and avoid such sins of Jainism as lying, stealing, sexual intercourse, and eating meals at night (for fear of inadvertently killing an insect or other small creature). Some monks have no possessions at all, not even clothing; others keep a few things—a robe, an alms bowl, a duster to sweep away insects in their paths, and a cloth to keep insects out of the mouth.

Lay members are expected to refrain from eating certain foods, limit their possessions, be content with their spouses, and avoid violence, lying, and stealing. They are also expected to avoid unnecessary travel and pleasure, to fast and control their diets, and to serve their fellow believers, especially the monks and the poor. Above all, they are expected to devote themselves to the stages of spiritual progress by means of various religious rituals and exercises.

Courtesy of the Government of India Tourist Office, London

A Tirthankara image is enshrined at the Dilwara Temple on Mt. Abu, India.

Temple worship plays a major role in Jainism. There is a large pantheon of lesser gods, goddesses, demons, and other divinities. The major objects of worship, however, are the Tirthankaras and other liberated souls who are called Lords of the Gods. Following these are the leaders of the monks, the teachers of sacred texts, and the rest of the monks.

History

Jainism was founded in the 6th century BC by Vardhamana Mahavira, a contemporary of Siddhartha Gotama, the Buddha (*see* Buddha). Mahavira is believed to be the last in a series of 24 Tirthankaras in the first age of the world. In the next age another 24 will live. Mahavira is regarded as a historical figure, as is his predecessor, Parsvanatha, who died 250 years before him. During Mahavira's lifetime a split occurred in Jainism, and over the next few centuries several more divisions took place. About AD 80 two principal sects emerged: the Svetambara, or "white-robed," and the Digambara, meaning "sky-clad" or "naked." In the 16th century two subsects opposed to image worship were organized: the Sthankakavasis, belonging to the Svetambara, and the Taranapantha, belonging to the Digambara. There are more than 2 million followers of Jainism in India and very few outside that country.

Jainism has an extensive canon, or body, of scripture. The Svetambaras recognize 45 agamas, collections that are supposedly based upon discourses of Mahavira made by his direct disciples. Digambaras recognize two works, the Karmaprabhrta and the Kasayaprabhrta, based on a work of the 1st century AD that is now lost.

© Luis Villota—The Stock Market

Modern office buildings line the broad boulevard Jalan Thamrin in downtown Jakarta. The towering National Monument with its gold pinnacle rises in the background.

JAKARTA, Indonesia.

The cultures of Java, India, China, and The Netherlands all contribute to the complex character of Jakarta, the capital city of Indonesia. Jakarta lies on the northwest coast of

the island of Java, in a marshy plain at the edge of the Java Sea. Its location is tropical, about 6 degrees south of the equator, and the climate is generally hot and humid. Normal temperatures range from 72° to 91° F (22° to 33° C) without great variation from season to season. Humidity of 60 to 90 percent prevails year-round. Heavy downpours are common in Jakarta during the wet season from November to March, and rain also falls occasionally in the dry season that makes up the rest of the year. Light winds blow inland from the ocean.

The heart of downtown Jakarta is Merdeka Square, site of the Independence Day parade every August 17. At the center of the square rises Jakarta's most famous landmark, the National Monument. The main structure is marble, on top of which is a flame covered with 1,125 ounces (32 kilograms) of gold leaf. Facing it from the north is the Presidential Palace, residence of the president of Indonesia. Along the west side of the square (and continuing to the south) runs the six-lane boulevard Jalan Thamrin. It is lined by modern hotels, banks, and embassies.

The part of the city nearest the waterfront is the colonial Kota, or Old City, section. It is the central business district and also Indonesia's financial capital. The Dutch had colonized Indonesia, formerly the Dutch East Indies, for several centuries before the country's independence. Gabled Dutch houses with doorsteps of black and white stone, walled gardens, and red tile roofs have been preserved and restored. The old port, Dutch town hall, and square have been renovated, as has the Portuguese Church completed by the Dutch in 1695.

Just south of Kota is the Chinese quarter, Glodok. It is notable for the many old temples scattered among its narrow, winding streets. Chinese restaurants face the central square of Glodok.

Life in Jakarta

Jakarta is a busy, crowded city surrounded by one of the most densely populated countrysides in the world. Tricycle taxis called *betjak*s tangle with other vehicles in traffic jams on busy thoroughfares. Vendors peddle their wares in the streets and sell fruits and orchids at Cikini Market. The many canals, dug in the 17th century to drain the marshy lowland, are used for bathing and laundry.

The common language of Jakarta's residents is Bahasa Indonesia, or standard Indonesian. Based on Malayan, it was created in the 20th century to provide a common language for a country in which many were spoken. It is the language of films and popular music and is in everyday use by the Jakartan middle

15

class. Recent migrants from rural areas, living in makeshift shanties on the edge of the city, often continue to use the local languages of their home regions.

In addition to Indonesians whose ancestors have lived on the islands for centuries, Jakarta has many citizens of Chinese, Indian, and Arab ancestry. The Chinese are particularly important in trade and commerce and in the professions. Traditional Chinese festivals such as the Chinese New Year are celebrated in Glodok. Descendants of the Dutch do not make up a significant part of the population.

Cultural life reflects the traditions of West Java, such as shadow puppetry and gamelan music. The Taman Ismail Marzuki (cultural center) features dance, drama, shadow puppet performances, art, and concerts by the Jakarta Symphony. Exhibits of ceramics and graphics are displayed at the Museum of Indonesian Culture, which was founded in 1778 and which also has a 360,000-volume library. The University of Indonesia, which was founded just after the country became independent in 1950, and the National Archives are also in Jakarta.

The Economy

Finance and commerce form the basis of Jakarta's economy. The Jakarta Stock Exchange was established in 1951. Tanjung Priok, the modern port a few miles east of the old Dutch port at Kota, handles most of Indonesia's imports and exports.

There are two airports. The older, Kemayoran, is near the waterfront three miles (five kilometers) from the city center. It serves domestic flights to all the major islands of Indonesia. International flights to Tokyo, Hong Kong, Bangkok, Singapore, and other cities use Halim International Airport, 9 miles (14 kilometers) southeast of the city center.

Although manufacturing remains secondary to commerce and trade, there is some industry, including many small batik factories, in which dyed fabrics are made, and a major metalworking enterprise. Agricultural products of the fertile hinterland include rice, copra, coffee, rubber, tapioca, tea, and quinine.

Since the late 1960s, government policy has emphasized tourism as a source of national income. Although most tourists are bound for more exotic places such as the Indonesian island of Bali, they often enter the country at Jakarta. Two amusement parks—Indonesia in Miniature and Ancol, both on the waterfront—are especially designed to attract foreign tourists.

As the national capital of Indonesia, Jakarta is the site of the national parliament. Greater Jakarta forms an administrative unit, Jakarta Raya, which is completely enclosed by the province of West Java. The mayor of the city has the same status as the governor of a province.

History

Before the 16th century, the port of Sunda Kalapa served the Sundanese Hindu kingdom of Pajajaran in West Java. The Hindu influence had been introduced by traders from India centuries before. In 1527, the Muslim sultan of Bantam defeated the Portuguese near Sunda Kalapa and renamed the port Jayakerta ("glorious fortress"). The name evolved and eventually became Jakarta.

The first Dutch ships reached Jakarta in 1596. The Dutch East India Company was formed in 1602 to trade in Indonesian spices. Eight years later the ruler of Jakarta allowed the Dutch East India Company to build a fort in the town; British traders built one as well. Rivalry between the two European powers led to a Dutch-British naval battle in the Java Sea. A few months later, in 1619, the Dutch seized and burned Jakarta and began construction of a new Dutch town on the same site. They called it Batavia.

The Dutch brought in Chinese slaves and settlers to help build the town and port. They dug the canals that still lace the city. They extended Batavia's rule over part of the surrounding area. The merchants' influence spread through the islands, and Batavia functioned as the capital of the Dutch East Indies.

The 18th century was a time of troubles in Indonesia. Health deteriorated, partly as a result of malaria carried by mosquitoes that bred in the stagnant canals. In 1740 anticipation of a rebellion by Chinese workers led to a massacre of the Chinese residents.

The Dutch East India Company ruled Batavia until 1799, when the company was dissolved and the Dutch government took over the colony. Batavia came under British rule in 1811, in connection with the Napoleonic Wars, but was returned to The Netherlands in 1816 after Napoleon's defeat. The main exports in the 19th century were plantation crops: sugar, coffee, indigo, and tobacco.

In the 20th century The Netherlands came under increasing pressure to give the people of the East Indies a greater voice in their own government. The People's Council of Indonesia first met in Batavia in 1918. An attack on Batavia Prison was part of an unsuccessful Communist rebellion in 1926.

World War II brought Japanese occupation from 1942 to 1945. By the end of the war, a nationalist party had declared Indonesian independence, published a constitution, and asserted control over much of Batavia. The Allies, having defeated the Japanese, returned the city to the Dutch, and the nationalists fled to establish the base of their republican regime elsewhere in Java. In 1949, when the Dutch agreed to transfer their authority to the new republic, the nationalists reclaimed Batavia as their capital and restored the name Jakarta.

Rapid, largely unplanned development followed, bringing new construction, mass migration to the city, and the spread of new suburbs. A series of attempts to overthrow the government and other problems in 1956 led to the expulsion of the remaining Dutch residents, followed the next year by the nationalization of Dutch businesses. (See also Indonesia.) The city grew rapidly after 1930, when the population was only 530,000. The population in 1981 was estimated to be 6,556,000.

JALAL UD-DIN RUMI (1207–73). The greatest of the Islamic mystic poets in the Persian language and the founder of an order of mystics known as Whirling Dervishes was Jalal Ud-Din Rumi. The basis of Islamic mysticism, called Sufism in Western languages, is the attempt, by meditation, to comprehend the nature of God and man and to experience the divine presence in the world.

Rumi was born in Afghanistan about Sept. 30, 1207. His father was a theologian and teacher. The family left their home about 1218 and traveled to Anatolia in Asia Minor to escape the threat of the Mongol invasion from the East. They settled at Konya, the capital, in 1228. Rumi's father taught at a religious school until his death in 1231, when Rumi took over the teaching. Rumi remained in Konya as poet and teacher until his death on Dec. 17, 1273.

Through the influence of his father and one of his father's disciples, Rumi's religious development became strongly oriented toward mysticism. His literary inspiration came from close personal companionships with three men in the last 30 years of his life. The first of these was a wandering mystic named Shams ad-Din, whom he met in 1244 and who disappeared in 1247. In his memory, Rumi wrote his first collection of poetry, 'The Collected Poetry of Shams', containing about 30,000 verses. The second companion was a goldsmith named Salah ad-Din Zarkub and the third was a mystic, Husam ad-Din Chelebi. The latter gave Rumi the literary and religious advice that inspired his greatest poetry, 'Masnavi-ye Ma'navi' (Spiritual Couplets), a work that conveyed all the aspects of 13th-century mysticism. Because of its influence on later Islamic literature and mysticism, the book has been called a poetic Persian Koran. (The Koran is the holy book of Islam.)

JAMAICA. The national motto of Jamaica is "Out of many, one people." In the early 19th century, however, the people of this Caribbean island were divided by color and class. Most were black slaves—treated more as property than as human beings. In fact, until slavery

was abolished in 1838, Jamaica served as the chief slave market of America. The transformation of the country into a multi-racial society with considerable social and political harmony, therefore, is a remarkable achievement.

Land and People

Jamaica is a mountainous island of 4,244 square miles (10,991 square kilometers). The Blue Mountains in the east, composed in part of ancient volcanic rock, contain the island's tallest peak at 7,402 feet (2,257 meters). The northern slopes of the Blue Mountains and the nearby John Crow Mountains are a completely uninhabited wilderness. Another un-

populated region is the Cockpit Country in the center of the island. A roadless jumble of limestone pinnacles and glades, the region is riddled with spectacular caves. In the west and along the coasts are attractive savannas, plains, and scattered trees. Most Jamaicans live on the coastal plains.

The climate is tropical, with temperatures higher along the coasts and cooler in the mountains. Rainfall, too, varies with region. Northeastern Jamaica receives over 100 inches (250 centimeters) of rainfall annually—making it one of the wettest regions in the world. Most of the country experiences severe fluctuations of drought and flood. Little rain falls on the hot, dry southern and southwestern plains. The average annual temperature at Kingston is 79° F (26° C).

For centuries Jamaicans have exploited their island for mahogany and other cabinet woods, leaving little of the natural rain forest still standing. Erosion of the hill slopes is one serious consequence of this exploitation. But there is still a rich flora of native orchids and ferns. Throughout the year the many species of tropical and subtropical plants produce a changing spectacle of colors. Among the plants are the vivid red poinciana, the yellow poui, and the blue lignum vitae, which is Jamaica's national tree. There are four major botanic gardens.

Jamaica has more than 200 species of birds, including a beautiful hummingbird—known locally as the "doctor bird"—which is the national bird. Also abundant are bats, mongooses, frogs, lizards, and crocodiles. There are no poisonous snakes on the island.

Most Jamaicans are of African origin. During the 18th century, more than 600,000 blacks were brought in to work the sugar, coffee, and other plantations. Through racial mixing a distinctive brown, or mulatto, type has emerged. There are also minorities of East Indian, Chinese, Amerindian, Syrian, Lebanese, and European ancestry, all with full and unqualified Jamaican citizenship. About half of the Jamaican population lives in urban areas.

The official language of Jamaica is English, but many people speak a popular and expressive Creole dialect. Originally developed as a means of communication between slaves, it contains elements from African languages as well as from English, French, and Spanish. Education is theoretically free, but illiteracy is still a problem. Near Kingston, the capital and chief port, is the main campus of the University of the West Indies and a technical college.

A religious people, Jamaicans enjoy complete freedom of worship. Many Christian denominations are represented—the majority belonging to the Anglican church—and there are small groups of Jews, Muslims, and Hindus. Two cults, *Kumina* (Revival) and *Rastafari*, have African links and are native to Jamaica. Rastafarians use ganja, a potent form of marijuana, as a sacrament and have special rules of dress, diet, and work. Jamaicans have developed a vibrant national culture, notably represented in such fields as reggae music, drama, and the visual arts and in the sport of cricket.

A Jamaican woman returning from market takes a path through the lush tropical vegetation of Castleton Gardens, near Kingston. She balances her day's purchases on top of her head, a customary way of carrying packages in Jamaica. Despite land clearing and erosion, the country still has a rich natural plant life.

Herbert Lanks—Black Star

Economy

About one third of the people depend upon agriculture for a living. Half the cultivated area is controlled by about 1,000 large estates, while the other half is divided into 185,000 small farms. The larger farms mainly produce sugarcane, citrus fruits, coffee, bananas, pimentos, and cattle—often for export. The small farms grow a variety of crops and raise goats and pigs for subsistence and for local markets.

A tourist paradise, Jamaica depends on tourism to maintain its economy. A string of beautiful resorts extends all along the north coast. Montego Bay and Ocho Rios are towns with many large hotels, but there are also simpler types of accommodations set in small coves and secluded bay areas. Among the popular attractions are water sports and game fishing.

Five international aluminum companies mine deposits of bauxite on the central limestone plateaus; three of them also process the ore into alumina. The aluminum industry causes environmental pollution, but it is also vital to the national economy. Among the top five producers of bauxite and alumina in the world, Jamaica derives essential foreign exchange from the industry. Workers in the bauxite industry are among the highest paid in the country.

The Kingston metropolitan area dominates the country commercially and industrially (see Kingston). Spanish Town (the capital from 1534 to 1872), May Pen, and Mandeville are smaller industrial and commercial centers. Jamaica has a good road network. Public transport is mainly by minibus. Air Jamaica links the country with other Caribbean islands, the United States, Canada, and Europe.

History and Government

When Christopher Columbus landed in Jamaica in 1494, the island was inhabited by the gentle Arawak people. During 150 years of Spanish rule, the Arawaks were virtually exterminated, and African slaves were brought to the island. A British force invaded successfully in 1655, and Jamaica remained a British colony until 1962. The slave trade expanded during the 18th century as Africans were shipped under appalling conditions to Jamaica.

Slavery was abolished by stages in the 1830s, and between 1839 and 1844 indentured laborers from India were brought in to replace the blacks, many of whom moved to the new free settlements that had developed in the hills. In 1865 there was an uprising within the country, which the British governor Edward John Eyre repressed so severely that he was recalled and put on trial. In the 1930s Sir Alexander Bustamante—a colorful figure who later led the country to independence—was prominent in a vigorous labor movement. He founded the Jamaica Labour party, while his cousin Norman Washington Manley formed the People's National party.

Jamaica is a parliamentary democracy, with a lower house elected by universal suffrage and an appointed senate. It belongs to the Commonwealth, and the head of state is the governor-general, who is appointed by the monarch of England. The prime minister is the leader of the majority party in the House of Representatives. In the late 1970s Jamaica moved toward closer ties with Cuba under Michael Manley, who was prime minister from 1972 to 1980. Under Manley the country was brought to the verge of economic collapse. After 1980 ties with the United States were strengthened with the election of the conservative Edward Seaga. During his term there were problems of overpopulation, limited resources, and inequitable distribution of land and wealth. Manley was again elected prime minister in 1989. A devastating hurricane in September 1988 caused widespread damage. Population (1988 estimate), 2,407,000.

JAMES, Kings of England.

JAMES, Kings of England. Only two rulers of England have borne the name James. The hatred felt for the second of these, because of his attempts to rule despotically and to restore the Roman Catholic religion, is probably the most important reason why the name fell into disuse.

JAMES I (born 1566, ruled 1603–25) was already King James VI of Scotland when he came to the English throne as the first of the Stuart line (*see* Stuart). He was the son of Mary, queen of Scotland, and of her second husband, the feeble Henry Stuart, Lord Darnley. He became king of Scotland the year after he was born when his mother was forced to abdicate. During his childhood a succession of regents struggled to assert his authority. He was a puppet of contending intriguers and faction leaders until 1582 when he was seized by Protestants and held captive for a year. Upon his escape he began to pursue policies of his own.

As a boy the king was sickly and had a weakness of the legs. He became a bold horseback rider, even though for many years he had to be tied into the saddle. He was well educated, especially in theology, and, although the son of a Catholic mother, remained through life a staunch Protestant.

When James succeeded to the English throne in 1603, on the death of Queen Elizabeth I, he was nearly 37 and prided himself on what he called his "kingcraft." In reality he so lacked political discretion that a French statesman once characterized him as "the wisest fool in Christendom."

The English people were displeased by his vain attempt to bring about a closer union of his two kingdoms of England and Scotland. He alienated both the Puritans and the Catholics (*see* Puritans). Some of the Catholics engaged in the Gunpowder Plot to blow up Parliament and the king and bring in a Catholic ruler (*see* Fawkes). Only one of his acts pleased the Puritans—at his instruction, scholars prepared a new translation of the Bible, called the "King James Version." Published in 1611, it remains in common use today.

James I also quarreled with Parliament over taxation and political matters. He believed in the "divine right of kings"; that is, that they receive their powers from God, and are responsible to Him alone. Thus it was not surprising that he took the position that Parliament owed all its powers and privileges to the graciousness of the king; while Parliament claimed that these powers and privileges were the "birthright and inheritance of the subjects of England." James wished to ally with the Catholic country of Spain and to marry his son Charles to a Spanish princess. Parliament wanted to fight Spain at sea and thus aid the German Protestants in the Thirty Years' War (*see* Thirty Years' War). Not until James's plans for a Spanish alliance failed and he decided to make war upon that country did he and Parliament agree. A year after the war began, James I died, leaving his son Charles I the problems he himself had been unable to solve.

King James II of England

JAMES II (born 1633, ruled 1685–88) was a grandson of James I. His ideas of the "divine right of kings" were the same as those of his grandfather and his father, Charles I. He obstinately attempted to carry out these ideas in spite of the fact that his father had been beheaded by Parliament. It has been said of James II that he alienated "not only the classes which had fought *against* his father, but also those that had fought *for* his father."

James was created duke of York in 1634. When he succeeded to the throne on the death of his brother, Charles II, the people welcomed him and fought for him against a rebellion led by the duke of Monmouth. But the cruelty that was shown to the followers of Monmouth at their trials—called the "Bloody Assizes" because of their vindictiveness—turned many against the king.

Then James angered the nation by trying to restore Catholicism as the religion of England. He set aside or "dispensed" with the laws against Roman Catholics and Dissenters. He appointed many Catholics to office and even named some as bishops in the Church of England.

At first there was no organized opposition since James was 51 when he came to the throne and his two daughters by his first wife, Anne, were both Protestants. But in 1688 a son was born to him by his second wife, Mary of Modena, a devout Catholic. Afraid that the boy would become another Catholic king, Protestant nobles unjustly claimed that the child was not really the son of James and the queen, but was fraudulently smuggled into the palace. They used this excuse to invite James's daughter Mary and her husband, William of Orange, to come from Holland and take the throne of England. When William landed, James lost his supporters and fled to France. This was the "Glorious Revolution." of 1688.

James was cordially received by Louis XIV, who had been furnishing him money to carry on his fight for absolute power and Catholicism. The French king now gave James a pension and support in trying to recover his throne. But James was defeated in Ireland at the battle of the Boyne (July 1, 1690) and the French fleet was crushed at La Hogue in 1692. James then gave up actively trying to regain his throne. He lived quietly in France, where he died in 1701. (*See also* Pretender; William, Kings of England.)

JAMES, Henry (1843–1916). One of the most productive and influential American writers, Henry James was a master of fiction. He enlarged the form, was innovative with it, and placed upon it the mark of a highly individual method and style.

James was born on April 15, 1843, in New York City, the younger brother of William James (*see* James, William). He had two other brothers and one sister. His father, Henry, had inherited wealth, and the family enjoyed a life of leisure. The elder James lectured and wrote, largely about religious matters.

The James children were educated by private teachers, and Henry entered Harvard Law School in 1862. At first Henry seemed to have no definite idea of how he would use his many talents. He was just as interested in drawing and mathematics as he was in writing. At Harvard, however, under the influence of Charles Eliot Norton and William Dean Howells, he decided that literature would be his life's work.

From 1865 to 1869 he wrote criticism and short stories. After much travel, he decided in 1875 to live in Europe. He went first to Paris but in 1876 settled in London. James received an honorary degree from Harvard in 1911 and one from Oxford in 1912. Angry at the United States for not entering World War I at its start, he became a British citizen in 1915.

Henry James; painting by John Singer Sargent

Courtesy of the National Portrait Gallery, London

Because he wrote of a society of sophistication and culture, Henry James was accused of being a snobbish writer. He maintained, however, that it was only this kind of society that had the leisure to indulge in the delicate personal relationships in which he was interested. He wrote of these relationships with great psychological skill and in precise language, usually seeking to involve the reader in the thoughts and outlook of one character.

James wrote 20 novels, 112 shorter works, and 12 plays. The theme of much of his writing was the clash between the innocence and exuberance of the New World with the corruption and wisdom of the Old. His themes also included personal relationships, which he explored in 'The Portrait of a Lady,' published in 1881, and social reform, of which he wrote in 'The Bostonians' and 'The Princess Casamassima' (both 1886). Some of his other works included 'Daisy Miller' (1878), 'Washington Square' (1880), 'The Turn of the Screw' (1898), 'The Wings of the Dove' (1902), and 'The Ambassadors' (1903). James died on Feb. 28, 1916, in London. His ashes were taken to the United States and buried in Cambridge, Mass. (*See also* American Literature.)

JAMES, Jesse (1847–82). Celebrated in song, story, and movies, the legend of outlaw Jesse James has become a permanent part of the lore of the 19th-century American West. For 16 years, from 1866 to 1882, the James gangs were the scourge of banks and stagecoaches and trains carrying gold.

Jesse Woodson James was born near present-day Kearney, Mo., on Sept. 5, 1847. His brother Frank was 4 years old at the time. Their father abandoned the family when Jesse was 2 in order to seek gold in California. When the Civil War started in 1861, the James family, along with many other Missourians, was on the side of the Confederacy. At 15 Jesse joined Frank as a member of a gang of raiders led by William C. Quantrill. These guerrilla fighters raided communities in Kansas and Missouri, killed pro-Northern citizens, and robbed mail coaches. After the war the raiders disbanded.

Jesse turned to crime as a way of life and in 1867 became the leader of a gang that specialized first in bank robberies, then in holding up trains. The membership of the gang varied over the years. Its earliest members were the Younger brothers—Cole, James, and Robert; Andy McGuire; Wood and Clarence Hite; George and Oliver Shepherd; Tom Little; and Frank James. All of these men were former raiders under Quantrill.

Their first bank robbery was at Liberty, Mo., on Feb. 14, 1866. Several more banks were robbed during the next seven years, usually many months apart in order to let the public outcry die down. On July 21, 1873, the gang robbed its first train at Adair, Iowa. Robbing trains and stagecoaches of their gold greatly enhanced the reputation of the James gang among Westerners. Whereas bank robberies affected the savings of ordinary people, stealing gold promoted a

Robin Hood image—that is, stealing from the rich to give to the poor—though how much giving the gang did is uncertain.

In September 1876 the gang was nearly destroyed in an attempt to rob a bank at Northfield, Minn. Only the James brothers escaped death or capture. All three Younger brothers were wounded, captured, and imprisoned. Frank and Jesse were not heard of again until 1879 when, with the gang reconstituted, they robbed a train in Glendale, Mo.

The often senseless killings and other violence that went along with the robberies finally prompted Governor Thomas T. Crittenden of Missouri to offer a reward of $10,000 for the capture of the James brothers, dead or alive. Robert Ford, a member of the gang, paid a secret visit to the governor and ascertained that the reward would be his if he killed Jesse. On April 3, 1882, when Jesse had his back turned, Ford shot him. With Jesse dead, Frank James turned himself in to the authorities. He was tried for his crimes but was acquitted, probably owing to public sentiment. He lived out his life on a Missouri farm, where he died in 1915. Robert Younger died in prison in 1889. James Younger killed himself in 1902. And Cole Younger was pardoned in 1903. He returned to Missouri, where he died in 1916.

JAMES, William (1842–1910). The American philosopher and psychologist William James had a remarkable variety of talents. Most notably he was a leader in the movement known as pragmatism, which stresses that the value of any idea or policy is based entirely on its usefulness and workability.

James was born on Jan. 11, 1842, in New York City. His early education, like that of his brother Henry, was varied (*see* James, Henry). Although William's first ambition was to be an artist, he entered Harvard Medical School in 1864. He was granted a degree in medicine in 1869, but by that time had decided that he would not practice medicine. He had studied chemistry, comparative anatomy, and physiology. In 1865 he went on a geological expedition to Brazil with Louis Agassiz (*see* Agassiz). James had also read widely in literature, history, and philosophy. He wrote literary criticism and became interested in psychology.

Outwardly a friendly, warm, and happy person, James was subject to periods of deep depression, partly because of constant ill health and partly because of his inability to find a suitable profession or philosophy. In 1870, however, he had an experience that gave him a sense of direction. He read Charles Renouvier's essays and gained a new insight into the power of free will as a moral force.

James was appointed an instructor in physiology at Harvard in 1872. He later taught psychology and philosophy and became famous as one of the outstanding teachers of his time.

In 1884 the "James-Lange theory" was published. It set forth James's belief that emotions are organic sensations aroused by bodily expression—that we feel

William James
Harvard University News Service

sorry because we cry, and angry because we strike. William James's most important work, 'The Principles of Psychology', was published in 1890. In this book, James advocated the new psychology that acknowledged a kinship with science as well as with philosophy. The book immediately became popular with laymen as well as with psychologists.

James's increasing fame made him much in demand as a lecturer. He also wrote 'The Varieties of Religious Experience', published in 1902, and 'Pragmatism' (1907). In the latter book, he expounded the theory that man knows the true meaning of an idea only when he sees what its effects are. In 1907 James taught his last course at Harvard. He died in Chocorua, N.H., on Aug. 26, 1910.

JAMESTOWN, Va. The first permanent English colony in America was founded on May 14, 1607, on a peninsula of the James River in what is now the state of Virginia. The colony was named after King James I of England. Here the first representative government in America was begun, and here the first black people were brought to the American Colonies.

In the spring of 1606 the king granted a charter to the Virginia Company of London. The charter granted to the company the rights to settle, explore, and govern limited parts of the New World. On Dec. 20, 1606, an expedition of about 100 men, commanded by Captain Christopher Newport, sailed from London.

On May 13 the expedition arrived at a marshy peninsula 30 miles (48 kilometers) up the James River. The men anchored their three small ships—the *Godspeed*, the *Discovery*, and the *Susan Constant*—and landed on May 14.

The settlers had been instructed, in London, to choose the site of their settlement with care, making certain that the location was healthful and easily defended. The colonists unfortunately ignored these instructions.

The site was low, damp, swampy, and unhealthful and many soon died. A supply ship bringing additional colonists eight months later found only 38 of the original 105 settlers alive. Famine, attacks by Indians, and trouble over the system of holding property in common added to the settlers' difficulties. Only the efforts of the boastful but efficient Captain John Smith had kept the colony together. A disastrous fire swept the town in 1608. During the winter of 1609, after Smith left Jamestown to return to England, many of the settlers died.

Disheartened, the colonists sailed for England in the spring of 1610. A few miles down the river, however, they met the supply ship of the new governor, Lord De la Warr (later spelled Delaware), and returned to the colony. In 1612 they began growing tobacco and thereafter fared better.

In 1619 three important events occurred. The first legislative assembly in America was formed. Two women had come in 1608, but now a shipload of prospective wives was on the way. The first blacks arrived and became indentured servants.

In 1624 the Virginia Company's charter was revoked and Virginia became a royal colony, controlled by the king. Jamestown remained the capital, but as agriculture became increasingly important in Virginia, the city declined in importance.

A rebellion against the government of the royal governor, Sir William Berkeley, swept Virginia in 1676. Nathaniel Bacon, leader of the rebellion, attacked Jamestown and burned it (*see* Bacon's Rebellion). The town was rebuilt, but in 1698 another fire destroyed the statehouse. In 1699 the government was moved to Williamsburg.

Since 1934 archaeologists have explored the site of Jamestown, uncovering many objects. Since 1893 the Association for the Preservation of Virginia Antiquities has worked to preserve Jamestown. It owns a 20-acre (8-hectare) tract. The remainder of the site is now part of the Colonial National Historical Park. (*See also* America, Discovery and Colonization of; National Parks, United States; Smith, Captain John; Virginia.)

A number of old Jamestown buildings have been reconstructed or reproduced near the site of the original settlement of 1607.

Thomas Williams

JAMMU AND KASHMIR. Located in the northern part of the Indian subcontinent in the area of the western Himalayas, the territory of Jammu and Kashmir has been in dispute between India and Pakistan since the partition of India in

1947. The territory is bounded on the northwest by Afghanistan, on the north and east by China, on the south by India, and to the west by Pakistan. Jammu and Kashmir has an area of 86,023 square miles (222,798 square kilometers), which is divided into regions of Indian and Pakistani control. The administrative capital of the Indian sector is Srinagar in summer and Jammu in winter. Muzaffarabad is the administrative capital of the Pakistani sector.

The territory is comprised of various geographic zones, including the plains, the foothills, the Pir Panjal Range, the Vale of Kashmir, the central Himalayan zone, the Upper Indus Valley, and the Karakoram Range. Wild animals found in Jammu and Kashmir include ibex, urial (a kind of wild sheep), the Kashmir stag, black and brown bears, and many varieties of game birds.

The population of this territory is as varied as its geographic zones. Farmers are settled in the plains and foothills. Following the late summer harvest of maize and millet, many of the hill people return to lower areas to work in forests and lumber mills. The city of Jammu contains mostly Hindus, whereas the people living in the Vale of Kashmir are mainly Muslims. Across the main Himalayan divide, in the smaller towns of Ladakh and Baltistan, are Tibetans who practice either Buddhism or Islam.

From the 9th to the 12th century, the region of Jammu and Kashmir was a center of Hindu culture. It was brought under Muslim rule in the 14th century and remained so until the Sikhs of Punjab and then the ruling prince of Jammu, Raja Gulab Singh, assumed control in the 19th century. The state then formed part of a buffer zone that was imposed by the British between their Indian empire and the empires of Russia and China to the north. When the British withdrew from South Asia in 1947, the maharaja of Kashmir sought independence but then chose to make the country part of India. The Pakistanis intervened militarily, claiming that the region was a natural extension of their country. Although a cease-fire line was established in 1948, the border dispute continued into the 1980s. Occasional incursions by Chinese forces after they conquered Tibet in 1951 complicated the situation. Today most of the population and the major portion of territory are in the Indian sector. (*See also* India; Pakistan.) Population (1981 preliminary census), 5,981,600.

JANUARY *see* FESTIVALS AND HOLIDAYS.

Before the snow-clad summit of Mount Fuji, the eternal symbol of Japan, a classic pagoda overlooks a bustling modern city.

JAPAN

JAPAN. The leading industrial nation of the Orient and the non-Western world, Japan also rivals the most advanced economic powers of the West. It rose rapidly from a crushing military defeat in World War II to achieve the fastest-growing economy of any major nation in the postwar period. Today only the United States and the Soviet Union outproduce it.

The Meiji Restoration of the 1860's launched Japan onto the road of modernization. The Japanese skillfully developed the technological base for modern industry and built their nation into a leading world power. Set back temporarily by wartime destruction and the consequences of military defeat, Japan has again become a world power. This time, however, its reputation is based not on armed might but on the productivity of its peacetime industry.

The Japanese people enjoy an unprecedented supply of goods, though their living standards are still behind those of the United States and Western Europe. Their swelling cities, paced by the giant

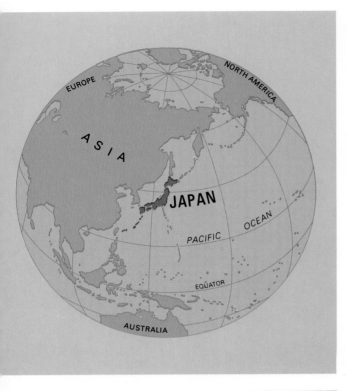

metropolis of Tokyo, are as modern as urban centers anywhere in the world. And they face the problems of great cities everywhere—overcrowded housing, inadequate waste-disposal facilities, air and water pollution, and traffic congestion.

In few other places in the world do the values and traditions of the past continue to flourish so strongly alongside the ideas and practices of the present. The persisting contrast between the new and the old, the modern and the traditional, is one of the most characteristic features of present-day Japan.

Urbanization, industrialization, and modern transportation and communication are rapidly changing the Japanese way of life. The impact of these developments is being keenly felt not only in the cities but in the countryside as well. However, beneath Japan's "new look" lie the deep-seated customs and institutions of traditional Japanese culture—in religion, in politics, and especially in family life. The people of Japan largely continue to respect and honor their past. Their society as a whole continues to adhere to the concepts of personal loyalty and obligation that have been a tradition through the ages.

Japan comprises an island chain along mainland Asia's east coast. The four main islands—Hokkaido, Honshu, Shikoku, Kyushu—stretch some 1,200 miles from northeast to southwest. Including the more than 3,900 smaller islands, Japan is about 1,800 miles long. Its maximum width is about 200 miles.

Japan has no land border with any other nation. Across the Sea of Japan to the west is Korea; across the Sea of Japan to the northwest and the Sea of Okhotsk to the north is the Soviet Union; across the East China Sea to the west is China; along the Ryukyu Islands of Japan to the southwest are Taiwan and the Philippines. The open waters of the vast Pacific Ocean wash Japan's eastern and southeastern shores. Across the Pacific, more than 4,000 miles away, is the United States mainland.

Japan is 145,842 square miles in area, about the size of Montana. Its largest island by far is Honshu, with about three fifths of the total area. On Honshu are most of Japan's principal cities and about four fifths of its more than 118 million people. Japan ranks high in population density and seventh in population among the world's nations. Its capital, Tokyo, is one of the world's largest cities.

The following contributors and consultants assisted in the preparation of this article: Michael Berger, Correspondent, *Stars and Stripes* (Tokyo); Peter Duus, Associate Professor of History, Claremont Graduate School; Earle Ernst, Senior Professor and Chairman, Department of Drama and Theatre, University of Hawaii; John D. Eyre, Professor of Geography, University of North Carolina; Yoshio Hiyama, former Professor, Faculty of Agriculture, Graduate School Division of Agricultural Science, University of Tokyo; Yoshiyuki Noda, Professor, Faculty of Law and the Graduate School Division of Law and Politics, University of Tokyo; Kazuo Okochi, former President, University of Tokyo; John Roderick, Foreign Correspondent; Jack Sewell, Curator of Oriental Art, The Art Institute of Chicago.

Preview

The article Japan is divided into the following sections:

Included in the article are the following special features:

At the end of the sections "People," "Government," "Economy," "Culture," "Natural Features," and "History" are two study aids—"Words to Remember" and "Questions to Think About."

Facts About Japan

Official Name: Nihon.

Capital and Largest City: Tokyo.

Population: (1980 census) 117,060,396; (1982 estimate) 118,830,000.

Area: Total, 145,842 square miles (377,728 square kilometers); Honshu, 89,199 square miles (231,025 square kilometers); Hokkaido, 32,246 square miles (83,517 square kilometers); Kyushu, 16,268 square miles (42,133 square kilometers); Shikoku, 7,260 square miles (18,803 square kilometers); Okinawa, 869 square miles (2,250 square kilometers).

Population Density (1982): 815 persons per square mile (315 persons per square kilometer).

Form of Government: Constitutional monarchy (head of state—emperor; head of government—prime minister).

Flag: *See* Flags of the World.

Major Political Subdivisions: 47 prefectures.

Extent: Point Soya (Hokkaido) to Cape Sata (Kyushu), 1,200 miles (1,900 kilometers).

Highest Elevation: Mount Fuji, 12,389 feet (3,776 meters).

Climate: North—short, cool summers and long, cold, snowy winters; southwest—warm, humid summers and mild, humid winters.

National Anthem: *Kimigayo.*

Monetary Unit: Yen.

Major Language: Japanese.

Major Religions: Shintoism, Buddhism.

Everyday Expressions in Japanese

Yes. *Hai.*
No. *Iie.*
Please. *Dozo.*
Thank you. *Arigato.*
You're welcome. *Do itashi-mashite.*
Excuse me. *Gomen kudasai.*
Hello. *Konnichi-wa.*
Good-bye. *Sayonara.*
I understand. *Wakari-masu.*
I don't understand. *Wakari-masen.*
What's your name? *Anata-no namae-wa nan desu ka?*
My name is Kenneth. *Watakushi no namae wa Kenneth desu.*
What time is it? *Nan-ji desu ka?*
What's this? *Kore-wa nan desu ka?*
This is _____. *Kore-wa _____ desu.*
Where is it? *Doko desu ka?*
It's here. *Koko desu.*
It's over there. *Soko desu.*
How are you? *Gokigen ikaga desu ka?*
I am well. *Watakushi-wa genki desu.*
To the left. *Hidari e.*
To the right. *Migi e.*
Straight ahead. *Massu gu.*

PREFECTURES AND DISTRICTS OF JAPAN

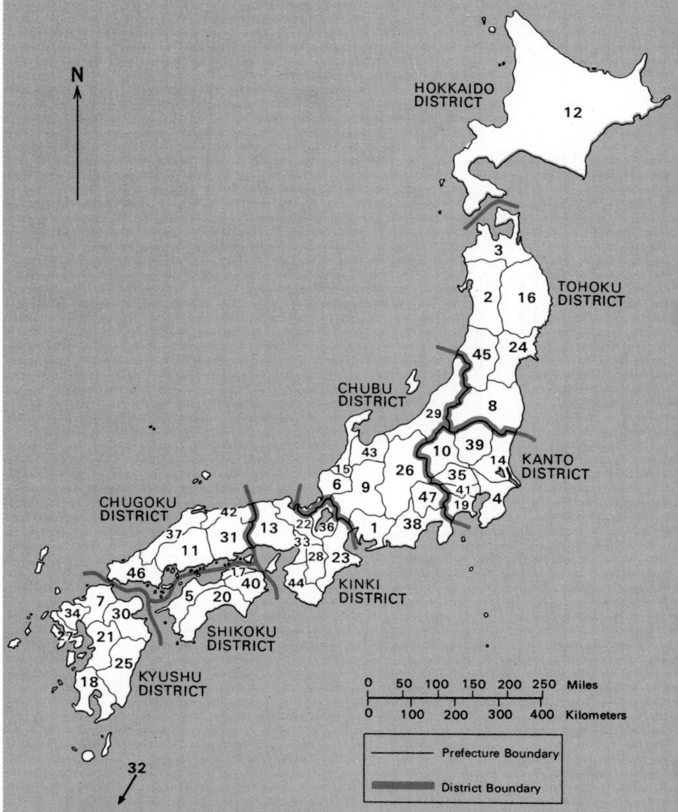

Prefecture Populations (1980 census)

1. Aichi	6,221,638	25. Miyazaki	1,151,587
2. Akita	1,256,745	26. Nagano	2,083,934
3. Aomori	1,523,907	27. Nagasaki	1,590,564
4. Chiba	4,735,424	28. Nara	1,209,365
5. Ehime	1,506,637	29. Niigata	2,451,357
6. Fukui	794,354	30. Oita	1,228,913
7. Fukuoka	4,553,461	31. Okayama	1,871,023
8. Fukushima	2,035,272	32. Okinawa	1,106,559
9. Gifu	1,960,107	33. Osaka	8,473,446
10. Gumma	1,848,562	34. Saga	865,574
11. Hiroshima	2,739,161	35. Saitama	5,420,480
12. Hokkaido	5,575,989	36. Shiga	1,079,898
13. Hyogo	5,144,892	37. Shimane	784,795
14. Ibaraki	2,558,007	38. Shizuoka	3,446,804
15. Ishikawa	1,119,304	39. Tochigi	1,792,201
16. Iwate	1,421,927	40. Tokushima	825,261
17. Kagawa	999,864	41. Tokyo	11,618,281
18. Kagoshima	1,784,623	42. Tottori	604,221
19. Kanagawa	6,924,348	43. Toyama	1,103,459
20. Kochi	831,275	44. Wakayama	1,087,012
21. Kumamoto	1,790,327	45. Yamagata	1,251,917
22. Kyoto	2,527,330	46. Yamaguchi	1,587,079
23. Mie	1,686,936	47. Yamanashi	804,256
24. Miyagi	2,082,320		

Source: Statistics Bureau, Prime Minister's Office

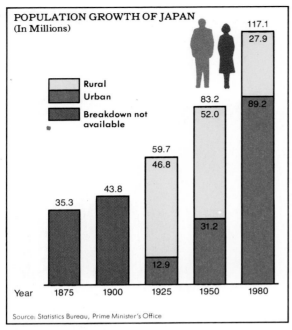

POPULATION GROWTH OF JAPAN
(In Millions)

Legend:
- Rural
- Urban
- Breakdown not available

Year	1875	1900	1925	1950	1980
Total	35.3	43.8	59.7	83.2	117.1
Rural			46.8	52.0	27.9
Urban			12.9	31.2	89.2

Source: Statistics Bureau, Prime Minister's Office

AGE AND SEX OF JAPAN'S POPULATION

Age in Years

Male — Female

85+
80–84
75–79
70–74
65–69
60–64
55–59
50–54
45–49
40–44
35–39
30–34
25–29
20–24
15–19
10–14
5–9
0–4

5 4 3 2 1 0   0 1 2 3 4 5

Percent of Total Population

Source: Statistics Bureau, Prime Minister's Office

JAPAN—People

Japan is the world's seventh most populous nation. In 1982, Japan had an estimated population of 118,830,000. Its population went beyond the 100 million mark in 1967 and at the 1980 census it had reached 117,060,396. Yet Japan has one of the lowest population growth rates in the world—about 1 percent per year.

Japanese population data is incomplete for the period before 1868, when the nation's modern era began. However, the population of Japan is believed to have reached 5 million in the 7th century and 10 million in the 14th century. Official estimates placed the number of Japanese in the mid-19th century at over 30 million. In 1920, when Japan's first census was taken, it had a population of 55,963,000. In 1940 its population was 73,114,000.

Japan experienced a brief baby boom after World War II, but then the nation's birthrate dropped from a high of 34 per 1,000 in 1947 to about 13 per 1,000 in the early 1980s. This is one of the fastest declines that has ever been experienced by any nation. Japan's death rate has also fallen—to about six per 1,000—largely because of improvements in public health measures, advances in medicine, and the greater availability of modern medical facilities. Average life expectancy in Japan reached 73 years for men and 79 years for women in 1980. In 1890 it was 43 years for men and 44 years for women.

The proportion of young people in Japan has been decreasing. Average family size has also been shrinking: It dropped from about five members in 1955 to about three members per family in 1980. This drop occurred in part because a growing number of young married couples were establishing their own households instead of living with their parents in the traditional fashion. Another reason was that young couples in Japan were having fewer children. In Japan, abortion is an accepted and widely used means of controlling family size. It is permitted under a 1952 law. Contraception, however, is not popular.

The Japanese are a fairly homogeneous people—both culturally and racially. They have a single language, and almost all are of Mongoloid racial stock. Koreans, the largest alien group in Japan, number about 667,000. The Ainu, a native people of northern Japan, have been almost completely assimilated into the general population of the country.

Japan is one of the world's most thickly populated nations. In 1982 the population density of the country as a whole was about 815 persons per square mile, but if only the urban land area is considered, the density becomes several times greater than it is for the entire land area. The bulk of Japan's people live in the coastal lowlands, which comprise a relatively small part of the nation's total area. The mountainous interior is sparsely populated.

Japan is one of the most urbanized major nations in Asia. In 1920, over four fifths of its people still lived in rural areas. In 1980, however, about three out of every four Japanese lived in cities.

Japan's greatest concentration of population is in a 350-mile-long belt that extends from Tokyo and the Kanto Plain westward along the Pacific coast through Nagoya and Kyoto to Osaka and Kobe on the eastern edge of the Inland Sea. Within this belt, called the Tokaido Megalopolis, live about 42 percent of Japan's people. The belt comprises the six largest cities and a large percentage of the 180-odd cities with more than 100,000 population. A western extension of the Tokaido Megalopolis has been developing along the Inland Sea and as far as the city of Kagoshima at the southern tip of Kyushu.

The Tokaido Megalopolis includes the metropolitan clusters of Tokyo-Kawasaki-Yokohama, Nagoya, and Osaka-Kobe-Kyoto. The largest and fastest growing of these is around Tokyo. Population growth within the city limits of Tokyo has slowed, but in its suburbs—where open land is available for the construction of new homes and apartments—the number of people is increasing rapidly.

The Tokaido Megalopolis comprises the principal Japanese centers of industry, business, and finance and Japan's major international ports. It provides most of the job opportunities for migrants from the farms and small towns of Japan. For this reason, perhaps, Japan's difficulties in providing adequate housing, transportation, and social services of all kinds are greatest in the Tokaido Megalopolis.

Many prefectures outside the Tokaido Megalopolis and the few other large metropolitan centers have been losing population through out-migration, especially since 1950. The heaviest losses have occurred along the Sea of Japan coast and in rural areas north and west of Tokyo, in Honshu, in western and eastern Kyushu, and on Shikoku. Hokkaido, the northernmost island, was an area of pioneer settlement until the 1930s. It has the lowest population density of any Japanese prefecture.

Four fifths of Japan's people—98,116,000 in 1981—were living on the island of Honshu. Three other major islands of Japan—Kyushu, Hokkaido, and Shikoku—had populations of 13,044,000; 5,607,000; and 4,175,000, respectively.

EVERYDAY LIFE IN JAPAN

Japan has been modernizing rapidly. Yet there are still great contrasts in the everyday life of the Japanese people. Especially striking are the contrasts between the tradition-bound countryside and the bustling urban centers.

Over one fourth of the Japanese people live in small farming villages called *buraku*. The way of life of these people is changing, but the traditional patterns established centuries ago are still widespread.

Rural homes are generally small. The walls are made of clay. Some rooms have earthen floors, while the floors of others are covered with wood or straw

WHERE THE JAPANESE PEOPLE LIVE

- · = 50,000 people
- ◦ = 500,000 people
- ◉ = 1,000,000 people
- ● = 2,000,000 people
- ● = 4,000,000 people
- ● = 8,000,000 people

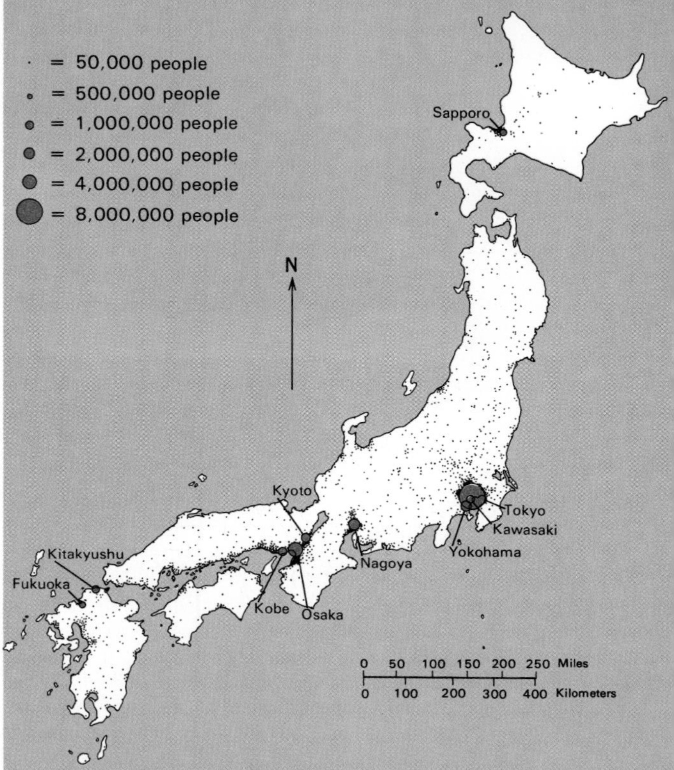

Japan's Ten Largest Cities: 1980 census (1982 est.)

Tokyo	8,351,893 (8,340,177)
Yokohama	2,773,674 (2,841,170)
Osaka	2,648,180 (2,625,624)
Nagoya	2,087,902 (2,092,183)
Kyoto	1,473,065 (1,480,278)
Sapporo	1,401,757 (1,433,355)
Kobe	1,367,390 (1,375,006)
Fukuoka	1,088,588 (1,104,483)
Kitakyushu	1,065,078 (1,065,038)
Kawasaki	1,040,802 (1,045,244)

Source: Statistics Bureau, Prime Minister's Office

In the late 1960's, nearly a million dwelling units were built in Japan each year with government aid. Much of the new housing was put up in the suburbs of the major cities.

mats. The stoves used for cooking are made of clay or brick. They are heated with such materials as straw or with compressed gas, which has come into widespread use. The toilet facilities are separate from the house. Water is usually obtained from wells.

The villagers usually live in households that include grandparents and grown sons with their families, as well as the farmer, his wife, and his younger children. When a farmer dies or grows old, his land is passed on to a son, traditionally the eldest. His other sons may inherit money and may stay on the farm. However, most enter occupations in the village or a city.

Each member of a farm family has certain responsibilities. The most important involve work in the fields. The men spend long days planting, tilling, and harvesting their crops. During the time in each growing season when the paddies are flooded, the men work knee-deep in water. Most farmers tend and harvest their crops by hand, but modern farm machinery is also being used. Rice is the principal food crop.

The women often help in the fields after they have finished their usual household tasks of cooking, cleaning, weaving straw mats, and gardening. Although older children go to school, they also work in the fields or take care of younger brothers and sisters. Grandparents no longer able to do field work weave mats and look after their grandchildren.

After a hard day's work, the entire family enjoys an evening bath. The large earthen or cedar bathtub stands in a bathhouse or in the kitchen near the stove. A fire kindled beneath the tub keeps the water hot. Then each family member in turn—beginning with the father—washes and rinses thoroughly before getting into the tub. The water in the tub is used only for soaking since it is shared by all members of the family. On winter days the hot bath gives the farm family its first chance to get really warm.

Japanese villagers are neighborly. They share many of their joys and sorrows. The whole village may partake in a wedding or a funeral. All the women prepare food for a village celebration, and every family brings its share. Most village business is handled through social and economic cooperatives. The farmers sell their produce in a common market.

Life in the Cities

Japanese city life is much more Westernized than that of the countryside. The cities have modern housing and modern transportation systems. Many Japanese city dwellers live in high-rise apartment buildings and take subways or buses to their jobs in offices and factories. The daily lives of city dwellers have been transformed by modern conveniences, such as automobiles, electric household appliances, and central heating. Yet many traditional practices survive. Bath facilities even in modern apartment houses may be much like those in the villages, and many city dwellers still use public bathhouses.

In the cities, fewer marriages are arranged by parents and fewer young people live with their parents after marriage. Since more of the young men and women attend universities or work away from home, they have more opportunities to meet socially and to choose their own husbands and wives.

Entertainment in the cities is not as dependent upon family activity as is that of the villages. Women enjoy shopping in markets and department stores. Men are attracted by teahouses and beer halls. Wealthy men may banquet friends and business associates in *geisha* restaurants. Here they are entertained by geisha, highly trained girls who dance, sing, recite poetry, play a banjolike instrument called the *samisen*, and chat with the guests. The geisha are gowned richly in silk costumes, and their hair is elaborately styled. City dwellers can also attend a wide variety of theatrical performances and sports events.

Growing Up in Japan

When a baby is about seven days old, his father places a paper bearing the child's name before a household shrine. He does this to inform the ancestors of the family that another member has been added to it. Friends and relatives attend, bringing gifts for the child. When the child is about a month old, he is taken to the nearest Shinto shrine. There the priest may record his name and birthday, and the child formally becomes a member of the community.

A Japanese baby is often carried on the back of his mother, grandmother, or sister, safely fastened with broad sashes. From early infancy a child is trained in obedience. Spankings are rarely used, but a child may be ridiculed and shamed if he acts badly.

After World War II, the status of Japanese men and women began to be equalized. Prior to that time, boys and girls were treated very differently. Parents thought it so important to have sons to carry on the family name that boys were preferred and pampered. They could "boss" their older sisters and even their mothers. Girls, on the other hand, had to defer not only to their elders but even to younger brothers. However, a father expected his sons to achieve more than his daughters, and boys were brought up with the obligation to do nothing to harm the family's reputation. Japanese boys are still often favored above their sisters and more is still expected of them, but the disparities in the treatment of boys and girls are not as great as they used to be.

When a boy is about 21, his family may take steps to find a suitable wife for him. When friends have recommended a young lady with a similar family background, the prospective couple are introduced. If neither the boy nor the girl objects strongly to the proposed marriage, the boy's family chooses a go-between to carry on discussions with the girl's parents and make arrangements for the exchange of presents.

There are religious and regional variations in the forms of the marriage ceremony in Japan. In the Shinto ceremony, the bride and groom take three sips of *sake*, a rice wine, from three cups. The bride wears the elaborate clothing and the complicated hairstyle that are traditional on this occasion. The marriage ceremony may be followed by feasting and dancing.

The Japanese mark a man's entry into old age with a special ceremony which occurs between his 59th and 60th birthdays. At that time he dons a red kimono, a color not usually worn by adult males, to signify that he has shed the responsibilities of maturity.

Most Japanese funerals are marked by Buddhist or Shinto rites. The body is borne in a procession to a crematory or a cemetery. The period of mourning may last as long as 50 days.

Inside a Japanese Home

Japanese homes are rather small by Western standards. They generally have a kitchen and three or four rooms that serve as living and sleeping quarters. The walls are lined with thin bamboo strips. The floors are covered with *tatami*, woven straw mats six feet by three feet in size. A room's size is stated in terms of the number of tatami required to cover the floor. Among the most common sizes are 6-, 8-, and 12-tatami rooms. To keep the tatami clean, the Japanese remove their shoes when entering a house.

Most houses perch on two-foot-high posts set on rock foundations. A narrow porch on the sunny side serves as a hall onto which the rooms open. Permanent partitions are rare. *Fusuma*, or sliding screens made of paper-covered frames, may be closed to create separate rooms or opened to convert the entire house into a single room. *Shoji*, or sliding outer doors, are pushed back on summer days to let in air and are shut for protection at night.

The light, open construction of such Japanese houses is well suited to a warm climate and to a region where earthquakes destroy heavier structures. However, these houses do not keep out the damp chill of winter. A *hibachi* (charcoal brazier) gives some warmth. Sometimes a *kotatsu* (burner) is set into the floor and a table draped with quilts is placed over it. The family gather around the table to warm their feet.

Furniture in the Japanese home generally consists only of storage chests and low tables. In most homes

Traditional dress may be worn in Shinto and Buddhist wedding rites. A *montsuki* (crested coat) tops the groom's kimono. A *tsunokakushi* (hood) accents the bride's elaborate hairdo.

the family sit on *zabuton* (low cushions) and sleep on *futon* (cotton-filled mattresses about four inches thick). However, many city families have replaced the futon with beds. Both the zabuton and the futon are stored in wall closets when they are not being used.

The most important spot in the house is the *tokonoma*, an alcove containing a low platform which holds a flower arrangement. Above the platform hangs a painted scroll. When callers come, the most honored guest is seated near the tokonoma. Except for the embellished parchment doors between rooms, scrolls and flower arrangements are usually the only decoration found in Japanese homes.

Carefully tended gardens demonstrate the Japanese love of nature. The rooms of a home often open onto a garden through a sliding door. Many Japanese gardens are actually miniature landscapes, with small trees, flowering bushes, pools, streams, and bridges.

Food for the Japanese Family

Most Japanese eat three meals a day. Rice, the mainstay of the Japanese diet for centuries, is eaten at almost every meal. At breakfast it is usually supplemented by *misoshiru* (a bean-paste soup) and *tsukemono* (pickled vegetables). In the cities, some Japanese have replaced these dishes with bread, butter, and eggs. Lunch is a light meal and may consist of salted fish, tsukemono, and *tsukudani* (seafood or vegetables cooked and preserved in soy sauce), in addition to rice or noodles. Supper is the most important meal of the day. In most homes it includes fish, beef, pork, or chicken with vegetables and rice. Meat is usually cut into thin strips and fried. It is not as important in the Japanese diet as in that of Western nations. Until the late 19th century, Buddhist practice discouraged eating the flesh of four-legged animals. Fish is often served raw.

The two most popular beverages in Japan are tea and sake. Tea is drunk during and after meals. It is also served to guests with such snacks as *soba* (buck-

Continued on page 32

RURAL HOUSE STYLES

MAGARIYA

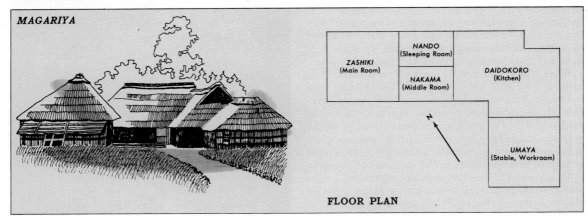

FLOOR PLAN

A stable to the right of the living quarters is the distinctive feature of the L-shaped magariya-style farmhouse. This type of Japanese home is common in the wild grasslands of mountainous areas in the Tohoku Region, where horse raising has been important. Linking the stable with the living quarters is a working and cooking area which provides warmth for the horses and storage space for their equipment. If the family has no horses, the stable is used as a workroom.

YAMATO

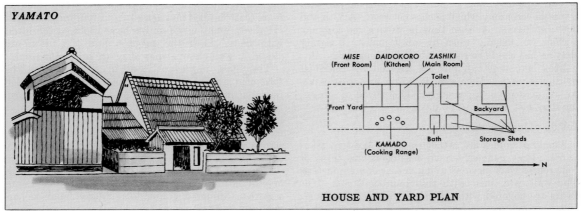

HOUSE AND YARD PLAN

Yamato-style farmhouses are common in the Nara Basin and are generally found densely clustered in villages. In the string-shaped villages that wind along Japanese highways, the houses, outbuildings, and plots are unusually long and narrow. The gabled roofs of neighboring houses nearly touch one another. An important feature of the Yamato farmhouse is the large cooking area. It has a huge range, called a *kamado*, which may have as many as 11 cooking units of different sizes.

MITSUNARABE

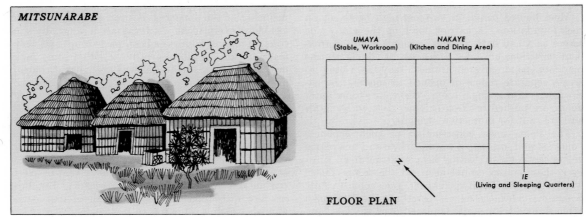

FLOOR PLAN

The small, simple Mitsunarabe-style farmhouse is generally found in southern Japan—particularly in Kagoshima Prefecture and on the Okinawa Islands. It is composed of a row of three individually roofed units enclosing living and sleeping quarters; a kitchen and dining area; and a stable, storage, and work area. The units may be joined, or they may be separated by narrow open spaces. Scattered outbuildings may house storage space and bath and toilet facilities.

The styles of traditional Japanese farmhouses were developed centuries ago and are adapted to the climate, economy, and customs of the regions in which they are located. As a result, the farmhouses in a given area tend to resemble one another. Japanese farmhouse styles include the *magariya*, the *Yamato*, and the *Mitsunarabe*.

The roof design of a traditional Japanese farmhouse expresses both the artistry of the architect and the individuality of the owner. Several distinct types of roofs have evolved. They include the *irimoya*, the *yosemune*, and the *kirizuma*. Like traditional Japanese house styles, individual roof types are often particularly common in certain regions. Thatch is the usual roof covering. Other roofing materials include wood shingles weighted by rocks, and decorative tiles—either alone or combined with thatch. *Chigi* (crossed ornamental rafters) may be placed on the roof crest. A ridge pole may run along the crest alone or supported by chigi.

ROOF STYLES

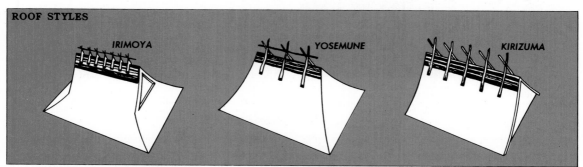

IRIMOYA   YOSEMUNE   KIRIZUMA

The irimoya (gabled-and-hipped) roof is found in Kinki Region, especially in the Kyoto area. It usually has long, low eaves and is large in relation to the rest of the building. Its crest is often beautifully ornamented.

The yosemune (hipped) roof is found throughout Japan. Its design, suited to areas with heavy rainfall, allows the rapid run-off of water in four directions. A variation of this roof type is slightly pyramidal or cone shaped.

The kirizuma (gabled) roof is common in central and western Honshu. Its structural simplicity shows the modesty which many Japanese believe to be proper for farmhouses. The gables are often ornamented with symbolic designs.

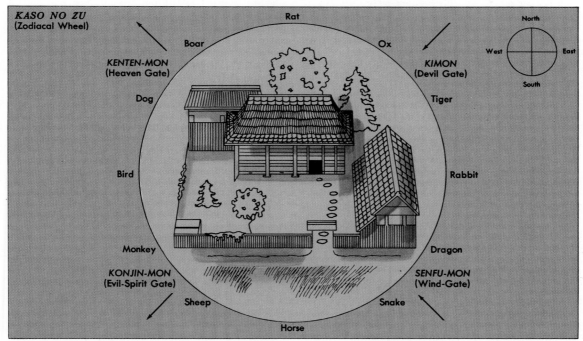

KASO NO ZU (Zodiacal Wheel)

Rat · Boar · Ox · KENTEN-MON (Heaven Gate) · KIMON (Devil Gate) · Dog · Tiger · Bird · Rabbit · Monkey · Dragon · KONJIN-MON (Evil-Spirit Gate) · SENFU-MON (Wind-Gate) · Sheep · Snake · Horse

North · West · East · South

Many Japanese farmyards look alike because the buildings are arranged according to *hogaku*, a system of traditional rules governing lucky and unlucky directions. Twelve primary directions, each bearing the name of an animal, form a zodiacal wheel. The wheel, called *kaso no zu*, may be inscribed on the farmhouse's *daikokubashira*, or main supporting pillar.

No important part of the house should face northeast (*kimon*, or devil gate), considered an unfavorable direction. Since ill fortune is thought to flow from northeast to southwest (*konjin-mon*, or evil-spirit gate), spaces should be provided in these directions to allow bad influences to leave the farmyard. The southeast (*senfu-mon*, or wind gate) is considered a lucky direction. Income is believed to flow from southeast to northwest (*kenten-mon*, or heaven gate), where a strong room should be located to collect it.

In modern Japan the rules of hogaku are not always strictly followed. However, in many areas total disregard for hogaku may still invite public scorn.

Young pupils in modern Japanese schools are taught general science in well-equipped classrooms. About one third of the college students specialize in some branch of the sciences.

wheat noodles) and *udon* (wheat noodles). Sake is served with meals, at dinner parties, and especially at celebrations such as weddings or holiday feasts.

Chopsticks are the only eating utensils—knives, forks, and spoons are not used. Food is served in china or lacquer bowls and in dishes. On important occasions, individual trays are provided. Usually a Japanese family sits around a low table for meals.

Japanese Clothing Styles

Modern Japanese dress incorporates both Eastern and Western styles. Western clothes, worn by both men and women, are seen most frequently on city streets. The traditional *kimono*, a loose-fitting garment with wide sleeves, is now worn principally at home. Men's kimono differ from women's primarily in color and fabric. Women wear their kimono at ankle length, bound with a sash called an *obi*. Men's kimono are shorter and on formal occasions are worn with a wide, divided skirt called a *hakama*. A kimono-shaped cloak called a *haori* may be worn over a kimono by both sexes.

The clothes Japanese children wear are much like those worn by children in the United States. Boys wear short or long pants and shirts or sweaters. Girls wear skirts with blouses or sweaters. Japanese girls still wear kimono for festivals, however.

The Japanese usually wear shoes like those worn in Western nations. However, *geta* (wooden clogs) and *zori* (rubber or straw sandals) are still worn with kimono. Socks called *tabi* are worn with geta and zori. The tabi have a separate place for the big toe—the geta or zori strap is held between it and the other toes.

Japanese men and women now wear Western hairstyles. The elaborate hairstyles Japanese women formerly wore are now used only at weddings or by entertainers in the theater and hostesses at geisha houses.

Education

Nearly all of Japan's school-age children attend school regularly. Attendance is compulsory through the lower level of secondary school. Children begin

nursery school when they are about 3. At 6, they begin elementary school; at 12, lower-secondary school. Any student who has completed lower-secondary school may enroll in an upper-secondary school. The Japanese upper-secondary school is comparable to the United States high school. It offers either a technical or a college preparatory course of instruction.

Japanese students, especially those who plan to attend college, strongly compete with each other for grades and honors. In school competitions, however, all participants usually receive some sort of recognition. All students are promoted at the end of each term. To go beyond high school, Japanese boys and girls must pass difficult college entrance examinations. There are junior colleges, four-year universities, and graduate schools. Before World War II Japanese colleges and universities stressed technical education. In recent decades, however, they have given greater emphasis to the liberal arts.

Recreation

Japanese recreational activities take place indoors and outdoors. Young children fly kites, spin tops, play baseball, watch television, and build plastic models. In the summer they watch fireworks, a pastime the Japanese have enjoyed for centuries.

With higher incomes and more leisure time, the Japanese have adopted a number of new outdoor sports. Blessed with high mountains and heavy snows, Japan has become one of the world's most popular ski areas. Most of the nation's major cities have indoor skating rinks. At Sapporo, outdoor ice-sculpture festivals attract many entrants each year. The 1972 winter Olympics were held in Sapporo.

Competitive sports have a wide following among the Japanese. Baseball—with two professional

SCHOOL ENROLLMENT IN JAPAN		
	NUMBER OF STUDENTS	
	1971	1977
Primary, elementary........	9,595,021	10,819,656
General and vocational (high school, middle school, secondary school)........	10,096,016*	9,156,883
Higher professional school, teachers college, university	1,791,514	2,093,935
Total.................	21,482,551	22,070,474

*Number of vocational students is for 1972.
Source: Ministry of Education

leagues—is one of Japan's most popular spectator sports. Other sports enjoyed by the Japanese include basketball, lawn and table tennis, volleyball, bicycling, hockey, and swimming. *Sumo, judo, kendo, karate,* and other traditional Japanese martial arts are now regarded primarily as competitive sports.

The Japanese go on frequent family outings. Parents take their children to shrines and temples and to parks and zoos. Excursions into the country to view the spring cherry blossoms or the autumn foliage are very popular.

Religious Practices

Most Japanese people follow either the Buddhist or the Shinto religion. There are fewer than one million Christians in Japan. Many families combine Buddhist and Shinto practices. These families have two separate altars in their homes, one for the family ancestors, in accordance with Buddhist teachings, another for the Shinto gods. Upon awakening, members of the family burn incense in honor of the dead and clap their hands in tribute to the Shinto gods.

Shinto is the only religion that originated in Japan. Buddhism was introduced into Japan from Korea in

At the November 15 Shichigosan Festival, parents give thanks at a shrine—these are at Tokyo's Meiji Shrine—that their children have safely reached ages three, five, and seven.

NATIONAL HOLIDAYS OF JAPAN

Jan. 1—Ganjitsu (New Year's Day). Celebrated by decorating the home, sending greeting cards, and visiting friends.

Jan. 15—Seijin-no-Hi (Adult's Day, or Coming-of-Age Day). Dedicated to those who reached the age of 20 during the previous year.

Feb. 11—Kenkoku Kinen-no-Hi (Day to Commemorate the Founding of the Nation).

March 20, 21, or 22—Shumbun-no-Hi (First Day of Spring).

April 29—Tenno Tanjobi (Emperor's Birthday).

May 3—Kempo Kinembi (Constitution Memorial Day). Marks the adoption of the 1947 constitution.

May 5—Kodomo-no-Hi (Children's Day). Dedicated to boys and girls, who celebrate it by decorating their homes with paper carp.

Sept. 15—Keiro-no-Hi (Respect for the Aged Day). Honors senior citizens.

Sept. 23 or 24—Shubun-no-Hi (First Day of Autumn).

Oct. 10—Taiiku-no-Hi (Health-Sports Day). Celebrates traditional sports and games.

Nov. 3—Bunka-no-Hi (Culture Day). Dedicated to the advancement of the arts.

Nov. 23—Kinro Kansha-no-Hi (Labor-Thanksgiving Day). Gives thanks to labor and for a successful harvest.

the 6th century, and Portuguese and Spanish missionaries brought Christianity to Japan in the 16th century. Shinto received the support of the Japanese government until 1947, when the emperor disclaimed his divinity. The present Japanese constitution guarantees complete freedom of religion.

Health and Welfare Services

Japanese medicine is administered by the Ministry of Health and Welfare. The ministry operates health centers throughout the nation. At these centers doctors examine patients and, when necessary, refer them to hospitals for treatment. The health centers are also responsible for dealing with sanitation and public health problems.

Most of the citizens of Japan are protected by a form of health insurance that is available on an occupational or a regional basis. The insured person pays a monthly premium. He is charged a small consulting fee for the treatment of each illness. The rest of his medical care is either furnished without charge or for only a fraction of its actual value. Members of the family other than the insured person are entitled to receive medical care for half the fees usually charged.

Words to Remember

buraku—a small farming village.

geisha—a female entertainer.

sake—a rice wine.

tatami—a straw mat, six feet by three feet in size.

fusuma—a sliding screen separating rooms.

shoji—a sliding outer door.

hibachi—a charcoal brazier.

kotatsu—a burner set into the floor.

zabuton—a low cushion used for seating.

futon—a cotton-filled mattress.

tokonoma—an ornamental alcove in a Japanese home.

tsukemono—pickled vegetables.

tsukudani—seafood or vegetables cooked and preserved in soy sauce.

kimono—a traditional loose-fitting garment worn by Japanese men and women.

obi—the sash used with a kimono.

geta—wooden clogs.

zori—rubber or straw sandals.

tabi—socks with the big toe separate, worn with geta and zori.

Questions to Think About

1. Give possible reasons why Japan has a low rate of population growth.
2. Which elements in traditional Japanese life may change as Japan continues to modernize? Which may remain unchanged? Why?
3. Half of the Japanese people live in the Tokaido Megalopolis. How might this urban concentration affect Japan's rural areas?
4. Give possible advantages and disadvantages in the way a traditional Japanese home is built and furnished.

JAPAN—Government

Source: Ministry of Foreign Affairs

The crest of the Japanese imperial family is a 16-petaled chrysanthemum. Most Japanese family crests have plant motifs.

NATIONAL ANTHEM
'Kimigayo'

Source: Ministry of Foreign Affairs

Kimigayo (Reign of Our Emperor) was adopted as the national anthem of Japan in 1888. Its words come from an ancient, anonymous Japanese poem. The Japanese court musician Hiromori Hayashi composed the melody. A revised version for Western instruments was written by Franz Eckert, a German who served as bandmaster of the Japanese army. Basil Hall Chamberlain, a British scholar at the Imperial University of Tokyo, translated the anthem into English.

The present, Showa constitution of Japan became law on May 3, 1947, as an amendment to the Meiji constitution of 1889. It is based on a draft prepared in English by the Allied occupation forces after World War II. A Japanese version was debated and approved by the Japanese Diet, or parliament. In some quarters, the Showa constitution has been regarded as an American-imposed document, untrue to Japanese traditions and political realities. However, moves to revise it have made little headway.

Government Organization

Under the constitution the emperor is "the symbol of the State and of the unity of the people." His duties are largely ceremonial, such as opening the Diet or receiving ambassadors. The emperor acts only on the initiative of responsible government officials. His appearances in public are carefully directed by the Kunaicho, or Imperial Household Agency.

The two-house Diet has the sole constitutional power to make laws. The upper house, or House of Councillors, has 252 members elected for six-year terms. Of these, 100 are elected by the nation at large and 152 by prefectural constituencies. The lower house, or House of Representatives, has 511 members elected for four-year terms. They represent districts that return from three to five members each.

All bills approved by both houses of the Diet become law, but a bill rejected in the upper house can become law if it is approved by a two-thirds majority in the lower house. A simple majority in the lower house is sufficient to ensure the selection of a prime minister or the ratification of a treaty even over the opposition of the upper house. In practice, however, the two houses are usually in agreement. The budget originates in the lower house.

The principal executive body is the cabinet. It is headed by the prime minister, who is chosen by the Diet. Ministers heading the major administrative agencies are named by the prime minister. They must all be civilians, and a majority of them must be members of the Diet. The cabinet is responsible to the Diet. If the House of Representatives passes a no-confidence resolution or rejects a confidence resolution, the cabinet must resign or the prime minister must dissolve the Diet and call a new election.

The judiciary is separate from both the legislative and executive branches. Fourteen Supreme Court justices are appointed by the cabinet, and the emperor appoints a chief justice nominated by the cabinet. An appointee to the Supreme Court is reviewed by the voters at the next general election for the House of Representatives. A Supreme Court justice is again reviewed at the elections following each of the ten-year periods that he remains on the bench. The Supreme Court has administrative control over lower courts. It is the court of last resort, with power to decide the constitutionality of laws, cabinet orders, regulations, and official acts.

Voters in each of Japan's 47 prefectures elect a governor and a one-house legislature. Voters in each city, town, and village elect a mayor and a one-house legislature. They have the powers of initiative, referendum, and recall. The governors and mayors can dissolve their legislatures, and the legislatures can, in turn, pass votes of no-confidence in their executives. Local governments adopt budgets and levy taxes. Routine national and local government business is handled by a professional civil service. It is estimated that more than one out of nine employed persons in Japan works for a governmental agency.

Politics

Since the end of World War II, Japan's most successful political organization has been the conservative Liberal-Democratic party (LDP). In general elections it regularly wins almost half of the vote and a majority of seats in the House of Representatives. In the 1983 elections, however, the party lost its absolute majority when a former prime minister was convicted of bribery. It was able to form a coalition with the New Liberal Club—a breakaway group formed by LDP dissidents, who rejoined the major party in 1986. The opposition includes the left-wing Socialist, Democratic Socialist, and Communist parties and the Komeito, or Clean Government, party, which is affiliated with a Buddhist sect, the Soka Gakkai.

Japanese political parties are mostly combinations of *habatsu,* or small factions centered on strong individual leaders. Local political organizations usually consist of small support groups for local Diet members. However, the Komeito party has a mass membership and an extensive organizational structure.

Japan has universal, equal, and direct suffrage. All Japanese citizens who are 20 years of age and over have the right to vote. In Japan, especially in rural areas, voting is regarded as a duty, and participation in elections is high. In ten national elections between 1949 and 1976 about 75 percent of qualified voters went to the polls. In local elections voter participation may go up to 90 percent. Candidates for office receive some financial aid from the government, but governmental attempts to limit campaign spending have been unsuccessful.

Interest groups play a major role in Japanese politics. National federations of labor unions are closely linked to the left-wing parties. Large industrial concerns, national federations of farm cooperatives, businessmen's associations, and professional groups have close links with the Liberal-Democrats. The relations between special-interest groups and government officials or political parties sometimes lead to bribery and corruption.

Demo, or mass demonstrations, are another means of influencing government policy. They are usually employed by the left-wing parties, which are able to mobilize the support of students and union members.

GOVERNMENT ORGANIZATION

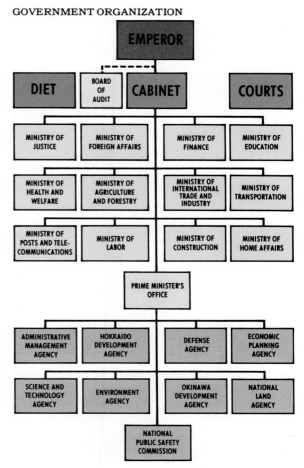

Source: Ministry of Foreign Affairs

Consulate General of Japan (Chicago)

Japan's longest-reigning emperor was Hirohito, shown here in an official portrait of the imperial family. After his death in 1989, he was succeeded by Prince Akihito (far left).

ELECTIONS TO HOUSE OF REPRESENTATIVES*

Party	Year	Number of Votes	Percent of Total Votes	Seats Won
Liberal-Democratic	1980	28,262,441	47.9	284
	1983	25,982,781	45.8	250
	1986	29,875,496	49.4	304
Socialist	1980	11,400,747	19.3	107
	1983	11,065,080	19.5	112
	1986	10,412,583	17.2	86
Communist	1980	5,803,613	9.8	29
	1983	5,302,485	9.3	26
	1986	3,895,857	6.4	26
Komeito	1980	5,329,942	9.0	33
	1983	5,745,750	10.1	58
	1986	5,701,277	9.4	57
Democratic Socialist	1980	3,896,728	6.6	32
	1983	4,129,907	7.3	38
	1986	5,313,246	8.8	27
Independents and minor parties	1980	4,335,363	7.4	26
	1983	4,553,687	8.0	27
	1986	5,250,139	8.8	12
TOTALS	1980	59,028,834	100.0	511
	1983	56,779,690	100.0	511
	1986	60,448,598	100.0	512

* June 22, 1980; Dec. 18, 1983; and July 6, 1986.

Sources: Election Bureau, Ministry of Home Affairs; and
Consulate General of Japan.

Nobuyuki Masaki

In 1970 these Japanese students protested the renewal of the security treaty between the United States and Japan. Demonstrations on political issues are common in Japan.

Frequently, large delegations of workers demonstrate in front of the Diet building or government ministries. In 1960 massive demonstrations against the renewal of Japan's mutual security treaty with the United States led to the resignation of the cabinet.

The expression of public opinion is protected by the constitution. Japanese citizens are guaranteed freedom of speech, religion, assembly, and association and take full advantage of these rights. Newspapers and magazines are uncensored and are often critical of the government and of its policies.

The former, discredited nationalist ideology of Japan's military-imperial system was known as *kokutai*, or "national essence." It was based on deep devotion to the emperor and submission to authority.

Defense and Foreign Relations

The Japanese constitution renounces "war as a sovereign right of the nation and the threat or use of force as means of settling international disputes." Nevertheless, since 1950 Japan has developed its own land, naval, and air arms into a National Self-Defense Force. In 1979 the National Self-Defense Force consisted of about 297,000 men, supplied with modern weapons and equipment. All members of the force are volunteers.

Foreign affairs and the negotiation of treaties are handled by the cabinet. The prime minister reports on foreign relations to the Diet and must obtain its approval of treaties. Routine administrative business with foreign nations, such as granting visas, is handled by a professional diplomatic corps.

Japan is a member of the United Nations and many other international organizations. Since regaining full sovereignty in 1952, its foreign policy has been based on close ties with the United States. A mutual security treaty between the two countries affords Japan the protection of American nuclear weapons.

Words to Remember

Showa constitution—Japan's present constitution.
Diet—the Japanese parliament.
Soka Gakkai—the Buddhist sect which supports the Komeito (Clean Government) party.
habatsu—the factions that make up Japanese political parties.
kokutai—Japan's former nationalist ideology, based on submission to authority.
National Self-Defense Force—the armed services of Japan.

Questions to Think About

1. How are the Japanese Diet and the United States Congress similar? How do they differ?
2. What are the advantages and disadvantages of having voters review Supreme Court appointments?
3. Under what circumstances might Japan renounce the "no war" clause in its constitution?

JAPAN—Economy

The growth of the Japanese economy is one of the most remarkable success stories of recent decades. Though Japan was already a modern industrial nation in the 1930's, its economy was shattered by its defeat in World War II. Japan emerged from the war shorn of its colonial empire, shunned by its former trading partners, and occupied by foreign troops. Much of its industrial plant had been destroyed. Yet by the late 1960's Japan ranked third among the industrially advanced nations of the world, surpassed only by the United States and the Soviet Union.

Japan's gross national product soared to almost 700 billion dollars—about $6,000 per capita—in 1977. For the seven-year period 1970–77 its annual economic growth rate averaged more than 18 percent. By the late 1970's the Japanese labor force totaled more than 53 million. The number employed in the primary industries (agriculture, fishing, forestry, and mining) fell from more than 14 million in 1962 to about 6.5 million in 1977. However, the number employed in the secondary industries (manufacturing and construction) and the tertiary industries (trades and services) rose from more than 31 million in 1962 to nearly 47 million in 1977. Despite the rapid growth of the Japanese labor force, the nation suffered from a labor shortage.

The Japanese economic miracle was based primarily on the application of modern technology and business methods and on a large, skilled, and hardworking labor force. In addition, the Japanese government encouraged new industry with subsidies, and more money was available for investments in industry and education because very little was being spent on defense. Japan's achievement was also spurred by a resurgence of national pride.

Agriculture

Japan has one of the world's most productive agricultural systems. Yet only 15 percent of the nation's total land area is under cultivation. A shift from subsistence to commercial farming has been taking place. Large crop surpluses in Hokkaido, northern and western Honshu, and central Kyushu are now shipped to the heavily populated, urbanized belt that stretches from Tokyo westward to northern Kyushu.

Rice, the staple food in Japan, is by far the largest crop in acreage, tonnage, and value. Irrigated rice fields, or paddies, occupy more than half the cultivated area of Japan. Most rice fields in Hokkaido and northern Honshu bear only one crop a year. To the south, where the winter is milder and the growing season longer, multiple cropping is used. Under this system, paddies produce a summer rice crop and a winter crop of dry grains or vegetables. As a result of government price supports and the use of modern farming methods, rice production rose steeply in the

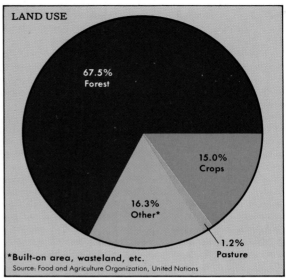

LAND USE

67.5% Forest

15.0% Crops

16.3% Other*

1.2% Pasture

*Built-on area, wasteland, etc.
Source: Food and Agriculture Organization, United Nations

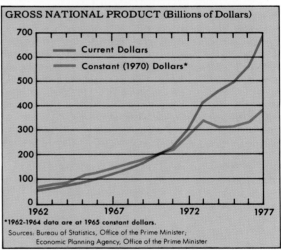

GROSS NATIONAL PRODUCT (Billions of Dollars)

Current Dollars

Constant (1970) Dollars*

*1962-1964 data are at 1965 constant dollars.
Sources: Bureau of Statistics, Office of the Prime Minister;
Economic Planning Agency, Office of the Prime Minister

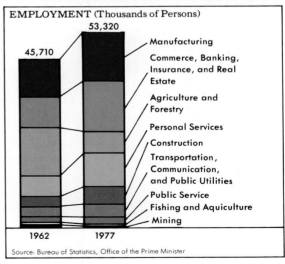

EMPLOYMENT (Thousands of Persons)

45,710

53,320

Manufacturing

Commerce, Banking, Insurance, and Real Estate

Agriculture and Forestry

Personal Services

Construction

Transportation, Communication, and Public Utilities

Public Service

Fishing and Aquiculture

Mining

1962   1977

Source: Bureau of Statistics, Office of the Prime Minister

Tea production in Japan increased by more than one third between 1950 and 1977. These women are cutting quality tea leaves by hand. Tea is Japan's most popular drink.

1960's. With bumper harvests in the late 1960's, when 14 to 15 million tons were raised yearly, the Japanese produced more rice than they consumed. Production fell in the 1970's.

Leading Japanese crops in addition to rice include wheat, barley, soybeans, sweet potatoes, white potatoes, sugar beets, and vegetables. Mandarin oranges are a major Japanese fruit crop. Sericulture—the production of silk from silkworms—provides income to only 5 percent of all Japanese farm households, a sharp drop from the 50 percent of the 1930's. A small but growing number of cattle and hogs are raised. Farm mechanization, however, has brought a decline in the number of horses and draft cattle. Large market-gardening belts lie outside the main cities, and many agricultural districts specialize in industrial crops, such as tea, tobacco, pyrethrum, hops, and reeds.

The average size of Japanese farms is only about 2.5 acres. About two fifths of all farms are less than

1.2 acres in size; less than one tenth, 5 acres or more in size. Average farm size increases from southwest to northeast. Only in Hokkaido, with its short growing season and relatively low productivity, does farm size average about 12 acres or more. The typical Japanese farm consists of several small fields located at some distance from the farmhouse. Farmhouses are usually clustered in hamlets surrounded by the fields of their inhabitants.

The percentage of the total labor force engaged in farming has been falling sharply. Before World War II, Japan's farmers comprised more than half of the total working population. Their proportion had declined to less than one fourth by 1965 and to less than one seventh by the late 1970's.

A large number of farm households are more dependent for a living on jobs in nearby cities than they are on farming. But many farmers who have taken city jobs are holding onto their farms because they regard them as a hedge against unemployment and inflation. The outflow of young men to the cities has been particularly great. This has led to an increase in the proportion of women and older men in the farm labor force. By 1976, women comprised 52 percent of all farm workers, and 22 percent of the men who worked on farms were at least 60 years old.

Prior to 1947, more than half of the farm families did not own the land they farmed. Under the Allied occupation, a Japanese government land reform abolished absentee ownership and transferred many farms to the tenant farmers who had been cultivating them. As a result, tenant-operated land was reduced to only 13 percent of the total cultivated area.

Farming was done mainly by manual labor before World War II, but since the 1950's mechanization has made spectacular headway. Most farm households now use power tillers or tractors; and power pumps, threshing machines, and other farm machinery have become commonplace. Mechanization has helped boost farm output despite the decline in the farm labor supply.

The amount of fertilizer used per acre by Japanese farmers is among the world's largest. Organic fertilizers—including night soil, or human waste—have been largely replaced by low-priced chemical fertilizers. Insecticides have reduced crop damage from insect pests such as the rice borer.

Funds needed by farmers to modernize their operations are provided by government agencies and by farm cooperatives. The cooperatives also help market the farmers' produce.

Fishing and Forestry

By the 1970's Japan had become the world's largest fishing nation. Its annual fish catch is more than 10 million tons. Japan also leads the world in the value of its fish catch, estimated at more than 12 billion dollars a year, and is second in tonnage.

Most Japanese fishermen work in shallow coastal waters. The typical coastal fishing craft have a capacity of less than ten tons. "Sea farming"—the

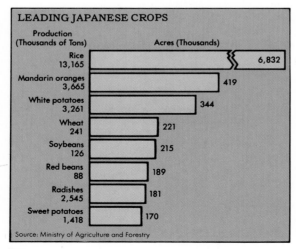

LEADING JAPANESE CROPS

Production (Thousands of Tons) — Acres (Thousands)

Crop	Acres (Thousands)
Rice 13,165	6,832
Mandarin oranges 3,665	419
White potatoes 3,261	344
Wheat 241	221
Soybeans 126	215
Red beans 88	189
Radishes 2,545	181
Sweet potatoes 1,418	170

Source: Ministry of Agriculture and Forestry

culture in shallow coastal bays of prawns, sea bream, edible seaweed, oysters, pearls, and other marine products—has grown rapidly in recent years. The value of the coastal catch is about one fourth that of Japan's total catch. Offshore fishing, for which somewhat larger boats are used, also accounts for about one fourth of the value of Japan's catch.

Pelagic, or deep-sea, fishing, which accounts for the balance, is done in waters far from Japan by large modern fleets. Mother ships serve the fleets as floating processing and canning plants. The Japanese government is a party to international treaties and conventions regulating the use of international waters for fishing.

The Japanese have traditionally depended on the sea for much of the protein in their diet. Though labor shortages are severe in the fishing industry, enough fish are caught to satisfy most domestic needs and to permit some exports. Many of the fish products used for fertilizer and animal feed are imported.

Forests occupy about two thirds of Japan's land area. Nearly three fifths of the forested land is privately owned, mostly in small plots of less than ten acres. These are usually a part of normal farming operations and a source of household fuel.

Planted forests, many of them publicly owned, occupy about one third of the total forested area. Cedar, cypress, and pine are the leading species. Sawlogs are obtained mainly from Hokkaido, the mountains of northern and central Honshu, Shikoku, and Kyushu. Both conifers and broadleaf trees are harvested for pulpwood. Charcoal was formerly an important source of income for mountain villagers, but it has been largely replaced by gas and electricity as the main household fuel.

Lumber production has fallen below the peak years of the early 1960's. Since the demand for lumber continues to rise, Japan has relied increasingly on imports. The government has been trying to increase domestic production by opening roads to remote forest stands, securing top-grade tree seeds, promoting tree planting by private owners of woodland, and mechanizing tree-felling equipment.

Minerals and Energy

Japan's mineral and energy base is small compared with that of other major industrial nations. Its mineral deposits are limited both in quality and in quantity. The supply of ordinary coal, limestone, chromite, magnesium, pyrites, sulfur, lead, and zinc is nearly adequate, but large amounts of such minerals as iron ore, coking coal, petroleum, tin, nickel, nitrate, and phosphate must be imported.

In both volume and value, coal is the main domestic mineral resource. Northern Kyushu, Hokkaido, the east coast of central Honshu, and extreme southwestern Honshu account for most of Japan's coal output. Because of high production costs, however, Japan's total coal production declined more than 60 percent from the mid-1960's to the mid-1970's. The production of coking coal also declined, and by the mid-

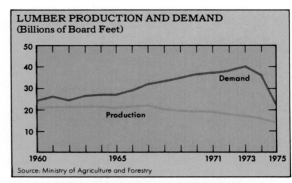

LUMBER PRODUCTION AND DEMAND
(Billions of Board Feet)

Source: Ministry of Agriculture and Forestry

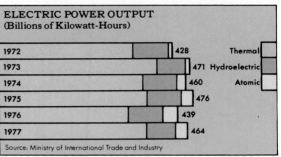

ELECTRIC POWER OUTPUT
(Billions of Kilowatt-Hours)

Year	Output	
1972	428	Thermal
1973	471	Hydroelectric
1974	460	Atomic
1975	476	
1976	439	
1977	464	

Source: Ministry of International Trade and Industry

1970's nearly three fourths of the coking coal used by the nation's rapidly expanding iron and steel industry had to be imported. The small, scattered deposits of iron ore in Hokkaido and northern Honshu also met only a small part of the nation's needs.

The consumption of petroleum increased greatly during the 1960's. Japan's domestic reserves, largely in northwestern Honshu, are meager and must be supplemented with enormous imports from the Persian Gulf and other areas. Near Tokyo and on the central Sea of Japan coast are natural-gas deposits.

The availability of large supplies of electric power has been a key to Japan's industrial growth and rising living standards. Japan ranks third in the world both in electric power output and in installed capacity. Hydroelectric power made up almost

Small fishing boats unload on a beach near Tokyo. Fish, served at most meals, is the main source of protein in Japan. The average Japanese eats nearly 80 pounds of seafood a year.

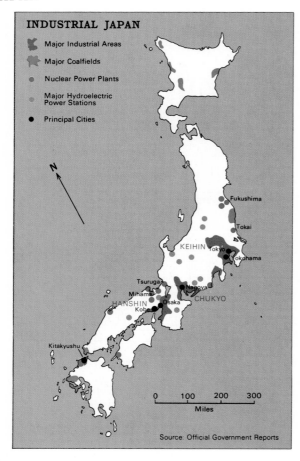

INDUSTRIAL JAPAN

- Major Industrial Areas
- Major Coalfields
- Nuclear Power Plants
- Major Hydroelectric Power Stations
- Principal Cities

Fukushima
Tokai
KEIHIN Tokyo
Yokohama
Tsuruga
Mihama Nagoya
HANSHIN CHUKYO
Osaka
Kobe
Kitakyushu

0   100   200   300
Miles

Source: Official Government Reports

Famous throughout the world, Japan's electrical and electronic products contribute significantly to the nation's economy. Here delicate parts are soldered under microscopes.

two thirds of the total electric supply in the early 1950's, and hydroelectric dams have continued to be built, mostly in central Honshu. However, there has been a much greater emphasis on the construction of coal- and oil-burning thermal power plants. Giant thermal power plants have been built along the coasts, near urban and industrial markets. Tokyo Bay has the largest concentrations of such plants. The first Japanese nuclear-powered thermal electric plant, situated at Tokai, went into full production in 1967. By the late 1970's thermal power plants were contributing about four fifths of the total electric power generated in Japan.

Manufacturing

More than one fourth of Japan's labor force is employed in manufacturing. Most Japanese manufacturing units are small workshops employing only up to three workers. These enterprises tend to be inefficient, to pay low wages, and to turn out goods of uncertain quality. But factories employing more than 300 workers—less than one percent of the total number—account for about 50 percent of Japan's industrial production. Prior to the 1950's, Japan had a reputation for low-priced, shoddy goods. In recent years, however, the quality of Japanese merchandise has met the highest standards in world markets.

Many large manufacturing firms have merged into *zaibatsu* (giant business combines). In many cases—in the manufacture of machinery, for example—large factories subcontract to small workshops.

Manufacturing is heavily concentrated in the Tokaido Megalopolis—the heavily populated urban-industrial belt extending westward from Tokyo and the Kanto Plain along the Pacific coast and the Inland Sea to northern Kyushu. The megalopolis comprises 80 percent of Japan's workers and manufacturing plants and contributes 85 percent of the value of its manufactured goods. Japan's major international ports, its best overland transportation facilities, and the headquarters of its leading banks and trading companies are in the megalopolis. Most of the industrial complexes are on the coast where they have access to ocean shipping and imported fuel and raw materials.

Within the Tokaido Megalopolis are several major clusters of manufacturing activity. The largest—the Keihin industrial area—is centered upon the urban core of Tokyo, Kawasaki, and Yokohama, on the Kanto Plain. Within the Keihin area, large-scale heavy industry lines the western and northern shores of Tokyo Bay. The area is also a center for printing and publishing and for the manufacture of machinery. Yokohama provides international port services.

The Nagoya cluster—the Chukyo industrial area—is noted for its production of textiles, ceramics, and machinery. The postwar expansion of local automobile plants and the port of Nagoya, new steelworks, and a small-scale revival of the aircraft industry have provided a base for further growth. Here also, in the Kuwana-Yokkaichi area, is one of Japan's largest oil-refining and petrochemical centers.

The Hanshin industrial area includes the cities of Osaka and Kobe. It led the nation in industrial output until the 1930's and now ranks second. Osaka has chemical and textile plants and an electronics industry. Kobe is a major international port and produces ships and railway rolling stock.

Another industrial area is centered on Kitakyushu, in northern Kyushu. It developed around Japan's first steel mill, established in 1901, at Yawata. The Kitakyushu area specializes in the manufacture of iron and steel and has other heavy industries.

The Japanese government is encouraging the growth of industrial centers outside the Tokaido Megalopolis. Its aim is to diversify the economy of predominantly agricultural regions and to reduce the concentration of people and manufacturing capacity in the megalopolis.

Japanese industrial production increased more than threefold between 1967 and 1976. Heavy industry, led by machinery, scored the biggest gains. In the late 1960's machinery—electrical and nonelectrical—accounted for one third of manufacturing output. The growing purchasing power of the Japanese people has led to a great increase in the production of consumer goods, such as electrical appliances and automobiles. The output of ceramics, glass, rubber, and petroleum products has also increased greatly. However, the output of textiles and food products has not, reflecting the shift from light to heavy industry.

The Japanese iron and steel industry, vital to the development of all manufacturing, has grown spectacularly since the 1950's. Crude-steel output surpassed the prewar high of 7.6 million tons in 1953 and reached 62 million tons in 1967; 93 million tons in 1970; and 102 million tons in 1977. The industry's modern equipment helps make it a strong competitor in international trade. Its plants are among the largest and most efficient in the world. In 1977, 80 percent of Japan's steel was made in oxygen furnaces, 19 percent in electric. Specially designed ships deliver imported iron ore and coking coal to coastal steel mills.

Five corporations account for more than four fifths of Japan's steel output. The largest plants are in the Tokyo and Osaka areas of the main manufacturing belt; in Kamaishi in northern Honshu; and in Muroran in Hokkaido. The output of copper, aluminum, and titanium has also expanded. Aluminum output, which reached 1,200,000 tons in 1977, still fell short of domestic demand, however.

Great advances have been made in the manufacture of machinery, electrical goods, and transportation equipment. New factories use the latest assembly-line techniques for the mass production of high-quality goods. A home-electrification boom has resulted in a great demand for radios, televisions, rice cookers, washing machines, electric fans, refrigerators, vacuum cleaners, and other household appliances. Also widely used are stereophonic equipment, tape recorders, home freezers, hot-water heaters, air conditioners, and cameras. There is a large output of telephones, watches and clocks, sewing machines, fluorescent lamps; textile machinery, construction equipment,

Japan's advanced and efficient iron and steel industry is largely dependent upon imported iron ore and coking coal. Japan is one of the world's leading steel producers.

agricultural machinery, metalworking machinery; computers and copying machines; and electrical equipment, such as motors, generators, and transformers. Japan is the leading producer of pianos.

The shipbuilding industry has thrived upon both the postwar worldwide demand for super oil tankers and specialty ships and government-sponsored programs for expanding the Japanese merchant fleet. Since the 1950's Japan has led the world in ship tonnage launched—in many years building fully one half of the world total. Japanese ships are noted for their advanced design, automation, and high speeds. Japanese shipbuilders have won foreign contracts be-

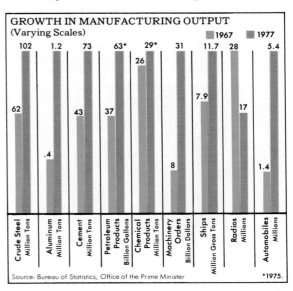

GROWTH IN MANUFACTURING OUTPUT
(Varying Scales) ▮ 1967 ▮ 1977

	1967	1977
Crude Steel Million Tons	62	102
Aluminum Million Tons	.4	1.2
Cement Million Tons	43	73
Petroleum Products Billion Gallons	37	63*
Chemical Products Million Tons	26	29*
Machinery Orders Billion Dollars	8	31
Ships Million Gross Tons	7.9	11.7
Radios Millions	17	28
Automobiles Millions	1.4	5.4

Source: Bureau of Statistics, Office of the Prime Minister   *1975.

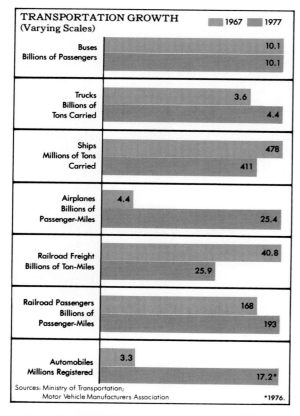

TRANSPORTATION GROWTH
(Varying Scales)

■ 1967 ■ 1977

Category	1967	1977
Buses — Billions of Passengers	10.1	10.1
Trucks — Billions of Tons Carried	3.6	4.4
Ships — Millions of Tons Carried	478	411
Airplanes — Billions of Passenger-Miles	4.4	25.4
Railroad Freight — Billions of Ton-Miles	40.8	25.9
Railroad Passengers — Billions of Passenger-Miles	168	193
Automobiles — Millions Registered	3.3	17.2*

Sources: Ministry of Transportation;
Motor Vehicle Manufacturers Association

*1976.

The growing use of the automobile has spurred the construction of such modern highway facilities as the Wakato Bridge (top), which spans Dokai Bay in Kitakyushu. Subways in Tokyo (bottom) and elsewhere serve Japan's city dwellers.

cause of their reputation for high quality, rapidity of construction, and relatively easy terms of payment.

It was not until the 1960's that Japan, already a major producer of trucks and buses, turned to the mass production of motorcycles and automobiles. American technology, styling, and selling methods were so successfully applied that in 1980 Japan for the first time surpassed the United States in the production of automobiles.

Japan is a leading producer of industrial chemicals, pharmaceuticals, chemical fertilizer, and petrochemical products, such as plastics, synthetic fibers, and synthetic rubber. Japanese oil-refining capacity has grown to third largest in the world. Japan is also a leading world producer of cement. Large amounts of Japanese-made plate glass, firebrick, asbestos products, fiberboard, and other construction materials find ready markets in the nation's fast-growing cities.

Textile manufacturing was Japan's first modern industry. As recently as the 1930's the textile industry employed one fourth of the Japanese industrial labor force. Outpaced by other industries, its relative position has slipped since then. Yet the textile industry remains one of Japan's leading employers. Cotton textiles, an early specialty, have lost ground to synthetics. Japan's output of synthetics is second only to that of the United States and comprises nearly four fifths of all Japanese textile production.

Transportation

Modern transportation facilities link all parts of Japan and facilitate the swift, efficient movement of people and goods. Railways are the main form of land transportation. Railway stations are the hubs of mass-transportation systems which also include buses, taxis, subways, and the vanishing trolleys.

The first Japanese railway was laid in 1872 between Tokyo and Yokohama. By 1930 a rail network covered the four main islands. Most private lines were nationalized in 1906 and passed to a public corporation, the Japan National Railways (JNR), in 1949. The JNR operates about four fifths of Japan's 17,000 miles of railway lines, including all long-distance trunk lines. It owns about 90 percent of all rolling stock. The private railways operate commuter lines in the metropolitan areas. Japanese railways use narrow-gauge track—3 feet 6 inches—and relatively small and light rolling stock. About three fifths of the JNR lines are double-tracked or electrified. Diesel and electric units have replaced coal-burning locomotives.

Postwar population and economic growth, most marked in the Tokyo-Osaka axis, has placed an enormous strain on the carrying capacity of Japan's railways. The high-speed, broad-gauge New Tokaido Line went into operation in 1964. Its fastest express trains make the 320-mile run from Tokyo to Osaka in a little more than three hours. An extension known as the New Sanyo Line was completed from Osaka to Okayama in 1972. The railways of Honshu are linked to Kyushu by undersea tunnel and to Hokkaido and

Shikoku by ferry service. Tokyo, Osaka, Nagoya, Kobe, Sapporo, and Yokohama have subways.

Modern highway construction has lagged badly behind the needs of automobile and truck traffic. Only one tenth of the total mileage of national, prefectural, and local roads is paved. The government's road-building program has been relying upon expressways to ease intercity traffic. The Meishin Expressway (1964) from Kobe to Nagoya, the Tomei Expressway (1969) from Nagoya to Tokyo, and other superhighways provide for uninterrupted high-speed movement through Japan's most densely settled areas. City traffic is speeded by street widening and the construction of elevated expressways.

Domestic air service links all major cities. Japan Air Lines (JAL), the Japanese international flag carrier, operates round-the-world service. The new Tokyo International Airport at Narita, more than 40 miles from downtown Tokyo, was completed in 1973. Its opening was delayed until 1978 because of protests by opponents of the facility.

Retail Trade

About four fifths of Japan's retail stores have fewer than four employees each. These small stores, many of which have a small stock and make little profit, are usually operated by an owner and members of his family. They generally live in quarters to the rear of or over the store. In good weather, storefronts are open and goods are within easy reach from the street. Merchandise is also sold by peddlers who circulate in residential neighborhoods.

Western-style stores with plate-glass windows and window displays are becoming common in the cities. Supermarkets based on American models have also sprung up. Japanese department stores are among the largest in the world. They have prime locations in the downtown areas and near key railway terminals. The typical department store has a wide selection of goods and offers many services, including a children's playground on the roof, cultural events, beauty parlors, dining facilities, and delivery services.

Foreign Trade

Japan is one of the world's leading trading nations. The value of its annual exports and imports reached more than 140 billion dollars by the late 1970's. Japan imports a huge volume of fuels and raw materials, upon which its manufacturing industries are greatly dependent. It exports great quantities of manufactured goods. Japan's domestic market is too small to absorb its entire output of manufactured goods.

Manufactured items account for more than 95 percent of Japan's exports. Textiles comprised half of its exports before World War II but less than 6 percent in the late 1970's. Machinery, transportation equipment, and metals—especially steel—now make up about four fifths of Japan's exports. Raw materials, such as iron ore, coking coal, and scrap metal account for about half the value of Japanese imports; foodstuffs, such as wheat and meat, for about 15 percent;

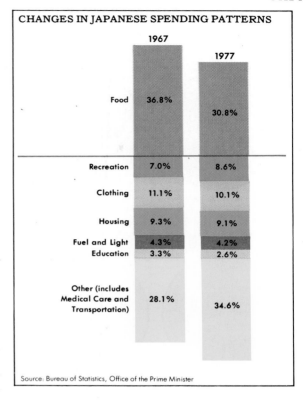

manufactured goods, including textiles, machinery, metals, and chemicals, for about 20 percent. Japan has had a favorable trade balance since 1964, exports having consistently exceeded imports.

Japan's principal trading partner is the United States, the supplier of about 18 percent of its imports and the market for about 25 percent of its exports. In this exchange, Japan's most important imports include foodstuffs, machinery, and coal; its most important exports, steel, metal products, and machinery. Nearly 30 percent of Japan's exports, largely machin-

Customers stroll in a covered shopping arcade in Osaka. Western-style department stores and supermarkets are providing strong competition for Japan's traditional small shops.

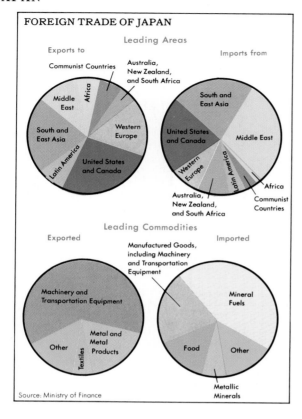

FOREIGN TRADE OF JAPAN

Leading Areas

Exports to

Communist Countries

Australia, New Zealand, and South Africa

Middle East

Africa

South and East Asia

Latin America

Western Europe

United States and Canada

Imports from

South and East Asia

United States and Canada

Middle East

Western Europe

Latin America

Australia, New Zealand, and South Africa

Africa

Communist Countries

Leading Commodities

Exported

Machinery and Transportation Equipment

Other

Textiles

Metal and Metal Products

Imported

Manufactured Goods, including Machinery and Transportation Equipment

Mineral Fuels

Food

Other

Metallic Minerals

Source: Ministry of Finance

These merchant ships are berthed at Yokohama, one of Japan's busiest ports. Japan has one of the world's largest merchant fleets and is the world's leading shipbuilder.

ery, iron and steel, chemicals, and textiles, go to the countries of southern and eastern Asia. Petroleum and petroleum products, foodstuffs, sawlogs, and other products and raw materials from this region constitute about 20 percent of its imports. Japan's trade with Western Europe is also strong and includes the export of ships and the import of machinery. The Middle East is a major source of oil.

Most of Japan's foreign trade is handled by large firms that are part of the zaibatsu. Shipping is channeled through seven main international ports: Chiba, Yokohama, Nagoya, Kobe, Kawasaki, Osaka, and Tokyo. The deepwater ports of Chiba, Yokohama, Nagoya, Kobe, and Kawasaki handle four fifths of Japan's exports and one third of its imports.

To guarantee its supply of raw materials, Japan has invested heavily in overseas developments. Its interests abroad include oil fields in Alaska and on Sakhalin and Sumatra; pulp mills in Alaska and British Columbia; copper mines in Peru, Canada, and South Africa; iron mines in Australia, Brazil, and India; and coking coal and bauxite mines in Australia. Japan gives other countries economic aid either directly or through the Asian Development Bank. It belongs to the Organization for Economic Cooperation and Development, the General Agreement on Tariffs and Trade, and other international economic organizations.

Communications and Information Media

Japan has one of the world's most advanced mass-communications systems. The Nippon Hoso Kyokai (NHK), or Japan Broadcasting Corporation, operates the nation's sole public broadcasting system. The NHK radio and television programs reach all parts of Japan through two television networks, three radio networks, and thousands of local television and radio outlets. Television programs are financed through monthly license fees paid by each household owning a set—85 percent of all Japanese households. The NHK broadcasts emphasize cultural and educational topics. The more than 700 commercial broadcasting stations in Japan receive advertising revenue and stress entertainment in their programming. In most areas, viewers can watch television on three or more channels.

The Japanese are among the world's most ardent newspaper readers. Average daily newspaper circulation in Japan was about 57.8 million in 1977. The nation has more than 180 newspapers, nearly two fifths of which publish both morning and evening editions. Magazines, books, and other reading matter are printed and sold in huge quantities.

Japan's government-owned telephone system is second only to that of the United States in size. Almost one fifth of its 48 million telephones are in the Tokyo-Yokohama metropolitan area. The government also operates the postal and telegraph services.

Finance, Labor, and Technology

The Bank of Japan is the core of Japan's banking system. The bank's purpose is to stabilize the value of the country's currency and to foster credit. The bank issues *yen* notes; the government mints coins. The country's commercial banks receive savings deposits and provide funds for private industry.

The Japanese government stimulates industry and foreign trade by providing funds through such agencies as the Japan Import-Export Bank, the Housing Finance Bank, and the Finance Bank for Small and Medium Enterprises. Credit associations, cooperatives, and the postal savings system are widely patronized. There are large stock exchanges in Tokyo, Osaka, Sapporo, Hiroshima, and Nagoya.

The Japanese labor movement flourished in the postwar period. About one fourth of all Japanese workers—12.4 million—are union members. Most unions are organized by single enterprises rather than by industry or craft. However, local unions have combined to form nationwide federations. The largest are Sohyo (the General Council of Trade Unions of Japan) and Domei (the Japanese Confederation of Labor). Management is organized in Nikkeiren (the Japan Federation of Employers' Association).

Japanese businesses take a keen interest in their employees. They provide many benefits, including low-cost housing, medical care, insurance, paid vacations, and huge year-end bonuses. There is a rigid system of promotions and salary increases in Japanese industry. Employees are traditionally very loyal to their companies, and job turnover is low. A Japanese is likely to spend his entire working life on the job he takes when just out of school.

Japan's success in economic development is based in part upon its many highly trained scientists, engineers, and technicians. The Japanese keep abreast of scientific advances in other countries through professional journals, foreign study and inspection tours, and international conferences. Many large Japanese firms share technical information with companies in the United States and Europe—particularly in the chemical, communications, electronics, synthetic fiber, machinery, steel, and rubber industries.

Japan's investment in basic and applied research has lagged behind that of the leading Western nations despite governmental efforts to promote technological innovation. Japan has been playing a growing role, however, in transmitting modern technology to other Asian nations, especially in Southeast Asia. Many Japanese technicians go abroad to teach or to help assemble Japanese-made plants. Groups of Asians attend Japanese universities and receive advanced scientific and technical training from Japanese firms.

Tourism

The number of foreign visitors to Japan—especially from the United States—has been increasing steadily. Japan abounds in natural scenic beauty, offers a charming combination of traditional and modern facilities, and has a great variety of cultural attractions. Tourism is well organized. There are many modern high-rise hotels, especially in Tokyo, Osaka, and Kyoto, and *ryokan* (Japanese-style inns) may be found throughout the country.

Japan's scientists have boosted its economic development. Shin-Ichiro Tomonaga (1965) (left), Hideki Yukawa (1949) (right), and Leo Esaki (1973) won the Nobel prize in physics.

An increasing number of international gatherings are being held in Japan. Special events have attracted many additional visitors. The most well received of these were the summer Olympics at Tokyo in 1964; Expo '70, Japan's first world's fair, near Osaka in 1970; and the winter Olympics at Sapporo in 1972.

Tourists in search of unspoiled natural scenery can choose from among a large number of national and prefectural parks. There are sweeping views from mountaintops reached by ropeways, cable cars, and automobile toll roads. Other tourist attractions in Japan include the many ancient temples and shrines, the Japanese theater and festivals, and the restaurants and night life of the big cities.

Words to Remember

zaibatsu—the giant business combines of Japan.
Keihin—the industrial area centered upon Tokyo, Kawasaki, and Yokohama.
Chukyo—the industrial area centered upon Nagoya.
Hanshin—the industrial area centered upon Osaka and Kobe.
Sohyo—the General Council of Trade Unions of Japan.
Domei—the Japanese Confederation of Labor.
Nikkeiren—the Japan Federation of Employers' Association.
ryokan—a Japanese-style inn.

Questions to Think About

1. What might be the effect of industrialization on living conditions in Japanese cities? In Japanese rural areas?
2. Spending money on defense is often thought to stimulate a nation's economy. Why then is Japanese industry believed to have benefited from *low* military expenditures?
3. How could the Japanese government induce industries to locate in areas other than the Tokaido Megalopolis?
4. Can Japan's economy continue to maintain its rapid rate of growth? Why or why not?

A Tour of Japan

1. **THE SAPPORO SNOW FESTIVAL,** held in February, is highlighted by a snow sculpture contest.

2. **NIKKO NATIONAL PARK** is the site of spectacular Kegon Falls. Boating is popular on Lake Chuzenji.

3. **THE GINZA** is the world-famous entertainment and shopping district of Japan's capital city, Tokyo.

4. **THE IMPERIAL PALACE,** completed in 1968, replaced the Tokyo palace destroyed in World War II.

5. **THE GREAT BUDDHA** at Kamakura, a huge bronze sculpture, was cast in the mid-13th century.

6. **MOUNT FUJI,** Japan's sacred volcano, is a favorite subject of artists. A Tokaido express streaks past.

7. **THE KINKAKUJI TEMPLE** (Gold Pavilion) in Kyoto was a villa of the Muromachi period.

8. **THE TENJIN FESTIVAL** is held in Osaka each July. A sacred litter is carried to its boat procession.

9

6

7

9. **THE CHILDREN'S PEACE MONUMENT** in Hiroshima commemorates the atomic bombing of the city at the end of World War II.

10. **THE TORII OF THE ITSUKUSHIMA SHRINE** is the largest shrine gateway in Japan. It was erected on Miyajima Island, near Hiroshima, in 1875. Ancient bugaku dances are performed at the shrine.

8

10

KANJI CHARACTERS

橋
Bridge

花
Flower

月
Moon

友
Friend

目
Eye

色
Color

Kanji characters stand for words.

KANA CHARACTERS

	HIRAGANA	KATAKANA
ha	は	ハ
na	な	ナ
ta	た	タ
ba	ば	バ
mi	み	ミ
shi	し	シ
ru	る	ル
ku	く	ク

Kana characters stand for the sounds of syllables.

THE JAPANESE LANGUAGE

The language of Japan has many dialects, and speakers of different dialects do not always understand each other. But almost everyone in Japan uses standard Japanese as well as the dialect of his home area. Standard Japanese, originally the dialect spoken by the educated people of Tokyo, is now taught and understood throughout the country.

Broadly speaking, the accent in Japanese is musical. To say "bridge" (*hashi*) in standard Japanese, the voice begins with a low pitch on *ha* and rises on *shi*. If the voice is high for *ha* and low for *shi*, the word means "chopsticks." The pitch of a word can also change in a sentence. As a word, *hi* (fire) has a low pitch. But in the sentence *Hi ga deta* (Fire has broken out), the pitch pattern is high for *hi*, low for the rest of the sentence.

Japanese sentences are not put together in the same way as sentences in English. For one thing, the verb comes at the end of a statement in Japanese. In Japanese, the word order for "Kenji read the book" is "Kenji the book read." In addition, two language particles—*wa* and *wo*—are added. *Wa* often follows the subject of a clause (Kenji). *Wo* follows the direct object of a verb (the book). So the sentence in Japanese is *Kenji wa hon wo yomimashita*. To make a question of a statement, the particle *ka* is usually added. Thus *Kenji wa hon wo yomimashita ka* means "Did Kenji read the book?"

In Japanese, different styles of speech are used to show degrees of politeness and familiarity. A plain style is generally used in speaking to close friends. For strangers, a polite style may be used. To show honor and respect, a deferential style is often used toward parents, older people, teachers, and so on. Different styles are also used in talking *about* people and things. One of them, the exalted style, is almost entirely limited to references to the emperor and the imperial family.

The Japanese writing system is unique. Chinese characters, called *kanji*, were adopted by the Japanese more than 1,500 years ago. Because Japanese is very different from Chinese, however, additional sets of characters, called *kana*, were developed. After World War II the Japanese government modified the system of writing. Kanji were reduced from many thousands of characters to 1,850 basic characters, and their forms were simplified. Many words are written with kanji only. Some words are written with kana (*hiragana* or *katakana*) only. But most Japanese writing is a mixture of kanji and kana. In newspapers and magazines, Japanese is usually printed from top to bottom, in columns running from right to left. But in many textbooks, Japanese is printed horizontally from left to right. In the Japanese culture, the surname, or family name, comes before a person's given name.

THE LITERATURE OF JAPAN

Poetry is an important part of Japanese culture. Occasions of many kinds are celebrated with poems, and thousands of poems are submitted for the poetry prize awarded by the emperor each New Year. Most Japanese compose short poems, called *haiku* and *tanka*. Japanese poems, which usually do not rhyme, are based on a syllable count. A haiku is a three-line poem, with 5 syllables in the first line, 7 syllables in the second, and 5 syllables in the third. A tanka has five lines, with 5, 7, 5, 7, and 7 syllables. Because haiku and tanka are short, they can only suggest a mood or a picture; the listener or reader has to fill in the details. Basho (1644–94), who has been regarded by many as Japan's greatest poet, was a master of haiku. A notable tanka poet was Tsurayuki Ki-no (884–946), one of Japan's "thirty-six poetic immortals."

Japanese literature is noted for distinctive forms of drama as well as of poetry. The *no*, or *noh*, play combines recitation, music, and slow dancing. No plays can be considered scenes from the ceremonious life of lords and ladies during Japan's Middle Ages. The mood of these plays is usually serious—often tragic—and they are noted for their fine poetry, which is chanted by the actors and chorus. Because no plays are short, five different types of plays are presented at a time, each with its own music. The first is usually about a god, the second about a warrior, the third about a woman. Japan's outstanding no dramatists were Motokiyo Zeami (Seami) (1363–1443) and his father, Kiyotsugu Kanami (1333–84).

Like the no, the Japanese puppet play is serious drama combining words, music, and dancing. Perhaps the greatest writer of puppet drama, called *bunraku*, was Chikamatsu (1653–1725). His plays fall into two groups: heroic plays, often set in Japan's Middle Ages, and domestic tragedies—for example, 'The Love Suicides at Amijima'—which give a naturalistic picture of middle-class life.

For elaborate spectacle, *Kabuki* drama has no rival. Kabuki plays are distinguished by sensationalism and melodrama. One of the most famous Kabuki plays is 'Chushingura', about 47 *samurai* who avenge their lord's death and then commit *hara-kiri* as required by the law of the time. (*See also* subhead "The Performing Arts of Japan" later in this section.)

Japanese prose works tend to be series of loosely connected episodes. Diaries and books of random thoughts, which lend themselves to this style, are typical of Japanese prose literature. Early Japanese novels consisted of series of incidents, each incident built around a poem. Perhaps the greatest work of Japanese literature is 'The Tale of Genji', an episodic novel by Lady Murasaki (975?–1025?). Most of the works of Saikaku (1642–93), the outstanding novelist of the Tokugawa period, are really collections of short stories based on a single theme. In many modern novels it is common to find loosely related incidents. (*See also* Japanese Literature.)

Yasunari Kawabata (center, facing camera) was awarded the 1968 Nobel prize in literature. He is pictured at an outdoor tea ceremony in a Kyoto temple.

Shown below are part of a poem scroll by a 17th-century poet, a section from the 'Pages of Collected Poems by Thirty-Six Poetic Immortals', and an illustration from the novel 'The Tale of Genji'.

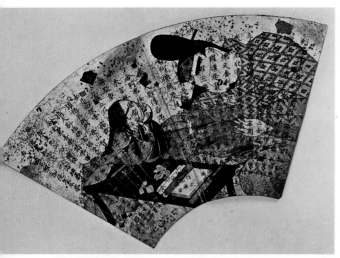

The 'Hokekyo Sutra', upon which the Nichiren sect of Buddhism is based, adorns this painted fan. A Japanese national treasure, it is kept at Shitennoji Temple in Osaka.

'Girl with a Maple Branch', by Katsukawa Shunsho (1726–93), is a kakemono painted on silk. Shunsho's famous paintings of Kabuki actors became woodcuts.

THE FINE ARTS OF JAPAN

The fine arts of modern Japan are similar to those of many Western countries. However, Japanese classical works of art are unique in the philosophy, methods, and materials used in their creation. These works include paintings and sculptures, as well as products of the decorative arts, such as pottery and porcelains, lacquers, textiles, and woodcuts.

Painting

In classical Japanese painting, black ink and watercolors were used on tissue-thin silk or *washi* (Japanese paper). Often the artist used only black ink, achieving a sense of color in the gradations from deep, luminous black to silvery gray. One-color paintings made in this way are called *sumi-e*.

Although classical Japanese paintings were realistic, they were never photographic. Instead, the artist used only a few brushstrokes to suggest the crumbly texture of a boulder; a hard-edged, rocky cliff; the gnarled trunk and rustling foliage of a tree; or the feathers of a bird. Unpainted areas of silk or paper created a sense of space and depth. Through economy of line and careful composition, the artist presented a distillation of his subject, leaving the viewer to fill in the details.

Classical Japanese paintings were "studio pictures." The artist did not go into the countryside with paints and easel. Instead, following a walk in the hills or along a stream, he returned to his studio to paint his impressions. The paintings usually took the form of hanging scrolls called *kakemono*, hand scrolls called *emakimono*, large folding screens, sliding doors, or fans. The hand scrolls, often 30 feet or more in length, are unrolled from right to left, the viewer enjoying only as much of the painting as may be exposed between his outstretched hands.

After Buddhism was introduced in Japan in the mid-6th century, great temples were built. These served not only as religious shrines but also as centers of art and learning. The numerous deities of Buddhism were depicted in paintings and sculptures. Artists, governed by precise descriptions in the *sutras* (holy texts) created likenesses of the Buddha, his disciples, and minor deities, as well as complex map-like representations of gods surrounding a central Buddha. These figures were painted or carved to embellish the temples and instruct the devout. Long narrative hand scrolls record in fine line and rich color the lives, journeys, and campaigns of important Buddhist priests and nobles. The names of most early painters, many of them priests, are no longer known.

Sumi-e developed rapidly during the Muromachi period (1392–1573) of Japanese art. It was fostered by Zen Buddhism, which stressed simplicity and was influenced by similar examples from China. However, while Japan was subjected over the centuries to successive waves of influence from China, the artists assimilated the foreign styles and in almost every instance made them uniquely their own.

During the Muromachi period and the Momoyama period (1573–1615), distinctive schools of painting emerged and individual artists established their fame. The Buddhist monk Sesshu (1420–1506) perfected black-and-white landscape painting in the Chinese tradition. The Kano school, founded by Masanobu Kano (1434–1530) and continued by his family, developed a distinctively Japanese style. Folding screens and sliding door panels in rich colors and patterns, often on a ground of gold or silver, were created to enliven the austere grandeur of 16th- and 17th-century castle interiors. The creators of these works were called "the great decorators." The Kano school remained dominant well into the Edo, or Tokugawa, period (1615–1867). It shared favor with traditional Chinese-style ink painting as well as a new artistic style called *ukiyo-e*, paintings depicting the life of common people.

Woodcuts

Woodcuts were made in Japan as early as the 11th century. But this art form enjoyed its greatest popularity from the mid-17th through the 19th centuries. The earliest woodcuts, which portrayed Buddhist patriarchs and deities, were executed in black with strong, rhythmic lines and areas of simple pattern. Occasionally, rich red-oranges, mustard yellows, and greens were added by hand. Early color prints, developed around 1740, were also restricted to three colors, usually green or pinkish-red, and sometimes yellow. True color prints, using many wood blocks and called *nishiki-e* (brocade pictures), were developed in 1765. A print bore the name of the artist who designed it. The carving and printing, however, were done by two other craftsmen.

Japanese woodcuts are probably the finest expression of the ukiyo-e movement. Courtesans, Kabuki actors, and scenes from Kabuki dramas were popular subjects. Moronobu Hishikawa (1618–94) is credited with beginning the ukiyo-e tradition of printmaking. The era of the full-color print starts with the work of Harunobu Suzuki (1725–70). The early 19th century brought both the full maturity and the gradual degeneration of this art form. The landscape artists Hokusai Katsushika (1760–1849) and Hiroshige Ando (1797–1858) were the last outstanding woodcut artists of the ukiyo-e. In the 20th century a modern movement in printmaking developed, called *sosaku hanga* (creative prints).

Sculpture

Japanese sculpture of the pre-Buddhist period is perhaps best represented by the *haniwa* (clay cylinders), which date from the 3d to the 5th century. These images of red clay were sometimes elaborately modeled in the forms of animals, birds, and human figures. Placed fencelike around tomb mounds of the imperial family and important court figures, the haniwa seem to have served the dual function of preventing soil erosion and providing the deceased with objects they had enjoyed during their lives.

Traditional woodcuts are still produced in modern Japan. The printing blocks, usually cherry wood, are carved with the grain rather than across it as is done in Western nations.

This haniwa warrior figure dates from the 5th century A.D. The cylindrical bases of the haniwa were used to hold the images firmly in the ground.

Following the introduction of Buddhism to Japan, the development of sculpture paralleled that of painting. Numerous icons depicted the growing number of deities. Sculpture closely followed earlier Chinese examples which had been transmitted through Korea. Important images were cast in bronze, though wood was also favored. In later periods, wood and clay were increasingly preferred, as was dry lacquer. This consisted of successive coats of lacquer applied to cloth over a clay or wood core that was later removed. Since stone was scarce and of poor quality, it was almost never used in sculpture. Most of the best surviving sculptures were made by unknown masters.

A noteworthy 8th-century tendency, which continued through the Kamakura period (1185–1392), was the portraitlike quality of much of the sculpture. This may in part be attributed to the growing preference for the dry-lacquer technique, which allowed greater inventiveness on the part of the artist. The finished product was light but durable. An innovation in wood sculpture—the use of small blocks ingeniously fitted together, rather than a single block or log—also provided the artist with greater freedom of expression.

Japanese sculpture reached its peak during the Kamakura period. Although distinctive pieces were made in later eras, sculpture never again attained the position it had enjoyed in the preceding seven centuries. Most of the important sculptures have remained in the temples for which they were created.

Decorative Arts

The Japanese decorative arts include the making of pottery, porcelains, lacquers, and textiles. It is

The woodcut 'Winter' was made by Kunihiro Amano in 1957. All but a small part is shown here. Modern Japanese printmakers carve and print their blocks as well as design them.

for such works that Japan is perhaps best known.

The earliest examples of Japanese artistic expression are earthenware vessels called *jomon* (rope-patterned) and the later, but still archaic, *yayoi* pottery. Some jomon specimens may date as far back as 6000 B.C. The style continued until about the 2d century B.C., when it was supplanted by the more finely executed yayoi.

The process of making true porcelain was not introduced into Japan until the 16th century. Elegantly patterned products found favor with the nobility and court circles. By contrast, native rough pottery enjoyed great popularity in intellectual circles and was especially favored for use in the tea ceremony.

Many well-known painters also applied their skills to allied arts. Koetsu Honnami (1558–1637), famed for his calligraphy, or decorative writing, was also a gifted potter and lacquer designer. Kenzan Ogata (1663–1743) executed in pottery the designs of his brother Korin (1658–1716), who was renowned for bold decorative paintings.

The dry-lacquer technique was used not only for sculpture but also for decorative accessories such as trays, tables, small chests, containers for tea and candy, and sumptuously fitted picnic boxes. Sprinklings of gold and silver powder and burnished and cut-gold foil—alone or combined with inlays of shell, mother-of-pearl, or metal—provided a bold contrast to the red, black, brown, and green lacquer surfaces. The 18th- and 19th-century love of splendor and rich decoration was mirrored in handsomely brocaded silks favored by the court and clergy. The latter, under vows of poverty, cut brocades into small squares and pieced them together again so that their fine garments would simulate the patched clothing of leaner years. Even the simple folk designs worn by the poor reflected the taste of Japanese weavers.

Architecture and Gardens

Japanese architecture, like painting and sculpture, made its greatest advances following the introduction of Buddhism. As with sculpture, wood was the primary material. The design of traditional Japanese architecture emphasizes horizontal lines. Even in taller structures like pagodas, the use of sloping roofs helps minimize the impression of height.

Great temples and monasteries and feudal castles and palaces are the major architectural monuments. The temples are characterized by vast halls and soaring roofs. Based on Chinese examples, the temples and storied pagodas feature elaborate bracketing systems to support their roofs. Major constructions mirror the taste of the periods which produced them. Horyuji Temple near Nara reflects the simple elegance favored in the 7th century. The Toshogu Shrine in Nikko illustrates the opulence of the Edo period.

Secular architecture of nearly all periods reveals the Japanese love for refined simplicity. Interior and exterior finishes depend on the fine grain of wood and textured stucco.

Origami—Japanese Paper Folding

Origami, the Japanese art of paper folding, may have originated in the 8th century in connection with the Dolls' Festival, now celebrated annually on March 3. On this day children would make paper dolls which they threw into a river to carry away the evil spirits hiding in their bodies. Today both adults and children enjoy making origami decorations, puppets, dolls, and animals.

Origami figures can be made with any thin, crisp paper that takes a sharp crease. Origami paper is usually square, brightly colored on one side, and lightly colored or white on the other side. Colored inks or paints may be used to decorate a completed origami figure. Origami figures can be so constructed that they seem to move and fly.

Modern origami is a symbolic art as well as a hobby. A paper crane or a tortoise attached to an important gift signifies a wish for good fortune and long life. Paper carps, signifying persistence and aspiration, are flown during the May 5 Children's Day festival.

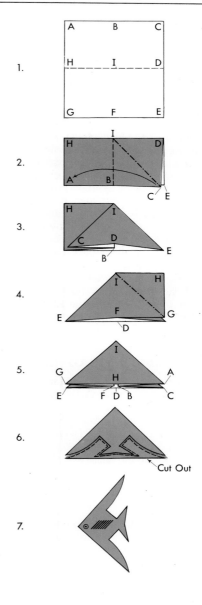

HOW TO MAKE AN ORIGAMI FISH

1. Place a sheet of square origami paper on a table with the light side up. Lettering may be added lightly as shown for aid in folding.

2. Fold the top half of the sheet over the bottom half so that the colored side appears. Fold the right side over the left side. Unfold, leaving creases IB and IF (in back). Fold corner D under so that it meets point F. Unfold, leaving creases IC and IE (in back).

3. Bring corner C up and over to corner A so that point D meets point B, refolding creases IB and IC. Press paper flat.

4. Turn paper over. Fold corner H under so that it meets point D. Unfold, leaving creases IG and IA (in back). Bring corner G up and over to corner E, refolding creases IF and IG.

5. Press paper flat.

6. Cut out shaded areas to form fins.

7. Decorate the completed figure if desired. Several fish can be fashioned into a mobile or used to make an ocean or aquarium scene.

53

Handsome gardens are created to so complement the buildings they surround that the landscape and structures appear to be part of one another. Moss, trees, pebbles, and rocks may be combined with artificial hills, ponds, and a stream to suggest the natural beauty of a lake, seascape, or mountain waterfall. Profound simplicity is achieved in the garden of Ryoanji Temple near Kyoto, for example, by the use of five artfully placed rock formations set in moss in a patterned field of white sand. Whatever its proportions or the materials used, the Japanese garden is designed to invite entry and inspire meditation.

Interior Decoration and Home Arts

The art of raising *bonsai* (dwarfed potted trees) has enabled the Japanese to admire nature in an indoor setting. Bonsai are able to bear fruit and to drop their leaves in season, thus reproducing nature in miniature. A skillful bonsai artist can prune, bend, and shape branches to suggest trees standing tall and upright in a field or bent and gnarled by age or weather. The beauty of a natural landscape is evoked in the viewer's imagination. (*See also* Bonsai.)

Another means of enjoying nature in the home is through the arrangement of flowers, which has been refined in Japan to an art known as *ikebana*. Unlike Western arrangements which emphasize the color and form of flowers, ikebana favors the flowing lines of stems, leaves, and branches. In any arrangement, the plant materials used must convey a feeling of continuing growth as well as be symbolic of time and the season. Full blossoms might suggest the past; buds, the future. A full and spreading arrangement might suggest summer; a sparse one, autumn. A graceful floral design and a symbolic ornamental scroll often decorate the alcove called the *tokonoma*, the place of honor in a Japanese home.

Chanoyu, the ceremonial art of making tea, is a notable aesthetic discipline in Japan. Through the delicate flavor of the tea and the simplicity of the ceremony, participants in the ritual hope to achieve serenity and an understanding of true beauty. (*See also* Tea.)

THE PERFORMING ARTS OF JAPAN

The Japanese have great respect for their ancient, traditional performing arts. At the same time they are attracted by new, more modern forms. As a result, a Japanese who enjoys a performance of *bugaku*, an ancient musical dance of the imperial court, may also take pleasure in a concert of contemporary Western music played by an excellent Japanese symphony orchestra.

One reason for the vitality of the performing arts in Japan is that "performance" is an essential part of the nation's life. The ceremonies of the native Shinto religion include music and dance. A Japanese wanting to honor the gods pays for a performance of the sacred dance *kagura* at a shrine. During the *bon* festival, a Buddhist celebration for the souls of the dead, the young people of a community dance in a circle around a drum tower. In the summer, groups of young men carrying a portable shrine dance and chant through the city streets. All such dances are related to the Japanese love and worship of nature.

Rhythm, singing, and chanting are also part of everyday work in Japan—pulling a net from the sea, felling timber, even erecting a telephone pole. Ancient music and dance accompany the planting and harvesting of rice. Music and rhythmical movement closely combine dancing, acting, and instrumental and vocal music. In any traditional Japanese stage performance, it is difficult to say where the dancing stops and the acting begins.

The Japanese performing arts differ greatly from those of the West. Traditional Japanese music does not use Western keys and scales. The drums, stringed instruments, and flutes produce sounds not usually heard from Western instruments, though the *koto* (Japanese harp) comes close to sounding Western. Traditional Japanese singing uses a different system of voice production than that of the West, and the traditional dance employs patterns of body movement unfamiliar in the West. A traditional Japanese actor does not think he should look like a "real person" when he is performing. From his youth the Japanese performing artist is trained in the strict imitation of his teacher. This method insures that traditional techniques of performance are preserved in a continuous, almost unchanged, artistic heritage.

Before 1640, foreign influences on the Japanese performing arts came only from the Asian mainland. But, as is typical in Japan, the borrowed materials were refined into a principally Japanese expression.

Gagaku and Bugaku

Classical *gagaku* music was introduced into Japan from China in the 8th century A.D. It combined musical forms absorbed from Korea, Manchuria, Persia, India, and Indochina. Gagaku merged with Japanese music around 850.

Wind, stringed, and percussion instruments are used in gagaku performances, which are known as *kangen* when performed alone. When gagaku is accompanied by dancing, it is called bugaku. A single dancer or one or more pairs of dancers perform with great symmetry of movement. The dances may be slow or spirited depending on whether they are ceremonial dances, military dances, or dances for children. A bugaku may tell a story, but the story is generally not learned from a view of the dance alone.

No Plays

The medieval dance drama of the no theater came in part from Chinese sources. Actors in no plays perform on a usually bare stage about 18 feet square and on a narrow runway leading to the stage from the dressing room. They are accompanied by drums, a high-pitched flute, and chanting by a chorus of six or eight men. All parts, including female roles, are played by men and boys. There are only two important roles—the *shite* (principal character) and the *waki* (subordinate character).

Both the shite and the waki wear handsomely embroidered costumes patterned upon medieval court dress. The shite usually wears a painted mask carved from wood. Joy, sorrow, or anger may be represented by slightly changing the position of the mask on the actor's face. Different masks are used to represent men, women, elderly persons, gods, and demons. In most of the 240 no plays performed in Japan today, the shite changes his costume and mask for the second half of the performance to reveal his true character. He may change, for example, from a beautiful woman to a demon or from a boy to a warrior. Often, the waki is a Buddhist priest and the shite is the ghost of a person who, suffering for evil he committed during his lifetime, seeks and obtains help from the priest for the peace of his soul.

A no performance neither looks nor sounds like real life. Movement is extremely slow. If the play requires, for example, a boat or a hut, these are represented by a skeletal framework which only suggests their shape. A folding fan in the hands of an actor may represent a variety of objects—a sword, a letter, the rising moon, or falling rain. The text is ancient poetry, difficult even for many Japanese to understand.

The traditional no program consists of five plays with short comic pieces called *kyogen* performed between them. The usual program is now three plays, each lasting an hour or longer, and two kyogen. The kyogen are a complete contrast to the serious no plays, for they are acted vigorously and amusingly and deal with such matters as servants outwitting their masters or husbands their wives.

Bunraku

Toward 1700 a new form of theater appeared in Japan. Called bunraku, it combines the manipulation of puppets with a narrative accompanied by music played on the *samisen*, a three-stringed, banjo-shaped, plucked instrument. Each puppet is about half life-size and is handled by a team of three men in a fashion unique to Japan. By means of strings inside the puppet's head, the chief manipulator controls the movable mouth, eyebrows, and eyelids, as well as the right arm and hand of the doll. His assistants animate the rest of the puppet. The operators are silent but visible to the audience throughout the play.

Unlike the no stage, the bunraku stage uses elaborate scenery and various techniques and devices for changing scenes rapidly. At one side of the stage are seated one or more samisen players and the narrator-singer, who chants both the descriptive passages and the spoken words of all the characters. Such precise coordination and teamwork is demanded among the operators, the musician, and the narrator that they must all have many years of training.

Bunraku developed two kinds of plays. *Jidaimono* deals with historical materials and the warrior class, while *sewamono* is concerned with the life of the commoner. Some of the greatest Japanese dramatists wrote bunraku plays. Among them was Chikamatsu, who is sometimes called "the Shakespeare of Japan."

Hayashi-kata (no accompanists) sit before the rear stage wall, which is decorated with a painting of an ancient pine. The *ji-utai* (no chorus) sits to the left of the actors.

The body of a bunraku puppet is a hollow, cloth-covered bamboo frame. The puppet heads are varied to portray characters of different sexes, ages, and personalities.

The Kabuki drama 'Kagami-jishi' is patterned after a no play. A shy young maiden performs a lion dance and, overcome by the animal's spirit, becomes the lion itself.

Another was Izumo Takeda (1691–1756), whose 'Kanadehon Chushingura' (1748), or 'Chushingura' for short, is a popular Japanese play in both the bunraku and Kabuki theaters. Its theme—loyalty to a master— is a common one in the puppet theater.

Bunraku declined in popularity after the mid-1700's. It survives only in Osaka, though tours are made to other cities. It is regarded as a "cultural property" by the Japanese government, which supports it through the Japan Broadcasting Corporation.

Kabuki

Kabuki, a form of Japanese theater using live actors, began around the same time as bunraku. It originated in Kyoto with new kinds of dances performed by a woman named Okuni in the early 1600's. These became highly popular, and Okuni was imitated by other actresses and actors. But the Japanese government, deciding that the performances were immoral, decreed in 1629 that women could no longer appear on the stage. Women's roles were taken over by men, and this practice continues in modern Kabuki.

A typical Kabuki program may include a dance based upon a no play or a kyogen, part of doll theater jidaimono, and acts from plays written especially for the Kabuki in the 18th and 19th centuries. No important Kabuki plays were written after 1900, and this theater is in many ways a living museum of the Japanese performing arts. It is now based in Tokyo theaters and attracts large audiences.

The performance of a Kabuki program requires highly skilled actors, trained from childhood in dance, voice, and acrobatics, who are capable of playing a wide variety of parts, including female roles. An actor who plays the part of a woman is called an *onnagata*. Among the Kabuki characters are horses, foxes, dogs, and demons, all played by actors.

Kabuki visual effects are varied and spectacular. Huge settings change on a revolving stage in plain view of the audience. Scenery and actors rise from or disappear into the stage floor on elevators. Actors perform portions of the program in the midst of the audience on the *hanamichi*, a runway about six feet wide extending from the rear of the auditorium to the stage. Music, most frequently that of the samisen, is used throughout, the musicians performing either on the stage or in a room at the side of it.

In some Kabuki plays the actors wear striking white, red, and black makeup to create the effect of power and strength. Elaborate costumes, which can be changed on stage, may weigh as much as 50 pounds. Masses of warriors dance and somersault in scenes of battle. The dramatic poses of an actor are accompanied by the beating of wooden clappers on the stage.

Television, Western Music, and Motion Pictures

Thanks to television, no, bunraku, and Kabuki are now seen by larger audiences than ever. The Japanese government television station regularly broadcasts performances, from short excerpts to long Kabuki programs. The entire nine-hour bunraku production of the 11-act 'Kanadehon Chushingura' has been televised. The national network also televises modern plays, opera, modern dance, ballet, and the programs of its own symphony orchestra.

Western music, which has been taught in Japanese schools since the 1870's, is as popular as the traditional music of ancient Japan. Many Japanese cities have permanent orchestras and thriving musical conservatories. Internationally known orchestra, ballet, and opera companies visit Japan. Similarly, the works of contemporary Japanese composers trained in Western music, such as Toru Takemitsu and Toshiro Mayazumi, are played in Europe and the United States.

Motion pictures have been another Western influence on the Japanese performing arts. Film making in Japan began early in the 20th century with screen adaptations of traditional literary masterpieces and Kabuki drama. The cinematic art declined during the war years of the 1930's and 1940's.

After World War II many Japanese films became internationally famous for their artistic and technical quality. Akira Kurosawa's 'Rashomon' won the grand prize at the Venice Film Festival in 1951. Other notable films are 'The Rickshaw Man', 'Bushido: Samurai Saga', 'Seven Samurai', and 'Kagemusha'. Styles ranged from the avant-garde 'Woman in the Dunes' to the violent 'In the Realm of the Senses'.

THE MARTIAL ARTS

The martial arts in Japan originated with medieval warriors, the samurai, who mastered at least one or two of them for use in battle. Today they are more important as competitive sports and as aids to physical and mental fitness. The martial arts were traditionally acquired through the family, but schools to teach them now thrive in Japan.

Sumo (Japanese wrestling) is one of the country's most popular sports. Professional sumo matches are held in rings of sand between two huge wrestlers dressed only in *mawashi* (loincloths). The actual bout is preceded by a ritual during which the wrestlers face each other, squatting and touching the ground with their fists. The match does not begin until both wrestlers come up at the same time. It ends only when a wrestler has been pushed out of the ring or when any part of a wrestler's body except his feet touches the ground. Several professional sumo tournaments are held each year in Japan. A grand champion wrestler is called *Yokozuna*.

Judo developed from *jujitsu*, an art of self-defense that was popular during the Tokugawa period. Judo has three basic strategies—attacking the opponent's vital points, throwing the opponent, and grappling. One referee and two assistants preside at a judo match. The winner is the first man to throw his opponent to the floor, to lift his opponent over his shoulders, to pin him down until he gives up, or to pin him for at least 30 seconds. If neither contestant accomplishes any of these goals, the match is awarded to the more aggressive of the two. Colored belts are worn to indicate degrees of mastery in judo.

During the Ashikaga period (1340–1540) kendo, then called *kata-kenjutsu*, stressed form over action. After about 1700, however, it became the lively sport that it is today.

Aikido also developed from jujitsu. In aikido, the purpose is to throw the opponent to the floor or to attack him at his weakest point by applying a painful hold. The opponent is then easier to overcome. Opponents in aikido, unlike judo contestants, try to stay apart from each other as much as possible. Aikido does not require great muscular strength. It is practiced to enhance body flexibility and to foster graceful movement.

Karate evolved in ancient China and was introduced into Japan in the 17th century. Only in the 20th century, however, did it gain wide popularity. Karate involves jabbing, hitting, and kicking at the most vulnerable parts of the opponent's body. One of the most destructive of the martial arts, karate is usually practiced on tiles, boards, and other hard objects rather than on human opponents.

Kendo (Japanese fencing) developed in ancient Japan. In kendo, two opponents hit or jab at each other with bamboo swords. Both wear protective bamboo armor, leg padding, and thick gloves. In a match, a point is given to the fencer who makes a clean hit on the throat, head, body, or hand of his opponent. The first to make two points is declared the winner.

Kyudo (Japanese archery) was used in early Japan for fishing and hunting. Later it became a military art. In medieval times, samurai displayed their skill as bowmen in exhibitions. After the introduction of firearms in the 16th century, however, kyudo declined as an effective technique of combat and became a sport. Kyudo archers use a seven-foot bow made of wood glued to bamboo. Arrows consist of a bamboo shaft, three feathers, and an arrowhead. Each contestant in a match usually shoots 10 to 20 arrows. The contestant hitting the target with the greatest number of arrows is the winner.

JAPANESE PHILOSOPHY AND RELIGION

Japan's religious philosophy derives from both native and foreign sources. Shinto originated in early Japan as a combination of nature and ancestor worship. Among its many gods were the creator, the moon, stars, mountains, rivers, seas, fire, and some animals and vegetables. Modern Shinto teaches that the gods are present in the mind of the individual.

Shinto became the state religion after the Meiji Restoration of 1868. As such, it assumed that the

A Buddhist monk meditates near a peaceful garden. There are more than ten leading Buddhist sects in Japan. Each differs in its rituals and its beliefs about the path to salvation.

Japanese were descendants of the sun-goddess Amaterasu and members of one family headed by the emperor. The nationalists and militarists who rose to power in the 1930's adapted Shinto to their purposes, telling the Japanese that they were destined to rule the world. After World War II, state support of Shinto was abolished and the emperor disclaimed his divinity.

Shinto is now split among many sects. Some of them place greater stress on rituals than on philosophic content. Shinto is also valued because it is unique to Japan and creates a bond between the individual, his ancestors, and his nation.

Confucianism, which originated in China, was introduced into Japan from Korea around the 3d century A.D. Its ethical teachings were adopted primarily by the aristocracy, though the principles of absolute obedience to one's father and lord also greatly influenced the samurai. During World War II, Confucian rules of obedience were used to arouse patriotism. After the war, Confucianism was excluded from the Japanese educational curriculum. (*See also* Confucius.)

Buddhism arose in India and was introduced into Japan from Korea in the 6th century. Japanese Buddhism teaches that all men should aim to become Buddha. The worship of ancestors through funeral and memorial rites are the most universal practices of the many Buddhist sects.

Christianity was introduced into Japan in the 16th century by Francis Xavier, a Spanish Jesuit. During the Tokugawa shogunate, Japanese Christians were severely persecuted. After Japan was opened to the West in the 19th century, Japanese Christians became involved in social-welfare movements. Many prominent Japanese intellectuals are Christians.

Words to Remember

kana—Japanese characters for syllable sounds.
haiku—a 17-syllable Japanese poem.
tanka—a 31-syllable Japanese poem.
no, or *noh*—medieval Japanese dance drama.
bunraku—a Japanese puppet drama.
Kabuki—a traditional form of Japanese drama.
ukiyo-e—art movement of Edo period depicting everyday life, places, and people in Japan.
ikebana—the Japanese art of flower arrangement.
samisen—a banjolike, three-stringed instrument.
sumo—Japanese wrestling.
judo—a martial art based on holds.
karate—a martial art based on jabs and kicks.

Questions to Think About

1. In what ways do Japan's traditional fine arts resemble and differ from those of the West?
2. Give reasons why the traditional Japanese performing arts do not strive for realism.
3. Compare the traditional Japanese martial arts with those of the medieval European knights.
4. Has modernization made religion less important to the people of Japan?

JAPAN — Natural Features

Land

The islands of Japan are the exposed tops of massive undersea ridges that rise from the floor of the Pacific Ocean on the eastern edge of the Asian continental shelf. The islands lie between the Japan Deep—a north-south, 28,000-foot-deep trench in the Pacific—and the 10,000–12,000-foot-deep Sea of Japan. The Japan Deep is east of the islands; the Sea of Japan, west of the islands.

The islands of Japan are geologically young and unstable. They have been subjected to considerable folding, faulting, and volcanic activity. As a result, the land surface of the Japanese islands is dominated by mountains and hills which divide them into hundreds of subunits. This creates a landscape of great variety and beauty and gives Japanese life a small-scale compactness. The largest and highest mountain mass, part of which is known as the Japanese Alps, is in central Honshu. From it mountain chains extend northward to Hokkaido and southwest to Shikoku and Kyushu. These mountain chains are gouged by many short river valleys and interrupted by many small lowland plains.

Only one fourth of Japan's land surface has a slope of less than 15 degrees. Most Japanese plains have been formed by river deposits and lie along the seacoast. The largest lowland, the Kanto Plain of east-central Honshu, has an area of only about 6,000 square miles. It contains the city of Tokyo. Among the nation's smaller plains are the Nobi (Nagoya) Plain and the Kansai (Osaka, Kyoto, and Kobe) Plain.

The numerous rivers of Japan are short and have small drainage basins. Only two of them are more than 200 miles long—the Shinano and the Tone, both on Honshu. Of the two, the Shinano is the longest (228 miles) and the Tone drains the largest area (about 7,100 square miles).

Japan's rivers generally have steep gradients and carry heavy loads of sediment from the mountains to the lowlands. On the lowlands they are usually shallow and braided and flow through gravel-filled beds. Often they have built-up natural levees and are elevated above the river plains. Their flow rates vary greatly with the seasonal rain.

Although of little use for navigation, the rivers of Japan are used intensively for irrigation, urban water supply, and the generation of electricity. Floods are common, especially during the typhoon season, and are highly destructive in the heavily populated river valleys and plains. Japan has few lakes. The largest is Lake Biwa, in west-central Honshu.

Japan's coastline is unusually long in relation to the nation's total land area. The Pacific coast has many deep indentations, among them Tokyo and Ise bays on Honshu and the Inland Sea between Honshu and Shi-

Sea of Okhotsk
Pt. Soya
HOKKAIDO
MT. DAISETSU (7,513 FT.)
Tsugaru Strait
HONSHU
Sea of Japan
Shinano R.
Tone R.
Hida R.
MT. FUJI (12,389 FT.)
L. Biwa
Inland Sea
MT. ISHIZUCHI (6,499 FT.)
SHIKOKU
MT. KUJU (5,866 FT.)
KYUSHU
PACIFIC OCEAN
East China Sea

0   100   200
Miles

| Sea Level | 100 m. 328 ft. | 200 m. 656 ft. | 500 m. 1,640 ft. | 1,000 m. 3,281 ft. | 2,000 m. 6,562 ft. | 5,000 m. 16,404 ft. |

Much of Japan's coast is hilly and heavily forested. The country contains thousands of small islands, like these along the northwest coast of Kyushu.

koku. The indentations are separated by rugged peninsulas and headlands. Among them are the Boso and Izu peninsulas. The west coast of Kyushu is also deeply indented, and there are many small offshore islands. The Sea of Japan coast of Honshu, however, is much straighter and has long stretches of sand dunes and beach ridges.

Japan's numerous volcanoes and frequent earthquakes are evidence of the instability of the rocks underlying the country. It has about 200 volcanoes and volcanic groups, of which about 60 have been active in recorded history. Some of the volcanoes are cone-shaped and rise to the highest elevations in Japan, while others are calderas, or lake-filled depressions where cones once stood.

Mount Fuji (12,389 feet), the famous volcanic cone, is the highest peak in Japan. It has been dormant since 1707. Mount Asama in central Honshu and Mount Sakurajima in southern Kyushu are well-known active volcanoes. Among the most notable calderas are Mount Aso in Kyushu and Mount Akan in Hokkaido. There are hot springs in the volcanic zones.

In Japan, the heaviest winter snows fall in mountain areas, on Hokkaido, and on the northwest coast of Honshu.

Undersea earthquakes in the northern Pacific basin stir up unusually large *tsunamis*, or "tidal waves," which are very destructive when they reach the Japanese coast. Severe earthquakes that do damage over small areas occur about every five or six years in Japan. One of the worst was the Great Kanto Earthquake of 1923, which combined with fire and tsunami to wipe out much of Tokyo and Yokohama. More than 100,000 lives were lost.

Climate

For a small nation, Japan has a great variety of climatic conditions. This is because its islands have a long latitudinal spread and are in the zone where the conflicting air masses of the Asian continent and of the Pacific Ocean meet and interact. The continental air masses make for more extreme temperatures, both in winter and in summer, and result in large annual temperature ranges. But their effect is moderated by the strong marine influence, which also produces high humidity and abundant rainfall. Japan's rugged topography also makes for many local variations in weather and climate.

During the winter, Japan is primarily under the influence of cold air masses moving out of Siberia, deep in the Asian interior. Biting northwest winds pass over the Sea of Japan and cross the islands of Japan. Moisture picked up over the Sea of Japan is deposited on Japan's west coast in the form of heavy snows that are among the deepest in the world.

During the summer, Japan is under the influence of air moving in from the Pacific Ocean. Southeast winds prevail, making the summer months warm and humid. The cycle of the seasons brings frequent, often sharp, changes in the weather, especially during the spring and autumn months.

Japan's climate, especially along the coasts, is also affected by two ocean currents—the warm Kuroshio, or Japan Current, from the south, and the cold Oyashio, or Okhotsk Current, from the north. The two currents meet off northeastern Honshu. The Kuroshio, on the lee side of Japan in winter, has little warming effect on land temperatures. The Tsushima Current, a branch of the Kuroshio, passes into the Sea of Japan by way of Korea Strait and slightly warms offshore waters. The Oyashio reduces summer temperatures and creates dense fog banks off the coasts of northeastern Honshu and Hokkaido.

Virtually all of Japan except parts of eastern Hokkaido averages more than 40 inches of precipitation annually. Several coastal mountain areas in Honshu get more than 120 inches. Areas around the Inland Sea, in eastern Honshu north of Tokyo Bay, and in western Hokkaido average 40 to 60 inches. The Sea of Japan coast gets more precipitation in winter, largely in the form of snow, than it does in summer. The reverse is true for the Pacific coast, where summer precipitation exceeds that of winter. In northern Hokkaido, snow falls an average of 130 days per year; along the Sea of Japan, 80 days; on the Pacific coast south and west of Tokyo Bay, only 10 days.

Climate Patterns of Japan

Japan has a wide range of climate. Winters are long and cold in Hokkaido and in the mountains of northern Honshu. They are short and mild along the southern and southwestern shores of Kyushu and Shikoku. Summers are short and cool in the far north but long and hot in the south. Winter snows are heavy along the north and central coasts of the Sea of Japan. Summer rains are heavy along the south and southwest coasts. In general the climate of Japan is much like that of the United States East coast, from the continental coolness of northern Maine to the humid subtropics of northern Florida.

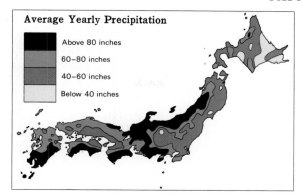

Average Yearly Precipitation

Above 80 inches
60–80 inches
40–60 inches
Below 40 inches

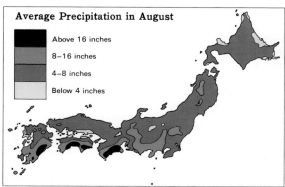

Average Precipitation in August

Above 16 inches
8–16 inches
4–8 inches
Below 4 inches

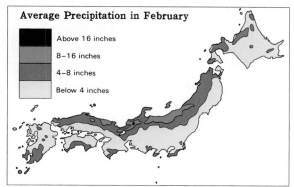

Average Precipitation in February

Above 16 inches
8–16 inches
4–8 inches
Below 4 inches

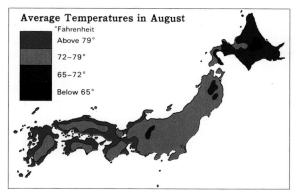

Average Temperatures in August

°Fahrenheit
Above 79°
72–79°
65–72°
Below 65°

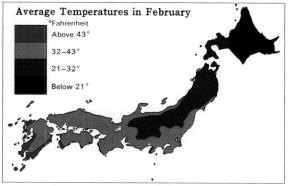

Average Temperatures in February

°Fahrenheit
Above 43°
32–43°
21–32°
Below 21°

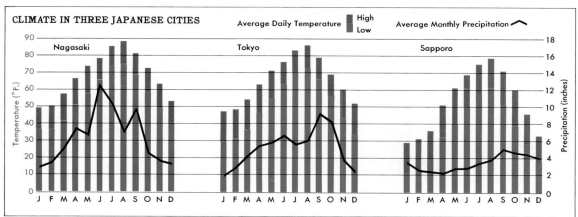

CLIMATE IN THREE JAPANESE CITIES

Average Daily Temperature — High / Low   Average Monthly Precipitation

Nagasaki   Tokyo   Sapporo

Temperature (°F.)   Precipitation (inches)

Japan contains hundreds of wild-bird species. Peacocks live in the southernmost part of the country.

Japan has rainy seasons in June and in September, though there is some precipitation throughout the year. The main, June rainy season is called the *baiu*, or *tsuyu*, and has many days of continuous rain. The September rainy season is called the *shurin*. It is associated with occasional typhoons, tropical storms like the hurricanes of southeastern North America. These move to the north and northeast in a clockwise arc from their spawning grounds east of the Philippines. When they strike Japan, their furious winds and heavy rains cause destructive floods and landslides. However, they also restore water levels in rivers and reservoirs, which drop during the dry days of late summer.

Typhoons bring roughly one third of the rain that falls annually on the Pacific coast. In 1959, one of the worst typhoons of modern times tore through the city of Nagoya and across central Honshu. Approaching typhoons are carefully watched by the Japan Meteorological Agency, and special radio and television bulletins are issued on their progress.

Seasonal temperatures in Japan increase from north to south. Average January temperatures are 15° to 20° F. in Hokkaido; 35° to 40° in central Honshu; and 45° in southern Kyushu. There is little difference in winter temperatures between the west and east coasts, though the skies are more overcast on the west coast and clearer and sunnier on the east coast. Summers are sultry throughout Japan. July temperatures average 77° to 80° in Kyushu, Shikoku, and southern and central Honshu; 72° to 75° in northern Honshu; and a cooler 65° to 70° in Hokkaido.

The clear, hot weather of summer arrives in mid-July, following the baiu rains. It is ended by the shurin rains. The length of the frost-free, or growing, season ranges from 250 days or more along the Pacific coast south from Tokyo Bay to only 120 days in central Hokkaido. Early autumn frosts in northern Japan and late spring frosts in central and southern Japan pose a seasonal threat to farming.

Plant and Animal Life

The trees, shrubs, and flowering plants of Japan are as varied as its topography and climate. Forests cover most of the land surface that has not been cleared by man. Coniferous, broadleaf, and mixed forests are the three main types. Among the conifers, pine, cypress, hemlock, cedar, fir, and spruce are commercially valuable. The numerous broadleafs include oak, maple, ash, birch, beech, poplar, chestnut, and horse chestnut. Subtropical forms such as bamboo and palms grow as far north as central Honshu.

The native plant life of Japan has been severely modified by man over the centuries. Many native species have been destroyed or reduced in extent, and new species from the Asian mainland have been introduced as a result of reforestation. Large virgin-forest areas have been preserved in parks.

Japan is rich in both land and marine animal life. Large mammals include bear, badger, otter, mink, deer, fox, and walrus. One monkey, the Japanese macaque, is found as far north as Hokkaido. Adjacent seas are the home of whales and porpoises. The hundreds of Japanese bird species include many water and wading birds, hawks, pheasants, peacocks, doves, owls, and woodpeckers. Among the reptiles are sea turtles, tortoises, lizards, and snakes. The sea abounds with hundreds of fish species. Salmon, sardine, sea bream, tuna, trout, mackerel, cod, and mullet are among those caught by commercial fishermen. Tropical varieties accompany the warm waters of the Kuroshio as far north as Tokyo Bay. The raising of goldfish for decorative purposes is a Japanese specialty.

Words to Remember

Kanto Plain—the lowland around Tokyo.
Shinano—Japan's longest river.
Biwa—Japan's largest lake.
Mount Fuji—Japan's highest mountain.
tsunami—a huge wave caused by an undersea earthquake.
Kuroshio and Oyashio—two major ocean currents which affect the climate of Japan.
baiu, or *tsuyu*—the June rainy season of Japan.
shurin—the September rainy season of Japan.

Questions to Think About

1. Japan and the United Kingdom are island nations situated just off continental mainlands. In what ways might this explain the industrialization of both nations?
2. How has the geologic instability of Japan influenced Japanese architecture?
3. Is Japan's varied climate more desirable than a climate that remains much the same all the time? Why or why not?

JAPAN—History

Ancient Japan (to 1185)

Men have lived in Japan since the Stone Age. The early Japanese were primitive hunters, gatherers, and farmers. They lived in small villages, growing rice in paddies and irrigated fields. They had no writing system, and they worshiped nature gods and family ancestors. Chieftains headed small, clanlike tribal units.

According to legend, the Japanese state was founded in 660 B.C. by Jimmu, the first emperor. In fact, it emerged by the 6th century A.D., when one family of chieftains became dominant. Their base was the Yamato region at the eastern end of the Inland Sea. Claiming the sun-goddess Amaterasu as their ancestor, this family founded the imperial dynasty which has reigned in Japan ever since.

The Japanese made borrowings from the civilization of the T'ang Dynasty in neighboring China. These included the Buddhist religion, Confucian ethics, and Chinese writing, art, architecture, and dress. In 604 the Yamato ruler Prince Shotoku (573–622) began to infuse the life of the imperial court with Chinese ideals, and in 607 the court's first official emissaries were sent to China.

The Chinese model of government was also imported. The Taika reforms, beginning in 645, transformed the Yamato ruler into an absolute sovereign —the emperor. An elaborate bureaucracy was established. Large landholdings were abolished; some farmland was redistributed among the peasants; and regular tax collections were begun. However, in order to encourage agricultural development, the Yamato regime allowed tax exemptions on newly cultivated land. This practice actually stimulated the growth of huge estates called *shoen*. Similar to the manors of medieval Europe, the shoen were owned by powerful families, court aristocrats, or religious institutions and worked by thousands of peasants.

In 710 an imperial capital was built at Nara on the model of Ch'ang-an, the Chinese capital. In 794 the capital was moved to Heian-kyo (Kyoto). From the 8th to the 11th century an aristocracy controlled by the Fujiwara family dominated Japan. This period was a classic age of art and literature. Japan's culture was no longer one largely borrowed from China but had become distinctively Japanese.

The Feudal Age (1185–1600)

Beginning in the 11th century the *samurai*, provincial warriors who resembled medieval European knights, began to assume power. They often managed the estates of aristocrats, and sometimes they held land in their own right. Rivalry between two warrior clans—the Taira and the Minamoto—led to the Heiji War (1159–60). The Taira won, but a revolt begun in 1180 ended in 1185 with the victory of the Minamoto.

Yoritomo Minamoto (1147–99) then established a new government at Kamakura, and in 1192 he was named *shogun*, or chief military commander, by the imperial court. He was authorized to appoint military governors (*shugo*) in the provinces and land stewards (*jito*) on many private estates. His administrative organization, called the *bakufu* (camp government), served as a model for a series of later regimes.

The Kamakura shogunate successfully repelled Mongol invasions in 1274 and in 1281. It was overthrown by a domestic revolt in 1333, and Takauji Ashikaga (1305–58) established a new regime. A dispute between rival families over the succession to the shogunate led to the Onin War (1467–77). Centralized control disappeared as the country was plunged into civil wars which lasted until the late 1500's.

During this period, warrior leaders fought each other for land and vassals. The emperor and shogun became politically insignificant. Local lords known as *daimyo* divided the country into feudal domains. Their vassals served both as warriors and as government officials. The daimyo taxed the peasantry, who made up the bulk of the population.

Mongols invading Japan in 1274 are shown in the medieval Japanese Mongol Scroll. Japanese archers and swordsmen triumphed despite the explosive missiles used by the invaders.

Before his death in 1616, Ieyasu Tokugawa defeated the forces of Hideyori, heir to Hideyoshi Toyotomi, at Osaka. Over two centuries of Tokugawa supremacy were thus ensured.

Meanwhile, Japan was developing trade contacts with the outside world. Official trade missions to China had begun in 1404. Japanese traders were active along the coasts of Korea and China. Japanese adventurers and pirates also operated in eastern Asian waters, some reaching Siam and the Philippines.

Later in the feudal period, the first Europeans arrived in Japan, known to them as Xipangu from the tales of Marco Polo. Portuguese traders came first, in 1543. They were soon followed by Spanish, English, and Dutch traders. In the hope of attracting European trade, the Japanese encouraged conversions to Christianity. After the arrival of the Jesuit priest Francis Xavier in 1549, the Christian missionary movement enjoyed great success in Japan.

National Unification (1600–1853)

Feudal division and disorder in Japan ended in the late 16th century. The powerful daimyo leader Nobunaga Oda (1534–82) began to subdue the smaller daimyo. By 1590 Hideyoshi Toyotomi (1536–98), one of his generals, succeeded in defeating the rival Hojo family. Although he never became shogun, Hideyoshi took control of the whole country. In 1592–93 and in 1597–98 he led invasions of Korea as part of an unsuccessful plan to conquer China.

The political consolidation of Japan continued under Ieyasu Tokugawa (1542–1616), one of several men

Mutsuhito became the emperor of Japan in 1867. As the Meiji emperor, he symbolized Japan's modernization.

chosen to govern the country after Hideyoshi's death in Korea in 1598. After winning a battle against his rivals at Sekigahara in 1600, Ieyasu organized the daimyo into a federation under a new bakufu at Edo, the present city of Tokyo. He was named shogun in 1603.

For the next two centuries, under the Tokugawa shogunate, Japan enjoyed extraordinary peace and stability. Ieyasu and his successors built an elaborate system of controls over the daimyo, including limits on their military strength. The country was closed to all outside contact. Fearing that Japan was being prepared for foreign conquest, the government expelled the Christian missionaries, prohibited the Christian religion, and persecuted many Japanese converts to Christianity. It gradually cut back foreign trade until by 1641 only Dutch and Chinese merchants were permitted to trade—at the single port of Nagasaki. Japanese were forbidden under pain of death to leave the country.

As a result of internal peace, a national market developed and the economy flourished. New rice lands were cultivated, and advances were made in farming techniques. Osaka and Edo became great commercial centers. By the 18th century Edo, with a population of more than 500,000, was larger than any city in Europe. A new urban culture, reflecting the tastes of merchants, shopkeepers, and artisans, emerged in both Osaka and Edo. The cultural standards of the peasantry rose as well, and by the middle of the 19th century almost half of the entire male population of Japan could read and write.

The Modernization of Japan (1853–1905)

The seclusion of Japan ended in 1853 with the arrival of a United States naval fleet commanded by Commo. Matthew C. Perry. He had been instructed to open Japan to foreign trade and diplomatic contact. The Edo bakufu, afraid of United States military superiority, signed a treaty of friendship during a second visit by Perry in 1854.

The Netherlands, Russia, Great Britain, and France followed the lead of the United States. By 1859 the bakufu had been pressured into signing a series of "unequal treaties" opening several Japanese ports to foreign trade. Western nationals were given the right of extraterritoriality, or exemption from local law. Tariff rates that the Japanese government could not alter were established.

Many Japanese regarded the surrender to the West as a national humiliation, and the bakufu's authority declined rapidly. There were growing demands for the expulsion of the foreigners and for the restoration of political power to the emperor. These demands were supported by the court and two powerful daimyo domains in western Japan—Satsuma and Choshu. In 1868 the Tokugawa shogun was forced to abdicate. A new government was established under the young emperor Mutsuhito, who took the reign name of Meiji ("enlightened government"). This transfer of power from the Tokugawa shogunate to the Meiji emperor is known as the Meiji Restoration. It is regarded as the beginning of Japan's modern era.

Leaders of the new government were former samurai of Satsuma and Choshu, such as Toshimichi Okubo (1830–78), Koin Kido (1833–77), and Takamori Saigo (1827–77). They wished to end the "unequal treaties" and to catch up militarily with the Western nations. Their first task, however, was to create internal order. A centralized administration replaced the daimyo system; many class distinctions were abolished; and a conscript army was built up. In 1868 Edo was renamed Tokyo ("eastern capital") and designated the new imperial capital.

During the 1870's the army quelled a number of rebellions by former samurai who objected to rapid modernization. The ill-fated Satsuma rebellion of 1877 was led by Saigo, who had resigned from the government in 1873. It was the last major challenge to the new regime.

The imperial government also laid the foundations for an industrial economy. Modern money and banking systems were introduced. Railroads, telegraph and telephone lines, and factories using the newest technology were built. Private enterprises were subsidized, and laws permitting the private ownership of land were enacted.

Leaders like Arinori Mori (1847–89) helped create a modern educational system. Compulsory universal education was instituted in 1872. By 1905 nearly 95 percent of Japanese school-age children were in school, and Japan soon achieved one of the highest literacy rates in the world.

A constitution was drafted in the 1880's under the direction of the political leader Hirobumi Ito (1841–1909), who took as his model the institutions of the German empire. The constitution, finally promulgated in 1889, gave strong executive powers to the emperor and a privy council. A prime minister headed a cabinet whose members were individually responsible to the emperor. Legislative powers were exercised by a two-house parliament, or Diet. The upper house, or House of Peers, consisted mainly of a new nobility created in 1884. The lower house, or House of Representatives, was elected by male taxpayers over 25 years of age.

By the 1890's Japan's rapid modernization had made it the most powerful nation in Asia. Extraterritoriality was relinquished by Great Britain, the United States, and the other Western powers by 1899. But Meiji leaders like Ito and Aritomo Yamagata (1838–1922) remained suspicious of Western imperialism. Using its growing economic and military power, Japan sought to build an empire of its own.

To achieve this objective Japan fought two major wars. After its victory in the first, the Sino-Japanese War of 1894–95, Japan forced the enormous but weak Chinese empire to cede Taiwan (Formosa) and the Penghu Islands (Pescadores). Japan was also supposed to get the Liaotung Peninsula in Manchuria, but Russia forced Japan not to accept it. Instead, in 1898, Russia took the peninsula itself.

The second war was fought in 1904–5 against Russia, now Japan's chief rival in eastern Asia. Japan won from Russia the southern half of Sakhalin Island and a leasehold in Liaotung, together with the South Manchurian Railway. In 1910 Japan annexed Korea. In 1915 Japan extended its hold in Manchuria after presenting "Twenty-one Demands" to the Chinese government. The empire of Japan had become a recognized world power.

Imperial Japan (1905–45)

After 1905 Japan faced a change in national leadership. The Meiji emperor died on July 30, 1912, and was succeeded by his son Yoshihito, who became known as the Taisho emperor. Yoshihito soon showed signs of mental illness, and Crown Prince Hirohito served as regent from November 1921 until he became the Showa emperor on Dec. 25, 1926.

More important, the original Meiji leaders had all died by the early 1920's. At first they were replaced by younger protégés, such as Taro Katsura (1848–1913) and Kimmochi Saionji (1849–1940). Gradually, however, under the leadership of men like Kei Hara (1856–1921) and Komei Kato (1860–1926), political parties in the Diet gained increasing control over the government. Between 1918 and 1932 most Japanese prime ministers were leaders of political parties in the lower house of the Diet.

The emergence of party government was accompanied by a flourishing of democratic ideas. Intellectuals like Sakuzo Yoshino (1878–1933) advocated greater attention to the needs of the common man. Some social-welfare legislation was approved, and in 1925 universal manhood suffrage was instituted.

By the 1920's Japan had begun to encounter severe economic problems. The rate of economic development was beginning to slow down. Agricultural production had reached a plateau, and domestic food supplies were no longer adequate. Imports of rice had to be increased greatly. By the late 1920's and early 1930's the countryside faced hard times.

World War II ended with Japan's surrender to the Allies. General Yoshijiro Umezo signed the surrender document on Sept. 2, 1945, aboard the USS *Missouri* in Tokyo Bay.

Continued on page 68

Japan and China

For nearly 2,000 years an intimate relationship existed between Japan and China. In the late 19th century and the first half of the 20th century that relationship was disrupted by Japanese wars of conquest waged against imperial and republican China. In recent years the rift between the two countries has been prolonged by basic political differences, and it was not until 1978 that a formal peace treaty finally was concluded.

Historical Background

During much of Japan's history its relationship to China was that of pupil to teacher. As early as the 1st century A.D., Japanese travelers visited the Chinese imperial court. They brought back treasures that enriched Japanese life—the Buddhist religion, Confucian ethics, written language, literature, art, architecture, music, and methods of government.

In the late 19th century the coming of the Industrial Revolution to Asia changed this relationship. Japan emerged from more than two centuries of self-imposed isolation, recognizing that industrialization was a means of gaining equality with the Western powers. Mastering Western techniques, it soon built factories and created a modern army and navy.

China was slower in acquiring the new technology. It was hampered by the actions of competing industrial nations which, eager to get its markets and raw materials, carved China into spheres of influence.

In 1894–95, armed with modern weapons, Japan warred China and seized Taiwan (Formosa). In the 1930's Japanese armies conquered Manchuria and carved from it a puppet state called Manchukuo. Japan's greed for the resources of China led to its brutal conquest and occupation of a large part of northern and eastern China before and during World War II.

The Japanese today have mixed feelings toward China. They are grateful for their rich inheritance from ancient China. They are also torn by feelings of guilt and shame over the indignities Japan's armies committed against the Chinese during the war years. Some Japanese are convinced that their country's old associations with China make Japan the one nation that knows China best. Others believe that the Japanese do not truly understand the type of leaders who now govern China.

It is an irony of history that Japan is today the custodian of the old Chinese virtues, the elaborate system of interpersonal obligations prescribed by Confucius. Within this framework, the Japanese have built a stable industrial, political, and social structure. Their skills and hard work have helped Japan become the world's third-ranking industrial power.

The situation in China has been different. New ideas have stirred the Chinese imagination. First democracy and then Communism gained ascendancy. Under the leadership of Mao Tse-tung, China was torn by revolutionary change and Communism has been the sole political system since 1949. Confucianism, with its accent on the family, has been shattered on the Chinese mainland. It has survived, however, on the island of Taiwan, where the defeated Nationalist leader Chiang Kai-shek established a Chinese government-in-exile—the Republic of China.

Present Relations

Japan's official posture toward Communist China since the end of World War II has generally been supportive of and consistent with American policy. In early 1952 Japan had little choice but to conclude a peace treaty with the Nationalist regime, thereby recognizing the government on Taiwan as the legitimate government of China.

The Japanese are bound to the United States by a security treaty that guarantees Japan protection against outside attack. Air and naval bases authorized by the treaty have been established by the United States on Japanese soil. A primary concern of successive Japanese governments seems to have been the avoidance of any official position on China that might jeopardize this alliance.

The present conservative government of Japan seems inclined to continue a close relationship with the United States well into the 1980's, and perhaps beyond. It has taken steps to expand and strengthen Japan's military establishment, the National Self-Defense Force, to a quota of about 270,000 men, with a total defense budget that amounted to some $6\frac{1}{2}$ billion dollars (1,690 billion yen) in 1977. However, Japan's leaders have refused to become upset over Communist China's possession of nuclear weapons, a situation that many observers believed would create new tensions between the two countries. The Japanese government has said that it would not retaliate by equipping Japan with nuclear weapons. Whatever Communist China has hitherto believed about the possibility and danger of a remilitarized Japan, it cannot deny that since 1945 no Japanese soldier has been involved in an overseas conflict. And until Japan's no-war constitution is revised, none can be.

War—Japanese capture Shanghai, China (1937).

Communist China's sensitivity to the alliance of Taiwan and South Korea with Japanese security interests was heightened when Okinawa reverted to Japan in 1972. China feared that the return of the island to Japanese control would further Japan's economic and political influence on Taiwan.

Japan's continued recognition of the Republic of China was also deeply resented by the People's Republic of China. By pursuing a policy that claimed to separate politics from economics, however, Japan was able to develop lucrative trade relations with both Chinas. Carried out through unofficial agreements between Communist China and leading members of Japan's Liberal-Democratic party, the value of Japan's trade with mainland China almost equaled that of Japan's official trade with Taiwan.

In late 1971, when United States President Richard M. Nixon announced an impending visit to the People's Republic of China, the news was received with shock by the Japanese government of Eisaku Sato. A reappraisal of Japan's own policy toward China, as well as a change in Japan's political leadership, was inevitable. When a new cabinet was formed under Prime Minister Kakuei Tanaka the following summer, Communist China responded favorably, and Japan acted quickly on the conciliatory gestures. In September 1972 a Japanese mission headed by Tanaka visited Peking, and a joint communiqué normalizing relations between the two countries was signed. Following the agreement with mainland China, the 1952 peace treaty between Japan and the Nationalist government on Taiwan was no longer considered in force, and the Japanese embassy in Taipei was closed.

Six years elapsed before the Chinese-Japanese agreement to sign a treaty of peace and amity was fulfilled. During the intervening years agreements on trade, navigation, and civil aviation were reached. But the actual peace treaty talks, begun in 1974, soon became stalled and were not resumed until the summer of 1978. At this time a compromise was reached between the government of Prime Minister Takeo Fukuda and the new Chinese leadership headed by Chairman Hua Kuo-feng. The treaty was signed in Peking on Aug. 12, 1978.

The basic disagreement that had delayed progress in the peace negotiations centered around the so-called *hegemony* clause. Even in their earliest drafts, the Chinese had expressed opposition to attempts of other countries—particularly the Soviet Union—to establish hegemony, or domination, in the Pacific region. The Soviet Union, meanwhile, had repeatedly warned Japan against conclusion of the pact with China.

Future Prospects

Although the new peace treaty does not in itself directly affect Chinese-Japanese economic relationships, there can be little doubt that a rapid expansion of trade will follow. After the normalization of Sino-Japanese relations in 1972, there was a marked increase in the volume of two-way trade. In Mao's last years, however, bitter internal struggle wrought havoc on China's industrial economy, and the country's foreign trade actually decreased. By 1977, nonetheless, the value of Japanese exports to China amounted to about 1,940 million dollars, and Japanese imports exceeded 1,547 million dollars. China's trade with Japan now makes up more than a quarter of its external trade, but represents less than $2\frac{1}{2}$ percent of Japan's total trade.

Abandoning the populist policies of the Cultural Revolution, the Chinese Ministry of Foreign Trade now plays a key role in the country's modernization drive, and the new leaders have given priority to economic development. The Japanese government is willing to make available long-term, low-interest loans to enable the Chinese to buy Japanese goods, particularly steel, chemicals, and machinery—including contracts for complete processing plants.

The peace treaty also provides a basis for widening human contacts. In 1969, before the normalization agreement, some 2,600 Japanese went to China. By 1977 this figure had grown almost tenfold, and there should be a much bigger increase in the future. The number of Chinese visitors to Japan has consistently been low in comparison, but China has already begun to dispatch large-scale economic and other fact-finding missions to Japan. In the academic and cultural fields, personal contacts are also expected to expand, reaffirming the long history of cultural interchange between the two nations.

Because the new treaty stipulates only the general principles of the two nations' foreign policies, it should give both Japan and China more leeway to take bolder diplomatic initiatives on their own. With more stable Japanese-Chinese ties, Japan can now begin to conduct a more independent diplomacy both with the Soviet Union and with the United States. China itself launched an unusual diplomatic offensive during the summer of 1978. Top officials, including Chairman Hua, visited 25 countries, many of them nations that the Chinese had earlier denounced as capitalist foes.

Peace—Japanese visit a trade fair in Canton, China (1963).

The cities remained relatively prosperous, however, and industry continued to grow. Employees of the *zaibatsu* (large urban business combines) enjoyed secure jobs and rising wages. The growth of labor unions led to the rise of a left-wing political movement in the 1920s, but the Peace Preservation Law was passed in 1925 to curb left-wing activities.

The party governments of the 1920s tried to follow a peaceful foreign policy. Men like Foreign Minister Kijuro Shidehara (1872–1951) advocated cooperation with Great Britain and the United States and nonintervention in Chinese affairs. But Japanese economic interests in southern Manchuria were threatened by the Soviet Union and China.

In September 1931 the Japanese army engineered a takeover of Manchuria, and in 1932 a puppet state, renamed Manchukuo, was established there. Ultranationalist military officers and civilians began to attack leading Japanese government officials. Prime Minister Tsuyoshi Inukai (1855–1932) was assassinated in 1932. A rebellion by military extremists in February 1936 was defeated, but the political parties were losing control of the government. Cabinets were increasingly dominated by militarists, and Japanese military involvement on the Asian mainland grew.

Undeclared war with China broke out in July 1937. Prime Minister Fumimaro Konoe (1891–1945) refused to negotiate with the Chinese government. But the Japanese armies, penetrating deep into China, were unsuccessful in forcing a Chinese surrender. In 1940 Japan moved troops into French Indochina and signed the Tripartite Pact with Nazi Germany and Fascist Italy. The United States attempted, unsuccessfully,

to curtail Japan's aggressive policy through economic sanctions. In October 1941 Gen. Hideki Tojo (1884–1948) became prime minister. Fearing that its plans to dominate Eastern and Southeastern Asia were in danger, the Japanese government decided to go to war against the United States. On Dec. 7, 1941, the Japanese air force attacked the United States fleet at Pearl Harbor, Hawaii.

By mid-1942 Japanese forces had occupied the Philippines, the Dutch East Indies, Malaya, and Burma and had reached into the Aleutian Islands of Alaska. Japan's leaders hoped to achieve a favorable negotiated peace with the United States by a series of quick victories.

But the United States was determined to win an unconditional surrender. Beginning with the defeat in naval battles in the Coral Sea and off the Midway Islands in 1942, Japan's fortunes declined. The United States, which enjoyed a superior industrial capacity and employed a strategy of island hopping, penetrated Japan's defense perimeter in the Pacific. In July 1944 the Tojo cabinet fell, and later in the year massive air raids began to destroy Japan's industry and cities. (*See also* World War II.)

Postwar Japan

Japan surrendered in 1945 after United States atomic bombs had destroyed the cities of Hiroshima on August 6 and Nagasaki on August 9. The Soviet Union had entered the war against Japan on August 8. Under the terms of surrender, all territory acquired by Japan since 1895 was given up and Japan was restricted to its four home islands. United States forces under the command of Gen. Douglas MacArthur began a military occupation of Japan.

The United States demobilized Japan's military forces and destroyed its arms. Many civilian and military leaders were tried as war criminals. Seven of the chief wartime leaders, including Tojo, were convicted and executed in December 1948. Thousands of lesser officials, military officers, and business executives were removed from their jobs because they had supported Japan's war policies.

To encourage the growth of democracy in Japan, the United States occupation authorities pressured the new Japanese government into accepting a series of political, social, and educational reforms. A new constitution became effective in 1947, and the educational system was reorganized.

On Sept. 8, 1951, Japan signed a peace treaty at San Francisco, Calif., with the United States and 47 other nations. The occupation formally ended when the treaty went into effect on April 28, 1952. Only Okinawa and several smaller Japanese islands remained under United States control. Shigeru Yoshida (1878–1967), prime minister during much of the occupation, was instrumental in the negotiation of the treaty. In 1956 Japan joined the United Nations.

When Japan regained full sovereignty in 1952, the political reforms of the occupation had taken effect. Political leadership rested in a cabinet based on a

LEADERS OF MODERN JAPAN
Emperors Since the Meiji Restoration

Mutsuhito	1867–1912 (Meiji Reign)
Yoshihito, son of Mutsuhito	1912–26 (Taisho Reign)
Hirohito, son of Yoshihito	1926–89 (Showa Reign)
Akihito, son of Hirohito	1989– (Heisei Reign)

Prime Ministers After World War II

Kijuro Shidehara	1945–46
Shigeru Yoshida	1946–47
Tetsu Katayama	1947–48
Hitoshi Ashida	1948
Shigeru Yoshida	1948–54
Ichiro Hatoyama	1954–56
Tanzen Ishibashi	1956–57
Nobusuke Kishi	1957–60
Hayato Ikeda	1960–64
Eisaku Sato	1964–72
Kakuei Tanaka	1972–74
Takeo Miki	1974–76
Takeo Fukuda	1976–78
Masayoshi Ohira	1978–80
Zenko Suzuki	1980–82
Yasuhiro Nakasone	1982–87
Noboru Takeshita	1987–89
Sousuke Uno	1989–

popularly elected Diet. Conservative political parties, which had led the country almost continuously since 1947, combined in 1955 to form the Liberal-Democratic party. The occupation reforms also strengthened the labor unions and the Socialists, whose popular vote and strength in the Diet increased during the 1950s and the early 1960s.

A bilateral security treaty signed on Sept. 8, 1951, permitted the United States to retain military bases and troops in Japan. The treaty enabled Japan to rely on the so-called "atomic umbrella" of the United States for effective defense. The Socialists and other left-wing groups objected to the treaty and demanded that Japan adopt a policy of neutrality. In 1960, after the Liberal-Democratic government of Nobusuke Kishi (1896–1987) had agreed to a renewal of the security treaty, there were widespread demonstrations. The treaty was renewed in 1970.

The most far-reaching developments in postwar Japan were economic. Freed from the burden of heavy military expenditures, the Japanese could pour most of their resources into peacetime industrial production. Between 1955 and 1967 the economy more than tripled in size. By 1970 Japan had become the third largest industrial nation, outranked only by the United States and the Soviet Union. In the late 1980s disputes over trade became heated between Japan and the United States.

Economic progress helped bring a return of Japanese national confidence. The 1964 Summer Olympics at Tokyo, the Meiji Centennial of 1968, the world exposition held near Osaka in 1970, and the return of Okinawa to Japanese sovereignty in 1972 all were expressions of renewed national pride.

Economic progress and reviving nationalism served to weaken the Japanese Socialists. In the 1969 election their popular vote declined and they lost a large number of seats in the Diet. In 1972, however, growing criticism of the ruling conservatives was reflected in the resignation of Eisaku Sato (1901–75), the prime minister since 1964. He was succeeded by Kakuei Tanaka (born 1918), president of the Liberal-Democratic party. In new elections later in the year, the Liberal-Democrats retained their majority but suffered a setback as both the votes and the number of seats won by the Socialists and the Communists rose to almost one third of the total. Tanaka resigned under pressure in November 1974 and was succeeded by Takeo Miki (born 1907). In the December 1976 election the Liberal-Democratic party lost its parliamentary majority for the first time in 21 years. Miki soon resigned, and Takeo Fukuda (born 1905) was elected prime minister. In 1978, however, Fukuda lost the presidency of the Liberal-Democratic party to Masayoshi Ohira (1910–80), who then became prime minister. In 1979 Ohira, hoping to increase party strength in the Diet, called for elections a year early. Although his party lost a seat, he refused to resign from office. Ohira was forced to call another election in 1980 but died ten days before the vote. The Liberal-Democrats won majorities in both houses. On July 15 Zenko Suzuki (born 1910) was selected president of the Liberal-Democratic party and became prime minister on July 17.

Japan's economy remained strong under Suzuki, whose main goal was to reform the government in order to reduce the staggering national debt. The Suzuki administration was shaken in mid-1982 when former government officials were convicted in a bribery scandal that involved the United States Lockheed Aircraft Corporation and former Prime Minister Tanaka, who was convicted the following year. In October 1982 Suzuki suddenly announced that he would not run again. A Liberal-Democratic party primary held in November was won by Yasuhiro Nakasone (born 1918), a cabinet member, who became Japan's prime minister. The continuing issue of political corruption marred the elections in 1983, when his party lost its majority, but Nakasone won a second term. In September 1986 the Diet voted to extend his term one year. Nakasone chose Noboru Takeshita (born 1924) to succeed him as president of the Liberal-Democratic party in October 1987. Takeshita had been secretary-general of the party. In November Takeshita was elected prime minister by the Diet.

Emperor Hirohito, the world's longest-reigning monarch, died in January 1989 after a 62-year reign. His son, Crown Prince Akihito, automatically became emperor. In April of that year Takeshita announced his resignation in order to accept responsibility for a stock-trading and bribery scandal that had plagued his administration for nine months. In May Nakasone resigned from the Liberal Democratic party to take responsibility for the scandal. Foreign Minister Sousuke Uno (born 1922) was elected by the Diet in June to replace Takeshita. (*See also* Hirohito; Akihito.)

BIBLIOGRAPHY FOR JAPAN

Beasley, W.G. The Modern History of Japan, 3rd ed. (St. Martin, 1981).
Bolitho, Harold. Meiji Japan (Lerner, 1980).
Buck, P.S. The Big Wave (Harper, 1986).
Crush, Margaret. Japan (Silver, 1986).
Davidson, Judith. Japan: Where East Meets West (Dillon, 1983).
Dunn, C.J. Everyday Life in Traditional Japan (Tuttle, 1977).
Epstein, Sam and Beryl. A Year of Japanese Festivals (Garrard, 1974).
Namioka, Lensey. Valley of the Broken Cherry Trees (Delacorte, 1980).
Roberson, J.R. Japan from Shogun to Sony (Macmillan, 1985).
Tames, Richard. Japan: the Land and Its People, rev. ed. (Silver, 1987).
Thurley, E.F. Through the Year in Japan (David & Charles, 1985).
Uchida, Yoshiko. Samurai of Gold Hill, rev. ed. (Creative Arts, 1985).

Words to Remember

Jimmu—the mythical first emperor and founder of the Japanese nation.

Amaterasu—the mythical sun-goddess claimed as ancestor of Japan's imperial dynasty.

shoen—a large medieval agricultural estate.

samurai—a medieval provincial warrior.

shogun—the chief military ruler and commander in Japan from 1192 to 1868.

bakufu—the military government of a shogun.

daimyo—a feudal lord of medieval Japan.

Notable Events in Japan's History

A.D. 593–622—Prince Shotoku rules Japan. In 604, reforms are begun to establish a Chinese-style form of government.

1854—Commodore Matthew C. Perry negotiates treaty opening ports of Shimoda and Hakodate to United States ships; treaty of 1858 opens more Japanese ports to United States.

600 **1150** **1850**

1159–60—Taira family defeats Minamoto family in Heiji War; Taira then control Japanese imperial court for 20 years; Minamoto revolt, launched in 1180, destroys Taira in 1185.

THE JAPANESE PEOPLE BUILD THEIR NATION

A.D. 300–500—Yamato state established.

600–622—Japan makes extensive borrowings from Chinese culture under Prince Shotoku.

710—Imperial capital established at Nara; moved to Heian-kyo (Kyoto), 794.

1156–85—Conflicts between Taira and Minamoto families: Heiji War (1159–60), Minamoto revolt (1180–85).

1192—Yoritomo Minamoto establishes Kamakura shogunate.

1274–81—Mongol invasions repelled.

1333—Kamakura shogunate overthrown.

1400–1500—Daimyo regimes emerge.

1543—Portuguese land in Japan.

1560–90—Military reunification achieved under Nobunaga Oda and Hideyoshi Toyotomi.

1889—Meiji constitution is promulgated on February 11, anniversary of legendary founding of Japan in 660 B.C.; it creates the Diet, Japan's first representative national assembly.

1592–98—Hideyoshi conducts expeditions against Korea.

1600—Ieyasu Tokugawa victorious at Sekigahara.

1603—Ieyasu establishes Tokugawa shogunate.

1633–41—Seclusion policy isolates Japan.

1853—United States Commo. Matthew C. Perry arrives in Japan.

1854—Japan signs treaty of friendship with United States; treaty of trade, 1858.

1867—Mutsuhito becomes emperor; Meiji Restoration ends Tokugawa shogunate, Edo (Tokyo) replaces Kyoto as capital, 1868.

70

1905—Japan defeats Russia at Mukden, Manchuria, in final battle of Russo-Japanese War, 1904-5.

1970—Expo '70, Asia's first universal exposition, is held near Osaka; Tower of the Sun symbolizes exposition's theme—"Progress and Harmony for Mankind."

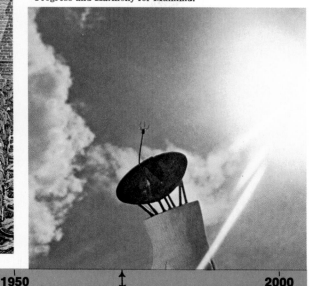

1900　　　　　　　　　　　　　**1950**　　　　　　　　　　　　　**2000**

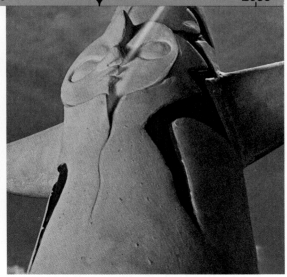

1944-45—Tokyo is nearly destroyed by Allied air raids during World War II; Japan's defeat in war is followed by United States military occupation.

1877—Satsuma rebellion put down.
1889—Meiji constitution promulgated.
1894–95—China defeated in Sino-Japanese War.
1904–5—Russia defeated in Russo-Japanese War.
1926—Hirohito becomes Showa emperor.
1931–32—Japan occupies Manchuria.
1936—February Rebellion defeated.
1937—War with China begins.
1940—Japan concludes alliance with Germany and Italy; enters World War II, 1941; defeated, 1945.
1945–52—Japan occupied by United States troops.
1956—Japan admitted to United Nations.
1960—Widespread demonstrations against United States-

Japan mutual security treaty.
1964—Asia's first Olympic Games held in Tokyo.
1970—Expo '70 held near Osaka.
1972—Japan and China reestablish diplomatic relations. Winter Olympic Games held near Sapporo.
1974—Former Japanese Prime Minister Eisaku Sato awarded Nobel peace prize. Gerald R. Ford is first United States president to visit Japan.
1975—Emperor Hirohito is first reigning Japanese monarch to visit United States.
1978—New Tokyo International Airport opened.

71

JAPAN—Fact Summary

HOW JAPAN COMPARES...
...IN AREA AND POPULATION

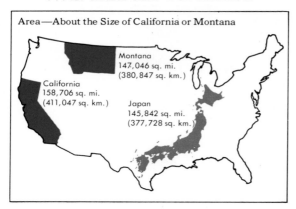

Area—About the Size of California or Montana

Montana
147,046 sq. mi.
(380,847 sq. km.)

California
158,706 sq. mi.
(411,047 sq. km.)

Japan
145,842 sq. mi.
(377,728 sq. km.)

Population—7th Largest Country[1]

1.	China	982,550,000
2.	India	683,810,000
3.	U.S.S.R.	267,700,000
4.	United States	229,805,000
5.	Indonesia	150,520,000
6.	Brazil	121,547,000
7.	Japan	117,645,000
8.	Bangladesh	89,000,000

Source: Statistical Office, United Nations

—Comparative Population Density[2]

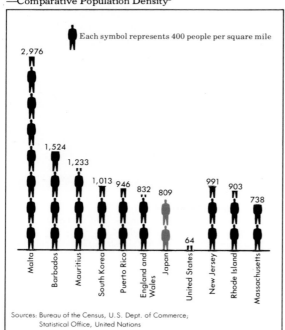

Each symbol represents 400 people per square mile

Malta	2,976
Barbados	1,524
Mauritius	1,233
South Korea	1,013
Puerto Rico	946
England and Wales	832
Japan	809
United States	64
New Jersey	991
Rhode Island	903
Massachusetts	738

Sources: Bureau of the Census, U.S. Dept. of Commerce;
Statistical Office, United Nations

HOW JAPAN COMPARES...

Rapid Increase in Gross National Product (GNP)[3,4]

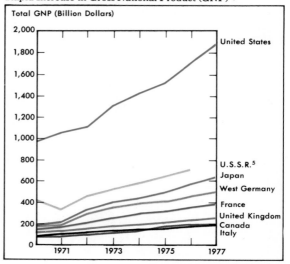

Total GNP (Billion Dollars)

United States
U.S.S.R.[5]
Japan
West Germany
France
United Kingdom
Canada
Italy

1971   1973   1975   1977

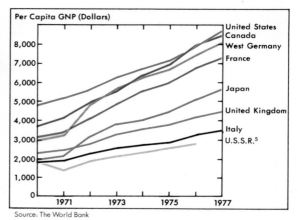

Per Capita GNP (Dollars)

United States
Canada
West Germany
France
Japan
United Kingdom
Italy
U.S.S.R.[5]

1971   1973   1975   1977

Source: The World Bank

Annual Rate of GNP Growth Compared with Rivals[4,6,7,8]

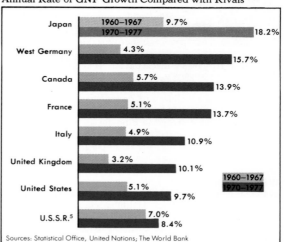

Japan	1960–1967	9.7%
	1970–1977	18.2%
West Germany		4.3%
		15.7%
Canada		5.7%
		13.9%
France		5.1%
		13.7%
Italy		4.9%
		10.9%
United Kingdom		3.2%
		10.1%
United States		5.1%
		9.7%
U.S.S.R.[5]		7.0%
		8.4%

1960–1967
1970–1977

Sources: Statistical Office, United Nations; The World Bank

How have the Japanese been able to achieve such a high rate of economic growth?

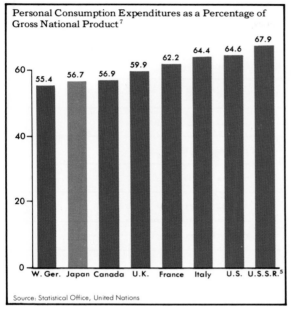

Personal Consumption Expenditures as a Percentage of Gross National Product[7]

W. Ger. 55.4 | Japan 56.7 | Canada 56.9 | U.K. 59.9 | France 62.2 | Italy 64.4 | U.S. 64.6 | U.S.S.R.[5] 67.9

Source: Statistical Office, United Nations

A smaller proportion of Japan's gross national product than that of other leading industrial nations is used for personal expenditures. Thus more money is available for investments in industrial plant and equipment.

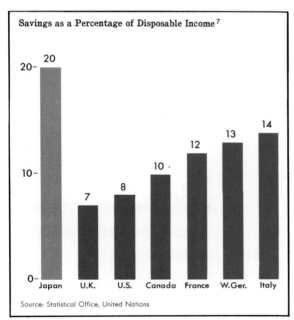

Savings as a Percentage of Disposable Income[7]

Japan 20 | U.K. 7 | U.S. 8 | Canada 10 | France 12 | W.Ger. 13 | Italy 14

Source: Statistical Office, United Nations

The Japanese save a larger proportion of their disposable income than the people of other leading industrial nations. These savings are then used for further investments in industrial plant and equipment.

Japan Ranks High in the Output of Many Products[9]

Product	Japan's World Rank	Japan's Share of World Output
Commercial Vehicles	1	41.6%
Crustacean and Mollusk Catch	1	25.9%
Fish Meal	1	18.2%
Men's and Boys' Suits	1	13.3%
Merchant Vessels	1	33.8%
Passenger Cars	1	24.1%
Television Sets	1	21.1%
Transistors	1	65.8%
Whale Catch	1	47.1%
Cement	2	10.2%
Fish Catch	2	29.8%
Radios	2	10.6%
Silk, Raw	2	29.1%
Synthetic fibers	2	12.8%
Zinc, Primary	2	12.1%
Aluminum, Primary	3	6.9%
Caustic Soda	3	9.2%
Copper, Refined	3	10.5%
Electric Energy	3	7.3%
Fish, Canned	3	12.9%
Macaroni and Noodle Products	3	17.1%
Newsprint	3	10.5%
Steel, Crude	3	15.0%
Eggs	4	7.5%
Gasoline	4	3.9%
Sulfuric Acid	4	5.2%
Wheat Flour	4	3.0%

Source: Statistical Office, United Nations.

Notes for Fact Summary

1. United Nations 1981 midyear estimate.

2. Based on 1981 population estimates of selected countries, regions, and states.

3. Leading countries in GNP.

4. Excludes the People's Republic of China.

5. Includes production of goods, not services.

6. Represents GNP at current market prices.

7. Selected countries.

8. Apparent growth in GNP reflects change in local currency in comparison with U.S. dollar for period indicated.

9. Based on latest available data.

10. Data not available.

11. Excludes Northern Ireland.

HOW JAPAN COMPARES ... IN TRANSPORTATION, COMMUNICATION, DEFENSE

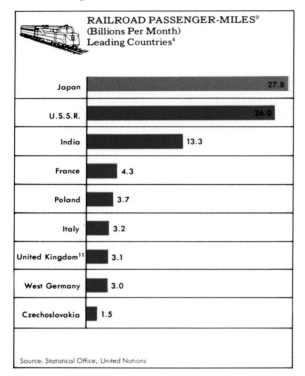

RAILROAD PASSENGER-MILES[9]
(Billions Per Month)
Leading Countries[4]

Japan	27.8
U.S.S.R.	26.0
India	13.3
France	4.3
Poland	3.7
Italy	3.2
United Kingdom[11]	3.1
West Germany	3.0
Czechoslovakia	1.5

Source: Statistical Office, United Nations

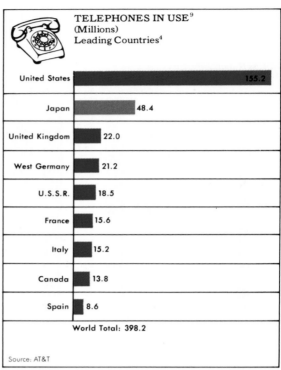

TELEPHONES IN USE[9]
(Millions)
Leading Countries[4]

United States	155.2
Japan	48.4
United Kingdom	22.0
West Germany	21.2
U.S.S.R.	18.5
France	15.6
Italy	15.2
Canada	13.8
Spain	8.6

World Total: 398.2

Source: AT&T

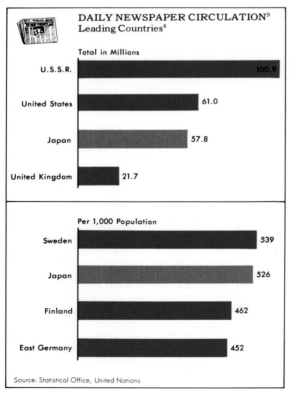

DAILY NEWSPAPER CIRCULATION[9]
Leading Countries[4]

Total in Millions

U.S.S.R.	100.9
United States	61.0
Japan	57.8
United Kingdom	21.7

Per 1,000 Population

Sweden	539
Japan	526
Finland	462
East Germany	452

Source: Statistical Office, United Nations

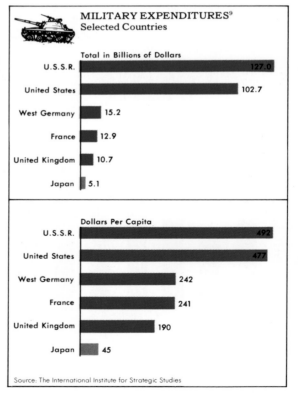

MILITARY EXPENDITURES[9]
Selected Countries

Total in Billions of Dollars

U.S.S.R.	127.0
United States	102.7
West Germany	15.2
France	12.9
United Kingdom	10.7
Japan	5.1

Dollars Per Capita

U.S.S.R.	492
United States	477
West Germany	242
France	241
United Kingdom	190
Japan	45

Source: The International Institute for Strategic Studies

JAPAN

PREFECTURES

Aichi, 6,221,638 ......H 6
Akita, 1,256,745 ......J 4
Aomori, 1,523,907 ......K 3
Chiba, 4,735,424 ......P 2
Ehime, 1,506,637 ......F 7
Fukui, 794,354 ......G 5
Fukuoka, 4,553,461 ......D 7
Fukushima, 2,035,272 ......K 5
Gifu, 1,960,107 ......H 6
Gumma, 1,848,562 ......J 5
Hiroshima, 2,739,161 ......E 6
Hokkaido, 5,575,989 ......K 2
Hyogo, 5,144,892 ......H 7
Ibaraki, 2,558,007 ......K 5
Ishikawa, 1,119,304 ......H 5
Iwate, 1,421,927 ......K 4
Kagawa, 999,864 ......G 6
Kagoshima, 1,784,623 ......E 8
Kanagawa, 6,924,348 ......O 2
Kochi, 831,275 ......F 7
Kumamoto, 1,790,327 ......E 7
Kyoto, 2,527,330 ......J 7
Mie, 1,686,936 ......H 6
Miyagi, 2,082,320 ......K 4
Miyazaki, 1,151,587 ......E 8
Nagano, 2,083,934 ......J 5
Nagasaki, 1,590,564 ......D 7
Nara, 1,209,365 ......J 8
Niigata, 2,451,357 ......J 5
Oita, 1,228,913 ......E 7
Okayama, 1,871,023 ......F 6
Okinawa, 1,106,559 ......N 6
Osaka, 8,473,446 ......J 8
Saga, 865,574 ......E 7
Saitama, 5,420,480 ......O 2
Shiga, 1,079,898 ......J 7
Shimane, 784,795 ......F 6
Shizuoka, 3,446,804 ......H 6
Tochigi, 1,792,201 ......K 5
Tokushima, 825,261 ......G 7
Tokyo, 11,618,281 ......O 2
Tottori, 604,221 ......G 6
Toyama, 1,103,459 ......H 5
Wakayama, 1,087,012 ......G 6
Yamagata, 1,251,917 ......K 4
Yamaguchi, 1,587,079 ......E 6
Yamanashi, 804,256 ......J 6

CITIES and TOWNS

Abashiri, 44,777 ......M 1
Ageo, 166,243 ......O 2
Aikawa, 12,721 ......H 4
Aizuwakamatsu, 114,528 ......J 5
Ajigasawa, 17,402 ......J 3
Akashi, 254,869 ......H 8
Aki, 25,022 ......F 7
Akita, 284,863 ......J 4
Akkeshi, 15,940 ......M 2
Akune, 29,527 ......E 7
Amagasaki, 523,650 ......H 8
Amagi, 42,863 ......E 7
Anan, 61,253 ......G 7
Aomori, 287,594 ......K 3
Asahi, 35,721 ......K 6
Asahikawa, 352,619 ......L 2
Ashibetsu, 32,946 ......L 2
Ashikaga, 165,756 ......J 5
Ashiya, 81,745 ......H 8
Atami, 50,082 ......J 6
Atsugi, 145,392 ......O 2
Awaji, 9,082 ......H 7
Ayabe, 42,552 ......G 6
Beppu, 136,485 ......E 7
Bibai, 38,552 ......L 2
Chiba, 746,430 ......P 2
Chichibu, 61,285 ......J 5
Chigasaki, 171,016 ......O 3
Chitose, 66,788 ......K 2
Chofu, 180,548 ......O 2
Choshi, 89,416 ......K 6
Daito, 116,635 ......J 8
Ebetsu, 86,349 ......K 2
Eniwa, 42,911 ......K 2
Esashi, Hokkaido, 10,076 ......L 1
Esashi, Hokkaido, 13,930 ......J 3
Esashi, Iwate, 35,738 ......K 4
Fuchu, Hiroshima, 49,026 ......F 6
Fuchu, Tokyo, 192,198 ......O 2
Fuji, 205,751 ......J 6
Fujieda, 103,225 ......J 6
Fujisawa, 300,248 ......O 3
Fukagawa, 35,376 ......L 2
Fukuchiyama, 63,788 ......G 6
Fukue, 32,135 ......D 7
Fukui, 240,962 ......G 5
Fukuoka, 1,088,588 ......D 7
Fukuyama, 346,030 ......F 6
Funabashi, 479,439 ......P 2
Furukawa, 57,060 ......K 4
Gifu, 410,357 ......H 6
Gobo, 30,398 ......G 7
Gose, 37,387 ......J 8
Gosen, 39,936 ......J 5
Goshogawara, 50,632 ......K 3
Gotsu, 28,264 ......F 6
Habikino, 103,181 ......J 8
Haboro, 13,254 ......K 1
Hachinohe, 238,179 ......K 3
Hachioji, 322,580 ......O 2
Hadano, 123,133 ......O 3
Hagi, 53,693 ......E 6
Hakodate, 320,154 ......K 3
Hakui, 28,784 ......H 5
Hamada, 50,799 ......E 6
Hamamatsu, 490,824 ......H 6
Hanamaki, 68,873 ......K 4
Hanno, 61,179 ......O 2
Haramachi, 46,052 ......K 5
Hayama, 28,359 ......O 3
Higashiosaka, 521,558 ......J 8
Hikone, 89,701 ......H 6
Himeji, 446,256 ......G 6
Himi, 62,413 ......H 5
Hino, 145,448 ......O 2
Hirakata, 353,358 ......J 7
Hirara, 32,924 ......L 7
Hirata, 31,067 ......F 6
Hiratsuka, 214,293 ......O 3
Hiroo, 11,512 ......L 2
Hirosaki, 175,330 ......K 3
Hiroshima, 899,399 ......E 6
Hitachi, 204,596 ......K 5
Hitachiota, 35,980 ......K 5
Hitoyoshi, 42,236 ......E 7
Hofu, 111,468 ......E 6
Hondo, 42,460 ......D 7
Honjo, 53,531 ......J 4
Hyuga, 58,347 ......E 7
Ibaraki, 234,062 ......J 7
Ibusuki, 32,855 ......E 8
Ichihara, 216,394 ......P 2
Ichikawa, 364,244 ......P 2
Ichinohe, 20,861 ......K 3
Ichinomiya, 253,139 ......H 6
Ichinoseki, 60,214 ......K 4
Ide, 9,258 ......J 7
Iida, 78,515 ......H 6
Iizuka, 80,288 ......D 7
Ikeda, Hokkaido, 11,902 ......L 2
Ikeda, Osaka, 101,121 ......J 7
Ikoma, 70,461 ......J 8
Ikuno, 5,988 ......G 6
Imabari, 123,234 ......F 6
Imari, 61,243 ......D 7
Imazu, 12,282 ......J 7
Ina, 56,086 ......H 6
Isahaya, 83,723 ......D 7
Ise, 105,621 ......H 6
Ishigaki, 38,819 ......K 7
Ishige, 20,374 ......P 2
Ishinomaki, 120,699 ......K 4
Ishioka, 47,829 ......K 5
Itami, 178,228 ......H 7
Ito, 69,638 ......J 6
Itoigawa, 36,080 ......H 5
Itoman, 42,239 ......N 6
Iwaizumi, 18,236 ......K 4
Iwaki, 342,074 ......K 5
Iwakuni, 112,525 ......E 6
Iwami, 15,969 ......G 6
Iwamizawa, 78,311 ......L 2
Iwanai, 22,373 ......K 2
Iwasaki, 4,061 ......J 3
Iwata, 75,810 ......H 6
Iwatsuki, 94,696 ......O 2
Iyo, 29,725 ......F 7
Izuhara, 18,564 ......D 6
Izumi, 124,322 ......J 8
Izumiotsu, 67,474 ......J 8
Izumisano, 90,684 ......J 8
Izumo, 77,303 ......F 6
Joetsu, 127,842 ......H 5
Joyo, 74,350 ......J 7
Kadoma, 138,902 ......J 7
Kaga, 65,282 ......H 5
Kagoshima, 505,360 ......E 8
Kaizuka, 81,162 ......H 8
Kakogawa, 212,233 ......G 6
Kamaishi, 65,250 ......L 4
Kamakura, 172,629 ......O 3
Kameoka, 69,410 ......J 7
Kamiiso, 29,944 ......K 3
Kaminoyama, 38,533 ......J 4
Kaminoyaku, 8,368 ......E 8
Kamo, 8,970 ......J 7
Kanazawa, 417,684 ......H 5
Kanonji, 44,927 ......F 6
Kanoya, 73,242 ......E 8
Kanuma, 85,159 ......J 5
Karatsu, 77,710 ......D 7
Kaseda, 25,392 ......D 8
Kashihara, 107,316 ......J 8
Kashiwa, 239,198 ......P 2
Kashiwara, 69,836 ......J 8
Kashiwazaki, 83,499 ......J 5
Kasugai, 244,119 ......H 6
Kasukabe, 155,555 ......O 2
Katsuta, 92,621 ......K 5
Katsuura, 25,462 ......K 6
Kawachinagano, 78,572 ......J 8
Kawagoe, 259,314 ......O 2
Kawaguchi, 379,360 ......J 6
Kawanishi, 129,834 ......H 7
Kawasaki, 1,040,802 ......O 2
Kesennuma, 68,551 ......K 4
Kikonai, 9,514 ......K 3
Kimitsu, 77,286 ......O 3
Kiryu, 132,889 ......J 5
Kisarazu, 110,711 ......P 3
Kishiwada, 180,317 ......J 8
Kitaibaraki, 47,670 ......K 5
Kitakami, 53,647 ......K 4
Kitakata, 37,553 ......J 5
Kitakyushu, 1,065,078 ......E 6
Kitami, 102,915 ......L 2
Kizu, 16,049 ......J 7
Kobayashi, 40,033 ......E 8
Kobe, 1,367,390 ......H 7
Kochi, 300,822 ......F 7
Kodaira, 154,610 ......O 2
Kofu, 199,262 ......J 6
Koga, 56,657 ......J 5
Koganei, 102,456 ......O 2
Kokubu, 35,433 ......E 8
Komagane, 31,179 ......H 6
Komatsu, 104,329 ......H 5
Koriyama, 286,451 ......K 5
Koshigaya, 223,241 ......P 2
Koyama, 16,498 ......E 8
Kubokawa, 17,646 ......F 7
Kuji, 39,013 ......K 3
Kuki, 54,410 ......O 2
Kumagaya, 136,806 ......J 5
Kumamoto, 525,662 ......E 7
Kumano, 26,062 ......G 7
Kumiyama, 16,345 ......J 7
Kurashiki, 403,785 ......F 6
Kurayoshi, 52,270 ......F 6
Kure, 234,549 ......F 6
Kuroiso, 46,574 ......K 5
Kurume, 216,972 ......E 7
Kushikino, 30,747 ......E 8
Kushima, 29,420 ......E 8
Kushimoto, 18,852 ......G 7
Kushiro, 214,694 ......M 2
Kyonan, 12,843 ......O 3
Kyoto, 1,473,065 ......J 7
Machida, 295,405 ......O 2
Maebashi, 265,169 ......J 5
Maihara, 12,633 ......H 6
Maizuru, 97,578 ......G 6
Makubetsu, 20,084 ......L 2
Makurazaki, 30,060 ......D 8
Mashike, 8,319 ......K 2
Masuda, 52,756 ......E 6
Matsubara, 135,849 ......H 8
Matsue, 135,568 ......F 6
Matsumae, 17,524 ......J 3
Matsumoto, 192,085 ......H 5
Matsusaka, 113,481 ......H 6
Matto (Matsuto), 43,766 ......H 5
Matsuyama, 401,703 ......F 7
Mihara, 84,450 ......F 6
Miki, 70,201 ......H 7
Mikuni, 22,030 ......G 5
Minamata, 37,150 ......E 7
Minobu, 9,807 ......J 6
Minoo, 104,112 ......J 7
Misawa, 39,962 ......K 3
Mitaka, 164,526 ......O 2
Mito, 215,566 ......K 5
Mitsukaido, 40,435 ......P 2
Miura, 48,687 ......O 3
Miyako, 62,478 ......L 4
Miyakonojo, 129,009 ......E 8
Miyazaki, 264,855 ......E 8
Miyazu, 28,881 ......G 6
Miyoshi, 37,877 ......F 6
Mizusawa, 55,226 ......K 4
Mobara, 71,521 ......K 6
Mombetsu, 33,860 ......L 1
Monbetsu, 15,222 ......L 2
Mooka, 52,764 ......K 5
Mori, 17,061 ......K 2
Moriguchi, 165,630 ......J 7
Morioka, 229,114 ......K 4
Motobu, 15,307 ......N 6
Muko, 50,604 ......J 7
Murakami, 33,540 ......J 4
Muroran, 150,199 ......K 2
Muroto, 26,086 ......G 7
Musashino, 136,910 ......O 2
Mutsu, 47,610 ......K 3
Nachikatsuura, 23,006 ......H 7
Nagahama, Ehime, 12,314 ......F 7
Nagahama, Shiga, 54,935 ......H 6
Nagano, 324,360 ......J 5
Nagaoka, Kyoto, 71,445 ......J 7
Nagaoka, Niigata, 180,259 ......J 5
Nagaokakyo, 71,445 ......J 7
Nagasaki, 447,091 ......D 7
Nagato, 27,574 ......N 6
Nago, 45,991 ......N 6
Nagoya, 2,087,902 ......H 6
Naha, 295,778 ......N 6
Nakaminato, 33,324 ......K 5
Nakamura, 35,466 ......F 7
Nakasato, 14,270 ......K 3
Nakatane, 12,297 ......E 8
Nakatsu, 63,941 ......E 7
Nanao, 50,394 ......H 5
Nankoku, 44,866 ......F 7
Nara, 297,953 ......J 8
Narashino, 125,155 ......P 2
Nayoro, 35,032 ......L 1
Naze, 49,021 ......O 5
Nemuro, 42,880 ......M 2
Neyagawa, 255,859 ......J 7
Nichinan, 52,949 ......E 8
Niigata, 457,785 ......J 5
Niihama, 132,339 ......F 6
Niimi, 28,933 ......F 6
Niitsu, 62,282 ......J 5
Nishinomiya, 410,329 ......H 8
Nishinoomote, 23,537 ......E 8
Nobeoka, 136,598 ......E 7
Noboribetsu, 56,503 ......K 2
Noda, 93,958 ......P 2
Nogata, 62,595 ......D 7
Nose, 10,024 ......J 7
Noshiro, 60,674 ......J 3
Noto, 15,480 ......H 5
Numata, 47,150 ......J 5
Numazu, 203,695 ......J 6
Obama, 34,049 ......G 6
Obihiro, 153,861 ......L 2
Oda, 38,026 ......F 6
Odate, 72,478 ......K 3
Odawara, 177,467 ......J 6
Ofunato, 40,023 ......K 4
Oga, 38,940 ......J 4
Ogaki, 143,151 ......H 6
Ogi, 4,593 ......J 5
Ohata, 12,328 ......K 3
Oita, 360,478 ......E 7
Ojiya, 44,963 ......J 5
Okawa, 49,537 ......E 7
Okaya, 62,210 ......H 5
Okayama, 545,765 ......F 6
Okazaki, 262,372 ......H 6
Omagari, 41,764 ......K 4
Omiya, 354,084 ......O 2
Omu, 7,041 ......L 1
Omura, Bonin Is., 1,507 ......M 3
Omura, Nagasaki, 65,538 ......D 7
Omuta, 163,000 ......E 7
Onagawa, 16,105 ......K 4
Ono, 41,901 ......E 6
Onoda, 44,803 ......E 6
Onomichi, 102,056 ......F 6
Osaka, 2,648,180 ......J 8
Ota, 123,115 ......J 5

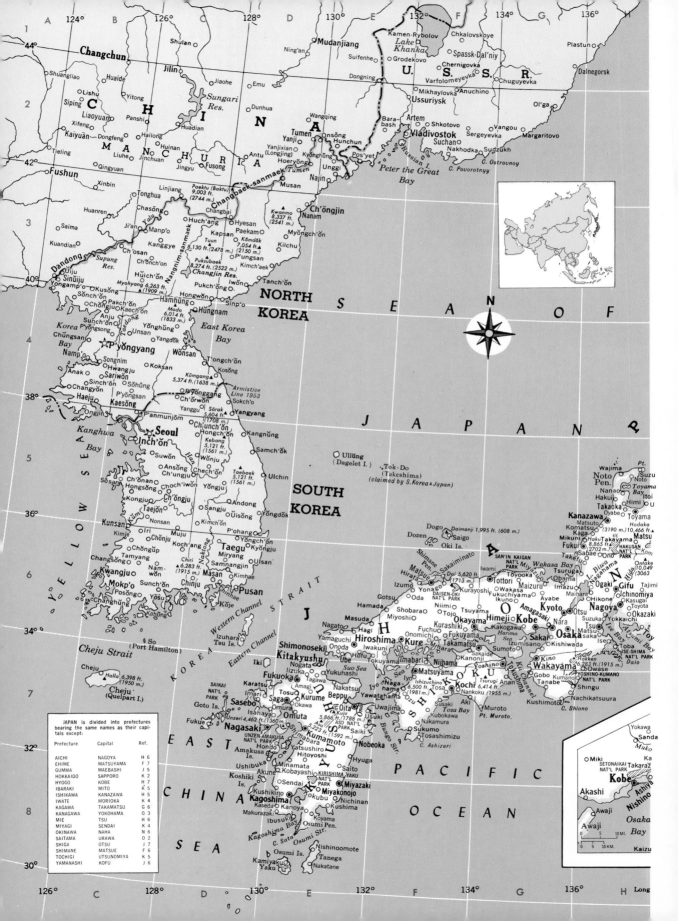

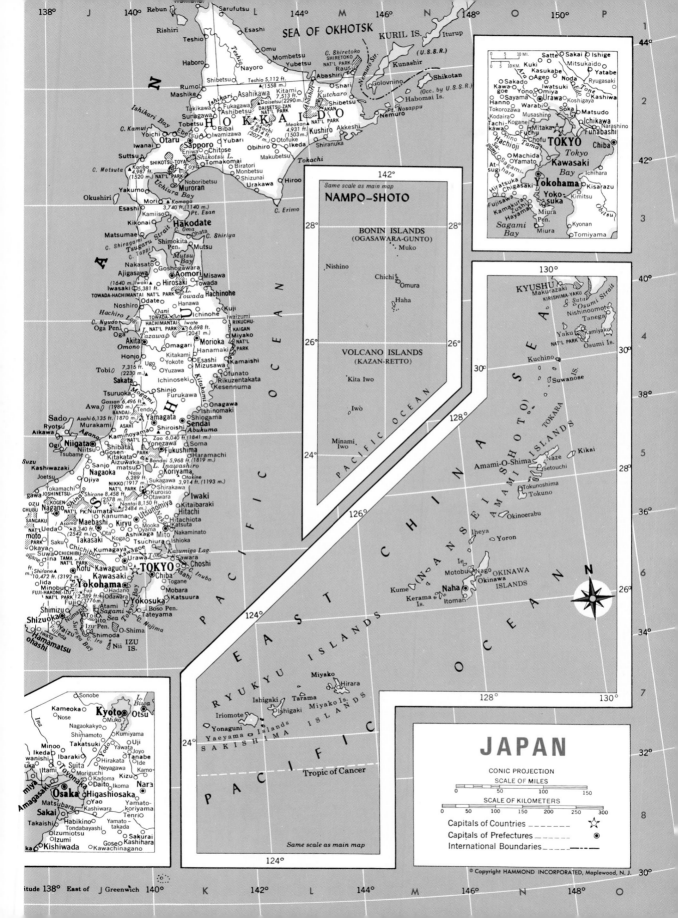

JAPAN, SEA OF. Located at the western edge of the Pacific Ocean, the Sea of Japan is bounded by Japan and the Soviet island of Sakhalin to the east and by the Soviet Union and Korea on the Asian mainland to the west. Its area is 389,100 square miles (1,007,800 square kilometers). The sea's average depth is 4,429 feet (1,350 meters), with a maximum depth of 12,276 feet (3,742 meters). The sea is separated into three underwater basins, the Japan Basin, the Yamato Basin, and the Tsushima Basin.

Japan's mild climate is greatly affected by the warm waters of the Sea of Japan. From December to March the prevailing northwest monsoon wind carries cold and dry polar air over the sea's warm waters, which results in persistent snowfall along the mountainous coasts of Japan. The winter monsoons bring rough seas and cause erosion along the coast. Also in winter, the northern part of the sea off the Siberian coast freezes. In summer the southerly tropical monsoon blows into the Asian mainland, causing dense fog. Typhoons occasionally occur in summer and fall.

Fishes and mineral deposits are the sea's main economic resources. Squid fishing is carried on in the central part of the sea, salmon fishing in the north and southwest shoal areas, and crustaceans are caught in the deeper parts of the sea. Seals and whales also abound, as well as such crustaceans as prawns and crabs. Natural gas and petroleum are among the sea's mineral resources. With increasing trade between Asian countries, the Sea of Japan is developing as a commercial waterway.

JAPANESE LITERATURE. Rich in sensitivity, quality, and variety, Japanese literature ranks as one of the great literatures of the world. Some of its collections of mythological history have survived for 1,300 years. Yet even the most ancient writings have a universal significance because they contain a sensory appeal that transcends the boundaries of time and cultural differences.

Ancient Literature

The earliest Japanese writers were greatly influenced by the Chinese. Without a writing system of their own, the Japanese adopted and adapted Chinese characters to their own needs. This is shown clearly in the most ancient complete works, the 'Kojiki' (Records of Ancient Matters), which was completed in 712, and 'Nihon shoki' (Chronicles of Japan), completed eight years later. In both of these collections, many sections of history, myth, legend, and songs are written entirely in Chinese.

The greatest literary achievement of the ancient period was the 'Manyo-shu' (Collection of Myriad Leaves), a magnificent anthology of more than 4,500 poems. It was compiled after 759, though it included poetry written a century or more earlier.

The 'Manyo-shu' is remarkable in several ways. Its poetry is memorable for its imagery, emotional power, and evocative appeal. The compiler of the anthology was probably the poet Yakamochi Otomo (716–

85?), but other poets such as Hitomaro Kakinomoto (died 710) and Tabito Otomo (665–731) also contributed to making this work a literary landmark.

Most of the poems in the collection are tanka, or short poems, one of the uniquely Japanese forms of poetry. A tanka always consists of five lines that follow a strict pattern of syllables: five, seven, five, seven, seven. This classic Japanese verse form is still in use today.

The masterpieces of the 'Manyo-shu' are its 260 choka, longer poems ranging up to 150 lines. These are also written in alternating lines of five and seven syllables, with the concluding line in seven syllables.

Classical Literature

In the 9th century the invention of the kana system of phonetic syllables greatly increased the ease of writing in Japanese and lessened Chinese influence (*see* Japan, section on Culture, subhead "The Japanese Language"). In 905 the 'Kokin-shu', the first great anthology of kana literature, was compiled. It consists of more than 1,100 poems, divided into 20 books that have been arranged according to topics, such as nature, the seasons, travel, love, congratulations, and mourning.

The chief compiler of the anthology was Tsurayuki Ki, or Ki-no, (884?–946?), a noted poet and prose writer of the period. In its memorable preface, which was perhaps the first complete prose in kana, he set forth the reasons that move people to write poetry. According to Tsurayuki, melancholy is the inspiration, and it is true that most of the love poems, which fill five books of the anthology, are sad.

Many of the tanka in the 'Kokin-shu' are beautifully lyric and perceptive. But their flawless symmetry often inhibited spontaneity. While these miniatures may lack the lively variety of the longer choka in the 'Manyo-shu', they were tremendously popular because skill in composing tanka was one way to win favor at the royal court.

Court opinion also affected early Japanese poetry in another way. Because they lived in a society that was strongly traditional, the court critics praised stylized perfection of language and disapproved of originality. These attitudes and restrictions made the 'Kokin-shu' the standard by which Japanese poetry was composed for centuries.

Tsurayuki had another lasting influence on Japanese literature. His 'Tosa nikki' (The Tosa Diary) is a vivid account of his travels from Tosa, where he had served as a governor, to his home in Kyoto. While most men at that time wrote in Chinese, he broke tradition by writing the diary in Japanese. His diary also created a tradition: It was the earliest ex-

---

In the Japanese culture, it is traditional for a person's surname to precede the personal name—for example, Mori Ogai. The literary figures in this article are cited in Western style, with the family name last—Ogai Mori. It should be noted that Japanese writers are often referred to by only their given name—Ogai, rather than Mori.

In an illustration from the
'Tale of Genji' (left) Prince
Genji is holding the infant
Kaoru. A page of text from
the book is also shown.

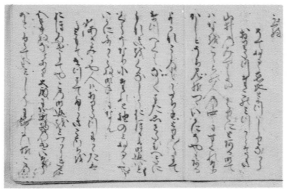

ample of the literary diary, one of the characteristic genres in Japanese literature.

Throughout the diary, Tsurayuki maintained the pretense that it was written by one of the women in the governor's entourage. In fact, most of the literary diaries that helped make the classical age of Japanese literature outstanding were written by women, the court ladies. The author of 'Kagero nikki' (The Gossamer Years) was the second wife of a 10th-century prime minister. Known only as "the mother of Michitsuna," she complained graphically about her unhappy life with her husband.

Another absorbing diary was 'Murasaki Shikibu nikki', a lively and realistic account of court life by the court lady who was later to write the immortal 'Genji monogatari' (The Tale of Genji). Critics have claimed that Lady Murasaki's 'The Tale of Genji' (about 1010) was the first major novel written in any language. It is almost universally acknowledged that this book is the finest flower of all Japanese literature, past or present.

Prince Genji, the hero of this sparkling chronicle of court life, is a complex personality and peerless lover. It is on the field of love, not on the fields of battle or politics, that the romantic Genji excels. With consummate sensitivity, he responds differently to meet the needs of each woman he captivates. That his character has enthralled readers ever since the tale first appeared is a tribute to its long-ago author, Shikibu Murasaki (978?–1014?), whose real name is un-

known. But the novel is also unforgettable for its rich poetry, imagery, and imaginative wordplay.

An instant success, 'The Tale of Genji' exerted wide influence over Japanese literature for centuries. This influence was both good and bad. The novel set a standard for excellence, but it also spawned a multitude of imitations and derivative books based on the story. Because it was so highly esteemed and widely imitated, its immediate effect was to inhibit innovative writing by the court society.

Another masterpiece of this period was 'Makurano-soshi' (The Pillow Book of Sei Shonagon), also written by a lady of the court. Witty and brilliant, it created a different mood than 'The Tale of Genji'. Unlike the romantic and sensitive Prince Genji, the 'Pillow Book' lover is fumbling and comic; the book irreverently portrays the ribald comedy that was also typical of court life.

By the middle of the 11th century, the court and its courtiers began to lose power as the authority of the emperors diminished. But even after political power passed to the new masters of society, the military, court society retained its privilege of claiming to be the arbiter of all culture.

In the 12th century, this too began to change. A new literary tradition appeared, a tradition based not on the aristocratic life of the court but on the ordinary life of the other social classes.

A striking example was the 'Konjaku monogatari', a mammoth collection of religious lore and folktales. The tales were drawn from the Japanese countryside and from the folklore of India and China. One strong element bound all the stories together; they portrayed the kind of people who had never been mentioned in the literature of the court society. These tales, though often crudely written, present illuminating insights into how the common people of Japan lived and thought and survived in a time when war ravaged the land.

Further evidence of the rise of a literature of the people was found in a collection of folk songs, 'Ryojin hisho', compiled in 1179. The fact that these folk songs were compiled by the emperor Shirakawa II signaled clearly that the new popular culture was gaining a permanent foothold, even at court.

Medieval Literature

The 12th century was a period of war, and the samurai, an aristocracy of military men, were in power. Emperor Shirakawa II abdicated, and power passed to the military. Women had little authority in a society dominated by warriors, and this may explain why writing by women dwindled in importance. In fact, there were few outstanding Japanese women writers between the 13th and 19th centuries.

Despite the waning of the political power of the court society, however, court poets remained active and new anthologies of poetry appeared. The finest of these anthologies was the 'Shin kokin-shu', compiled in 1206 by Teika Fujiwara (1162–1241) and others. By calling this anthology the "New Kokin-shu," the compilers boldly asserted their conviction that the poets represented in it compared favorably with the contributors to the original 'Kokin-shu' of 905.

Many critics consider the 'Shin kokin-shu' to represent the highest point of tanka composition. The poets collected in the anthology included the famed Teika Fujiwara himself; his father, Toshinari Fujiwara; the priest Saigyo; and the former emperor Toba II. These poets searched for symbolic meanings—not the appearance of the bright flower but the significance of the flower. They turned inward, trying to sense a deeper meaning that they felt but could not clearly define or express.

Teika Fujiwara and his poetic concepts dominated the direction of Japanese poetry. He was able to exert a strong influence through his own poems, his essays on poetry, and through the poetry of the past that he chose as most worthy of preservation.

In prose during this early medieval period, collections of Buddhist and popular tales flourished. One of the most enjoyable collections was the 'Ujishui monogatari', which showed considerable literary skill.

An even more distinctive literary genre was the war tale. The most famous was 'Heike monogatari', which was apparently begun by a nobleman at the court in about 1220. It was based upon a feud between two prominent families in the previous century. The work was expanded through the years as it was recited with improvisations by priest-entertainers and did not reach its final form until the mid-13th century. Perhaps because of its mixture of written and oral presentation, the 'Tales of the Heike' is sometimes vivid and effective, sometimes dull. But, despite its uneven style, it was highly popular, and many later writers used its characters and incidents to embellish their own novels and plays.

The reflective essays of Buddhist priests formed another important medieval genre. In 'Hojo-ki' (The Ten Foot Square Hut) by Chomei Kamo (1155–1216), the priest-author describes his disillusionment with the world and the contentment he finds in solitude. The beauty and profundity of this brief work made it a classic. The priest was also a noted poet and his essay 'Mumyo-sho' (1210–12) is a distinguished example of traditional Japanese poetic criticism.

In the 15th century a new poetic form became popular. Called renga (linked verse), it began as the composition of a single tanka by two people. For a while it was only a popular pastime, particularly among the common people in rural areas, or a competition. But as soon as renga reached the court poets, they formalized the patterns, and the poetry lost much of its freshness and vitality.

The greatest literary works of the 15th century were the No dramas. A traditional form of Japanese theater, they usually deal with well-known historical themes. The acting is highly stylized, and the masks, the rich costumes, the music, and the chorus make the performances highly effective. One of the most distinguished of the creators of No plays was Motokiyo Zeami (1363–1443), who was also an actor. His plays, written in magnificent poetry, often dealt with Zen Buddhist themes.

In the early 17th century Japan was restored to peace and unified under the Tokugawa shogunate, a family of military rulers. This peace was to last almost 250 years. Another event influenced Japanese literature even more strongly. From 1638 to 1853 Japan was closed to contact with the outside world. At first this encouraged the growth of a distinctly native literature, but later writing became provincialized and imitative.

Another event that influenced the country's literature was the adoption of printing. Commercial publication began in 1609, and soon presses were printing works of even slight literary value to satisfy the needs of a public eager for new books.

The haiku, a new form of short verse, developed. As was customary in Japanese literature, this became stylized, and even today haiku follows a formal pattern in which there are seventeen syllables in a sequence of five, seven, five. Each haiku strives to express a single and complete mood, such as sadness. Basho Matsuo (1644–94) was the writer who perfected the haiku into a form capable of expressing poetry of sensitivity and beauty.

The first influential novelist of this period was Saikaku Ihara (1642–93). Some Japanese critics rank him second only to Shikibu Murasaki in stature, but this probably would have surprised him since he wrote rapidly and with little regard for critical review. His first novel, 'Koshoku ichidai otoko' (The Life of an Amorous Man), opened a new dimension to Japanese writers as the erotic world of pleasure became a new field to explore. In his most famous novel, 'Koshoku gonin onna' (Five Women Who Loved Love), Saikaku Ihara broke another tradition: for the first time a writer dealt with women of the merchant class and their desires and dreams. His warm sympathy for his characters and his brilliant style raised his novels to the quality of art.

Monzaemon Chikamatsu (1653–1725) also wrote about unhappy women. He is often considered the greatest writer of Kabuki plays, and his historical dramas made superb acting vehicles. But he also wrote highly acclaimed plays for the puppet theater.

A brush painting showing crows perched in a tree during an autumn evening was painted by Japanese artist Itcho Hanabusa to illustrate a poem by Basho Matsuo.

Courtesy of Donald Keene

Modern Literature

In 1853 a United States naval fleet under the command of Commodore Matthew C. Perry arrived in Japan, with instructions to open the country to the Western world. After 1868, when the emperor Meiji announced that he would seek knowledge from the entire world, a new era in Japanese literature began. Translations of European works appeared, but they were often inaccurate and Japanese writers discovered that Western literature had qualities unknown to Japanese works of the the past.

The literary scholar Shoyo Tsubouchi (1859–1935) was a leader in influencing Japanese writers to accept change. His essay 'Shosetsu shinzui' (The Essence of the Novel) emphasized the role of realism in fiction, as well as the artistic value of novels, which had been considered mere entertainment.

The first modern Japanese novel was 'Ukigumo' (The Drifting Cloud) by Shimei Futabatei (1864–1909). Influenced by Russian literature, he wrote the book in the colloquial language of ordinary people because he was convinced that only in this way could a writer capture the essence of his own society. With the traditional Japanese reluctance to abandon tradition, however, most writers continued to use stylized literary language until the end of the century.

Another writer who was influenced strongly by the West was the poet and novelist Toson Shimazaki (1872–1943). His novel 'Hakai' (The Broken Commandment) deals with the outcast eta class (a minority at the lowest level of society) and was one of the first Japanese novels to confront social problems.

Because of his knowledge of English, Toson Shimazaki also helped to modernize Japanese poetry. Yet, though his "Song of the Autumn Wind" echoes Shelley in its attitude toward nature, the irregular lines of the poem fall into the traditional Japanese pattern of five and seven syllables.

The traditional forms of the tanka and haiku were not forgotten. Instead they were given new freshness and vitality by Shiki Masaoka (1867–1902). He was an outstanding poet of both verse forms, but was perhaps more important as a critic.

Akiko Yosano (1878–1942) was one of the most successful writers in the new style of tanka. Her lyrical collection 'Midaregami' (Tangled Hair) had special appeal for women because it seemed to glorify a new age of romantic love.

Takuboku Ishikawa (1886–1912) was one of the most popular tanka poets in the history of Japanese literature. His poetry reveals the many facets of his strongly individualistic character.

Sakutaro Hagiwara (1886–1942) is often considered the greatest Japanese poet of the 20th century. He created musical rhythms that brilliantly celebrated modern language patterns. In doing this, he was striking out on a new path while most of the contemporary tanka and haiku poets still clung to the literary language of the traditional past.

While the dominant theme in early 20th-century Japanese literature was naturalism, two prominent novelists worked outside the movement. Ogai Mori (1862–1922) was noted for his autobiographical fiction and historical novels. Soseki Natsume (1867–1916) wrote a humorous masterpiece, 'Wagahai-wa Neko-de aru' (I Am a Cat).

Jun-ichiro Tanizaki (1886–1965) and Ryunosuke Akutagawa (1892–1927) showed sensitive awareness to the new streams of thought that were flooding in from the West and yet were drawn also to the traditional past and the heritage that was uniquely Japanese. In novels such as 'Tade kuu mushi' (Some Prefer Nettles) Tanizaki used this conflict between the old and the new ways of life as a central theme. One of Akutagawa's short stories was made into the award-winning film 'Rashomon'.

In 1968 Yasunari Kawabata (1899–1972) became the first Japanese to win the Nobel prize in literature (see Kawabata). According to the citation, the award was bestowed "for his narrative mastery, which with great sensibility expresses the essence of the Japanese mind." It is characteristic that his first literary successes were the tiny vignettes he called "palm-of-the-hand" stories. Even one of his major novels, 'Yukiguni' (Snow Country), began as a short story that gradually evolved into a novel.

One of the most influential authors was Naoya Shiga (1883–1971). If not the initiator, he was one of the leading writers of the autobiographical story, known as the "I novel," and did much to make it a dominant genre in Japanese writing.

Even Akira Abe (born 1934), one of the most imaginative and lyrical young writers of Japan, worked mainly in the "I novel" tradition. His literary career began with a moving tale of growing up with a retarded brother. One of his major novels deals with his father's death.

Many of the modern Japanese novelists have been experimentalists. Kobo Abe (born 1924) set his most famous novel, 'Suna no onna' (The Woman in the Dunes), in a sand pit; it later was adapted as a highly successful film.

Traditionally Japanese writers have been masters of brevity, and they still are today. In 1980 a poignant collection of short stories by Tatsuo Nagai (born 1904), entitled 'Aki: Sono ta' (Autumn and Other Pieces), appeared.

Theater also remains a creative force in modern Japan. The brilliant Yukio Mishima (1925–1970) created many modern Kabuki and No dramas, and many of the younger writers have won international recognition for their screen plays. (*See also* Japan, section on Culture, subheads "The Literature of Japan"; "The Performing Arts of Japan.")

BIBLIOGRAPHY FOR JAPANESE LITERATURE

Algarin, J. P. Japanese Folk Literature (Bowker, 1982).

Braisted, W. R. Meiroku: Journal of the Japanese Enlightenment (Harvard Univ. Press, 1976).

Hibbett, Howard. Contemporary Japanese Literature: an Anthology of Fiction, Film and Other Writing Since 1945 (Knopf, 1977).

Hibbett, Howard. The Floating World in Japanese Fiction (Tuttle, 1974).

Kato, Shuichi. A History of Japanese Literature (Kodansha, 1982).

Keene, Donald, ed. Anthology of Japanese Literature: From the Earliest Era to the Mid-Nineteenth Century (Grove, 1955).

Lippitt, N. M. Reality and Fiction in Modern Japanese Literature (Sharpe, 1980).

Page, C. H. Japanese Poetry (Folcroft, 1976).

Ury, Marian, trans. Tales of Times Now Past (Univ. of Calif. Press, 1979).

JAURÈS, Jean (1859–1914). Until he was assassinated in 1914, Jean Jaurès was the most effective leader of the French Socialist movement. He was a great scholar, a brilliant orator, and an adept political organizer.

Jaurès was born in Castres, France, on Sept. 3, 1859. He attended college in Paris and was a teacher there and in Toulouse from 1881 to 1885. He was elected to the French Chamber of Deputies in 1885 without any party affiliation. He lost the election of 1889, but was returned to office in 1893. By this time he had become a Socialist, although he belonged to the least revolutionary of the five schools of French Socialism. He and his associates believed that they should work for the gradual adoption of democratic Socialism. By 1905 the two remaining Socialist parties had joined together under his leadership, forming the Section Française de l'Internationale Ouvrière (French Section of the Workers' International).

In the 1890s Jaurès, like all Frenchmen, was involved in the tragic affair of Captain Alfred Dreyfus, who was convicted of treason in 1894 on the basis of forged evidence. In this, one of the most explosive events of modern French politics, Jaurès was convinced of Dreyfus' innocence, a position that lost him the election of 1898. He was reelected in 1902.

Another unpopular position, and the one that cost him his life, was his desire for friendly relations with Germany in the years before World War I. His passion for a French-German reconciliation when most Frenchmen were eager for war with Germany led to his assassination by an anti-German fanatic on July 31, 1914, three days before the war began.

JAVA *see* INDONESIA.

JAY, John (1745–1829). Like George Washington, John Jay was a man pursued by public office. For a quarter of a century after the start of the Revolutionary War he was given diplomatic missions, appointed to high offices, and elected to others. Jay could render this public service freely because his father was a successful and wealthy merchant.

Jay was born in New York City on Dec. 12, 1745. He was a serious-minded, studious boy. In 1764 he was graduated from King's College (now Columbia University). He became a lawyer in 1768, and soon became one of the most respected lawyers in the American Colonies.

When the Revolutionary War began, Jay was made a member of the New York Committee of Correspondence, the Continental Congress, and the New York Provincial Congress. He helped draft a constitution for New York and served as the state's chief justice until 1779. He was president of the Continental Congress until that body sent him to Spain to obtain a loan and an endorsement of American independence. Spain, a colonial power, refused to support the American Colonies.

In 1782 Jay went to France to help Benjamin Franklin—and later John Adams—negotiate a peace treaty with Great Britain. After the peace was signed, Jay declined appointment as minister to Britain or France. He returned home in 1784 to find that Congress had named him secretary of foreign affairs.

When a new government was formed under the Constitution, Jay became the first chief justice of the United States. Because of fears of war with Britain, in 1794 he was sent to London to settle many problems remaining from the Revolution. An agreement, known as Jay's Treaty, was drawn up. It provided that by June 1, 1796, the British would withdraw from the forts they still held in the Northwest Territory. The United States was to pay debts contracted by its citizens before the Revolution. Commissions were provided to settle disputed parts of the boundary between the United States and Canada. Thomas Jefferson and his fellow Democratic-Republicans assailed Jay, and also Washington's Administration, for having failed to secure Britain's promise to cease interfering with United States ships at sea.

In Jay's absence he was elected governor of New York. He served two terms, then retired to his estate near Bedford, N.Y. He died on May 17, 1829.

Tulane Jazz Archive

Tulane Jazz Archive

King Oliver's Creole Jazz Band (left) was the first black group to record. King Oliver, background, played cornet as did Louis Armstrong, kneeling with a slide trumpet. Jelly Roll Morton (right), who claims to have "invented" jazz, was the first great jazz composer.

JAZZ. In the early decades of the 20th century the word jazz was used to mean most kinds of American popular and dance music. Since the 1920s, however, jazz has usually signified a tradition in Afro-American music that began as a folk music in the South and developed gradually into a sophisticated modern art. While many other kinds of music, from classical to rock, have often borrowed features of jazz, they remain outside the jazz tradition.

Unique features of jazz are its sounds and its rhythms. Basically jazz is an improvised kind of music, and the goal of jazz musicians has always been to express strongly felt emotions. So jazz improvisers adapted standard band and orchestra instruments such as the trumpet and trombone to their expressive purposes. They also rediscovered neglected or forgotten instruments such as the saxophone. Instruments such as the violin, tuba, and flute have been used much less often because they are less able to express the feelings of jazz. Unlike most classical music, jazz features syncopated rhythms—rhythms with stimulating, offbeat accents. The several instruments in jazz groups are usually played in separate rhythms that unite to create an uplifting effect.

The jazz improviser creates and plays music simultaneously, unlike the composer who creates music at leisure and may never perform it. The improvised jazz solo may be variations on a theme, or it may consist of entirely new melodies. In either kind of solo, the player tries to create natural, flowing melodies. A solo, say jazz musicians, should "tell a little story." Typically jazz band compositions and arrangements

leave many spaces in which improvisers tell their stories, using the language of music.

Beginnings

The first jazz was played in the early 20th century. The work chants, spirituals, and folk music of black Americans are among the sources of jazz. Some of this music reflects the rhythms and expressive features of West African song. The earliest jazz musicians also drew upon marches, opera arias, popular songs, ragtime, and blues for their inspiration. Ragtime, an Afro-American music that first appeared in the 1890s, was composed for the piano, and each rag is a composition with several themes. The leading ragtime composer was Scott Joplin.

Originally a blues was a song of sorrow, sung slowly to the accompaniment of piano or guitar. A blues is 12 measures long, and typically the first line is repeated. For example,

The blue sky is my blanket, and the moonlight is my spread,
Blue sky is my blanket, and the moonlight is my spread,
A rock is my pillow, that's where I lay my head.

A blues tradition developed separately from that of jazz, but blues harmonies and the 12-measure form have always enriched the jazz tradition.

Early Jazz

According to legend, the first improvising jazz musician was the cornetist Buddy Bolden, leader of a band in New Orleans. The first jazz bands were usually made up of one or two cornet players who played the principal melodies, a clarinetist and trombonist who improvised countermelodies, and a rhythm section (piano, banjo, string bass or tuba, and drums) to accompany the horns. These bands played for dancers or marched in parades that were held almost all year long in the warm Southern climate.

This article was contributed by John Litweiler, jazz critic, a director of the Jazz Institute of Chicago, and author of 'The Freedom Principle: Jazz After 1958'.

The "divine" Sarah Vaughan (left), a major influence in jazz singing, began her career with bop bands in the 1940s. At Toronto's Massey Hall in 1953, Max Roach, Dizzy Gillespie, and Charlie Parker, left to right, play in *The Greatest Jazz Concert Ever.*

Some of the first New Orleans musicians were among the most stirring of all jazz artists. They include clarinetist Johnny Dodds, clarinetist-soprano saxophonist Sidney Bechet, pianist Jelly Roll Morton, and cornetist King Oliver. The first jazz record was made in 1917 by a New Orleans band—the Original Dixieland Jass Band, made up of white musicians who copied black styles.

The New Orleans musicians discovered that audiences were eager for their music in the cities of the North and the Midwest. In the 1920s Chicago became the second major jazz center—the new home for Morton and Oliver, among others. White Chicago youths, such as tenor saxophonist Bud Freeman and clarinetist Benny Goodman, were excited by the New Orleans masters—including the thrilling Louis Armstrong, who played in King Oliver's band—and formed their own Dixieland jazz bands. Pee Wee Russell (clarinet), Jack Teagarden (trombone), and the gifted melodic cornetist Bix Beiderbecke went to Chicago to help create this new hot jazz.

The third major jazz center was New York City, and it became the most important. In New York, pianists such as James P. Johnson created the "stride" piano style by transforming rags and Southern black folk dances into jazz. Big band jazz was first played in the ballrooms and theaters of New York. The cornets, clarinets, and trombones of Dixieland became trumpet sections, saxophone sections, and trombone sections in Fletcher Henderson's ensemble. Big band jazz was smoother, with lighter rhythms, but no less exciting than Dixieland.

Swing Era

Armstrong was the first great jazz soloist. He played vividly dramatic cornet and trumpet solos with his Hot Five and Hot Seven from 1925 to 1928 and then with a series of big bands. His rhythmic feeling was a rare combination of tension and relaxation that inspired the word swing. The free, loose feeling of music that swings became the major feature of the swing era, which lasted from about 1930 to 1945. Radio popularized the sounds of swing bands.

"It don't mean a thing (if it ain't got that swing)," according to a 1932 Duke Ellington piece of the same title. Ellington composed music full of colorful sounds and imaginative melodies. The soloists in his big band were very individualistic, playing clarinet cries, saxophone moans, and trumpet growls to his hundreds of compositions. Again and again Ellington portrayed Afro-American life in song suites such as 'My People' and 'Black, Brown and Beige' and in short masterpieces such as 'Main Stem' and 'Mood Indigo'. Ellington's career lasted for over a half century. In the 1960s he began performing his original concerts of sacred music in churches in the United States and Europe.

Coleman Hawkins, who made the tenor saxophone one of the foremost instruments in jazz, played with a full, strong sound, creating dramatic solos such as his moving version of 'Body and Soul'. Fine pianists flourished in the swing era. They included the dazzling Art Tatum, the profound Jimmy Yancey, and Earl (Fatha) Hines, who invented a daring style that replaced stride piano rhythms with appealing melodies. Yancey's simple blues were reflected in boogie-woogie, with its heavy, rolling bass rhythms.

Louis Armstrong was among the jazz musicians who accompanied Ma Rainey and the rich-voiced Bessie Smith, the classic blues singers of the 1920s. When Armstrong began singing, too, he scatted songs by improvising his own phrases and nonsense syllables. Ella Fitzgerald was the popular favorite among later swing scat vocalists. Billie Holiday was only a teenager when she began her singing career. She subtly changed the notes and rhythms of popular songs to give them new, often ironic meanings. Despite her small voice, she could swing as powerfully as Armstrong or Hawkins. Another swing era favorite was Fats Waller, who sang hilarious parodies of popular songs while playing stride piano.

Jimmy Rushing and Big Joe Turner were among the shouting blues singers of Kansas City, where another new kind of jazz began. Count Basie's Kansas City big band featured swinging blues melodies over the evenly syncopated beat of a hot rhythm section.

The exotic Art Ensemble of Chicago uses obscure instruments to create surreal effects. Art Pepper's emotional style is captured in one of his last performances (right).

The star Kansas City soloist was the graceful tenor saxophonist Lester Young. His sound was smooth, and his fanciful melodies floated over the dynamic rhythms of Basie's band.

Bop Era

Bop blossomed out of informal performances—jam sessions—in New York City's Harlem in the early 1940s. Among these new musicians, Charlie Parker was the leading personality. His exciting alto saxophone flights won him the popular nickname of Bird, yet he played equally creatively in ballads and in heartfelt blues such as 'Parker's Mood'. His broken melodies were rich with surprising accents and highly contrasted rhythms. Bop required extremely fine, indeed almost virtuoso, technique to play, and Parker was the most skillful of all bop musicians.

Many bop pieces were played at the fastest tempos yet heard in jazz. Bop featured many-noted solos and unusual, quickly changing harmonies; also, bop drummers began playing startling accents, "dropping bombs" on bass drums. Dizzy Gillespie and Fats Navarro played soaring high notes on their trumpets, while Bud Powell created long, uninterrupted streams of piano melody. Even though bop was difficult to sing, a few vocalists such as Sarah Vaughan had the necessary control and wide voice range.

The bop era, which lasted from about 1945 to 1960, was also the period of cool jazz. This was a music that offered the harmonic discoveries of bop while avoiding bop's most irregular rhythms. The leaders of the cool jazz movement were piano player Lennie Tristano, who believed in completely spontaneous improvisation, and his students Lee Konitz and Warne Marsh, who both played saxophones. The white West Coast musicians of the 1950s were inspired by cool jazz to create a soft, quiet kind of improvisation. Among them Art Pepper was most unusual for his boldness and for the strong emotional quality of his alto saxophone improvising.

The opposite of cool jazz was hard bop, which was played in the Eastern cities. Hard bop was vigorous and energetic and emphasized the Afro-American basis of jazz. Hard bop songs were enriched by the soulful harmonies of blues and black church music, and as a result the electronic organ became a popular jazz instrument. Like bop, hard bop was played not by big bands but by small instrumental groups. Hard bop composers such as the prolific Horace Silver wrote arrangements that attempted to make five musicians sound as powerful as an 18-piece big band. The aggressiveness of Silver's quintets was matched by the quintet headed by Clifford Brown on trumpet and Max Roach on drums. Art Blakey played powerful drum syncopations, inflaming the players in successive groups of his Jazz Messengers.

Many swing and bop musicians rejected pianist Thelonious Monk because of his harsh, zigzagging melodies and startling blues discords. Yet Monk was respected for the songs he composed, many of which were played by virtually all 1950s musicians: 'Round Midnight', 'Blue Monk', and 'Rhythm-a-ning'. And some musicians understood Monk's subtle style of improvising. Sonny Rollins was a forceful, dramatic tenor saxophonist who was originally inspired by Parker, Hawkins, and Young, the greatest swing and bop saxophonists. He became Monk's student and featured a cruel, Monk-like sense of humor and sudden, breathtaking melodies.

There was one musician who played in almost every possible kind of bop era ensemble—Miles Davis. When Davis was 19, he became trumpeter in one of Parker's bop groups. Then Davis led one of the first cool jazz groups and began leading a quintet of hard bop musicians in the 1950s. Sometimes Davis' trumpet playing was fast and angry; often it was lonely and haunting, in echoes of the sound of Spanish folk music. Davis liked to play pieces in which the basic patterns of harmony remained unchanging for long periods of time. This kind of harmonic structure was

SOME INNOVATIVE JAZZ MUSICIANS

Some prominent persons are not included below because they are covered in the main text of this article or in other articles in Compton's Encyclopedia (see Fact-Index). At the end of each profile a definitive record album is listed.

Air. Avant-garde "collective" formed by **Henry Threadgill** (born 1944) on flute, Hubkaphone, and alto, tenor, and baritone saxophones; **Fred Hopkins** (born 1947) on bass; and **Steve McCall** (born 1933) on drums and percussion. McCall helped organize the seminal, nonprofit Association for the Advancement of Creative Musicians (AACM) in Chicago in 1965. Threadgill worked with a gospel music group and a blues band. Hopkins was a member of the Chicago Civic Orchestra. The trio evolved from working together in a pit band, playing Scott Joplin rags, in late 1972. The original members (McCall left in 1982) defined Air as a "cooperative effort"—both in its composition and performance. Air's style was multi-textured, yet effervescent. (*Air Lore*, Arista.)

Basie, Count (1904–84). Swing pianist, composer, and bandleader. Born William Basie on Aug. 21, 1904, in Red Bank, N.J. Second pianist in Bennie Moten's Kansas City Orchestra, he reorganized the big band to perform in his polished, precisely phrased style after Moten's death in 1935. His light touch on the piano was delightfully witty. (*The Best of Count Basie*, Roulette.)

Bechet, Sidney (1897–1959). Traditional soprano saxophonist and clarinetist. Born on May 14, 1897, in New Orleans. Began playing his brother's clarinet at age 6. During a 1919–20 tour of Europe with a concert group, became probably the first jazzman to gain classical recognition. On the soprano, which he discovered in Europe, he was a pioneer. His style was emotional, direct, with a heavy and wide vibrato. Autobiography, 'Treat It Gentle' (Da Capo, 1975). Died in Paris, his home for many years, on May 14, 1959. (*Master Musician*, Bluebird.)

Blakey, Art (born 1919). Hard bop drummer and bandleader. Born on Oct. 11, 1919, in Pittsburgh, Pa. Adopted the name Abdullah Ibn Buhaina in the late 1940s during a search for his African roots. In 1954, with pianist Horace Silver, formed the Jazz Messengers. Alumni of the Messengers powerhouse include saxophonists Jackie McLean, Wayne Shorter, Billy Harper, Johnny Griffin, and Benny Golson; and trumpeters Clifford Brown, Donald Byrd, Lee Morgan, Freddie Hubbard, Woody Shaw, and Wynton Marsalis. Blakey was a master of the drum roll. (*Reflections in Blue*, Muse.)

Blanton, Jimmy (1918?–42). Swing bassist. Probably born in October 1918 in Chattanooga, Tenn. His pianist mother led her own band for many years. His first gig, at age 8, was on violin. Switched to string bass while at Tennessee State College. Signed by Duke Ellington in 1939, he emancipated the bass to solo status and sometimes used it like a horn. His plucking was melodic, yet driving. Died in Los Angeles on July 30, 1942. (*The Indispensable Duke Ellington*, RCA Victor.)

Brown, Clifford (1930–56). Hard bop trumpeter. Born on Oct. 30, 1930, in Wilmington, Del. As a child was fascinated by the trumpet his father, an amateur musician, played. Sat in with bop groups in Philadelphia in 1948. Toured with a rhythm-and-blues band in 1952–53. Had a lyrical style marked by double-tempo runs and soaring sustained improvisations. His imaginative work with drummer Max Roach, beginning in 1954 in California, popularized hard bop. Involved in three serious automobile accidents. After one, in June 1950, his career was interrupted by a year of recuperation. En route to an engagement with Roach in Chicago, he died in an accident on the Pennsylvania Turnpike on June 26, 1956. (*The Quintet*, EmArcy.)

Condon, Eddie (1904–73). Dixieland guitarist, banjoist, and impresario. Born Albert Edwin Condon on Nov. 16, 1904, in Goodland, Ind. Catalyzed Chicago's so-called Austin High School Gang (Bud Freeman, Jimmy McPartland, Dave Tough, Frank Teschemacher) with other white Midwesterners (Pee Wee Russell, Muggsy Spanier, Art Hodes, Wild Bill Davison). In 1942 organized the first televised jam session. Brought respectability and a wider audience to jazz with improvised concerts at New York City's Town Hall in the 1940s. Autobiography, 'We Called It Music' (Holt, 1947). Died in New York City on Aug. 4, 1973. (*The Best of Eddie Condon*, MCA.)

Gillespie, Dizzy (born 1917). Bop trumpeter and composer. Born John Birks Gillespie on Oct. 21, 1917, in Cheraw, S.C. Studied

trombone at 14, but switched to trumpet at 15. Gained his nickname from onstage antics while touring with Teddy Hill's band in the late 1930s. His beret, goatee, and horn-rimmed glasses became symbols of the bop era he pioneered with Charlie Parker in the mid-1940s. Since 1954, when his horn was accidentally damaged, his bent trumpet has been a trademark. A brilliant technician, he expanded the trumpet's range. Autobiography, 'To Be or Not to Bop' (Doubleday, 1979). (*In the Beginning*, Prestige.)

Henderson, Fletcher (1897–1952). Swing bandleader, pianist, and arranger. Born on Dec. 18, 1897, in Cuthbert, Ga. Earned a degree in chemistry but became a song demonstrator when he went to New York City for postgraduate work in 1920. With Don Redman, pioneered big band swing in mid-1920s. First orchestrator to use written arrangements that preserved the spirit of improvisation. Became Benny Goodman's pivotal staff orchestrator. Died in New York City on Dec. 29, 1952. (*Swing's the Thing*, MCA.)

Johnson, James P. (1891?–1955). Traditional pianist and composer. Born on Feb. 1, 1891 or 1894, in New Brunswick, N.J. Schooled in classical techniques by an Italian piano teacher. Played at Harlem rent parties before he was 21. The father of stride piano, he taught Fats Waller. To improve his dexterity, he sometimes practiced in the dark and played exercises through a sheet. Composed several black musical comedies. His style was flamboyant and physically powerful. Died in New York City on Nov. 17, 1955. (*The Original James P. Johnson*, Folkways.)

Pepper, Art (1925–82). So-called "cool" saxophonist, clarinetist, and composer. Born on Sept. 1, 1925, in Gardena, Calif. An instinctive musician, he began playing clarinet at age 9 and took up alto at 12. On the road with Stan Kenton's band in 1950 he became a drug addict. Prison terms for narcotics convictions included several years at San Quentin. Career resurged in the mid-1970s after drug therapy. His bittersweet style became increasingly intense and personal. Autobiography, 'Straight Life' (Schirmer, 1979). Died in Los Angeles on June 15, 1982. (*Living Legend*, Contemporary.)

Reinhardt, Django (1910–53). Traditional guitarist. Born Jean-Baptiste Reinhardt on Jan. 23, 1910, in a Gypsy caravan in Liberchies, Belgium. First influential non-American jazzman. Forced to give up the violin after a caravan fire in 1928 mutilated his left hand. In 1934, with violinist Stéphane Grappelli, became coleader of the Quintette du Hot Club de France. His style was ornate, a beguiling blend of black and Gypsy traditions. Died in Fontainebleu, France, on May 16, 1953. (*The Best of Django Reinhardt*, Capitol.)

Rivers, Sam (born 1930). Avant-garde saxophonist, flutist, pianist, and composer. Born on Sept. 25, 1930, in El Reno, Okla. Pioneered "loft" jazz in New York City in the 1970s with Studio Rivbea, where younger musicians were free to rehearse and experiment. His music, an astonishing collage of sound clusters, reflected a determination not to sound like anybody else. (*Streams*, Impulse.)

Roach, Max (born 1925). Bop and avant-garde drummer and educator. Born on Jan. 10, 1925, in New York City. His career has transcended his classic bop groups, with Charlie Parker and Clifford Brown, to free playing in multiple meters. Formed the percussion ensemble M'Boom in 1972. One of the most prominent jazzmen to become an educator, he was a professor at the University of Massachusetts after 1972. (*Drums Unlimited*, Atlantic.)

Rollins, Sonny (born 1929). Hard bop tenor saxophonist. Born Theodore Walter Rollins on Sept. 7, 1929, in New York City. Often played long runs of linear improvisation in odd rhythmic patterns, occasionally unaccompanied. His tonal distortions foreshadowed the free jazz revolution. He moved about as he played, angling his horn for new resonances. Often "on sabbatical," he sometimes practiced by night on New York City's Williamsburg Bridge or by day in the woods. (*Saxophone Colossus and More*, Prestige.)

Shepp, Archie (born 1937). Avant-garde saxophonist, pianist, composer, educator, and playwright. Born May 24, 1937, in Fort Lauderdale, Fla. Majored in dramatic literature at Goddard. Emerged as a controversial spokesman for the black protest movement in the 1960s. Experimented in every type of black music, using unorthodox instrumentation and sometimes his own poetry as counterpoint. His style, an amalgam of generations of jazz innovators, was sometimes savage, sometimes sentimental. After teaching drama at the University of Buffalo, he became a professor of black music history and theater at the University of Massachusetts. (*Trouble in Mind*, Steeplechase.)

called "modal." Much of the new jazz of the 1960s was based on modal structures.

The 1950s also brought forth composers who were not considered either bop or hard bop creators. The Modern Jazz Quartet offered the delicate, almost cool, compositions of its pianist, John Lewis, and became one of the most popular of all jazz groups. In contrast Herbie Nichols was neglected until after his death in 1963 and only recorded a few albums of his many sharp-witted, brisk piano portraits. The traditional forms of jazz songs were abandoned by Lewis, Nichols, and George Russell, who wrote complex, brightly colorful works for big bands. Written themes were only a small part of Charles Mingus' compositions. He built instead grand, highly emotional pieces out of blocks of music by mixing his soloists, rhythms, accompaniments, and sound colors.

Modern Era

"I believe music is really a free thing," said alto saxophonist Ornette Coleman. He abandoned the harmonic structures of the bop era and instead improvised melodies based only on the themes he composed. Coleman's music was emotionally impulsive. Often the sound of his saxophone changed from one phrase to the next as he played in and out of tune with completely unpredictable accents. Bop and swing musicians thought Coleman's music was impossibly discordant and difficult. Yet in his 'Free Jazz' a double quartet of musicians improvised at once, each supporting or inspiring the others in turn.

Because Coleman's music was so excitingly expressive, it led to the discoveries of Eric Dolphy and John Coltrane. Dolphy imitated birdcalls on his flute, played wild, fast, lurching alto saxophone solos, and made his bass clarinet sound like people talking. Coltrane played long tenor saxophone solos that began with hard bop phrases and moved to harsh, guttural sounds and high screams. A religious man, he took his music on a spiritual search that included the difficult, often violent, sounds of 'A Love Supreme' and the serene beauty of 'Dear Lord'.

With his piano, electronic organ, and synthesizer, the mystic Sun Ra led his Arkestra of space-suited musicians on imaginary journeys to distant stars. Cecil Taylor's piano music was the most complex jazz of all. His long solos were constructed in near-symphonic fashion, with many themes and many rhythms building to grand climaxes at tornado-fast tempos. Like Taylor, tenor saxophonist Albert Ayler believed emotional excitement was more important than melody. Ayler's songs began as simple marches but turned into extremely discordant honking, wailing, and screaming at the fastest possible tempos.

Chicago revived as a jazz center in 1965 when a cooperative, the Association for the Advancement of Creative Musicians (AACM), was formed to produce concerts and to teach music to inner-city youths. It generated Anthony Braxton's groups, the trio Air, and the Art Ensemble of Chicago. AACM artists played hundreds of instruments, many of which had never been used in jazz before. These included bells, sirens, whistles, musical toys, African drums, and instruments that they built themselves.

Audiences in Europe were especially enthusiastic about post-1960 jazz, leading to two important trends of the 1970s and 1980s. First, improvising musicians from many countries were inspired to draw on their individual musical heritages to create new kinds of jazz. Second, American jazz musicians such as Don Cherry, master of the pocket trumpet, discovered ways of joining Afro-American musical traditions with musics from around the world. The most popular result of this trend to variety has been "fusion" music, which joins jazz, rock, and Latin-American rhythms. (*See also* Armstrong, Louis; Beiderbecke, Bix; Joplin, Scott.)

BIBLIOGRAPHY FOR JAZZ

Collier, J. L. The Making of Jazz (Dell, 1978).
Feather, Leonard. The Encyclopedia of Jazz (Horizon, 1960).
Gitler, Ira. Jazz Masters of the Forties (Macmillan, 1966).
Gridley, M. C. Jazz Styles (Prentice, 1978).
Hadlock, Richard. Jazz Masters of the Twenties (Macmillan, 1965).
Litweiler, John. The Freedom Principle (Morrow, 1984).
Shapiro, Nat and Henthoff, Nat. Hear Me Talkin' to Ya (Dover, 1966).
Stearns, M. W. The Story of Jazz (Oxford, 1970).
Terkel, Studs. Giants of Jazz, rev. ed. (Harper, 1975).
Wilmer, Valerie. As Serious as Your Life (Lawrence Hill, 1980).

JEANS, James (1877–1946). One of the great astronomers and physicists of modern times was also one of the most enjoyable and interesting writers on science. Sir James Jeans expressed complex astronomical and physical concepts in simple words. He was the first to propose that matter is created continuously throughout the universe.

James Hopwood Jeans was born on Sept. 11, 1877, at London, England, the son of a newspaperman. He early developed a love for mathematics and mechanisms, especially clockworks. He also liked music, took piano lessons, and became an amateur organist.

He entered the ancient Merchant Taylors' School in London when he was 13, and at 18 won a scholarship to Trinity College, Cambridge University. After graduation Jeans taught mathematics at Trinity College. In 1905 he went to the United States to teach at Princeton University for four years. He taught at Cambridge for a few years more, then retired. From 1923 to 1944 Jeans was a research associate at Mount Wilson Observatory in Pasadena, Calif. He was knighted in 1928. After the death of his first wife, an American, in 1934, he married Susi Hock, an Austrian organist. His science posts included the secretaryship of the Royal Society and presidency of the Royal Astronomical Society of England.

After compiling learned books and papers on thermodynamics, kinetics, mechanics, and electricity and magnetism, Jeans began writing for a wider audience. His books include 'The Universe Around Us', published in 1929, 'The Mysterious Universe' (1930), and 'Physics and Philosophy' (1942). He died in Surrey, England, on Sept. 17, 1946.

THOMAS JEFFERSON—

3d President of

the United States

JEFFERSON, Thomas (1743–1826; president 1801–09). The third president of the United States was Thomas Jefferson. He had been the author of the Declaration of Independence and the Virginia Statute for Religious Freedom. In an age of great men Jefferson was outstanding. He helped the United States get started, and his plans for the future helped it grow. Many of the good things Americans enjoy today have come from Jefferson's ideas for his country.

The Man and His Ideas

Jefferson was a tall, straight-bodied, loose-jointed man. He stood and walked straight and his shoulders were always square. He was hazel-eyed and freckle-faced; he had a long, high nose; and no one ever thought of him as handsome. His hair was reddish, becoming sandy as he grew older. Even when he was an old man his hair was plentiful. Unlike other gentlemen of his day, he never wore a wig.

In the fashion of his time, Jefferson dressed in a long, dark coat (usually blue, and in the summer generally of silk), a ruffled stock, or cravat (in place of the modern necktie), a red waistcoat, short knee breeches, and shoes with bright buckles. Except in his days of courtship and married life, he paid little attention to clothes. When he was president of the United States he made a habit of plainness, both in dress and in matters of ceremony.

He was a courteous person, bowing to everyone he met. He was reserved, and no one ever called him by his first name. He was a very poor public speaker in a day of great orators. He talked in a thin, fine voice, and with his arms folded. He loved music, played

the violin well, liked to sing, and usually hummed or sang as he walked or rode. A good horseback rider, he often rode for pleasure in a day when men generally rode only as a means of travel.

Jefferson is often called the founder of the Democratic party. Many other groups also claim to follow his principles. He developed the theory of states' rights, which was against giving much authority to the federal government. He is known to everyone as the author of the ringing statement in the Declaration of Independence that all men are created equal, that among their inalienable rights are life, liberty, and the pursuit of happiness. His writings have stood as a torch to the defenders of individual freedom, in spiritual as well as in worldly affairs.

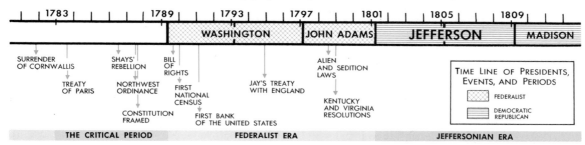

1783	1789	1793	1797	1801	1805	1809
	WASHINGTON		JOHN ADAMS	JEFFERSON		MADISON

SURRENDER OF CORNWALLIS

TREATY OF PARIS

SHAYS' REBELLION

NORTHWEST ORDINANCE

BILL OF RIGHTS

FIRST NATIONAL CENSUS

CONSTITUTION FRAMED

FIRST BANK OF THE UNITED STATES

JAY'S TREATY WITH ENGLAND

ALIEN AND SEDITION LAWS

KENTUCKY AND VIRGINIA RESOLUTIONS

TIME LINE OF PRESIDENTS, EVENTS, AND PERIODS

▨ FEDERALIST

▤ DEMOCRATIC REPUBLICAN

THE CRITICAL PERIOD   **FEDERALIST ERA**   **JEFFERSONIAN ERA**

Jefferson was the chief thinker and writer among a group of men who risked their lives, their fortunes, and their honor in fighting against a tradition. This tradition was that people need to be protected against themselves by the rich, the wellborn, the educated, or the powerful. Jefferson was foremost among the influential men who believed that laws should be made by those who are to obey them.

About 37 years after Jefferson's death Abraham Lincoln, in his Gettysburg Address, described the American government as "of the people, by the people, for the people." He was defining the kind of government that Jefferson, more than any other man, made possible. Even Jefferson's closest co-workers thought of the rights of man as including the protection of life and liberty and, above all, of private property. Their use of the words "all men are created equal" left out racial minorities. There is much evidence that Jefferson did not exclude them.

Give the people light, said Jefferson, and they will find their own way. He meant *all* the people.

Boyhood in Virginia

Jefferson's father, Peter Jefferson, was a land surveyor of Welsh ancestry who moved west from the Virginia tidewater settlements toward the frontier. His mother, Jane Randolph, was of the old Virginia aristocracy. Jefferson was the third child and eldest son in a family of four sons and six daughters. Most of his brothers and sisters died in infancy. He was born April 13, 1743, at Shadwell, in the red western hills of what is now Albemarle County, Virginia, near the mountain on which he later built his home, Monticello (pronounced *mon-ti-chel'lo*). Seven of his first nine years were spent at Tuckahoe, the Randolph estate on the James River near Richmond. He remembered, as a two-year-old, being handed up to a slave on horseback, who carried him on a pillow as they rode down the river road.

When Jefferson was nine, his family moved back to Shadwell. From his father and in the English school at Tuckahoe he had already learned to read and write.

By this time he could ride a horse. He learned to become a strong swimmer and to shoot straight. When not at school, he went with his father to hunt the plentiful deer and wild turkeys along the Rivanna River. He was first permitted to hunt by himself with a gun when he was ten, but before this he had been out alone at night hunting 'possum with his dogs.

Jefferson had started school when he was five, and at nine he entered a boarding school. This was conducted by the Rev. William Douglas, a Scottish clergyman, whose pies he remembered as moldy and whose teaching (except in the classics) he remembered as excellent. When he was 14, his father died. He was then sent to the classical school of the able and learned Rev. James Maury. There he studied until he was ready for college.

At this time his outdoor sports were long walks in the mountains, hunting, riding, and swimming. He played the violin, danced, and very early formed the habit of reading for his own amusement. He learned classical and modern languages as a child. Later he said that this was the best time to learn them.

At 17 he entered William and Mary College (at Williamsburg, colonial capital of Virginia). For two years he studied mathematics, literature, and philosophy under Dr. William Small, a stimulating Scotsman. Small then arranged for him to study law privately under George Wythe. Wythe, later one of the signers of the Declaration of Independence, led Jefferson into law practice. He continued this work until the Revolution. Then the demands of public service interfered, and he never resumed regular private practice.

While Jefferson was studying law at Williamsburg, the 1765 resolutions against the Stamp Act were proposed. From the door of the Virginia House of Burgesses the young law student heard Patrick Henry make his "If this be treason" speech (*see* Henry, Patrick). Jefferson later said that "Mr. Henry . . . appeared to me to speak as Homer wrote."

Pre-Revolutionary War Offices and Marriage

Elected to the Virginia legislature in May 1769, Jefferson served in it until the Revolution. There he was recognized as one of the outstanding young revolutionists. He was a member of the 1774 Virginia convention. Although he was unable to attend because of illness, his resolutions written for this convention resulted in the publication of his first work, 'A Summary View of the Rights of British America'. He did attend the Virginia Convention of 1775, and he was a delegate to the Continental Congress in both 1775 and 1776. It was this Congress that declared the independence of America in Jefferson's undying words (*see* Declaration of Independence).

When Jefferson was 28 he married a 23-year-old widow, Martha Wayles Skelton, on New Year's Day, 1772. During their 11 years of happy married life, his wife bore six children. Only two of them, Martha (nicknamed Patsy) and Maria (baptized Mary, but called Polly by her father), lived through the rigors of 18th-century childhood. Patsy, tall like her

Virginia Conservation Commission

Thomas Jefferson drew the plans and superintended the construction of Monticello (Italian for "little mountain"). He based the design on the architectural principles of Palladio. He chose the highest hill on his estate and leveled off the top for the site. All building materials except hardware and glass came from the estate. Planning and building took about 25 years.

father, married and had 11 children. During the winter of 1805–6 the young family stayed with the president, and Patsy's second son was the first baby to be born in the White House. Polly was small and pretty like her mother. She died in her mid-20s after the birth of her second child.

Martha Jefferson had never recovered from the birth of her sixth child. She died on Sept. 6, 1782, and Jefferson inscribed on her tombstone (in the Greek original) two lines from the 'Iliad':

> If in the house of Hades, men forget their dead,
> Yet will I even there remember my dear companion.

He never remarried.

State Government and First Retirement

In September 1776 Jefferson left the Continental Congress and at once reentered the Virginia House of Delegates. He served until he was elected governor of Virginia in June 1779. As a lawmaker he started with a broad program of reform. He had served only five days in the legislature when he moved for a complete revision of the laws. He was immediately elected to the Board of Revisors. For the next two years he worked with thoroughness and success, helping to build a set of laws in which he hoped "every fiber of ancient or future aristocracy" would be erased and a foundation laid for a government of the people.

Jefferson proposed many bills that struck at the old aristocracy of wealth and family in favor of government by those of talent and virtue. They included:

The bill abolishing entails—that is, repealing laws permitting land and other wealth to be set aside for the benefit of one line of descendants, who might enjoy the profits but who could never sell or divide the estate. Jefferson considered that this bill saved the land of his country from the dead hand of the past.

The bill abolishing primogeniture—that is, repealing laws giving an eldest son all his father's property and leaving nothing to the other children.

The statute for religious freedom, separating church and state and removing the private right of religious belief from control by public law. This statute has come down to present generations as one of the timeless declarations of intellectual freedom.

The bill for general education, allowing everyone, without regard to birth or wealth, to have as much free education as each person was fitted for.

All these bills were not immediately passed, and Jefferson's general plan for education has not yet been completely put into action. However, elements of the plan are at the root of all the public school and free library systems in the United States.

As governor of Virginia during the Revolution, Jefferson was unable to use his talents as well as he could as a legislator. He took formal possession of the vast Northwest Territory won by George Rogers Clark. He did his best to raise supplies and men for the army. He moved the capital of Virginia from Williamsburg to Richmond, but he could not defend the state from British invasion. (*See also* Virginia.)

Monticello, now maintained by the Thomas Jefferson Memorial Foundation, is much as it was in Jefferson's time. It may be visited by tourists. Here is one of the rooms on display. It shows Jefferson's skill at adapting classic decorative themes; and many examples of Jefferson's ingenuity are present. The clock weight in the right corner tells the day of the week.

His hesitancy in taking unconstitutional steps in a time of crisis cost him popular support. However, his influence remained strong enough to overcome the movement by Patrick Henry and Richard Henry Lee to appoint a dictator. In 1781 Jefferson retired to his home, his books, and his family, intending never to re-enter public life. It was in this period that he began writing his only full-length book, 'Notes on the State of Virginia'.

Congress Again—and France

This first retirement was brief. In a year his wife died. Jefferson re-entered Congress, throwing himself into the work of lawmaking, this time for the national government. Within two years he wrote some of the most meaningful state papers of the Continental Congress. Three reports were especially good:

1. *On Government for the Western Territory*, the basic document for the growth of the United States, in which Jefferson's effort to abolish slavery failed by one vote.

2. *The provision in the 1784 Instructions to the Ministers*, in which he proposed that new treaties specify that in wartime unfortified towns remain unmolested by enemy armed forces.

3. *The Notes on the Establishment of the Money Unit*, which led to the adoption of our present decimal system of copper pennies, silver dimes, and dollars. Neither the 2-dollar bill nor the common 5-cent piece, both of which carried pictures of Jefferson and of his home, was among the money units he proposed.

In 1784 Jefferson sailed for Europe with his daughter Patsy. Polly joined them later. With Franklin and John Adams he was one of the ministers who were to make treaties of commerce. In 1785 he was appointed to succeed Franklin as minister to France. Jefferson stayed in Europe until the fall of 1789,

Typical of Jefferson's clever devices is this table used at Monticello. The table top revolves and the wedge-shaped drawers, each alphabetically labeled, serve as filing cabinets.

skillfully practicing the diplomatic arts of peace.

He worked out a plan for collective action against the Barbary states, whose piracies in the Mediterranean were threatening the peace. This plan was adopted by Congress but was doomed to failure because Europe would not co-operate. He smuggled rice seed out of Italy for planting in South Carolina and Georgia. He drew an architectural plan based on the Maison Carrée at Nîmes for the new State Capitol at Richmond. He conspired with Lafayette to introduce republican government into France. Finally, with his usual zeal and foresight, he notified Congress of the French invention of a stamping press that could mass-produce machine parts.

Secretary of State and Vice-President

Jefferson returned to Monticello just before Christmas 1789. He brought Patsy and Polly home and saw Patsy married soon after their homecoming. The slaves at Monticello gave the travelers a rousing welcome.

The Federal Constitution had been adopted in Jefferson's absence. Upon his return he was offered a post in Washington's Cabinet. Jefferson accepted with great hesitancy. He became the first secretary of state under the new constitution. From then until his final retirement, with only one intermission, Jefferson was at the center of a whirlwind of complex and bitter politics.

During his stay in Europe, the reaction from revolutionary liberalism had been severe. Jefferson viewed the rising power of the conservatives, especially as represented first by Alexander Hamilton and later by John Adams, with dread. To him this mounting power meant overthrow of republican government in favor of rule by an upper class. He always believed that the defeat of the Federalists (as the conservatives were called) saved the United States from a rule by monarchy. (See also Hamilton, Alexander; Adams, John.)

In spite of his open and growing hostility to Hamilton, his loyalty to George Washington persuaded him to stay in the Cabinet until the end of 1793. In his 51st year he again retired to his home, his farm, and his debts.

Although Jefferson thought of this retirement as final, it actually lasted less than three years. In 1796 he was elected vice-president when John Adams was elected president. As presiding officer of the Senate he wrote the 'Manual of Parliamentary Practice', still used in modified form by Congress today.

While vice-president he secretly helped draft the Resolutions of 1798 for the Kentucky and Virginia legislatures against the Alien and Sedition Acts (see Alien and Sedition Acts). These Kentucky Resolutions claimed the right of the states to nullify acts of the Federal Constitution believed to be unconstitutional. They were especially remembered during the Civil War for their advocacy of states' rights principles; but their central purpose —as Jefferson saw it—was the defense of personal liberty and individual freedom.

Third President

By 1800 Jefferson's break with the Federalists was final. He and Aaron Burr both ran for president against John Adams, once his old friend but now his political opponent. Jefferson's new Republican (or Democratic-Republican) party, as the Liberals were then called, won the election; but under the original system of electoral votes both the party's candidates were considered to be running for president. The one who won the most votes became president; the other candidate became vice-president. There was a tie between Jefferson and Burr for the presidency. The tie was resolved in Jefferson's favor by vote in the House of Representatives after more than 30 ballots (see President). Jefferson's election to a second term in 1804 was virtually without opposition.

Jefferson was the first American president to be elected in a two-party campaign; he was the first president to be inaugurated in Washington, D. C.; and he was the first to start his term in the new White House. He had much to do with the design of the capital. Jefferson's presidency helped shape the destinies of the nation for more than a century, guaranteeing not only its greatness, but also some of its disasters.

In an effort to restore a balance of Republicans in government office, Jefferson started what came to be known as the "spoils system." He tried in vain to control the Supreme Court in the interests of the will of the people. He negotiated the purchase of the vast Louisiana territory on doubtful constitutional grounds (see Louisiana Purchase). He launched the Lewis and Clark Expedition (see Lewis and Clark

The frame of the Jefferson bed at Monticello is a pair of rails attached to the walls of the passageway. The frame's design makes it possible for the bed to be dismantled quickly. The writing table and the chair, with its comfortable leg support, were also designed by Jefferson.

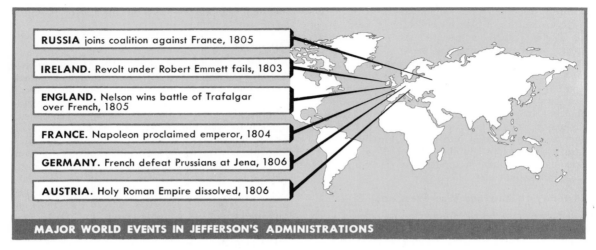

RUSSIA joins coalition against France, 1805

IRELAND. Revolt under Robert Emmett fails, 1803

ENGLAND. Nelson wins battle of Trafalgar over French, 1805

FRANCE. Napoleon proclaimed emperor, 1804

GERMANY. French defeat Prussians at Jena, 1806

AUSTRIA. Holy Roman Empire dissolved, 1806

MAJOR WORLD EVENTS IN JEFFERSON'S ADMINISTRATIONS

Expedition). He was responsible for the fighting of our first war as a nation, on the shores of Tripoli against the Barbary pirates. His efforts to prevent a second war with England only postponed it until 1812 (*see* War of 1812).

Jefferson was slow but successful in meeting the first real threat to the new American union. Aaron Burr was accused of making a treasonable effort to set up an independent government in the Southwest. This was halted when it had scarcely begun (*see* Burr). However, in the trial that followed the suppression of this Burr conspiracy, Jefferson's personal animosity toward Burr and toward Chief Justice John Marshall did him little credit (*see* Marshall, John).

His Embargo Act was a daring and original, but eventually unsuccessful, means of keeping the peace (*see* Embargo Acts). However, it may have been one of the most successful and inspired diplomatic moves of the young republic. In effect it applied economic pressures against Britain and France, who were at war with each other. It was Jefferson's answer to the British Orders in Council and the Impressment Acts, directed against neutral (in this case, mainly American) shipping. The Embargo Act stopped American shipping, thus in intent depriving European nations (particularly Britain) of some of the raw materials needed for war.

The act also had the effect of destroying the Southern economy, thus alienating Jefferson's chief supporters. It also forced his political enemies in New England into substituting—against their will—a manufacturing economy for their shipping trade. Thus one far-reaching effect of the Embargo Act was to give New England an economic supremacy which it enjoyed for more than a century. From this economic power came money to establish political power and to build the great universities which made New England a center of intellectual activity.

Best of all Jefferson's performances as president was his unwavering insistence on the freedom of the press. He stood firm in this even when he himself was the object of the most slanderous and malicious suc-

cession of personal libels ever unleashed by irresponsible newspapers.

With the failure of the Embargo Act, Jefferson finally and permanently retired from public life to his home at Monticello. There he spent the last 15 years of his life, devoting himself to his lands, his friends, his correspondence, his books, and his financial problems. He also devoted himself to the establishment of the University of Virginia at Charlottesville, which opened in 1825. Jefferson died July 4, 1826, exactly 50 years after the adoption of the Declaration of Independence and on the same day as his old friend and political rival, John Adams.

Jefferson's Versatility

In his long lifetime of public service, Jefferson played the major part in planning the principles of American democracy. He laid the cornerstone of the expansion of the United States, and so he has become the hero of many states outside the original 13. His support of individual rights, of religious freedom, of freedom of speech, and of free intellectual inquiry have made him much more than a national hero. With Washington, he is one of the two heroes of the American Revolution whose fame has spread around the world.

Most people tend to think of Jefferson as a statesman only. Actually he was one of the most versatile and accomplished men who ever lived. As an agriculturist, he invented a mold board plow that was widely used for many years. He introduced the threshing machine into the United States, and he encouraged Robert Mills in the development of his mechanical reaper. He was one of the first Americans to employ crop rotation and contour plowing.

As a scientist he suggested the invention of the stop watch, in which he was interested not for timing races but for making astronomical observations. He was one of the earliest believers in the submarine, and he was one of the first prominent men in the United States to submit to inoculation for smallpox. He had his children inoculated as well.

As an architect, Jefferson designed the 35-room Monticello, one of the most beautiful historic homes in America. He also designed the capitol at Richmond and the original buildings for the University of Virginia. He used elevators and conveyors in his own flour mill and nail factory. Among the mechanical contrivances at Monticello were dumbwaiters, hidden staircases, and an interior weather vane connected with one on the roof. In Monticello's 13 bedrooms, all the beds were simply mattress supports hung on wall hooks. He is said to have invented the lever-operated double door opener, seen today on streetcars and buses, and the folding chair both of the common type and of the walking-stick type, now used at field sports. Even in his own day he was "accused" of inventing the swivel chair. He is often called the Father of the Patent Office, because the nation's first patent laws were administered by him as secretary of state. One of his official acts was to grant Eli Whitney a patent for the cotton gin.

Jefferson was an able linguist. In addition to mastering Greek and Latin at school, he learned several modern languages, especially Spanish. He made pioneer studies of American Indian languages. He collected books all his life—and read them as well. Late in life Jefferson sold his cherished library of 10,000 volumes to the United States government. His books replaced the government collection which was burned by the British during the War of 1812. The Jefferson collection became the nucleus of the vast modern Library of Congress.

A plaster mask was made directly from Jefferson's features by John H. I. Browere, who then modeled it as a sculptured bust. It was the last likeness made of Jefferson.

No one with a knowledge of only a few aspects of Jefferson's life can have any grasp of the depth and complexity of his character. Jefferson was at the same time one of the simplest and most complicated men in history. It is completely characteristic that a man who had held the highest offices in his

This monument to the memory of President Thomas Jefferson stands on the Tidal Basin in the national capital, with the Washington Monument and the Lincoln Memorial. The splendid colonnaded structure was designed by John Russell Pope in the classic Greco-Roman style that Jefferson admired. Its exterior material is shining marble. The building was completed in 1942.

state and nation should ask that his tombstone be inscribed with these simple words:

Here was Buried
THOMAS JEFFERSON
Author of the
Declaration
of
American Independence
of the
Statute of Virginia
for
Religious Freedom
and Father of the
University of Virginia

BIBLIOGRAPHY FOR THOMAS JEFFERSON

Boorstin, D. J. The Lost World of Thomas Jefferson (Univ. of Chicago Press, 1981).

Brodie, F. M. Thomas Jefferson: an Intimate History (Norton, 1974).

Commager, H. S. Jefferson, Nationalism, and the Enlightenment (Braziller, 1975).

Dabney, Virginius. The Jefferson Scandals: a Rebuttal (Dodd, 1981).

Kimball, Marie. Jefferson, the Road to Glory, 1743–1776 (Greenwood, 1977).

Malone, Dumas. Jefferson and His Time, 6 vols. (Little, 1948–81).

Mayo, Bernard, ed. Thomas Jefferson and His Unknown Brother (Univ. Press of Virginia, 1981).

Smith, Page. Jefferson: a Revealing Biography (McGraw, 1976).

Richards, Norman. Story of Monticello (Childrens, 1970).

JEFFERSON CITY, Mo. When selected in 1821 as the site for the capital of the state of Missouri, Jefferson City was known as Lohman's Landing. It lay on the south bank of the Missouri River, near the center of the state, and had only a mission, a tavern, and a blacksmith shop. The town, named for Thomas Jefferson, was incorporated in 1825. The next year, when the legislature first met there, it had 31 families, a general store, a hotel, small tanneries, a gristmill, and a distillery. In 1839 it was incorporated as a city.

Modern Jefferson City, a trade center for a fertile farming region, is dominated by the great gray dome of the Capitol, rising from a riverside bluff. From this bluff the city extends east, south, and west over ridges and valleys paralleling the south bank of the river. The Capitol, which was completed in 1917, is particularly noteworthy for its museums of state resources and history and murals by Missouri-born painter Thomas Hart Benton.

Across a park from the Capitol lies the three-story Governor's Mansion, which was completed in 1871. Nearby are the 14-story Jefferson Building (1952), the eight-story State Office Building (1938), and the Supreme Court Building (1906). Lincoln University was opened as a school for blacks in 1866. The school has been state-operated since 1879 and now admits students of all races.

The city's industries include the manufacture of electrical appliances and shoes, bookbinding, and steel fabrication. Government, however, is the city's principal business. Jefferson City has a mayor-council form of government. (*See also* Missouri.) Population (1980 census), 33,619.

JEHOVAH'S WITNESSES. The religious organization known as Jehovah's Witnesses since 1931 was originally called the Russellites after its founder, Charles Taze Russell. It has also been known as the Millennial Dawnists and the International Bible Students. The group's central belief is that the Bible, when it is literally interpreted, can be used to predict God's plan of salvation with precision. Jehovah's Witnesses believe that the end of the world is near and that there will be a great "battle of Armageddon" between the forces of God and Satan; in this conflict God will be victorious and will set up an earthly paradise for all believers.

Russell, a native of Pittsburgh, renounced the teachings of Christian denominations because he could not accept what he saw as the conflicting ideas of eternal damnation and a merciful God. He started a Bible class in 1872, and in 1879 he began publishing a magazine entitled *Zion's Watch Tower and Herald of Christ's Presence*, now published as *The Watchtower*. When Russell died in 1916 he was succeeded as leader of the organization by Joseph Franklin Rutherford, a former circuit judge from Missouri. Rutherford molded the organization in his image, discarding some of Russell's ideas and publishing a voluminous outpouring of books and tracts. The group became highly centralized, with Rutherford directing all of its activities from his headquarters in Brooklyn, N.Y. It was at the annual convention of the society in 1931 that he announced the name change to Jehovah's Witnesses. Rutherford was succeeded as leader of the Witnesses by Nathan H. Knorr, who governed from 1942 to 1977. In 1977 the directors elected Frederick W. Franz to be the fourth president.

Three corporations direct the activities of Jehovah's Witnesses: the Watch Tower Bible and Tract Society of Pennsylvania, the Watch Tower Bible and Tract Society, Inc., of New York, and the International Bible Students Association. Local congregations are called Kingdom Halls. Members are expected to spend several hours a week at the halls in meetings and Bible study and as much time as possible in door-to-door preaching and distribution of Watch Tower literature. Each hall has a board of elders that elects a presiding minister for a one-year term. Only men are qualified to hold teaching or administrative positions in the society.

The Watch Tower Society also maintains Bethel residences around the world, the largest of which is in Brooklyn. Workers at the Brooklyn Bethel conduct the business of the society, including writing the books, publishing the magazines, and operating the printing presses. Some workers raise food for the society on Watch Tower farms.

Jehovah's Witnesses hold beliefs that differ markedly from those in traditional Christian denominations. They believe in a God, Jehovah, who sent Michael the Archangel to Earth as Jesus Christ to make it possible for mankind to obtain eternal life. The divinity of Jesus is denied, as is the existence of the Holy Spirit as a separate person of the Trinity.

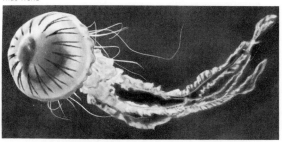

An almost transparent species of jellyfish is found in the cold waters of the North Sea. Its tentacles are about six inches (15 centimeters) long.

The major emphases of the Witnesses are on the invisible beginning of the Kingdom of God on Earth, the final Armageddon conflict, the Last Judgment, and the reconstitution of Earth as a paradise for believers only. This emphasis on God's kingdom as the primary reality leads Witnesses to dissociate themselves from all civil societies. They refuse to vote, run for public offices, serve in the armed forces, or take part in any patriotic exercises. This stand has frequently brought them in conflict with governments in many countries. During World War II thousands of Witnesses were interned in Nazi concentration camps, and they are still persecuted in the Soviet Union and its Eastern European satellites. In the United States the Witnesses have also run afoul of the law on many occasions, and they have taken many cases to the United States Supreme Court and won significant victories in the areas of freedom of religion and freedom of speech.

In the 1980s the Witnesses had about 2,200,000 members worldwide and were doing work in more than 200 countries and territories. The society has, over the years, distributed more than 4 billion copies of *The Watchtower* in 210 languages. Total distribution of its modern English Bible was more than 43 million by the early 1980s.

JELLYFISH. Among the most unusual of sea animals are the jellyfishes. Cousins of the jellyfishes are the corals and sea anemones. These three belong to the great group of animals known as Coelenterata.

The jellyfish has none of the characteristics of fishes. It has no skeleton, and more than nine tenths of its body is jellylike. In some forms not much more than one percent is living matter. There are a thousand kinds, varying in form, size, and color. A typical jellyfish may be umbrella-shaped, with few or many feelers, or tentacles. Sometimes it has simple eyes around the edge of the umbrella. The mouth and stomach are in the "handle" of the umbrella. Simple muscles on the underside contract the body much like the closing of an umbrella and enable the jellyfish to swim. The tentacles have explosive cells that produce poisons that paralyze other small animals. Then the tentacles draw them into the mouth of the jellyfish. A network of nerves runs beneath the lining of the umbrella and coordinates the muscles.

During most of their lives, the larger jellyfishes swim about freely. Many reproduce by the process shown in this article. Some smaller jellyfish spend most of their lives as attached polyps. A new individual develops from a fertilized egg and swims about for a short time. Then it attaches itself to rocks or seaweeds and develops an internal cavity, a mouth, and tentacles. From each polyp others develop as buds. Some of them remain attached to the parent and

The development of an aurelia, the common form of jellyfish, begins when the fertilized egg that is lodged in the mouth folds of the female develops into a larva, the planula. The larva breaks away from the female and swims to a spot where it becomes fixed. There it turns into a polyp with growing tentacles and forms buds from which new polyps develop. Then it elongates, and a series of horizontal segments resembling a pile of saucers appears. One by one the "saucers" break off and swim away as young jellyfish. The stages are known as the polyp, hydra, strobila, ephyra, and medusa. At the right are aurelias in various stages of development. One ephyra is swimming away.

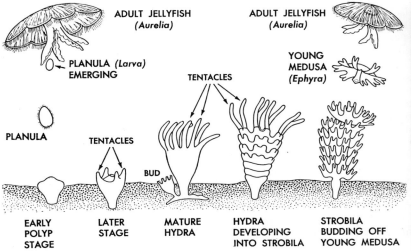

ADULT JELLYFISH (Aurelia) · ADULT JELLYFISH (Aurelia) · PLANULA (Larva) EMERGING · TENTACLES · YOUNG MEDUSA (Ephyra) · PLANULA · TENTACLES · BUD · EARLY POLYP STAGE · LATER STAGE · MATURE HYDRA · HYDRA DEVELOPING INTO STROBILA · STROBILA BUDDING OFF YOUNG MEDUSA

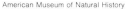American Museum of Natural History

Douglas P. Wilson, Marine Biological Laboratory

form a colony. Others break away and become jelly-fish. The budding process, following reproduction by fertilized eggs, is called alternation of generations.

Some jellyfishes are scarcely large enough to be seen. Others are 2 feet (.6 meters) or more in diameter. Some are delicate. Others are almost as firm as gristle. Jellyfish may be transparent or brown, pink, white, or blue. Some are egg-shaped or ribbonlike. Others, such as the Portuguese man-of-war, are more complex. Most jellyfishes live at or near the surface of the sea, though a few live at the bottom. Some are phosphorescent, glowing eerily in the sea.

JENNER, Edward (1749–1823). For centuries smallpox was a scourge. The dread disease killed or left weakness and hideous scars. When late in the 18th century Edward Jenner, a young physician, startled the medical profession by claiming that people who had had cowpox would not get smallpox, his theory was scorned. After many years, however, doctors began using Jenner's method, based upon his theory, of preventing smallpox. He called the method vaccination. By the late 1970s the disease was thought to be eliminated (see Vaccine).

Edward Jenner was born on May 17, 1749, in Berkeley, Gloucestershire, England, the son of a parish vicar. When he was 13 he decided to be a physician and began as an apprentice to Dr. Daniel Ludlow, who lived near Bristol. One day he heard a young farm girl tell the doctor that she could not contract smallpox because she had once had cowpox. This was the beginning of Jenner's theory and experiments related to it. In 1770 he became the house pupil of the eminent London surgeon and anatomist John Hunter. Hunter was the ideal inspiration for Jenner, with his critical mind, broad interest in biology, disciplined powers of observation, and interest in and skill for scientific experimentation and investigation. The two men formed a lasting friendship, though in 1773 Jenner returned to Berkeley in order to begin his own medical practice.

Jenner continued to experiment with cowpox. He found that there were two forms but that only one provided immunity against smallpox. This one—true cowpox—was a modified form of the more infectious and contagious smallpox. At last he was ready to test his theories.

In 1796 Jenner inoculated a healthy eight-year-old boy, James Phipps, with cowpox. Two months later he exposed the child to smallpox, but the boy did not get the disease. Jenner wrote a paper in 1798 explaining his experiments, but it was received coldly in medical circles. He then went to London to demonstrate his theory. No one would submit to vaccination. Discouraged, Jenner returned to Berkeley. Meanwhile, a successful vaccination by a London physician revived interest in Jenner's theory. The medical world was finally convinced.

Many honors came to Jenner. The British government granted him large sums of money to carry on his work. Jenner died in Berkeley on Jan. 26, 1823.

JEREMIAH (650?–570? BC). In the early decades of the 6th century BC, the prophet Jeremiah tried to help his nation of Judah adjust to the political conflicts between the superpowers of the day—Assyria, Babylonia, and Egypt. Sometimes called "the father of personal religion," he also preached the ideal of religious individualism.

Jeremiah was born about 650 BC in the village of Anathoth, near Jerusalem. He is reported to have started his prophetic work under King Josiah about 626 BC. Josiah had achieved independence from Assyria for Judah, and in 621 BC instituted extensive religious reforms. After Josiah's death in 609 BC, Judah soon found itself darkening under the growing shadow of Babylonian power, which caused many of Josiah's reforms to be ignored.

Jeremiah's early messages to the Judean people were condemnations of their false worship and social injustice, and he summoned them to repent. He preached against the policies of Josiah's successors and was often punished for his efforts. His warnings that Judah should cooperate with Babylonia to avoid conquest and exile went unheeded. After Judah was made a province of Babylonia, continued revolts led the Babylonians to ravage it in 586 BC.

Against his will, Jeremiah was carried into exile in Egypt by some Judeans who were escaping the Babylonians. He died there about 570 BC. According to tradition, Jeremiah was stoned to death by other exiles who were exasperated by his rebukes.

As a prophet, Jeremiah pronounced God's judgment upon the people of his time for their wickedness.

A fresco of Jeremiah in the Sistine Chapel in Rome was painted by Michelangelo in about 1512.

A rooftop panorama of Jerusalem reveals the Muslim shrine the Dome of the Rock, lower right, the Redeemer's Church, center, and modern high-rise buildings in the background.

He was concerned especially with false and insincere worship and failure to trust God in national affairs. He found the source of sin to be in what he often called "the stubbornness of the evil heart." He considered sin to be unnatural. He emphasized that some foreign nations were more loyal to their pagan, or false, deities than Judah was to Yahweh, the real God. He often contrasted nature's obedience to law with man's disobedience to God.

JERSEY CITY, N.J.

Jersey City is on the Hudson River across from the southern tip of New York State. On the north the city adjoins Hoboken and on the south, Bayonne. The Port Authority Trans-Hudson (PATH) system provides rapid transit service to and from New York City. The Holland

Tunnel is the road link for motor traffic. In Jersey City it connects with the Pulaski Skyway, which leads to Newark, N.J. Several trunk-line railways end in Jersey City. Ferries carry the freight cars across the Hudson to New York. Jersey City is also a terminus for oceangoing and coastal vessels.

Industries include meat-packing, oil refining, and the manufacture of electrical equipment, wearing apparel, iron and steel goods, chemicals, soap, paint, and cosmetics. Higher education is provided by Saint Peter's and Jersey City State colleges.

The Dutch made the first settlement, Paulus Hook, on the waterfront, in 1630. The name was changed to Jersey City in 1820. The seat of Hudson County, it is now the state's second largest city. It has a mayor-council government. (*See also* New Jersey.) Population (1980 census), 223,532.

JERUSALEM.

Three major world religions regard Jerusalem as a holy city. To Christians it is sacred because of its associations with Christ. For Jews it serves as the center of both their national and their religious life. In the religion of Islam, Jerusalem ranks in importance after Mecca and Medina as a holy city.

Jerusalem's importance as a religious center and its location at an ancient Middle Eastern crossroads have made it the prize of many conflicts throughout history. Since 1948, when the state of Israel was founded, the city has been a battleground whenever war erupted between Israel and Jordan. The Arab-Israeli war of 1948 left the city divided by an armistice line. Eastern Jerusalem, called the Old City, became part of the Hashemite Kingdom of Jordan. Western Jerusalem became part of Israel.

Western Jerusalem was made the capital of Israel in 1950. After Israel occupied Jordanian Jerusalem in the Israeli-Arab war of 1967, Israel proclaimed the unification of the city under Israeli rule. Neither Jordan nor the United Nations recognized this Israeli action. (*See also* Israel; Jordan.)

Location, Climate, and Water Supply

Jerusalem stands on a rocky spur of the Judaean Hills about 2,500 feet (762 meters) above sea level. On the west the stony hills merge into a fertile coastal plain. On the east the desert reaches almost to the walls of the Old City. The surrounding land is not very fertile. The heat is oppressive in spring and autumn, but in summer—the dry season—a Mediterranean Sea breeze tempers the climate.

Viewed from across a pool and fountain is the administrative headquarters of the Hebrew University in the western part of Jerusalem known as the New City. The university is situated in the corridor that connects western Jerusalem with the Israeli plain.

The water supply has always been poor. Houses in the Old City have rock-cut cisterns to catch rainwater. Water for the New City is piped from the Mediterranean plain and lifted by pumping stations.

The New City

Even before old Jerusalem was annexed to the New City in 1967, western Jerusalem was the third largest city in Israel. In the New City there are modern apartment houses and shopping centers as

The massive stones of the Wailing Wall, in the former Jewish quarter of the Old City, are believed to be the remains of the Second Temple of Jerusalem.

well as attractive suburban homes. The oldest section, the Orthodox Jewish quarter, was the first Jewish suburb outside the Old City walls. It was established in 1860. The New City also includes Mount Zion.

Since the founding of Israel the New City has expanded rapidly into the corridor that connects western Jerusalem with the Israeli plain. Surrounding Jerusalem and the corridor is Arab territory. In the corridor, government buildings and the new Hebrew University are included in one design. Still farther west is the Hadassah Medical Center.

The Old City

There was a fortified city on the site of old Jerusalem at the beginning of history. Many times it was destroyed and rebuilt. The wall that now surrounds it was built by a Turkish sultan, Solyman the Magnificent, in the 16th century. Wall gates open into streets so narrow that no wheeled vehicle can pass through. They are paved with uneven, slippery cobblestones. Some are covered over for shade. Others are arched overhead to support old buildings on either side. They are lined with slum dwellings, cavelike shops, and open-air bazaars. The streets are crowded with long-robed Arabs, on foot or riding on donkeys.

The Dome of the Rock and the Wailing Wall

On the supposed site of Solomon's splendid Temple stands a beautiful Mohammedan mosque, built of marble and colored tiles. This is the Dome of the Rock, usually (but incorrectly) called the Mosque of Omar. Under the great dome is a massive rock, traditionally regarded as the altar for burned sacrifices in Old Testament times. Moslems believe that Mohammed, after

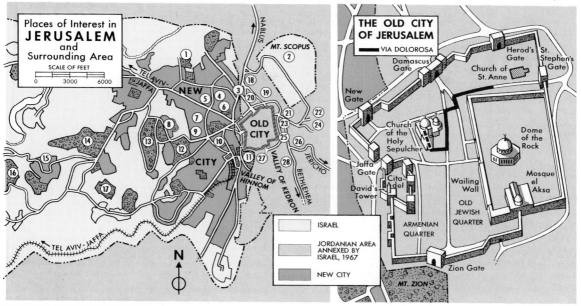

GUIDE TO PLACES OF INTEREST

IN ISRAELI TERRITORY

1. Biblical Zoo
2. Former Hebrew University and Medical Center
3. Mandelbaum Gate
4. Orthodox Jewish Quarter
5. Histadrut
6. Russian Compound
7. Knesset (Parliament)
8. Government offices
9. Jewish Agency Building
10. Y.M.C.A.
11. Mount Zion: Abbey of the Dormition; Cenaculum
12. Monastery of the Cross
13. Hebrew University Campus
14. Mount Herzl: Herzl's Tomb
15. Ein Karem: Christian churches and monasteries
16. Hadassah Medical Center
17. B'nai B'rith Children's Home

IN ANNEXED TERRITORY

18. Tomb of the Kings
19. Rockefeller Museum
20. St. George's Cathedral
21. Mary's Tomb
22. Mount of Olives
23. Garden of Gethsemane
24. Church of the Ascension
25. Absalom's Tomb
26. Jewish Cemetery
27. House of Caiaphas
28. Benedictine Monastery

praying at this rock, was carried up by the angel Gabriel for a visit to heaven.

The Dome of the Rock stands in a vast walled courtyard called the Haram esh-Sherif. Part of the western wall is believed to be a relic of the wall that surrounded Solomon's Temple. It is called the Wailing Wall because for centuries Jews made pilgrimages to it to lament the destruction of the Temple by the Romans. The whole quarter in which Jews once lived was destroyed by the Arabs in 1948.

Christian Shrines in the Old City

North of the Haram esh-Sherif begins the Via Dolorosa (Street of Sorrows), also called the Way of the Cross. This is believed to be the path Christ trod on his way to Calvary. It ends at the Church of the Holy Sepulcher, built over the supposed tomb of Jesus. This is the place most visited by Christians. Part of the church was built by the Crusaders in the 12th century (see Crusades).

Just outside the walls, to the east, Franciscan friars tend the ancient Garden of Gethsemane. Still farther east, Christian holy places are scattered up the slope of the Mount of Olives.

Early History of Jerusalem

The first historical mention of Jerusalem is in Egyptian texts written about 1900 B.C. At the time of the Israelites' entrance into Palestine, the city was held by the Jebusites, a Canaanite tribe. David,

king of the Israelites, captured it about 1000 B.C. and established the Ark of the Covenant there. King Solomon, his son, built a great temple for the Ark as well as a splendid palace for himself.

Solomon's Temple stood until 586 B.C. Then King Nebuchadnezzar II of Babylon destroyed it and carried off the Israelites. In the 50 years of their famous Babylonian captivity they remembered Jerusalem and sang the songs of Zion: "If I forget thee, O Jerusalem, let my right hand forget her cunning."

Rome took Jerusalem in 63 B.C. From 40 to 4 B.C. its Roman ruler was King Herod the Great. Herod was an enthusiastic builder. He put up a palace for himself and constructed new walls with three great towers. He even rebuilt the Temple, following Jewish laws. This was the Jerusalem Christ knew.

In A.D. 66 the Jews revolted against Roman rule. In A.D. 70 the Roman emperor Titus cruelly crushed the rebellion and destroyed the city. Jews were forbidden to live there or to visit the Temple site.

The Roman emperor Hadrian built a new city on the ruins; but the temples he put up were to Roman gods. All that remained of Herod's city were three towers and part of the wall.

Long Centuries Under Moslem Rule

Constantine, Rome's first Christian emperor, put up the first Church of the Holy Sepulcher in Jerusalem. Omar, the second caliph after the prophet Mohammed, ousted the Romans in A.D. 637.

AP/Wide World

Ewing Galloway

A chapel (left) under the dome of the Church of the Holy Sepulcher is the final station of the Way of the Cross. Jesus went to his death along the Way of Sorrows (right).

The Crusaders took Jerusalem in 1099, but the Moslem leader Saladin won it back in 1187. The city remained in Moslem hands, passing from the Arabs to the Turks, until World War I. Then the British captured it in 1917. After the war the British continued to administer Palestine under a mandate from the League of Nations. Jerusalem was its capital. (*See also* Crusades; Palestine.)

Modern Jerusalem

During the years of the mandate, many Jews settled in Palestine. After two decades of uneasy rule the British withdrew in 1948, and the Jews established the State of Israel. War immediately broke out with the Arab states. When it ended, Israel was in possession of the New City of Jerusalem; the country of Jordan held the Old City. The United Nations voted in 1949 to make Jerusalem an international city. Jordan and Israel, however, agreed on a boundary along the armistice line through the city's center. Jews were thus denied access to the Wailing Wall.

In June 1967, during the Six-Day War between Israel and the Arab states, Israel occupied western Jordan, including Jordanian Jerusalem. On June 28, 1967, Israel proclaimed a unified Jerusalem under Israeli administration. The barriers dividing the city were removed for the first time in 20 years. Israel guaranteed the accessibility of religious shrines to members of all faiths.

In 1968, despite the United Nations call for internationalization, Israel expanded the city by annexing adjacent Arab territories. In 1988 the Palestine Liberation Organization (PLO) declared Palestine an independent state. The PLO envisioned the new state as consisting of the Israeli-occupied West Bank and the Gaza Strip, with Jerusalem as the capital. Population (1986 estimate), 457,700.

JESPERSEN, Otto (1860–1943). A linguist and a foremost authority on English grammar, Otto Jespersen helped to revolutionize language teaching in Europe. He contributed greatly to the advancement of linguistic theory, the history of English, and the knowledge of phonetics, or the sounds of speech. He also originated an international language that was known as Novial.

Otto Jespersen was born on July 16, 1860, in Randers, Denmark. As a boy he was inspired by the accomplishments of the famed Danish linguist Rasmus Rask, who influenced Jespersen in his study of Icelandic, Italian, and Spanish. Jespersen decided to explore the study of language at a time when phonetics and reform in language were important concerns. He received his master's degree in French from Copenhagen University in 1887. As a professor of English there from 1893 to 1925, he led a movement for basing foreign-language teaching on everyday speech. In the course of his career he wrote a number of textbooks used in Denmark and other countries. One of his most vital works, 'Growth and Structure of the English Language', was published in 1905 and reprinted in 1969. His greatest work in this area was the encyclopedic 'A Modern English Grammar on Historical Principles', published in seven volumes (1909–49).

Jespersen gave special attention to the relationship between sound and sense in language. His book on phonetics, 'Fonetik' (1897–99), was the best scientific treatment of general phonetics for many years. His principal work on linguistic evolution and probably his most brilliant achievement was 'Language: Its Nature, Development, and Origin' (1922). He presented his international language, Novial, in a work entitled 'International Language' (1928). A lexicon for this language followed in 1930. Jespersen died in Roskilde, Denmark, on April 30, 1943.

"The child Jesus tarried behind in Jerusalem; and Joseph and his mother knew not of it. . . . And when they found him not, they turned back again to Jerusalem, seeking him. . . . After three days they found him in the temple, sitting in the midst of the doctors, both hearing them, and asking them questions. And all that heard him were astonished at his understanding and answers" (Luke ii, 43, 45-7). The picture is from a painting by Heinrich Hofmann, 'The Finding of Christ in the Temple'.

JESUS CHRIST. Nearly all that we know about the life of the founder of Christianity is contained in the four Gospels of the New Testament. These accounts were written from 60 to 100 or more years after the birth of Christ by men of different temperaments. So they differ in some details, but agree in all essentials. Aside from mere mention by two Roman historians, in works written within a century after his death, the secular historians of his time said nothing about this Man who has had such a profound influence on the life and thought of the world.

Although in most countries today time is reckoned from the birth of the founder of Christianity, a mistake occurred in fixing the date of this event. We have no record of the exact date of Jesus' birth. But we do know that the date adopted several centuries later as the beginning of the Christian Era was at least three years too late; that is, Jesus was born in 3 B.C., or earlier, according to our reckoning.

The Birth of Jesus

Jesus was born in Bethlehem of Judea, about six miles from Jerusalem. To his mother Mary an angel foretold that she, a virgin, should bring forth a child who should be the Son of God. When her time was fulfilled Mary and her husband Joseph, a poor carpenter from Nazareth in the northern province of Galilee, went to Bethlehem to be taxed by the Roman governor. Because there was no room for them in the inn they had to lodge in a cave hollowed in a hillside and used as a stable. Yet the babe born in this lowly place was descended from David, the great king of Israel; and his birth was heralded by signs and wonders. Guided by the words of an angel, shepherds came to the cave and knelt in adoration before the holy child lying in swaddling clothes in a manger.

Soon afterward wise men, or Magi, as they were called, came from the East, saying, "Where is he that is born King of the Jews? for we have seen his star in the East, and are come to worship him." The chief priests of Herod, king of Jerusalem, said the child would be found in Bethlehem. The Magi continued their journey, with the bright star—now traditionally called the Star of Bethlehem—moving ahead of them till it stopped above the place where the child lay.

Herod feared his throne would be endangered by the child if he grew to manhood. To remove the threat, Herod ordered all children two years old or younger

Rembrandt, the master of light and shade, depicted Jesus as a humble and simple man, and yet a striking and noble figure.

to be slain. But Joseph, having been warned by an angel in a dream, fled with Mary and the child to Egypt, where they lived until the cruel Herod died. Then they returned and took up their abode in Nazareth. Here Jesus passed his boyhood. Of these years, the Bible tells only one incident. When he was 12 years old, Jesus went with his parents to Jerusalem to celebrate the Passover. His parents had traveled a long distance on their way when they noticed that Jesus was not with them. Anxiously returning to the Temple, they found him in the midst of the doctors, who were astonished by his wisdom.

From boyhood to manhood Jesus grew in wisdom. When he was about 30 years of age, he was ready for his great mission. A short time before, a prophet had appeared, announcing the near approach of the long-awaited Messiah or Christ. From the fact that he baptized his followers in the Jordan River, he is known as John the Baptist. Jesus himself came for baptism, and John recognized in him the one mightier than himself, whose coming he had foretold.

Preparation for His Great Work

In order to prepare himself for the great work that now lay before him, Jesus went into the wilderness. For 40 days and 40 nights he fasted and prayed, struggling with temptation. After his return there gathered about him a group of disciples who recognized him as the Messiah. Gradually the number of these followers increased, and from them were chosen 12 apostles to spread his message (see Apostle).

Jesus showed miraculous powers in turning water into wine at the wedding at Cana, in healing the sick, in feeding 5,000 with five loaves and two fishes, and in performing many other wonders. Wherever he went he sought out the lowly, associating with publicans (the despised tax-gatherers), with the poor and the maimed, even sinners.

To all who were suffering he brought a message of comfort: "Come unto me, all ye that labour and are heavy laden, and I will give you rest." Love was the keynote of his preaching. "Thou shalt love the Lord thy God with all thy heart, and with all thy soul, and with all thy mind, and with all thy strength; this is the first commandment. And the second is like, namely this, Thou shalt love thy neighbour as thyself." He bade men follow the law of Moses and the words of the prophets. "Think not I come to destroy the law, or the prophets," he said; "I am not come to destroy, but to fulfill." But he saw that many of the Pharisees followed only the letter of the commandments and forgot the spirit. For this he denounced them; while they in turn looked upon him as a revolutionary, accused him of breaking the Sabbath because he healed the sick on the day of rest, and regarded as blasphemy his claim to be the Son of God.

Jesus knew when he went to Jerusalem that he must suffer and die. On Passover Eve, he ate his last supper with his 12 disciples and retired for prayer to the Garden of Gethsemane. There he was betrayed by Judas Iscariot, one of the Twelve. He was arrested and brought before the Sanhedrin, the Jewish council of priests and elders. After a hasty trial, they pronounced him "guilty of death" for blasphemy. They had no authority to pass the death sentence, so they delivered him to Pontius Pilate, the Roman governor. Pilate, after washing his hands to show that he was innocent of the blood of the prisoner, yielded to the demands of the multitude and gave him up to be crucified. With a crown of thorns upon his head and arrayed in a purple robe, which the soldiers placed upon him in mockery, Jesus was led to Golgotha, the place of execution. There, with a criminal on either side of him suffering the same punishment, he died upon the cross, crying in his last agony, "My God, my God, why hast thou forsaken me?"

Jesus' body was taken from the cross and placed in a tomb by Joseph of Arimathea and Nicodemus. Three days later, when some women came with spices to embalm the body, they found the tomb empty. An angel who kept watch told them that Christ had arisen from the dead. The risen Christ appeared first to Mary Magdalene, the once sinful woman from whom he had cast out seven devils and who had become one of his followers; and then to others who had been close to him. He spent 40 days on earth after his resurrection, and then from the midst of his disciples he was taken up to heaven. He left no writings. From recollections of his teachings his followers put together the record of his ministry, as it is stated in the New Testament, and with it there slowly took shape the doctrine and organization of the Christian church. (See also Bible.)

Boeing Co.

The Boeing 727 jet airliner is the "workhorse" of the airways. In 1972 total sales of all versions of the 727 surpassed 1,000 aircraft, the first time that number was reached by a commercial plane.

JET PROPULSION. Near the end of World War II, Allied pilots were startled by a new German fighter plane. It had no propeller, flew with a deep roar, and flashed through the air at a speed of more than 500 miles (800 kilometers) per hour. This amazing airplane was a jet-propelled Messerschmitt Me-262.

Today jet fighters fly through the stratosphere more swiftly than sound. Jet airliners fly higher, faster, and farther than ever before. Jet propulsion speeds missiles to their targets (*see* Guided Missiles). In addition, rockets boost Earth satellites into orbit.

Although most uses of jet propulsion have been for flight, it can also be applied to hydraulic jet propulsion for small, high-speed boats and pleasure craft. In such applications water is taken in at the forward end of the boat, compressed by high-pressure pumps, and discharged through a nozzle at the rear of the craft. The need for efficient pumps and the limitations of boat speeds have not made hydraulic jet propulsion an attractive or economic alternative to propeller-driven vessels.

Jet propulsion is the driving forward of a body by means of a jet of gas or fluid. The idea dates back to the 1st century AD when Hero of Alexandria built an engine called an aeolipile. He mounted a hollow metal globe with projecting tubes between two pipes so it could spin. Steam entered the globe through the pipes. As it escaped through the bent tubes, the jets of steam spun the globe.

Hero's machine illustrates a scientific principle that Sir Isaac Newton formulated in 1687. Newton's third law of motion states that for every action there is an equal and opposite reaction. In Hero's machine the jets of steam escaping from the tubes are the action, the spinning of the globe the reaction. The same principle applies to jet engines, and for this reason they are called reaction engines.

Newton himself designed a jet-propelled carriage called Newton's Wagon. A water-filled sphere was heated by fire, creating steam. A large nozzle projected back from the sphere. As the steam escaped from the nozzle, it propelled the wagon forward.

Principle

There are many everyday examples of jet propulsion. A blown-up toy balloon with its neck closed shows no tendency to move because the air inside is pressing equally in all directions. If the neck is opened suddenly, the balloon shoots away. The escaping air relieves pressure at the neck, and there is a reaction from the air opposite the neck. It is not the air rushing out of the neck and pushing against the outside air, however, that drives the balloon ahead. It is the air pushing against the inside front wall of the balloon that propels it forward. In fact, a jet would operate more efficiently in a vacuum because there would be no air to obstruct the escaping gases.

A blown-up balloon darts away in jet-propelled flight when released with its neck open. As air escapes, pressure against the balloon's inside front wall propels it.

HOW A JET WORKS

Escaping air **does not** thrust balloon forward by pushing against atmosphere

Air pressing
HERE
pushes balloon
forward

105

TYPES OF JET PROPULSION

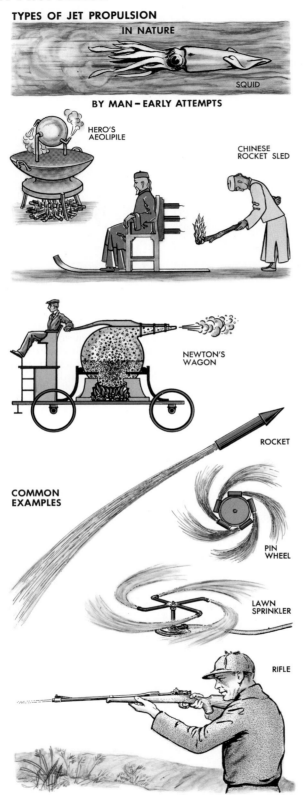

IN NATURE

SQUID

BY MAN — EARLY ATTEMPTS

HERO'S
AEOLIPILE

CHINESE
ROCKET SLED

NEWTON'S
WAGON

ROCKET

COMMON
EXAMPLES

PIN
WHEEL

LAWN
SPRINKLER

RIFLE

The recoil of a rifle also illustrates action and reaction. Expanding gases propel the bullet out of the barrel at high velocity. The rifle in response to the force of the gases "kicks back." Another example of jet action is the garden hose whose nozzle jumps back when the water is suddenly turned on full force.

Types

There are two general types of jet propulsion—air-breathing and nonair-breathing engines (see Airplane). Air-breathing engines use oxygen from the atmosphere in the combustion of fuel. They include the turbojet, turboprop, ramjet, and pulse-jet. The term jet is generally used only in reference to air-breathing engines.

Nonair-breathing engines carry an oxygen supply. They can be used both in the atmosphere and in outer space. They are commonly called rockets and are of two kinds—liquid-propellant and solid-propellant. (For a complete description, see Rocket.)

Air-breathing engines may be further divided into two groups, based on the way in which they compress air for combustion. The turbojet and turboprop each has a compressor, usually turbine-driven, to take in air. They are called gas-turbine engines. The ramjet and the pulse-jet do not have compressors.

Turbojet engines. The most widely used air-breathing engine is the turbojet. After the air is drawn into the engine through an inlet, its pressure is first increased by a component called a compressor. The air then enters the combustion chamber, where it is burned with fuel to increase its temperature. The hot, high-pressure gas then expands through a wheel-like device called a turbine, where it produces power. The turbine is connected to the compressor by a shaft, and the power output of the turbine drives the compressor. At the turbine outlet the hot-gas pressure is still above that of the surroundings, and the final expansion takes place through an exhaust nozzle where the speed of the exhaust gas is increased. It is the final high-velocity jet that produces the thrust to push the plane through the air. Although in concept a jet engine is much simpler than a reciprocating engine that turns a propeller, the actual design for efficient operation is complex, and large jet engines are extremely costly.

Today almost all airborne jet engines utilize axial-flow compressors. In these devices the air flows generally in one direction along the shaft that connects the compressor and the turbine; it moves through alternate rows of stationary and rotating sets of blades called stators and rotors respectively. The blades are arranged so that the entering air is slowed while passing through them and its pressure increased. Modern axial-flow compressors can increase the pressure 25-fold in about 16 "stages," each stage consisting of a set of rotor and stator blades.

Centifugal compressors, which were used in early aircraft jet engines, take air in at the center of an impeller, or vaned wheel, and compress it in a radial, or outward, direction. Lower efficiencies, a limited pressure rise, and large diameters that add to the drag of the engine assembly now limit the use of centrifugal compressors to small engines and to non-flight applications.

When the air in a turbojet engine leaves the compressor and enters the combustion chamber, it is mixed with a finely atomized kerosene-like fuel and burned. In theory, for best performance the burning temperature should be as high as can be achieved from the complete combustion of the fuel and the oxygen in the air. This would, however, make the turbine inlet temperature much too high for operation, and at present turbine inlet temperatures are limited to about 1,900° to 2,200° F (1,040° to 1,200° C). The temperature is controlled by burning only part of the compressor discharge air, while the rest is diverted past the burning section and mixed with the high-temperature gases farther along the combustion chamber.

Combustion chambers can be composed of individual cans, or cylinders, arranged around the turbine shaft. Another approach is the use of an annular chamber in which a liner, or tubular sleeve, surrounds the shaft.

Special alloys that are both strong and lightweight are required in turbine blades in order to withstand the high temperatures and stresses there. Among those under study are combinations of metals and ceramics called cermets. Turbine blades can be cooled by diverting some of the unburned compressor air and feeding it through internal passages to small holes at the front, or leading edge, of the turbine blades. This provides a film of cool air that protects the blade wall from the hot gases.

High-pressure ratio engines are built with dual spools, two shafts rotating within each other. The outer one is a high-speed shaft, which can operate at about 11,000 revolutions per minute (RPM). It connects the high-pressure turbine and compressor stages. The inner shaft, operating at about 3,000 RPM, connects a low-pressure turbine and compressor portions of the engine.

TYPES OF JETS AND ROCKETS

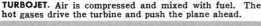

AIR-BREATHING ENGINES

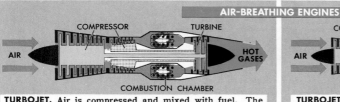

TURBOJET. Air is compressed and mixed with fuel. The hot gases drive the turbine and push the plane ahead.

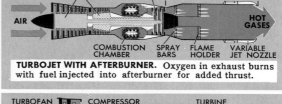

TURBOJET WITH AFTERBURNER. Oxygen in exhaust burns with fuel injected into afterburner for added thrust.

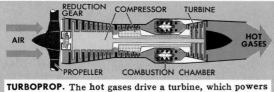

TURBOPROP. The hot gases drive a turbine, which powers the compressor and propeller, and provide jet thrust.

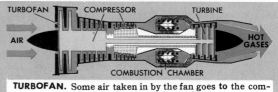

TURBOFAN. Some air taken in by the fan goes to the compressor; the rest bypasses the main engine.

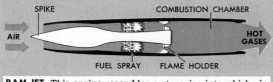

RAM JET. This engine resembles a stovepipe into which air is rammed, or compressed, by the vehicle's forward motion.

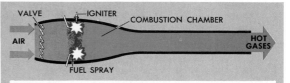

PULSE JET. A series of rapid explosions causes the valve shutters to open and shut, creating thrust in bursts.

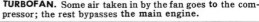

NONAIR-BREATHING ENGINES

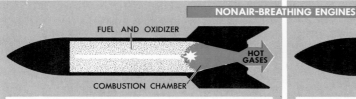

SOLID-PROPELLANT ROCKET. The combustion chamber carries the fuel and oxidizer mixed together in a solid state.

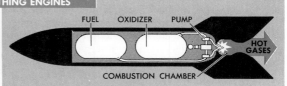

LIQUID-PROPELLANT ROCKET. The pump forces fuel and oxidizer from their tanks into the combustion chamber.

TURBOFAN JET ENGINE PROPULSION SYSTEM

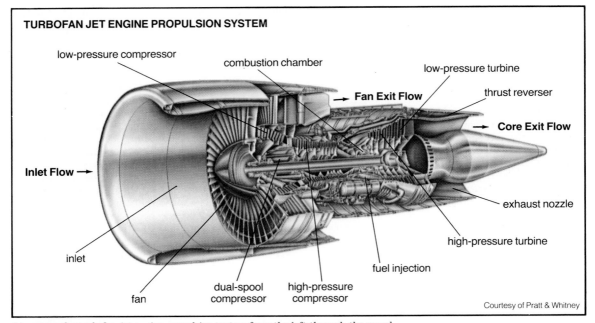

low-pressure compressor

combustion chamber

low-pressure turbine

Fan Exit Flow

thrust reverser

Core Exit Flow

Inlet Flow →

exhaust nozzle

high-pressure turbine

inlet

fuel injection

fan

dual-spool compressor

high-pressure compressor

Courtesy of Pratt & Whitney

Air enters the turbofan jet engine propulsion system from the left through the sound-proofed inlet. Once the air is in the system it slows down as it reaches the fan. Most of the air that is compressed by the fan is bypassed through to the rear of the engine and out of the system. A smaller portion of the air (shown in blue) is compressed in the dual-spool compressor until it enters the combustion chamber (bright orange). From there it passes through the turbine (dark red) to exit out the exhaust nozzle.

The greatest thrust would be obtained if the exhaust nozzle could expand the gas to the pressure of the surrounding air. However, a nozzle that is capable of doing this would be too large and heavy, and so the shorter nozzles that are used cause small losses in engine performance.

A turbojet engine cannot be started directly from rest. An external starting motor starts the unit spinning. The fuel is then ignited by a heated spark plug. Once the engine is running, combustion can be maintained without a spark plug.

The useful output of the turbojet is its thrust, which is proportional to the mass flow rate of air through the engine and the change in velocity between the exit and the inlet. (Mass flow rate is the mass of a fluid in motion that crosses a given area per unit of time.) This makes it desirable to achieve a high velocity at the nozzle exit.

Two performance characteristics are commonly used to describe turbojets: the specific thrust and the specific fuel consumption. The specific thrust produced (units of thrust per unit of engine gas flow per second) increases with the turbine inlet temperature. For this reason engineers continuously seek higher turbine inlet temperatures by means of improved materials and better blade cooling. The specific fuel consumption (unit of thrust produced per unit of fuel burned per second), which is lowered as the engine efficiency is increased, improves with increasing pressure ratio. This requires more and more compressor stages. In an actual jet engine there must be a trade-off between high pressures and high temperatures for best overall performance.

Another important performance factor of the turbojet engine is the in-flight propulsion efficiency. In this case, the best performance is obtained if the jet exit (from the nozzle) velocity is about twice the flight velocity of the aircraft. As the thrust is increased by raising the turbine inlet temperatures, the turbine exit velocity also increases and the jet exit velocity becomes too high. In such a case, propulsion performance can be increased by adding bypass air, as discussed later in this article.

Maximum thrust is usually required at takeoff, while maximum efficiency is desired at the aircraft's cruising speed, which is about 500 to 550 miles (800 to 880 kilometers) per hour for most commercial airliners. For takeoff from a high-altitude airport on a hot summer day, the lower air density results in a lower mass flow rate of air through the engine and thus decreases the available thrust. In such a case, the plane may have to fly partially empty.

Since the combustion products leaving the turbine still have a large amount of oxygen contained in them (from the mixing of additional compressed air in the combustion chamber), it is possible to put another combustion chamber at the turbine exit. This so-called afterburner is used in some military aircraft to provide emergency bursts of speed. The fuel consumption in an afterburner is very high, however, so this thrust augmentation, or increase, is not practical for cruising or for commercial aircraft.

Water injection consists of introducing water into the compressor. This increases the thrust by cooling the air and thereby increasing both its density and the mass that can be passed for a given air velocity. Water injection can be used for emergency takeoff thrust, but the weight of water that is required to be carried on a plane does not make it desirable for in-flight operation.

As indicated above, it is desirable to have the average jet exit velocity about twice the air speed of the plane. A direct expansion of all the gases through the turbine would result in a jet velocity that would be too high for effective in-flight performance. Most modern aircraft jets now employ a turbofan, in which much of the air is only slightly compressed by a propeller-like compressor device at the front of the engine and then is passed around the engine core for mixing with the turbine exhaust gases, therefore bypassing the main engine. Bypass engines provide increased thrust for takeoff and climb, and they reduce jet noise. Modern engines may bypass five or six times the flow that goes through the engine core, and even higher bypass ratios are anticipated in the future for engines operating at higher turbine inlet temperatures.

In most commercial aircraft engines, the initial compression for both core and bypass flow is achieved by a large fan consisting of one or two compressor-like stages. After the flow has been divided, the core flow is further compressed, and the bypass flow is directed around the engine.

Turbojet engines tend to be noisy, which creates a problem in the neighborhood of airports. There is both a high-frequency noise, or whine, emanating from the compressor and a lower-frequency noise from the exit jet as it mixes with the surrounding air and produces turbulence. Compressor noise can be reduced by placing sound-absorbing material into the inlet ducting. The jet mixing noise is reduced by increasing the bypass air and by special mixers in the exhaust pipe. These mixers are corrugated to increase the area over which the hot and cool gases are in contact as they begin to mix.

At the tail of the engine is the thrust brake, or thrust reverser. This is a clamshell-like device activated by the pilot after landing. It closes over the jet exit nozzle to deflect the flow outward and slightly forward so that the thrust exerted on the plane is now backward, helping to brake the craft. With thrust reversers on, a jet plane can be made to roll backward on the ground.

The most serious problem a jet plane can encounter is the breaking off of a turbine or compressor blade if it is struck by a foreign object or if it breaks loose because of an internal engine failure. All engines must be designed with a casing strong enough to contain failing blades and to prevent a broken blade from cutting through the engine and damaging vital parts or from penetrating into the passenger space.

The most serious problem facing the compressor is posed by birds. All engines must be able to "swallow"

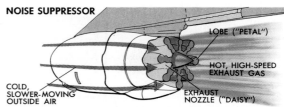

NOISE SUPPRESSOR

Enlarging the mixing area and slowing the exhaust reduces noise caused by hot gases "rubbing" against cold air.

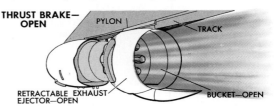

THRUST BRAKE—OPEN

A thrust-reverser brake slows the jet airplane. Here the pilot has moved the exhaust ejector back down the pylon track.

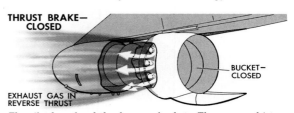

THRUST BRAKE—CLOSED

The pilot has closed the doors, or buckets. The rearward jet blast hits them and is forced forward to slow the plane.

a heavy bird without catastrophic failure, since birds can be unpredictably sucked into jet engines at low altitudes or on the ground.

In the event of engine failure in flight, the engine must be shut down. All multi-engine planes can land safely on one engine so that there is little more than inconvenience to the passengers involved if the plane must turn back for safety reasons.

Turboprop engines. In turboprop engines a conventional aircraft propeller is usually mounted in front of the jet engine and in one type of engine is driven by a second, or free, turbine. This is located behind the turbine that is driving the compressor. In other designs the power is obtained by additional stages on the main turbine.

Since turbine speeds are much higher than propeller speed, a reduction gear is required between the turbine and the propeller. About 90 percent of the energy in the hot gases is absorbed in the turbine, and only about 10 percent remains to increase the speed of the exhaust jet. Accordingly, only a very small portion of the overall thrust is produced by the jet; most of it comes from the propeller.

Turboprops are advantageous for small- and medium-sized planes and at air speeds from 300 to 400 miles (480 to 640 kilometers) per hour. They cannot compete with turbojets for very large planes or at higher speeds.

Ramjet engines. The air into which an engine rushes at high flight speeds is partially compressed by the

U.S. Air Force

1939—German Heinkel He-178—was the world's first successful gas-turbine jet airplane.

British Information Services

1942—German Messerschmitt Me-262—was the only jet fighter plane in combat service during World War II.

U.S. Air Force

1942—American Bell XP-59 Airacomet—was the first jet airplane to fly in the United States.

Hawker Siddeley Aviation Ltd.

1949—British De Havilland DH-106 Comet—was the first commercial jet airliner to fly, entering service in 1952.

Novosti/Sovfoto

1968—Soviet TU-144—was the first supersonic transport (SST) airplane to fly in the stratosphere.

Boeing Co.

1970—American Boeing 747—was the first jumbo jet airplane to begin flying.

110

so-called ram effect. If the speed is high enough, this compression can be sufficient to operate an engine with neither a compressor nor a turbine. A ramjet has been called a flying stovepipe because it is open at both ends and has only fuel nozzles in the middle. A straight stovepipe, however, would not work; a ramjet must have a properly shaped inlet diffuser that produces low-velocity, high-pressure air at the combustion section, and it must also have a properly shaped exhaust nozzle to increase the speed of flow.

Ramjets can operate at speeds above 200 miles (320 kilometers) per hour, but they become practical only at very high speeds, which must be greater than that of sound. Rockets or other similar devices are needed to produce the initial speed at which a ramjet can begin to operate.

Pulse-jet engines. A pulse-jet is similar to a ramjet except that a series of spring-loaded, shutter-type valves is located ahead of the combustion section. In a pulse-jet the combustion is intermittent or pulsing rather than continuous as in a ramjet. Air is admitted through the valves, and combustion begins. This increases the pressure and closes the valves, preventing backflow through the inlet. As the gases expand through the rear nozzle to produce thrust, the pressure in the combustion section drops to the point where the valves open again to admit fresh air. This cycle is then repeated.

The most widely known pulse-jet was the German V-1 missile, or "buzz bomb," which was used near the end of World War II and which fired at a frequency of about 40 cycles per second. Pulse-jets are inefficient, noisy, and subject to severe vibration. Their use is now limited to low-cost pilotless vehicles.

Nonair-breathing, or rocket, engines. Rocket engines carry both fuel and oxidizer on board, and they are therefore not dependent on the surrounding atmosphere for the needed supply of oxygen. Accordingly, they provide the primary means of propulsion in outer space.

Rockets are usually classified by the type of fuel burned; solid-propellant rockets carry a solid mixture of fuel and oxidizer. This mixture is similar to gunpowder and burns completely after ignition. The burning generates a large volume of high-pressure gas in the combustion section. This gas is then expanded into a high-velocity jet as it leaves the exhaust nozzle. The burning rate is controlled by shaping the solid fuel in such a fashion that the combustion gases are released at a nearly uniform rate. The control of the thrust, however, is limited, making solid-propellant rockets only suitable for the first, or takeoff, stage of space rockets.

Better control can be obtained in liquid-propellant rockets. In these, both fuel and oxidizer are stored in separate tanks and are then pumped in a carefully metered fashion into the combustion chamber. There they are atomized, mixed, and burned. Because liquid-propellant rockets can be restarted and fully adjusted, they have become the primary propulsion systems in space programs.

History

Hero of Alexandria applied the principle of jet propulsion in his aeolipile in the first century AD. The Chinese probably invented rockets about 1100. About 1400 a wealthy Chinese developed a rocket-propelled sled-chair, but it exploded when tested.

Leonardo da Vinci in the 16th century used the jet engine principle to design a mechanism for turning a roasting spit. In 1629 Giovanni Branca, an Italian engineer, built a steam turbine that drove a stone-crushing mill. John Barber of England was issued the first patent for a gas turbine in 1791.

Sanford A. Moss in 1902 was probably the first to develop a gas turbine in the United States. Working for the General Electric Company, he designed an aircraft gas turbine in 1918.

In England A. A. Griffith of the Royal Aeronautical Establishment experimented with gas-turbine compressors in 1927. In 1930 another Englishman, Frank Whittle, patented a design for a jet engine, and in 1937 such an engine was successfully tested and in 1941 achieved its first flight.

In Germany the Ernst Heinkel aircraft company produced in 1939 the first successful gas-turbine jet plane, the Heinkel He-178. The next year the Caproni-Campini CC2 was flown in Italy. A reciprocating engine, not a gas turbine, was used to provide the exhaust jet.

In 1941 the British flew their first jet airplane, the Gloster E28/39, powered by a Whittle engine. In the United States the General Electric Company built an engine based on Whittle's design. It powered the Bell XP-59 Airacomet in 1942—the first jet airplane to fly in the United States.

In the same year the Germans produced the first successful jet combat plane, the Messerschmitt Me-262. Germany was the only nation with jets in combat during World War II, but they were introduced too late to be decisive.

After the war jet research continued. In 1947 the American rocket-powered Bell X-1 became the first airplane to fly faster than sound. The next year Britain flew its first supersonic plane, the De Havilland DH-108. In 1959 the American F-106, built by Convair, flew at more than twice the speed of sound.

Britain began the first jet airline service in 1952 with the De Havilland Comet serving scheduled flights from London to Johannesburg, South Africa. This service was stopped, however, after two serious accidents in 1954. In the United States the first jet plane to be commercially tested in 1954 was the Boeing 707, which began regular airliner service in 1958. Since then numerous jet liners, both large and small, have been developed, and today the major portion of all commercial air fleets throughout the world use jet planes.

The British- and French-built Concorde, the first supersonic transport made in the non-Communist world, entered commercial service in 1976. Flying at 2.5 times the speed of sound, the plane seats only about 100 passengers. Because of its high fuel consumption and low seating capacity, it has not proven to be a commercial success.

While the original Boeing 707 and Douglas DC-8 planes utilized four engines, increasing engine size and improved performance have allowed the use of fewer engines. The Lockheed L-1011 and the McDonnell Douglas DC-10 are large three-engine planes with two engines under the wing and one centered at the tail. More recently medium-size twin-engine planes such as the Airbus, built by several European firms, and the Boeing 767 have been introduced with fuel-efficient engines. They are competing with the Boeing 727, a three-engine plane that has become one of the most widely used aircraft in the free world.

The East Pass jetties near Destin, Fla., direct the currents between Choctawhatchee Bay and the Gulf of Mexico.

JETTY. A jetty is a structure that extends from the shore into a body of water in order to influence the current or tide, often to protect a harbor or shoreline. Most jetties resemble either small breakwaters or piers, and they may be built straight or curved. Jetties may be built into rivers to narrow a wide channel so that the current is concentrated, deepening the channel and making it navigable. They can also be built in appropriate places on a river to help control erosion of the river banks.

Entrance jetties are constructed at bay inlets, entrances to lagoon-type harbors, and the mouths of rivers. They are sometimes called training jetties because they "train"—confine and direct—the water currents in order to prevent the buildup of sand and silt that might block the entrance and also in order to protect ships from bothersome crosscurrents. Entrance jetties are usually built in pairs that are either parallel or converge toward the seaward ends. Jetties are made of a variety of materials, including concrete, stone, steel, and timber.

JEWELRY AND GEMS

JEWELRY AND GEMS. Men, women, and children in every part of the world wear some sort of jewelry either as ornament or for "magic." Some pieces, made of gems and precious metals, are almost priceless. Much, however, is only *costume jewelry*—fashioned from imitation gems and the cheaper metals and manufactured in large quantities. Among primitive peoples, as in Africa and on the Pacific Islands, jewelry is largely oddments of wood, bones, shells, or animal hair; yet many of the designs are graceful. For some tribes "jewelry" is only a wooden lip plug.

As far back as the Old Stone Age, men made jewelry. In their cave dwellings they fashioned amulets and necklaces of teeth and animal bones to ward off evil spirits. By Babylonian times, men had learned to work with gold, and jewelry making had become a craft. The Sumerian jewelers had their workshops within the temple grounds. Jewelers in ancient Egypt developed jewelry enamels, or cloisonné, and produced magnificent gold and silver pieces. The Etruscans have never been equaled for their work in granulation—fusing tiny pellets of gold onto a metal surface to form a raised design. (*See also* Enameling.)

The ancient Greeks worked chiefly in enamel and *filigree*—gold or silver wire shaped into lacelike openwork. Jewelers of the Roman Empire added gems to gold and silver pieces. Enameling and heavy design characterized the elaborate Byzantine jewelry.

In ancient Hebrew times, bracelets were the insignia of kings. The Bible frequently mentions jewelry. The design for the breastpiece of Aaron, the high priest, for example, appears in Exod. xxviii, 15, and was to have 12 gems—sardius (ruby), topaz, carbuncle, emerald, sapphire, diamond, jacinth, agate, amethyst, beryl, onyx, and jasper, all set in gold filigree.

Medieval nobles delighted in jeweled religious objects, and in robes and gloves sewn thick with gems (for picture, *see* Charlemagne). In the brilliant, florid days of the Renaissance, jewelry designs were made by such great artists as Dürer in Germany and Botticelli, Ghiberti, and Cellini in Italy.

Except in Japan, peoples of the Orient have long loved jewelry and worn a great deal of it. In the bazaars of India today artisans still make pieces from designs that may be 2,000 years old. The Chinese too display great skill and artistry, especially in the classical wedding headdresses. Chinese so prize jade that many carry a piece of it in their pocket to stroke.

Medieval artists carved this superb medallion from rock crystal, probably for Lothair II, king of Lorraine. It depicts the story of Susannah and is now in the British Museum.

Instead of the brilliant green jade, they prefer more rare colors, such as white mottled with grass green or red spots and green flecked with gold.

Gem Superstitions and Gem Materials

Superstition surrounds some gems. As late as the 18th century many people used powdered gems to "prevent" or "cure" disease. They thought sapphire would relieve insanity, powdered jet would kill toothache, and topaz ease asthma. Even today some superstitious people wear amber beads to "cure" goiter; others fear that opals bring bad luck.

Most gem stones are hard minerals. Their colors range from the colorless transparency of diamonds to pure black. Some are mottled or banded. Others reflect light waves in sparkling brilliance.

Gem minerals are usually crystal. Mineral crystals vary in size from huge blocks weighing many tons to tiny specks that can be seen only under a microscope. Rock crystal, a common gem material, is found in chunks large enough to be carved into massive vases and plates. The crystals of chalcedony are so tiny that this mineral was long thought to be noncrystalline. Minerals such as chalcedony are called *cryptocrystalline* (Greek for "hidden crystal"). A very few gem materials, including opal and turquoise, seem to be *amorphous* (Greek for "without form").

A few gem materials are organic substances or have an animal or vegetable origin. The pearl, for example, is formed from secretions of mollusks. The pearls of great value come only from the pearl oyster (*see* Pearls). Amber is a fossilized tree resin; jet, a compact form of lignite (brown coal); and coral, the skeletons of tiny sea animals (*see* Amber; Coral).

through an intense oxyhydrogen flame, and the fused material drops down on a sticklike support. A lump (*boule*) is gradually built up, cooled, and cut.

Pure alumina yields white sapphire. Mixed with a small amount of chromium oxide, it makes synthetic ruby. Other mixtures yield blue, green, rose, or violet sapphires. A variation of the Verneuil process, developed in the United States in World War II, produces slender rods up to 30 inches long. They are especially useful in the manufacture of jeweled bearings for precision instruments. Synthetic gems are used principally in industry. They have replaced natural stones in the manufacture of most watches.

Chemically, synthetic gems and natural gems are identical. An expert, however, can tell a synthetic gem by physical differences. The thin layers formed by the material as it builds into a boule may be seen under a microscope. Gas bubbles are sometimes found in synthetic gems, whereas natural gems may have bubbles of liquid.

Other manufactured types are *imitation* gems and *doublets*. For transparent imitation gems—such as ruby, diamond, or sapphire—glass is used. It is a very hard variety called *paste*, or *strass*—giving the name "paste" to imitation gems. A real gem can also be combined with less valuable material. A thin slice of ruby, for example, may be cemented to a base of red paste or of garnet. The ruby forms the top of the cut stone and the combination is a *doublet*.

The beauty of all gems is increased by cutting and polishing. In ancient times and in the Middle Ages, stones were merely smoothed and rounded. From this treatment developed the *cabochon cut* of today. Stones cut *en cabochon* are oval or round in outline and have a polished, domed surface. The bottom is usually flat.

In the late Middle Ages or early Renaissance, men discovered the art of cutting stones in a complex of flat surfaces, or *facets*. Earliest was the *table cut*. This was a simple pattern with a rectangular principal face, or *table*, on top, surrounded by four sloping quadrilateral facets. The base facet, the *culet*, was much smaller than the table. Typical modern cuts are shown later in this article.

The diamond's hardness makes it an extremely difficult gem to cut, and diamond cutting is a specialized craft in the gem-cutting industry (*see* Diamond). Cutters of other gems (also called *lapidaries*) use a sandstone or carborundum grindstone. For faceted cuts the grindstone is flat surfaced; for cabochon cuts, it

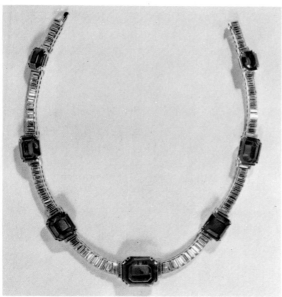

The platinum setting of this emerald and diamond necklace is simple, emphasizing the beauty of the stones. It is set with 7 emeralds in graduated sizes and 105 baguette diamonds.

There are also *manufactured* gems. Early in the 19th century several experimenters successfully produced artificial reproductions of rare stones, such as the ruby. In 1902 Auguste Verneuil of Paris established the first commercially successful process for making such *synthetic* gems. The chief raw material is extremely pure, powdered aluminum. This is sifted

The coronation crown of England is St. Edward's crown. Almost priceless, it is studded with diamonds, rubies, sapphires, emeralds, and pearls. Shown with it here are the orb, the scepters with dove and cross; and the coronation ring.

GARNET
January

AMETHYST
February

AQUAMARINE
March

DIAMOND
April

EMERALD
May

PEARL or ALEXANDRITE
June

RUBY
July

PERIDOT
August

SAPPHIRE
September

OPAL or TOURMALINE
October

TOPAZ
November

TURQUOISE or ZIRCON
December

Traditions and superstitions about the various gem stones have led to assigning certain of them to each of the 12 months. These stones are popular birthday gifts. Because superstition associates pearls with tears and opals with bad luck, alternate stones are assigned those months. The popularity of zircon in recent years has led to its wide use as a December birthstone.

is grooved. While grinding, some lapidaries hold the gem in their fingers; others use a lapidary's stick (*dop*), to which the gem is cemented. They polish the gems by holding them against a canvas-covered wheel, impregnated with *jeweler's rouge*, ferric oxide.

Jewelry making is a popular hobby. Gem materials and cutting equipment are available in most large cities, and many organizations, such as the YMCA, give courses in gem cutting and jewelry making. The science of gems is called *gemmology*.

Gem stones were formerly classed as *precious*, *semiprecious*, and *ornamental* stones. Today this classification is largely replaced by the broader term *gem*

materials. The following list includes the major gem materials and some of the less important ones.

Achroite. A colorless variety of tourmaline.

Agate. A type of chalcedony, with colored bands, first found on the banks of the river Achates; hence the name agate. The markings of moss agates occasionally resemble natural objects and so were much prized in the past. Most agates are naturally grayish and are artificially colored. They are usually soaked in solutions of sugar or honey and acid or salt solutions and then heated.

Alexandrite. Named after Alexander II of Russia. A variety of chrysoberyl, grass green in color. Shows a red hue in artificial light.

Amazonite, or Amazonstone. A feldspar, jadelike in color. Found in Russia (Ural Mountains), Virginia, and Colorado.

Amethyst. A transparent violet-to-purple quartz. Believed by the ancient Greeks to prevent intoxication. Amethysts were used in both Greek and Roman jewelry. Under certain conditions the color of some amethysts may be improved by heating. Under others heating may turn them yellow, then clear. Found in quantity in southern Brazil and northern Uruguay. Smaller amounts come from India, Sri Lanka, and Madagascar.

Aquamarine. Transparent sea-blue or sea-green beryl; of the same family as the emerald but far less valuable. Found in many parts of the world, particularly Brazil, Sri Lanka, Russia, Madagascar, and in Maine and North Carolina. An aquamarine crystal found in Brazil in 1910 weighed about 220 pounds.

Aventurine. A quartz spangled with yellow mica or other mineral. Imitation aventurine is called goldstone.

Azurite. An azure-blue copper carbonate found in most copper mines. Pliny called it *caeruleum* ("like the sky"). Used for tabletops, vases, and jewelry. Found in Russia (Ural Mountains), Chile, Zaire, Arizona, Utah, and Montana.

Beryl. A silicate occurring in several forms. Includes the emerald, aquamarine, golden beryl, morganite, and goshenite.

Bloodstone, or Heliotrope. A dark-green chalcedony (quartz) spotted with red jasper. Prized in the Middle Ages for carvings of martyrs, with the red flecks representing blood spots. Was called "St. Stephen's Stone." Widely used in signet rings, cuff links, tiepins. Found in Russia, India, and western United States.

Cairngorm. A smoky yellow to smoky brown quartz, readily decolorized by heating. Very popular in Scotland, it is sometimes called *Scotch topaz*. Used for pins, brooches, and similar jewelry.

Carbuncle. A garnet cut *en cabochon*; that is, flat on the bottom, rounded above, without facets. In ancient times any red stone was called a carbuncle, and a mythical "carbuncle" was said to give out light in darkness.

This is a *boule* for a synthetic gem, here a ruby, as described in the text. Until World War II, the United States was almost entirely dependent on Europe for synthetic gems.

Carnelian, or Sard. Name given to orange-red chalcedony. Used for ornamental carvings. Chief sources are Russia, India, and Brazil.

Cat's-Eye. The cheaper cat's-eye is of quartz, the more highly valued is of chrysoberyl. Colors range from apple green to olive, from yellow to brown, but each color has a streak or line through the middle, of varying brilliance, like a cat's eye. Found in Sri Lanka, India, Brazil, and Bavaria.

Chalcedony. A cryptocrystalline quartz, used by gem engravers since ancient times. Bible has many references to it. Color usually white, pale blue, or gray. Varieties include carnelian (or sard), chrysoprase, prase, plasma, bloodstone (or heliotrope), agate, onyx, sardonyx, jasper. Used chiefly for ornamental carvings. Widely distributed. Excellent stones are obtained from Russia, Uruguay, and Rumania.

Chrysoberyl. A rare, unusually hard stone. One variety, the alexandrite, green by day and red by lamplight, had a great vogue among aristocrats of czarist Russia. Other varieties include chrysolite and cat's-eye.

Chrysolite. An olive-green vitreous magnesium iron silicate, also called olivine and peridot. It is crystalline and, when transparent, used as gem.

Chrysoprase. An apple-green type of chalcedony.

Citrine. A clear yellow quartz resembling topaz. Used for pendants, bracelets, earrings, and pins.

Coral. Precious coral is red and branching, found in the Mediterranean. Black coral has been found in the Persian Gulf and on the Great Barrier Reef off Australia (*see* Coral).

Diamond. Pure crystallized carbon, the most highly esteemed of all gem stones (*see* Diamond).

Emerald. A deep-green brilliant emerald is one of the costliest of gems. The emerald is a variety of beryl. The finest stones come from Colombia. Other sources are Brazil, Egypt, Australia, Russia, and North Carolina.

Feldspar. Silicate feldspar produces several gem stones: amazonite, a bright green; moonstone, opalescent; sunstone, reddish; labradorite, gray with play of colors in blue and green and sometimes yellow or red. Feldspars are widely distributed.

Garnet. A gem, usually deep red, of several varieties, including the almandite and pyrope. When cut *en cabochon* garnets are called carbuncles. Garnet is found in nearly all colors but blue. Rarest of garnets is the green demantoid, found only in Russia. Others come from Brazil, India, Sri Lanka, and United States.

Girasol. A variety of opal. Iridescent.

Heliotrope. Same as bloodstone.

Hematite. Black crystalline iron; when finely divided, streaked with red. Popular for costume jewelry. Found in England, Norway, Sweden, island of Elba, and Lake Superior region.

Hyacinth, or Jacinth. Variety of zircon.

Jade. A name applied to jadeite and nephrite. The color is usually green but sometimes a whitish cast appears. The stone takes a high polish. Jewelry, cups, and bells are made of it, and poems of Chinese emperors have been carved in priceless jade bowls. In China jade is considered the most precious gem stone.

Jasper. An opaque ornamental chalcedony, in red, yellow, brown, green, or gray-blue, used for vases, tables, mantels, and pillars. Jasper is often striped. Swiss or German lapis is jasper artificially colored.

Jet. A hard, black lignite (variety of coal). Takes high polish. Popular for ornaments and costume jewelry. Many jet articles manufactured in Yorkshire, England,

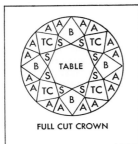 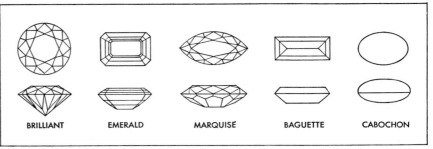

One of the most popular gem cuts used in jewelry is the full cut crown (left). The crown has 33 facets—1 table facet; 8 star facets (S); 4 bezel facets (B); 4 top corner facets (TC); and 16 top half facets (A). The pavilion, or base, of the diamond has 25 facets. For large stones the brilliant cut is increased, by groups of 8 facets, up to 82 total facets. The emerald cut has a large, rectangular table; the marquise is a pointed oval; the baguette, a narrow rectangle; the cabochon, round or oval.

from local lignite and imports from Spain. Pennsylvania anthracite and Scottish cannel coal are often used in place of jet.

Labradorite. A pearl-gray or brown feldspar, showing many colors in light. Takes high polish.

Lapis Lazuli. The blue mineral lazurite. Mines in Afghanistan, worked for 6,000 years, probably world's oldest mines. Called "sapphire" by ancient world. Also found in Chile, Siberia, and southern California. Used for jewelry, mosaics, inlaid work, vases. Best varieties are gold flecked with iron pyrites.

Malachite. A green copper carbonate; used for ornaments.

Marcasite. Differs from pyrite only in crystal structure; often set as brilliants in costume jewelry.

Moonstone. A milky, translucent feldspar. The finest specimens are found in Sri Lanka.

Morganite. A rose-colored beryl. Named for J. Pierpont Morgan.

Obsidian. A smoky natural glass of volcanic formation, abundant in Yellowstone National Park.

Olivine. A silicate of iron and magnesium. Bottle-green varieties are peridot and chrysolite.

Onyx. The cameo carver's favorite material, chalcedony, with horizontal stripes of black and white. Also used for tabletops, lamps, and decorations (*see* Onyx).

Opal. Noncrystalline silica, often combining several colors and frequently opalescent (*see* Opal).

Pearl. Not a true gem stone (*see* Pearls).

Peridot. A yellowish-green olivine. Found in St. John's Island (Red Sea), Australia, Arizona, and Hawaii.

Plasma. A variety of green chalcedony.

Prase. A dull-green chalcedony.

Precious Serpentine. Translucent and rich green.

Pyrite. A pale yellow opaque iron disulfide.

Pyrope. A variety of garnet, often deep red.

Quartz. Crystalline silica, the commonest of all minerals. Gem varieties include rock crystal, amethyst, citrine, siderite, aventurine, chalcedony, cat's-eye, and rose, smoky, milky, and rutilated quartz.

Rhinestone, or Brilliant. Imitation gem made from special kinds of glass called *paste*, or *strass*. Colorless, sparkling, in imitation of diamonds. Rhinestone glass made from heating mixture of quartz, red lead, potassium carbonate, borax, white arsenic.

Rhodolite. A pink or purple variety of pyrope.

Rock Crystal. A clear quartz much used for beads, vases, goblets, and crystal balls.

Ruby. A transparent red corundum valued according to shade of color. Large rubies are often worth more than fine diamonds of the same size. Pigeon-blood (deep carmine-red) rubies, which seldom exceed three carats, are obtained from Burma. Darker rubies come from Thailand. Rubies also occur in Sri Lanka, Afghanistan, and North Carolina.

Sapphire. A transparent corundum, or aluminum oxide. Sapphires range from white through blue, violet, yellow, and green to near black. Blue star sapphires with six rays are favorite stones. Fine sapphires are equal in value to diamonds of equal size. Found in Burma, Thailand, Sri Lanka, and Jammu and Kashmir.

Sardonyx. A variety of onyx with parallel layers of white, brown, black, and red sard. Chief sources are Brazil, Uruguay, Madagascar, India, and Russia.

Spinel. A red, violet, blue, green, or yellow magnesium aluminate. Sometimes called "mother of ruby." Found in Burma, Thailand, Sri Lanka, and Madagascar.

Sunstone. A reddish feldspar with fiery reflections.

Tigereye. Like cat's-eye, a chatoyant stone; that is, when polished, the interior shows an undulating light.

Topaz. An aluminum fluosilicate occurring in tawny yellow, blue, green, reddish violet, pink, and colorless varieties. Found in Brazil, Russia, Sri Lanka, and United States.

Tourmaline. A complex aluminum borosilicate occurring in great variety—colorless, rose red, green, blue, yellowish, green, honey yellow, violet, and dark blue. Most tourmaline is obtained from Brazil, Elba, Madagascar, and Maine, Connecticut, and California.

Turquoise. A hydrous copper aluminum phosphate ranging from sky blue to greenish gray. Often cut *en cabochon*. Widely used for bracelets, earrings, pins, belt buckles, and saddle studdings. Faded by heat and sunlight. Found in Iran, New Mexico, and Nevada.

Zircon. A zirconium silicate usually occurring in brownish, gray, or brownish-red varieties, but sometimes in yellows and greens. Colorless and blue varieties are usually produced by heating brown zircons. Zircons come chiefly from Sri Lanka and Indochina.

A late Incan armlet of gold is embossed with figures of birds, monkeys, and a man riding a horse.

The Art Institute of Chicago

JEWS *see* JUDAISM.

JIANGSU, or **KIANG-SU.** One of the 21 provinces of China, Jiangsu is located on the east coast and is bounded by the Yellow Sea on the east, Zhejiang Province on the south, Anhui Province on the west, and Shandong Province on the north. Its area is 39,600 square miles (102,600 square kilometers), and the provincial capital is Nanjing (Nanking) (*see* Nanjing).

Jiangsu's wide, low, alluvial plain is divided by the Yangtze and Huang rivers. Yuntai Shan, near the Yellow Sea, is the highest point at 2,034 feet (620 meters). Jiangsu has two types of climate: humid and subtropical in the southern and central parts and cool, temperate, and continental in the north.

Fish farming is highly developed in Jiangsu. Important food sources include fish, duck, crab, and shrimp. Primary food crops are rice and wheat. Secondary crops include barley, corn (maize), and sweet potato. The Yangtze Delta is a major cotton region. Livestock raised in Jiangsu are cattle, pigs, and poultry. Industries include automobile works, chemical fertilizers, steel, machine tools, electrical supplies, cameras, textiles, farm machinery, and oil refining.

Except for its northernmost portion, Jiangsu was a part of the ancient state of Wu. In the 13th century there was a large migration from the north. During the Ming Dynasty it was under the jurisdiction of the imperial capital of Nanjing until 1421. Jiangsu became a separate province in 1667. The Yangtze Delta was invaded by British forces during the Opium War of 1839 to 1842. The province was occupied by Japan during the Sino–Japanese War of 1937 to 1945. (*See also* China.) Population (1986 estimate), 62,130,000.

JIANGXI, or **KIANG-SI.** One of the 21 provinces of China, Jiangxi is in the southeastern part of the country and is bounded by the provinces of Hubei and Anhui on the north, Zhejiang and Fujian on the east, Guangdong on

the south, and Hunan on the west. Jiangxi's area is 63,600 square miles (164,800 square kilometers). The provincial capital is Nanchang. The most common language is Mandarin.

Jiangxi is rimmed by mountains. The principal river, the Gan, crosses the province from south to north. It is located in a subtropical weather belt and therefore has hot, humid summers and cool winters.

Jiangxi is one of China's richest agricultural provinces. Its food crops include rice, wheat, sweet potatoes, and an enormous variety of fruits. Tea, cotton, tobacco, sugarcane, peanuts, and soybeans are commercial crops. Jiangxi exports wood to all parts of China. Other industries include food processing, fishing, and the manufacture of farm machinery, textiles, paper, electrical supplies, chemicals, and porcelain.

Jiangxi was ruled by various dynasties from as early as 770 BC. There was an extended period of peace during the Ch'ing Dynasty (1644–1911), which ended in revolution. Warlord rule continued until Chiang Kai-shek and the Nationalists achieved control of the province in 1926. Jiangxi was under Japanese occupation from 1938 to 1945. Communist forces took control in 1949. (*See also* China.) Population (1986 estimate), 34,600,000.

JIDDAH, or **JIDDA, Saudi Arabia.** A major commercial port on the Red Sea, Jiddah is located in the central Hejaz region of western Saudi Arabia west of Mecca. It is one of the country's largest cities and busiest seaports, as well as its diplomatic capital.

After World War II Jiddah was completely modernized and expanded with the new wealth acquired by Saudi Arabia from the profits brought by spiraling oil prices. The once famous *suqs* (bazaars) were demolished and the old town walls disappeared. Old, picturesque buildings were replaced by modern concrete high rises and shops. Jiddah's harbor was deepened and enlarged to accommodate large vessels, and a plant to make fresh water from seawater was built.

The economic life of the city expanded to include steel rolling; oil refining; cement, clothing, and pottery manufacturing; and dairying. Jiddah houses the Saudi ministry of foreign affairs as well as the embassies and missions of foreign governments. Higher education is provided by King Abdul University, founded in 1967. The city is served by King Abdul Aziz International Airport and highways radiate to Mecca and Medina. Tourism has become increasingly popular in Jiddah.

Jiddah first began to develop under 17th-century Turkish rule as a transit center for Muslims making their pilgrimage to the holy cities of Mecca and Medina. It formed part of the Kingdom of the Hejaz until 1925 when it was captured by Ibn Saud, the Muslim leader who formed the modern state of Saudi Arabia. (*See also* Saudi Arabia.) Population (1981 estimate) 1,308,000.

JILIN, or **KIRIN.** One of the 21 provinces of the People's Republic of China, Jilin lies in the central region of a part of China known as the Northeast, or Manchuria. Jilin is bordered on the east by the Primorsky Kray (Maritime Province) of the Soviet Union, on the southeast by North Korea, on the south by Liaoning Province,

on the west by the Inner Mongolian Autonomous Region, and on the north by Heilong jiang Province. The province occupies an area of 72,200 square miles (187,000 square kilometers). The provincial capital of Jilin is Changchun.

The province may be divided into three parts: the eastern mountains, the western plains, and a zone of rolling hills that lies between them. The Songhua River, flowing for almost 500 miles (805 kilometers) within the province, is Jilin's main stream. During the winter the ice on the Songhua is thick enough to support mule carts. There are five warm and rainy months from May to September.

Jilin is the most urbanized province in China. Almost all of the inhabitants of the province are Chinese except for a small percentage that consists of Koreans and Manchus.

Many valuable wild animals and medicinal plants are found in Jilin's forested mountain areas. The Songhua Valley is a rich agricultural region. The province is well served by extensive highway and railway networks.

Jilin became a province in 1907. It was occupied by the Japanese army in 1931. Just before Japan's surrender to the Allies in August 1945, Soviet forces entered the region. Following their withdrawal, Chinese Nationalists moved in, but by 1948 they were driven out by Chinese Communists. (*See also* China.) Population (1982 census), 22,560,053.

JIMÉNEZ, Juan Ramón (1881–1958). One of the Spanish-language poets strongly influenced by the Modernist movement of Rubén Darío, Jiménez rejected his early sentimental and ornate poetry in the middle of his career and favored, instead, a sparse, free verse form. He was awarded the Nobel prize for literature in 1956.

Jiménez was born at Moguer, Spain, on Dec. 24, 1881, and attended the University of Salamanca. At the invitation of Darío he went to Madrid to write. His first two books, 'Almas de violeta' (Souls of Violet, published in 1900) and 'Ninfeas' (Water Lilies, 1900), are so sentimental that he later came to despise them. His other early works—'Jardines lejanos' (Distant Gardens, 1905), 'Elegías' (Elegies, 1908), and 'Pastorales' (Pastorals, 1911)—reflect the influence Darío had on him.

In 1916 Jiménez went to the United States where he married Zenobia Camprubi Aymar, a poet and translator. In 1917 he published 'Diario de un poeta recién casado' (Diary of a Poet Recently Married), the volume that marks his transition to free verse. After the Spanish Civil War ended in 1939, he and his wife went into voluntary exile in Puerto Rico. He achieved popularity in the United States with an English translation of his novel 'Platero y yo' (Platero and I, 1957), the story of a man and his donkey. His later books of poetry include 'Poesía en prosa y verso' (Poetry in Prose and Verse, 1932) and 'Voces de mi copla' (Voices of My Song, 1945). Jiménez died in San Juan, Puerto Rico, on May 29, 1958.

JINNAH, Mohammed Ali (1876–1948). The founder of Pakistan was Mohammed Ali Jinnah. Frustrated in his desire to get Hindus and Muslims to work together, he succeeded in getting India partitioned in 1947 so that Pakistan could emerge as a separate Islamic nation.

Jinnah was born in Karachi on Dec. 25, 1876. After attending school in the province of Sind, he studied law in London, England, from 1892 to 1896. He practiced law for ten years before entering politics. Because of his conviction that Muslims and Hindus could work together for the independence of India, he remained aloof from the All-India Muslim League until 1913, at which time he felt assured of the League's intent to cooperate with the Hindu Indian National Congress.

The emergence of Mahatma Gandhi and a series of Hindu revivalist movements drove a wedge between the two religious factions in the 1920s and 1930s (*see* Gandhi, Mahatma). Jinnah and his fellow Muslims persistently attempted to resolve the conflict, but to no avail. Relations between the Hindu majority and Muslim minority deteriorated rapidly in the late 1930s, and by March 1940 the Muslim League had passed a resolution calling for a separate Islamic state. In 1947 the British government and the Indian National Congress agreed, and when India became independent from Britain on Aug. 15, 1947, Pakistan was born. Jinnah served as Pakistan's first head of state until his death on Sept. 11, 1948, in Karachi.

JOAN. Through the writings of two 13th-century Dominican priests, there developed a legend that a woman using the name John VIII had once been a pope of the Roman Catholic church. The name Joan (probably derived from Johannes, or John) for the legendary pontiff was not finally adopted until the 14th century.

The French Dominican Stephen of Bourbon, who dated a nameless female Pope's election at about 1100, declared that she was pregnant at the time. She supposedly gave birth during the procession to the Lateran (Roman Catholic ecumenical council), whereupon she was immediately dragged out of Rome and stoned to death.

According to a later version of the story, spread by the Polish Dominican Martin of Troppau, her election occurred in 855. He named her Johannes Angelicus and said she was an Englishwoman. She supposedly fell in love with an English Benedictine monk and, dressed as a man, accompanied him to Athens. From there, having acquired great learning, she moved to Rome, where she became a cardinal and then pope for about 25 months.

Until the 17th century, Joan's existence was regarded as fact and the myth perpetuated. It has since been proved, principally through the work of the Calvinist David Blondel in 1647, that there was no interval between the reigns of popes Leo IV (847–55) and Benedict III (855–58) during which the fictional Joan could have reigned.

JOAN OF ARC (1412–31). One of the most romantic figures in European war history is Joan of Arc, a girl who saved France from English domination. Although only 17 years old, Joan inspired a French army to break the English siege of the French city of Orléans and to win other important victories. She is known variously as the Maid of Orléans and as the Maid of France.

Joan of Arc (the French form is *Jeanne d'Arc*) was born in the tiny village of Domrémy, in the valley of the Meuse, on Jan. 6, 1412. She was the daughter of a wealthy peasant farmer. From her pious mother she learned the arts of spinning, sewing, and cooking and to love and serve God. With her brothers and sisters she herded cattle and sheep and cut ripe grain in her father's fields. Busy as these tasks kept her, there was still time for singing and dancing, for playing games with other children, and for gathering flowers for the church altars. There was seldom a day that she did not kneel in prayer in church.

The Hundred Years' War

For almost a hundred years France and much of Europe had been fighting in what has become known as the Hundred Years' War. The English occupied much of northern France and the Duke of Burgundy was their ally. The impoverished French king, Charles VII, had not yet been crowned and so was called the Dauphin. Reims, where the coronation ceremonies for French kings had been held for a thousand years, lay in enemy hands (*see* Reims). The valley of the Meuse, where Joan lived, was constantly overrun by armies and guerrilla bands.

Joan's "Visions" Command Her

The pious girl was only 13 years old when she first saw a heavenly vision. Saint Michael, she later said, told her to be a good girl, to obey her mother, and to go to church often. For some time she told no one of the visions. When Saint Catherine and Saint Margaret commanded her to journey to the Dauphin so that she might inspire his armies to clear the way to Reims for the coronation, she told her parents and others. Her father refused to let her go.

Joan's visions continued to command her. Her friends, who believed her truly inspired, secured boy's clothing and a horse for her. Several rode with Joan on the long trip to the Dauphin's court at Chinon. Perhaps as a test, the Dauphin made one of his courtiers pretend to be the king. Joan, however, went directly to the true king and greeted him.

The Dauphin and his councilors were not entirely convinced of her mission, however. Months of doubt and indecision followed while the Maid was questioned. Slowly an army was gathered.

She Raises the Siege of Orléans

The Dauphin equipped her with armor, attendants, and horses. A special banner was made. One side

bore a figure of God, seated on clouds and holding a glove, with kneeling angels at His side, and the words "Jesus Maria." The other side had a figure of the Virgin and a shield, with two angels supporting the arms of France. Joan carried this banner into battle.

The army at last moved toward Orléans. Joan was not its commander, but her presence inspired officers and men with confidence of victory. At Orléans Joan disapproved of the plans made for entering the besieged city. Her suggested plan was adopted and the entrance safely made. From the city she led a series of sallies that so harassed and discouraged the Eng-

Joan of Arc saw many visions, the first when she was only 13 years old. The painter Eugene Thirion depicts Joan's awe as Saint Michael tells her she is commanded to inspire and lead the Dauphin's army to victory over the English.

lish that they withdrew. In one of the skirmishes Joan was wounded. On May 8, 1429, the victory was celebrated by the first festival of Orléans.

The army of the Maid entered Reims on July 14. Two days later the Dauphin was crowned king. The Maid with her banner stood at his side. (*See also* France; Hundred Years' War; Orléans.)

Captured by the English

It was decided to attack Paris, but the new monarch's hesitation and indecision prevented the Maid's soldiers from concerted attack. Nevertheless, Compiègne and other nearby towns were taken. A

Giraudon

Joan of Arc is portrayed on horseback in an
illustration from a manuscript of about 1505.

French attack on a Paris salient was driven back and
Joan was again wounded. Charles VII disbanded his
army for the winter and retired southward. Through
the cold months Joan chafed at royal delay.

In the spring she returned to Compiègne, now besieged by forces of the Duke of Burgundy. On May
23, 1430, Joan on a sortie into the Burgundian lines
was separated from her soldiers and captured.

Trial and Execution

As a prisoner at Beaurevoir, she attempted to escape, but was injured in the leap from the donjon
tower. Later she was sold to the English, who vowed
that she would be executed. They removed her to
Rouen, where she was held in chains.

Although the English wanted Joan's death, they
desired her to be sentenced by an ecclesiastical court.
The Burgundian-controlled University of Paris provided the charges of heresy and witchcraft. It also
provided some of the members of the court. Other
members came from areas under English occupation.
Chief of the court was the bishop of Beauvais.

Joan was handed over to this bishop on Jan. 3,
1431. The sittings began on February 21 and continued intermittently for months. Joan's appeal to be
sent before the pope for judgment was denied. On
May 23 she was condemned to be burned unless she
recanted. She had been held for many months in
chains, threatened with torture, and harassed by
thousands of questions. In spite of all this, she had
maintained her shy innocence, often confounding her
oppressors with simple, unaffected answers to tricky
questions. Saint Catherine and Saint Margaret, she
said, still counseled her.

Faced with death in the flames, she recanted, but
many historians think she did not understand what
was meant in the statement of recantation. As a result of her submission, her punishment was commuted from death to life imprisonment. This lenien-
cy enraged the English, however, and it was not long before she was accused of relapsing from her submission. On May 30, 1431, when she was only 19 years
old, Joan was turned over to civil authority and
burned to death at the stake.

Charles VII had made no effort to save Joan. Some
25 years later he did aid her family to appeal the case
to the pope, and in 1456 a papal court annulled the
judgment of 1431. On May 16, 1920, Joan of Arc was
canonized a saint by the Roman Catholic church.

Joseph-Jacques-Césaire
Joffre in a portrait
painted in 1915

H. Roger-Viollet

JOFFRE, Joseph-Jacques-Césaire (1852–1931).
Because Marshal Joffre halted the German invasion
of 1914 on the Marne River he has been called the
"victor of the Marne." He was born on Jan. 12, 1852,
in southern France. His father made wine casks. The
boy, however, had little interest in this work so he
was sent to prepare for a military career at the École
Polytechnique in Paris.

Before he completed the course, Joffre was called
into service in the Franco-Prussian War of 1870 and
1871. He saw the victorious Germans march into Paris. In the next 40 years he prepared himself and
France for the next Prussian blow. He spent some of
those years in the French colonies in Africa and Asia,
and superintended the building of many important
defenses. In 1914 at the outbreak of World War I he
was the French chief of staff. Subsequently, he was
made supreme commander of the French forces on
the Western front.

Before the powerful German thrust, Joffre retreated from Belgium into France. Joffre, however, was
choosing his own time and his own ground for battle.
On Sept. 6, 1914, after five weeks of retreating, he
gave the command for attack. The result was the
victory of the Marne. Joffre was acclaimed as the
savior of France.

His country made him marshal of France and decorated him with the grand cross of the Legion of Hon-
or. Joffre's removal from supreme command came in
December 1916, after losses at Verdun. Later he
served on the French High Commission as technical
adviser. He died in Paris, on Jan. 3, 1931.

JOGGING. Running for fitness, exercise, and pleasure is commonly called jogging. It became very popular in the 1970s and 1980s.

The popularity of jogging today stems from several factors. First, jogging is one of the most efficient forms of exercise. Generally, a person jogging burns up more calories per minute than in most other sports. Running, like biking, swimming, and brisk walking, is an aerobic exercise. Such an exercise uses a great deal of oxygen and is described as nonstop exercise for 30 minutes or more that brings the heart rate up to 60 to 80 percent of its maximum. This strengthens the heart muscle so that it pumps more efficiently. Aerobic exercise is also one of the best ways to improve the general health and capacity of the lungs. Thus, jogging improves cardiovascular and pulmonary health, which involves the condition and interaction of the body's heart, lungs, and blood vessels.

Studies have shown that aerobic exercise is likely to reduce the risk of heart attack and stroke; help weight loss; increase body flexibility, muscle tone, and strength; alleviate moderate depression; increase self-esteem; and improve sleep.

Jogging is also popular because almost everyone—regardless of age, sex, athletic experience, or income—can participate. Jogging is an ongoing, noncompetitive activity that doesn't require any unusual skills or specific coordination. Jogging is relaxing and fun. Finally, it can be done alone, with another person, or in a group.

Since the same number of calories (about 100 for most men and 80 for most women) is burned walking a mile as running a mile, one of the best ways to begin a jogging program is to combine it with a walking program. Increases in the amount jogged should come gradually. The jogger who experiences dizziness, tightness of the chest, or nausea should slow down. If the discomfort is great, the jogger should consult a doctor before running again.

Aerobic authorities state that a person should ultimately run for 30 minutes or more three to five times a week to attain aerobic fitness. How long and how often a person does an aerobic exercise are more important than speed or distance.

For anyone who runs more than 10 miles (16 kilometers) a week, it is important to have a good pair of running shoes, not tennis shoes or sneakers. At each foot strike running produces stress that is 300 percent of the stress produced by standing or walking. With this added stress to the feet and legs, it is important to wear good shoes and replace them when they are worn out or worn unevenly.

A running shoe should have a thick layered sole the full length of the shoe with a soft inner layer for cushioning and a tough outer layer for shock absorption. The shoe should be flexible enough to let the foot bend naturally with each step and have an ele-

This article was written by Liz Elliott, Executive Director, American Running and Fitness Association.

Julie Widdifield-Brown

A family activity for some, jogging gained greatly in popularity during the 1970s and 1980s.

vated heel stabilizer so the foot will strike the ground firmly and not roll to one side or the other. The most important consideration, however, is comfort; running shoes should fit comfortably.

Cold weather poses few problems for joggers. The main hazard in winter running is slipping on ice or snow. There is no danger of freezing the lungs, because the body warms the air well before it reaches the lungs. Winter joggers should be sure to cover the head and extremities, keep feet as dry and warm as possible, and wear layers of clothing.

In summer, joggers must be careful not to get dehydrated. Drinking before, during, and after running on hot, humid days is important. The best summer running wear is loose fitting and light colored.

Although jogging is a healthful sport, injuries do occur. Aside from biomechanical problems, the most common jogging injury comes from overexertion. Too many joggers try to run too far, too fast. As a good rule of thumb, joggers should never increase distance by more than 10 percent a week, nor should they increase distance the same week they increase speed. The best method is to alternate hard and easy days of jogging. A few simple safety precautions should also be observed. When running along a road, joggers should face traffic, they should be in single file, and they should wear reflective clothing at dusk.

There are several good books and other publications on running. Just a few include 'Complete Book of Running' by Jim Fixx, published by Random House in 1977; and 'Guidelines for Successful Jogging', a book, and *Running and Fitness*, a bimonthly newspaper, both from the American Running and Fitness Association.

Ed Mullis/CLICK

Tall and modern buildings line the streets of downtown Johannesburg, the largest city in South Africa.

JOHANNESBURG, South Africa.

The largest city in South Africa is Johannesburg. It is sometimes called the "city of gold" because gold was discovered on the site in about 1885. The gold-bearing reef, the Witwatersrand (ridge of white waters), is commonly

called the Rand. It extends to unprobed depths over an area that is more than 50 miles (80 kilometers) long. Mine shafts and tunnels penetrate deeply, some reaching under the city itself. When miners explode dynamite in these tunnels, the city quivers as though shaken by a slight earthquake.

Johannesburg is the only city of its size that is not situated on a coast, a lakeshore, or a river. It lies on rolling veld, or prairie, in the southern part of the Transvaal province. It is a center for international air travel and for an extensive network of rail lines.

The city's latitude and elevation provide a mild climate. In July the mean temperature is about 50° F (10° C); in December it is 68° F (20° C). Rainfall averages about 30 inches (760 millimeters) a year. Little remains of the area's original plant and animal life, except in the Melville Kopje (small hill) Reserve northwest of the city. Suburban gardens flourish and are often elegant.

In accordance with South Africa's policy of apartheid, Johannesburg is a segregated city (see Apartheid). The predominant groups in the cosmopolitan city are English- and Afrikaans-speaking whites and African blacks who speak Zulu, Xhosa, Pedi, Venda, and Tswana. The Asian population includes Japanese, Chinese, and Indians. Among the Europeans are Germans, Hungarians, Italians, and French.

With the city's rapid urbanization and industrialization between the two World Wars, a large influx of blacks from the rural areas set up squatter camps and shanty towns. Because of the tremendous pressure that they exerted on the city's services—including health, water, and transportation—Johannesburg undertook a massive slum-clearance program. In the 1950s the separate area of Soweto (southwestern townships) was established exclusively for the blacks. It now houses more than a million people and offers subsidized housing and various health, education, and welfare facilities supported by the municipal government. Other townships are Coronationville and Westbury, reserved for the coloreds, and Lenasia, a township for Asians about 20 miles (32 kilometers) away. Whites live in exclusive suburbs in the northern part of the city.

Tall buildings overlook Johannesburg's narrow downtown streets. Streets in the suburbs are more spacious and treelined. The city is the administrative headquarters of the gold mining companies located in the vicinity. A financial center, it houses the Stock Exchange, established in 1887, and several banks and insurance companies.

The University of Witwatersrand for English-speaking students was founded in Johannesburg in 1922. Rand Afrikaans University provides higher education in Afrikaans. The Transvaal College of Education is for Asians. Rand College of Education was established for coloreds. There are numerous primary and secondary schools, technical and other colleges, and training and research institutions.

Every phase of South African life and history, including the material culture of the early natives, is illustrated in the Africana Museum of the Johannesburg Public Library. The Zoological Gardens in Herman Eckstein Park also house the Museum of South Africa Rock Art. Joubert Park, which covers 15 acres (6 hectares), is one of the most ornamental parks in the city. The 42-acre (17-hectare) Wilds, close to the center of the city, has a lovely garden.

When gold was discovered, the site of Johannesburg held only a few shanties. The townsite laid out in 1886 was named for Johannes Rissik, the surveyor general of the Transvaal. Johannesburg grew quickly. In 1896, when the Transvaal (which was then independent) permitted it a municipal government, it had about 102,000 people. Half were Europeans. Johannesburg was a center of the Boer-English conflict that started the Boer War, fought from 1899 to 1902. During much of the war the city was occupied by English troops. (*See also* Boer War; South Africa.) Population (1980 census), 1,536,400.

JOHN XXIII (1881–1963). On Oct. 28, 1958, Angelo Giuseppe Cardinal Roncalli was elected the Supreme Pontiff of the Roman Catholic church. He succeeded Pius XII, who died on Oct. 9, 1958. The new pope chose his father's name, Giovanni (John).

He was the first pontiff to use the name John since 1334, when John XXII died. In the early 15th century Baldasarre Cossa called himself Pope John XXIII. According to the Vatican, however, he was an antipope (*see* Papacy). A previously listed 8th-century pope, Stephen II, was dropped from the 1961 Pontifical Yearbook's official roster of popes because he had never been formally installed as pope. His successor was given the name Stephen II. Thus John XXIII became the 261st pope.

John XXIII was born Angelo Giuseppe Roncalli in a stone farmhouse in the tiny northern Italian village of Sotto il Monte, near Bergamo, on Nov. 25, 1881. He was the third child and eldest son in a family of 13. His father was a sharecropper who had saved enough money to buy a plot of his own. He hoped his son would help him in the fields, but when Angelo was 11, he told his father he wanted to become a priest.

Angelo studied at the Bergamo Seminary from 1892 to 1900. He did so well in his studies that his teachers recommended him to church officials in Rome. When he was 25 he was graduated from the Apollinare Seminary in Rome and ordained a priest.

From 1905 to 1914 Father Roncalli was the personal secretary of the Bishop of Bergamo. During this

Pope John XXIII posed for his first formal photograph as pope in his Vatican Palace study shortly after his election by the College of Cardinals on Oct. 28, 1958.

Wide World

period he became active in historical research and wrote several books. Part of his research work was done at Milan's Ambrosian Library, whose prefect later became Pope Pius XI.

In World War I Father Roncalli served in the Italian army as a medical corps sergeant and later as a chaplain with the rank of lieutenant. After the war he founded Italy's first students' home for poor youths working their way through school.

His work in education and in the Catholic Action movement brought him to the attention of Pope Benedict XV. Called to Rome, Father Roncalli was named a domestic prelate of the pope and given the title of monsignor.

Pope Pius XI appointed him apostolic visitor to Bulgaria and titular archbishop of Areopolis in 1925. In 1935 Archbishop Roncalli was promoted to apostolic vicar and delegate to Turkey and apostolic delegate to Greece. In December 1944 he was appointed papal nuncio, or ambassador, to France. This was regarded as one of the most difficult diplomatic assignments in Vatican history.

Archbishop Roncalli thought there had been some mistake when he heard of his appointment. "Do you know what you are doing?" he asked a papal official. "I am not worthy of the job."

The new nuncio's role was to smooth relations between France and the Vatican. Premier Charles de Gaulle's government resented the fact that the Vatican had had official diplomatic relations with the wartime regime of Marshal Henri Pétain. Nuncio Roncalli made it clear to them that the only reason the Vatican had worked with Pétain was that his government was the established French government at that time.

In addition to smoothing diplomatic relations between Paris and Rome, Archbishop Roncalli made friends with all the top-ranking French officials. With his wit, humor, and tact he came to be dearly loved in Paris.

When Pius XII named him a cardinal on Jan. 12, 1953, French President Vincent Auriol placed the red cardinal's hat on the prelate's head (*see* Pius). Auriol and Cardinal Roncalli remained friends long after the cardinal left Paris. Also in 1953 Cardinal Roncalli was appointed Patriarch of Venice. He served in this capacity until his elevation to the papacy in 1958.

In 1960 Pope John met with Archbishop Geoffrey F. Fisher, primate of the Church of England. This first meeting of a bishop of Rome and an archbishop of Canterbury in over 400 years was a historic event.

Pope John raised the number of cardinals to a record 87 and appointed the first black African, Japanese, and Filipino cardinals. His decrees were generally popular. His major undertaking was the 21st Ecumenical Council. The first to be held at the Vatican since 1869, it is known as Vatican II. Its opening session was held in 1962.

Pope John XXIII issued his final encyclical, 'Pacem in Terris' (Peace on Earth), on April 10, 1963. He died on June 3, 1963, in the Vatican.

JOHN OF ENGLAND

JOHN OF ENGLAND (1167–1216). Vicious, shameless, and ungrateful, King John has been called the worst king ever to rule England. Yet the very excesses of his reign proved positive in that they provoked such a violent reaction that his subjects revolted and forced him to put his seal on the Magna Carta. This document became the safeguard of English liberty. John's nickname was Lackland because at first he owned no land. Later his father, King Henry II, gave him castles, lands, and revenues in both England and France. John plotted against his father, however, and the discovery of this conspiracy was a factor in the king's death. John's brother, Richard the Lion-Hearted, became king and added to John's possessions (*see* Richard, Kings of England). While Richard was absent from England on the Third Crusade, John conspired against him also.

When Richard died in 1199, the barons selected John to be their king. This denied the royal claim of Arthur, son of another brother, Geoffrey. Two French provinces fought for young Arthur, but the boy fell into the hands of John and died soon after. During the war John lost all his French possessions except Aquitaine. John then quarreled with Pope Innocent III about the appointment of Stephen Langton as archbishop of Canterbury. John was excommunicated, and England was forbidden all religious services except baptism and extreme unction. The growing discontent of his subjects finally forced John to recognize the new archbishop.

When John went to France seeking to regain his lands in Normandy, the barons marched against the king and demanded a charter of liberties. All but a handful of followers deserted John. He was forced to meet the barons at Runnymede on June 15, 1215, and to sign the Great Charter (*see* Magna Carta).

John had no intention of supporting the charter, however. He recruited a new army and destroyed the estates of the barons. The barons then offered the English crown to Louis, a French prince. In the midst of a war for the throne, John died of a fever. The task of restoring the torn kingdom fell to his nine-year-old son, Henry III (*see* Henry, Kings of England).

JOHN PAUL, Popes. Two popes have borne the name John Paul, both in the 20th century.

JOHN PAUL I (pope 1978) died suddenly only 34 days after his election. Although he had one of the shortest reigns in Roman Catholic history and did not affect church doctrine, John Paul I had a humble and friendly manner that won him great affection. He was born Albino Luciani on Oct. 17, 1912, to poor parents in a small town in northeastern Italy. At the age of 10 he began religious studies.

As a priest in northern Italy, he was known for his charity towards the poor and his defense of strong family life. He was appointed patriarch (archbishop) of Venice in 1969, and he became a cardinal in 1973.

Upon his election as the 263rd pope on Aug. 26, 1978, he chose the name John Paul in honor of his predecessors, John XXIII and Paul VI. He was the first pope to choose a double name and the first in a millenium to take a new name. John Paul I set other precedents by rejecting much of the pomp and formality of the papacy. He declined the tiara, the symbol of his earthly powers. John Paul I preferred to walk rather than to be carried on his throne. In public audiences he often used the personal "I." John Paul I saw himself as a pastor rather than a ruler.

JOHN PAUL II (pope 1978–) was the first Polish prelate elected to the papacy, and he was the first non-Italian pope in more than 450 years. He was born Karol Wojtyla on May 18, 1920, to working-class parents in Wadowice. His mother died when he was 9; his father was killed in World War II.

Karol entered Jagiellonian University in Kraków in 1938 to study literature and philology. He wrote poetry and acted in a theater group. When the Nazis closed the university, he worked as a laborer and began studying for the priesthood in an illegal seminary. Karol also belonged to an underground theatrical group that performed anti-Nazi plays, and he helped Polish Jews escape persecution. After World War II Karol studied at a seminary in Kraków, and in 1946 he was ordained.

After receiving a Ph.D. degree in philosophy from Pontifical Angelicum University in Rome in 1948, Father Wojtyla returned to Poland to become a parish priest and a student chaplain. He continued the study of ethics and taught ethics and theology at the Catholic University of Lublin. In 1958 he became the

John Paul II, the first Polish pope, was also the first non-Italian pontiff in more than 450 years and, at the time of his election, the youngest pope in more than a century.

youngest Polish bishop when he was appointed auxiliary bishop of Kraków. In 1964 he was named archbishop. After becoming a cardinal in 1967, he studied philosophy in Belgium and France.

Throughout his years as a leader in the church, Wojtyla continued his interest in athletics and in writing. Fluent in six languages, he wrote poetry; and his books included 'Love and Responsibility', a work on sexual morality. As a spokesman for the large Roman Catholic population of Poland, he defended the church and the right to freedom of worship.

Upon his election as the 264th pope on Oct. 16, 1978, he was only 58. John Paul II adopted both the name and the style of his predecessor. To avoid a conflict with a soccer match, he scheduled his coronation for noon. He became the first pope to wear trousers under his vestments. He performed a rare wedding ceremony for commoners. In his official statements, however, John Paul II supported traditional church doctrines. An exception was the customary Vatican policy of neutrality, which he abandoned as he became involved in international political controversy.

In January 1979 John Paul II attended a conference of Latin American bishops in Mexico. The first pope to visit a Communist country, he returned to his native land in June. He was also the first pope to visit a United States president in the White House. In October he addressed the United Nations General Assembly while on his six-city tour of the United States. The pope's travels in 1980 included visits to six African countries, Brazil, and West Germany. Dubbed the "pilgrim pope," he journeyed to the Philippines and Japan in early 1981.

The pope survived an assassination attempt by a Turkish political dissident in Saint Peter's Square on May 13, 1981. On May 12, 1982, when he went to Portugal's Shrine of Our Lady of Fátima to give thanks for his recovery from the gun wounds, another attack on his life was attempted. A rebel Spanish priest, carrying a bayonet, was subdued by security guards.

During the war between Great Britain and Argentina to determine sovereignty over the Falkland Islands, the pope visited both countries in June 1982. John Paul II toured eight Central American and Caribbean nations in March 1983.

On Jan. 25, 1983, the pope approved the first revision of the Roman Catholic church's canon law since it had been codified in 1917. The new code, however, did not change any of the more controversial prohibitions of the church.

ANDREW JOHNSON—
17th President of
the United States

JOHNSON, Andrew (1808–75, president 1865–69). Andrew Johnson became a public figure during the nation's greatest crisis—the Civil War. Although he came from the slave state of Tennessee, Johnson refused to resign as United States senator when the state seceded; he worked to preserve the Union. For his efforts he won the vice-presidency, taking office in March 1865. Six weeks later Abraham Lincoln was assassinated and Johnson became president.

In his time Johnson's Administration was widely condemned. His reconstruction policies were bitterly opposed in Congress by the Radicals, the majority faction of the Republican party. The resulting political struggles led to an unsuccessful attempt in the United States Senate to remove him from office.

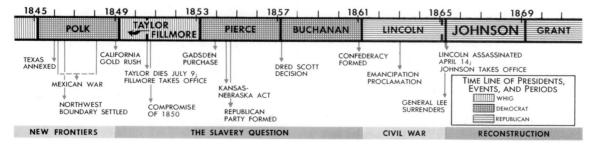

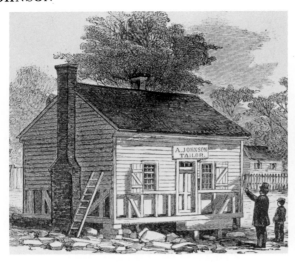

President Johnson's old tailor shop at Greeneville, Tenn., is now part of the Andrew Johnson National Historic Site. Here the future president set up his tailoring business in 1826.

In May 1865 President Johnson pardoned many Confederates. Officers and persons of wealth, however, had to go to the White House to receive a personal pardon, as shown here.

Boyhood in North Carolina

Andrew Johnson was born in Raleigh, N. C., Dec. 29, 1808. He was the younger son of Jacob Johnson and Mary (Polly) McDonough Johnson. His father, a bank porter and sexton, died three years after Andrew was born. The family remained very poor even though the boys' mother later married again.

Unable to attend school, young Andrew was hired out to a tailor at an early age. He learned the trade but was so unhappy at his job that he refused to serve out his apprenticeship.

Marriage and Home in Tennessee

In 1826 the Johnsons moved to Tennessee, and Andrew finally settled at Greeneville. The following year he married Eliza McCardle, daughter of a Scottish shoemaker. They had five children—Martha, Charles, Mary, Robert, and Andrew. Eliza was a great help to her husband in improving his reading, writing, and general education. (*See also* White House, section "Hostesses of the White House.")

Meanwhile Johnson had become a successful tailor and an important figure in Greeneville. He was elected a city alderman three times and then mayor. In 1835 he was elected to the state legislature where he served two terms in the House of Representatives and one term in the Senate. Politically, he was a Jacksonian Democrat.

Congressman and Governor

In 1843 Johnson began his first of five consecutive terms in Congress. His most notable achievement here was the introduction of the first "homestead bill." This would have cut up Western public lands into many small holdings for the free farmers. Johnson's bill was defeated by Southern representatives.

Johnson was elected governor of Tennessee in 1853 and re-elected in 1855. In this position he secured

the passage of the first tax in Tennessee to be levied in support of popular education. He also directed the creation of a state board of agriculture and a state library.

Throughout his career Johnson fearlessly championed the cause of the workingman against the interests of the slaveholders. He always fought against any claim of superiority based on birth or wealth.

Senator and Military Governor

In 1857 Johnson became a United States senator from Tennessee. He again tried to enact a homestead law but the measure was vetoed by President Buchanan. (Such a bill was not passed until 1862, after the secession of the slave states.)

When secession came in 1860–61, Johnson attracted the attention of the North by his arguments for the Union. He was the only Southern senator who did not resign and go with his state when it seceded.

In March 1862 President Lincoln appointed Johnson military governor of Tennessee. Although the state had seceded in 1861 eastern Tennessee remained loyal

---

JOHNSON'S ADMINISTRATION
1865–1869
Amnesty Proclamation issued (1865)
13th Amendment ratified (1865)
Civil Rights Act passed over president's veto (1866)
Cable to Great Britain completed (1866)
Reconstruction bills passed over vetoes (1867)
Nebraska admitted to the Union (1867)
Tenure of Office bill passed over veto (1867)
Alaska purchased from Russia (1867)
French forced to quit Mexico (1867)
14th Amendment ratified (1868)
President acquitted in impeachment trial (1868)

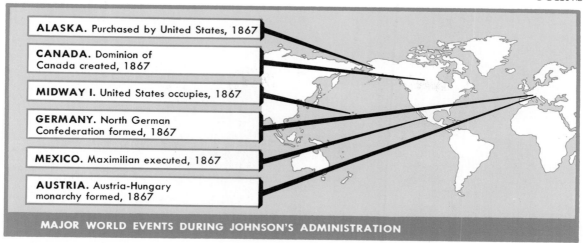

ALASKA. Purchased by United States, 1867

CANADA. Dominion of Canada created, 1867

MIDWAY I. United States occupies, 1867

GERMANY. North German Confederation formed, 1867

MEXICO. Maximilian executed, 1867

AUSTRIA. Austria-Hungary monarchy formed, 1867

MAJOR WORLD EVENTS DURING JOHNSON'S ADMINISTRATION

to the Union. Johnson set out to restore civil government in Tennessee after the defeat in 1863 of the last remaining Confederate forces there. (*see* Civil War, American).

As Vice-President He Succeeds Lincoln

In the Republican convention of 1864 Lincoln's renomination for president was assured. In choosing a vice-presidential candidate the convention wanted to name a man who would appeal to Democrats and Republicans alike. Johnson was selected because of his work for the Union and his political label as a "war Democrat." Under the name Union party, this ticket won an easy victory.

Upon the assassination of Lincoln, April 14, 1865, Johnson was elevated to the presidency. He now had to face a series of difficult problems. The Civil War was over but its damages were still to be repaired and the Union restored. The bitterness of the people in the North was increased by the death of Lincoln. Many held the South responsible for this tragedy, and a majority in both houses of Congress were demanding harsh measures against the defeated states.

At first many Congressional leaders liked the idea of Johnson as president. They felt that Lincoln would have been too merciful to the South and that Johnson would be more unforgiving. During his early weeks in office the new president seemed to justify this belief. He denounced Confederates as traitors, saying they must be punished and "impoverished."

Johnson's Quarrels with Congress

Soon Johnson changed his attitude. Before Congress met in December 1865 he had recognized state governments in nearly all the seceding states that had not been reconstructed under Lincoln. But Congress refused to seat men from these states, claiming its right to judge the qualifications of prospective Southern members. The remainder of Johnson's administration was dominated by a long and bitter struggle with Congress about the supremacy of legislative over executive rule.

Johnson believed firmly in states' rights. Consequently, he vetoed a bill that would have increased the powers of the Freedmen's Bureau, established as a guardian of the freed slaves. He also vetoed a Civil Rights bill that placed all cases involving the rights of blacks in the federal rather than state courts. Congress passed both of these bills over his veto and then proposed the 14th Amendment to the Constitution. This would deprive the Southern states of their full share of representation in Congress unless they gave blacks the right to vote. It also excluded from office all who had taken part in the rebellion until they were pardoned by a two-thirds vote of each house.

Politics and Impeachment

Before the Congressional elections of 1866 the president appealed to the people to support his policies. He made a tour through the country—called a "swing around the circle"—in which he spoke bitterly of Congress. The effort proved to be a complete failure. His personal abuse of his opponents lost Johnson what little support he had.

In 1867 and 1868 Congress passed a series of four reconstruction acts establishing military rule and conditions of readmission for ten Southern states. Johnson vetoed every one of these measures, but each time Congress overrode the president's disapproval.

In 1868 the quarrel between Johnson and the Radical Republicans in Congress came to a head. The president sought to remove Edwin M. Stanton as his secretary of war (*see* Stanton). This action violated a Tenure of Office Act passed by Congress in 1867 to limit the powers of the presidency. Stanton refused to give up the office, and the Senate supported him. Charges of impeachment were then brought against Johnson by the House of Representatives. The grounds of the charges were clearly political. Acting as a court of trial the Senate voted 35 for removal from office and 19 against it. As 36 votes—two thirds of the membership—were necessary for conviction, Johnson's impeachment was not upheld (*see* Impeachment; Reconstruction Period).

127

In a painting, Secretary of State William H. Seward sits with a map in his lap and a Russian envoy points to a globe as aides draw up the papers with which the United States purchased Alaska from Russia. The year was 1867. The price was $7,200,000.

Brown Brothers

Progress in Foreign Affairs

The struggle over reconstruction overshadowed two important international developments. During the Civil War the French emperor, Napoleon III, had installed Archduke Maximilian of Austria on the Mexican throne. In 1867 Johnson forced the French troops to withdraw. Maximilian was then overthrown by Mexican patriots. (*See also* Mexico.)

In 1867 Alaska was purchased from Russia for $7,200,000 on the advice of Secretary of State William H. Seward. Gold had not yet been found there, and many people thought it a bad bargain. They called it "Seward's folly." (*See also* Alaska; Seward.)

Retirement and Election to the Senate

Johnson left office in 1869 under a storm of abuse. He was a stubborn fighter, however, and refused to quit politics. In 1872 he ran for congressman-at-large from Tennessee but was defeated. Two years later he campaigned for senator and this time he won. In 1875 he took his seat in the Senate, which he had left 13

President Johnson campaigns to win support in the Congressional election of 1866.

The Bettmann Archive

years before. Johnson thus became the only ex-president ever elected to the Senate. He suffered a paralytic attack several months later and died on July 31, 1875. He was buried at Greeneville.

BIBLIOGRAPHY FOR ANDREW JOHNSON

Benedict, M. L. The Impeachment and Trial of Andrew Johnson (Norton, 1973).

Castel, Albert. The Presidency of Andrew Johnson (Univ. Press, Inc., 1979).

Dickinson, J. N., comp. Andrew Johnson, 1808–1875 (Oceana, 1970).

Nash, H. P., Jr. Andrew Johnson: Congress and Reconstruction (Fairleigh Dickinson Univ. Press, 1972).

JOHNSON, Jack (1878–1946). The first black to hold the heavyweight boxing championship of the world was Jack Johnson. His success as a boxer angered many prejudiced people and his free-wheeling, flamboyant lifestyle enraged them. At one time Johnson owned as many as six automobiles and traveled with several servants. He was also severely criticized by the press for having twice married white women.

John Arthur Johnson, also called Li'l Artha, was born March 31, 1878, in Galveston, Tex. He fought professionally from 1897 to 1928, and engaged in exhibition matches as late as 1945. He won the heavyweight title in 1908 by knocking out champion Tommy Burns in Sydney, Australia. He lost the title on a knockout by Jess Willard in 26 rounds in Havana, Cuba, in 1915.

In 1912 Johnson was convicted of violating the law for having taken his wife across state lines before their marriage. He was sentenced to a year in prison and was released on bond. He then disguised himself as a member of a black baseball team and fled to Canada, after which he went to Europe. He later agreed to the fight with Willard in Cuba. Many people thought Johnson lost deliberately, because he mistakenly believed that the charges against him would be dropped if he lost to a white man. In 1920 he surrendered to United States marshals and served his sentence. He died in an automobile accident in Raleigh, N.C., on June 10, 1946.

LYNDON B. JOHNSON—
36th President of
the United States

JOHNSON, Lyndon B. (1908–73; president 1963–69). At 2:38 P.M., on Nov. 22, 1963, Lyndon B. Johnson took the oath of office as 36th president of the United States. On his right stood his wife, Lady Bird. On his left stood Jacqueline Kennedy, stony-faced with shock. Less than two hours earlier, President John F. Kennedy had died in a Dallas, Tex., hospital from an assassin's bullets. He had been shot while riding in a motorcade through downtown Dallas. Johnson, riding two cars behind Kennedy, was unhurt. (*See also* Kennedy.)

As vice-president of the United States, Lyndon Johnson immediately became president. He was the fourth vice-president to be thrust into the nation's top office by the assassination of his predecessor. The new president's first message to the nation, televised the evening of that fateful day on his arrival at Andrews Air Force Base, near Washington, D. C., was brief. "I will do my best. That is all I can do. I ask for your help, and God's."

On Nov. 3, 1964, the voters of the nation elected Johnson to a full term. He overwhelmingly defeated Republican Senator Barry M. Goldwater of Arizona. Senator Hubert H. Humphrey of Minnesota was elected vice-president. Johnson called his landslide victory "a tribute to the program that was begun by our beloved president, John F. Kennedy."

A Son of Texas Pioneers

Johnson, a six-foot-three-inch Texan, had an air of the frontier even when he was not wearing his ten-gallon hat. Visitors to his LBJ Ranch, near Johnson City, Tex., were shown two stone forts built by his grandfather, Samuel Ealy Johnson, founder of Johnson City. They were constructed to protect the first

settlers from Indian raids. His grandmother once saved her life in a surprise Indian raid by hiding in a flour barrel. Grandfather Johnson served in the Texas state legislature and became Texas secretary of state. When he first saw the infant Lyndon, he is said to have prophesied that his grandson would someday be a United States senator.

Johnson's father, Samuel Ealy Johnson, Jr., was a farmer and schoolteacher. He too was a member of the state legislature, where he was a colleague and

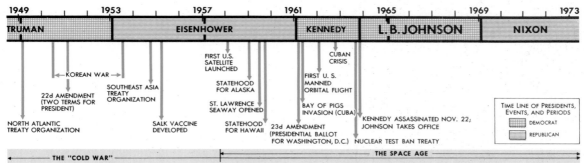

1949	1953	1957	1961	1965	1969	1973
TRUMAN		EISENHOWER		KENNEDY	L. B. JOHNSON	NIXON

KOREAN WAR

22d AMENDMENT (TWO TERMS FOR PRESIDENT)

SOUTHEAST ASIA TREATY ORGANIZATION

FIRST U.S. SATELLITE LAUNCHED

STATEHOOD FOR ALASKA

ST. LAWRENCE SEAWAY OPENED

CUBAN CRISIS

FIRST U. S. MANNED ORBITAL FLIGHT

NORTH ATLANTIC TREATY ORGANIZATION

SALK VACCINE DEVELOPED

STATEHOOD FOR HAWAII

BAY OF PIGS INVASION (CUBA)

23d AMENDMENT (PRESIDENTIAL BALLOT FOR WASHINGTON, D.C.)

KENNEDY ASSASSINATED NOV. 22; JOHNSON TAKES OFFICE

NUCLEAR TEST BAN TREATY

TIME LINE OF PRESIDENTS, EVENTS, AND PERIODS
DEMOCRAT
REPUBLICAN

◄— THE "COLD WAR" —► ◄————— THE SPACE AGE —————►

close friend of Sam Rayburn, who later became speaker of the United States House of Representatives.

Johnson's mother was Rebekah Baines Johnson. Her family also were pioneers of central Texas. Her grandfather was the Rev. George W. Baines (the name was originally spelled Bains). He was a Baptist leader in Texas during the Civil War and was president of Baylor University for two years (1861–63). Mrs. Johnson's father, Joseph W. Baines, was a representative in the state legislature. Her mother was a niece of a member of the first Congress of the Republic of Texas. Her forebears for generations had represented their home district in the Scottish Parliament. Rebekah Baines was a graduate of Baylor University and taught school before her marriage.

A Hardworking, Active Youth

Lyndon Baines Johnson was born on Aug. 27, 1908, on a farm near Stonewall, Tex. He was the eldest of five children. He had three sisters and a brother, Sam Houston Johnson. When Lyndon was five, the family moved to Johnson City. To help earn his way, young Lyndon shined shoes in the "city's" only barber shop and herded goats for the ranchers.

He finished high school in 1924 and with a group of friends worked his way on freight trains to California. Odd jobs provided scarcely enough food for the rapidly growing, lanky youth. Hungry and homesick, he hitchhiked back to Johnson City and took a job on a road-building gang. By this time he began to realize that his parents were right in insisting on a college education. "It became increasingly apparent

---

JOHNSON'S ADMINISTRATIONS
1963–1969
Johnson assumes presidency on Kennedy's assassination (1963)
24th Amendment signed (1964)
Civil Rights Act bans discrimination in private employment (1964)
War on poverty launched (1964)
Johnson elected president (1964)
United States forces begin combat in Vietnam; North Vietnam bombed (1965)
Voting Rights Act for Negroes passed (1965)
Medicare established (1965)
11th Cabinet post added—Department of Housing and Urban Development (1965)
First Negro Cabinet member, Robert C. Weaver, appointed (1966)
12th Cabinet post added—Department of Transportation (1966)
25th Amendment passed (1967)
First Negro Supreme Court justice, Thurgood Marshall, appointed (1967)
Fair Housing Act passed (1968)
Vietnam peace talks begin in Paris (1968)
Bombing of North Vietnam halted (1968)
Declines renomination; Humphrey nominated his successor; Nixon elected (1968)
United States astronauts first to orbit moon (1968)

---

to me," he said later, "that there was something to this idea of higher education."

College and Teaching

With a little borrowed money he set out for Southwest Texas State Teachers College, in San Marcos. He paid his expenses with part-time jobs as janitor, secretary to the college president, and door-to-door hosiery salesman. Forced to quit school temporarily when his money ran out, he taught Mexican children in the small southern Texas town of Cotulla.

A year later he was able to repay the money he had borrowed. He bought some athletic equipment for the underprivileged children of the town and took one small boy back home with him for private instruction by his mother. Cotulla has a Lyndon Johnson Alumni Club of Mexican-Americans who claim to have been taught by the famous Texan. Johnson returned to the teachers college and got his degree in 1930. He then taught public speaking and debate at a Houston high school for two years.

Johnson Enters Politics and Gets Married

Johnson entered politics at the age of 24, when Congressman Richard M. Kleberg, one of the owners of the famous King Ranch, took him to Washington, D. C., as his secretary (1932–35). His political ability was recognized even then. He was elected speaker of the "Little Congress," an organization of Congressional secretaries.

In 1934 Johnson met Claudia Alta Taylor, daughter of a wealthy Marshall, Tex., rancher. He knew immediately that she was the girl he wanted. They were married on Nov. 17, 1934. When Mrs. Johnson was a baby, she was nicknamed Lady Bird by a family servant who declared she was "purty as a ladybird." She was never called by any other name. The Johnsons had two daughters—Lynda Bird, born in 1944, and Luci Baines, born in 1947. Johnson belonged to the Christian church, his wife and Lynda to the Episcopalian. Luci became a member of the Roman Catholic church in 1965.

Mrs. Johnson was an astute businesswoman who built up the family fortune while her husband occupied himself in public office. With an inheritance from her parents she bought a radio station in Austin which was losing money. Eventually the LBJ Company, Inc., came to control several radio-television stations, a bank, large real-estate holdings, and other valuable properties. When Johnson became vice-president in 1960, he and Mrs. Johnson transferred the control of this company to trustees.

First Public Offices

Sam Rayburn, the old family friend, got Johnson his first important public job, as Texas director of the National Youth Administration. This was in 1935. Two years later Johnson, a Democrat, was elected to the United States House of Representatives to fill a vacancy left by the death of James P. Buchanan. His victory on an all-out New Deal platform attracted the

Lyndon B. Johnson stands in front of a reconstruction of the simple frame house in which he was born. The house, rebuilt in 1964, is now a part of the Lyndon B. Johnson National Historic Site.

to enter active duty in World War II. A lieutenant commander in the Navy, he was stationed in New Zealand and Australia. General Douglas MacArthur decorated him with the Silver Star for gallantry in action on a flight over enemy territory.

Senator and Party Leader

Johnson served five successive full terms in the House. During one year of this time he also studied at the Georgetown University Law School. In 1948 and 1954 he was elected to the United States Senate. Here Johnson quickly established himself as one of the most effective and persuasive party leaders in memory. The 18-hour working day he put in may have contributed to a severe heart attack which he suffered in the summer of 1955. By the next session of Congress, five months later, he was back at work.

In 1953 he became minority leader in a Republican Senate, and in 1957 he was made Senate majority leader. He followed a policy of compromise which resulted in unusual cooperation between Republican and Democratic senators. His greatest accomplishment was to obtain passage through the Senate of the first civil rights bill since 1875. He was a member of the Senate Armed Services Committee and the Appropriations Committee.

Vice-President of the United States

Johnson was a candidate for the presidential nomination in 1960, but he accepted second place on the ticket with John F. Kennedy. His vigorous campaign through the Southern states is credited with winning the 81 Southern electoral votes cast for the Democrats in the election. Johnson was reelected to the Senate at the same time he was chosen vice-president. He resigned from the Senate after the November elections to take up his new duties.

Kennedy lived up to his campaign promise to make his vice-president an active partner. Johnson attended Cabinet, National Security Council, and special White House meetings. He was chairman of the President's Committee on Equal Employment Opportunity, which sought to end racial discrimination in the hiring practices of government contractors. He also headed the National Advisory Council for the Peace Corps and was chairman of the National Aeronautics and Space Council.

attention of President Franklin D. Roosevelt, who was vacationing in Texas at the time. Roosevelt asked the new congressman to return to Washington with him on the presidential train. He then became identified as one of the "Young Guard" of Roosevelt supporters.

The day following the Japanese attack on Pearl Harbor, Johnson became the first member of Congress

Johnson represented the president on goodwill missions throughout the world, explaining the Administration's foreign-aid policy. As a "global politician," he showed the same persuasive charm so familiar in the Senate. Secret Service agents assigned to guard him disapproved strongly of the way he plunged into crowds to shake outstretched hands. He was determined to "meet the people," to "get the feel of the folks." In October 1962 he was awarded the Grand Cross of Merit of the Sovereign Order of

As a lieutenant commander in the Navy, Johnson served for seven months in the South Pacific before he was recalled to Congress. Here he tours the New Guinea front.

131

Malta for his "significant humanitarian contributions," the first American to be so honored by the knights of one of the oldest Roman Catholic orders.

The Vice-President Becomes President

In November 1963 Mr. and Mrs. Johnson flew to Texas with President and Mrs. Kennedy on a political trip, looking forward to the 1964 presidential campaign. The Kennedys were to have vacationed at the LBJ Ranch after the Dallas visit. The assassination of President Kennedy plunged Johnson into the office which he had sought three years earlier.

On the evening of November 25, after the Kennedy funeral services, Johnson held a reception in the State Department Building for the 220 government leaders who had gathered from all parts of the world to honor the late president. The Johnson family moved into the White House on December 7.

President Johnson's first address to a joint session of Congress, on November 27, emphasized the theme of continuity in United States government. Regarding foreign policy, he declared that "this nation will keep its commitments from South Vietnam to West Berlin." He pledged continuation of foreign aid to Africa, Asia, and Latin America. In addition, he promised continued support of the United Nations by the United States. In domestic affairs, he asked Congress to enact a tax-cut bill and stressed economy in government spending.

Johnson Takes a Firm Hold

When Johnson became president, he took firm command of the government, reassuring a worried world of the continuity of United States policy and leadership. Addressing the United Nations General Assembly on December 17, he reaffirmed his nation's dedication to world peace and called for a "peaceful revolution" that would forever wipe out hunger, poverty, and disease.

Johnson moved quickly to gain support among the nation's businessmen while maintaining his party's traditionally friendly ties with organized labor. In

In the presidential jet plane, at Dallas, Tex., Johnson takes the oath of office, administered by Federal District Judge Sarah T. Hughes. By his side are his wife (left) and Mrs. John F. Kennedy (right), widow of the slain President Kennedy.

his State-of-the-Union message to Congress on Jan. 8, 1964, Johnson announced a cut in the federal budget. He called for increased spending on education, health, and manpower training but for reduced military spending.

Johnson's great popularity was partly the result of the nation's continuing business upswing. Hailing it as a major stimulus to the economy, Johnson signed a multibillion-dollar tax-cut bill on February 26. He also urged a war on poverty reminiscent of President Franklin D. Roosevelt's New Deal.

The legislation enacted during Johnson's first year was largely based on groundwork laid by the Kennedy Administration. Among the first measures signed by the new president were bills authorizing almost 3 billion dollars for aid to education, more than $1\frac{1}{2}$

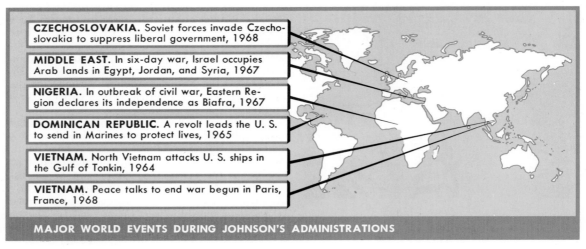

CZECHOSLOVAKIA. Soviet forces invade Czechoslovakia to suppress liberal government, 1968

MIDDLE EAST. In six-day war, Israel occupies Arab lands in Egypt, Jordan, and Syria, 1967

NIGERIA. In outbreak of civil war, Eastern Region declares its independence as Biafra, 1967

DOMINICAN REPUBLIC. A revolt leads the U. S. to send in Marines to protect lives, 1965

VIETNAM. North Vietnam attacks U. S. ships in the Gulf of Tonkin, 1964

VIETNAM. Peace talks to end war begun in Paris, France, 1968

MAJOR WORLD EVENTS DURING JOHNSON'S ADMINISTRATIONS

With President and Mrs. Johnson are their daughters—Luci Baines, the younger, at left, and Lynda Bird, at right. The two girls shared the LBJ initials made famous by their father.

billion dollars for public works, and more than 3 billion dollars for foreign aid. In February he signed the document that added to the Constitution the 24th Amendment, banning the poll tax as a prerequisite for voting in federal elections.

Johnson's persuasive skills were shown when he helped settle a five-year-old work-rules dispute in the railway industry. When he intervened, on April 9, 1964, union and company officials agreed to postpone a threatened strike. Johnson took part in subsequent negotiations. On April 22 he announced that a "just and fair" settlement had been reached.

Crises in Panama and Southeast Asia

The new president faced grave problems in his conduct of the nation's foreign affairs. One of them grew out of clashes between Panamanian demonstrators and United States troops in January 1964. More than 20 persons were killed. Panama then severed diplomatic relations with the United States, demanding the revision of the 1903 Panama Canal Treaty. Johnson offered a "full and frank review" of the issues but refused to make any more definite commitment. Diplomatic ties with Panama were not restored until early April.

Relations with the Soviet Union improved somewhat, but Johnson was unable to bridge the growing gulf between United States and French policies. The rift was most noticeable in Southeast Asia, where France advocated the neutralization of South Vietnam. Instead, the United States—committed to help fight a growing Communist insurrection—sharply boosted military aid to the South Vietnamese government. Furthermore, after North Vietnam attacked United States destroyers in the Gulf of Tonkin in

August 1964, Johnson ordered retaliatory attacks. France extended diplomatic recognition to the People's Republic of China, a policy opposed by the United States.

The 1964 Civil Rights Act

A major event in Johnson's first year as president was Congressional passage of the most far-reaching civil-rights bill in the nation's history. Backed by President Kennedy, the measure had been introduced into Congress in June 1963 in the wake of nationwide civil-rights demonstrations. When Johnson assumed office, he firmly supported the bill.

The bill passed the House of Representatives in February, but Southern opponents blocked its passage in the Senate. On June 10, after a record 75-day filibuster, a bipartisan coalition voted cloture— the first time in history that the Senate had voted to cut off debate on a civil-rights measure. The bill then passed the Senate, 73 to 27. On July 2 President Johnson signed the historic measure. His antipoverty legislation was also passed that summer.

Landslide Election Victory

After his nomination as the Democratic party's presidential candidate in 1964, Johnson plunged into the campaign. Attacking the so-called "extremism" of his Republican opponent, Senator Barry M. Goldwater of Arizona, he called for a continuation of bipartisan "peace and prosperity" policies.

In November Johnson was elected president by what was then the greatest landslide in the nation's history. He won 61 percent of the total popular vote and a plurality of nearly 16 million votes. He carried every state except Arizona and five in the Deep South, with 486 electoral college votes.

The Great Society

On Jan. 20, 1965, Johnson was inaugurated for his first full presidential term. The first change in the Cabinet he had inherited from Kennedy became official in January. John T. Connor was sworn in as secretary of commerce, succeeding Luther H. Hodges. Nicholas deB. Katzenbach was named attorney general to succeed Robert F. Kennedy. In April Henry H. Fowler replaced C. Douglas Dillon as secretary of the treasury. Other new Cabinet members in 1965 were Lawrence F. O'Brien, who succeeded John A. Gronouski as postmaster general, and John W. Gardner, who replaced Anthony J. Celebrezze as secretary of health, education, and welfare.

In domestic affairs, Johnson expanded his concept of the Great Society, the name he used to distinguish his administration from Kennedy's New Frontier. The legislative program proposed by Johnson concentrated on antipoverty, health, education, conservation, and urban planning measures.

Deeply involved in civil-rights issues, Johnson pressed Congress for—and obtained—legislation assuring voting rights for blacks (see Black Americans). Legislation passed in July raised social security payments and taxes. The bill also provided for hospital benefits (medicare) for most persons 65 years of age and over (*see* Social Security).

Johnson won excellent cooperation from the 89th Congress, in which Democrats outnumbered Republicans by more than two to one. A 1.3-billion-dollar measure to aid public schools and a bill creating a Cabinet-level Department of Housing and Urban Development (HUD) were passed though similar legislation urged by other presidents had been rejected. Other major measures enacted in 1965 included the easing of immigration procedures, a highway beautification act, aid to higher education, and an omnibus housing bill (*see* Housing). In January 1966 Johnson named as secretary of HUD Robert C. Weaver—the first black to head a Cabinet department. (*See also* United States History.)

1966 Domestic Program

The president curtailed his schedule for several weeks after he underwent surgery for removal of his gall bladder in October 1965. His third State-of-the-Union message was delivered in January 1966. He pledged United States support in Vietnam "until aggression has stopped" and a continuation of his Great Society programs.

Congress approved many of Johnson's 1966 legislative proposals—notably the creation of a Cabinet-level Department of Transportation (DOT). Among the president's proposals rejected by Congress were a civil rights bill with an open-housing provision and Constitutional amendments to abolish the electoral college and to lengthen to four years the terms of members of the House of Representatives.

International Problems and Events

The United States role in South Vietnam changed in 1965. In March United States planes began bombing military targets in North Vietnam. In June American forces in South Vietnam joined in the fighting. Throughout the year, numerous proposals for discussions to end the conflict were made directly by Johnson or through private diplomatic talks; all were rejected by North Vietnam. In a major peace-seeking effort, Johnson suspended bombing raids late in 1965 and sent personal representatives on peace missions to capitals throughout the world. North Vietnam's rejection of these efforts led to the resumption of bombing on Jan. 31, 1966.

In February 1966 Johnson and his military and political advisers conferred in Honolulu, Hawaii, with South Vietnamese government officials. They issued a "Declaration of Honolulu," outlining policies for winning the conflict. Bipartisan criticism of Johnson's policies in Vietnam grew during 1965. It also increased in 1966 when the United States role in the fighting was intensified, especially in the bombing of North Vietnam. (*See also* Vietnam Conflict.)

When a reportedly Communist-led revolt had broken out in the Dominican Republic in April 1965, Johnson had dispatched Marines and other forces to

President Johnson (right), elected to the nation's top office, confers with his running mate, Hubert H. Humphrey.

protect Americans and other non-Dominicans there. Later a force of the Organization of American States —including United States troops—took over peace-keeping duties. Troop withdrawal began in 1966 after the Dominicans elected a new government. (*See also* Dominican Republic.)

In April 1966 Johnson visited Mexico City for the unveiling of a statue of Abraham Lincoln, given to Mexico by the United States. It was his first visit to a foreign capital since his becoming president.

Johnson made his first major overseas journey in October. In the Philippines he discussed the Vietnam conflict and other Asian problems with heads of government from South Vietnam, Australia, New Zealand, Thailand, South Korea, and the Philippines. He visited these nations as well as Malaysia. He returned home just before the November elections. A minor operation prevented him from campaigning.

Vietnam Overshadows Domestic Issues in 1967

Johnson dwelt heavily on the Vietnam problem in his 1967 State-of-the-Union message. As the United States expanded its participation in the warfare, domestic affairs tended to take a secondary place.

Nevertheless, the president made many legislative proposals to the first session of the 90th Congress. These included a civil rights bill similar to that rejected in 1966, suggestions for expanding social security and for controlling crime, and a request for an income tax surcharge.

The 25th Amendment to the Constitution, ratified in February, settled questions that were unresolved when Johnson succeeded Kennedy. It clarified the role of a vice-president in the event of a president's death or disability and that of a president in filling a vice-presidential vacancy.

In 1967 Johnson appointed Alan S. Boyd as the first secretary of DOT; Alexander B. Trowbridge as secretary of commerce, succeeding Connor; and William Ramsey Clark as attorney general, succeeding Katzenbach. Johnson filled Supreme Court vacancies by appointing Abe Fortas in 1965 and Thurgood Marshall, the court's first black justice, in 1967.

Meetings Abroad and at Home

On a visit to Guam in March 1967, Johnson held strategy sessions on Vietnam and talked with officials of the United States Pacific island possessions. In April he participated in a Latin American summit conference on inter-American trade and economics. The meeting was held in Punta del Este, Uruguay.

Later in April the president flew to Bonn, West Germany, for the funeral of Konrad Adenauer, the nation's first chancellor. While there, he talked with France's President Charles de Gaulle, whose policies had posed many diplomatic problems for the Johnson Administration. (*See also* De Gaulle.)

The outbreak of the Israeli-Arab war in June 1967 led to conferences between Johnson and the premier of the U.S.S.R., Aleksei N. Kosygin. Kosygin went to the United States to support the Arab position at the United Nations. He met with Johnson on June 23 and June 25 at Holly Bush, home of the president of Glassboro State College, in Glassboro, N.J. The talks were cordial but ineffectual. (*See also* Israel.)

1968: Dissent and Steps Toward Peace

As 1968 began, Johnson was faced with growing dissent in the nation and in Congress over the conduct of the war in Vietnam. In addition, serious urban riots in 1967 had raised the question of national priorities, and the nation's balance of payments was increasingly threatened by an outflow of gold. To meet these problems, the president's State-of-the-Union message renewed his request for an income tax surcharge; called for a repeal of the 25 percent gold cover for dollars; and proposed housing, job, and urban-affairs legislation to help alleviate poverty and ghetto conditions. Congress enacted laws to cover these proposals, including a civil rights act with open-housing provisions.

Under the pressure of domestic problems and increasing antiwar sentiment, the president on March 31 announced a curtailment of bombing in North Vietnam and once again proposed peace talks to North Vietnam. He renounced his candidacy for a second presidential term to free his hand for peace negotiations. Peace talks began in Paris, France, in May but quickly became stalemated. Johnson broke the impasse by ordering a total cessation of the bombing of North Vietnam, effective November 1.

In April the president met in Hawaii with military commanders from South Vietnam. In July Johnson traveled to El Salvador, where he discussed Central American economic integration with the presidents of El Salvador, Costa Rica, Honduras, Nicaragua, and Guatemala.

UPI

Johnson speaks with Premier Aleksei N. Kosygin of the Soviet Union at a summit meeting in Glassboro, N.J., in June 1967.

In 1968 Johnson worked to improve United States-Soviet relations. A nuclear nonproliferation treaty was proposed. The Soviet-led invasion of Czechoslovakia in August was condemned by Johnson, and his hopes to visit the Soviet Union were foiled.

Johnson's Retirement

The crowning event of Johnson's presidency was man's first flight around the moon, achieved by the spacecraft Apollo 8. Johnson was succeeded by Richard M. Nixon, a Republican, on Jan. 20, 1969. Johnson retired to his Texas ranch, where he devoted himself to the establishment of a library to house his presidential papers and the Lyndon Baines Johnson School of Public Affairs at the University of Texas in Austin. The library was dedicated in May 1971.

On Jan. 22, 1973, Johnson was stricken with a heart attack at his ranch. He was pronounced dead at Brooke Army Medical Center in San Antonio, Tex. His death occurred just a few days prior to the signing of the agreement to end the war in Vietnam. Later in 1973 the space center at Houston was renamed the Lyndon Baines Johnson Space Center in his memory.

BIBLIOGRAPHY FOR LYNDON B. JOHNSON

Barton, T. F. Lyndon B. Johnson: Young Texan (Bobbs, 1973).
Caro, R. A. The Path to Power (Knopf, 1982).
Cormier, Frank. LBJ the Way He Was (Doubleday, 1977).
Dugger, Ronnie. The Politician: the Life and Times of Lyndon Johnson (W. W. Norton, 1982).
Kearns, Doris. Lyndon Johnson and the American Dream (Harper, 1976).
Miller, Merle. Lyndon: an Oral Biography (Putnam, 1980).
Mooney, Booth. LBJ: an Irreverent Chronicle (Crowell, 1976).
Newlon, Clarke. L. B. J., the Man from Johnson City, rev. ed. (Dodd, 1970).
Reedy, George. Lyndon Johnson: a Memoir (Andrews & McMeel, 1982).
Rulon, P. R. The Compassionate Samaritan (Nelson-Hall, 1981).

Courtesy of the National Portrait Gallery, London

Samuel Johnson in a painting by Sir Joshua Reynolds

JOHNSON, Samuel (1709–84). The most famous writer in 18th-century England was Samuel Johnson. His fame rests not on his writings, however, but on his friend James Boswell's biography of him.

Samuel Johnson was born on Sept. 18, 1709, in Lichfield, England. In infancy he had scrofula, a disease that left its effect on his skin and eyesight. His father was a bookseller, and the boy read widely. His family had only enough money to send him to Oxford University for a year. There he was known for skill with Latin and Greek and for his ready wit.

The young man struggled for several years at a series of menial jobs. When he was 26 he married Elizabeth Porter, a widow 20 years older than he. The two remained devoted to each other until her death in 1752. They had no children. After marriage Johnson started a school, but it soon closed. He and a student, David Garrick, went to London to find work.

His early days in London were extremely hard, and he was barely able to support himself and his wife. He reported parliamentary speeches, taking care, as he frankly said, "that the Whig dogs should not have the best of it." He did translations for publishers and made catalogs for booksellers.

Gradually Johnson's reputation grew. A combination of booksellers offered him about $7,800 to prepare an English dictionary. The venture took almost eight years. The 'Dictionary' brought him an honorary Doctor of Laws degree from Oxford, well-paying editorial posts, and a government pension. Today this dictionary seems old-fashioned and unscientific, but it is far better than any earlier works in its field. Johnson sometimes permitted his own feelings to color his definitions. An example:

Lexicographer: A writer of dictionaries; a harmless drudge, that busies himself in tracing the original, and detailing the signification of words.

In 1763 James Boswell, a 22-year-old Scottish lawyer of good family, went to London and met Johnson. At once Boswell became devoted to the older man. They remained good friends until Johnson's death. Boswell remembered nearly everything Johnson said and recorded their conversations in his journal.

Johnson died on Dec. 13, 1784. In 1791 Boswell's 'Life of Samuel Johnson' was published. It has 200 pages covering Johnson's life before he met Boswell and 1,100 pages on the 21 years of their friendship. It is considered one of the greatest of biographies. (*See also* Boswell; Biography.)

Johnson's other chief works are: poems—'London' published in 1738 and 'The Vanity of Human Wishes' (1749); a play—'Irene' (1749); essays—'The Rambler' (1752) and 'The Idler' (1761); a novel—'Rasselas' (1759); and a criticism—'Lives of the Poets' (1781).

JOINT. The skeletons of animals would be too stiff to move or would fall in a disorderly heap if they were not carefully fitted with joints. A joint is a connection that holds together two or more bones or other hard structures. Joints have two main purposes: They give support, and they allow movement where it is needed.

All animals that have segments have joints. The joints of arthropods—insects, spiders, crabs, and similar creatures—connect the external skeleton, which is made of a shell-like substance called chitin. (The word *arthropod* means "joint-footed" in Greek—from *arthron*, meaning "joint," and *pod*, meaning "foot.") The joints of vertebrates—fishes, reptiles, birds, and mammals—connect the parts of the internal skeleton made of bone and cartilage (*see* Skeleton; Bone).

This article describes the joints in the human body. They provide a good example of the joint types found in mammals, and they are similar to the joints of birds and reptiles.

Types

The body has three main joint types: joints that are fixed, or that do not move, such as the seams between the pieces of bone that make up the skull; joints that have limited movement, such as those in the spine; and joints that allow a good deal of movement, such as those at the knee, elbow, and shoulder.

In the immovable joints the bones have united, or fused, after having been separate early in life. The joining is called synarthrosis (in Greek, *syn* means "together"). In a newborn baby the six skull bones have room to squeeze closer together. This allows for an easier passage through the birth canal. Later the bones grow toward each other until the gaps are sealed. Another example of fixed joints is at the bottom of the spine, where five bones gradually fuse to form the sacrum, a strong attachment for the hips.

The joints of the spine allow a slight tilt in any direction around a compressed jelly-like disc between the vertebrae. These joints belong to the second type of joint, amphiarthrosis (in Greek, *amphi* means "both sides," or "around"). When the back bends, each joint makes only a small movement, but the total effect is that of a single large movement. Along the front and back of the spinal column, long straps of ligaments, tough fibrous tissues, hold the joints and bones together and also limit their movement.

The joints in the arms, legs, hands, feet, hips, and shoulders can move quite freely because the ends of the bones are separated. This type of joint is called diarthrodial (in Greek, *di* means "separate"). The space between the bones is the joint cavity. It is formed by the joint capsule, a sac covering the bone ends. The cavity often extends into pouches, or bursas. Lining the capsule is the synovial membrane. It secretes a fluid that keeps the bone ends from rubbing against each other and brings the joints nutrients. The fluid is spread by movement; to remain in good condition, a joint must be moved regularly. (Another name for the diarthrodial joints is synovial joints.) Movement is also helped by the smooth bone ends. They are made of cartilage, a softer and springier material than bone. While tough ligaments wrap and bandage the joints in various formations, a more elastic connective tissue, the tendons, connect the joints with muscles. Muscles are arranged around the joints in opposing pairs. When one set of muscles shortens, the joint bends and the opposite set of muscles stretches (*see* Muscle).

Diarthrodial joints are classified according to the way they move. The joints at the fingers and knee move back and forth, or open and close like the hinge on a door. They are called hinge joints. The very flexible joint that connects the thumb to the hand is a saddle joint, so named because of the shape of the ends. This joint allows the thumb to move from side to side, and from back to front. The forearm can turn at the elbow joint so that palm faces up or down. The elbow is thus a combined hinge and pivot. A pure pivot joint is found in the spine between the two top vertebrae; it permits the head to turn from side to side. Examples of joints that allow the most motion are at the shoulders and hips. They are called ball-and-socket joints because the head of one bone is round and fits into a cuplike depression on the other bone.

Disorders

The joints are prone to injury because they are in the less protected places of the body and are subject to great stresses. Sprains are common at the ankle, wrist, knee, and back, usually from putting weight on the joint while it is not in a weight-bearing position. Dislocations, where the bone slips out of position, are most common at the shoulder.

Bursitis is a painful inflammation of a pouch in the joint cavity, caused by mechanical irritation. It is often associated with occupations and has been known by such colorful names as housemaid's knee, soldier's heel, and tennis elbow. It is one of many kinds of arthritis, a group of inflammatory disorders resulting in pain, stiffness, and enlargement of the joints (*see* Arthritis). Joints may ache during viral and bacterial infections; the reason is not clear. Joints severely damaged by injury or arthritis can sometimes be rebuilt or even replaced with fittings of steel and other materials (*see* Bioengineering).

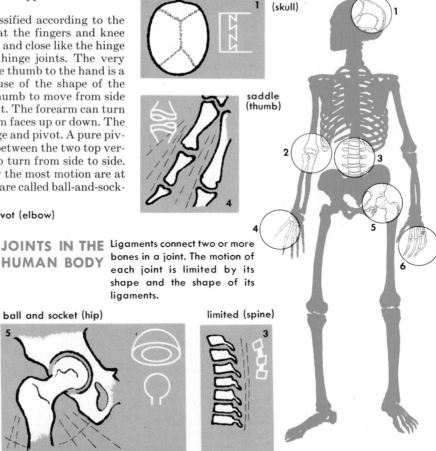

fixed (skull)

saddle (thumb)

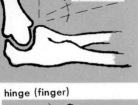

pivot (elbow)

JOINTS IN THE HUMAN BODY Ligaments connect two or more bones in a joint. The motion of each joint is limited by its shape and the shape of its ligaments.

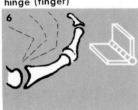

hinge (finger)

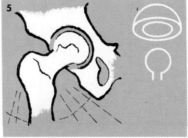

ball and socket (hip)

limited (spine)

JOLLIET, Louis (1645–1700). Two men share the honor of discovering and exploring the upper Mississippi River—Father Jacques Marquette and Louis Jolliet. They were the first white men to travel the giant river after the Spaniard Hernando de Soto found the lower Mississippi in 1541.

Jolliet was born near Quebec, Canada, in September 1645. He studied for the priesthood at the Jesuit seminary in Quebec. Before taking the final vows he changed his mind and went to France for a year's study in science.

Back in Canada he was a fur trader, traveling through the wilderness around the Great Lakes. He became an expert map maker and was skilled in Indian languages. In 1672 Count Louis de Frontenac, governor of New France (France's possessions in North America before 1763), selected Jolliet and Father Marquette to find the great river in the west. At that time the river was known only by rumor (*see* Mississippi River; Marquette).

During their journey Jolliet's maps and papers were lost when his canoe upset. However, Marquette's account was of help to La Salle, who explored the Mississippi to its mouth in 1682 (*see* La Salle).

Jolliet was granted the feudal rights to several islands in the lower Saint Lawrence River. After his marriage in 1675 he established his home on Anticosti. He made further explorations for New France and was appointed royal cartographer. He died in 1700 in a Quebec province.

JONES, Bobby (1902–71). Regarded as the greatest amateur golfer of modern times, Bobby Jones is the only player to have won the grand slam in golf. In one year, 1930, he won the four major tournaments of the time: the British Amateur, the British Open, the United States Amateur, and the United States Open. From 1923 through 1930, Jones won 13 championships in those four annual tournaments, a record that stood until it was surpassed by Jack Nicklaus, a professional, in 1973. During his career Jones won the British Open three times, the British Amateur once, the United States Open four times, and the United States Amateur five times. He played for the United States against Britain in the Walker Cup team matches in 1922, 1924, 1926, 1928, and 1930, winning nine of ten matches.

Born on March 17, 1902, in Atlanta, Robert Tyre Jones became a practicing lawyer in that city. He never became a professional golfer and rarely played in championship competition after he completed his grand slam in 1930. Afterward he helped to organize the annual Masters Tournament, first held in 1934, at the Augusta National Golf Club in Georgia. In 1958 Jones received the freedom of the burgh of Saint Andrews, Fife, Scotland, home of the oldest golf club of the world; he was pronounced honorary burgess and guild brother of the city. He was the first American recipient of this award since Benjamin Franklin was so honored in 1759. He died in Atlanta on Dec. 18, 1971. (*See also* Golf.)

JONES, Inigo (1573–1652). Founder of the English classical school of architecture, Inigo Jones was surveyor of works, or official architect, to James I and Charles I and exerted a wide influence in his own time. He left his mark on London by designing the first of its civic squares. His work became even more highly regarded in the 18th century.

Jones was baptized on July 19, 1573, in the church of Saint Bartholomew the Less in London. He was the son of a clothworker and was probably apprenticed to a kind of woodworker called a joiner to learn the trade; little else is known about his early life. By 1603 he had visited Italy and had studied painting and design. Before his return to England he worked for Christian IV of Denmark. In 1605 he was employed by Anne, sister of Christian IV and queen of James I of England, to design the scenery and costumes for a masque, the first of at least 25 of these elaborate dramatic works that Jones worked on for the royal courts of England. His visual effects for the masques were ingenious and spectacular.

In 1610 Jones became surveyor of works to the prince of Wales, but Jones did no actual building for him. In 1613 Jones again visited Italy, where he studied both antique ruins and the works of the Renaissance architects of the day, especially Andrea Palladio. In 1615 he was appointed surveyor of works to King James I, continuing in the position under Charles I until 1642.

Jones built, rebuilt, and improved many royal buildings. Only three, however, survive: the Queen's Chapel at Saint James's Palace; the Queen's House at Greenwich, which is now the National Maritime Museum; and the Banqueting House at Whitehall. When the original Banqueting House was destroyed by fire, Jones replaced it in 1622. Considered to be his greatest work, the structure is one large chamber. In 1635 Peter Paul Rubens painted allegorical, or symbolic, scenes on the main panels of the ceiling.

The Banqueting House at Whitehall in London is usually considered the masterpiece of Inigo Jones.

A. F. Kersting

Nearly 20 years after the Banqueting House was built, Charles I instructed Jones to prepare designs for rebuilding the whole of Whitehall Palace. These designs by Jones still exist and are among his most interesting creations.

In 1630 Jones introduced town planning to London when he designed the city's first square, Covent Garden. Only the church of Saint Paul survives of Jones's original work. From 1633 to 1642 he restored St. Paul's Cathedral and built a new portico, but his work on the cathedral was destroyed in the 1666 London fire. Sir Christopher Wren knew his predecessor's work, however, and Jones's influence can be seen in Wren's rebuilding of the cathedral after the fire.

The last few years of Jones's life were affected by political events and by civil war. In 1642, when war broke out between Charles I and the Parliamentarians, Jones fled London. He was captured and fined, and his property was confiscated. But in 1646 he was pardoned and his property returned. In 1649 he again began working for lesser royalty. He died in London on June 21, 1652.

John Paul Jones in 1781 portrait

JONES, John Paul (1747–92). The first great American naval hero was Captain John Paul Jones. Strong, resourceful, and skilled in seamanship, he loved a battle almost as much as he loved freedom. His words, "I have not yet begun to fight," are famous throughout the world.

John Paul Jones was born on July 6, 1747, near Kirkcudbright, Scotland. His father, John Paul, was a gardener. The boy was christened John Paul, Jr.; he added the "Jones" later. When only 12 years old, he was signed on as an apprentice aboard the *Friendship,* a merchant vessel sailing from England to the American Colonies.

When the youth finished his apprenticeship, he joined the British navy. He did not stay long. At once he saw that no gardener's son, however capable, could rise in the British service. He became first mate on a slaver, a ship that carried slaves, but soon quit. Ashore in the West Indies, he became an actor. In a season he earned enough to sail home as a passenger. On the way, however, the captain and first mate died of typhoid fever. John Paul was the only man aboard who could navigate. He took the ship into port and the grateful owners kept him on as captain.

At port in the West Indies Captain Paul had a man flogged for mutinous conduct. The man left the ship, took berth on another, and died some weeks later. Word circulated that he died as a result of the beating. A court of inquiry cleared Paul, but suspicion hung over him. Later, a drunken sailor attacked Paul in his cabin. Drawing his sword only in defense, Paul accidentally ran the man through. The two accidents troubled Paul, and he fled his ship. In Virginia and North Carolina he found old friends. Calling himself Jones, he led the placid life of a planter.

When the Revolution came he rode to Philadelphia and offered his services. He served as first lieutenant on the *Alfred.* His first command was the *Providence;*

in 1777 he became captain of the sloop *Ranger.* He carried the news of British General John Burgoyne's surrender to France.

From France he sailed to the west coast of England, destroying coastal shipping and capturing the sloop *Drake.* Back in France, he was given command of the converted merchant ship *Bonhomme Richard.*

Sailing from France he met a convoy off Flamborough Head on England's North Sea coast. The convoy was escorted by the British 44-gun frigate *Serapis.* On the afternoon of Sept. 23, 1779, the *Bonhomme Richard* engaged the *Serapis* in one of the most famous sea battles in history. For hours the ships blazed away at each other at short range. Then Jones maneuvered to lash the bowsprit of the *Serapis* to his own mizzenmast. The *Bonhomme Richard* was badly damaged, and the English captain called upon Jones to surrender. Jones's proud reply has become classic: "I have not yet begun to fight!" Victory came when an American sailor tossed a grenade into a temporary gunpowder magazine located just below the main deck of the *Serapis.*

After the war Jones served the new nation as agent in Europe, and for a brief time he was an admiral in the Russian navy. His health was poor and he retired to Paris, where he died on July 18, 1792.

JONES, Mother (1830–1930). When she was past 50, a labor organizer called Mother Jones became widely known as a fiery agitator for the union rights of American coal miners. In her 80s she was jailed several times for leading miners' strikes.

Mother Jones was born Mary Harris on May 1, 1830, in County Cork, Ireland. She emigrated to the United States as a child and later married an iron worker. In 1867 her husband and children died in an epidemic in Memphis, Tenn.

Jones opened a dressmaking shop in Chicago, but in 1871 she lost everything she owned in the great

Chicago fire. Turning for assistance to the Knights of Labor, she was attracted by their campaign for improved working conditions. By the 1880s Jones herself had become a highly visible figure in the American labor movement. She traveled across the country, organizing for the United Mine Workers and other labor unions and giving speeches on her own. Her slogan was "Join the union, boys." In 1886 she was a prominent figure in the Haymarket riot in Chicago (*see* Chicago).

Mother Jones was also an active supporter of legislation to prohibit child labor. She was one of the founders of the Social Democratic party in 1898 and of the Industrial Workers of the World in 1905. Her autobiography was published in 1925.

Mother Jones died at Silver Spring, Md., on Nov. 30, 1930, at the age of 100. A biography, 'Mother Jones, the Miner's Angel', by Dale Fetherling, was published in 1974.

Courtesy of the National Portrait Gallery, London

Ben Jonson

JONSON, Ben (1572?–1637). Few English poets or playwrights have led such adventure-filled lives or enjoyed such enduring fame as Ben Jonson. A bricklayer, soldier, and actor, he also wrote plays that have become classics.

Ben Jonson is thought to have been born on June 11, 1572, in or near London, England, two months after the death of his father. His stepfather was a bricklayer, but young Jonson attended the Westminster School. He was then apprenticed to his stepfather's trade but was unhappy and ran away to Flanders, where he joined the English troops.

He soon returned to London and began to work in the theater as a strolling player. In 1598 his first comedy was successfully produced. The play proved a turning point, and he gradually earned his place among the best of the Elizabethan dramatists. As such he was also the leader of the Mermaid wits, a

circle of poets and playwrights who met in London's Mermaid Tavern and later the Devil Tavern.

Jonson died on Aug. 6, 1637. The following epitaph is on his grave in Westminster Abbey: "O rare [supposed by some to be intended for *Orare*, meaning 'pray for'] Ben Jonson."

His works include 'Sejanus' (1603); 'Volpone, or the Fox' (1606?); 'Epicoene, or the Silent Woman' (1609); 'The Alchemist' (1610); 'Catiline' (1611); and 'Bartholomew Fair' (1614). His best-loved song is 'To Celia', which begins "Drink to me only with thine eyes." (*See also* Drama; English Literature.)

JOPLIN, Janis (1943–70). One of the most popular female vocalists in rock music was Janis Joplin. Her singing had a power and depth of feeling that earned her comparison with the greatest performers in the blues tradition.

Janis Joplin was born on Jan. 19, 1943, in Port Arthur, Tex. She spent much of her adolescence listening to the music of black recording artists such as Bessie Smith, Leadbelly, and Odetta. Joplin left home at age 17 to perform country and western music in Houston, then went to San Francisco where she lived in unconventional style. She enrolled at several California colleges and lived in communes. In 1966 she joined a local San Francisco rock group, Big Brother and the Holding Company, as its lead singer. A year later the group appeared at the Monterey International Pop Festival, the event that escalated Joplin to stardom. She stunned the audience with her classic rendition of 'Ball and Chain'. Excellent reviews, a recording contract, and national concert tours followed the Monterey festival.

Cheap Thrills, Joplin's first starring album, was recorded with Big Brother. She soon left the group to go solo and assembled her own backup group, the Full Tilt Boogie Band, in 1968. With it she recorded two more albums and toured the United States and Europe. Joplin was as flamboyant offstage as on; she drank heavily, and her death on Oct. 4, 1970, in Hollywood is attributed to an overdose of narcotics. Her albums include *I Got Dem Ol' Kozmic Blues Again, Mama,* released in 1969, *Pearl* (1971), *In Concert* (1972), and *Janis* (1975).

Janis Joplin in 1968

David Gahr

JOPLIN, Scott (1868–1917). A black composer and pianist, Scott Joplin was known as the King of Ragtime at the turn of the 20th century. His classic ragtime pieces for the piano—including 'Maple Leaf Rag' and 'The Entertainer', published from 1899 through 1909—were important factors in his fame. An interest in Joplin and ragtime was stimulated in the 1970s by the use of his music in the Academy award-winning score for the movie 'The Sting'.

Scott Joplin was born in Texarkana, Ark., on Nov. 24, 1868. He studied piano with teachers near his childhood home. From the mid-1880s, he traveled through the Midwest, performing at the Columbian Exposition in Chicago in 1893. In 1895 he settled in Sedalia, Mo., where he studied music at the George R. Smith College for Negroes.

Joplin's first published extended work was a ballet suite (1902), using all the rhythmic devices of ragtime. In 1907 he moved to New York City and wrote an instruction book, 'The School of Ragtime', which outlined his complex bass patterns, syncopation and breaks, and harmonic ideas. He produced his opera 'Treemonisha' in 1915 at his own expense. This work combined all his musical ideas into a conventional, three-act opera, which he was obsessed with producing. The obsession drove him to a nervous breakdown and collapse that same year. He was institutionalized in 1916 and died on April 1, 1917, in New York City.

JORDAN, Michael (born 1963). Both literally and figuratively, Michael Jordan soared higher than any National Basketball Association (NBA) guard before him. His exciting leaps to the basket and his tongue-wagging slam dunks inspired his nickname of Air Jordan. And only a few seasons after joining the Chicago Bulls in 1984 he was perhaps the most recognized athlete in the United States.

Michael Jeffery Jordan was born on Feb. 17, 1963, in Brooklyn, N.Y., but he grew up in Wilmington, N.C. At Laney High School he did not make the varsity basketball team until his junior year. He attended the University of North Carolina from 1981 to 1984. He made the winning shot for North Carolina in the 1982 national championship game and was All-America the next two seasons. After leading the United States basketball team to a gold medal in the 1984 Olympic Games, he left school after his junior year.

After his first year as a professional with the Bulls in 1985, Jordan was named rookie of the year. Wilt Chamberlain was the only other player to score 3,000 points in a season before Jordan did it in the 1986–87 season, with a league-leading average of 37.1 points per game. He led the league again in 1987–88 with a per-game average of 35 points, in a year when he failed to score more than 20 points in only three of 82 games. At the 1987 All-Star Game he won his second consecutive slam-dunk contest and was named the most valuable player. Jordan was only the second scoring leader to ever make the NBA's all-defense team. After the 1987–88 season he was named the most valuable player in the NBA.

JORDAN. The Hashemite Kingdom of Jordan is a small country with limited natural resources, but for years it has played a critical role in the struggle for power in the Middle East. Jordan's significance results partly from its strategic location at the crossroads of what most Christians, Jews, and Muslims call the Holy Land. The country is bounded by Syria on the north, Iraq on the east, Saudi Arabia on the southeast and south, and Israel on the west.

Jordan is famous for its historical relics, including ancient Roman ruins, beautiful crusader citadels such as the one at Al Karak, the remarkable rose-red city of Petra, and an active seaport and fishing resort at Al ʿAqabah. Jordanians are known for their hospitality, an outgrowth of their Bedouin heritage, and this trait has given the nation a new and growing status as a business center of the Middle East. A tremendous building boom in Amman, the capital and largest city, has expanded the city's boundaries from the seven small hills on which it was originally built to include large outlying suburbs (*see* Amman).

Land and Climate

In spring the rolling hills and valleys of Jordan are covered by grasses and wildflowers that provide food for grazing flocks. No fish live in the Dead Sea, which is known for its extreme saltiness. Many kinds of sea life, however, can be found in the waters of the Gulf of ʿAqaba at Al ʿAqabah, Jordan's only port and access to the sea.

The climate of western Jordan—separated from the sea only by the narrow width of Israel—is determined by mild Mediterranean winds and occasional rain, and the eastern part of the country has a desert-type climate. In the south the influence of the dry Saharan winds is felt, and the land is largely desert. The Jordan River, which provides water for Jordan's major agricultural region, the Jordan Valley, flows south into the Dead Sea. This depression along the border with Israel continues in a fissure known as the Wadi ʿAraba and into the Red Sea at Al ʿAqabah.

JORDAN

© Paolo Koch—Photo Researchers

Swimmers enjoy the warm waters of the Gulf of 'Aqaba at Al 'Aqabah, Jordan's only seaport.

People

After World War I ended in 1918, the region east of the Jordan River, then called Transjordan, became a British mandate. Its population consisted mostly of desert tribes, both settled and nomadic, and a small percentage of Circassians who had emigrated from the Caucasus in Russia since the 19th century. Today, Jordan has few nomadic or seminomadic peoples, most of the population having been given housing and land to raise crops or herd their flocks. This change in custom occurred mainly because the people realized the value of a formal education for their children and because they could benefit most from government assistance by settling in one place.

Jordan's labor force has a large number of Palestinians who fled to Jordan after the creation of Israel in 1948 and the 1967 Israeli occupation of the west bank of the Jordan River. In 1988 Jordan had a population of about 2,965,000, including people in occupied territories. About 99 percent are Arabs and fewer than 1 percent Circassians. Muslims make up more than 90 percent of the population. Arabic is the official language, and nearly 80 percent of the people are literate.

Economy, Transportation, and Communication

Jordan's economy has been greatly strained by the presence of a large number of refugees living in makeshift camps that the United Nations can only partially support. All the refugees have been granted Jordanian citizenship and have refugee status for

relief purposes. Nevertheless, Jordan has prospered greatly. Although a large part of the country consists of semidesert land, the fertile Jordan Valley provides such vital crops as vegetables, olives and other fruits, and grain. The economy depends largely on industries such as phosphate mining, petroleum refining, cement production, and tourism.

A major desert highway runs between Amman and the port at Al 'Aqabah. It serves as the main route through Jordan to the sea and is used to transport many goods for export. There is a railway, and many new highways are being built. Amman has a television station and a radio station, and another radio station broadcasts from near Jerusalem.

Government and History

Jordan is a constitutional monarchy ruled by members of the Hashemite family. The legislature, called the National Assembly, consists of a senate and a house of representatives. The king appoints the members of the senate, and the people choose the members of the house. Citizens who are more than 18 years old may vote if they are not members of the royal family.

Before World War I Transjordan formed part of an Ottoman Empire seriously weakened by internal discord (see Ottoman Empire). With British military assistance, Greater Syria was freed from Turkish domination by Arab nationalists led by the Sharif of Mecca and his four sons. The Arabs hoped to establish an independent Arab state in all of Greater Syria, but the French and British had divided this region into their own spheres of influence in the Sykes-Picot Agreement of 1916.

Nevertheless, one of the sharif's sons, Faisal I, went to Damascus and declared himself head of an independent Arab state. The French moved in to depose him in 1921, and Faisal's brother, Abdullah, started north from Arabia to assist him. When Winston Churchill, then the British colonial minister, learned of these events, he guaranteed Abdullah an emirate in Transjordan if he would seek no additional territory. Abdullah agreed. He became king of an independent Jordan in 1946.

FACTS ABOUT JORDAN

Official Name: Hashemite Kingdom of Jordan.

Capital: Amman.

Area: 36,659 square miles (94,946 square kilometers).

Population (1988 estimate): 2,965,000; 86 persons per square mile (33 persons per square kilometer); 70 percent urban, 30 percent rural.

Major Language: Arabic (official).

Major Religion: Islam (official).

Literacy: 79 percent.

Highest Peak: Jabal Ramm.

Major River: Jordan River.

Form of Government: Constitutional monarchy.

Chief of State and Head of Government: King.

Legislature: National Assembly.

Voting Qualifications: Citizens who are 18 years of age and are not members of the royal family.

Political Divisions: 8 governorates (*muhafazat*).

Major Cities (1986 estimate): Amman (833,500), Az Zarga' (285,000), Irbid (150,000).

Chief Manufactured and Mined Products: Cigarettes, beer, alcoholic beverages, phosphates, cement.

Chief Agricultural Products: *Crops*—tomatoes, eggplants, citrus fruits, melons, cucumbers, wheat, barley, lentils, peas, beans, maize. *Livestock*—chickens, sheep, goats, cattle, donkeys, camels.

Flag: *Colors*—red, white, black, and green (*see* Flags of the World).

Monetary Unit: 1 dinar = 1,000 fils.

142

King Abdullah was assassinated in 1951 while on a trip to Jerusalem. His son Talal ruled briefly until mental illness led to his removal from office. Talal's 17-year-old son, Hussein, became king in 1953. Jordan joined the United Nations in 1955. The special relationship between Great Britain and Jordan was officially terminated in 1957.

In 1967, as the result of the Six-Day War between the Arab states and Israel, the Israelis occupied all of Jordan west of the Jordan River and all of Jerusalem. In 1970 the Jordanian army defeated a Palestinian guerrilla force in a ten-day civil war. Jordan and other Arab nations fought another war against Israel in 1973. In 1974 the Arab governments recognized the right of the Palestine Liberation Organization (PLO) to establish an independent Palestinian state on the west bank of the river if Israel withdrew from the area. In agreeing to this, Jordan effectively gave up its claim to the West Bank; however, Jordan continued to fund social and economic development in the territory and to pay salaries to territorial civil servants. In 1978 Israel agreed to a freeze on new settlements in the West Bank. Jordan broke off diplomatic relations with Egypt in 1979 following the Camp David agreements between Egypt and Israel because Egypt had not affirmed the status of Palestinians in the West Bank and the Gaza Strip. Relations were restored in 1984. In 1988 Jordan announced that it would give up its involvement in the West Bank, thereby accepting the PLO's claims to the area. The action followed an eight-month Palestinian uprising in the occupied territories.

JORDAN RIVER. Flowing southward from Syria across Israel and into Jordan, the Jordan River is the lowest river in the world. It is more than 223 miles (359 kilometers) long. Over most of its course the river is shallow and rapid flowing. The Jordan has often served as an international boundary and since 1967 has marked the cease-fire line between Israeli-occupied territory to the west and Jordan to the east.

The headwaters of the Jordan originate on snow-covered Mount Hermon in southern Syria and Lebanon. These streams flow into the Hula Panhandle, a marshy region at the northern tip of Israel. Most of the basin has been drained for agriculture, but a small part has been preserved for the natural vegetation and animal life.

From the Hula Panhandle the river drops sharply to the Sea of Galilee, 686 feet (209 meters) below sea level. This lake serves to stabilize the river's rate of flow to the Dead Sea. Between these two lakes the river winds through a plain in a narrow, high-walled valley. The elevation at the Dead Sea, the lowest lake in the world, is 1,315 feet (401 meters) below sea level.

The Jordan is fed by rains falling on its neighboring plateaus, but little rain actually falls into the deep valley, so agriculture along the river is completely dependent on irrigation. The river is also fed by water from thermal springs that have a high mineral content. As a result, the river waters could not be used for farming until dams and drainage canals were built, ensuring a water supply adequate to dissolve and remove the poison salts from the soil.

In irrigated areas the Jordan Valley has been settled by Arab and Jewish agricultural communities. The Ghawr irrigation canal, which is 43 miles (69 kilometers) long, was completed in 1967 and has permitted the cultivation of oranges, bananas, early vegetables, and sugar beets. More than 11 billion cubic feet (311 million cubic meters) of the Jordan's water is pumped annually to the center and south of Israel.

The river was called the Aulon by the Greeks, ha-Yarden by the Hebrews, and ash-Shari'ah (Watering Place) by the Arabs. Christians, Jews, and Muslims alike revere the Jordan. (*See also* Israel; Jordan.)

Chief Joseph posed in 1878 for the photographer Charles M. Bell.

Courtesy of the Smithsonian Institution, Washington, D.C., Bureau of American Ethnology

JOSEPH, Chief (1840?–1904). In 1871, when he became chief of the Nez Percé Indian tribe in the American Northwest, Joseph led his people in an unsuccessful resistance to the white man's takeover of their lands. The land was in the Wallowa Valley of the Oregon Territory where he had been born in about 1840. Negotiations failed, and by 1877 the tribe was ordered to move to the Lapwai Reservation in Idaho. Joseph reluctantly agreed, but when three of his braves killed a group of white settlers, he attempted to escape to Canada with his followers.

They traveled more than 1,600 miles (2,500 kilometers), through Oregon, Washington, Idaho, and Montana. Although they were able to defeat the pursuing United States Army troops in several battles, the Indians finally surrendered on Oct. 5, 1877. The War Department, fearful of a general Indian uprising, ordered them to be taken to Indian Territory, now Oklahoma, where many became sick and died.

In 1885 Joseph and the remainder of his tribe were allowed to return to Washington and Idaho. Joseph ended up on the Colville Reservation in Washington Territory and was never allowed to return to Wallowa Valley. He died at Colville on Sept. 21, 1904.

JOSEPHINE (1763–1814). As the wife of Napoleon Bonaparte, Josephine became empress of the French in 1804. A widow after her first husband was guillotined during the French Revolution, she reluctantly agreed to marry Bonaparte, at the time a little-known artillery officer.

Josephine Tascher de la Pagerie was born on June 23, 1763, in Martinique, in the French West Indies. She went to France in 1779 after marrying a rich young army officer, Viscount Alexandre de Beauharnais. After he was killed, she was left to raise their two children. Her grace and charm attracted Bonaparte and in 1796, after he had been appointed commander of the Italian expedition, they married. When Napoleon was proclaimed emperor of the French at Notre Dame cathedral, Josephine was crowned empress.

The marriage was childless, and Napoleon wanted a son. In 1810 he arranged for the nullification of his marriage to Josephine on the grounds that a parish priest had not been present at the ceremony. Soon thereafter he married Archduchess Marie Louise of Austria. The French Senate awarded Josephine a large annuity, and she retired to the château at Malmaison, near Paris. Napoleon visited her there.

Josephine's children by her first marriage were named Eugène and Hortense. Eugène proved an able and loyal general under Napoleon and was for a time viceroy of Italy. Hortense married Louis Bonaparte, Napoleon's brother, and became the mother of Napoleon III. Josephine died at Malmaison on May 29, 1814. (*See also* Napoleon I.)

JOSQUIN (1440?–1521). A Flemish composer now considered the greatest of the Renaissance, Josquin was also widely acclaimed in his own lifetime. His full name takes many forms. There is evidence that he preferred Josquin Desprez, but the surname is often spelled des Prez and des Prés.

Josquin was born about 1440 in the province of Hainaut, now in Belgium, possibly at Condé-sur-L'Escaut. He was probably a chorister at the collegiate church of Saint Quentin and was a singer from 1459 to 1472 in the cathedral at Milan, Italy. He then served Duke Galeazzo Maria Sforza in Milan and later in the papal chapel. Before becoming choirmaster of the chapel of Ercole I, duke of Ferrara, in 1503, he seems to have been associated with the chapel of Louis XII of France and with the cathedral of Cambrai. At the duke's death in 1505, Josquin became provost of the collegiate church of Notre Dame in Condé, where he spent the remainder of his life.

Twenty of his masses survive in their entirety. Of these, 17 were printed in his lifetime, as were many motets and chansons. He developed methods inherited from the late Middle Ages, using imitative and antiphonal techniques. Martin Luther admired his music, calling him "master of the notes, which must do as he wishes; other composers must do as the notes wish." Josquin was also praised for his teaching. He died at Condé on Aug. 27, 1521.

JOYCE, James (1882–1941). The Irish-born author James Joyce was one of the greatest literary innovators of the 20th century. His best-known works contain extraordinary experiments both in language and in writing style.

In these works Joyce developed a technique of writing called "stream of consciousness." Using this technique, he ignored orderly sentence structure and attempted to reproduce in words the rambling processes of the human mind.

James Joyce, one of several children of John Stanislaus Joyce, was born in Dublin on Feb. 2, 1882. He was educated in Dublin at Jesuit schools and graduated from what was then known as Royal University. From boyhood he was fascinated by the sounds of words and by the rhythms of speech and song.

When he was in his early twenties, Joyce left Ireland to live in continental Europe. Although he divorced himself from both his homeland and his church, the major source of his literary inspiration was to be his early life in Dublin and the years he spent in its Jesuit schools.

He lived for a time in Paris and then settled in Trieste, Italy. Later he married Nora Barnacle, of Galway, Ireland. Their son and daughter, George and Lucia, were born in Trieste.

Joyce, who is said to have known 17 modern and ancient languages, at times eked out a living as a language instructor. During World War I he took his family to Switzerland, which was neutral in the war. There his struggle for recognition as a writer was complicated by near-blindness. He underwent a long series of operations and had to wear a patch over one eye, which was damaged.

'Chamber Music', a book of poems, was Joyce's first published work (1907). It was followed in 1914 by 'Dubliners', a collection of cruelly realistic short stories that deal with life in Joyce's native city. In 1916 Joyce's first full-length book in the stream of

James Joyce in 1939

Gisele Freund

consciousness technique, 'A Portrait of the Artist as a Young Man', was published as a novel. It is an autobiographical work, though Joyce named the central figure Stephen Dedalus.

Stephen Dedalus is also a central character in 'Ulysses', an enormous work printed in book form in 1922 in Paris, where Joyce made his postwar home. The book re-creates a single day in Dublin in 1904. The language of 'Ulysses' is often as disjointed as the images in a dream. It is full of puns, slang, and metaphors. Portions of the book were considered obscene and 'Ulysses' was banned for many years in English-speaking countries. Joyce's last work was 'Finnegans Wake', published in 1939 after parts of it had been serialized as 'Work in Progress'. It is written almost in an invented language. His critics complained that Joyce had reached the ultimate in obscurity in the writing of 'Finnegans Wake'.

Among other works by Joyce is a book of poems, 'Pomes Penyeach' (1927). Part of the first draft of 'A Portrait of the Artist as a Young Man' appeared in 1944 as 'Stephen Hero'.

Joyce spent his last months in Switzerland, where he went in 1940 to escape the German occupation of France. He died in Zurich on Jan. 13, 1941.

JUAN CARLOS I (born 1938). When Francisco Franco died in 1975, Spain once again became a monarchy, with the accession of Juan Carlos I of the House of Bourbon to the throne (*see* Bourbon; Franco). The transfer of power began in October 1975, when the future king took over the functions of head of state during Franco's last illness.

When Juan Carlos was born on Jan. 5, 1938, in Rome, his parents—Don Juan, count of Barcelona, and Doña María de las Mercedes de Borbón y Orleans—were living in exile. The family later moved to Lausanne, Switzerland, and then Estoril, Portugal.

In 1947 Franco announced that Spain was a kingdom and that he had decided that Juan Carlos should one day be king. (He is a grandson of King Alfonso XIII, who had been forced into exile in 1931.) Juan Carlos was prepared carefully for his future tasks, with special attention to a military education. He attended the Instituto San Isidro in Madrid, the Navy Orphans' College, and the Academia General Militar (General Military Academy) at Saragossa (Zaragoza). He was commissioned a lieutenant in the army in 1957. He attended the Naval Academy in 1957 and 1958 and the Aviation Academy in 1959. He followed up his military training with a general course of studies at the University of Madrid.

In May 1962 Juan Carlos married Princess Sophie, a daughter of King Paul and Queen Frederika of Greece. They have two daughters and a son, Felipe, who is heir to the throne.

In July 1969 the Spanish Cortes (legislature) declared Juan Carlos "Prince of Spain," and he took his oath as future king. From that time on he played a ceremonial role in the government on behalf of Franco. Juan Carlos was sworn in as king on Nov. 22, 1975, two days after Franco's death. As king, he exercises more power than most constitutional monarchs; he is head of the armed forces and has some say about the political direction of the country. In his inaugural he stated his intent to mold Spain into a broadly based democratic society.

JUÁREZ, Benito (1806–72). Mexico's national hero and its first president of Indian descent was Benito Juárez. During his years in government he succeeded in undermining the power of the Roman Catholic church and the wealthy landlords in order to make Mexico a constitutional democracy.

Juárez was born at San Pablo Guelatao in the state of Oaxaca on March 21, 1806. He studied law at the Oaxaca Institute of Arts and Sciences, receiving his degree in 1831. Politics became his life's work, and within a few years he had served in both state and national legislatures. In 1841 he became a judge and served as governor of his state. From his government service he gained many ideas for political and economic reform.

When liberals defeated conservatives in the elections of 1855, Juárez became minister of justice and public instruction. The new administration abolished special courts for the church and the military, forced the church to sell its enormous property holdings, and created a new, liberal constitution. In 1857 Juárez was chosen to preside over the Supreme Court and, in effect, to serve as vice-president. During a conservative revolt from 1858 to 1860, he acted as president. He was forced to flee Mexico City but held the government together.

He was officially elected president in January 1861, but Mexico's suspension of payments on foreign debts led France to land troops and, in 1864, to install Archduke Maximilian of Austria as ruler of Mexico. Maximilian was deposed and executed by the Mexicans in 1867, and Juárez returned to office. He was reelected in 1867 and 1871. The 1871 election was contested, and Juárez spent the last months of his life trying to keep peace. He died on July 18, 1872, in Mexico City. (*See also* Mexico.)

Benito Juárez

JUDAISM. Along with Christianity and Islam, Judaism is one of the three major religions of the Western world. With them, it has in common a belief in one God as creator and ruler of the universe and the lord of human history. Of the three, Judaism is much the oldest, having its roots in the history of Israel, a nation, or people, that traces its origins back at least 3,000 years to Abraham, the patriarch who is considered the father of the Jewish faith (*see* Abraham). Ancient Israel dwelled in the land of Palestine in the Middle East, and the modern state of Israel, founded in 1948, represents a return of the people to a homeland that had been under other domination for more than 20 centuries (*see* Israel; Palestine).

With the passing of centuries, any major religion develops within it a great deal of variety and numerous points of view: Islam is divided into several competing factions, and Christianity is made up of many denominations. So, too, Judaism in the modern period is not uniform (*see* below, subhead "Modern Judaism"). This article presents primarily the basic beliefs and institutions of Judaism as they emerged in the ancient world and have persisted in a fairly traditional manner for nearly two millennia.

Origins

The events of Israel's past are recounted in the Bible or, more properly, the Hebrew Bible, which the Christian church calls the Old Testament (*see* Bible). The period covered by the Biblical narratives is a long one—from about 2000 BC to the end of the 6th century BC, with the addition of some few occurrences from a later period. Within this time span, the story of Israel as a nation unfolds, beginning with the founding of the people by Abraham. Long after the time of Abraham, an economic crisis led the Israelites to move to Egypt, where they were originally made welcome but later turned into slaves. After more than 400 years they were freed from Egyptian bondage under the leadership of Moses and led back to Palestine, or Canaan, as it was called then (*see* Moses). This release from Egypt is believed to have taken place about the 13th century BC. Over the next several centuries Israel became a moderately powerful nation in the Middle East, particularly under its first three kings—Saul, David, and Solomon. After Solomon's death, the kingdom was divided in two parts. The northern segment of Israel was overrun by the Assyrian Empire late in the 8th century BC, and the southern part (known as the nation of Judah) was conquered by the Babylonians early in the 6th century. When the southern kingdom ended with the carrying off of most of the remaining Israelites to Babylon, the nation's days as a political and military power were virtually over. This Babylonian captivity began what is called the Diaspora, or dispersion. From that time until the present, the Jewish people were dispersed throughout the world, particularly in the Middle East and the Mediterranean region.

Some Jews were allowed to return to their homeland, Palestine, beginning in the 6th century BC.

Peter Southwick—Stock, Boston

A rabbi and one of his students, each wearing a yarmulke on his head, admire a handwritten scroll of the Torah.

From that time on, however, Palestine was under the domination of one foreign power after another, with the exception of a brief period of independence in the 2nd century. In the 1st century BC, Palestine was incorporated into the Roman Empire. Jewish revolts against Rome in the 1st and 2nd centuries AD proved fruitless, and from that time until the modern state of Israel, the Jewish people had no homeland.

The whole history of Israel may be viewed as the tale of a tiny nation caught up in the struggles between the great powers of the day. But Jews do not see it that way, and it is their view of Israel's past that sets them apart from other states and forged the nature of Judaism. It is Israel's firm conviction that the one God, creator of the universe, was active in every phase of its history: God called Abraham and told him to go to Canaan to become the father of a nation. God released the people from Egypt and led them back to Palestine. God did this because He chose to select Israel from all the nations of the world and use it as the vehicle for bringing knowledge of Him to the rest of the nations.

This arrangement between God and Israel is called a covenant (bargain). God promised to make Israel a great nation and, in response, Israel was to be obedient to Him forever (*see* below, "The Covenant").

Although there is a direct line of historical continuity from ancient Israel to modern Judaism, the two are not identical. The word Judaism is not to be found in the Hebrew Bible, nor is the word religion. Today it is impossible to do without the word religion when discussing the relationship of humans to God, but in ancient Israel life was not compartmentalized into the social, the political, the economic, and the religious. The people of Israel believed that all human activity—both individual behavior and community action—was under God's guidance. The notion of religion would have been incomprehensible to them.

Modern Judaism originated in the period after the return to Palestine from the Babylonian captivity in the 6th century BC. The days of Israel's political power were over. The people began to reflect on the meaning of their existence, in the light of their whole history from Abraham to the Diaspora. What direction the nation should take was unclear, since there seemed to be no new directives from God. If there were no new directives, the Israelites had to rely on what they knew—their history as it had been compiled in the many books that now make up the Hebrew Bible. Should Israel assert itself to become a political power again, or should it await some definitive action by God to restore its fortunes? Opinions were sharply divided, and, by the time of the early Roman Empire, a number of parties or sects had formed.

One party centered around the priestly cult of the Temple at Jerusalem. The Temple was the center of worship and sacrifice. Another major party consisted of the rabbis, teachers and interpreters of God's law. Some small sects withdrew from public life to await the coming of God's kingdom, while others organized to prepare a revolt against the Romans. When the Romans destroyed the Temple in AD 70 and ended Jewish opposition 60 years later, Jerusalem as the center of worship ceased to exist. The rebellious sects were smashed, and those who had withdrawn into the desert to await the action of God were of no effect. The one group that was left to fill the breach and provide guidance for the Jewish people was the party of rabbis. The program of the rabbis replaced Temple worship and pilgrimages to Jerusalem with the study of God's law, prayer, and good works. The new place of worship became the local synagogue (from a Greek word meaning "assembly"), where Jews could gather together and hear the Scriptures read and interpreted, sing the Psalms, and pray.

The rabbis attempted to standardize religious practices for the dispersed community and to build up a large body of interpretation of God's law. This collection of rabbinic law, called the Mishna, became the primary reference source in all rabbinic schools and the core around which the Talmud—the extensive commentaries on the Mishna—were later compiled. The rabbis also saw to it that the collection now known as the Hebrew Bible was carefully put together about the end of the 1st century AD.

Beliefs

The beliefs of Judaism rest upon the Hebrew Bible. Of particular significance is the Torah, the name of which comes from the Hebrew for "to point the way."

The Torah is the first five books of the Bible. Commonly called the books of Moses, they contain the early history of Israel and the laws of God. Jewish doctrines concerning God, man, the nature of Israel, obedience, and the end of the world are derived from the Torah and other writings.

God. The foundation on which the whole course of Israel's faith rests is the conviction that the one God, creator of the universe and absolutely unknowable in Himself, revealed Himself (revelation) to Abraham and his descendants. The concept of revelation is not an easy one to grasp: In the common understanding of the term, what is revealed is no longer hidden, but with reference to God, He always remains hidden in his revelation. He does not put Himself on display, but He acts within the course of events. His acts are perceived only by faith in those to whom He gives understanding. This means that all of His actions could be regarded from a completely secular point of view: There is no evidence available to the senses that can point to an event and say it is from God.

This God, Israel believes, was the one and only God; all other gods are but idols and fictions of the imagination. As stated in the basic creed of Judaism, derived from Deuteronomy 6:4–9: "Hear, O Israel! the Lord is our God, the Lord alone." This God created the universe and mankind, and He, for incomprehensible reasons, chose Israel to be His beacon light for the rest of the nations. He did this, because the world, as it exists, did not know Him: It was Israel's mission to call all people back to knowledge of Him and obedience to His precepts. God's law upholds and provides for the whole of creation. To go against the law, whether natural or moral, creates disorder, strife, wars, and many other evils.

The architectural style of synagogues varies greatly. The synagogue at Florence, Italy (right) shows Byzantine influences, while the one at the Hebrew University in Jerusalem (below) is quite contemporary in its design.

(Right) Courtesy of the Italian Government Travel Office; (below) © A. L. Goldman—Photo Researchers

The Torah scrolls are returned to the arc (top) in the center of the front part of the sanctuary in a sabbath service at a synagogue near Chicago. A congregation (above) celebrates the Jewish high holy days.

The Covenant. The arrangement God made with Israel is called a covenant. It was first stated to Abraham about 2000 BC in Mesopotamia: "The Lord said to Abraham, 'Leave your own country, your kinsmen, and your father's house, and go to a country that I will show you. I will make you into a great nation'." The obedience of Abraham was dependent upon God's fulfilling this promise. This covenant has been renewed time and again by God in Israel's history, always with the condition that the nation be obedient to His commands. After the escape from Egypt, God restated the covenant in more explicit terms (Deut. 7:6–11):

> For you are a people consecrated to the Lord your God: of all the peoples on earth the Lord your God chose you to be His treasured people.... Know, therefore, that only the Lord your God is God, the steadfast God who keeps His gracious covenant to the thousandth generation of those who love Him and keep His commandments, but who instantly requites with destruction those who reject Him—never slow with those who reject Him, but requiting them instantly. Therefore, observe faithfully the instruction—the laws and the rules—with which I charge you today.

Torah. "These commandments, statutes, and laws" find their fullest expression in the Torah. After Moses had led Israel out of Egypt, the people formed themselves into a nation. He became their lawgiver. According to the book of Exodus, Moses received the Ten Commandments, the basic moral law, directly from God on Mount Sinai. These laws were amplified by an extensive code providing statutes and regulations for all aspects of personal and communal life, including the manner of worship and sacrifice. The complete compilation of laws may be found in the book of Leviticus in the Hebrew Bible.

Torah, however, means more than law. In its broadest sense, it is the entire content of Judaism: its sacred Scriptures, its oral traditions, its theological affirmations, its ethical obligations, its historical recollections, its ritual and ceremonial observances, and its interpretations of authoritative texts. More specifically, Torah is the five books of Moses, the first books of the Hebrew Bible: Genesis, Exodus, Leviticus, Numbers, and Deuteronomy. From this core developed the rabbinic teaching and interpretations that formed the foundation for modern Judaism, which the rabbis elaborated upon in their teachings in the Mishna and explained in the Talmud.

The creation of the Mishna, an authoritative, post-Biblical collection of oral laws, was considered necessary by the rabbis in order that Jewish people dispersed throughout the Middle East and the Roman world would have one standard for the practice of their religion. The Mishna was given its final form by the 3rd century AD.

While there was one Mishna for all Jews, there developed two Talmuds, one in Palestine and the other in Babylon. Both places were at the time advanced centers of rabbinical learning; both Talmuds were compiled during the early centuries of the Christian era. In time the Babylonian Talmud became the standard work for all of Judaism. This happened in part because Babylon was a far more stable region than Palestine, but it also owed a great deal to the determination of the Babylonian school to displace the work of its Palestinian competitors.

The nature of man. Unlike the speculations of Greek philosophy that sought to arrive at a complete understanding of human nature, man in the Hebrew Bible is seen primarily as a creature of God, put on Earth to be free and responsible before Him. The long-held notions, devised by the Greeks and others, concerning man as a composite of material body and spiritual (or immortal) soul was foreign to Israel.

The book of Genesis presents mankind as created in the image of God. The meaning of this term is uncertain and has been the subject of debate for centuries. Presumably it means that as God's creature, man is able to be responsive to the Creator, yet he is free to make his own ethical choices. He is even free to choose disobedience to the will of God.

The issue of human death was never clearly defined in Israel. There was no question of the body's dying and an immortal soul's going off by itself, because the individual was believed to be a unit, not a composite of body, mind, and soul. The whole man died; but Israelites did not believe that death meant extinction. The dead continued to exist in a kind of netherworld called *sheol,* where they had no experience of any kind. This concept, while not very clear, laid the groundwork for the later belief in the resurrection of the body from the dead.

Ethical behavior. If Israel's ideas on the nature of man were not clearly defined, its ideas on man's responsibilities to God and his fellow creatures were spelled out in great detail. Mankind is, with no choice

148

(Top) Milt & Joan Mann; (above) © Katrina Thomas—Photo Researchers

The Passover seder, one of the main family observances of Judaism, is rich in tradition and ritual. A father (top) passes bitter herbs around the table. Another family (above) takes part in the washing ritual of the meal.

of its own, created by God and subject to His divine will. This will is expressed in the law—the moral law of the Ten Commandments and the hundreds of statutes that are meant to regulate daily life for the individual and the community. It is necessary to note here that individual and community always are together. There is no life for the individual outside the community: God called a whole people for Himself, not isolated individuals. A just society requires just individuals, and just individuals function best in a just community. The whole law can be summed up as total devotion to God and love for one's neighbor. The statutes, as collected in the book of Leviticus, specify all the many ways these two injunctions are to be carried out, and the regulations are extremely detailed, governing the minutest aspects of daily living along with the larger arena of social interaction.

In rabbinic Judaism, the supreme virtue for individuals and the community is the study of the Torah, for it is by careful scrutiny of God's laws that true obedience can be learned. The Torah is not only a guide to right attitudes but also a compendium of specific directives to be observed in detail.

The coming of God's kingdom. The promises made by God within the terms of the covenant were specific. They promised to make Israel a great nation with a land of its own. They also pointed to a time when Israel, under an ideal king, would draw all other nations together in a worldwide community of justice and peace under the guidance of God's law. After the exile in Babylon and the evident failure of Israel to become a holy people and witness to all nations, speculation arose about how God would in fact fulfill His

promises. The variety of speculation led to the emergence of a number of schools of thought.

One opinion held that there would be a gradual restoration of Israel to its promised land in Palestine. There, a divinely chosen ruler would exhibit his obedience to God and stimulate the obedience of the people. This holy community, in which economic, social, and political justice reigned, would be the inspiration to lure all nations to an imitation of Israel.

Another view put little faith in the gradual processes of history. It looked, rather, for a decisive act on the part of God whereby He would reassert His divine sovereignty over the whole creation. This expectation often looked for the appearance of a messiah figure, an individual chosen by God to inaugurate His reign on Earth. The messiah (meaning, "the anointed one," from the ritual of applying oil in the consecration of a king), would be a monarch after the style of David, Israel's greatest king (*see* David).

Other motifs were also woven into the hope for God's kingdom. It was expected by some that all the dead of Israel would be raised to enjoy life in the new community. But even the restored kingdom was not viewed as permanent. At some future date God would intervene to judge the wicked and transport the righteous to a new world—a transformed creation—where the rule of God would be direct and endure forever. Some believers held that the end of the present world would be preceded by a titanic struggle between the forces of good and evil. After the victory of the righteous the end would come.

Still other Jews abandoned hope of a redemption within the historical process. They emphasized instead a personal salvation through individual piety and scrupulous adherence to all tenets of the law.

Institutions and Practices

As had been true in ancient Israel, so too in rabbinic Judaism it was understood the life of the individual and the life of the community were bound up together. The institutions and practices of Judaism reflect this conviction. There are observations and rituals that take place within the family, ceremonies that pertain to the individual, and the pattern of practices within the synagogue—the community of the faithful. Many of the observances are bound up with the cycle of the religious year, with its feasts and its commemorations.

The rabbi. The term rabbi means literally "my teacher." It was used as a title of honor for graduates of Palestinian academies in the period after the exile. The graduates, who had studied the Torah, were normally appointed as legal officers and supervisors of local communities. They were not priests: All the priestly functions took place at the Temple in Jerusalem under the authority of a priestly class whose membership was strictly regulated. Nor were the rabbis a clergy in the modern sense: They were not ordained to serve their function. They were appointed scholars. A synagogue could actually call the rabbi it wanted to serve them.

In the modern period the rabbis have become similar to Christian clergy. They are college graduates who receive subsequent training in seminaries. After seminary graduation, they serve as congregational rabbis in much the same way as Roman Catholic priests and Protestant clergy serve their congregations.

The synagogue. The origins of this local house of worship and community center are obscure. It probably first made its appearance in the years after the Babylonian captivity, when Jews were dispersed throughout much of the Middle East, and later throughout the entire Roman Empire. The center of Israel's worship life was, of course, in the Temple at Jerusalem, and all Jews were expected to make at least one annual pilgrimmage to Jerusalem. But to maintain the quality and continuity of religious life, it was necessary that those who were far from Jerusalem have some place where they could study the Scriptures and hear them explained. After the destruction of the Temple in AD 70, the synagogue became the locus of worship life.

At the heart of synagogue worship is the public reading of the Scriptures, specifically the five books of Moses arranged in an annual cycle. These books, the Torah, are inscribed on a large scroll. The order of worship consists of preparatory prayers, the recitation of Psalms, the "Hear, O Israel" (the *Sh'ma,* from the Hebrew word that opens the passage in Deut. 6:4), a call to worship, a prayer of petition, the reading of Scripture, and concluding prayers.

Worship services take place on Friday evenings (the beginning of the Sabbath, or seventh day), on Saturday mornings, on holy days and festivals, on Monday and Thursday mornings, and on Sabbath afternoons. The Sabbath is derived from the creation story in the book of Genesis, where it is stated that, after the six days of creation, God rested. When, in later generations, the law was promulgated in Israel, it was commanded that the people observe the seventh day as a day of rest and, later, of worship as well.

The language of formal worship, at least for more orthodox Jews, is Hebrew. This language of ancient Israel was for a time replaced by Aramaic, a similar language, and by other local languages. In the modern period, Hebrew developed as a literary tongue, and its use has been restored in worship, as well as in the reading of the Scriptures.

Festivals and holy days. Judaism has two cycles of festival days in the year. One, beginning in the spring, observes occasions of historical or agricultural interest. Passover, for instance, commemorates the escape from Egyptian bondage. *Shavout,* or the Feast of Weeks, marks the end of the grain harvest as well as the giving of the law to Moses. *Succoth,* or the Feast of Tabernacles, is an autumnal harvest festival. The last of these holidays, *Simchat Torah,* marks the conclusion and new beginning of the annual cycle of Torah readings.

The other cycle begins in the fall with Rosh Hashanah, the new year, and a ten-day period of penitence that concludes with Yom Kippur, the Day of Atonement. In early winter the feast of Hanukkah commemorates a successful war for independence in the 2nd century BC. Purim, later in the winter, celebrates the deliverance of the Jews from potential extermination in Persia, as told in the book of Esther. In the summer a fast day commemorates the destruction of the Temple by the Romans in AD 70. All of the festivals and holy days combine synagogue worship and family observances and rituals.

Individual and family observances. Judaism considers that all of life is holy, that is, set apart for devotion to God. All the moments of an individual's daily life, therefore, are times when God is to be remembered and thanked. Every deed, no matter how trivial in appearance, reminds each person that the world and his life exist in the presence of God.

The family, too, is a locus of worship and devotion. Nearly every occasion of community worship in the synagogue has its counterpart in an observance by the family at home. One of the best known of these is the Passover Seder, or meal, with its symbols and the narration of the events surrounding the Exodus from Egypt. Most of the celebrations involve a careful and highly ritualized preparation of food.

The life of the individual and the family is marked by a series of rites of passage, rituals that single out notable events in the life of the person within the community. Infants are dedicated to God and named. At the coming of age, a young person accepts responsibility for following the Commandments in a ceremony called a Bar Mitzvah, or, in the case of girls, a Bas, or Bat, Mitzvah. In the ceremony, which is after a girl's 12th birthday and a boy's 13th birthday, the young person is called to read from the Torah. Betrothal, marriage, and death are also marked with observances in the community of the local synagogue.

Modern Judaism

Like all major religions, Judaism has always had within it a number of movements, points of view, and local emphases. These did not constitute sects as such historically, since rabbinic authority maintained itself intact until the 18th century. By that time, Jewish people had settled all over the Western world. In the Middle East and North Africa they were influenced by Islam, with its rich cultural and philosophic traditions. In Europe Jews came into contact with a modernizing society, new ideas in philosophy and religion, discoveries in science, European modes of living, and the Industrial Revolution.

These developments could not but influence the growth of Judaism in the modern era. The Enlightenment in Europe challenged traditional philosophical and religious views and promoted new ideas on the nature of human beings, society, and religion. One result of this was a demand for reform in Judaism, particularly in Western Europe.

In Germany during the 1840s, Reform Judaism became institutionalized. It asserted that since the Jews were no longer a nation, but citizens of the states where they lived, they were no longer bound

Mike Mazzaschi—Stock, Boston

Jewish children in Boston, Mass., take part in a parade honoring the anniversary of the founding of Israel.

by the whole religious code of law. Only the dictates of the moral law were necessary.

Reform Judaism never had any great success in Europe, but when millions of Jewish immigrants came to North America in the late 1880s, they brought it with them. By 1880 most of the synagogues in the United States had become Reform and were members of the Union of American Hebrew Congregations, which had been formed in 1873.

Conservative Judaism appeared in the 1840s. Although it did not adhere entirely to Orthodox standards, it clung more closely to the traditions of historic Judaism, while making some concessions to the spirit of reform.

Reconstructionism was founded in the United States in the 1920s and holds that Judaism is a religious civilization, and its religious elements are expressions of a specific culture. The movement rejects the notion of an all-knowing God who made a covenant with his chosen people, and it does not accept the Bible as the inspired word of God.

The most traditional adherents of rabbinic Judaism are commonly called Orthodox, those who uphold what they consider to be the unchanging faith of Israel. None of the major segments of modern Judaism can, however, be viewed as having complete uniformity within it.

Two major phenomena of the 20th century have deeply influenced modern Judaism: Zionism and the Holocaust. Zionism, the reassertion of Jewish nationhood and the goal of reestablishing the state of Israel, emerged in the late 19th century under the leadership of Theodor Herzl in Europe. Although not winning the loyalty of all Jews, Zionism gained momentum steadily after 1900. Whether a Jewish state would have been established without the occurrence of the tragic events in Nazi Germany during World War II is difficult to say. The systematic massacre by the Nazis of about 6 million Jews—the Holocaust—one of the most cataclysmic events in world history, spurred the proponents of a Jewish homeland to achieve their goal. Three years after the end of the war, the State of Israel was established in Palestine. For the first time in nearly two millennia, the Jewish people had their country again. (*See also* Herzl; Holocaust; Zionism.)

JUDSON, Adoniram (1788–1850). One of the outstanding Christian missionaries of the modern era, Adoniram Judson was also an accomplished linguist who translated the Bible into Burmese. He also wrote a Burmese dictionary that is still a standard work.

Adoniram Judson was born in Malden, Mass., on Aug. 9, 1788. He graduated from Brown University, in Rhode Island, in 1807 and returned to Massachusetts to Andover Theological Seminary, where he decided to become a missionary. In 1812, after he was ordained, he and his wife, Ann Hasseltine Judson, sailed for Calcutta, India, under the sponsorship of the Congregational church.

While on shipboard, they studied the doctrine of Christian baptism and were converted to the Baptist denomination (*see* Baptists). Their presence in India was opposed by the powerful British East India Company, which supported the Church of England. The Judsons therefore relocated to Rangoon, Burma, in 1813. Judson spent several years mastering the Burmese language and Pali, the Buddhist religious language. He opened a mission in 1819. His efforts there eventually resulted in a Burmese Baptist community of more than 500,000 people. In spite of imprisonment and torture during the First Burmese War with Britain, Judson survived to carry on his work until his death on April 12, 1850.

JUJITSU *see* MARTIAL ARTS; WRESTLING.

JULIUS II (1443–1513). The greatest of the Renaissance popes was Julius II. He was most notable as a patron of the arts and as a powerful ruler thoroughly devoted to establishing the church's earthly domain.

Born Giuliano della Rovere on Dec. 5, 1443, in Albisola, Italy, he was a nephew of Pope Sixtus IV. In 1468 he became a Franciscan monk, and three years later the pope made him a cardinal. When Rodrigo Borgia, who became pope as Alexander VI in 1492, plotted Giuliano's assassination, Giuliano escaped to France in 1494. He remained there in exile for almost ten years. Alexander VI died in 1503, and Giuliano returned to Italy. After the brief reign of Pope Pius III, Giuliano was elected pope in 1503.

The enduring contributions of Julius II can still be seen in Rome. It was he who authorized the building of St. Peter's Basilica in 1503. In 1508 he commissioned Michelangelo to create the paintings on the ceiling of the Sistine Chapel. In 1508 he also commissioned Raphael to paint frescoes in rooms of the Vatican Palace. These masterpieces, as well as works by Donato Bramante and Andrea Sansovino, remain as Julius II's permanent contribution to the church. He died in Rome on Feb. 21, 1513. (*See also* Michelangelo; Raphael; Vatican City.)

JULY *see* CALENDAR; FESTIVALS AND HOLIDAYS.

JUNCO *see* FINCH.

JUNE *see* CALENDAR; FESTIVALS AND HOLIDAYS.

JUNEAU, Alaska.

The picturesque city of Juneau is the capital of Alaska. It is situated on the mainland of the Panhandle (southeastern Alaska), about a thousand miles (1,600 kilometers) northwest of Seattle, Wash. Islands to the west

shelter it from the open Pacific Ocean, about 75 miles (120 kilometers) distant. The climate is mild but very damp. Annual precipitation averages over 90 inches (2,250 millimeters).

The city has a beautiful setting on the fjord-like Gastineau Channel. Its buildings climb the forested slopes of Mount Roberts and Mount Juneau, which rise steeply from the water's edge to more than 3,500 feet (1,060 meters). Behind them in the Coast Mountains are peaks more than twice as high. North of Juneau is Mendenhall Glacier. A bridge across Gastineau Channel connects the main part of the city with Douglas Island, a residential area of Juneau.

Juneau can be reached only by air or by water. The airport is 9 miles (14 kilometers) from the city. The harbor is excellent and ice-free the year round. Just north of the harbor begins Lynn Canal, a channel that leads to Haines and Skagway. The Alaska Marine Highway serves 14 Alaskan ports, including Juneau. Its ferries, carrying both passengers and cars, connect the Panhandle with Seattle, Wash., and Prince Rupert, B.C., by way of the Inside Passage. Northwest of Juneau, highways connect with the Alaska Highway (*see* Alaska Highway).

Juneau was settled by gold miners in 1881. It was named for Joe Juneau, who with Dick Harris discovered gold in the area in 1880. The settlement became the mining center of Alaska. Douglas was the site of the Treadmill gold mines.

Juneau was made the capital of Alaska in 1900, but the government offices were not moved from Sitka until 1906. When Alaska was admitted to the Union in 1959, Juneau became the state capital.

In 1974 Alaskans voted to move the capital to a site north of Anchorage. With the gold mines and lumbermills long since closed and the local fishing industries on the decline, Juneau's future, if indeed the capital is moved, is uncertain. Government and tourism now provide the area's economic base.

Juneau's skyline is dominated by several government buildings. The tallest is the Federal Building, followed by the State Office Building, the State Court Building, and the older brick and marble-columned Capitol. The Alaska State Museum near the waterfront has excellent Indian, Eskimo, and Aleut cultural displays; wildlife and mining exhibits; and art and totem poles.

The University of Alaska has its southeastern regional campus in nearby Auke Lake. The Alaska State Library is housed in the State Office Building. Juneau has a council-manager type of government. (*See also* Alaska.) Population (1980 census), 19,528.

152

JUNE BUG *see* BEETLE.

JUNG, Carl

(1875–1961). Early in his career the Swiss psychologist and psychiatrist Carl Jung was a friend and follower of Sigmund Freud, the founder of psychoanalysis. Jung, however, came to disagree with Freud and established an alternative school, which he called analytical psychology. Aside from Freud, probably no person had a greater influence on modern psychology and psychiatry than did Jung.

Carl Gustav Jung was born in Kesswil, Switzerland, on July 26, 1875. Jung studied medicine at the University of Basel and psychology in Paris. He was a physician in the psychiatric clinic at the University of Zurich from 1900 to 1909 and a lecturer in psychiatry from 1905 to 1913.

Jung met Freud in 1907 and became a devotee of his psychoanalytical theories and a member of the International Psychoanalytical Society, a group dominated by Freud and his followers. In 1912 he resigned from the society and founded his own school of psychology in Zurich. From 1933 to 1941 Jung was professor of psychology at the Swiss Federal Institute of Technology in Zurich and from 1943 at the University of Basel. He died in Zurich on June 6, 1961.

Jung rejected Freud's idea that sexual experiences during infancy were the principal cause of neurotic behavior in adults. Jung believed that Freud overemphasized the role of sexual drive. He developed an alternative theory of the libido, arguing that the will to live was stronger than the sexual drive. Jung also emphasized analysis of current problems, rather than childhood conflicts, in the treatment of adults.

His classification of personalities into two types—introverts and extroverts—became well known. He developed a theory of the unconscious mind, arguing that there were both personal, or individual, and inherited, or collective, elements. Jung wrote many books. 'Modern Man in Search of a Soul', published in 1933, became a classic statement of the problems of 20th-century life. His autobiographical 'Memories, Dreams, Reflections' was published after his death.

Carl Jung

Leni Iseley—Nancy Palmer Agency

A subtropical rainforest in the San Carlos Valley of Costa Rica fits the strictest definition of a jungle because it has a thick, tangled growth of small trees, vines, and other low-lying plants.

JUNGLE. A general, commonly used term for the dense rain forests of tropical regions of the world is "jungle." Certain forests of broad-leaved evergreen trees in subtropical or even warm temperate regions are also called jungles. An older, more precise definition of jungle is an area of thick, tangled plant growth at ground level. In this strict definition, jungle occurs in tropical or subtropical rain forests where a significant amount of light can reach the ground and promote the characteristic dense growth of vines, small trees, and other plants. This occurs in areas where forests have been cleared of trees by humans, under natural situations where tall trees have fallen, or along the margins of large water courses.

Distribution and Classification

Rain forests occur in a band around the Earth between the Tropic of Capricorn (23° S. latitude) and Tropic of Cancer (23° N. latitude). Some modern accounts restrict jungles to about 20° S. and 30° N. latitude. The major continental jungles are found in Central America and the northern half of South America, in the central two thirds of Africa, and in

This article was contributed by J. Whitfield Gibbons, Associate Director and Associate Research Ecologist, Savannah River Ecology Laboratory, Aiken, S.C., and Professor, University of Georgia.

India and Southeast Asia. The East Indies, particularly Sumatra, Borneo, and New Guinea have significant jungle regions. So also do parts of northern Australia, the Philippines, most of Madagascar, and the West Indies. Parts of Baja California and of Florida qualify as temperate rain forest areas.

Rain forests are sometimes categorized according to their latitudes, altitudes, and environmental conditions. Rain forests may be generally classified as either equatorial or subtropical.

Equatorial forests of South America, Africa, and the Malaysian region are the densest jungles. The largest continuous, intact rain forest is in Brazil, in a vast region surrounding the Amazon River. The largest tract of jungle in Africa is in a region around the Congo River, with a major portion being in the country of Zaire. Equatorial rain forests also occur through much of the East Indian region, with the most extensive natural forests remaining in New Guinea and parts of Borneo.

Subtropical forests are outside of the strict equatorial region and have more noticeable seasonal changes. Although temperatures may vary only slightly over a year, rainfall may be distributed unevenly so that wet and dry seasons occur, though annual rainfall is still high. Subtropical jungles occur in Central America and the West Indies, in India, Madagascar, Southeast Asia, and the Philippines. Small areas around the Everglades in southern Flori-

153

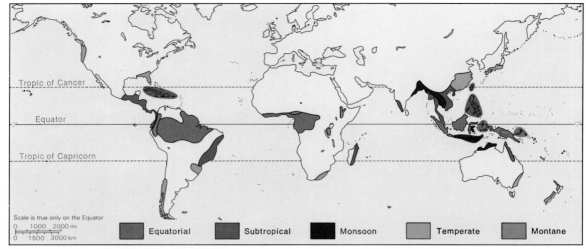

Tropic of Cancer

Equator

Tropic of Capricorn

Scale is true only on the Equator
0   1000   2000 mi
0   1500   3000 km

Equatorial   Subtropical   Monsoon   Temperate   Montane

Types and locations of the world's major jungles

da contain the only parts of the United States that can be classed as jungle.

Monsoon forests receive high amounts of annual rainfall distributed unevenly throughout the year. Monsoons of the Indian Ocean region characteristically create climatic situations of heavy and continual rainfall during spring and summer, followed by a distinct dry season in fall and winter. The canopy, or upper levels, of a monsoon jungle is not as dense as that of an equatorial rain forest, but the lower levels are denser. Monsoon forests are prevalent in Southeast Asia, Java, and northeastern Australia. Some of the jungles of West Africa and South America are also under the influence of monsoons.

Montane, or high-altitude, jungles do not meet the warm and unvarying temperature standards used to define typical rain forests. However, despite lower and wider-ranging temperatures, tropical forests in mountain regions are dense, constantly wet environments that qualify as jungles. These forests may range in altitude from about 3,000 feet (900 meters) to more than 5,000 feet (1,500 meters). Some of the most notable of them are in Central Africa and the New Guinea highlands, although high altitude jungles exist throughout the tropics.

Other areas sometimes are considered to be jungle. Some temperate zone lowland habitats such as the evergreen, broadleaf tree forests of the coastal areas of North and South Carolina and Georgia in the southeastern United States have dense undergrowth and a canopy of medium-sized trees. Rainfall is high and temperatures seasonally warm, though neither is equivalent to more tropical areas. Another habitat often considered jungle is that of the tropical and subtropical mangrove forests that grow along many coastlines of the world. While there are not a great number of different plant species and the trees are small compared to inland rain forests, the closeness of trees and roots creates an impenetrable jungle habitat in many instances.

Geological History

Warm, perpetually humid climatic conditions suitable for tropical and subtropical rain forests, which are most commonly called jungles, have existed on Earth since at least the middle of the Carboniferous Period (approximately 300 million years ago). Authorities disagree on the geographic extent and distribution of such areas during different geologic periods. Most agree that much of the equatorial region remained as a high-temperature, high-rainfall area during the Triassic Period (from 225 to 180 million years ago). Certain studies suggest that the Ice Ages (about 1 million years ago) during the Pleistocene Epoch and perhaps similar conditions in earlier times, resulted in worldwide conditions of decreased temperatures and increased dryness. According to these accounts some of the equatorial rain forests of that time became deserts.

Climatic Conditions

The jungle environment is characterized by high, constant temperatures and abundant rainfall. The amount of sunlight penetration is determined by the density of canopy vegetation, sometimes resulting in daytime semi-darkness at the ground level. The permanently wet conditions, coupled with the warm stable temperatures, have led to some of the most magnificent plant and animal communities in the world. The great number of different species of both plants and animals in a typical jungle is unrivaled by any other ecological community in the world.

Rainfall in a jungle is more than 60 inches (150 centimeters) a year and may be as high as 400 inches (1,000 centimeters). The relative humidity in a tropical jungle environment is normally from 75 to 100 percent. Near the equator the rainfall may be continual throughout the year with little variation in the amount from month to month. In subtropical regions, where slight seasonal changes are apparent, rainfall may be consistently higher at certain times of the year than at others. Even in areas where such wet-dry cycles occur, some rainfall occurs during the so-called dry season so that a high humidity is maintained. Such climatic conditions of rainfall and temperature are necessary for the luxuriant growth of trees and other vegetation that make up a jungle.

Temperatures in the jungle are always warm, never hot like those of the desert. Although temperatures may vary a few degrees during the day, the average temperature in a jungle from one month to the next may vary by only one or two degrees. Temperatures in tropical rain forests range from about 68° F (20° C) to above 90° F (32° C). Although conditions may vary from one region to another so that slightly lower or higher temperatures may occur, jungle temperatures remain constant and seldom go above or below these extremes. The average monthly temperatures of rain forests on the equator are generally between 75° and 82° F (24° and 28° C). With the exception of heavy rainstorms, extreme weather conditions such as high winds, sudden drops in temperature, or prolonged drought are unusual occurrences.

Soils and Hydrology

No single type of soil or topographic situation is characteristic of tropical or subtropical rain forests, but all are affected by the constant wetness. As water drains through the soil, a process known as leaching occurs in which certain minerals and nutrients are drained away. Soil weathering and erosion processes are highly complex in tropical rain forests and are not totally understood. Despite the wealth of vegetation in a jungle, the soils themselves are nutrient-poor. Rooted plants of a tropical jungle are dependent on decaying ground litter for most of their nutrients, which are maintained in the upper few inches of the soil and in the rich layer of decaying litter from falling vegetation. Most nutrient and mineral exchange in a rain forest occurs within this thin soil-litter layer. The myriad of simple and microscopic animals inhabiting the forest floor decomposes vegetation and recycles nutrients back into the trees and other plants of the community through their shallow root systems.

The constant passage of water through the upper soil layer results in the selective removal of certain elements. Calcium, magnesium, and silicon compounds are commonly leached out in highly drained tropical soils. Compounds of iron and aluminum often remain in the upper soil layers to form kaolinite, a type of clay. Many tropical soils with heavy concentrations of iron and aluminum compounds are called lateritic. Such soils may have distinct layers with a surface layer of red loam. Most jungle soils have not been investigated thoroughly enough to develop a general soil classification scheme for rain forests.

Plants

The diversity of higher plant life in a jungle is unrivaled by any other habitat in the world. As a consequence of millions of years of a relatively uniform warm, wet climate, jungles became the center of origin for many of the terrestrial species of plants and animals on Earth today. Although the number of species inhabiting the jungles of the world can only be estimated, one study found ten times as many kinds of trees in an acre of rain forest as in the same area of a typical temperate zone forest. If the herbaceous species, vines, fungi, and other plant types were considered, the tropical jungle would possibly have more than 100 times as many plant species as do other forest types. The jungles of the Amazon are believed to have more than 40,000 species of plants, many of them still undescribed.

One feature of the natural, undisturbed rain forest is the layering effect created by the different heights of trees and other vegetation. The tallest jungle trees are more than 150 feet (46 meters) high and are scattered throughout the forest. In parts of Asia and the East Indies, trees occasionally reach heights of 200 feet (61 meters). Below the giant trees are ones whose tops converge horizontally to form a dense upper canopy 60 to 100 feet (18 to 30 meters) above the ground. Many plants and animals live in the canopy and depend directly upon it for both their physical support and their nourishment.

Below the upper canopy there is often an open space and then a second canopy created by smaller trees and other understory vegetation. Below this second canopy the forest floor is dark, as most light has been blocked out by the layers of trees. It is estimated that less than 1 percent of the sunlight penetrates to the ground in a heavily vegetated rain forest. Therefore, the forest floor may be only lightly covered by ground vegetation with extensive spacing between the vines and tree trunks. Such natural forests can sometimes be traveled through with relative ease. It is only when the upper canopy is disturbed and sunlight penetrates to the forest floor, ground vegetation becomes thick and dense so that travel becomes difficult.

Many of the plant species in jungle canopies are not trees. Epiphytes, or air plants, live on tree trunks or branches and never touch the ground during their life cycle. Thousands of epiphytic species, which obtain nutrients directly from rainfall and sunlight, have evolved in the rain forests. These include types of ferns, bromeliads, and orchids. Each has a complex life cycle adapted to the environmental circumstances peculiar to its particular habitat. The life histories of fewer than 1 percent of the epiphytic species are understood.

Dense jungles have numerous species of vines, an evolutionary solution to overcome the minimal levels of sunlight on the forest floor. The large woody species are called lianas. Many of the trees in a rain forest are covered by lianas on their way to the top. Some species of vines and epiphytes have evolved mechanisms to extract nutrients directly from the host tree. One example of the complex life cycles found among jungle plants is that of the strangler figs whose wind-borne seeds land atop a tall tree. The

Robert Frerck

strangler sends roots toward the ground and, as the vine grows, the host tree is eventually killed by the combination of a loss of light, competition for nutrients, and actual physical pressure of the vine around the tree trunk.

Animals

There are an extraordinary number of different animal species in the jungle, and they often have complex life cycles. Because of the forest structure, many animal species characteristically are associated with either the soil-litter layer, the ground surface atop the litter, the undergrowth, the upper canopy, or the tops of the giant trees. Many species spend their entire lives only in one of these, including the upper canopy.

The variety of plant forms and lifestyles create a vast number of specific living places for animals, which depend on the plants for cover and food. Through a process called coevolution, however, many jungle plants have become dependent upon certain animals for pollination, seed dispersal, and even protection. For example, some bats routinely obtain nectar from the flowers of certain plants, at the same time pollinating them. Another well-known relationship is the one between acacia plants and ants. The ants raise their young inside acacia thorns by feeding them material harvested from the plant. In return for a guaranteed food supply, the ants constantly patrol the tree and will attack any animal or plant that touches it. Such a relationship, called mutualism, is common in tropical rain forests.

The numerous specific habitats available in the jungle have resulted in the great number of species representing most animal groups. This is most notable among insects, but included also are such tree-oriented mammals as orangutans, monkeys, lemurs, and marmosets. Several species of cats also inhabit jungles. Tropical forests harbor more species of bats than any other type of mammal. Despite the great number of different species of vertebrate and invertebrate animals, the density of a single species is generally low: A common saying about the jungle is that it is easier to collect 30 different species of a given group of plants or animals than 30 of the same kind. Social insects such as ants and termites are often the most prevalent animals in a jungle.

Bird diversity in the tropics is high, and the species include some of the most colorful in the world, such as the macaws, parrots, and birds-of-paradise. The jungles of South America, Africa, and the Philippines are inhabited by large birds of prey (harpy eagles, African-crowned eagles, and monkey-eating eagles, respectively) that devour animals, particularly monkeys, that live in the highest treetops.

Rain forests also contain the greatest number of species of terrestrial reptiles, the snakes and lizards, on Earth. The largest snakes on Earth, the pythons

The dense jungle on the west coast of New Zealand's South Island yields most of the native timber.

M.P.L. Fogden—Bruce Coleman, Inc.

Bromeliads, plants in the pineapple family, are epiphytes, which are abundant in the jungle.

of the Old World and the anaconda of South America, are characteristic jungle forms. Some amphibians also attain their highest species numbers in the tropical forests. Frogs are common tropical species throughout the world, but tropical salamanders are restricted primarily to the New World. Caecilians, an order of wormlike amphibians, are represented by about 150 species that are found only in the tropical and subtropical jungle environments.

Beetles, butterflies, spiders, centipedes, scorpions, and other members of the phylum Arthropoda reach their highest species diversity and greatest variety in the tropics. New species are described each year, but details of the life cycles and habits are known for only a small proportion.

Human Impact

Human activities have severely disrupted the jungles of the world. Recent estimates are that 19 to 50 million acres (7 to 20 million hectares) are lost each year to farming, logging, mining, and other human endeavors. The largest continuous rain forest area, the Amazon, is also the largest tract of unexploited, natural jungle. Most of the South American countries have undisturbed rain forest left, and some have made efforts to protect part of what remains; but in Central America, cattle ranching and cultivation have been primarily responsible for the loss of an estimated two thirds of the region's rain forests.

Much of the once vast jungle region in Africa has been destroyed by lumbering and slash-and-burn agriculture. Slash-and-burn farming consists of cutting away trees and other vegetation, burning what is left, and then planting crops. Because of poor soil, many such areas can support only two or three agricultural plantings before the thin veneer of nutrients is exhausted. Timbering and crop-clearing may eliminate the jungle forests of the Ivory Coast before 1993.

Already in Asia and Australia, most of the natural rain forests are gone or severely disrupted. Only a small proportion of the original jungle remains on the Indian subcontinent, and most of the rain forests of southern China are also greatly disturbed. Logging and clearing for rubber plantations have eliminated two thirds of the forests in Malaysia and Borneo. In the Philippines, which had a vast covering of forests in 1950, two thirds of the rain forests had been logged or cleared for farming by the 1980s.

Most of the timbering and clearing of jungle habitat throughout the world has occurred within the last century. These activities have caused unnatural breaks in the ecological balance of the jungle communities, and are progressing at a rate such that the final effect on the ecosystem cannot be estimated.

A tropical jungle is a delicate biological network comprised of numerous, ecologically fragile interrelationships. The disruption of a key species in one part of the system can affect other species and create an imbalance in jungle ecosystems. These same species dependencies, however, can also work together in such a way that, if left to themselves, they could in time recover to become once again a highly diverse jungle habitat.

BIBLIOGRAPHY FOR JUNGLE

Ayensu, Edward. Jungles (Crown, 1980).
Perry, Richard. Life in Jungle and Forest (Taplinger, 1975).
Pope, Joyce. A Closer Look at Jungles (Watts, 1978).
Seabrook, W. B. Jungle Ways (Folcroft, 1977).
Selsam, M. E. See Through the Jungle (Harper, 1957).
Soule, Gardner. Mystery Creatures of the Jungle (Watts, 1982).

JUNIPER. The juniper is an aromatic evergreen tree. Many species are widely distributed throughout the Northern Hemisphere. Some are called cedars. Junipers are conifers, which means they bear their seeds in cones, but their cones are fleshy and look like berries. The young leaves are needlelike. The mature leaves are scalelike. In form, the juniper may be tall and slender, a low pyramid, or a creeping shrub.

The best-known juniper in the United States is the eastern red cedar, whose scientific name is *Juniperus virginiana*. Its wood is so easily whittled that it was used for pencils, but its scarcity has led to substitution of imported woods. It is used for fence posts because the wood is durable in contact with the soil. Because of its fragrance and its reputation for keeping away moths, the heartwood is much used for lining wardrobes and closets. Farmers often cut down the tree because it is a host for cedar-rust fungus, which attacks apple trees.

The western juniper (*J. occidentalis*) of the Pacific coast is an especially rugged tree that grows even in the crevices of the granite ledges of the Sierra Nevada. Common, or dwarf, juniper (*J. communis*) is the most widely distributed of all conifers. Gin was once flavored with its berries. The Chinese juniper (*J. chinensis*), native to eastern Asia, is cultivated in America for ornamental purposes. The Japanese prune and train the limbs to fantastic forms.

157

JURY SYSTEM. Any panel of people that judges a beauty contest, music contest, art show, or other competition may be called a jury. But the predominant use of the word is as a legal term for a panel of people sworn to try to declare a verdict in a court trial. The jury system—using a jury to decide such verdicts—is used in several countries. (*See also* Courts of Justice.) The word jury is derived from the French *jurer*, which means "to swear an oath."

History

The jury system, as it exists now, is entirely the creation of the British and American legal systems. Efforts to introduce trial by jury into the legal systems of other nations had some limited success in the 19th century. Beginning about 1850, however, juries were gradually abolished or used far less throughout Europe. In the 20th century, with the rise of fascism, nazism, and communism in Europe and elsewhere, jury systems were abolished outright. They were done away with in Japan in 1943, during World War II. In the second half of the 20th century, more than 90 percent of all jury trials took place in the United States. Most of the remainder occurred in England and other nations of the British Commonwealth, especially Australia and Canada.

The ancient world. Although the modern jury system originated during the late Middle Ages in England, trial by jury was one of the most prominent features of public life in ancient Athens, probably the most democratic of the Greek city-states. In Aristotle's 'Constitution of Athens', there are some striking similarities to modern processes for assembling juries. The chief difference is that all matters pertaining to a trial in Athens were in the hands of nonprofessionals. There was no judge, well trained in all aspects of law, to guide the jurors in their deliberations. All jurors were chosen by lot for a particular trial, as was the magistrate who presided over the court.

In addition, there were no trial lawyers. During a trial, any citizen could prosecute a case and the defendant had to conduct his own defense. These were truly people's courts. Every year a jury list of several thousand names was made up from the census of citizens. Juries for ordinary cases consisted of from 200 to 500 members, much larger than the 12-member trial juries that are standard today. At the famous trial of the philosopher Socrates in 399 BC, there were 501 jurors (*see* Socrates).

After evidence was presented in such trials and speeches were made by the prosecutor and the defendant, there was no jury deliberation, as there is in modern trials. Each member of the jury was given two metal tokens before the trial began. One signified guilt and the other innocence. At the end of the trial, each juror put the token representing his decision into a brass urn and threw the other into a wooden box. The tokens in the urn were counted and the verdict rendered on the basis of a majority vote. Socrates, for example, was found guilty by a majority of 60 tokens. If there was a tie vote, the defendant was declared innocent. After the trial all jurors were paid for their services.

Although this system represented an advanced form of direct democracy, it had disadvantages: There were no legal experts to state legal precedents. The juries were too large, closer to the size of legislative bodies. And verdicts could easily be based on the whims and passions of the population at a given moment, instead of being derived from the practices of settled law. This is, in fact, what happened in the trial of Socrates.

England. In the Roman Republic juries were used for trials in much the same manner as in Greece. But under the emperors trial by jury was abolished and ceased to exist as a factor in Western law until it emerged in England after the Norman Conquest in AD 1066. The roots of the English jury system lie in a practice established by the emperor Charlemagne in early 9th-century France. He sent groups of citizens throughout his domain to inspect the courts of justice and to ascertain the rights of the monarchy in relation to the nobility. The custom passed into Normandy, on the northwestern coast of France, and from there to England with William the Conqueror, who used it in much the same way.

Under Henry II, who ruled from 1154 to 1189, the custom of using average citizens to pass judgment in civil matters, especially in controversies over property, came into use. The use of juries in criminal cases—murder, assault, treason, and others—came more slowly. In 1166 Henry established the practice that 12 men be present at all county court sessions to present to the justices the names of persons suspected of crimes. This was the beginning of the grand jury—the jury that indicts people, or charges them with a crime, but does not try them (*see* subhead "Grand Juries," later in this article). The distinction between the grand jury and the petit (meaning "small") jury, which is the jury that actually tries a case, emerged in 1194. And in 1219 Henry III ordered the substitution of judgment by neighbors for the previous methods of trying an individual. (Such methods included trials in which a defendant had to prove his innocence by combat or by enduring a painful, life-threatening ordeal.) By the middle of the 14th century trial juries had become completely separate from grand juries.

In these early centuries of the jury system, the jurors passed judgment on the basis of what they themselves knew about a defendant and the case. It was believed that one's neighbors and associates were the most competent to render a fair verdict. But if they were unfriendly or bore a grudge, the verdict could be unjust. By the end of the 17th century the principle that jurors must reach a verdict solely on the basis of evidence—the practice that is followed today—was established.

In 1367 the size of the petit, or trial, jury was fixed at 12. After the 14th century unanimous verdicts (verdicts in which all jurors agree) were required by law in England until the Criminal Justice Act of 1967 introduced majority jury verdicts. In the United

States today, a unanimous verdict is not always required in state courts. However, it is a requirement in the federal courts.

Until the early 17th century, in addition to the grand and petit juries, there was also an attaint jury. It consisted of 24 people whose duty was to decide whether the verdict of the trial jury was right. If the attaint jury decided against the verdict, the members of the petit jury could be punished by having their lands and property confiscated. The attaint jury was gradually abandoned in favor of the right of judges to declare new trials, as well as the right of defendants to appeal verdicts.

United States. Throughout the British colonies of North America, including Canada after the French and Indian War, juries were used in both civil and criminal trials. Jury trials were highly regarded by the colonists, because they served as a means of preventing enforcement of unpopular British laws. After 1776 the early state constitutions safeguarded the right to a jury trial in both criminal and civil cases, but the federal Constitution of 1789 guaranteed the right to a jury trial in criminal cases only. This was remedied by the Bill of Rights, which was adopted in 1791. The 7th Amendment guarantees the right of a jury trial in all civil cases in which the amount of judgment might exceed 20 dollars. The 6th Amendment guarantees the right of a jury trial in all criminal proceedings. The basic elements of English common law jury trials were carried over into American law: trial juries should consist of 12 persons; trials are to be supervised by a judge who can instruct juries in matters of law and evidence; and all verdicts are to be unanimous. State constitutions have generally followed these principles, although, as has been noted, some states allow for a less than unanimous verdict. Oregon, for instance, allows for a 10 to 2 majority verdict; and in 1968 England began following the prece-dent set in Oregon. In states that do not allow for a divided opinion, when one occurs the judge declares a mistrial and orders a new trial, unless the case is withdrawn by the prosecution. Divided opinions are commonly called "hung" juries. Some states deprive judges of the right to comment on evidence; they become simply umpires in the proceedings. It is also possible for defendants to waive the right to a jury trial in both civil and criminal cases, particularly if it seems that a judge would be fairer.

Grand Juries

Called "grand" because of their size, not their function, grand juries have from 12 to 23 members. The purpose of the grand jury is to inquire whether a crime has been committed. A grand jury does not decide upon the issue of guilt or innocence; it simply hears testimony and looks at evidence from any number of sources to decide if someone should be indicted for an offense.

Although grand juries are part of the court system, they are not presided over by a judge. The chief officer is a prosecutor from a federal, state, or local jurisdiction, depending on the nature of the offense being investigated. In their proceedings, grand juries have far more leeway than trial juries. Their inquiries may, in fact, become inquisitions because the normal protections afforded the person being questioned (such as the right to the presence of a lawyer) are not allowed. Refusal to answer questions may lead to the imposition of jail sentences for contempt of court.

Grand jury proceedings are informal and secret, although the veil of secrecy may be lifted by the court if it feels the interests of justice will be served. Any unauthorized disclosure of grand jury proceedings is itself, in some jurisdictions, an indictable offense.

If the jury decides, on the basis of testimony and evidence, that a crime has been committed, it pre-

Lawyers Clarence Darrow, left, and William Jennings Bryan opposed one another in the famous Scopes trial in 1925. Darrow defended John Scopes, a Tennessee high-school teacher on trial because he taught the Darwinian theory of evolution, while Bryan aided in the prosecution.

UPI

sents a bill of indictment. The next step in the justice system is trial in a criminal court.

While grand juries continue to function as part of the court system, particularly on the federal level in the United States, they have come under criticism. Because the rights that witnesses have in court trials are not present in grand jury hearings, the hearings seem to many people to deny those protections that are guaranteed by the Constitution. Prosecutors have sometimes used grand juries for political ends, manipulating them for personal goals or to serve the interests of a particular political party. Occasionally details of grand jury hearings are "leaked" to the media, resulting in widespread (and often unfavorable) publicity for some individual, even when no indictment has been handed down. In some parts of the United States, grand juries are bypassed completely by allowing prosecutions to be initiated directly by elected or appointed prosecutors.

Petit Juries

Selection. In the early centuries of the trial jury system there were some minimum requirements for service as a juror, such as ownership of property and clear mental competence. Women were not allowed to serve. This has changed in the 20th century. The principle of random selection from among qualified voters has come to be common in the United States, England, Canada, and Australia. Some Canadian provinces still have property qualifications, and in Quebec women are still not allowed to serve as jurors. In most places persons who are employed in certain professions—lawyers, physicians, clergy, police—are exempt from jury service.

To be called for jury duty does not necessarily mean that one will actually serve. Before the trial begins, potential jurors are questioned by the judge and by lawyers for the defendant and the plaintiff. The law allows the lawyer to challenge jurors for cause, such as a specific bias in the case. A limited number of peremptory challenges are also allowed; these are challenges for which no cause need be stated. This screening process is called voir dire, meaning "to say the truth." It can become very complex and time-consuming, especially in a case that has received a great deal of publicity.

Function. During a trial, whether civil or criminal, the jury is under the supervision of the judge. It is he who decides what evidence the jury may hear, according to complex and established rules of evidence. If the judge decides the evidence presented leaves no matter of fact to be resolved, he may direct a verdict of acquittal. This effectively ends the proceedings. In a civil trial the judge may, on his own, find in favor of the defendant or the plaintiff. But in a criminal trial he may not direct a guilty verdict; this is the responsibility of the jury. The judge, in most cases, also explains the legal aspects of the evidence and the duties of the jury. If the jury's verdict is completely at odds with the weight of the evidence, the judge may set it aside. The exception to this rule is acquit-

tal in a criminal trial: acquittal is final, and the persons cannot be tried again for the same crime. This is called the principle of double jeopardy.

If a verdict of guilty is rendered by a jury, its duties are not finished. In many jurisdictions the jury must also be present for a hearing on sentencing and may be asked to decide what the sentence should be. In civil cases, the jury is asked to decide on the damages to be awarded to the plaintiff. In some jurisdictions the awarding of damages or sentencing are part of the original trial. In other places they become the subject of what is virtually a second trial. Where the death penalty is in effect and could be a sentence, a jury is required at least to express an opinion on whether it should be used.

Merits and criticisms. Along with other parts of the political structure, the jury trial system has come under a great deal of criticism for its competence and performance. It has been claimed that because juries are drawn from such a wide range of the populace, they do not have the intelligence or sophistication to deal with the complexities of law. To counter this criticism, it is argued that a jury of nonexperts brings a good deal of common sense and openness to a trial. This results in cases being decided in the spirit of the law, rather than by the rigidity of individual statutes. A jury also may provide a useful counterweight to the biases (if any) of the judge and lawyers involved in a trial. Although juries are strictly confined by law to the finding of facts, their presence frequently injects a sense of justice into the proceedings, either on the side of the defendant or the plaintiff.

Alternatives to trial juries. Some countries have adopted what are called mixed tribunals to hear cases. These tribunals consist of trained judges and lay, or untrained, judges. Mixed tribunals have been adopted extensively in Eastern European nations, some Scandinavian countries, Austria, France, and West Germany. Another alternative, fast disappearing in the United States, is trial before a justice of the peace, one type of lay judge.

Coroner's Juries

Another type of jury, rapidly falling into disuse, is the coroner's jury, a group of people summoned from within a given district to inquire into the cause of a death. Numbering from 6 to 20 individuals, its function closely resembles that of the grand jury in that it does not try cases, but weighs evidence to determine whether a crime has been committed. The evidence it finds may, of course, eventually be used at a criminal trial. If the jury decides a crime has been committed, it may name suspects. The coroner, usually a legal or medical professional, has the power to arrest suspects pending a grand jury hearing. The findings of a coroner's jury are only admissible as evidence of the fact of death. All other evidence must be presented at the jury trial. As an instituition, the coroner's jury is being displaced by the office of the medical examiner, a non-elected official with great expertise in discerning causes of death under mysterious circumstances.

JUSTINIAN I (483–565). The most famous of all the emperors of the Byzantine, or Eastern Roman, Empire was Justinian the Great. Born a barbarian, he became a powerful ruler and law reformer. He is known today chiefly for his codification of law.

Justinian was born probably of Slavic parents in a place called Tauresium, in Illyria (now Yugoslavia and Albania). Nothing is known of his early years except that as a youth he was adopted by his uncle Emperor Justin I and was educated in Constantinople. In 527 Justin made him a co-ruler of the empire. When his uncle died four months later, Justinian became sole emperor. He was crowned together with his wife Theodora, a famous actress.

Justinian found the laws of the empire in great confusion. Many were out of date; some contradicted others; nowhere did a complete collection of them exist. Justinian appointed a commission to study the problem. The work of the commissioners resulted in the publication of the 'Code of Justinian'. The first book, 'Codex Constitutionum', is a collection of decrees of the emperors; the 'Digest', or 'Pandects', a summary of 9,000 extracts from the opinions of the lawyers and judges who had interpreted these decrees; and the 'Institutes', a textbook. The 'Institutes' stated legal principles in simple terms. A fourth book, the 'Novels' (*Novella constitutiones*), included the ordinances of Justinian after the codification. These four together constitute the 'Code of Justinian', or Civil Law (*Corpus Juris Civilis*).

Under Justinian the empire enjoyed its greatest glory. His armies, led by his generals Belisarius and Narses, drove the Ostrogoths out of Italy and the Vandals out of Africa, temporarily restoring those lands to the empire. Justinian also became a great builder. Throughout his vast empire he erected forts, aqueducts, and churches. The most splendid of these buildings is the church of Hagia (Santa) Sophia, now a museum (*see* Architecture).

Religion also was of extreme importance to Justinian throughout his life. A pious man, he tried to end the disputes between the eastern and western

Justinian I, in a 6th-century mosaic at the Basilica of San Vitale in Ravenna, Italy

Alinari/Giraudon

branches of the Christian church. He died on Nov. 14, 565. His only child, a son, had died in infancy, and Justinian was succeeded to the throne by a nephew, Justin II. (*See also* Byzantine Empire.)

JUTE. Burlap, low-grade twine, and many other products are made from a glossy fiber called jute, which comes from the jute plant. Because it is low-priced and adaptable, jute is second only to cotton in world consumption of natural fibers. India, China, and Bangladesh are the leading producers.

The jute plant is an annual that thrives best in moist soil in a hot, humid climate. Seeds are hand-sown, and plants mature in three months, often averaging a height of 10 to 12 feet (3 to 3.6 meters). Their light green leaves are arrow-shaped, and small yellow flowers bloom singly or in clusters. Jute is classified scientifically in the genus *Corchorus*.

The plants are harvested when the blossoms first begin to shed. The cut stalks are sorted according to length and gathered into bundles. They are then placed in shallow pools of stagnant water where they are allowed to ret, or ferment. When they have become soft enough, the fibers are separated from the stalks and then hung on lines to dry. After drying, the fibers are sorted, graded, and baled for export.

JUVENAL (55?–127?). Decimus Junius Juvenalis, commonly known as Juvenal, was the best of the Roman satiric poets. Unfortunately little is now known of his life. It is believed that he was born at Aquinum, near Rome, between AD 55 and 60. He served as an army officer under the Emperor Domitian (AD 81 to 96), but when the emperor was assassinated, Juvenal found himself without a career. He was forced to live off the charity of wealthy friends. Later in life, he apparently became prosperous, for he had a comfortable home in Rome and a farm at nearby Tibur (now Tivoli). He probably died in 127.

Juvenal's literary masterpiece is the 'Satires', a collection of 16 satiric poems that deal with life in Rome under the emperors Domitian, Nerva, Trajan, and Hadrian. The main themes of the 'Satires' are the corruption and degradation of life in the city of Rome and the follies and brutalities of mankind. The satires vary greatly in length, the sixth being the longest, with more than 600 lines, and the 16th and last the shortest, with only 60 lines. The 16th is unfinished.

Each satire has its own general theme. In the first, Juvenal explains his reason for writing, stating that vice, crime, and the misuse of wealth have reached such a peak that it is impossible not to write a satire. Every sordid aspect of Roman life is frankly, forcefully, and sometimes brutally described. Probably the best of the poems is the tenth, in which Juvenal examines the great ambitions of mankind and shows that they all lead to disappointment or danger.

The fine quality of the 'Satires' has not been lost in translation. The rhythmic poetry abounds in memorable phrases and aphorisms, and the vividness of his descriptions leaves little to the imagination.

JUVENILE COURTS. The purpose of juvenile courts is to establish and supervise a plan of control and rehabilitation for youths who have broken the laws of their community. Most juvenile courts are also responsible for legal matters involving dependent and neglected children.

The largest number of juvenile court cases involve juvenile delinquency (*see* Juvenile Delinquency). A juvenile court usually regards a young offender as one who is in trouble because of a situation beyond his control. Regardless of the offense the entire program is devised to reestablish the young offender as a good citizen of the community. Experience has shown that in dealing with young people under these circumstances the best results are achieved when the courts operate without a trial atmosphere.

After the original complaint and arrest the judge and his staff take over. The staff, which frequently includes psychologists, psychiatrists, social workers, and other specially trained workers, investigates the situation and the offender. On the basis of what it finds the judge and the staff establish and carry out a plan of rehabilitation. Such a plan may involve a period of residence in a corrective institution, medical treatment, a foster home for the youth, probation, which is continued supervision by the court, or any other corrective plan that seems desirable.

Probation is the least expensive means of supervision. Of the more than 1.3 million cases before the juvenile courts each year involving children ages 10 to 17, about two thirds of the cases are dismissed or the child is placed in the custody of a parent or guardian. Of the remaining one third, about 90 percent of those children are placed on probation and the other 10 percent on parole or in detention.

All this special work with children is done on the theory that the average boy or girl wants to be a useful and respected citizen, that no child is born wicked, and that he or she will usually make good if given a chance. Society now assumes a responsibility for children brought up in improper surroundings. Many experiments carried out along these lines have justified this faith in children.

In 1869 the city of Boston started separate sessions of court for juvenile offenders. The first court entirely for children, however, was established in 1899 in Chicago, by Judge Richard Tuthill. The Boston juvenile court was established in 1906. Under Judge Frederick P. Cabot it became one of the best courts in the country. The next year Denver opened its juvenile court, under Judge Ben B. Lindsey. He was a pioneer in the movement to have all cases involving children brought before a special court. Judge Lindsey served for 27 years and attained national recognition. He was one of the first to use a woman as assistant judge to deal with girl offenders. The first woman to serve as a juvenile court judge was Mary M. Bartelme, elected in Chicago in 1927. Juvenile courts now exist in most states and Europe, Latin America, Israel, Iraq, Japan, and other countries, though structure and procedure vary.

JUVENILE DELINQUENCY. Criminal acts of young persons are juvenile delinquency. In some countries delinquency includes conduct that is antisocial, dangerous, or harmful to the goals of society. But the general tendency is to limit the term to activities that if carried out by an adult would be called crimes. The age at which juveniles legally become adults varies from country to country, but it generally ranges from 15 to 18. The extent of the problem is great: Fully half of those arrested for serious offenses are between 11 and 17. Because of the serious nature of some of the offenses committed by juveniles, there has been a tendency in some places to try juveniles in court as adults for certain crimes.

There has been much sociological research on delinquency in an effort to predict and prevent it. This research has established such bases for prediction as the nature of a child's home environment, the quality of the neighborhood in which he lives, and his behavior in school. It has never been conclusively proved, however, that delinquency can be either predicted or prevented. It is far likelier that delinquency is an integral part of society and probably part of the maturation process that some children go through. As long as society has laws and tries to enforce them, delinquency will exist. There is also a tendency for delinquency, like all crime, to increase if it is perceived that laws are unfairly or inadequately enforced.

Social Bases

For the majority of young offenders, delinquency seems to be a phase passed through on the way to adulthood. Delinquent acts begin at about age 10 or 11, although there has been a substantial increase in even younger offenders in recent years. The more serious activities peak at 14 or 15 years of age and then begin to decline for the next several years. The exceptions to this generalization are among older youth who get involved in car theft, robbery, and burglary. They may well become adult criminals. For the majority, delinquent activities gradually decrease and may cease altogether as a young person enters his 20s and faces the prospect of full-time work and marriage. It does seem to be true, however, that the earlier in life delinquent activities are begun the likelier it is that the pattern will persist—particularly in offenders who are convicted and sentenced to juvenile correction institutions. Probably their enforced companionship with other offenders serves to reinforce already developed patterns of illegal behavior.

Criminal types. There has been much controversy among psychologists and sociologists in the late 20th century concerning whether some people are genetically disposed to crime or whether illegal acts have their origin in one's upbringing and environment. There is evidence to support both views.

Those who believe it probable that there is a genetic disposition to crime have noted certain physical and personality differences between delinquents and nondelinquents. Delinquents have been found to have sturdier bodies and to act in a more aggressive

Graffiti covers most of the surfaces in a New York City subway train. Such illegal disfiguring of public and private property is a common form of juvenile delinquency.

Mike Tappin

way than nondelinquents. In their personality traits, delinquents are more extroverted, narcissistic, impulsive, and less able to delay the satisfaction of desires. In addition to these outward characteristics, some psychologists believe that there is an inherited flaw in the genetic makeup of a criminal that leads to rejection of society's standards.

The contrary opinion tends to view delinquents as not substantially different from the remainder of the population. Not all sturdily built individuals, for instance, become criminals; many make their living as athletes or in a variety of professions. Studies in Great Britain have shown that delinquents tend to come from families where there is tension and much difficulty in interpersonal relationships. Similar research suggests that delinquents come from homes where the parents are often drunk or perform criminal acts. Poverty, parents with little respect for themselves, and erratic discipline patterns emerge as contributing factors in such research. Harsh punishments may also lead young people to run away from home and to react against society.

Social class. In the United States, Europe, and Japan, most delinquents are boys. Fully 80 percent of the delinquents in the United States are boys, and most of these come from the lower middle class and the poorest segments of society. One reason for this is the low esteem in which education is often held in these groups. Schooling seems boring and unchallenging, and the delinquent rebels against it by cutting classes or disrupting them and eventually may drop out altogether. Such poor or working-class boys find in each others' company a compensation for their educational failure by rejecting the social values to which they are supposed to adhere. To make up for this failure, and finding their job market limited, they live dangerously and show contempt for authority.

Another impetus to illegal behavior can be found in the economic aspirations and goals of society itself. The signs of affluence that boys in the poor and working classes see about them—money, power, and a large array of consumer goods—make them desperately want some of these things even though they may feel they will never be able to afford them.

Delinquency among middle-class boys has not been adequately researched. Therefore its causes are even less clear. One theory suggests that it is a form of masculine protest against the dominant mother figure in many middle-class homes. This may be true in

cases where the father is away at work most of the time and has little contact with his children in free time. In places where drug abuse has become an important social factor for the young, crime may increase because of the need to support the habit.

Gangs. The cliché that "birds of a feather flock together" has special relevance for the social situation in which delinquents find themselves. Alienated from society, they tend to form groups. Although nondelinquent boys also form gangs, delinquents are far likelier to do so. They are impelled by the need to belong and are drawn by the security that a gang offers its members. In belonging to a gang there is a solidarity that an individual fails to find as a loner in society. Gangs do, in fact, form a subculture of crime within the larger framework of the general society. This subculture has its own standards, obligations, and rights. It may also have its own dress code.

Urban gangs in the United States have a history going well back into the 19th century. Originally they had a uniform ethnic composition based on the neighborhoods where they formed. Immigrant families normally settled in neighborhoods of people from the same old-world background. There developed local gangs with Irish, Italian, Jewish, and other ethnic-group memberships. Not all of these gangs engaged in widespread criminal activity, though a number of them did survive into the 20th century and become the nucleus for organized crime groups that emerged in major cities during the 1920s.

Present-day gangs often have an ethnic basis as well. There are gangs of blacks, poor whites, Mexicans, Puerto Ricans, Cubans, and Chinese in many large American cities. Some gangs are small, but others have thousands of members with histories going back at least two generations. Gangs also exist in Europe and Japan.

Researchers in the United States have suggested that there are three types of gangs: criminal, conflict, and retreatist. Criminal gangs, probably the most dominant form in the late 20th century, thrive in slum areas that have a long tradition of criminal activity. These gangs are well organized and make their money through an array of illegal activities, including extortion, robbery, prostitution, and drug sales. Conflict gangs usually live in newer urban housing developments, where a strong crime tradition has not yet developed. They are likelier to deal in violence and vandalism than in well-organized activi-

163

Two members of rival gangs square off against each other in the motion picture 'West Side Story'. Originally a Broadway musical, this extraordinarily popular dramatization introduced millions to the big-city subculture of street gangs.

ties. Retreatist gangs are those that, generally living in slums, use various escape mechanisms—primarily drugs—because they are unable to find any other way to gain what they envision as the good life.

Society's Response

Society tries to deal with youthful offenders in a variety of ways. The most common unofficial means are through school counseling and sessions with psychologists and psychiatrists. Social workers who deal with family problems also attempt to sort out the difficulties of young potential delinquents.

Serious offenses are dealt with officially by the police and the courts (see Juvenile Courts). The courts try by various means to steer young people away from a life of crime, though the more serious offenses normally result in periods of confinement in juvenile halls or prisons for younger criminals. If possible, however, the courts try the more lenient methods of probation, juvenile aftercare, or foster care.

Probation means that the court suspends sentence and releases the offender on the condition of good behavior, subject to certain rules and under the supervision of the court. Probation is frequently granted to first offenders. Sometimes, in order to avoid bringing a case before the court, informal probation under the supervision of a probation officer is prescribed. Probation has proved to be the most successful way of dealing with very young offenders.

Juvenile aftercare is the equivalent of parole for an older criminal; it takes place after the young person has been released from an institution and is supervised by a youth counselor. The purpose of aftercare is to promote readjustment to society.

In foster care the juvenile is placed in a stable family situation with the hope that he will adjust to the positive values of society. It is often part of an effort to prevent institutionalization.

Dramatization. Of all aspects of juvenile delinquency, none has been so frequently dramatized in book, drama, and movie than gangs. Countless films have depicted the gangs of the American West, many of whose members were hardly more than juveniles. The series of "Dead End Kids" movies in the 1930s and 1940s softened the harsh realities of gang life by showing young men in escapades that were usually more humorous than harmful. By contrast, later films such as 'Blackboard Jungle', which appeared in 1955, 'The Warriors' (1979), 'Bad Boys' (1983), and 'The Outsiders' (1983) came closer to the truth in portraying the antisocial, criminal nature of gangs. But probably the most popular depiction of gangs in recent decades has been 'West Side Story', a stage musical that opened in 1957 and was made into a motion picture in 1961. Based on the plot of Shakespeare's 'Romeo and Juliet', it was a highly romanticized dramatization of conflict between ethnic gangs in New York City.

BIBLIOGRAPHY FOR JUVENILE DELINQUENCY

Asbury, Herbert. The Gangs of New York (Capricorn, 1970; repr. of 1927 ed.).

Belkin, Alison. The Criminal Child (Kendall & Hunt, 1978).

Davis, J. R. Street Gangs (Kendall & Hunt, 1982).

Eldefonso, Edward. Law Enforcement and the Juvenile Offender (Wiley, 1978).

Hoenig, Gary. Reaper: the Inside Story of a Gang Leader (Bobbs, 1975).

Langer, Sidney. Scared Straight (Univ. Press of America, 1981).

McGee, Mark and Robertson, R. J. The J. D. Films: Juvenile Delinquency in the Movies (McFarland, 1982).

Richards, Pamela et al. Crime as Play (Ballinger, 1979).

Whyte, W. F. Street Corner Society, 3rd ed. (Univ. of Chicago Press, 1981).

The lighter side of gang life was depicted in a number of "Dead End Kids" films made in Hollywood during the 1930s and 1940s.

The Bettmann Archive

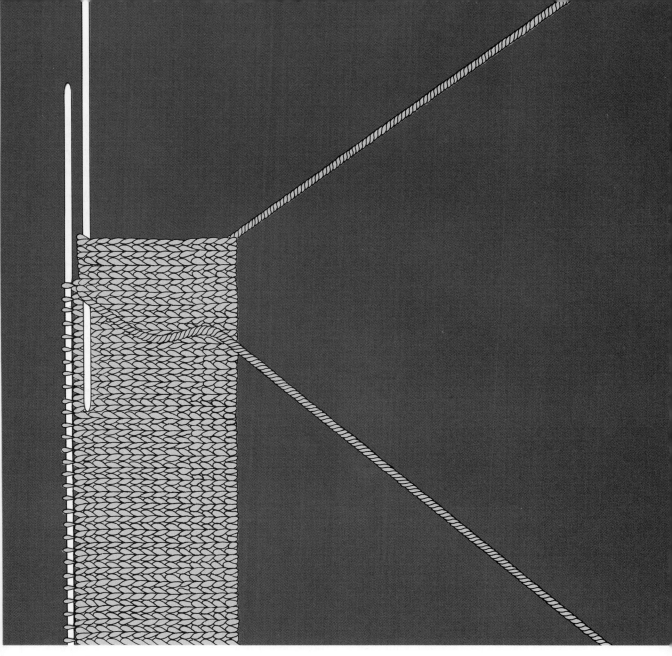

The letter K

may have started as a picture sign of the palm of the hand, as in Egyptian hieroglyphic writing (1) and in a very early Semitic writing used about 1500 B.C. on the Sinai Peninsula (2). About 1000 B.C., in Byblos and other Phoenician and Canaanite centers, the sign was given a linear form (3), the source of all later forms. In the Semitic languages the sign was called *kaph,* meaning "palm."

The Greeks changed the Semitic name to *kappa*. They also turned the letter around to suit the left-to-right direction of their writing (4).

The Romans took the sign over into Latin, but they used it sparingly. From Latin the capital letter K came into English unchanged.

The English small handwritten "k" is simply a capital K with small, straight strokes, which were gradually rounded. The printed "k" is similar to the handwritten form.

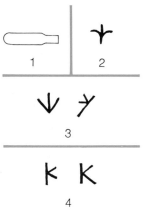

The jagged, snow-encrusted peak of K2 presents one of the world's most difficult challenges to mountain climbers.

K2, or MOUNT GODWIN AUSTEN. The Earth's second highest mountain, after Mount Everest, is K2, also known as Mt. Godwin Austen and as Dapsang. The peak, 28,250 feet (8,611 meters) high, is in the Karakoram mountain system of northern Jammu and Kashmir near the border of Pakistan and China.

K2 was long considered unclimbable because of its great height and almost unbroken slopes of rock and ice. The ascent is precipitous and full of overhangs, and there are few areas where climbers can camp.

The first of several attempts to reach K2's summit was made in 1902. Several persons were killed in these climbs. Finally, in 1954 an Italian expedition succeeded. It was led by geologist Ardito Desio and included four other scientists, a doctor, a photographer, and 12 others. Achille Compagnoni and Lino Lacedelli, the team chosen to attempt the final portion of the climb, are credited with having reached the summit.

KABUL, Afghanistan. The capital and largest city of Afghanistan, Kabul is the nation's leading cultural and economic center. The city lies on the Kabul River in a triangular-shaped valley between the steep Asmai and Sherdawaza mountain ranges.

Kabul is a blend of old and new buildings. In modern times the city has grown steadily. Roads connect it to most Afghan provinces, to the Soviet Union to the north, and to Pakistan to the east. Much of the old city has been destroyed and replaced with modern construction. Industries include food-processing plants, rayon and wool mills, a furniture factory, a foundry, and marble and lapis lazuli works.

Kabul has many historical monuments, including the tombs of some of its rulers, and a number of fine gardens. The Dar ol-Aman palace houses the parliament and government departments. The University of Kabul was founded in 1931. Most of the population speaks Dari, a Persian dialect.

Kabul has existed for more than 3,000 years. Its long prominence is due to its location, which commands the passes from both the north and south as well as from Pakistan and India through the Khyber Pass. The city first became a regional seat of government in the 8th century. In the 13th century considerable damage was inflicted on Kabul by the Mongol invader Genghis Khan. Kabul was the capital from 1504 to 1526 of the Mughal Empire, under the emperor Babur, and remained under Mughal rule until the city's capture in 1738 by Nader Shah of Iran. Kabul has been the nation's capital since 1776. Kabul was the site of hostilities during both the first and second Afghan Wars, from 1839 to 1842 and 1878 to 1880, with the British (*see* Afghan Wars).

More recently Kabul became the center of much military and guerrilla activity after the Soviet Union invaded Afghanistan when civil war broke out in that country in 1979. (*See also* Afghanistan.) Population (1979 estimate), 891,750.

KAFFIR WARS. Often called the Cape Frontier Wars, the Kaffir Wars were a series of intermittent conflicts from 1779 to 1879 in what is now South Africa. They were part of an effort on the part of the Xhosa, agricultural and pastoral peoples native to the Eastern Cape, to prevent the continued intrusion of Dutch settlers into their lands. In the later phases of these wars, the Xhosa had also to combat the British, who had taken over the Cape region during the Napoleonic Wars of the early 19th century. (*See also* South Africa, section on history.)

There had been trading contacts between the Dutch and the Xhosa since early in the 18th century, but friction developed between the two peoples in the last quarter of the century over grazing grounds, water rights, and the terms of the cattle trade. In 1778 the Great Fish River was declared the eastern boundary of the white colony. The Xhosa, however, were incensed when some of their tribesmen were expelled from west of the river in 1779. For revenge they began to kill and steal the Dutch colonists' cattle, and this led to the first war that year. This was followed by a second war in 1789 and a third from 1799 to 1802. The third was the most serious of the early wars, because it coincided with an uprising of the Khoisan servants, common in the area, against their Dutch masters. By this time the British controlled the colony. They achieved peace with the Khoisan peoples but were unable to dislodge the Xhosa from west of the Great Fish River.

Five more indecisive wars occurred between 1812 and 1853. The Xhosa slaughtered their own cattle and destroyed their own crops in 1857, believing a prophecy that this would ensure defeat of the British. This caused widespread starvation among the people and ended Xhosa military resistance to white settlement for nearly two decades. The last conflict, in 1877 and 1878, ended with the defeat of the tribesmen. They were disarmed, and their territory was gradually incorporated into the Cape Colony.

KAFKA, Franz (1883–1924). The credit for making Kafka internationally famous as a writer of visionary and imaginative fiction belongs to his friend, novelist Max Brod. In Kafka's will, Brod was asked to burn all unpublished manuscripts and to refrain from re-publishing those already in print. Brod instead edited the manuscripts and had them published.

Kafka was born into a Jewish middle-class family in Prague, Bohemia (now Czechoslovakia), on July 3, 1883. At the University of Prague he received his doctorate in 1906. After spending a short time as a legal apprentice, he went to work for an insurance company. When the long hours of work prevented him from writing, he took a less demanding job with another insurance business and remained there until forced to retire in 1922 because of ill health. He died in a tuberculosis sanatorium at Kierling, Austria, on June 3, 1924.

Kafka was in many ways a solitary figure, isolated in his own mind from any true community of friendship and alienated from his own Jewish heritage. This inner turmoil, as expressed in his continuously popular writings, promoted Kafka into a symbol of the anxiety and alienation that has pervaded much of 20th-century society.

Only a fraction of his total work was published in his lifetime. This includes sections from 'Beschreibung eines Kampfes' (Description of a Struggle, published in 1909), a chapter from his novel 'Amerika' (1913), and two stories: "Die Verwandlung" (Metamorphosis, 1915) and "In der Strafkolonie" (In the Penal Colony, 1919). His major novels, 'Der Prozess' (The Trial) and 'Das Schloss' (The Castle) were published after his death.

KALAHARI DESERT *see* AFRICA.

KALE *see* CABBAGE.

KALIDASA. The poet-dramatist Kalidasa was one of India's greatest writers and a master of the Sanskrit language. Unfortunately, so little is known about him that it is impossible to state with certainty in what century he lived. He probably lived during the Gupta dynasty, which ruled India from the 4th to the 6th centuries AD, and he may well have been associated with the emperor Candra Gupta II, who reigned from about 380 to 415. Kalidasa was a member of the aristocracy and possibly was a Hindu priest. His name means "servant of Kali" (one of the Hindu deities).

In his writings, Kalidasa attempted to fuse older religious traditions with the newer, and more secularized, Hinduism of his time. He is remembered for three major dramas, as well as epic and lyric poetry. His best drama, 'Sakuntala Recognized', recounts the legend of Bharata, the ancestor of the Indian nation. Another drama, 'Urvasi Won by Valor', deals with the love of a mortal king for a divine maiden. A third drama, 'Malavika and Agnimitra', is a comedy concerning intrigue within a king's harem.

In his epic poem 'Dynasty of Raghu,' Kalidasa recounts legends of the Indian hero-god, Rama. And in 'Birth of the War God' he tells the story of the god Kumara, son of the goddess Siva.

KALIMANTAN *see* BORNEO.

KAMEHAMEHA I (1758?–1819). The conqueror and king who united all the Hawaiian islands under his rule is Kamehameha I. Also known as Kamehameha the Great, he was the first of several rulers of Hawaii in the Kamehameha dynasty.

Kamehameha was probably born in 1758 on the island of Hawaii, the largest of the Hawaiian islands. Prophecies concerning his future as a leader frightened his grandfather King Alapai; so he ordered the infant put to death. However Kamehameha was raised secretly and, in 1782, he and a cousin became co-rulers of Hawaii. Through war, Kamehameha became sole ruler of the island in 1792, and by 1795 he had also brought the islands of Maui, Lanai, and Molokai under his control. In May 1795 his forces defeated the army of Oahu's chief on the site of present-day Honolulu, and that island became his as well. He acquired Kauai, the final island of the Hawaiian chain, through peaceful negotiations in 1809.

Kamehameha was a shrewd but fair king. He appointed governors to administer each island, outlawed ritual human sacrifice, and established laws to protect the people from the brutality of their chiefs. He died on May 8, 1819, in Kailua on Hawaii.

KAMPALA, Uganda. The capital and largest city of Uganda in East Africa, Kampala lies on a series of hills in the Central Province. It is the hub of the nation's road network and is served by the railway that connects Kasese to the west with Mombasa, Kenya, on Africa's east coast. The international airport is at Entebbe 21 miles (34 kilometers) southwest. Port Bell, six miles (ten kilometers) east on Lake Victoria also serves the city.

Kampala is located in its country's most prosperous agricultural section. The city exports coffee, cotton, tea, tobacco, and sugar. Numerous factories produce food, metal products, furniture, and tractors in Kampala, headquarters for most large Ugandan firms. Kampala has more than 20 schools and a technical institute and is the seat of Makerere University, which was founded in 1922. Mosques, Hindu temples, and Christian churches are widespread in Kampala.

Kampala was selected in 1890 as headquarters of the Imperial British East Africa Company. The name Kampala ("hill of the impala") comes from the custom of African rulers to graze herds of tame impala on the slopes. A fort, built by the British on Old Kampala Hill, remained the Ugandan colonial administrative headquarters until it was moved to Entebbe in 1905. In 1949 Kampala became a municipality, and in 1962 the city became the capital of independent Uganda. (*See also* Uganda.) Population (1980 census), 458,423.

The former Royal
Palace at Phnom Penh,
Kampuchea, was
constructed in 1919.

M. Mattson—Shostal

KAMPUCHEA. The small country of Kampuchea is a descendant of the Khmer Empire, which ruled much of Southeast Asia from the 9th to the 15th century. Formerly called Cambodia, the nation was a unit of French Indochina from 1887 to 1953, when it gained independence. During the 1970s rival factions engaged in a bloody struggle for control of the country. One faction, supported by China, took over the government in 1975, but another, backed by Vietnam, overthrew it in 1979. The country's political situation continued to be unstable.

The Land and Climate

Kampuchea has an area of 69,898 square miles (181,035 square kilometers). It is roughly circular in shape, and centers on a basinlike lowland that rises gently from sea level to the Dangrek Mountains on the north, the Elephant Mountains on the south, and the Cardamom Mountains in the southwest. The Dangrek range is more than 4,000 feet (1,200 meters) high, and elevations exceed 5,000 feet (1,500 meters) in the Cardamom range. To the west a low divide separates Kampuchea from Thailand. The Mekong River flows southward from Laos through eastern Kampuchea, and both the river and its basin drain through the Mekong Delta in southern Vietnam.

Approximately in the center of the lowland lies the Tonle Sap, meaning Great Lake, which serves as a natural flood reservoir for the Mekong River. From

This article was contributed by J. E. Spencer, Professor Emeritus, Department of Geography, University of California, Los Angeles, and author of 'Asia, East by South'.

Facts About Kampuchea

Official Name: People's Democratic Republic of Kampuchea.

Capital: Phnom Penh.

Area: 69,898 square miles (181,035 square kilometers).

Population (1982 estimate): 5,882,000; 84 persons per square mile (32 persons per square kilometer); (1970) 12 percent urban, 88 percent rural.

Major Languages: Khmer (official), French.

Major Religion: Buddhism.

Literacy: 54 percent of population age 10 and over is literate.

Mountain Ranges: Cardamom, Dangrek (Dong Rak).

Highest Peak: Phnum Aoral, 5,949 feet (1,813 meters).

Largest Lake: Tonle Sap.

Major River: Mekong.

Form of Government: People's Republic.

Chief of State: Chairman, Council of State (president).

Head of Government: Chairman, Council of Ministers (premier).

Legislature: National Assembly.

Voting Qualifications: Universal over 18 years.

Political Divisions: 17 provinces.

Major Cities: Phnom Penh (500,000), Batdambang (150,000), Kampong Saom (90,000).

Chief Manufactured Products: Fabricated metal, textiles, canned fish, plywood, paper, cement, sugar, tires, pottery, glass work.

Chief Mined Products: Phosphates, iron ore, gem stones, bauxite, silicon, manganese ore.

Chief Agricultural Products: *Crops*—rice, corn (maize), bananas, oranges, soybeans, rubber, tobacco, jute, peppers. *Livestock*—cattle, water buffalo, pigs, ducks.

Flag: Red with the temple of Angkor Wat in the center in yellow (*see* Flags of the World).

Monetary Unit: 1 riel = 100 sen.

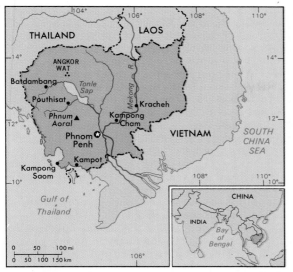

Thai forces in the 14th and 15th centuries cut the population by about half. Wars with the Thai and the Vietnamese from the 17th to the 19th century reduced the Khmer to about a million people by the mid-19th century. By 1960 the number of Khmer had again increased to almost 5 million.

About six aboriginal groups, totaling about 65,000 people, occupy the upland area around the borders of Kampuchea. About 70,000 Muslim Chams live in villages in the eastern part of the country. For centuries colonies of southern Chinese have made their homes in Kampuchean cities, and some have intermarried with Khmer. The Chinese population of Kampuchea was about 400,000 in 1980, of whom approximately one third lived in Phnom Penh, the capital and largest city. Vietnamese settlers began arriving in southeast Kampuchea in the late 17th century, and by 1960 their number had also reached about 400,000. A few thousand Thai live along the western fringes of Kampuchea, near the Thai border.

The Khmer are primarily an agricultural people. Almost all the Chinese live in cities and work in a wide variety of nonagricultural occupations. Some of the Vietnamese of Kampuchea are farmers or fishers, and others are craftworkers or merchants in the cities. In the rural lowlands, the Khmer live in villages of 300 to 800 people and build houses of bamboo and thatch that stand on stilts above the flood levels of the rainy season.

The Khmer have long been Buddhists, though many rural people follow ancient folk religions. During the 14th century the Khmer shifted from the Mahayana to the Theravada, or Hinayana, tradition, a southern version of Buddhism. Young Khmer men normally spend a period as priests associated with a temple.

The Economy

The Kampuchean economy is based on agriculture, chiefly rice growing. Rice is primarily a wet-field crop, grown with the aid of flooding during the rainy season, but some areas have irrigation facilities. A number of farmers grow "floating rice" on the deep-watered depressions paralleling the natural levees of the Mekong River and harvest the crop from boats. Corn ranks second in importance, and other crops include bananas, manioc, soybeans, sweet potatoes, chili peppers, sesame, sugarcane, sugar palm, and green vegetables.

Small amounts of tobacco, cotton, kapok, ramie, and raw silk are produced chiefly on the levee lands along the Mekong. These products are used both by domestic craftsworkers and for export. The French began to establish rubber plantations east of the Mekong in the 1920s, and Kampuchea is one of the chief rubber producers of the Far East. Almost every village home is surrounded by trees that produce such fruits as coconuts, mangoes, citrus fruits, jackfruit, betel nuts, guavas, and bananas, all for home use.

Livestock raising has a minor role in the economy, supplying draft animals for use in agriculture and

November to late April, the lake shrinks to about 1,000 square miles (2,600 square kilometers) in area, or about 20 by 60 miles (32 by 96 kilometers), and is no deeper than 5 feet (1.5 meters). Then, from July to late October, when the Mekong floods flow up the Tonle Sap River into the lake, the area expands and may cover almost 10,000 square miles (26,000 square kilometers), or about 50 by 220 miles (80 by 350 kilometers), and the depth may reach 45 feet (14 meters).

Kampuchea has a tropical climate. It is always warm to hot in the lowlands, with temperatures seldom below 80° F (26° C). The rainy season comes with the summer monsoon, and from May through October normally brings 50 to 80 inches (1,270 to 2,030 millimeters) of rain in the lowlands and about twice as much in the southwestern mountains.

About half of Kampuchea consists of thick tropical evergreen forests, and a fourth of the country has been transformed into a mixture of forest, parkland, and grassland. Away from the streams, the soils are chiefly sandy to coarse, eroded and infertile yellow to red earth. Along the many river-flooded plains are narrow strips of good alluvial soil. The annually flooded shores of the Tonle Sap and Mekong rivers have soils that are renewed by the silt of the flood season. Animals of Kampuchea include monkeys, buffalo, elephants, tigers, panthers, leopards, civet cats, crocodiles, pheasants, and jungle fowl.

The People

A large majority of the people are Khmer, a racially mixed group that arrived in Southeast Asia about 2000 BC. They speak the Khmer language, a member of the Malayo-Polynesian language family. Most Khmer are short, stocky, brown-skinned people with black hair that often is wavy. Men and women both generally wear an upper jacket and a saronglike lower garment called a *sampot.*

The Khmer Empire at its height during the 12th century AD had almost 4 million people. Conquest by local transportation, and small amounts of beef for the urban population. Fishes are a more commonly consumed product. They are dried, salted, or made into sauces and pastes. The supply exceeds domestic needs, and the surplus is exported to Vietnam.

A few types of light manufacturing had developed in Kampuchea prior to 1965, but political unrest from then until 1979 stopped almost all production. Handicrafts also declined during this period. The economy began to recover in 1980, with small operations in textiles, paper, cigarettes, glass, soft drinks, and rubber goods. Some timber and raw rubber were exported to the Soviet Union in exchange for road-building equipment. However, black-market dealing became more common than legal transactions.

Transportation, Communication, and Education

Transportation in Kampuchea is largely by water during the wet season and by ox cart in the dry months. Phnom Penh is a river port used by small seagoing ships, and small boats operate on the Mekong and Tonle Sap. A railroad connects Phnom Penh and Thailand, and another line runs between the capital and the port of Kampong Saom.

Kampuchea has about 2,000 miles (3,200 kilometers) of all-weather roads, but a lack of maintenance since 1960 has made them barely usable. A network of improved dirt roads serves the nation during the dry season. Kampuchea's communications system was largely destroyed or damaged between 1975 and 1979.

Political conflict also disrupted the educational system. The number of literate people in Kampuchea was increasing slowly before 1970 but was below that of other Southeast Asian nations except Laos. In 1970 elementary, high school, and university education was regularly available, but after the Khmer Rouge took over in 1975 only elementary classes were regularly scheduled. Little information about the educational system has been available under the regimes that have controlled the country since 1975.

History and Government

During the last five centuries the Khmer state lost both people and territory to Thailand on the west and Vietnam on the east. The country was almost divided between Thailand and Vietnam in the 19th century before the French made Cambodia a protectorate in 1863. The country formed part of French Indochina from 1887 until it became independent in 1953 under King Norodom Sihanouk. The next year at the Geneva Conference, Sihanouk's government was recognized as the sole legitimate authority in the country. Sihanouk abdicated in 1955, reorganized the government, and was elected chief of state in 1960. Cambodia tried to remain politically neutral in the fight for power between Communist and non-Communist nations during the 1960s. By 1965, however, Communist factions were competing in promoting revolution there.

In March 1970 Gen. Lon Nol, an anti-Communist, seized control of Cambodia. The Cambodian legisla-

ture abolished the monarchy and changed the name of the nation to the Khmer Republic. Sihanouk had been out of the country when Lon Nol took over the government. In late 1972, in Peking, Sihanouk organized a revolutionary government-in-exile. It was backed by China and opposed the Communist faction that was backed by the Soviet Union and Vietnam.

In January 1975 the Khmer Rouge, as the China-backed revolutionaries came to be called, launched a major offensive against the Vietnamese faction and the Lon Nol government. The Khmer Rouge, led by Pol Pot, occupied Phnom Penh in April. A new constitution legalized the Communist government and program and renamed the country Democratic Kampuchea. The Khmer Rouge turned all cultivated land into cooperatives and sent city people to rural areas to clear cropland; Phnom Penh became a ghost town. More than 2 million people were killed during brutal purges of opposing factions, former government officials, and the educated and middle classes. Thousands of people fled the country seeking refuge in neighboring countries, such as Thailand.

In December 1978 Vietnam invaded Kampuchea. The Vietnamese government said it wanted to save Kampuchea from further harshness and purges by the Khmer Rouge; its support went to the Soviet-Vietnamese Communist faction. By April 1979 the Vietnamese had taken Phnom Penh, installed a new government under Heng Samrin, and changed the name of the country to the People's Democratic Republic of Kampuchea. The Vietnamese army occupied the country and waged anti-Khmer Rouge campaigns in the western border areas.

The Vietnamese set up a People's Revolutionary Council to govern Kampuchea. In 1981 a 117-member National Assembly was elected to a five-year term, and it approved a new constitution. The Assembly that year appointed a seven-member Council of State and a 16-member Council of Ministers to replace the Revolutionary Council.

Kampuchean farmers harvested adequate rice crops in 1981 and 1982, and some community life returned to the countryside. Domestic recovery, however, was threatened by a lack of equipment, skilled labor, and trained administrative personnel.

The long-term intentions of Vietnam toward Kampuchea remained unknown, but such nations as Thailand, Malaysia, Singapore, and Indonesia were concerned because of Vietnam's traditional aggressiveness toward the Khmer. Thailand continued its indirect support of the Khmer Rouge. China bitterly opposed the new regime and in retaliation for the takeover briefly invaded Vietnam in 1979. In 1982 the principal anti-Vietnamese Khmer forces formed a coalition to combat Vietnam's continued military occupation of their homeland. Sihanouk resigned as head of the coalition and went into exile in July 1988. Peace talks were held later that month between all of the warring Kampuchean factions. In 1989 Vietnam announced that it would withdraw its remaining 50,000 to 70,000 troops by the end of September.

KANANGA, Zaire. The city of Kananga, formerly Luluabourg, is the capital of the Kasai-Occidental region of the central African country of Zaire. It lies on the Lulua River, in the south central part of the country on road and rail routes to Lubumbashi and the Kasai River port of Ilebo.

Kananga is a main commercial center that serves an area producing diamonds, livestock, and large quantities of coffee and cotton. Palm oil, rice, manioc, peanuts, bananas, and pineapples are processed in the capital. Other industries include brewing and printing. Kananga is the site of a national museum and a teacher-training college. The national broadcasting station has a radio station in Kananga that broadcasts in French and official Zairian languages.

Like the other cities in Zaire with populations greater than 100,000 Kananga developed during the colonial period, when there were separate sectors for the Europeans and the Africans. The European neighborhoods were characterized by big houses with large yards, wide and paved streets, and adequate electricity. The crowded African areas had smaller houses and yards, and poor or no electric service. These characteristics had changed little by the early 1980s, although upper income Africans have moved into traditional European sectors.

The city originated as Luluabourg, so named by a German explorer in 1884. It became a military post that was the scene in 1895 of a widespread revolt of African troops against the Belgians. Luluabourg succeeded Lusambo as the capital of the region in 1950 and received its present name in 1972. Since Zaire became independent in 1960, Kananga's population has more than quadrupled. (*See also* Zaire.) Population (1976 census), 462,621.

KANDINSKY, Wassily (1866–1944). Ranked among the artists whose work changed the history of art in the early years of the 20th century, the Russian abstract painter Wassily Kandinsky is generally regarded as one of the originators of abstract painting, or abstract expressionism (*see* Painting). In both his painting and his theoretical writings he influenced modern styles. Spending many years of his life in Germany, Kandinsky became an instrumental force in the development of German expressionism.

Kandinsky was born in Moscow on Dec. 4, 1866. He studied law and political economy at the University of Moscow, but after a visit in 1895 to an exhibition of French impressionist paintings in Moscow, Kandinsky decided to become a painter. Moving to Munich, Germany, he worked under Anton Azbé and Franz von Stuck, studying impressionist color and art nouveau (an ornamental style of about 1890 to 1910). From the very beginning Kandinsky's own work showed an interest in fantasy.

Between 1900 and 1910 Kandinsky traveled widely, including visits to Paris that put him in contact with the art of Paul Gauguin, the neoimpressionists, and fauvism (a style with aggressive use of brilliant colors). He began developing his ideas concerning the

'Improvisation No. 30', painted in oil by Kandinsky in 1913, hangs in the Art Institute of Chicago.

power of pure color and nonrepresentational painting. In 1909 Kandinsky helped found the New Artists' Association in Munich.

Kandinsky painted his first abstract watercolor in 1910 and began formulating his important theoretical study, 'Upon the Spiritual in Art', which was published originally in German in 1912. In this work he examined the psychological effects of color and made comparisons between painting and music. Together with the German painter Franz Marc, Kandinsky became a leader in the influential *Blaue Reiter* (Blue Rider) movement, an expressionist group. He and Marc edited 'Der blaue Reiter', an almanac in which they reproduced art from all ages.

Marc and Kandinsky organized avant-garde international exhibitions in Munich and elsewhere—exhibitions that proved to be major events in the development of German expressionism. With the outbreak of World War I, Kandinsky left Germany to return to Russia, where he taught and organized numerous artistic activities. He went back to Germany in 1921 and became one of the principal teachers at the Bauhaus school in Weimar, remaining with the school until it was closed by the Nazi regime in 1933. Kandinsky then moved to Paris, where he stayed until his death on Dec. 13, 1944.

A significant change took place in Kandinsky's work during the 1920s. From the romantic superabundance of his earlier abstract expressionism, his style evolved into geometric forms—points, bundles of lines, circles, and triangles. During the last decade of his life, Kandinsky blended the free, intuitive image of his earlier years with the geometric forms of his Bauhaus period.

KANGAROO. When Captain James Cook was exploring the coast of Australia in 1770, his men were amazed by a strange animal. At times the creature stood upright, braced firmly on its hind legs and huge tail. It moved by great leaps. Thus white men first met the great gray kangaroo, often called the "boomer" or "old man" of Australia.

More than a hundred species of the kangaroo family live in the open spaces of Australia, New Guinea, and nearby islands. They belong to the marsupial order, which are animals that carry their young in pouches. The kangaroo's body is specially built for jumping. In this way it differs from other marsupials. However, the kangaroo family should not be confused with kangaroo rats, jerboas, and similar jumping rodents of America, Africa, and Asia.

The great gray kangaroo reaches a weight of 200 pounds (90 kilograms) and a length of ten feet (three meters) from nose to tip of tail. The tail alone is about four feet (one meter) long, and the strong muscles at the base make it nearly as thick as the animal's body. There are four toes on each of the two hind feet. The second toe from the outside is much stronger and longer than the others and ends in a huge claw. This toe and the shorter outside toe are used in the great leaps that the kangaroo makes. It can leap along the ground at 30 miles (48 kilometers) an hour.

Three fourths of the animal's size and weight are in its hindquarters. The front legs are short and slender, with two small five-toed paws. These are used like hands in taking hold of food.

The female has a large pouch on the belly made by a fold in the soft furry skin. When the single, naked baby kangaroo is born it is only an inch (2.5 centimeters) long. It finds shelter in the pouch. There it attaches itself to one of the mother's nipples, which swells inside the baby's mouth. For several weeks it cannot loosen its grip. It is unable at first to draw out milk or to swallow it. The mother has muscles that pump her milk down the baby's throat.

The young kangaroo is called a joey in Australia. When the joey is about four months old, it is able to lean out of the sheltering pouch and nibble grass. Soon it climbs out and learns to hop around in search of food. It continues for several weeks longer to climb back into the pouch for sleep and safety. If sudden danger threatens while the young kangaroo is some distance away, the mother starts toward it at full speed, gathers it up, and tucks it into her pouch.

Other Kinds of Kangaroos

The red kangaroo and the wallaroo are nearly as large as the great gray kangaroo. Next in size are various species popularly known as wallabies. These larger types are usually found in small groups called mobs. They move from place to place, feeding on grass, shrubs, and the leaves of small trees. Their keen noses, ears, and eyes warn them of danger from hunters or wild dogs. Kangaroos are hunted because of the damage they do to crops and for their tender flesh and their skins, which produce fine leather.

Timid as it is, the kangaroo fights hard when cornered. It stamps its hind feet and growls. With its front paws it pushes its attackers within reach of a blow from its back feet. It can rip a dog to death with a single stroke. When chased by a pack, a kangaroo

will sometimes escape its danger by jumping into a lake or stream.

The smaller kangaroos include the rock wallabies, the hare wallabies, and the rat kangaroos. They live in hidden places in cliffs or in thick brush. A few species live in trees. These tree kangaroos have much shorter hind legs and longer forelegs than the others. They do not hop but climb among the branches like small bears. Some of these smaller kangaroos eat berries and small insects as well as grass and leaves.

Scientific Facts About Kangaroos

Fossil remains of about 30 different kangaroo species have been found in Australia. Among them were several giant types, one of which is estimated to have stood fully ten feet (three meters) tall.

Kangaroos make up the family Macropodidae of the marsupial order. The scientific name of the great gray kangaroo is *Macropus canguru* (sometimes called *M. giganteus*). Other marsupials are the phalangers, including the cuscus, koala, and several Australian opossums; wombats; bandicoots; Tasmanian devil; Tasmanian wolf; banded anteater; marsupial mole; and true opossums.

The young do not reach the same degree of development inside the mother's body as do the young of higher mammals. They are born sooner and complete the early growth stages in the mother's pouch.

The marsupials lie between the most primitive egg-laying mammals, such as the duckbill and the spiny anteater of the order Monotremata, and the higher orders, which include all remaining mammals.

A joey, or baby kangaroo, leans out of the pouch of its watchful mother to nibble on vegetation.

Australian Tourist Commission

Santa Fe Railway

A golden field of Kansas wheat, bending in the wind, awaits the harvest. Kansas is traditionally among the United States chief wheat producers.

KANSAS

KANSAS. One of the greatest farming states in the nation is Kansas. Its fertile prairies normally yield over 400 million bushels of wheat yearly. In most years this is more than is grown in any other state. The state's output is usually more than 10 percent of the total United States crop. Kansas is also among the leading states in corn (maize), sorghum, alfalfa, and hay production.

Kansas is the most centrally located state, not including Alaska and Hawaii. It lies halfway between Canada and Mexico. Until Alaska and Hawaii became states, the geographic center of the United States was in Smith County, two miles northwest of Lebanon. Just 42 miles to the south, in Osborne County, is the geodetic center of North America. All geodetic land surveys on the continent are controlled from this point. (*See also* Surveying.)

The state is named for the Kansa tribe of Sioux Indians who lived along the Kansas (or Kaw) River. *Kansa* is a Sioux word meaning "wind people." Because wild sunflowers grow profusely in the state, Kansas is nicknamed the Sunflower State. It is also called the Jayhawker State, from a Civil War term for Kansas troops and for guerrilla forces in the state.

Population (1980): 2,363,208—rank, 32nd state. Urban, 66.7%; rural, 33.3%. Persons per square mile, 28.9 (persons per square kilometer, 11.1)—rank, 37th state.

Extent: Area, 82,264 square miles, (213,063 square kilometers), including 477 square miles (1,235 square kilometers) of inland water surface (14th state in size).

Elevation: Highest, Mount Sunflower, 4,039 feet (1,231 meters), in Wallace County; lowest, Verdigris River at southern boundary of state, 680 feet (207 meters).

Geographic Center: 15 miles (24 kilometers) northeast of Great Bend.

Temperature: Extremes—lowest, −40° F (−40° C), Lebanon, Feb. 13, 1905; highest, 121° F (49° C) near Alton, July 24, 1936, and on earlier dates at other locations. Averages at Topeka—January, 28.0° F (−2.2° C); July, 78.2° F (25.6° C); annual, 54.5° (12.5° C). Averages at Yuma—January, 32.0° F (0° C); July, 80.9° F (27.1° C); annual, 57.1° F (13.9° C).

Precipitation: At Topeka—annual average, 33.03 inches (838 millimeters). At Wichita—annual average, 28.41 inches (721 millimeters).

Land Use: Crops, 60%; pasture, 30%; forest, 3%; other, 7%.

For statistical information about Agriculture, Education, Employment, Finance, Government, Manufacturing, Mining, Population Trends, and Vital Statistics, see KANSAS FACT SUMMARY.

173

Survey of the Sunflower State

Kansas is in the central region of the United States. It is bordered by four states—Oklahoma on the south, Colorado on the west, Nebraska on the north, and Missouri on the east. Its only natural boundary is in the northeast, where the Missouri River flows between Kansas and the state of Missouri before turning eastward at Kansas City.

The state is shaped like a rectangle, almost twice as long as it is wide. Its greatest length, from east to west, is 411 miles. Its greatest width, from north to south, is 207 miles. The total area of Kansas is 82,264 square miles, including 477 square miles of inland water surface.

The State's Four Natural Regions

Although Kansas is generally level, it consists of four distinct natural regions. In the east are the Osage Plains and the Glacial Plains. Both regions are part of the Central Lowland of the United States. Western Kansas, a part of the Great Plains, is divided into the High Plains and the High Plains Border.

In Wallace County, near the western border, is Mount Sunflower (4,039 feet), the highest point in the state. From here the surface slopes down to a low of 680 feet along the Verdigris River at the Kansas-Oklahoma boundary in the southeast.

The High Plains cover the western end of the state. This is a rolling tableland with little rainfall and few trees. From west to east the elevation slopes from 4,000 to 3,000 feet above sea level.

The High Plains Border occupies west-central Kansas. It is an intermediate zone between the high-

Castle Rock, a chalk spire, breaks the flat area near Utica. Such formations are common in Gove County.

Kansas Industrial Development Commission

er region of the west and the lower plains to the east. In the south-central part of this region are the prairies of the Great Bend of the Arkansas River.

The Glacial Plains lie in the northeastern corner of the state. During the Ice Age, glaciers deposited a layer of fertile soil in this region. To the southwest are the low, grass-covered Flint Hills.

The Osage Plains extend over southeastern Kansas. This is gently rolling, rich farmland. In Cowley and Butler counties and to the north are the Flint Hills. These hills extend across the state in a north-south direction.

Most of the rivers of Kansas flow from west to east. The northern half of the state is drained by the Kansas (Kaw) River, formed by the junction of the Republican and Smoky Hill rivers in Geary County. The chief river of southern Kansas is the Arkansas. Its tributaries include the Cimarron in the southwest and the Verdigris and Neosho in the east.

Climate and Weather

Because it is about 600 miles from any large body of water, Kansas has a continental climate. Summers are hot and winters are cold.

Greeley County receives the least precipitation (rain and melted snow)—about 16 inches a year. From west to east the rainfall gradually increases until it reaches a maximum of 40 inches in the extreme southeast. The growing season varies from 150 days a year in the northwest to 200 days a year along the southeastern border. As with the other states of the Great Plains region, Kansas is subject to occasional droughts and tornadoes.

Natural Resources and Conservation

The Sunflower State's chief natural resource is its soil. The flat plains of western Kansas are ideal for large-scale wheat growing. The fertile farmland of eastern Kansas produces corn and other crops. There are also extensive grazing lands, chiefly bluestem grass in the east and buffalo grass in the west.

Kansas farm products help make food processing one of the state's most important manufacturing industries. Petroleum and natural gas are the state's principal mineral resources.

The chief conservation problem in Kansas has been the protection of the soil from erosion by wind and water. This has been partly accomplished by improved farming practices and by the planting of trees. (*See also* Conservation.) In the northern half of the state the rivers of the Missouri Basin are being developed primarily for flood-control and irrigation purposes. Since 1925 many of the state's natural resources have been administered by the Kansas Fish and Game Commission.

People of the Sunflower State

What is now Kansas was the home of several tribes of Plains Indians. These included the Kansa (Kaw), Osage, Pawnee, and Wichita. Several tribes of eastern Indians arrived after 1830, when Congress or-

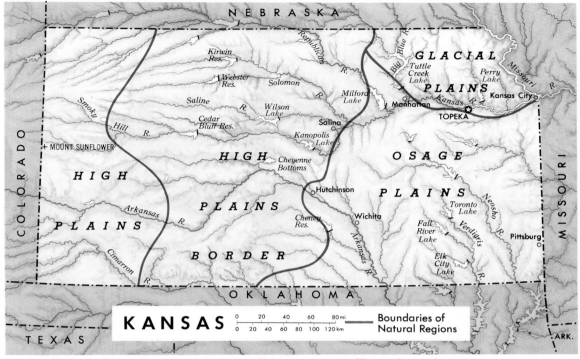

The relatively flat terrain of Kansas can be divided into four natural regions. The use that can be made of the land is determined by the physical features of each region.

dered them to be moved west of the Mississippi River. After Kansas was opened to white settlement in 1854, the Indians began to surrender their lands. By about 1880 most tribes had been resettled in Indian Territory (now Oklahoma). Today the state has about 15,300 American Indians.

The Kansas-Nebraska Act of 1854 brought a rush of settlers into the region. Proslavery men from Missouri and antislavery groups from as far away as New England fought for control of the territory. In 1855 there were only about 8,600 people in Kansas. Five years later the state's population had increased to more than 107,000.

The state's greatest growth in population came during the 25 years that followed the Civil War. Many of the new settlers were farmers who journeyed to Kansas from the eastern states. They took land opened up by the Homestead Law of 1862. Only a few foreign immigrants came to Kansas. Today the foreign-born make up about 2 percent of the population. Of the total foreign stock, Germans are the most numerous. Blacks make up about 5 percent of the state's population.

Products of the Land

About 90 percent of Kansas is cropland or pasture. The state's 75,000 farms occupy 48,300,000 acres. The average Kansas farm is about 653 acres.

The most important crop by far is wheat. Most of it is a hard, winter variety grown on large farms that are highly mechanized. The chief wheat-growing counties in Kansas are Sumner, Reno, Harper, Kingman, and McPherson.

Sorghum for grain is the second most valuable crop. It is produced largely in the southwest. Hay, especially alfalfa and sweet clover, is grown throughout the state. Other important crops are corn (maize), popcorn, soybeans, dry beans, and sugar beets. Of the state's livestock, cattle and calves produce the largest cash income. Cattle and sheep are grazed mainly in the central part of the state and in the west. Dairying and the raising of hogs and poultry are important in eastern Kansas.

Petroleum accounts for about three fifths of the value of the state's mineral production. The central part of Kansas is the most productive area. Next in value is natural gas. Other valuable minerals are cement, stone, and salt.

Manufacturing and Cities

Only about one out of every six workers in Kansas is engaged in manufacturing industries. The chief industry is the manufacture of aircraft, motor vehicles, and other transportation equipment. The manufacture of nonelectrical machinery, such as farm, garden, and construction equipment, is the second most important industry. Those industries that process foodstuffs, such as flour and meal, meat, bakery goods, and dairy products, also rank high in value in the state. Included among the other important industries in Kansas are petroleum refining and printing and publishing.

Cattle and petroleum comprise two of the most important sources of income in Kansas. A herd of Hereford cattle (left) is fattened in a feedlot before being shipped for slaughter elsewhere. Modern refineries at Augusta (right) process much of the state's petroleum.

The largest city in the state is Wichita, on the Arkansas River. Wichita is noted for its food processing, oil refineries, and aircraft manufacture (*see* Wichita). Kansas City, second in size, is a livestock and meat-packing center where the Kansas and Missouri rivers meet. Nearby is rapidly growing Overland Park. Across the state line is the twin city, Kansas City, Mo. (*see* Kansas City, Kan.). About 60 miles upstream from the mouth of the Kansas River is Topeka, which is the state capital and third largest city (*see* Topeka).

In the northeast are Lawrence, on the Kansas River, and Leavenworth, on the Missouri. Salina, a flour-milling and grain-storage city, is on the Smoky Hill River. Hutchinson is located on the Arkansas River. Hutchinson's industries are based on wheat, oil, and salt. Pittsburg and Coffeyville are the largest cities of the southeast. Manhattan lies near the coming together of the Big Blue and Kansas rivers.

The Development of Transportation

The first highway for wheeled vehicles across the Kansas region was the Santa Fe Trail, which was opened by William Becknell in 1821. It ran from Independence, Mo., west and south through Council Grove and Pawnee Rock to Santa Fe, N.M. The second great route to the West that passed through Kansas was the Oregon Trail.

Today the Sunflower State is served by a large network of modern roads. Kansas maintains some 10,000 miles of primary highways and other state roads. The chief east-west routes are Interstate 70 (which incorporates parts of US 40) and US 36, 24, 50, 54, and 160; the major north-south highways are Interstate 135 and US 83, 283, 183, 281, 81, 77, 75, 59, and 69. Interstate 35 extends southwestward from Kansas City through Emporia and Wichita and on to the Oklahoma border.

The first railroad in the state was a five-mile line from Elwood to Wathena, opened in 1860. By 1873 the Atchison and Topeka Railroad (now The Atchison, Topeka and Santa Fe Railway) had been completed across the state. Today more than a dozen railroads serve Kansas, with most of the trackage in the eastern half. Another important form of transportation is the barge line on the Missouri River.

Recreation in Kansas

Twenty-two state parks and 21 federal reservoirs have been established to provide fishing, swimming,

Assembly lines turn out military and commercial planes at Wichita, a major aircraft-production center. Transportation equipment manufacturing is the state's chief industry.

and other recreation for the people of the Sunflower State. Some of the leading points of interest in Kansas are mementos of pioneer days. Boot Hill Cemetery at Dodge City, the Pawnee Capitol at Fort Riley, Fort Scott, and Fort Hays are among these. Fort Larned, which once was an important military post on the Santa Fe Trail, is administered by the National Park Service.

At Abilene is the Eisenhower Center, which includes a museum, a library, and the president's boyhood home. Wichita is noted as the site of the annual National Semipro Baseball Tournament. The Kansas State Fair is held at Hutchinson, and the Sunflower State Exposition at Topeka.

Growth of the School System

The first schools in Kansas were religious missions established among the Indians in the 1820s. In 1827 the federal government sent Daniel Morgan Boone, son of Daniel Boone, to teach farming to the Indians in Jefferson County. In 1855 the first territorial legislature provided for a system of free public schools. From this law came the organization of school districts administered by county superintendents.

Compulsory attendance for children of school age has been in effect since 1874. The first high school was built in Chapman in 1889. Today the public educational system is directed by the State Board of Education, composed of ten members.

The largest school of higher learning is the University of Kansas, at Lawrence, with the University of Kansas Medical Center, at Kansas City. Also state supported are Kansas State University, at Manhattan; Wichita State University, at Wichita; and three other state universities, at Emporia, Pittsburg, and Fort Hays. Other schools of higher learning are Washburn University of Topeka; Benedictine College, at Atchison; Ottawa University, at Ottawa; and Bethany College, at Lindsborg.

Government and Politics

The capital of Kansas was chosen by popular vote in 1861. Topeka was the winner over Lawrence. The state is governed under its original constitution, adopted in 1859 and effective 1861.

The chief executive officer is the governor, elected every four years. Lawmaking is in the hands of the Senate and the House of Representatives. The judiciary is headed by the Supreme Court. Kansas pioneered in the development of a legislative council, which studies public problems and prepares bills for the legislature. The legislative coordinating council consists of three senators and four representatives.

Predominantly Republican Kansas has elected only seven Democratic governors. In presidential elections it voted Republican except in 1892, 1896, 1912, 1916, 1932, 1936, and 1964. Alfred M. Landon, governor from 1933 to 1937, was the unsuccessful Republican candidate for president in 1936. Dwight D. Eisenhower was elected the 34th president of the United States in 1952 and reelected in 1956.

The Shawnee Methodist Mission, which opened in 1839 to educate Indian children, is located just south of Kansas City. The first Kansas schools were religious missions.

HISTORY OF KANSAS

On May 30, 1854, Kansas was organized as a territory out of what had been the old Missouri Territory, sometimes called "Indian country." Three of its boundaries were the same as they are today—the state of Missouri on the east, the 40th parallel on the north, and the 37th parallel on the south. Its western border extended to the Rocky Mountains. When Kansas became a state, on Jan. 29, 1861, its western boundary was set at the "25th meridian of longitude west from Washington (D.C.)." The area west of this line was made a part of Colorado Territory. The sections that follow discuss the development of Kansas into a modern state.

Exploration to Statehood

In 1541 Francisco Coronado and his party of Spanish explorers became the first white men to enter what is now Kansas (see Coronado). Little was known of the region when the United States acquired all but the southwestern corner of the present state in 1803 (see Louisiana Purchase). The remainder was secured by the United States from Texas in 1850.

During the first half of the 1800s, the chief settlements in the Indian country were forts erected to keep peace on the frontier. Fort Leavenworth was built in 1827, Fort Scott in 1842, and Fort Riley in 1853. By 1850 the population numbered only about 1,500 whites and some 34,000 Indians.

In 1854 the territory was opened to white settlement by the Kansas-Nebraska Act (see Kansas-Nebraska Act). Congress left it up to the settlers to decide whether they wanted Kansas to become a free state or a slave state. The earliest arrivals were proslavery people from Missouri. They founded Leavenworth and Atchison. Later, free-state forces established settlements at Lawrence and Topeka.

For four years the two groups battled for control of "Bleeding Kansas." In 1856 Lawrence was sacked by a proslavery party. In revenge John Brown and his followers massacred five men along Pottawatomie Creek near Lane. Gradually the antislavery settlers became dominant. In 1859 a convention at Wyandotte (later Kansas City) adopted a free-state constitution that was ratified by popular vote. In 1861 Kansas was admitted to the Union as the 34th state.

Growth of the Modern State

In 1867 the first herd of Texas longhorn cattle was driven along the Chisholm Trail to the railroad at Abilene. This began the cattle boom that lasted until the 1880's. Meanwhile Mennonite pioneers from Russia introduced a hardy new type of wheat, called Turkey Red. First grown near Hillsboro in 1874, it provided the basis of today's bountiful crops of Kansas wheat.

During the 1890's farmers expressed their discontent with low farm prices by joining the Granger movement and the Populist party. This was also the era when Carry Nation became nationally famous for smashing Kansas saloons that disregarded antiliquor laws.

By 1900 most of the state's farmland had been claimed by settlers. Because of the drought-created Dust Bowl and low farm prices, Kansas lost almost 80,000 residents between 1930 and 1940. During the 1940's and 1950's this loss was more than made up by an increase of some 379,000 persons. Between 1970 and 1980 the population increased by 114,137 persons, a gain of 5.1 percent but 6.3 percent less than the national growth. During the 1960's the major industries of Kansas were expanding at a slow rate. They were unable to provide job opportunities for all of the Kansas farm workers who had been displaced by mechanization. (*See also* United States, sections "North Central Plains" and "Great Plains"; individual entries in the Fact-Index on Kansas persons, places, products, and events.)

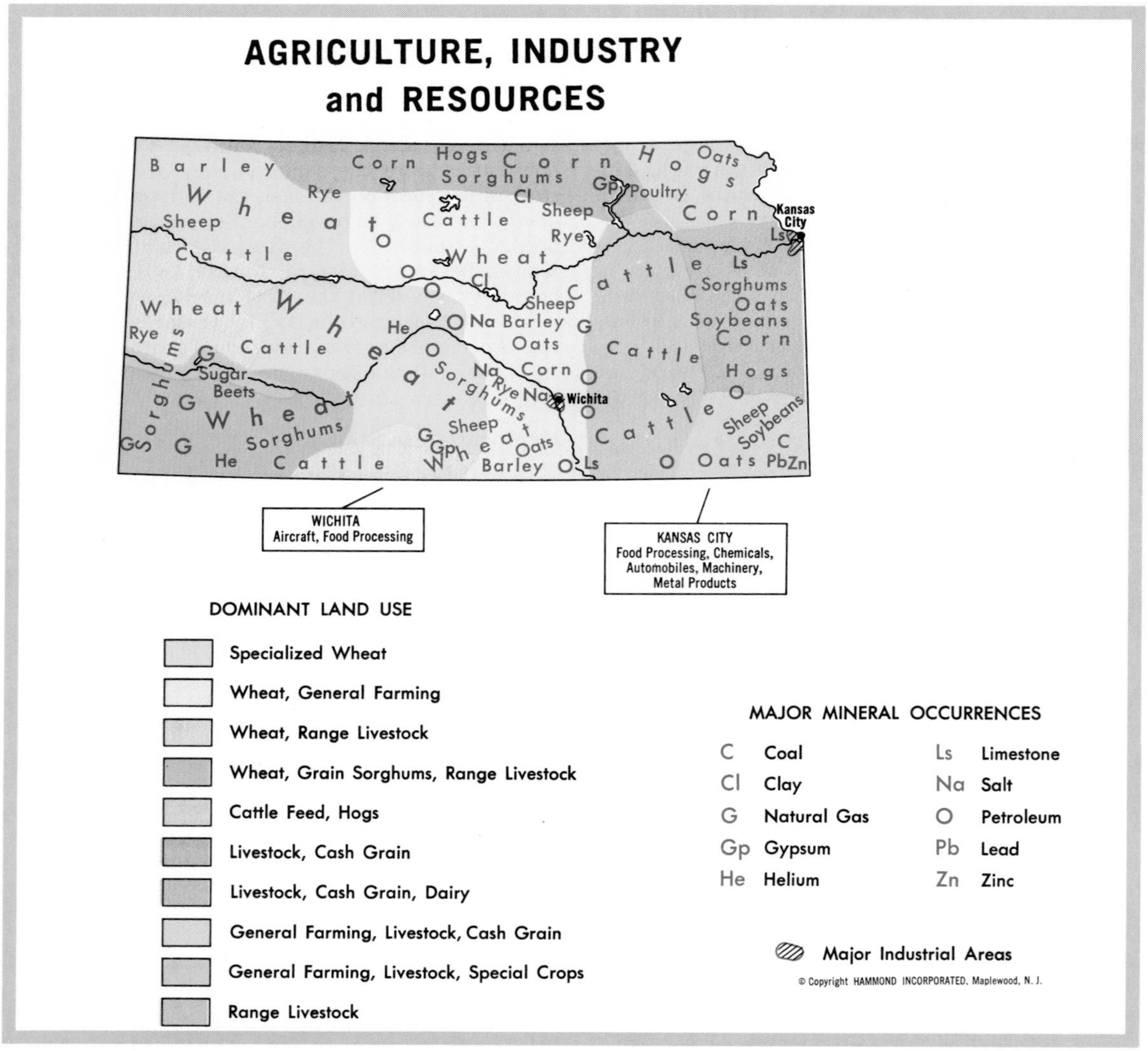

AGRICULTURE, INDUSTRY and RESOURCES

WICHITA
Aircraft, Food Processing

KANSAS CITY
Food Processing, Chemicals,
Automobiles, Machinery,
Metal Products

DOMINANT LAND USE

- Specialized Wheat
- Wheat, General Farming
- Wheat, Range Livestock
- Wheat, Grain Sorghums, Range Livestock
- Cattle Feed, Hogs
- Livestock, Cash Grain
- Livestock, Cash Grain, Dairy
- General Farming, Livestock, Cash Grain
- General Farming, Livestock, Special Crops
- Range Livestock

MAJOR MINERAL OCCURRENCES

C	Coal	Ls	Limestone
Cl	Clay	Na	Salt
G	Natural Gas	O	Petroleum
Gp	Gypsum	Pb	Lead
He	Helium	Zn	Zinc

Major Industrial Areas

© Copyright HAMMOND INCORPORATED, Maplewood, N. J.

Notable Events in Kansas History

1541—**Coronado, searching for city of Quivira, reaches central Kansas.**

1723—Étienne de Bourgmont builds Fort Orléans.

1803—France sells Louisiana, including most of Kansas, to U.S.

1804—Kansas included in District of Louisiana under Indiana Territory; made part of Louisiana Territory in 1805. Lewis and Clark enter Kansas.

1806—Zebulon M. Pike explores Republican River area.

1812—Territory of Missouri created.

1819—*Western Engineer,* first steamboat in Kansas, carries Stephen H. Long's expedition.

1821—William Becknell opens route of Santa Fe Trail.

1824—Presbyterian mission founded on Neosho River.

1825—Kansa (Kaw) and Osage Indians cede land.

1827—**Fort Leavenworth established.** Daniel Morgan Boone founds Indian school in Jefferson County.

1830—Shawnee Methodist Mission for Indians established near Turner; moved to site near Shawnee in 1839.

1842—John C. Frémont leads first of several expeditions through Kansas. Fort Scott established.

1843—Wide-scale migration to Oregon country begins.

1849—California gold seekers follow Kansas trails.

1853—Fort Riley established.

1854—Kansas-Nebraska Act creates Kansas Territory; temporary capital, Fort Leavenworth; governor, A.H. Reeder. Leavenworth, Lawrence, Atchison, and Topeka founded.

1855—First territorial legislature meets at Pawnee, then at Shawnee Mission; legalizes slavery. Free State party forms separate government. Wakarusa War occurs over slavery.

1856—Proslavery men sack Lawrence. **John Brown leads free-state raiders in massacre along Pottawatomie Creek.**

1857—Proslavery Lecompton Constitution rejected.

1859—Antislavery Wyandotte Constitution adopted. Atchison and Topeka Railroad chartered.

1860—Pony Express crosses Kansas en route to West. First oil well in Kansas drilled near Paola.

1861—Kansas becomes 34th state, January 29; capital, Topeka; governor, Charles Robinson.

1863—Confederates led by William Quantrill sack Lawrence.

1864—University of Kansas organized at Lawrence. Confederate Gen. Sterling Price raids Kansas.

1867—First herd of Texas cattle driven to Kansas.

1874—**Mennonites introduce Turkey Red wheat to U.S.**

1878—Cheyenne raid is last Indian skirmish in state.

1880—Kansas adopts state prohibition amendment.

1899—Carry Nation begins her saloon-smashing raids.

1903—Present State Capitol completed.

1948—Kanopolis Dam on Smoky Hill River completed; Fall River Dam, in 1949; Cedar Bluff Dam on Smoky Hill River, in 1951.

1951—Floods cause great damage.

1952—Dwight D. Eisenhower, who spent his boyhood in Abilene, elected 34th president of U.S.

1954—Eisenhower Museum, adjacent to boyhood home, opens in Abilene; Dwight D. Eisenhower Library founded in Abilene in 1962. In historic Brown *vs.* Topeka Board of Education decision, U.S. Supreme Court bans segregation in public schools.

1956—Construction of Kansas Turnpike completed.

1965—Agricultural Hall of Fame and National Center opened near Kansas City. Fort Scott designated national historic monument.

1976—Mid-American All-Indian Center opens in Wichita.

1988—Severe drought and wind erosion damaged more than 865,000 acres in state; harvests ruined.

1541

1827

1856

1874

STATE FLOWER:
Wild Sunflower

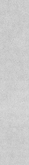

STATE TREE:
Cottonwood

STATE BIRD:
Western Meadowlark

STATE SEAL: Plowman represents
agriculture; steamboat symbolizes
commerce; wagon train, Indians,
and buffalo depict early history.

Kansas Profile

FLAG: *See* Flags of the United States.
MOTTO: Ad Astra per Aspera
(To the Stars Through
Difficulties).
SONG: 'Home on the Range'—words,
Brewster Higley; music, Dan Kelly.

Visitors to the Sunflower State are struck by the extent of its flat terrain. To many Kansans the vast plains are a blessing, for the wealth of the state lies in and under its soil. Record wheat crops are often harvested. Kansas is a leading producer of sorghum, hay, and corn. Plump cattle graze throughout the state. Kansas packinghouses prepare Kansas-bred livestock for national markets. In addition, rich petroleum and natural-gas deposits lie beneath the western part of the state.

The early settlers' conflicting views jeopardized the stability of young Kansas. Proslavery and abolitionist groups fought savagely during the brief territorial years of "bleeding Kansas." Then, after the Civil War, gunmen and outlaws terrorized the cow towns—Dodge City, Abilene, Wichita—that arose at railroad cattle-shipping terminals. With great determination, the people of Kansas survived these trials and brought peace to their land.

Before the settlers staked out Kansas, it was a windswept grassland across which great herds of buffalo roamed. These herds had vanished by the end of the 19th century, destroyed largely by hunters who furnished meat to transcontinental railroad workers. Much of the grass had also disappeared, plowed under by farmers who came to the state from New England and the South.

Modern Kansas has experienced floods and droughts, falling farm prices, and a dwindling of owner-operated farms. Steps have been taken to cope with these problems. Large reservoirs have been built for flood control and irrigation. These also serve as recreational sites. The state has made successful efforts to attract industry and thus provide jobs for displaced farmers. In such cities as Topeka, Kansas City, and Wichita flourishing manufacturing enterprises are preparing the way for the further urbanization of Kansas.

The University of Kansas, at Lawrence, was organized in 1864 and opened two years later. Its campanile, a 53-bell, 120-foot-high war memorial, has been a campus landmark since 1951. Kansas State University, at Manhattan, opened as an agricultural college in 1863.

The State Capitol, built between 1866 and 1903, is in Topeka, one of the largest cities in the Sunflower State. The state legislature has held its sessions at Topeka since 1861. During the restless territorial history of Kansas, lawmakers met at many different sites.

Wichita, the largest city in Kansas, is best known for its aircraft industry. The city is also an agricultural and petroleum center. This is a portion of downtown Wichita.

Kansas rail centers, known as cow towns, flourished until the great cattle drives ended in the 1880's. The jail of the famed Western lawman Wyatt Earp has been restored in Wichita, a former cow town.

181

Eisenhower Chapel

Eisenhower Home

Eisenhower Library

Dwight D. Eisenhower, the 34th president of the United States, spent his boyhood in Kansas. His home in Abilene, now part of the Eisenhower Center, has become a national shrine. The center also includes a chapel, a museum, and a library which houses Eisenhower's military and presidential papers.

Kansans can enjoy water-skiing, camping, and other outdoor activities at state, county, and city parks and lakes. Here a water-skier skims over the surface of Topeka's Shawnee Lake.

Dodge City, in southwestern Kansas, was one of the tough frontier towns that characterized the old West. Today it features replicas of the shops and saloons of the past.

Cavalry troops played an important part in the pacification of Kansas in frontier days. At Fort Riley, birthplace of the United States Seventh Cavalry, the Old Trooper monument honors the horse soldier.

Gypsum Hills, a cluster of curiously eroded rocks, stand in the south-central part of Kansas, near Medicine Lodge. This town became famous as the home of Carry Nation, the prohibitionist saloon wrecker.

During its brief life the Pony Express performed a valuable communications service. This Pony Express station at Hanover was one of the points where the mail-carrying riders changed their horses.

Winter wheat (below) is the most valuable Kansas crop. These huge grain elevators at Hutchinson (left) have a combined capacity of 27 million bushels.

KANSAS FACT SUMMARY

POPULATION TRENDS

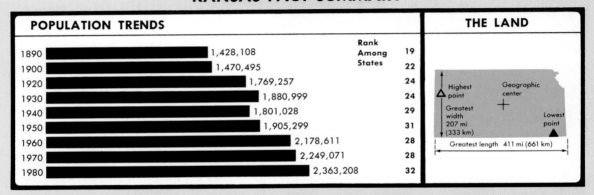

Year	Population	Rank Among States
1890	1,428,108	19
1900	1,470,495	22
1920	1,769,257	24
1930	1,880,999	24
1940	1,801,028	29
1950	1,905,299	31
1960	2,178,611	28
1970	2,249,071	28
1980	2,363,208	32

THE LAND

Highest point
Geographic center
Greatest width 207 mi (333 km)
Lowest point
Greatest length 411 mi (661 km)

LARGEST CITIES (1980 census)

Wichita (279,835): industrial center; flour mills, grain elevators, meat-packing plants, stockyards, oil refineries, airplane factories, railroad shops; Wichita State University; restoration of Wyatt Earp's jail (*see* Wichita).

Kansas City (161,148): industrial city across Missouri River from Kansas City, Mo.; stockyards; grain elevators; oil refineries; meat-packing; flour milling; soap; auto assembly plant (*see* Kansas City, Kan.).

Topeka (115,266): state capital; Kansas State Historical Museum; manufacturing city; railroad shops; flour mills; meat-packing; Menninger Foundation; (*see* Topeka).

Overland Park (81,784): community near Kansas City; dairying.

Lawrence (52,738): flour mills; canning; University of Kansas; Haskell Indian Junior College.

Salina (41,843): trade center; flour mills; Kansas Wesleyan University; Marymount College; Indian Burial Pit nearby.

Hutchinson (40,284): salt mines; oil refineries; flour mills; meat-packing plants; railroad shops.

Olathe (37,258): residential suburb of Kansas City; Mid-America Nazarene College.

Leavenworth (33,656): industrial city in farm area; Fort Leavenworth, federal penitentiary; Saint Mary College.

Manhattan (32,644): farm center; dairy products; Kansas State University; Tuttle Creek Dam nearby.

VITAL STATISTICS 1981 (per 1,000 population)

Birthrate:	16.9
Death Rate:	8.9
Marriage Rate:	11.0
Divorce Rate:	6.1

GOVERNMENT

Capital: Topeka chosen by popular vote in 1861.

Statehood: Became 34th state in the Union on Jan. 29, 1861.

Constitution: Adopted 1859. Amendment may be passed by two-thirds vote of State Legislature; ratified by majority voting on it in an election.

Representation in U.S. Congress: Senate—2. House of Representatives—5. Electoral votes—7.

Legislature: Senators—40; term, 4 years. Representatives—125; term, 2 years.

Executive Officers: Governor—term, 4 years; may succeed himself once. Other officials—lieutenant governor, secretary of state, attorney general; all elected; term, 4 years.

Judiciary: Supreme Court—7 justices appointed by the governor; run for reelection at large; term, 6 years. Court of Appeals—7 judges; term, 4 years. District courts—211 judges; term, 4 years.

County: 105 counties. Governed by a county board of 3 elected commissioners; term, 4 years. Other county officers elected; term, 4 years.

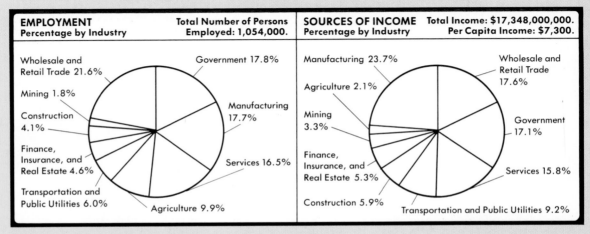

EMPLOYMENT
Percentage by Industry
Total Number of Persons Employed: 1,054,000.

- Wholesale and Retail Trade 21.6%
- Mining 1.8%
- Construction 4.1%
- Finance, Insurance, and Real Estate 4.6%
- Transportation and Public Utilities 6.0%
- Agriculture 9.9%
- Services 16.5%
- Manufacturing 17.7%
- Government 17.8%

SOURCES OF INCOME
Percentage by Industry
Total Income: $17,348,000,000.
Per Capita Income: $7,300.

- Manufacturing 23.7%
- Agriculture 2.1%
- Mining 3.3%
- Finance, Insurance, and Real Estate 5.3%
- Construction 5.9%
- Transportation and Public Utilities 9.2%
- Services 15.8%
- Government 17.1%
- Wholesale and Retail Trade 17.6%

MAJOR PRODUCTS

Agricultural: wheat, corn (maize), sorghum, hay, soybeans, beef cattle and calves, hogs, lambs, sheep, dairy cows.

Manufactured: aircraft; motor vehicles; transportation equipment; farm, garden, and construction equipment; food processing of flour, meal, meat, bakery goods; dairy products; printing and publishing of newspapers, periodicals, books.

Mined: petroleum, natural gas, propane, cement, sand and gravel, salt, coal, limestone, clay and shale.

EDUCATION AND CULTURE

Universities and Colleges: Benedictine College, Atchison; Bethany College, Lindsborg; Friends University, Wichita; Kansas State University, Manhattan; Kansas Wesleyan University, Salina; Marymount College, Salina; Mid-America Nazarene College, Olathe; Ottawa University, Ottawa; Saint Mary College, Leavenworth; University of Kansas, Lawrence; Washburn University of Topeka; Wichita State University, Wichita.

Libraries: Dwight D. Eisenhower Library, Abilene; Kansas State Historical Society Library, Topeka; Kansas State Library, Topeka; Wichita State University Library and Medical Resources Center, Wichita.

Notable Museums: Fort Leavenworth Museum, Leavenworth; Kansas State Historical Society and Museum, Topeka; Martin and Osa Johnson Safari Museum, Inc., Chanute; Museum of Natural History, Lawrence; Santa Fe Trail Center, Larned; Spencer Museum of Art, Lawrence; Systematics Museums University of Kansas, Lawrence; Wichita Art Museum, Wichita; Wichita-Sedgwick County Historical Museum Association, Wichita.

PLACES OF INTEREST

Atchison: historic railroading city; birthplace of Amelia Earhart; Atchison County Museum.

Cedar Bluff State Park: near Ellis; water sports; camping.

Cheyenne Bottoms: near Great Bend; wildlife refuge; hunting, fishing.

Clark State Lake: near Kingsdown; deep canyon of Bluff Creek; fishing, picnicking.

Council Grove: Indian treaty signed for survey of Santa Fe Trail (1825); Kaw Mission, opened in 1849.

Dodge City: former cowboy capital; Boot Hill, gunman cemetery; Front Street, 1870s historic reproduction of main street.

Eisenhower Center (boyhood home, museum, and library): in Abilene; papers and memorabilia of former president.

Fall River State Park: near Fall River; camping, picnicking, water sports.

Fort Hays Historic Site: in Hays; frontier military post (1865).

Fort Larned National Historic Site: in Larned; protected traffic along Santa Fe Trail (1859-78); military base (1868-69).

Fort Leavenworth: near Leavenworth; established in 1827; museum; federal penitentiary on grounds.

Fort Riley: Santa Fe Trail military post (1853); first territorial capitol (1855).

Fort Scott National Historic Site: in Fort Scott; military post established in 1842; restored buildings of U.S. frontier (1840-50s).

Garden City: Finnup Park; Lee Richardson Zoo; State Game Preserve, 4,000 acres (1,619 hectares) of buffalo reserve.

Garden of Eden: in Lucas; Biblical cement and stone figures, allegorical characters built by S. P. Dinsmoor.

Hollenburg Pony Express Station: near Hanover; only original unaltered station extant; museum.

Indian Burial Pit: near Salina; prehistoric artifacts and skeletal remains of Indians over 6 feet (2 meters) tall.

John Brown Memorial Park: in Osawatomie; log-cabin home of abolitionist (1850s).

Kansas Cosmosphere and Discovery Center: in Hutchinson; planetariumlike structure, exhibits on aeronautics, climate, and Earth science.

Kanopolis State Park: near Kanopolis; hiking, water sports, camping.

Kirwin National Wildlife Refuge: near Phillipsburg; recreational reservoir; habitat for various waterfowl species.

Lebanon: near geographic center of 48 contiguous states.

Little House on the Prairie: near Independence; reconstructed log cabin of author Laura Ingalls Wilder; one-room schoolhouse.

Meade: Dalton Gang Hideout, museum, and park; state park.

Meade's Ranch: near Osborne; geodetic center of North America.

Oakley: Fick Fossil Museum, local antiquities and rock collection; Chalk Pyramids, eroded chalk mounds containing reptilian fossils.

Neosho State Lake: near Parsons; artificial lake in deep ravine; water sports.

Pawnee Indian Village: near Courtland; museum built over original earth lodge floor, artifacts, dioramas.

Pawnee Rock: near Great Bend; sandstone cliff landmark on Santa Fe Trail.

Pioneer Adobe House and Museum: near Hillsboro; Mennonite home with antique furnishings, artifacts, farm implements (1880).

Rock City: near Minneapolis; eroded sandstone formations and balanced rocks.

Sedgwick County Zoo: in Wichita; 212 acres (86 hectares), educational zoo featuring simulations of world's wild regions, herpetarium.

Shawnee Methodist Mission: near Kansas City; Indian mission and school established in 1839.

Tuttle Creek State Park: near Manhattan; camping, fishing, picnicking.

BIBLIOGRAPHY FOR KANSAS

Bailey, Bernadine. Picture Book of Kansas, rev. ed. (Whitman, 1969).

Carpenter, Allan. Kansas, rev. ed. (Childrens, 1979).

Desmond, J. Patrick. Kansas Boy (Roush, 1979).

Ise, John. Sod and Stubble; the Story of a Kansas Homestead (Univ. of Neb. Press, 1967).

Unell, Barbara. Kansas City Kid's Catalog (Independence Press, 1980).

Wheeler, Keith. The Scouts (Time-Life, 1978).

Wilder, Laura I. Little House on the Prairie (Harper, 1953).

Writers' Program. Kansas: a Guide to the Sunflower State (Somerset, 1939).

Zornow, W. F. Kansas: a History of the Jayhawk State (Univ. of Okla. Press, 1969).

All Fact Summary data are based on current government reports.

KANSAS

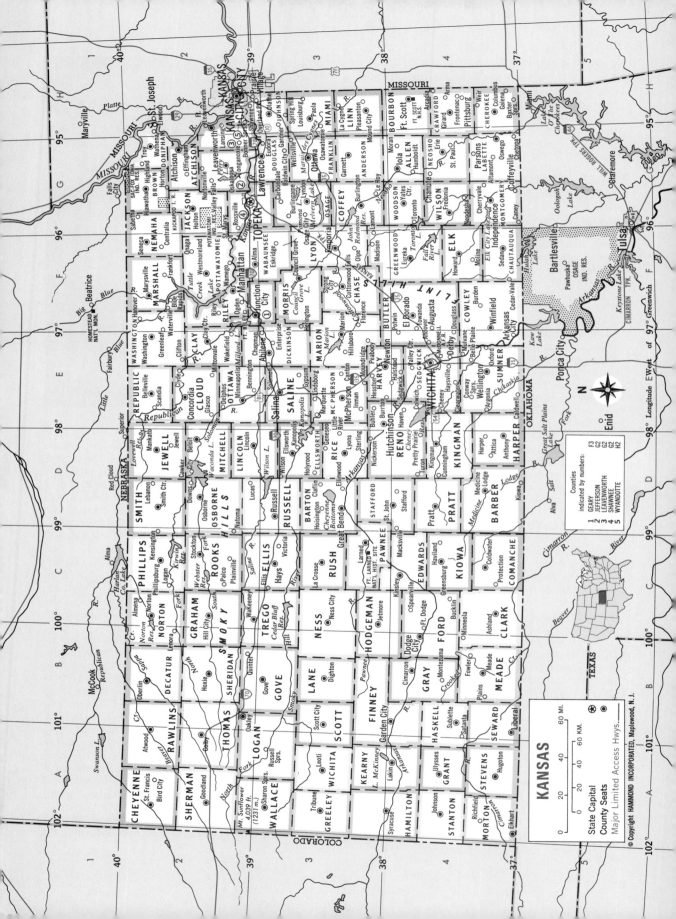

KANSAS

State Capital ⊛

County Seats ◉

Major Limited Access Hwys. ━━━

0   20   40   60 MI.

0   20 40 60 KM.

© Copyright HAMMOND INCORPORATED, Maplewood, N.J.

Counties
indicated by numbers:

1	GEARY	F3
2	JEFFERSON	G2
3	LEAVENWORTH	G2
4	SHAWNEE	G2
5	WYANDOTTE	H2

KANSAS CITY, Kan. Only the state line divides Kansas City, which is the second largest city of Kansas, from its twin city in Missouri. The two cities really comprise one industrial and commercial center. The Kansas metropolis is situated on both sides of the Kansas, or Kaw, River, which is west of Kansas City, Mo. It rises in the west to bluffs and hills where many residences have been built.

The bottomlands in the river valley are devoted to industries and factories. The slaughtering and meat-packing plants are important. Owing to their position among the southwestern corn and beef states, the two Kansas Citys rank high as a livestock market. They also make shortening, soap, and other important by-products of the meat-packing industry.

The advantages of nearby oil and natural gas, combined with excellent railway facilities, were significant in building up the industries of Kansas City, Kan. In addition to its stockyards it has flour and feed mills, grain elevators, and varied food-product plants. It also has oil refineries, iron- and steelworks, foundries, and auto assembly plants, electrical- and transportation-equipment plants, and lumber- and brickyards. There are numerous parks, totaling about 300 acres (121 hectares). Educational institutions include the University of Kansas Medical Center and the Kansas School for the Blind. West of the city the Agricultural Hall of Fame and National Center stands on a 275-acre (111-hectare) site. Modern Kansas City was formed in 1886 by a merger of eight towns. Urban renewal programs were carried out in the second half of the 20th century that modernized the downtown section. The city is governed by a commission form of government. (*See also* Kansas.) Population (1980 census), 161,148.

KANSAS CITY, Mo. Missouri's second largest city is the marketplace and manufacturing center for a vast area of the West and Southwest. It lies on the western boundary of the state, where the Kansas, or Kaw, River enters the waters of the Missouri.

Here the winding Missouri leaves the state border, checks its southward course, and turns sharply eastward. This location has been a natural trading center for more than 100 years. Fur trappers along both rivers brought their pelts to the bend where François Chouteau established a trading post in 1821. Westport Landing grew up nearby. At this transfer point, settlers coming upstream by boat outfitted their wagons for the long journey to the Far West over either the Santa Fe or the Oregon Trail. At first Independence, 10 miles (16 kilometers) to the east, was the main outfitting center. But the great Missouri flood of 1844 destroyed the Independence wharves, and Westport Landing gained most of the Santa Fe trade. In 1853 Westport Landing was renamed City of Kansas, and in 1889 it became Kansas City.

The Liberty Memorial, in Kansas City, Mo., is a 217-foot (66-meter) World War I monument.

Kansas City's industries have developed out of the rich agricultural lands that surround it. Lying between the Western range country, where cattle are raised in large numbers, and the corn belt, where they are fattened, it became a big livestock market and meat-packing center. Important by-products of the meat-packing industry include soap, gelatin, oleomargarine, and leather goods. It is the world's largest winter wheat market. With Kansas City, Kan., its twin city, it is a leading grain and livestock market. Other large industries include bakery and other food products, garmentmaking, printing and publishing, automobile assembling, petroleum refining, and the manufacture of iron and steel, machinery and equipment, cereals, stock feed, and chemicals.

Kansas City is situated on bluffs that rise in terraces above the river bottoms. An extensive boulevard and expressway system links the various parts of the city and the suburbs. In the heart of the city is the Municipal Auditorium, where conventions, stage productions, and sports events are held. The auditorium's Music Hall is the home of the Kansas City Philharmonic Orchestra. Baseball's Kansas City Royals and football's Kansas City Chiefs play in separate stadiums in the Harry S. Truman Sports Complex. The Kansas City Kings basketball team plays in Kemper Arena. The city's Union Station is one of the largest railway terminals in the country. Facing it across a plaza is the shaft of the Liberty Memorial.

The William Rockhill Nelson Gallery of Art and the Mary Atkins Museum of Fine Arts contain notable collections. Nearby is the Kansas City Art Institute and School of Design. Also in the city are the University of Missouri at Kansas City, Rockhurst College, Kansas City College of Osteopathy and Surgery, and Avila College. The Midwest Research Institute is noted for its scientific research. Kansas City International Airport serves the city.

An extensive rebuilding program was begun in the early 1960s. Many government buildings are concentrated in the Civic Center. Kansas City has a council-manager form of government. (*See also* Missouri.) Population (1980 census), 448,159.

KANSAS-NEBRASKA ACT. Passed by Congress in 1854, the Kansas-Nebraska Act has been called the most momentous piece of legislation in the United States before the Civil War. It set in motion events that led directly to the conflict over slavery.

In January 1854, with the support of President Franklin Pierce, Senator Stephen A. Douglas of Illinois laid before the Senate a report of the Committee on Territories. This provided for the organization of the territories of Kansas and Nebraska. The bill allowed the people of these regions to decide for themselves whether they would allow slavery within their borders. The bill as finally enacted into a law expressly repealed the Missouri Compromise, which had prohibited slavery north of latitude 36° 30'. A whole generation had regarded the Missouri Compromise as a binding agreement between the North and the South. (*See also* Missouri Compromise.)

The news that such an act was being considered fell like a thunderbolt upon the people of the North. Ministers preached against the "Nebraska iniquity," and Douglas was accused of weakly yielding to the South in the hope of winning the presidency.

In spite of Northern anger, Congress passed the bill on May 30, 1854. The fight over slavery was then transferred to the two territories. Proslavery men of the South and antislavery men of the North rushed into Kansas. Each side determined to win the state. The first elections, in 1855, were carried by the settlers from the South, aided by the "border ruffians" of Missouri. They crossed the border the night before election and seized the polls, illegally casting their votes for a proslavery candidate for governor.

The settlers from the North refused to accept the results of this fraudulent election. They held an election of their own, at which the proslavery men refused to vote. As a result two rival governments were set up in the territory, and a civil war began. The antislavery party under the leadership of John Brown returned violence for the violence of the proslavery men. The attention of the whole country was fixed on "bleeding Kansas."

The settlers from the South were supported by President Pierce. Eventually he sent United States troops into the territory to quell the disturbance and to disperse the free-state legislature. A new election was then called. Again the illegal methods of the proslavery party won the day. Congress refused to recognize the constitution adopted by such methods as legal, and Kansas was forced to remain a territory for a while longer.

As time went on, the free-state settlers became more numerous, and finally the South gave up the attempt to make Kansas a slave state. A new constitution was then drawn up, and on Jan. 29, 1861, on the eve of the Civil War, Kansas was admitted to the Union as a free state. (*See also* Kansas.)

KANT, Immanuel (1724–1804). The philosopher of the 1700s who ranks with Aristotle and Plato of ancient times is Immanuel Kant. He set forth a chain of explosive ideas that humanity has continued to ponder since his time. He created a link between the idealists—those who thought that all reality was in the mind—and the materialists—those who thought that the only reality lay in the things of the material world. Kant's ideas on the relationship of mind and matter provide the key to understanding the writings of many 20th-century philosophers.

Kant was born on April 22, 1724, in Königsberg, East Prussia, Germany. His father was a saddle and harness maker. Young Kant was the fourth of ten children. He attended school at the Collegium Fredericianum and studied religion and the Latin classics. When he was 16 years old Kant entered the University of Königsberg. He enrolled as a student of theology, but soon became more interested in physics and mathematics.

After leaving college he worked for nine years as a tutor in the homes of wealthy families. In 1755 he earned his doctorate at the university and became a lecturer to university students, living on the small fees his students paid him. He turned down offers from schools that would have taken him elsewhere, and finally the University of Königsberg offered him the position of professor of logic and metaphysics.

Kant never married and he never traveled farther than 50 miles (80 kilometers) from Königsberg. He divided his time among lectures, writing, and daily walks. He was small, thin, and weak, but his ideas were powerful.

Kant's most famous work was the 'Critique of Pure Reason' (published in 1781, revised in 1787). In it he tried to set up the difference between things of the outside world and actions of the mind. He said that things that exist in the world are real, but the human mind is needed to give them order and form and to see the relationships between them. Only the mind can surround them with space and time. The principles of mathematics are part of the space-time thoughts supplied by the mind to real things.

For example, we see only one or two walls of a house at any one time. The mind gathers up these sense impressions of individual walls and mentally builds a complete house. Thus the whole house is being created in the mind while our eyes see only a part of the whole.

Kant said that thoughts must be based on real things. Pure reason without reference to the outside

E. Aubert de la Rüe

world is impossible. We know only what we first gather up with our senses. Yet living in the real world does not mean that ideals should be abandoned. In his 'Critique of Practical Reason' (1788) he argued for a stern morality. His basic idea was in the form of a Categorical Imperative. This meant that humans should act so well that their conduct could give rise to a universal law. Kant died in Königsberg on Feb. 12, 1804. His last words were *Es ist gut,* "It is good."

KAOHSIUNG, Taiwan. A major international port and industrial city in southwestern Taiwan, Kaohsiung is the most rapidly developing urban center in the island country of Taiwan. With an area of 44 square miles (114 square kilometers), it has a splendid natural harbor, though the entrance is narrow, rock-strewn, and in need of dredging.

As an exporting center, Kaohsiung serves the rich agricultural interior of southern Taiwan, as well as the mountains southeast. Major raw material exports include rice, sugar, bananas, pineapples, peanuts (groundnuts), and citrus fruits. The 5,500-acre (2,200-hectare) Linhai Industrial Park, on the waterfront, was completed in the mid-1970s and includes a steel mill, shipyard, petrochemical complex, and other industries. The city has an oil refinery, aluminum and cement works, fertilizer factories, sugar refineries, brick and tile works, and salt-manufacturing plants. There is also a large canning industry that processes both fruit and fish.

In the late 17th century intensive settlement of Kaohsiung, then known as Ch'i'hou, began. Opened in 1863 as a treaty port, Kaohsiung became a customs station in 1864. Its real development started under the Japanese occupation between 1895 and 1945. It was chosen as the southern Taiwan port to serve the areas designated as a major source of raw materials and food for Japan. Kaohsiung became a municipality in 1920. Before and during World War II it handled a growing share of Taiwan's agricultural exports to Japan. It came under Chinese administration in 1945. Population (1980 estimate), 1,242,400.

KAPOK. From the branches of the ceiba tree dangle pods filled with silky fibers called kapok. These fibers are fine, air-filled tubes, valuable for making mattresses, upholstery, lifesaving equipment, and insulation. In life preservers kapok supports 30 times its own weight and is seven times more buoyant than cork. Fiberglass, foam rubber, and other substitutes are replacing kapok in some uses. Highly flammable, kapok can be made reasonably fireproof by a simple chemical treatment.

The ceiba tree grows in all tropical and semitropical climates. It thrives best at altitudes of less than 1,000 feet (300 meters) and on porous volcanic soil.

Almost all the kapok used in the United States is imported from Thailand. Other important producers are Indonesia, Vietnam, Ecuador, the Philippines, and Sri Lanka. Most kapok is obtained from wild trees. A mature tree yields about 7,000 pods, or 60

A mature ceiba tree may provide 7,000 pods filled with silky kapok. The pods can be harvested by cutting or when they fall off.

pounds (27 kilograms) of cleaned floss, and about 135 pounds (61 kilograms) of seeds. The seeds furnish oil for making soap. The down of milkweed can be used as a substitute for kapok (*see* Milkweed).

KARACHI, Pakistan. When Pakistan became a nation in 1947, Karachi in West Pakistan was chosen its first capital. A seaport and airport on the Arabian Sea, northwest of the Indus River Delta, the city grew rapidly as throngs of Muslim refugees arrived from  Hindu India. Today Karachi is the largest city in Pakistan and is the capital of the province of Sind. It is also the nation's principal commercial and industrial center and the terminus of the country's railway system, which mainly is used to transport goods.

The city and its natural harbor are protected from storms by Kiamari Island, Manora Island, and Oyster Rocks. Karachi has hot, humid summers with a mean maximum temperature of about 93° F (34° C) during May and June. The coolest months are January and February, during which the mean minimum temperature is about 56° F (13° C). The average an-

The Masjid-i-Tuba (Tuba Mosque) was built in the 1970s in the Defense Housing Society complex at Karachi.

William Macquitty—Camera Press, London

nual rainfall is about 8 inches (20 centimeters) and falls mostly during June, July, and August.

The chief industries are textiles, footwear, metal products, food and beverages, furniture, machinery, and chemicals. The city is an important center for handicrafts and cottage industries that produce hand-loomed cloth, lace, and carpets; articles made of brass and bell metal (an alloy of copper and tin); and pottery, leather goods, and gold and silver embroidery. Large industrial areas have developed on the western margin of the city. Several oil refineries are nearby, and there is a pipeline to Multan. Karachi handles most of Pakistan's seaborne trade. In the mid-1980s another deep-sea port opened at Qasim, which is 26 miles (42 kilometers) east of Karachi.

In the central part of the city the houses of the British colonial period are characterized by red tiles and deep verandas enclosed by latticed window screens. Some buildings built after independence in 1947 follow contemporary Western design, while others incorporate features of traditional Muslim architecture. Frere Hall, built in 1865, now houses the National Museum and Liaquat Memorial Library. Other libraries are the Karachi University Library and the National Archives Library. The Town Hall, built of red sandstone, is now the seat of city government. Memon Masjid (1960), also on Bundar Road, is a red sandstone mosque that is typical of Muslim architecture, with friezes and screens patterned in intricate mosaic designs.

Karachi has a public school system, but there are many private schools, some of which are associated with religious denominations such as Christianity, Zoroastrianism, and Islam. The University of Karachi (1951), located about 7 miles (11 kilometers) from the city, is the main educational institution. It has more than 20 graduate departments in arts and sciences as well as a school of business administration. In addition the city has colleges of medicine, engineering, home economics, and numerous polytechnic institutes.

Although there is a general shortage of open spaces, Bush Garden is famous for its coconut palms. A zoo is attached to Gandhi Garden. There are swimming and fishing beaches for recreation at Sandspit, Clifton, and Hawksbay. Major sporting events are held at the National Stadium.

In the early 18th century Karachi was a small fishing village called Kalachi-jo-Goth. A group of traders moved there from the decaying port of Kharak Bandar about 16 miles (26 kilometers) west. In 1839 it was captured by the British, who annexed it in 1842 together with the province of Sind. Between 1843 and 1864 a river-steamer service, port improvements, a railway, and a direct telegraph communications link with London were established. With the opening of the Suez Canal in 1869, Karachi became a principal seaport. When the adjoining region of the Punjab emerged as the granary of India in the 1890s, Karachi became the main outlet for its grain. By 1914 the city had become the largest grain-exporting port of the British Empire. Karachi became the provincial capital of Sind in 1936. From 1947 through 1958 it remained the capital of Pakistan. It also grew as an industrial and business center. In 1959 the capital was moved to Rawalpindi and in 1967 to Islamabad. (*See also* Pakistan.) Population (1981 census), 5,208,132.

KARAJAN, Herbert von (1908–89). One of the major conductors of the late 20th century, Herbert von Karajan led the Berlin Philharmonic from 1955 until ill health—and disputes over his responsibilities under a "lifetime" contract—forced him to step down in 1989. During much of that period he also headed the Vienna State Opera and the Salzburg Festival and conducted La Scala Opera in Milan, Italy, and the London Philharmonia. He was a perfectionist, noted for the precision and objectivity of his musical interpretations.

Karajan was born in Salzburg, Austria, on April 5, 1908, into a musically talented family. He played a public piano recital when he was 11 and studied at the Mozarteum in Salzburg and at the Vienna Academy. His early conducting was at the opera houses in Ulm and Aachen, Germany, and then at the Berlin State Opera from 1938 to 1944. Although he joined the Nazi party in 1933, Karajan was cleared of any crime by an Allied tribunal after World War II but was barred from conducting for two years. His first appearance in the United States in 1955, however, was greeted by public protest.

Karajan was one of the first conductors of the Austro-German school to perform a wide range of

191

repertory. He is particularly regarded for his recordings of all of the symphonies of Beethoven, Brahms, and Schumann, though his extensive recordings include a wide representation of all schools.

KARAKORAM RANGE. One of the highest mountain systems in the world, the Karakoram Range of Central Asia extends southeastward some 300 miles (480 kilometers) from the easternmost part of Afghanistan. The borders of the Soviet Union, China, Pakistan, Afghanistan, and India all converge within the system.

The range's average height is about 20,000 feet (6,100 meters), and four peaks exceed 26,000 feet (7,900 meters), the highest being K2 (Mount Godwin Austen) at 28,250 feet (8,611 meters) (*see* K2). The Karakorams are characterized by craggy peaks, steep slopes, and heavy glaciation. The melted water from snow and glaciers forms the headwaters of the Indus and Tarim rivers.

The high-altitude vegetation varies. On the drier northern-facing slopes, vast areas are completely devoid of vegetation. In scattered areas are found certain flowering plants, thickets of brushwood, some poplar trees, coarse grasses, and wintergreen. On the more moist, southern-facing slopes are forests of pine and Himalayan cedar, and higher up, alpine meadows. Near streams and lakes are willows and poplars, and some sections have been developed as pastures, crop farms, and apricot orchards. Animal life of the region includes the snow leopard, wild yak, and Tibetan antelope.

The Karakorams are extremely inaccessible. The exceptionally severe natural conditions make life hard for humans. Approximately 25,000 Tibetans live in villages at altitudes of up to 14,800 feet (4,500 meters). Most are farmers who grow barley, oats, and millet and who breed cattle. Some nomadic peoples also live on the Karakoram slopes.

KÁRMÁN, Theodore von (1881–1963). Scientist, teacher, research organizer, and promoter of international scientific cooperation, Theodore von Kármán was one of the great research engineers of the 20th century. He pioneered the use of mathematics and the basic sciences in aeronautics and astronautics.

Kármán was born on May 11, 1881, in Budapest, Hungary. He demonstrated a natural mathematical facility at an early age, and his father guided him toward a career in engineering. He completed his undergraduate education at the Royal Polytechnic University in Budapest in 1902. He did graduate work at the University of Göttingen, Germany, and at the University of Paris. He returned to Göttingen to assist with dirigible research. He became especially interested in the ideas of the renowned mathematician Felix Klein, who stressed mathematics and the basic sciences in engineering to increase technological efficiency. Kármán became one of the first to apply mathematics to the study of turbulence, or irregular motion of a gas or liquid.

In 1912 he became director of the Aeronautical Institute at Aachen, Germany. While serving at the Military Aircraft Factory at Fischamend, Austria, during World War I, he led the development of a helicopter having two propellers that rotated in opposite directions. As Kármán's international reputation grew after the war, the institute increasingly attracted more students. In 1922 Kármán organized an international congress on aerodynamics and hydrodynamics at Innsbruck, Austria. During the 1920s he traveled as a lecturer and consultant to industry.

In 1930 Kármán became director of the Guggenheim Aeronautical Laboratory at the California Institute of Technology (CIT), and it soon became a world center of aeronautical sciences. He also directed the Guggenheim Airship Institute at Akron, Ohio, and was a founder of the United States Institute of Aeronautical Sciences.

In 1941 Kármán participated in the founding of a corporation for the manufacture of liquid- and solid-propellant rocket engines. Three years later he became the cofounder of the Jet Propulsion Laboratory at CIT when it undertook the first governmental long-range missile and space exploration research program in the United States. The program was later to become part of the National Aeronautics and Space Administration (NASA). Kármán also conceived the idea of cooperation among aeronautical engineers of the member nations of the North Atlantic Treaty Organization (NATO). Between 1960 and 1963 he led NATO-sponsored studies on the interaction of science and technology. He made scientific contributions to the areas of fluid mechanics, turbulence theory, supersonic flight, mathematics in engineering, aircraft structures, and wind erosion of soil. Kármán became a United States citizen in 1936, and in 1963 Pres. John F. Kennedy presented him with the first National Medal of Science. Kármán died on May 6, 1963, in Aachen, West Germany.

KASHMIR *see* JAMMU AND KASHMIR.

KATHMANDU, Nepal. The capital of Nepal and the country's most important business and commercial center is Kathmandu. Located at the point where the Baghmati and Vishnumati rivers meet, the city lies at an altitude of 4,344 feet (1,324 meters).

Kathmandu was founded as Manju-Patan in 723. Its present name refers to a wooden temple said to have been built from the wood of a single tree in 1596. Supposedly the original building still stands in the central square. Another notable building is the 16th-century durbar, or palace, of the Malla kings. After a severe earthquake in 1934, many modern-style buildings were constructed in the city. Tribhuvan University was chartered in 1959.

In the 1970s, after construction of new roads and expansion of air service, Kathmandu became the hub of the national transportation system, which for centuries had been limited to footpaths. Population (1981 census), 235,211. (*See also* Nepal.)

KAUNDA, Kenneth (born 1924). When he was elected Zambia's first president in 1964, Kenneth Kaunda promised to establish a "color-blind society." But racial tensions in neighboring Rhodesia (now Zimbabwe) spilled over into Zambia, making the pledge difficult to keep.

Kenneth David Kaunda was born in 1924 in Chinsali, Northern Rhodesia (now Zambia). He was educated in mission schools where his parents taught, under the auspices of the Church of Scotland. He trained to be a teacher, but the racism he encountered among white settlers led him to become politically active by joining the African National Congress in 1949. Ten years later a clash over strategy split the Congress, and Kaunda founded the Zambia African National Congress. His inspired opposition to British colonial policies made him the leader of Zambia's independence movement.

In 1960 Kaunda, after a period of imprisonment, was elected president of the new United National Independence party. Within the year Britain had announced that the formal decolonization of Zambia would begin. Pressures from the white European settlers, numbering about 77,000, and the Asian community of 11,000 failed to delay decolonization, and Zambia became an independent nation in 1964.

As president, Kaunda faced a number of grave domestic problems: intertribal rivalries, civil wars in neighboring Angola and Rhodesia, and near economic collapse of his nation. In 1972 he imposed one-party rule, and in 1976 he was forced to assume emergency powers. Reelected for a fourth term in 1978, he played a mediating role in the conflicts in southern Africa, but failure to meet economic goals was a persistent cause of unrest within Zambia.

KAWABATA, Yasunari (1899–1972). The works of the Japanese novelist Yasunari Kawabata are filled with a sense of loneliness and thoughts of death. This melancholy type of writing probably stemmed from the fact that his parents and grandparents died when he was very young.

Kawabata was born near Osaka on June 11, 1899. His first novel appeared in 1925, shortly after he graduated from Tokyo Imperial University. Entitled 'The Izu Dancer', it is the story of a lonely university student who seeks friendship and consolation in the companionship of a strolling dancer. The book is a compilation of lyrical episodes without a clear beginning, middle, or end. It is full of abrupt transitions and startlingly contrasting images of the ugly and the beautiful. Kawabata apparently intended the reader to appreciate the quality of the episodes instead of viewing the work as a whole. His style is somewhat similar to post-World War I French impressionist writing as well as to Japanese literary prose and poetic traditions of earlier centuries.

Kawabata took a long time to write a book. His best novel, 'Snow Country', was begun in 1935 and completed in 1947. The sequel to it, 'Thousand Cranes', was started in 1949 and never completed.

'The Sound of the Mountain' took six years to complete, from 1949 to 1954. These novels, too, are stories of lonely and alienated individuals who seek comfort in occasionally unlikely relationships.

Kawabata was awarded the Nobel prize for literature in 1968. On April 16, 1972, in Zushi, he killed himself, perhaps because he was upset over the suicide of fellow writer Mishima Yukio.

KAZAKH SOVIET SOCIALIST REPUBLIC. The Kazakhs are a Muslim people who once wandered over the grasslands of Central Asia with their herds. In the 19th century the Russians invaded their territory, which eventually became the second largest republic of the Soviet Union. The Kazakh Soviet Socialist Republic, also known as Kazakhstan, has become an important agricultural, mining and industrial region with a large Russian population.

The Land and Climate

Kazakhstan covers a vast area of more than a million square miles (2.6 million square kilometers) and extends 1,200 miles (1,900 kilometers) from west to east. The northern part consists of grasslands, while most of the south and center is covered by semidesert and desert. The central and eastern areas contain the Kazakh Uplands and the western ranges of the Altay and other Central Asian mountains. In the south the Karatau Mountains divide two areas of sandy desert—the Kyzyl-Kum and the Muyun-Kum. In the southwest the Mangyshlak Peninsula extends into the Caspian Sea. Kazakhstan is crossed by several large rivers. The Irtysh flows north to Siberia; the Ili empties into Lake Balkhash; and the Syrdar'ya crosses the desert to reach the Aral Sea. The Ural and Emba rivers flow to the Caspian Sea.

The climate is continental, with warm summers and cold winters. July temperatures generally average between 70° and 80° F (21° and 27° C) and January temperatures between 20° and 0° F (-7° and -18° C). Precipitation in the north averages less than 15 inches (380 millimeters) and in the south less than 8 inches (200 millimeters) a year.

The People

The Kazakhs, a Turkic-speaking people, were traditionally nomads who grazed their horses, sheep, and camels on the northern grasslands during the summer and on the pastures to the south of the deserts in the winter. In the 1930s they resisted the collectivization of their herds by the Soviet authorities, and in the subsequent fighting many Kazakhs were killed. After the Soviet conquest, most gave up their nomadic life for work on farms and in industry.

Russians number about 5,991,000, or 41 percent, of the republic's population of 14,684,000 (1979 census). Only 5,289,000, or 36 percent, are Kazakhs. There are also 900,000 Germans and 898,000 Ukrainians in Kazakhstan. Some 1,267,000 Kazakhs live outside their republic in other parts of the Soviet Union.

The traditional culture of the Kazakhs consists of stories and folk poems. Because of their nomadic life they had little written literature and art, except carpet weaving. Now there are Kazakh writers and artists. The main center of culture is the capital city of Alma-Ata with its theaters, museums, libraries, and a university and technical institutes.

Economy and Transportation

Although herding of livestock still continues, the agriculture of Kazakhstan has changed dramatically since the Soviets established collective and state farms in the 1930s. In the 1950s large numbers of settlers emigrated from European Russia to plow up the "Virgin Lands," the untouched grasslands of northern Kazakhstan. This area has become a major producer of grain for the Soviet Union. In the south cotton is grown on irrigated land. Fruits and vegetables are also produced.

Kazakhstan is one of the richest areas of mineral deposits in the Soviet Union. Coal is mined at Karaganda and Ekibastuz, oil is extracted on the north Caspian coast and the Mangyshlak Peninsula, and some natural gas is exploited. Iron ore, copper, manganese, chromite, lead, zinc, bauxite, gold, and other minerals are also mined.

An iron and steel industry is located at Karaganda. The smelting of metallic ores is an important activity at Ust-Kamenogorsk, Chimkent, Aktyubinsk, and other towns. Engineering plants are located in Alma-Ata, Chimkent, and Pavlodar. The chemical fertilizer industry is also important. Electric power is supplied by hydroelectric plants on the Irtysh, as well as by coal-burning plants.

For such a large territory the transportation network is sparse. A line runs from the Trans-Siberian Railroad south to Karaganda and Alma-Ata. Another line from Alma-Ata joins Central Asia with the industrial area of western Siberia. A line links the port of Gur'yev on the Caspian Sea with the Ural region. The densest railroad network is in northern Kazakhstan and is used to transport grain. The highway system is not well developed, and most freight moves by rail. The Irtysh, Ili, and Ural rivers are navigable, and there is some shipping on the Aral Sea. The major port on the Caspian Sea is Gur'yev. Flights from Alma-Ata and Aktyubinsk link Kazakhstan with other cities of the Soviet Union.

Government and History

The Kazakh republic has its own government and Communist party, but they have little power and are directed by the central government at Moscow. Before the territory was invaded, the Kazakhs were organized in three major groups known as hordes.

These hordes were gradually pushed out of the grasslands by the advance of the Russians from the north.

In 1854 the Russians reached southern Kazakhstan and founded the fort of Verny, now Alma-Ata. After the October Revolution of 1917, the Kazakhs attempted to establish an independent state, but in 1920 the Red Army entered Kazakhstan and declared it an autonomous Soviet republic. In 1936 it became the Kazakh Soviet Socialist Republic.

KEAN, Edmund (1789–1833). One of the three great English tragic actors of all time was Edmund Kean. He ranked with actors David Garrick and Sir Henry Irving and was especially known for his portrayal of the title role in Shakespeare's 'Othello'.

Edmund Kean was born on March 17, 1789, in London. He had a troubled childhood and at 15 set off on his own, joining a theater company. Ten years later he made his Drury Lane Theatre debut as Shylock in Shakespeare's 'Merchant of Venice'.

Kean acted in the so-called naturalistic style: He rejected static poses in favor of ease of movement, and he preferred beautiful recitation to passionate speeches. He gave the illusion of being rather than playing a character. His performances were carefully planned and carried out, and he had a lasting and profound influence on the art of acting. His magnetic power and ability to dominate the stage has possibly never been equaled.

In 1808 he married actress Mary Chambers. They had two sons, Howard and Charles. Edmund led an unfortunate personal life that included alcoholism and well-known public emotional outbursts. He collapsed during a performance at London's Covent Garden on March 25, 1833, and died two months later at his home in Richmond, Surrey.

KEARNY, Stephen Watts (1794–1848). United States Army officer Stephen Watts Kearny seized New Mexico and helped capture California from Mexico. He was born in Newark, N.J., on Aug. 30, 1794. During service in the War of 1812 he was promoted to captain and thereafter made the army his career. He spent most of the next 30 years on frontier duty, and in 1846 he was made commander of the Army of the West and promoted to the rank of brigadier general. At the outbreak of the Mexican War in May 1846, he was ordered to conquer New Mexico and California. He and his 2,700 men entered Santa Fe unopposed on August 18, and he established a new civil government for the territory. On September 25 Kearny left for California to help Commander Robert F. Stockton and Colonel John C. Frémont deal with the territory, which they had already conquered. Clashes between Frémont and Kearny led to court-martial for Frémont (see Frémont).

Kearny was then ordered to Mexico to become military commander of Veracruz. While there he contracted yellow fever. He returned to the United States in 1848 as a major general, but poor health led to his death on Oct. 31, 1848, in St. Louis, Mo.

KEATS, John (1795–1821). "Here lies one whose name was writ in water." This is the epitaph that the poet John Keats prepared for himself. He thought of it in the dark days when he felt death drawing near and despaired of winning fame. His whole poetical career had lasted only seven years. During this brief period he had written some of the greatest poems in the English language.

John Keats was born in London, England, on Oct. 31, 1795. His father was a livery-stable keeper. He did not spend his early years close to nature, as did many poets, but in the city of London. There was, however, born in him an intense love of beauty. "A thing of beauty is a joy forever" is the first line of his 'Endymion'. In the "Ode on a Grecian Urn," in which he seems to have caught much of the ancient Greeks' worship of beauty, he declares:

> Beauty is truth, truth beauty,—that is all
> Ye know on earth, and all ye need to know.

Unlike his contemporaries Percy Bysshe Shelley and William Wordsworth, Keats had no desire to reform the world or to teach a lesson. He was content if he could make his readers see and hear and feel with their own senses the forms, colors, and sounds that his imagination brought forth.

Keats was apprenticed to a surgeon in his youth and studied surgery faithfully for six years, but his heart was elsewhere. "I find I cannot exist without poetry," he wrote, "—without eternal poetry." In 1816 he became acquainted with Leigh Hunt, and through Hunt with Shelley. The next year, at 22, he gave up his profession and devoted the rest of his short life entirely to the writing of poetry.

In 1818 his first long poem, 'Endymion', appeared. It was harshly attacked by the reviewers of the day, who failed to see that its faults were due to immaturity. Other troubles also crowded upon the young poet. He was in money difficulties, and he was tormented by a hopeless love affair. His health had begun to fail. He rapidly developed tuberculosis. In the autumn of 1820 he went to Italy with his friend Joseph Severn. He died in Rome on Feb. 23, 1821.

Keats's chief poems are: 'Endymion'; "Lines on the Mermaid Tavern"; "Isabella, or The Pot of Basil"; "On a Summer's Day"; "The Eve of Saint Agnes"; "La Belle Dame sans Merci"; "Ode to a Nightingale"; "Ode to Autumn"; "Lamia"; and 'Hyperion'. Among his sonnets are "On First Looking into Chapman's Homer" and "When I Have Fears That I May Cease to Be."

KEKKONEN, Urho (1900–86). When he stepped down from the presidency of Finland in 1981, Kekkonen was his nation's most popular political figure. His administration was most noted for its policy of "active neutrality," which enabled Finland to live peaceably with its powerful neighbor, the Soviet Union. His goal was to mesh his foreign policy with that of the Soviets in such a way as to leave Finland free to conduct its own affairs without undue outside influence. One of his major achievements was arranging the Conference on Security and Cooperation in Europe in August 1975, a meeting that produced the Helsinki Accords (*see* Bill of Rights).

Urho Kaleva Kekkonen was born on Sept. 3, 1900. He studied law at the University of Helsinki and held many elected and appointed posts including serving as a member of parliament from 1936 to 1956, prime minister for five terms, minister of the interior, and minister of justice.

It was during World War II, when Finland was invaded twice by the Soviet Union, that Kekkonen began to realize the need for a policy that would guarantee his country's independence, while not causing any unnecessary irritation to the Soviets. This view had become the basis of Finnish foreign policy under Kekkonen's predecessor, President Juho Paasikivi, after Finland signed a friendship treaty with the Soviet Union in 1948. When Kekkonen was elected president in 1956, he carefully followed the same pattern of diplomacy. Kekkonen was reelected to three six-year terms. His third term was extended four years by an act of parliament. He resigned in 1981 because of declining health.

KELLER, Helen (1880–1968). "Once I knew only darkness and stillness. . . . My life was without past or future. . . . But a little word from the fingers of another fell into my hand that clutched at emptiness, and my heart leaped to the rapture of living." This is how Helen Keller described the beginning of her "new life," when despite blindness and deafness she learned to communicate with others.

Helen Adams Keller was born on June 27, 1880, in Tuscumbia, Ala. Nineteen months later she had a severe illness that left her blind and deaf. Her parents had hope for her. They had read Charles Dickens' report of the aid given to another blind and deaf girl, Laura Bridgman. When Helen was six years old, her parents took her to see Alexander Graham Bell,

Helen Keller

Courtesy of the American Foundation for the Blind

famed teacher of the deaf and inventor of the telephone (*see* Bell, Alexander Graham). As a result of his advice, Anne Mansfield Sullivan began to teach Helen on March 3, 1887. Until her death in 1936 she remained Helen's teacher and constant companion. Sullivan had been almost blind in early life, but her sight had been partially restored.

Helen soon learned the finger-tip, or manual, alphabet as well as braille. By placing her sensitive fingers on the lips and throat of her teachers, she felt their motions and learned to "hear" them speak. Three years after mastering the manual alphabet, she learned to speak herself.

At the age of 20 she was able to enter Radcliffe College. She received her Bachelor of Arts degree in 1904 with honors. She used textbooks in braille, and Sullivan attended classes with her, spelling the lectures into her hand.

Keller helped to found the Massachusetts Commission for the Blind and served on the commission. She raised more money for the American Foundation for the Blind than any other person. She lectured widely and received honors and awards from foreign governments and international bodies.

At her home near Easton, Conn., she wrote and worked for the blind and deaf. She died at her home on June 1, 1968.

Keller's writing reveals her interest in the beauty of things taken for granted by those who can see and hear. Her books include 'The Story of My Life' published in 1903; 'Optimism' (1903); 'The World I Live In' (1908); 'Out of the Dark' (1913); 'Midstream: My Later Life' (1929); 'Journal' (1938); and 'Let Us Have Faith' (1940).

KELLY, Ned (1855–80). The most notorious of the Australian outlaws known as bushrangers, Kelly was a gang leader who started his criminal career by stealing horses and cattle. The bushrangers lived in the Australian Outback, or bush, and traveled on horseback to raid country towns and isolated settlements.

Ned Kelly was born at Wallan, Victoria, in June 1855, the son of a criminal who had been transported from Belfast, Ireland (now in Northern Ireland) in 1842. Wanted for horse stealing in Victoria in 1877, Ned fled to New South Wales and joined his brother Dan, also a fugitive. Together with two other bushrangers, Joe Byrne and Steve Hart, they formed what became known as the Kelly gang.

These men, like other bushrangers, were motivated by a desire for gain and by a great hatred of the police. In October 1878 the gang killed three policemen in a patrol party. In spite of a large reward offered for their capture, they roamed New South Wales and Victoria for two years, robbing banks and small towns. In June 1880 they took possession of the town of Glenrowan. They were besieged by police, and all members of the gang were killed except for Ned Kelly. He was captured and sent to Melbourne for trial. He was executed there on Nov. 11, 1880.

KELVIN, Lord (1824–1907). William Thomson, who became Lord Kelvin of Largs (Scotland) in 1892, was one of Great Britain's foremost scientists and inventors. He published more than 650 scientific papers and patented some 70 inventions. He is known for developing a temperature scale in which $-273.15°$ C ($-459.67°$ F) is absolute zero. The scale is known as the absolute, or Kelvin, temperature scale.

William Thomson was born on June 26, 1824, in Belfast, Ireland. The family moved to Glasgow, Scotland, in 1832, and young Thomson entered the university there when he was 10. He was a brilliant student. By the time he was 21 he had studied in Glasgow, Cambridge (England), and Paris and had published 12 scientific papers.

In 1846 he became a professor of natural philosophy at Glasgow. There he established the first physics laboratory in Great Britain. His investigations into the properties of matter made him famous.

Thomson supervised the laying of the first transatlantic cable in 1866. To improve cable communication, he also invented and put into use the mirror galvanometer for signaling and the siphon recorder for receiving. For his work he was knighted by Queen Victoria. (*See also* Cable.)

Sir William traveled widely in Europe and the United States, lecturing at Johns Hopkins University in Baltimore, Md., in 1884. He had an interest in yachting and the sea that inspired him to invent, patent, and manufacture a compass used by the British admiralty, a calculating machine that measured tides, and sounding, or depth-measuring, equipment. He co-authored the textbook 'Treatise on Natural Philosophy', which was published in 1867 and was a major influence on future physicists.

Before his death at Largs on Dec. 17, 1907, Lord Kelvin had become an honorary member of many foreign academies and held honorary degrees from many well-known universities. He served as president of the Royal Society from 1890 to 1895.

Lord Kelvin in a painting by Elizabeth King

Courtesy of the National Portrait Gallery, London

JOHN F. KENNEDY—
35th President of
the United States

KENNEDY, John F. (1917–63; president 1961–63). In November 1960, at the age of 43, John F. Kennedy became the youngest man ever elected president of the United States. Theodore Roosevelt had become president at 42 when President William McKinley was assassinated, but he was not elected at that age. On Nov. 22, 1963, Kennedy was shot to death in Dallas, Tex., the fourth United States president to die by an assassin's bullet.

Kennedy was the nation's first Roman Catholic president. He was inaugurated in January 1961, succeeding Republican President Dwight D. Eisenhower. He defeated the Republican candidate, Vice-President Richard M. Nixon, by little more than 100,000 votes. It was one of the closest elections in the nation's history. Although more than 68 million votes were cast, Kennedy and his vice-presidential running mate, Lyndon B. Johnson, got less than half of them. Kennedy thus became the 14th minority president.

Because of the close vote, election results were challenged in many states. The official electoral vote was Kennedy 303, Nixon 219, and Senator Harry F. Byrd of Virginia 15.

Kennedy's Family

President Kennedy's great-grandparents immigrated to the United States from Ireland in 1858. They settled in Boston, Mass. His grandfathers, Patrick J. Kennedy and John F. ("Honey Fitz") Fitzgerald, were born there. Both men became influential in state politics. "Honey Fitz" served several terms as Boston's mayor and as a member of the United States House of Representatives. Patrick Kennedy was a powerful ward boss and served in both houses of the Massachusetts legislature.

Patrick's son, Joseph, was a brilliant mathematician. At the age of 25 he became the youngest bank president in the United States. His fortune continued to grow, and he was one of the few financiers to sense the stock market crash of 1929. He made hundreds of millions of dollars.

Joseph married Rose Fitzgerald, daughter of Honey Fitz, Oct. 7, 1914. Their first child, Joseph, Jr., was born in 1915. John was born May 29, 1917. Seven other children followed: Rosemary, Kathleen,

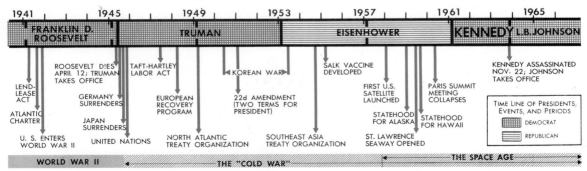

An active athlete, John Kennedy played football (left) at Dexter School, in Brookline, Mass., and was a star swimmer (cen-ter) at Harvard University in 1938. He served courageously as a naval officer (right) during World War II.

Eunice, Patricia, Robert, Jean, and Edward (called Teddy). All were born in Brookline, Mass., which is a suburb of Boston.

Training Pays Off

Joseph Kennedy, Sr., set up a million-dollar trust fund for each of his children. This freed them from future financial worry and allowed them to devote their lives to public good, if they desired. As the children grew, their parents stressed the importance of competitive spirit. One of their father's favorite mottoes was: "Second place is a loser." The drive to win was deeply embedded in the children, and they never did anything halfheartedly.

Their parents were careful to neglect neither the intellectual nor the physical development of the children. As they grew older, the children would eat their evening meals in two groups, divided by age. Mr. and Mrs. Kennedy ate at both meals. This allowed them to discuss subjects which were of interest to each group. All the children attended dancing school while very young, and all, with the exception of Rosemary, loved sports activities. Rosemary did not take part in rough-and-tumble play. The other children, however, thrived on it. Even when they were adults, one of their favorite pastimes was a rousing and often bruising game of touch football.

On pleasant days, Mrs. Kennedy took her children for long walks. She made a point of taking them into church for a visit each day. "I wanted them to form a habit of making God and religion a daily part of their lives," she said later in life.

With this background, it was quite natural for John Kennedy and his brothers and sisters to excel in school and in sports. John attended public schools in Brookline. Later he entered private schools in Riverdale, N. Y., and Wallingford, Conn. In 1935 and 1936 he studied at the London School of Economics. Then he followed his older brother, Joe, into Harvard University. An excellent athlete, John was a star swimmer and a good golfer. His athletic activities, however, were cut down after he suffered a back injury in a Harvard football game. The injury was to plague him later in life.

John and his older brother were very close. While a young boy, Joe said that someday he would be president of the United States. The family took him at his word. Of all the children Joe seemed the one most likely to enter the political field.

Joseph, Sr., was named ambassador to Great Britain in 1937. John and his older brother then worked as international reporters for their father. John spent his summers in England and much of the rest of his time at Harvard. The brothers often traveled to distant parts of the world to observe events of international importance for their father. The clouds of World War II were hovering over Europe at that time.

Return to the United States and College

The senior Kennedy was a controversial ambassador. His candid remarks about the progress of the

KENNEDY'S ADMINISTRATION
1961–1963

Peace Corps established (1961)
Alliance for Progress announced (1961)
23d Amendment adopted (1961)
First United States astronaut orbits earth (1962)
Trade Expansion Act passed (1962)
Nuclear test ban treaty (1963)
Kennedy assassinated (Nov. 22, 1963)

war in Europe earned him the disfavor of the English and of some of his countrymen in the United States. His family returned home in 1939, and he followed the next year.

John finished his studies at Harvard and was graduated with honors in 1940. Later that same year he did graduate work in economics at Stanford University. He also expanded a college thesis into a full-length book entitled 'Why England Slept'. It dealt with England's unpreparedness for World War II and was based on John's own experiences while working for his father. The book became a best seller.

Serves with Navy in the Pacific

A few months before the Japanese attacked Pearl Harbor in December 1941, John attempted to enlist in the United States Army. His old back injury kept him from being accepted. After several months of exercise, he was granted a commission in the Navy. Eventually he became the commander of a torpedo boat and saw extensive action in the South Pacific.

In August 1943, during a night action in the Solomon Islands, John's torpedo boat was rammed and cut in half by a Japanese destroyer. The force of the collision threw him to the deck, reinjuring his back. Despite this, he gathered the ten members of his crew together. One of the crew members was so badly injured that he was unable to swim. He was put into a life jacket.

Kennedy gripped one of the jacket's straps between his teeth and towed the man as the crew swam to a nearby island. It took them five hours to reach it. For his heroism, Kennedy was awarded the Navy and Marine Corps medal, the Purple Heart, and a citation. The back injury, however, put him out of action for the remainder of the war.

Nearly one year after John's narrow escape, Joe, Jr., a Navy pilot, was killed when his plane exploded in the air over the English coast. To his brother's memory John wrote 'As We Remember Joe', a collection of tributes. In 1948 John's sister Kathleen died in an airplane crash in the south of France. She

In his father's spacious summer home (bottom center) at Hyannis Port, Mass., on Cape Cod, Kennedy spent the early years of the 1930's. Later he occupied the home at top center with his own family.

was the widow of the marquess of Hartington of England. He too had been killed in action during World War II, while leading an infantry charge in Normandy, France.

Begins Political Career

The death of his brother deeply affected John Kennedy. Before the war Joe had decided to carry on with his ambition to enter politics. This caused a certain degree of disappointment for John, because he too had considered that field. He felt, however, that one Kennedy in politics was enough and determined to become a newspaperman. After his discharge from the Navy he worked for a short time as a correspondent for the *Chicago Herald American* and the International News Service. In 1946 he decided to take up where his older brother had left off

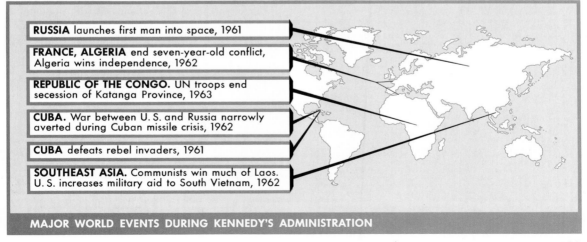

RUSSIA launches first man into space, 1961

FRANCE, ALGERIA end seven-year-old conflict, Algeria wins independence, 1962

REPUBLIC OF THE CONGO. UN troops end secession of Katanga Province, 1963

CUBA. War between U. S. and Russia narrowly averted during Cuban missile crisis, 1962

CUBA defeats rebel invaders, 1961

SOUTHEAST ASIA. Communists win much of Laos. U. S. increases military aid to South Vietnam, 1962

MAJOR WORLD EVENTS DURING KENNEDY'S ADMINISTRATION

and enter politics. To the family this was the most natural thing for him to do.

For his first target, Kennedy chose to try for a seat in the United States House of Representatives. He would represent the 11th Massachusetts Congressional District. His family rallied to his side as he began his campaign for the nomination. Because the 11th district was predominantly Democratic, the candidate for the office would have no trouble being elected once he had gained the nomination. Kennedy and his family worked tirelessly. Their efforts, Kennedy's own impressive war record, and his family's political background greatly aided his campaign. He easily defeated eight other candidates running for the same nomination.

In office, Kennedy quickly established himself as a moderately independent thinker. Occasionally he voted against proposed measures which had met with the approval of his own Democratic party. He was re-elected in 1948 and 1950. An accomplished orator, the young congressman became a popular speaker.

His back injury, however, continued to bother him. He often appeared on the House floor and at speaking engagements supported by crutches. In 1946 he was named by the United States Chamber of Commerce as one of the nation's outstanding men of the year.

Elected to the Senate

In 1952 Kennedy decided to run for the United States Senate. His opponent was Republican senator Henry Cabot Lodge, Jr. Again the Kennedy family worked side by side to get John elected. Kennedy defeated Lodge by more than 70,000 votes. The victory was particularly impressive because across the rest of the nation Republican candidates were swept into office along with the landslide of votes for the new Republican president, Dwight D. Eisenhower.

During their courtship, John Kennedy and his fiancée, Jacqueline Lee Bouvier, enjoyed sailing this small boat.

In the Senate Kennedy had woolen textile tariffs raised and urged President Eisenhower to obtain an agreement with Japan to cut textile imports. The president agreed to do so. Kennedy helped pass several other measures important to Massachusetts' textile industry. He also sponsored bills which improved his state's conservation programs.

One of the many committees Kennedy served on was the Select Committee of the Senate to Investigate Improper Activities in Labor-Management Relations. His younger brother Robert was chief legal counsel for this group. The two Kennedys were frequently in the public eye in 1959 as the committee investigated racketeering among top labor union officials. As a result of these hearings, John sponsored a labor bill which did a great deal to eliminate criminal practices in unions.

Weds Long Island Beauty

Kennedy met his future wife, Jacqueline Lee Bouvier, at a Washington, D.C., party shortly after his election to the Senate. Described as a cameo beauty, "Jackie" was the daughter of a Long Island family. At the time they met, she was a photographer and a pen-

The president chats with his younger brothers, Robert (left) and Teddy (center). The oldest Kennedy son, Joseph, was killed in action in World War II.

and-ink artist for a Washington, D. C. newspaper. They were married on Sept. 12, 1953. Their daughter, Caroline, was born in 1957. Their son, John Fitzgerald, was born on Nov. 25, 1960, 17 days after Kennedy was elected president of the United States. As wife of the president, Jackie became one of the most gracious and most beautiful White House hostesses.

Jackie was born on July 28, 1929, at Southampton, Long Island. She attended several private American schools and the Sorbonne, in Paris, France. She was graduated from George Washington University, in Washington, D. C. (See also White House, sections "Hostesses of the White House" and "Children in the White House.")

Back Surgery

Kennedy's old back injury still gave him a great deal of pain. Beginning in October 1954 he underwent a series of spinal operations.

While he was recuperating in 1955 he decided to write a book he had been contemplating for several years. It was a series of portraits of eight of the most courageous senators in the nation's history. Entitled 'Profiles in Courage', it became a best seller and won Kennedy the 1957 Pulitzer prize for biography.

Misses Vice-Presidential Nomination

During his campaign for the 1960 Democratic nomination, Kennedy often began his speeches with this remark: "Thanks for not voting for me in 1956." That was the year he barely missed being nominated vice-president on the Democratic ticket. Senator Estes Kefauver of Tennessee, who won the nomination, and Adlai E. Stevenson, the presidential nominee, were defeated in the election. Had Kennedy won the nomination and been defeated in the election, his chances for the presidency might have been lost.

The Presidential Nomination

Following the 1956 national election, Kennedy began an elaborate campaign for the 1960 Democratic presidential nomination. His popularity increased. In 1958 he was re-elected to the Senate by a margin of some 874,000 votes, more than any other Massachusetts senator had ever received. His brother Robert managed John's senatorial campaign. In 1958 Teddy, the youngest of the Kennedy family, worked with Robert in managing John's campaign for the Democratic nomination.

In the early months of 1960 Kennedy entered and won seven primary elections across the nation. At the 1960 Democratic convention in Los Angeles he received his party's nomination on the first ballot.

During the campaign Kennedy and Vice-President Richard M. Nixon met in four nationally televised "debates." It was generally conceded that these televison appearances helped Kennedy more than Nixon.

Problems Facing the New President

As Kennedy took office, cold-war tensions between Communist and Western nations increased. Com-

munist forces pushed into Laos and threatened South Vietnam. The new president pledged strong efforts to halt the spread of Communism. As one step toward this end, he created a Peace Corps of young American men and women to work in underdeveloped countries.

After Russia successfully launched the first man into outer space in April 1961, Kennedy asked for a greatly increased budget for space research. This new phase of the cold war was called the "space race." The first United States manned space flight was in May.

Kennedy and Johnson confer before making their acceptance speeches at the 1960 Democratic National Convention.

Jacqueline Kennedy, wife of the president, poses with their children, John, Jr., and Caroline.

In the spring of 1961 Cuba was invaded by opponents of its Communist premier, Fidel Castro. The rebels were defeated quickly. The invasion had been aided by the United States Central Intelligence Agency (CIA). Kennedy was criticized by some for having approved the CIA's support of the invasion. Others blamed him for the operation's failure.

Kennedy met with Premier Nikita Khrushchev of Russia in Vienna in June to discuss world problems. The conference apparently did not alter Communist goals. Khrushchev immediately made new attempts to drive the Western powers from Berlin.

Domestic and Latin American Affairs

At home Kennedy won Congressional approval of a number of his proposals, including greater social security benefits, a higher minimum wage, and aid to economically depressed areas in the country. The 23d Amendment to the Constitution was ratified early in Kennedy's Administration. It gave Washington, D. C., citizens the right to vote in presidential elections. (*See also* United States Constitution.)

In March 1961 Kennedy proposed an Alliance for Progress in the Americas. In August a conference of the Organization of American States formally ratified the charter for the Alliance for Progress (*see* South America, subhead "Alliance for Progress").

Events of 1962

In March 1962 Kennedy used his influence to get a steel-industry wage settlement generally regarded as noninflationary. Early in April, however, several companies announced increases in their steel prices. Kennedy was angered. He exerted unusual pressure by shifting government orders to rival steel manufacturers and by threatening tax and antitrust suits. Within four days the price increases were canceled.

Kennedy's most important legislative success of 1962 was the passage of the Trade Expansion Act. It gave the president broad powers, including authority to cut or eliminate tariffs. The act was designed to help the United States compete or trade with the European Economic Community (Common Market) on equal terms. Kennedy's medical care project was defeated in Congress. Under this plan certain hospital expenses for most elderly persons would have been paid through the social security system.

In October 1962 Kennedy faced the most serious international crisis of his Administration. Aerial photographs proved that Russian missile bases were being built in Cuba. Declaring this buildup a threat to the Americas, Kennedy issued an ultimatum to Russia. He warned that any attack by Cuba would be regarded as an attack by the Soviet Union and the United States would retaliate against Russia. He also imposed a quarantine on ships bringing offensive weapons to Cuba. Negotiations were carried on between the president and Premier Khrushchev. By the end of November the missiles had been shipped back to the Soviet Union, the United States had lifted the quarantine, and the month-long crisis had abated. (*See also* Cuba.)

The Civil Rights Crisis of 1963

In 1963, clashes between the police and demonstrating Negroes in Birmingham, Ala., and elsewhere induced the president to stress civil rights legislation. Kennedy's new civil rights message was sent to Congress in June. It included bills to ban discrimination in places of business; to speed up desegregation of public schools; and to end discrimination in the hiring of workers on federal construction projects.

An agreement to set up a teletype link between Kennedy and Khrushchev was signed in June 1963. This limited but promising achievement was intended as a precaution against war by accident or miscalculation.

The president also paid increasing attention to strengthening the North Atlantic Treaty Organization (NATO). Visiting Europe early in the summer of 1963, he conferred with government leaders in West Germany, Italy, and Great Britain. In West Germany, the president pledged that United States military forces would remain on the European continent. Kennedy also visited Ireland, from which his great-

Chancellor Konrad Adenauer welcomed President Kennedy to Bonn, the West German capital, in June 1963. They discussed a unified nuclear missile force.

grandparents had emigrated to the United States.

A limited nuclear test ban treaty was signed by representatives of the United States, Russia, and Britain in the summer of 1963. The agreement permitted underground nuclear tests, and signatory nations could withdraw after 90 days' notice. Kennedy called the treaty a "victory for mankind."

Mrs. Kennedy gave birth to her second son, Patrick Bouvier, on Aug. 7, 1963. Born prematurely, the infant died after only 39 hours of life.

Kennedy was assassinated on Nov. 22, 1963. With Mrs. Kennedy frantic, secret serviceman Clinton J. Hill leaps onto the back of the car to fling himself over her and the dying president. Kennedy is slumped in the back seat. Governor Connally and his wife have fallen to the floor of the car.

The Last Campaign

In November, looking forward to the 1964 presidential election, Kennedy made a political visit to Florida and Texas, the two most populous Southern states. His wife, Vice-President Johnson, and Mrs. Johnson accompanied him on the Texas trip.

He had been warned that Texas might be hostile. In Dallas, only a month earlier, Adlai Stevenson, United States ambassador to the United Nations, had been spat upon and struck with a picket's placard. In San Antonio, Houston, and Fort Worth, however, the crowds were friendly, and obviously delighted with the charming young Jacqueline Kennedy.

Kennedy Is Assassinated

A large and enthusiastic crowd greeted the presidential party when it arrived at the Dallas airport on the morning of November 22. Along the route of the motorcade into downtown Dallas the people stood 10 to 12 deep, applauding warmly. Next to the president in the big open limousine sat his wife. In front of them, on "jump seats," were John B. Connally, the governor of Texas, and his wife, Nellie. The third car in the procession carried Vice-President and Mrs. Johnson. As the cars approached a triple underpass, Mrs. Connally turned around and said, "You can't say Dallas doesn't love you, Mr. President."

At that moment three shots rang out. The president, shot through the head and throat, slumped over into his wife's lap. The second bullet hit Governor Connally, piercing his back, chest, wrist, and thigh. A reporter, glancing up, saw a rifle slowly disappear into a sixth-floor corner window of the Texas School Book Depository, a textbook warehouse overlooking the highway. It was 12:30 P.M. in Dallas.

President Kennedy died in Parkland Memorial Hospital without regaining consciousness. The time of death was set at 1:00 P.M. Governor Connally recovered from his multiple wounds.

Six minutes after the shooting, a description of a man seen leaving the textbook warehouse went out over the police radio. At 1:18 P.M. patrolman J. D. Tippit stopped and questioned a man who answered the description. The man shot him dead. At 1:35 P.M. Dallas police captured Lee Harvey Oswald in a motion-picture theater, where he had hidden after allegedly killing patrolman Tippit.

At the slain president's funeral procession John F. Kennedy, Jr., salutes the American flag, as his father had taught him. Behind him is Robert F. Kennedy. Behind Caroline, standing next to her mother, is Edward M. Kennedy.

LEE HARVEY OSWALD

Although a mass of circumstantial evidence, including ballistics tests, pointed to Oswald as the slayer of President Kennedy, the 24-year-old professed Marxist and Castro sympathizer never came to trial. On Sunday, November 24, as he was being led across the basement of the City Hall for transfer to another prison, Jack Ruby (born Rubenstein), a Dallas nightclub owner, broke through a cordon of police and shot Oswald. The murder was committed in full view of television cameras as millions watched.

The Return to Washington

The casket bearing Kennedy's body was removed to the presidential jet plane, Air Force One, where Lyndon B. Johnson took the oath of office as president of the United States (for picture, *see* Johnson, Lyndon B.). Only 98 minutes had elapsed since Kennedy's death.

All that long afternoon and into the early morning of the next day, Mrs. Kennedy refused to leave her husband's body. Close by her side at all times after her return to Washington, D.C., was her husband's

brother and closest adviser, Attorney General Robert F. Kennedy. Mrs. Kennedy directed the details of the funeral, consulting with historians as to the burial procedures for other presidents who had died in office.

Burial at Arlington

The body lay in repose for a day in the East Room of the White House. On November 24, in a solemn procession to the slow beat of muffled drums, the casket was removed to the rotunda of the Capitol and placed on the catafalque which had borne President Abraham Lincoln's casket.

The following day the funeral procession moved from the Capitol to the White House and then to St. Matthew's Cathedral. Here Richard Cardinal Cushing, Roman Catholic archbishop of Boston, celebrated Low Mass. From the White House to the cathedral, Mrs. Kennedy walked in the procession between her husband's brothers, Robert and Edward. In a scene unduplicated in history, 220 foreign leaders followed them.

Burial was at Arlington National Cemetery, on a hillside overlooking the Potomac and the city of Washington. At the conclusion of the service Mrs. Kennedy lighted an "eternal flame" at the grave.

Two Kennedy infants were later reburied on either side of their father. They were Patrick Bouvier and an unnamed daughter who was stillborn in 1956.

On June 8, 1968, the Kennedy family and a host of other mourners again gathered at the Kennedy gravesite—this time for the burial of Robert F. Kennedy. The president's brother, who had become a United States senator, was shot on June 5 in Los Angeles, Calif., while campaigning for the Democratic presidential nomination. He died on June 6 of brain damage. Sirhan Bishara Sirhan, a Jordanian immigrant who was seized at the scene of the shooting, was indicted for the murder.

For the second time President Johnson declared a day of mourning for a Kennedy. Many Americans who honored Robert Kennedy's memory on June 9, 1968, were reminded of an earlier day of mourning.

In his proclamation declaring November 25, 1963, a "National Day of Mourning" for John Kennedy, President Johnson paid this tribute to the slain president, quoting in conclusion from Kennedy's inaugural address of January 1960: "As he did not shrink from his responsibilities, but welcomed them, so he would not have us shrink from carrying on his work beyond this hour of na-

The flag-draped casket holding the body of John F. Kennedy is borne on a caisson drawn by six gray horses. It is followed by the traditional riderless black horse, the empty boots turned backward in the stirrups, the sword sheathed in its scabbard.

tional tragedy. He said it himself: 'The energy, the faith, the devotion which we bring to this endeavor will light our country and all who serve it—and the glow from that fire can truly light the world'."

Warren Commission

On Nov. 29, 1963, President Johnson created the President's Commission on the Assassination of President John F. Kennedy to investigate and report on the facts relating to the tragedy. It functioned neither as a court nor as a prosecutor. Chief Justice Earl Warren was appointed chairman. Other members of the bipartisan commission were Senators Richard B. Russell of Georgia and John Sherman Cooper of Kentucky, Representatives Hale Boggs of Louisiana and Gerald R. Ford of Michigan, Allen W. Dulles, and John J. McCloy. J. Lee Rankin was the general counsel. The report was published on Sept. 24, 1964.

Since Oswald was unable to stand trial and defend himself, and in fairness to him and his family, the commission requested Walter E. Craig, president of the American Bar Association, to participate in the investigation and to advise the commission whether the proceedings conformed to the basic principles of American justice.

The commission found that the shots that killed President Kennedy and wounded Governor Connally were fired by Lee Harvey Oswald. There was no evidence at that time that either Oswald or Jack Ruby was part of any conspiracy, domestic or foreign, to assassinate President Kennedy. No direct or indirect relationship between Oswald and Jack Ruby had been uncovered. On the basis of the evidence before it, the commission concluded that Oswald acted alone. Despite the findings of the commission, conspiracy theories persisted for decades.

The commission criticized both the Secret Service and the Federal Bureau of Investigation (FBI). Some of the advance preparations and security measures in Dallas made by the Secret Service were found to have been deficient. In addition, though the FBI had obtained considerable information about Oswald, it had no official responsibility to refer this information to the Secret Service. "A more carefully coordinated treatment of the Oswald case by the FBI might well have resulted in bringing Oswald's activities to the attention of the Secret Service," the report stated.

The commission made suggestions for improved protective measures of the Secret Service and better liaison with the FBI, the Department of State, and other federal agencies. Other recommendations were:

That a committee of Cabinet members, or the National Security Council, should review and oversee the protective activities of the Secret Service and other agencies that help safeguard the president.

That Congress adopt legislation that would make the assassination of the president and vice-president a federal crime.

That the representatives of the bar, law-enforcement associations, and the news media establish ethical standards concerning the collection and presentation of information to the public so that there will be no interference with pending criminal investigations, court proceedings, or the right of individuals to a fair trial.

BIBLIOGRAPHY FOR JOHN F. KENNEDY

Bradlee, B.C. Conversations with Kennedy (Norton, 1984).
Hurt, Henry. Reasonable Doubt: an Investigation into the Assassination of John F. Kennedy (Holt, 1987).
Lowe, Jacques. Kennedy, a Time Remembered (Quartet, 1983).
Manchester, William. One Brief Shining Moment: Remembering Kennedy (Little, 1988).
Martin, R.G. A Hero for Our Time: an Intimate Story of the Kennedy Years (Fawcett, 1984).
Parmet, H.S. JFK: the Presidency of John F. Kennedy (Penguin, 1984).
Reston, James, Jr. The Great Expectations of John Connally (Harper, 1989).
Schlesinger, A.M. A Thousand Days: John F. Kennedy in the White House (Houghton, 1965).

Chief Justice Earl Warren, chairman, hands the report of the President's Commission on the Assassination of President John F. Kennedy to President Lyndon B. Johnson. Others, left to right, are John J. McCloy, J. Lee Rankin, Senator Richard B. Russell, Representative Gerald R. Ford, Allen W. Dulles, Senator John Sherman Cooper, and Representative Hale Boggs.

AP/Wide World

KENNEDY FAMILY.

KENNEDY FAMILY. Apart from the Roosevelts of New York, no family played a more prominent role in American political life during the 20th century than the Kennedys of Massachusetts. One son, John (1917–63), became president (*see* Kennedy). Another, Robert Francis (1925–68), served as attorney general of the United States and as senator from New York. The youngest son, Edward Moore (born 1932), became a senator from his home state.

The father, Joseph P. Kennedy (1888–1969), was the grandson of an Irish immigrant. He was born in Boston and graduated from Harvard University in 1912. In 1914 he married Rose Fitzgerald (born 1890), daughter of John F. Fitzgerald, the mayor of Boston. Kennedy had a remarkable knack for making money. At 25 he was a bank president, and by age 30 he had become a millionaire. By means of shrewd stock investments during the 1920s, he made enough money to retire and set up million-dollar trust funds for his children. During the administrations of Franklin D. Roosevelt, Kennedy served as chairman of the Securities and Exchange Commission from 1934 to 1935 and as ambassador to Great Britain from 1937 to 1940. He later lived in retirement at Hyannis Port, Mass., where he died in 1969.

Rose and Joseph Kennedy had nine children: Joseph P., Jr.; John Fitzgerald; Rosemary; Kathleen; Eunice; Patricia; Robert Francis; Jean; and Edward Moore, commonly known as "Ted."

Joseph P., Jr., whom his father had intended for public office, was killed while serving in World War II. Rosemary was discovered to be mentally retarded and was put into a private institution. Kathleen died in a plane crash in Europe in 1948. Eunice married R. Sargent Shriver, who became head of the Peace Corps under President Kennedy. Patricia married actor Peter Lawford (since divorced). Jean married businessman Stephen Smith.

Robert F. Kennedy was born in Brookline, Mass., on Nov. 20, 1925. He attended Harvard University and the University of Virginia Law School. He worked in the Justice Department and served on several Senate committee staffs before being named attorney general by his brother John in 1961. He resigned the post in 1964, nearly a year after his brother's assassination. In 1964 he was elected in New York to the United States Senate. In 1968 he campaigned for the presidency in opposition to the Vietnam War. On June 5, during a victory celebration following the California primary, he was assassinated by Sirhan Sirhan, an Arab immigrant. His wife, Ethel, was left with their 11 children, the last of whom was born after Robert's death.

Edward M. "Ted" Kennedy was born in Brookline on Feb. 22, 1932. His college education at Harvard spanned 1950 to 1956, being interrupted by two years of military service. He graduated from the University of Virginia Law School in 1959 and worked on his brother John's presidential campaign in 1960. In 1962 he was elected in Massachusetts to the United States Senate. Throughout his senatorial career, he was considered to be a potential presidential candidate. In the summer of 1969 his career suffered a setback when he was involved in an automobile accident at Chappaquiddick Island in Massachusetts. This incident led to the death of a young woman. The suspicious circumstances surrounding the accident caused a scandal, but Kennedy was nevertheless reelected in 1970. He refused to accept either the presidential or vice-presidential nomination in 1972, and in 1976 the presidential nomination went to Jimmy Carter.

Disagreement with Carter's economic policies and style of leadership inspired Kennedy to campaign for the presidency in 1980. Carter successfully staved off the Kennedy drive, but the split in the Democratic party probably helped Ronald Reagan defeat Carter in the fall elections. Kennedy remained in the Senate and was considered one of the champions of liberal policies that were the legacy of Roosevelt, Harry Truman, John Kennedy, and Lyndon Johnson.

Rose Fitzgerald Kennedy
and Joseph Patrick Kennedy

Photos, (far left) Sir Cecil Beaton, (left) Wide World

KENNY, Sister (1886–1952). The Australian nurse who developed a method for treating victims of the dreaded disease infantile paralysis, or poliomyelitis, was Sister Kenny. She was also the author of several works about the disease and her experiences in dealing with it, including her autobiography, 'And They Shall Walk', published in 1943.

Elizabeth Kenny was born on Sept. 20, 1886, in Warialda, New South Wales, Australia. She graduated from college in 1902 and from 1911 to 1914 was a nurse in the bush country districts of Queensland. During this time she developed her treatment method for infantile paralysis, an acute infection by a virus involving paralysis of the muscles. The treatment consisted basically of stimulating the affected muscles using hot, moist packs and passive exercise in the early stages, followed by active exercise as soon as possible. Sister Kenny spent most of the years of her life working to cure the disease.

At first the method was found unfavorable by a royal inquiry commission, but in 1939 it was accepted for use in Australian hospitals and later approved by medical associations in the United States. In 1942 Sister Kenny established the Kenny Institute in Minneapolis, Minn., to train practitioners in her method. She died on Nov. 30, 1952, in Toowoomba, Queensland, Australia. Other of her publications include 'Physical Medicine Concerning the Disease Infantile Paralysis', published in 1945, and 'My Battle and Victory' (1955).

KENT, James (1763–1847). One of the foremost influences on the shaping of American law in the 19th century was Kent's book entitled 'Commentaries on American Law'. It was published in four volumes between 1826 and 1830.

Kent was born at Fredricksburgh, New York, on July 31, 1763. He graduated from Yale in 1781, after which he studied law and was admitted to the bar in 1785. His first practice was at Poughkeepsie. He moved to New York City in 1793 when he was appointed first professor of law at Columbia University. Five years later he was appointed a justice of the New York Supreme Court. He remained on the court until 1814, the last ten years as chief justice. That year he was named chancellor of the state Court of Chancery, making him New York's highest judicial officer. While on the bench, Kent's decisions were recorded and published as 'Reports for New York' and widely circulated among other states.

In 1823 Kent returned to teaching law at Columbia. He revised and expanded his lectures for publication as the 'Commentaries on American Law'. This work dealt with American constitutional law within the federal system, international law, the laws of the states, individual rights, and the laws of property. It was the first major systematic treatment of Anglo-American law. Kent re-edited the work for five subsequent editions during his lifetime, and translations were made of portions of it. He died in New York City on Dec. 12, 1847.

KENT, Rockwell (1882–1971). Few modern artists can claim a more adventurous life than Rockwell Kent. In search of subjects for his pictures, he lived in such faraway places as Newfoundland, Alaska, and Tierra del Fuego. Once he was shipwrecked off Greenland. A talented author, he wrote and illustrated books of his travels.

Born on June 21, 1882, in Tarrytown, N.Y., Kent grew up there and in New York City, attending the Horace Mann School. He studied architecture at Columbia University but left in his junior year. He had already begun to study painting. Not until 1914, however, was he able to make a living in art. Meanwhile he had worked as a carpenter, gravedigger, lobster fisherman, draftsman, engraver, and illustrator—painting all the time.

His early works are mostly highly stylized landscapes and seascapes that feature dramatic contrasts of light and dark. His scenes of nature and adventure were very popular in the first half of the 20th century. Kent illustrated special editions of 'Moby Dick', 'Candide', 'Leaves of Grass', and Shakespeare. He also illustrated a number of his own books, including 'Wilderness', published in 1920, 'Voyaging' (1924), and 'Rockwellkentiana' (1933). The Soviet Union elected him to its Academy of Arts in 1966. In 1955, when he was 73, he wrote a long autobiography, 'It's Me, O Lord'. Kent died in Plattsburgh, N.Y., on March 13, 1971.

A Kent drawing for Melville's novel 'Moby Dick'

Kentucky Department of Public Information

Thoroughbred horses graze peacefully in pastures rimmed with trim white fences and spacious barns that mark the horse farms of Kentucky's Bluegrass section.

KENTUCKY

KENTUCKY. The oldest state west of the Appalachian Highlands is Kentucky. Originally a part of the western lands of Virginia, Kentucky had its first permanent white settlement in 1774. During the next 15 years its population grew to more than 73,000. In 1792, with the permission of Virginia, Kentucky was admitted to the Union as the 15th state.

Kentucky has a well-balanced economy. Its chief source of income is manufacturing, which amounts to more than 5.7 billion dollars a year. Tobacco farming, coal mining, and the bourbon whiskey industry have been traditionally important in the economy.

The state is noted for its many political leaders. Henry Clay, author of the Compromise of 1850, served in Congress for more than 30 years (*see* Clay, Henry). The two opposing leaders of the Civil War, Abraham Lincoln and Jefferson Davis, were both born in Kentucky (*see* Lincoln, Abraham; Davis, Jefferson). The state has also had three vice-presidents of the United States—Richard M. Johnson, John C. Breckinridge, and Alben W. Barkley.

The state's name probably comes from the Indian word *Kentake,* meaning "meadowland" or "prai-

Population (1980): 3,661,433—rank, 23rd state. Urban, 50.8%; rural, 49.2%. Persons per square mile, 92.3 (persons per square kilometer, 35.0)—rank, 23rd state.

Extent: Area, 40,395 square miles (104,623 square kilometers), including 745 square miles (1,930 square kilometers) of water surface (37th state in size).

Elevation: Highest, Black Mountain, 4,145 feet (1,263 meters), near Lynch; lowest, Mississippi River near Hickman, 257 feet (78 meters); average, 750 feet (229 meters).

Geographic Center: 3 miles (5 kilometers) northwest of Lebanon.

Temperature: Extremes—lowest, −34° F (−37° C), Cynthiana, Jan. 28, 1963; highest, 114° F (46° C), Greensburg, July 28, 1930. Averages at Lexington-Fayette—January, 34.4° F (1.3° C); July, 76.3° F (24.6° C); annual, 55.4° F (13.0° C). Averages at Louisville—January, 35.7° F (2.1° C); July, 78.5° F (25.8° C); annual, 56.9° F (13.8° C).

Precipitation (annual average): At Lexington-Fayette—46.09 inches (1,171 millimeters). At Louisville—42.64 inches (1,083 millimeters).

Land Use: Crops, 39%; pasture, 6%; forest, 47%; other, 8%.

For statistical information about Agriculture, Education, Employment, Finance, Government, Manufacturing, Mining, Population Trends, and Vital Statistics, see KENTUCKY FACT SUMMARY.

rie." During pioneer days, Kentucky was called the "dark and bloody ground," for the many battles between the settlers and the Indians. The nickname Bluegrass State is from the unusual grass that grows in various parts of Kentucky and is most abundant in the Lexington area.

Survey of the Bluegrass State

Kentucky lies in the south-central section of the United States. On the north the Ohio River separates the state from Ohio, Indiana, and Illinois. To the northeast is West Virginia, separated from Kentucky by the Big Sandy River and its Tug Fork. Virginia is to the southeast. To the south is Tennessee. On the west the Mississippi River is the boundary between Kentucky and Missouri.

The state's greatest length, from east to west, is 425 miles. Its greatest width is 182 miles, from north to south. The area of Kentucky is 40,395 square miles, with 745 square miles of inland water surface.

The State's Three Natural Regions

From highlands in the southeast the surface of Kentucky slopes generally north and west. The highest point in the state is Black Mountain (4,145 feet), at the Virginia border. Here the average elevation is about 2,800 feet. Central Kentucky has an average elevation of about 1,000 feet; western Kentucky, about 400 feet. The lowest point in the state is 257 feet, along the Mississippi River near Hickman. There are three distinct natural regions.

The Appalachian Plateau covers the eastern fourth of Kentucky. The southeastern edge of this region is formed by the Cumberland and Pine Mountain ranges, known also as the Cumberland Mountains. From these highlands a series of sharp ridges and narrow valleys extend north (Kanawha section) and west (Cumberland Plateau section). Another name

that is sometimes used to designate the Appalachian Plateau is the Eastern Coal Field.

The Interior Low Plateaus extend from the eastern mountains to the Tennessee River in the west. This region is by far the largest in the state. It contains four separate areas. In the northern bulge of Kentucky is the *Bluegrass* area, named for its bluish-tinted grass. The area is also known as the Lexington Plain. Around the edge of the Bluegrass is a semicircle of rounded hills called the *Knobs*. To the south and west is the *Pennyroyal* (Pennyrile) Plateau, named for a variety of the mint plant found here. Another low plateau, the *Western Coal Field*, lies on both sides of the Green River, from Edmonson County north to the Ohio River.

The Coastal Plain occupies the eight westernmost counties. It is part of the great lowland that sweeps north from the Gulf of Mexico. This region is also called the Jackson Purchase, or Purchase. It is so named because Andrew Jackson helped buy the land between the Mississippi and Tennessee rivers from the Chickasaw Indians in 1818.

Most of Kentucky's rivers flow north and west into the Ohio. These include, from east to west, the Licking, Kentucky (with its branch, the Dix), Salt, and Green. The Cumberland River rises in the southeast, makes a loop in Tennessee, then reenters Kentucky to join the Ohio. The Tennessee flows through the western end of the state. Along the northern and western boundaries are the Ohio and Mississippi rivers (*see* Ohio River; Mississippi River).

Climate and Weather

Kentucky has a continental climate, with warm summers and cool winters. The coldest part of the state is the far north, which has an average annual temperature of about 55° F. This is about five degrees lower than that of the extreme southwest, the

Early in May the spectacular Kentucky Derby is run at Churchill Downs in Louisville. The racing event attracts people from many states and countries. First held in 1875, it is for three-year-olds over a distance of 1¼ miles.

The Louisville Courier-Journal

A map of Kentucky shows the state's three natural regions and surface features. How the land is used is related to the physical features of each region.

warmest section. The growing season varies from 176 days a year in the eastern highlands to 197 days in the western part of the state.

The average precipitation varies from 40 inches a year in the extreme north to 52 inches in the extreme south-central part of the state. The heaviest rainfall falls along the southern border between Allen and Bell counties. Boone, Kenton, and Campbell counties in the far north area of the state receive the least.

Natural Resources and Conservation

Kentucky's chief agricultural resources are fertile soil, a favorable climate, and plenty of rainfall. Almost half of the land is forested, with the heaviest stands of timber in the east. About 600 million board feet of hardwood and softwood lumber are cut each year in the state.

Deposits of coal, petroleum, and natural gas provide fuels for manufacturing. The state's rivers are an important means of transportation. Kentucky has pure water for making distilled and malt liquors. Horse farms and horse racing are tourist attractions.

A major problem has been the erosion of topsoil. This condition is being corrected by crop rotation, cropland terracing, and reforestation.

Several large dams have been built, primarily to improve navigation and to supply power. The lakes formed by these dams also offer boating, fishing, and swimming, and facilities for camping are available along their shores. Kentucky Dam, on the Tennessee River, is part of the Tennessee Valley Authority (*see* Tennessee Valley Authority). Barkley Dam, on the Cumberland River, was built and is maintained by the United States Army Corps of Engineers. Wolf Creek Dam, on the Cumberland, and Dale Hollow

Dam in Tennessee, on the Obey, a branch of the Cumberland, have aided the economy of the Cumberland Basin. Other important dams are the Rough River, Nolin, Green River, Buckhorn, and Dewey.

The Department of Natural Resources and the Environmental Protection Cabinet are concerned with all aspects of controlling pollution and preserving resources. The conservation work is shared by the Department of Fish and Wildlife Resources.

People of the Bluegrass State

Kentucky was a hunting ground and battlefield for such Indian tribes as the Shawnee from the north, the

The City Hall, left, of Louisville was completed in 1873. It faces the Jefferson County courthouse.

210

Iroquois from the east, and the Cherokee from the south long before white men entered the region. The only tribe the white men found living in the region was the Shawnee.

The first pioneers to settle in Kentucky came from Virginia and North Carolina. Until about 1830 the state was settled largely by people of English and Scottish descent who worked their way over the Appalachian Mountains. Then, as new routes to the West came into use (by way of the Deep South and the Great Lakes), the mountain region became somewhat isolated. It was not until the 1900s that improved methods of transportation and communication forged a close link between eastern Kentucky and the rest of the state. One of the greatest aids to the people in the isolated areas was the Frontier Nursing Service, a public health agency founded by Mary Breckinridge in 1925.

Kentucky has attracted few immigrants from abroad. Today only less than one percent of its people are foreign born. Of the total foreign stock the Germans and the English are the largest groups. Seven percent of the people are black.

Manufacturing and Cities

During World War II the value of manufacturing in Kentucky increased almost four times, reaching a total of some 740 million dollars. Today the value of work done in the state's mills, factories, and processing plants is more than 5.7 billion dollars a year. Most of the state's large manufacturing centers are located on the Ohio River.

The most important industry in Kentucky is the production of construction equipment, conveyors, and other nonelectrical machinery; and the manufacture of transportation equipment. Next in value are the manufacture of chemicals and allied products and the tobacco industry. Also important is the manufacture of electrical machinery.

The largest city and chief industrial center is Louisville, on the Ohio River (*see* Louisville). Lexington-Fayette, the second largest city, is a tobacco and livestock market in the heart of the Bluegrass region (*see* Lexington-Fayette). Owensboro, the third largest city, and Paducah, Ashland, and Henderson are industrial cities on the Ohio River. Covington, fourth in size, is a manufacturing city upstream on the Ohio opposite Cincinnati, Ohio. It stands at the Ohio's juncture with the Licking River. Nearby is Newport, a residential city with metal-manufacturing plants.

Bowling Green and Hopkinsville are farm centers in the west-central part of the state. Middlesboro, in the southeast, is noted for its mountain resorts and nearby coal mines. Frankfort, on the Kentucky River, is the state capital (*see* Frankfort).

Products of the Land

About 8 percent of all the workers in Kentucky are engaged in agriculture. The state has about 101,000 commercial farms. The average size of these farms is about 144 acres. Tobacco, the principal cash crop,

Towering Chained Rock, once seeming a constant menace to Pineville, now is held safely in place by a huge chain.

accounts for about two fifths of the total farm income. The chief growing region is between the Green and Cumberland rivers. Only North Carolina produces more tobacco than Kentucky.

Corn, the second most valuable field crop, is grown throughout the state. Other important crops are soybeans, hay, wheat, barley, potatoes, sorghum, and oats. Kentucky also raises many cattle (for beef and milk), hogs, chickens, and sheep.

The Bluegrass State ranks first nationally in the breeding of Thoroughbred horses. Breeders have produced strains of saddle horses that combine speed with endurance. The chief breeding area, which also develops horses for harness racing and for show, is around Lexington-Fayette.

Coal is by far the most valuable mineral. Kentucky mines more coal than any other state. The major coal-mining counties are Hopkins and Muhlenberg in western Kentucky and Pike and Harlan in the eastern part of the state. Other important minerals are stone, petroleum, natural gas, sand and gravel, natural-gas liquids, and clays.

Development of Transportation

The first "highway" into Kentucky was the Wilderness Road blazed by Daniel Boone in 1775. It led through Cumberland Gap northwest to Boonesborough, Harrodsburg, and later to Louisville. The second important "road" into the state was the Ohio River, which carried flatboats down to landings at what later became the cities of Maysville, Louisville, and Owensboro.

The state's chief cash crop is tobacco. Here buyers (left) bid for lots of loose-leaf tobacco sold by an auctioneer. A large amount of Kentucky's coal is obtained by strip mining. The huge electric shovel (right) can handle 30 cubic yards at one bite.

Railroad transportation began in 1832 with the opening of the Lexington and Ohio line between Lexington and Frankfort. This route is now part of the Louisville and Nashville Railroad. Today the state is served by nearly 30 railroads and several airlines.

Kentucky has an extensive multilane highway system. Interstate 64, a major east-west route, extends east from Louisville into West Virginia. Western Kentucky Parkway begins at Princeton and extends northeast to Elizabethtown. Interstate 75 crosses the state from north to south, skirting Lexington. Interstate 65, which extends south through Louisville, incorporates a 40-mile turnpike from Louisville to Elizabethtown.

Recreation in Kentucky

The state's scenic mountains, valleys, and historical landmarks are visited by many tourists. Three of the chief attractions are maintained by the federal government—Mammoth Cave National Park, Abraham Lincoln Birthplace National Historic Site, and Cumberland Gap National Historical Park (see National Parks, United States).

Man-made lakes such as Kentucky, Cumberland, and Herrington are noted for fishing and other sports. Louisville is the site of the Kentucky State Fair and the Kentucky Derby. There are a variety of state parks.

Growth of the Educational System

The first school in what is now Kentucky was opened in the fort at Harrodsburg in 1775. By 1800 many private academies had been established. One of these schools was Transylvania Seminary, which was founded at Danville in 1780. Moved to Lexington in 1788, it was one of the first schools of higher learning west of the Appalachians.

The state legislature passed the first public school law in 1838. There was little progress, however, until 1847, when Robert Breckinridge became superintendent of education. By 1853 a public school system had been established in every county. The Civil War temporarily halted further development. Since that time Kentucky has continued to improve its schools.

Fort Boonesborough State Park's natural sandy beach beside the Kentucky River is near the site where Daniel Boone built his famous homestead fort.

The state's largest schools are the University of Kentucky, at Lexington-Fayette, and the University of Louisville, at Louisville. Other state-supported universities are Western Kentucky University, at Bowling Green; Eastern Kentucky University at Richmond; Murray State University, at Murray; Morehead State University, at Morehead; and Kentucky State University, at Frankfort. Other schools include Bellarmine College and Spalding University, both at Louisville; Cumberland College, at Williamsburg; Georgetown College, at Georgetown; and Berea College, at Berea.

Ewing Galloway

Billions of dollars in gold are stored in the Gold Bullion Depository built by the United States at Fort Knox in 1936.

Government and Politics

When Kentucky was admitted to the Union on June 1, 1792, the capital was Lexington. Later in 1792 Frankfort was selected as the permanent seat of government. Although generally referred to as a state, Kentucky calls itself a commonwealth. It is governed under a constitution adopted in 1891.

The chief executive officer is the governor, elected every four years. Lawmaking is in the hands of the General Assembly, made up of the Senate and the House of Representatives. The judiciary is headed by the Supreme Court.

Kentucky usually votes Democratic in both local and state elections. In presidential campaigns it has supported the Democratic candidate in every election since the American Civil War except those of 1896, 1924, 1928, 1956, 1960, 1968, 1972, 1980, 1984, and 1988. Kentucky was the second state, after Georgia, to lower the voting age from 21 to 18.

HISTORY

The Big Sandy River, its Tug Fork, and the Cumberland Mountains have formed the eastern boundary of Kentucky since 1776. The state's western boundary, the Mississippi River, was fixed by the peace treaty of 1783. Its northern border, along the Ohio River, was established by the Northwest Ordinance of 1787. Although Kentucky was admitted to the Union in 1792, its boundary with Tennessee was not settled until 1820. This line was based upon two earlier surveys—from Cumberland Gap to the Tennessee River and from the Tennessee to the Mississippi River. The sections below tell the history of Kentucky to the present.

Exploration and Settlement

For almost 150 years the American Colonies were blocked from expanding westward by the mountain ranges of the Appalachians. Then, in 1750, Dr. Thomas

Walker led a party of Virginians into what is now Kentucky through a pass in the Cumberland Mountains. He named the pass Cumberland Gap.

Later John Finley, Daniel Boone, and others came through the Gap looking for fertile land (*see* Boone). Many of these adventurers stayed in Kentucky so long that they were called "long hunters." Meanwhile the region was organized by Virginia as Fincastle (later Kentucky) County.

In 1774 James Harrod and a group of Virginians made the first permanent settlement in the region at Harrodstown (now Harrodsburg). The next year Daniel Boone led a party from North Carolina along the famous Wilderness Road from Cumberland Gap. He founded Boonesborough (now Boonesboro) on the Kentucky River in what is now Madison County. There was some rivalry between the two settlements of Boonesborough and Harrodstown, but they united their efforts in fighting off Indian attacks.

Ewing Galloway

Abraham Lincoln Birthplace National Historic Site, near Hodgenville, reputedly houses the log cabin where he was born.

Much of the danger from Indians was removed by the victories of George Rogers Clark in the Revolutionary War (*see* Clark). The last Indian battle in the state was at Blue Licks (near Mount Olivet) in 1782. The Indians retreated across the Ohio River.

Statehood to the Civil War

In 1784 a group of Kentuckians meeting at Danville asked to be separated from Virginia. This was the first of ten such conventions that prepared the way for statehood. Finally, on June 1, 1792, Kentucky was admitted to the Union.

The new state joined with Virginia in 1798 in passing the resolutions denouncing the Alien and Sedition Acts (*see* Alien and Sedition Acts). The resolutions were guided through the state legislature by John Breckinridge of Lexington.

The name Breckinridge became one of the most famous in Kentucky. Three of John's sons—Joseph, John, and Robert—were noted as either lawyers or Presbyterian clergymen. Robert served as Abraham Lincoln's Kentucky adviser during the Civil War. Two grandsons, however, fought for the Confederacy—John C. Breckinridge, son of Joseph and vice-president of the United States under James Buchanan; and William C. Breckinridge, son of Robert.

During the Civil War Kentucky was as divided as the Breckinridge family. A slave state, it tried to remain neutral. Some of its men joined the Confederacy, others fought for the North. Late in 1861 a separate state government at Bowling Green was recognized by the Confederate government. The following year Gen. Braxton Bragg led a Southern army into Kentucky. He was turned back at the battle of Perryville by a Union force under Gen. Don Carlos Buell. (*See also* Civil War, American.)

Growth into a Modern State

Following the reconstruction period, Kentucky showed a steady growth in agriculture and manufacturing (*see* Reconstruction Period). Coal mining on a large scale was started during the 1870's. There were a number of clashes between miners and operators until the United Mine Workers of America won recognition as the miners' bargaining agent in 1939.

The first Kentucky Derby was held at Louisville's Churchill Downs in 1875. Another major attraction, Mammoth Cave, became a national park in 1936. In the same year the nation's gold reserve was moved to Fort Knox for safekeeping. In 1962 the Kentucky legislature passed a law regulating the strip mining of coal. Unchecked, this mining technique ravages the soil. The law was made more comprehensive in 1965. (*See also* United States, section "The South"; individual entries in the Fact-Index on Kentucky persons, places, products, and events.)

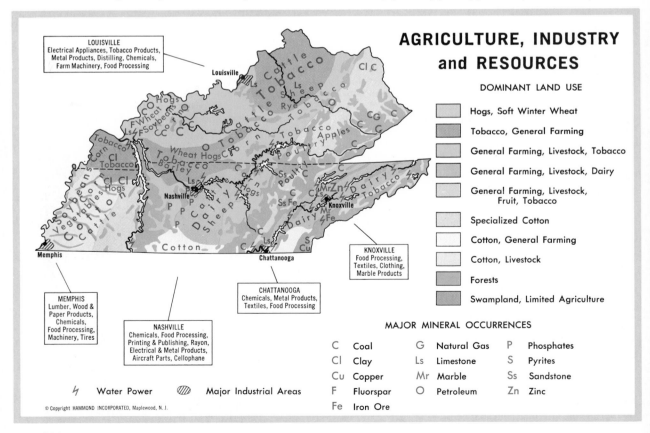

Notable Events in Kentucky History

1671—Thomas Batts and Robert Fallam of Virginia reach Ohio Valley.

1739—Capt. Charles de Longueuil discovers Big Bone Lick, near Walton.

1750—Dr. Thomas Walker discovers Cumberland Gap.

1751—Christopher Gist explores area along Ohio River.

1763—France cedes area including Kentucky to Britain.

1769—Daniel Boone and John Finley explore Kentucky.

1774—James Harrod starts building Harrodstown (Harrodsburg); Indians force settlers to withdraw; settlers return in 1775.

1775—Boiling Springs and St. Asaph settled. Indians give Richard Henderson land between Ohio and Cumberland rivers for Transylvania Land Company. **Boone blazes Wilderness Road; Boonesboro founded.**

1776—Harrodsburg settlers, jealous of Boonesboro, send George Rogers Clark and John Jones to ask Virginia's aid; Virginia declares Transylvania Land Company illegal; creates Kentucky County.

1778—Indian siege of Boonesboro repulsed. Clark organizes expedition against British beyond the Ohio.

1782—**"Last battle of American Revolution" fought at Blue Licks, near Mount Olivet.**

1784—First of ten conventions held to prepare way for separation of Kentucky from Virginia.

1792—Kentucky becomes 15th state, June 1; governor, Isaac Shelby; capital, Lexington, then Frankfort.

1794—Gen. "Mad Anthony" Wayne's victory at Fallen Timbers in Ohio ends Indian attacks in Kentucky.

1796—Wilderness Road opened to wagons.

1798—Legislature passes Kentucky Resolutions opposing U.S. Alien and Sedition Laws.

1811—Henry Clay elected to Congress from Kentucky. *New Orleans*, first steamboat on Ohio River, stops at Louisville; *Enterprise* reaches Louisville from New Orleans, La., in 1815.

1812—Kentuckians bear brunt of war with England north of the Ohio and in New Orleans.

1830—Louisville and Portland Canal, around Falls of Ohio River, opened.

1849—Zachary Taylor, Kentucky hero of Mexican War, becomes 12th president of U.S.

1861—Kentucky declares its neutrality in Civil War.

1862—Last major Civil War battle in state fought near Perryville.

1865—University of Kentucky founded at Lexington.

1875—**First Kentucky Derby run at Churchill Downs.**

1891—Present state constitution adopted.

1909—Present State Capitol completed.

1936—U.S. gold depository built at Fort Knox. Mammoth Cave National Park established.

1937—Worst Ohio River flood occurs.

1944—**Kentucky Dam on Tennessee River completed by Tennessee Valley Authority.**

1946—Frederick M. Vinson, born 1890 in Louisa, is appointed chief justice of the U.S.

1950—Atomic energy plant built near Paducah.

1951—Wolf Creek Dam on Cumberland River dedicated.

1959—Cumberland Gap National Historical Park dedicated.

1962—Kentucky is first state given control of certain nuclear energy materials by federal government.

1964—Western Kentucky Parkway opened; Kentucky Central Parkway, in 1965.

1966—Kentucky is first Southern state to pass a comprehensive civil rights law. Barkley Dam on Cumberland River dedicated.

1977—Nightclub fire in Southgate kills 164 persons.

1988—Voters approved the establishment of a state lottery.

1775

1782

1875

1944

STATE FLOWER:
Goldenrod

STATE TREE:
Kentucky Coffee Tree

STATE BIRD:
Cardinal

**STATE SEAL: Two friends shaking
hands, surrounded by state motto.**

Kentucky Profile

FLAG: *See* **Flags of the United States.**
**MOTTO: United We Stand, Divided
We Fall.**
**SONG 'My Old Kentucky Home'—
words and music by Stephen
Collins Foster.**

When Daniel Boone explored the Kentucky region in 1769, herds of bison roamed the grassy areas and its forests offered a seemingly unlimited supply of bear, deer, and wild turkey. Describing his determination to settle in this lush, wild country, the great woodsman called Kentucky "a second paradise."

Today the bison are gone, and the bear, deer, and wild turkey populations survive only through careful restocking. Kentucky is well on its way to becoming an industrial state. Yet Daniel Boone's paradise lives on in the tough, individualistic spirit and strong feeling for tradition that continue to characterize its citizens. The mountains near the West Virginia border are still home to descendants of such famous feuding families as the Hatfields and the McCoys. Although the shotgun is rarely used to settle disputes, family loyalties and antagonisms among families remain extremely strong.

Kentucky is still a decidedly rural state, but it is developing a rich manufacturing industry that yields more income and becomes increasingly varied with each passing year—as the burgeoning Louisville aluminum industry and the new chemical plants on the Ohio River testify. Yet farming is also vital to the economy of the Bluegrass State. Tobacco is the leading crop. Increasingly, however, farms are becoming larger and their number fewer. The high cost of labor is driving many small tobacco farmers out of business, and agriculture is diversifying as many farms change over to crops more easily managed by machines than tobacco.

The automation of the large coal mines and the consequent unemployment of the miners, especially in the eastern part of the state, is probably the state's major problem. Efforts are being made to attract tourists and industry to Kentucky, so that the economic level of this area can be raised.

Louisville, Kentucky's largest city, is noted for tobacco products, fine whiskey, and the Kentucky Derby. Founded in 1778 by George Rogers Clark, the city was later named in honor of Louis XVI of France.

The State Capitol at Frankfort was completed in 1909. It stands on a wooded slope overlooking the Kentucky River. The dome is a reproduction of the dome over Napoleon's tomb.

The University of Kentucky, at Lexington, was chartered as the Kentucky Agricultural and Mechanical College in 1865 and opened at its present location in 1881. Shown is the university's Medical Center.

Cumberland Gap, a famous pass through a range of the Appalachian Highlands, is in Cumberland Gap National Historical Park, one of two such parks in Kentucky. The first settlers from Virginia entered Kentucky through this pass.

Kentucky picture profile

The 68-foot-high waterfall is the most impressive sight in Cumberland Falls State Park. A beautiful moonbow often forms over it. The park occupies nearly 2,000 acres on the Cumberland River.

Boating is popular on Kentucky Lake, one of the longest man-made lakes in the world. This Tennessee Valley Authority project is about 180 miles long and encompasses some 2,400 miles of shoreline.

This is the central attraction at Natural Bridge State Park, a 1,372-acre area in the Red River valley near Slade. There are more than 30 state parks in Kentucky.

Much-visited Mammoth Cave National Park is noted for its more than 150 miles of charted underground passageways. The cave's high, vaulted rooms are filled with unusual onyx and limestone formations.

Every October the Daniel Boone Festival is held in Barbourville. The town is on the Wilderness Road, the trail that the famous frontiersman blazed in 1775.

The museum in Audubon State Park is a tribute to John J. Audubon, the renowned artist and ornithologist. It houses many of his works as well as relics of the period in which he lived. The park is also a bird sanctuary.

Ashland, in the city of Lexington, was the home of Henry Clay, for whom it was built in 1806. In 1857, five years after Clay's death, the mansion was rebuilt. Clay raised cattle and horses on his estate.

In Pioneer Memorial State Park at Harrodsburg stands a reconstruction of Fort Harrod. It was erected on the site of the first permanent white settlement in Kentucky, established by James Harrod in 1774.

Tobacco is Kentucky's chief field crop. The buds are usually cut off to give the leaves more nourishment. The green leaves turn brown in curing.

219

KENTUCKY FACT SUMMARY

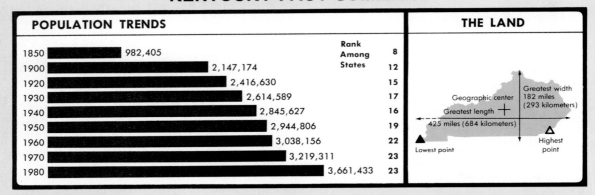

POPULATION TRENDS

Year	Population	Rank Among States
1850	982,405	8
1900	2,147,174	12
1920	2,416,630	15
1930	2,614,589	17
1940	2,845,627	16
1950	2,944,806	19
1960	3,038,156	22
1970	3,219,311	23
1980	3,661,433	23

THE LAND

Geographic center
Greatest length
425 miles (684 kilometers)
Greatest width 182 miles (293 kilometers)
Lowest point
Highest point

LARGEST CITIES (1980 census)

Louisville (298,694): industrial center at Falls of the Ohio; port; railroad shops, distilleries, cigarette plants; chemicals; University of Louisville; Churchill Downs racetrack; J. B. Speed Art Museum (*see* Louisville).

Lexington-Fayette (204,165): in bluegrass region; horse farms; Keeneland Race Course; tobacco and livestock market; University of Kentucky; Transylvania University; Ashland, Henry Clay's home; Gen. John Hunt Morgan House; Kentucky Horse Park with Man O' War Monument (*see* Lexington-Fayette).

Owensboro (54,450): major tobacco market; varied industries; Kentucky Wesleyan College.

Covington (49,574): industrial city on Ohio River; Cathedral Basilica of the Assumption; Carroll Chimes Bell Tower in Goebel Park.

Bowling Green (40,450): farm center; livestock and tobacco market; Western Kentucky University.

Fort Knox (31,055): U.S. Gold Bullion Depository; Patton Museum of Cavalry and Armor; historical armored-vehicle show.

Paducah (29,315): port on Ohio River; tobacco market; rail shops; near atomic plant.

Pleasure Ridge Park (27,332): suburb south of Louisville.

Hopkinsville (27,318): industrial center; manufacture of precision springs, lighting fixtures, wire; tobacco auctions; Fort Campbell military installation.

Ashland (27,064): industrial center; steel, oil, and chemical products.

Frankfort (25,973): state capital on Kentucky River; distilleries, quarries; State Capitol; historic homes; Frankfort Cemetery; Kentucky State University (*see* Frankfort).

VITAL STATISTICS 1981 (per 1,000 population)
Birthrate:	15.9
Death Rate:	9.1
Marriage Rate:	9.6
Divorce Rate:	4.8

GOVERNMENT

Capital: Frankfort (since 1792).

Statehood: Became 15th state in the Union on June 1, 1792.

Constitution: Adopted 1891. Amendment may be passed by three-fifths vote of both houses; ratified by majority voting on it in an election.

Representation in U.S. Congress: Senate—2. House of Representatives—7. Electoral votes—9.

Legislature: Senators—38; term, 4 years. Representatives—100; term, 2 years.

Executive Officers: Governor—term, 4 years; may not succeed self. Other officials—lieutenant governor, secretary of state, attorney general; all elected; terms, 4 years.

Judiciary: Supreme Court—7 justices; elected; term, 8 years. Court of Appeals—14 judges; elected; term, 8 years. Circuit courts—91 judges; elected; term, 8 years.

County: 120 countries; governed by fiscal courts consisting of judge and magistrates or a judge and commissioners; all elected; term, 4 years.

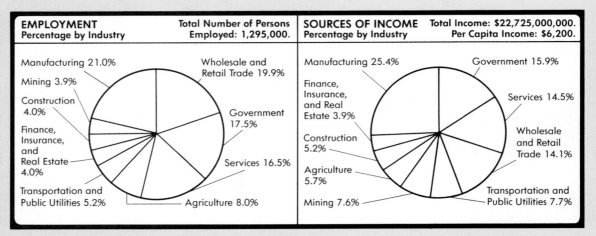

EMPLOYMENT
Percentage by Industry
Total Number of Persons Employed: 1,295,000.

- Manufacturing 21.0%
- Mining 3.9%
- Construction 4.0%
- Finance, Insurance, and Real Estate 4.0%
- Transportation and Public Utilities 5.2%
- Agriculture 8.0%
- Services 16.5%
- Government 17.5%
- Wholesale and Retail Trade 19.9%

SOURCES OF INCOME
Percentage by Industry
Total Income: $22,725,000,000.
Per Capita Income: $6,200.

- Manufacturing 25.4%
- Finance, Insurance, and Real Estate 3.9%
- Construction 5.2%
- Agriculture 5.7%
- Mining 7.6%
- Transportation and Public Utilities 7.7%
- Wholesale and Retail Trade 14.1%
- Services 14.5%
- Government 15.9%

MAJOR PRODUCTS

Agricultural: Tobacco, corn, soybeans, hay, wheat, barley, potatoes, sorghum, oats, racing and show horses, beef and dairy cattle, hogs, chickens, sheep.

Manufactured: Construction equipment, conveyors, transportation equipment, farm and garden machinery, plastics materials and synthetics, industrial inorganic chemicals, paints and allied products, electric distributing equipment, electrical industrial apparatus, household appliances.

Mined: Coal, stone, petroleum, natural gas, sand and gravel, natural-gas liquids, clays.

EDUCATION AND CULTURE

Universities and Colleges: Bellarmine College, Louisville; Berea College, Berea; Cumberland College, Williamsburg; Eastern Kentucky University, Richmond; Georgetown College, Georgetown; Kentucky State University, Frankfort; Morehead State University, Morehead; Murray State University, Murray; Spalding College, Louisville; Transylvania University, Lexington-Fayette; University of Kentucky, Lexington-Fayette; University of Louisville, Louisville; Western Kentucky University, Bowling Green.

Libraries: Eastern Kentucky University Library, Richmond; Kentucky Department for Libraries and Archives, Frankfort; Louisville Free Public Library, Louisville; Morehead State University Library, Morehead; University of Kentucky Library, Lexington-Fayette; University of Louisville Library, Louisville; Western Kentucky University Library, Bowling Green.

Notable Museums: Barton Museum of Whiskey, Bardstown; Berea College Museums, Berea; International Museum of the Horse, Lexington; Kentucky Historical Society, Frankfort; J. B. Speed Art Museum, Louisville; The Kentucky Museum, Bowling Green; Patton Museum of Cavalry and Armor, Fort Knox.

PLACES OF INTEREST

Abraham Lincoln Birthplace National Historic Site: near Hodgenville; memorial building encloses Lincoln's reputed birthplace cabin.

Ancient Buried City (King Mounds): in Wickliffe; 5 of 40 prehistoric Indian mounds explored; museum.

Audubon State Park: near Henderson; museum.

Bardstown: Georgian colonial homes; paintings in St. Joseph's Cathedral; John Fitch Monument; Knob Creek farm, a Lincoln home (1811–16), nearby.

Berea: Berea College, mountain school; Boone Tavern, college hotel; Churchill Weavers.

Blue Licks Battlefield State Park: near Carlisle; site of "last battle of American Revolution" (1782).

Breaks Interstate Park: in mountains bordering Kentucky and Virginia; area of rugged scenic beauty.

Columbus-Belmont Battlefield State Park: on Mississippi River bluff near Columbus; fortified in Civil War.

Constitution Square State Shrine: in Danville; site of framing of Kentucky's first constitution, in 1792.

Cumberland Gap National Historical Park: in Kentucky, Virginia, and Tennessee; near Middlesboro; pass used by Daniel Boone and pioneers.

Dr. Thomas Walker Memorial State Shrine: near Barbourville; first white man's cabin in Kentucky (1750).

Fort Knox: U.S. gold depository housing major part of gold reserve of U.S.; Patton Museum of Cavalry and Armor.

Harlan: coal capital of Kentucky; in heart of magnificent mountain scenery.

Herrington Lake: near Danville: Dix River Dam; fishing.

Horse Farms: in Bluegrass area near Lexington-Fayette.

Isaac Shelby State Shrine: near Danville; grave of first governor of Kentucky.

Jefferson Davis Monument State Shrine: near Hopkinsville; honors Confederate president; 351-foot (107-meter) shaft.

Land Between the Lakes: wooded peninsula between Barkley and Kentucky lakes; TVA-owned and operated national demonstration area for recreation, environmental education, and resource management; museum.

Levi Jackson Wilderness Road State Park: near London; Indian massacre site (1786); pioneer buildings.

Lincoln Homestead State Park: near Springfield; museum.

Mammoth Cave National Park: near Cave City; more than 150 miles (240 kilometers) of passages; stalactites and stalagmites in vast chambers.

My Old Kentucky Home State Park: near Bardstown; Stephen Foster said to have written song here.

Old Fort Harrod State Park: in Harrodsburg; replica of Fort Harrod, state's first white settlement (1774).

Old Mulkey Meeting House State Shrine: near Tompkinsville; oldest log meetinghouse in Kentucky (1798).

Paris: Duncan Tavern, built in 1788; Claiborne Farm, famous Thoroughbred horse farm, nearby.

Perryville Battlefield State Shrine: near Perryville; site of bloody Civil War battle (1862).

Shaker Village of Pleasant Hill: near Harrodsburg; communal town founded by Shakers in 1805.

William Whitley House State Shrine: near Stanford; first brick house west of Alleghenies.

BIBLIOGRAPHY FOR KENTUCKY

Bailey, B. F. Picture Book of Kentucky, rev. ed. (Whitman, 1967).

Carpenter, Allan. Kentucky, rev. ed. (Children's, 1979).

Channing, S. A. Kentucky: a Bicentennial History (Norton, 1977).

Clark, T. D. The Kentucky (Henry Clay, 1969).

Clark, T. D. Kentucky: Land of Contrast (Graphic Arts, 1982).

Coleman, W. J. Kentucky; a pictorial history (Univ. Press of Ky., 1971).

Filson, John. The Discovery and Settlement of Kentucky (Univ. Microfilms, 1966).

Fradin, Dennis. Kentucky In Words and Pictures (Children's, 1981).

Giles, J. H. The Kentuckians (G. K. Hall, 1980).

Neal, Julia. Kentucky Shakers (Univ. Press of Ky., 1977).

Steele, W. O. The Old Wilderness Road (Harcourt, 1968).

Stuart, Jesse. The Thread That Runs So True (Scribner, 1958).

Writers' Program. Kentucky: a Guide to the Bluegrass State (Somerset, 1939).

All Fact Summary data are based on current government reports.

221

KENTUCKY

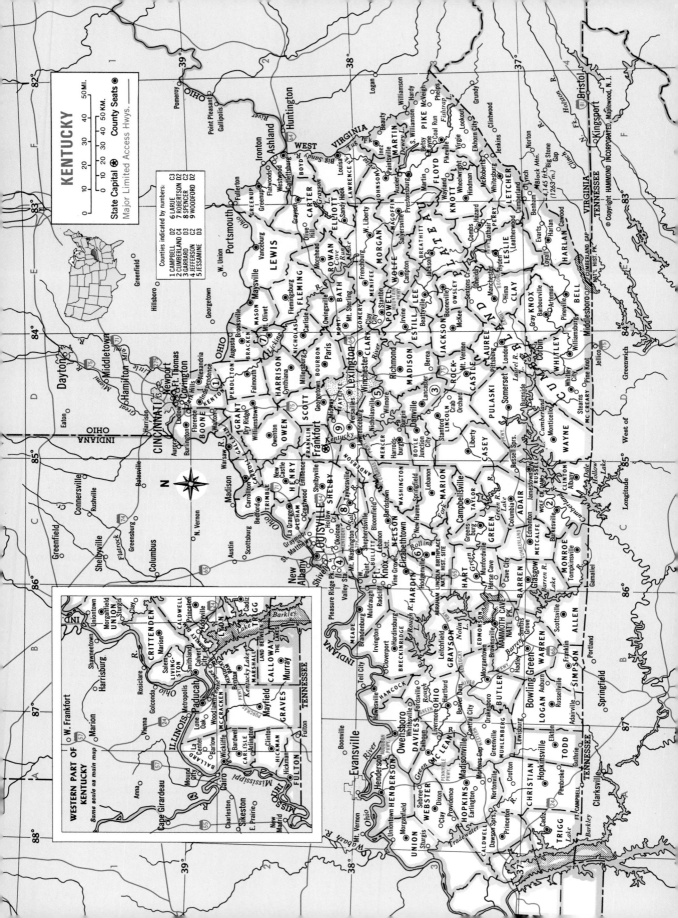

Kenya's Amboseli National Park spreads out before Mt. Kilimanjaro rising in Tanzania.

KENYA.

A republic of Africa, Kenya is located on the equator on the continent's east coast. The country is well known for its scenic beauty and varied wildlife. Although only about 20 percent of the land is suitable for cultivation, the majority of Kenyans are farmers who produce crops mainly for their own needs. Coffee and tea, grown for export on large plantations and on small farms, together with tourism are Kenya's most important sources of foreign exchange—money used to buy foreign goods. The nation imports all of its petroleum and most manufactured products. Kenya is a poor country by comparison with industrialized countries such as those of Western Europe.

Climate and Geographic Regions

Kenya has two wet seasons and two dry seasons. The rainy seasons extend from March to May and from November to January. The amount of rainfall is greatest in the highlands of Kenya, which are located in the west. The lowland deserts of the north receive the least amount of rain. Occasionally the rains fail or are below normal for consecutive seasons, leading to drought. During excessive periods of drought, such as in 1960 and 1961 and 1972 to 1976, crop production is low and many animals die.

Because of the uneven distribution of rainfall and the variation in land elevation ecological conditions differ throughout the country. There are three main geographic zones: the highlands, the semiarid lowlands, and the deserts. A fourth, the coastal zone, occupies a narrow strip along the Indian Ocean.

The highlands. In the western part of Kenya the land rises to more than 5,000 feet (1,500 meters) above sea level. These highlands, which represent less than 25 percent of Kenya's land area, are divided

This article was contributed by David John Campbell, Assistant Professor, Department of Geography and African Studies Center, Michigan State University.

by the Great Rift Valley. In the eastern part of this region, Kenya reaches its highest point at the peak of Mount Kenya, 17,058 feet (5,199 meters) high. The highlands are the only part of the country where rainfall is sufficient—over 50 inches (1,270 millimeters) a year—and reliable enough to support farming. Because most Kenyans depend on agriculture for a living, it is in these highlands that the majority of the population lives. Most of the forest that once covered the land has been cleared for crop production. Some of Kenya's forest does remain, and national parks have been created by the government to protect the local vegetation and the wildlife.

The semiarid lowlands. Much of Kenya is semiarid, receiving between 15 and 30 inches (380 and 760 millimeters) of rainfall a year. This amount of rainfall is insufficient for production of crops, so cultivation is limited to the borders of rivers and swamps where irrigation is possible. In the past there was little farming in the lowlands, and most of the inhabitants were nomadic or seminomadic herders. The number of lowland farmers has increased, however, as people have moved from the overcrowded highlands in search of land.

The main economic activities are livestock raising by Kenyans and wildlife viewing by foreign tourists. Both the wildlife and the livestock are able to graze on the vegetation that grows under the dry conditions. Trees, such as the acacia, are scattered throughout the bushy grasslands. The herders, such as the Masai (Maasai), raise cattle, goats, and sheep and move them seasonally from place to place to give them access to water and pasture.

The wildlife includes large numbers of gazelles, zebras, and wildebeests and predators such as the lion and cheetah. Also common are the predatory leopard and wild dog and other grazing animals such as the antelope, elephant, buffalo, and rhinoceros. National parks have been created where these animals are found in large numbers. Unfortunately, water is scarce, and there is increasing competition for it.

The deserts. The deserts of Kenya are not so extensive as other deserts in Africa. They are located in the north of the country. The vegetation is sparse, consisting of hardy grasses and occasional bushes. Desert peoples are few, but the area includes some nomadic people, such as the Somali and the Gabbra, who raise herds of camels and goats. On the edge of the desert region is Lake Rudolf (Turkana), which stretches down from the border with Ethiopia. It is the site of a small fishing industry. Archaeologists working on the shores of the lake have found evidence of some of the Earth's earliest people, dating the ancestors of man back some 4 to 5 million years.

The coast. Stretching along the shores of the Indian Ocean is a narrow strip of land 10 to 15 miles (16 to 24 kilometers) wide that separates the dry interior from the sea. It is an area with relatively heavy rainfall, 40 inches (1,000 millimeters) a year, and is an important crop-producing area. Cash crops such as coconuts and cashews are produced.

For centuries the coast has been important in trade across the Indian Ocean, and ancient ports, such as Lamu, remain as evidence of the early coastal trade cities. Today, Mombasa is the largest coastal city and Kenya's largest and busiest port. It has modern facilities, an oil refinery, and a variety of light industries. The port also serves the landlocked countries of Uganda, Rwanda, and Burundi. The long and beautiful white coral sand beaches are the basis of Kenya's coastal tourist industry. Hotels serve tourists along the entire length of the coast.

Population and Economy

Kenya has more than 100 different ethnic groups. This poses a potential problem of communication. Swahili and English have been selected as national languages and most people speak at least one of these as well as their own local language.

The people are also divided among many religious groups. African traditional religions are widespread as is Christianity, which was spread by missionary groups in the 19th and early 20th centuries. Islam is particularly well established along the coast; the Kenyans of Asian origin are predominantly Hindus.

Kenya's artistic heritage is represented by a variety of crafts. Among them are matweaving on the coast, wood carving by the Kamba people, and beadwork jewelry made by groups such as the Masai and the Samburu.

Among the nation's 17 million people, the most populous groups are the Kikuyu, the Luhya, the Luo, and the Kamba. There are just over one million herders such as the Masai and the Somali living in the semiarid and desert areas. An increasing number of people live in the capital city of Nairobi and in other large cities. In the early 1980s it was estimated that Kenya's population was increasing at the rate of about 4 percent a year. This growth rate, one of the world's highest, greatly increases the people's demand for land, housing, food, jobs, education, medical care, and other services. These conditions place a severe strain on the economy of Kenya, a country whose resources are extremely limited.

One reason that Kenya has remained heavily dependent on agriculture is its lack of fuel resources, such as petroleum. Totally reliant on foreign countries for oil, Kenya's manufacturing industries have developed slowly. Some energy is forthcoming from hydroelectric projects, but it is inadequate, and additional electric power must be imported from neighboring countries. To remedy this situation, especially in light of oil-price increases, the government has accelerated development of alternative sources of energy. Kenya now produces power from geothermal (natural heat from the Earth's interior) sources, and plans are to increase the number of geothermal units. The sugar industry, which can produce alcohol for fuel, is another developing source. The Kenyan economy receives minimal support from such other resource areas as mining, forestry, and fisheries.

Agriculture. The most rapidly growing population group in Kenya is the farmers. In many areas, however, there is insufficient land available, and some farms have been subdivided into several units. These are often unable to produce sufficient crops to meet the needs of the families tending them. Increasing numbers of people are migrating to areas where more land is available. Most of the areas where people can find land are on the dry edges of the highlands. In these areas soils may be less fertile and the rainfall less certain, making farming risky.

The vast majority of Kenya's farmers own only about seven acres (three hectares) of land. On these small farms most of what they produce is to meet their family's needs. Some crops are grown for sale to raise money to buy consumer items. Typically a farmer grows several different crops together in the same field: a grain such as corn; a legume such as beans; and perhaps a few trees producing coffee, bananas, or mangoes. This allows the family to harvest

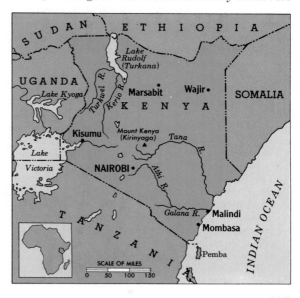

G. Ricatto—Shostal Associates

Nairobi's Kenyatta Conference Center hosts international meetings. It is named for Jomo Kenyatta, Kenya's independence leader and first president.

a variety of foods for a balanced diet. In order to increase production, the government sponsors agricultural experiments and encourages farmers to try different production methods. Some farmers also keep a few animals such as cattle and goats, and many raise poultry. Tea and coffee, raised for cash and export, are two of Kenya's major sources of income.

The herders raise such animals as cattle, camels, sheep, and goats. These produce milk and meat for the family and some to be sold for cash. Herding families use the cash to buy grains to supplement the meat and milk in their diet. As the human population grows so have the number of animals, and there is concern that they may be overgrazing the land. In many parts of the country the government is promoting better use and management of the grazing land.

Tourism. The other major earner of foreign exchange, the tourist industry, does not bring income to as many people as coffee or tea sales. Tourist facilities are concentrated in Nairobi, along the coast, and in the national parks. The industry is largely owned by foreign companies, however, and relatively few Kenyans benefit from it.

Tourists visit Kenya for a number of reasons. Its beaches are beautiful and uncrowded, and hotels are of high quality and serve good food. Kenya has one of the world's largest wildlife populations, and a wide variety of animals can be seen in national parks. There, excellent hotels with special viewing facilities have been built for tourists. The parks protect the wildlife, but some species, such as the rhinoceros and elephant, are still hunted by poachers for their horns and tusks. Nairobi also attracts tourists, and it has become a site for international conferences.

Cities and industry. The cities of Kenya have been growing partly because of emigration from the countryside. Most salaried jobs in the cities are in the government bureaucracy, in industry, and in occupations such as sales and domestic services.

Kenya's industries include food processing, brewing, clothing and textiles, transport equipment, and refined petroleum and petrochemicals. The majority of companies are located in or near Nairobi, but the government is encouraging new firms to locate in other towns so that more of the country can benefit from industry. Nairobi, the capital city of Kenya, is located on the railway line at the junction between the lowlands and the highlands. More than 60 percent of Kenya's salaried workers live in the city, which dominates the nation's economy. It is an important commercial center and many foreign firms base their east African operations there. Most government employees also work in Nairobi.

The Kenyan economy is supported by one of the best transportation systems in Africa. The railway links the main towns and paved roads reach all but the most inaccessible towns. The main roads to Tanzania and Uganda are paved and the one to Ethiopia is almost completely paved. Nairobi's modernized airport is one of Africa's busiest. Flights connect the city to other African cities, and to Europe, the United States, and Asia.

Government and Education

When Kenya became independent in 1963 it was ruled as a constitutional monarchy, but in 1964 it declared itself a republic within the Commonwealth of Nations. The one-house parliament, the National Assembly, is led by a president. The president chooses the vice-president and ministers from among the members of the assembly. The dominant political party since independence, the Kenya African National Union, is now the only legal party.

Education has been strongly supported by the government and nearly all children go to primary school, which is free. The adult literacy rate increased from 20 percent in 1960 to 45 percent in 1976. After primary school the educational system becomes highly competitive and few of those who go on to secondary school gain admittance to the University of Nairobi or any of the country's smaller colleges.

History

As recently as the 1880s there was no country known as Kenya. At the beginning of the 20th century the British colonized East Africa and drew boundaries around the country they named Kenya. Prior to the arrival of the British each of Kenya's peoples had its own form of government, culture, and economy. The British imposed their own administration and through their economic, religious, and educational activities they transformed the Africans' way of life.

The colonial administration encouraged British and South African white people to move from their homeland to settle in Kenya. To promote this settlement, they reserved a large area exclusively for whites, and made generous offers of land. Eventually this area totaled about 16,000 square miles (41,400 square kilometers) and contained about one half of the country's land suitable for crops. In the highlands the settlers grew tea and coffee for export, while in the lowlands they raised livestock.

The loss of land to the British brought resentment against the colonial administration, and in 1952 a war of liberation began. A guerrilla group called the Mau Mau made up of members of several ethnic groups led the struggle. The Mau Mau rebellion, as it was called, took place mainly in the highlands, where the Kikuyu people claimed that much of this land had been stolen from them.

Eleven years later, in 1963, independence for Kenya was won. Many Kenyans who fought in the war looked forward to a redistribution of land from European to African farmers. More than 1 million acres (400,000 hectares) were redistributed to 45,000 Kenyans, but many large farms were left intact and taken over by powerful Kenyans. The problem of land shortage continued to be an issue.

The new country adopted a democratic parliamentary form of government, and Jomo Kenyatta was elected president. He held the position until his death in 1978, when he was succeeded by the vice-president, Daniel arap Moi. (*See also* Kenyatta.)

Moi was supported by all of Kenya's leading politicians. He faced a major threat to his government in 1982, however, when air force personnel attempted a coup. The army, which remained loyal to Moi, halted the rebellion. In 1985–86 Kenya recovered from three years of drought. By following a stabilization program prepared by the International Monetary Fund, the country was able to maintain economic growth. Kenya experienced border disputes with Uganda and Tanzania into the late 1980s that resulted in periodic closings of the borders.

BIBLIOGRAPHY FOR KENYA

Collier, Paul and Deepak, Lal. Labour and Poverty in Kenya, 1900–80 (Oxford, 1985).
Kennedy, Dane. Islands of White: Settler Society and Culture in Kenya and Southern Rhodesia, 1890–1939 (Duke Univ. Press, 1987).
Lerner Publications. Kenya in Pictures (Lerner, 1988).
Livingstone, Ian. Rural Development, Employment, and Income in Kenya (Gower, 1985).
Lye, Keith. Take a Trip to Kenya (Watts, 1985).
Miller, Norman. Kenya: the Quest for Prosperity (Westview, 1984).
Schatzberg, M.G., ed. The Political Economy of Kenya (Praeger, 1988).
Stein, R.C. Kenya (Children's, 1985).
Trzebinski, Errol. The Kenya Pioneers (Norton, 1988).

Kenya Fact Summary

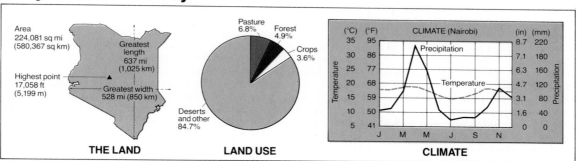

THE LAND   LAND USE   CLIMATE

Official Name : Republic of Kenya.
Capital: Nairobi.

NATURAL FEATURES

Mountain Ranges: Highlands associated with the Great Rift Valley (Aberdare Range, Cherangany Hills, Mau Escarpment).
Highest Peaks: Mount Kenya (Kirinyaga), 17,058 feet (5,199 meters); Mount Elgon, 14,178 feet (4,321 meters).
Largest Lakes: Lake Rudolf (Turkana), Lake Victoria.
Major Rivers: Galana, Tana, Turkwel.

PEOPLE

Population (1988 estimate): 22,919,000; 104 persons per square mile (40 persons per square kilometer); 19.7 percent urban, 80.3 percent rural.
Major Cities (1984 estimate): Nairobi (1985 estimate, 1,162,000), Mombasa (425,600), Kisumu (167,100), Nakuru (101,700).
Major Religions: Christianity, traditional African religions, Islam.
Major Languages: Swahili, English, Kikuyu, Luo.
Literacy: 59 percent.
Leading University: University of Nairobi.

GOVERNMENT

Form of Government: Republic.
Chief of State and Head of Government: President; elected by popular vote.

Legislature: Unicameral (single house) National Assembly; members elected by popular vote for a five-year term (202 members, including 14 nonelective seats).
Voting Qualification: Age 21.
Political Divisions: 8 provinces:

Central	Nairobi	Rift Valley
Coast	North Eastern	Western
Eastern	Nyanza	

Flag: Five horizontal stripes: black, white, red, white, green; shield in center (*see* Flags of the World).

ECONOMY

Chief Agricultural Products: *Crops*—coffee, corn (maize), cotton, pyrethrum, sisal, sugar, tea, tobacco, wheat. *Livestock*—camels, cattle, goats, sheep.
Chief Mined Products: Cement (limestone), flourspar, salt, soda ash.
Chief Manufactured Products: Beverages and tobacco; canned vegetables, oils, and fats; clothing and textiles; metal products; nonelectrical machinery; paper and paper products; refined petroleum and petrochemicals; rubber and plastic products; sugar and confectionery; transport equipment.
Chief Imports: Chemicals, corn (maize), crude petroleum, fertilizers, iron and steel, medicinal products, paper and paper products, petroleum products, plastic materials, vegetable oils and fats.
Chief Exports: Cement, coffee, hides, petroleum products, pyrethrum extract and flowers, sisal fiber, tea, tinned pineapple.
Monetary Unit: 1 Kenya pound = 20 Kenya shillings; 1 Kenya shilling = 100 Kenya cents.

Jomo Kenyatta
John Moss—Black Star

KENYATTA, Jomo (1894?–1978). When the East African nation of Kenya gained its independence from Great Britain in 1963, Jomo Kenyatta became its first prime minister. His adult career, from 1922 onward, had spanned the whole period of Kenya's pursuit of independence—a movement for which he was the chief spokesman for 30 years.

Kenyatta was born in about 1894 in Ichaweri, in the East African highlands. His parents, members of the Kikuyu tribe, gave him the name Kamau. Childhood fascination with the life of European settlers led him to run away from home and study in a Christian mission school. As a young man he went to live in Nairobi, the capital, where he worked for the colonial government. In 1922 he joined the East Africa Association, and when that was disbanded, he helped organize the Kikuyu Central Association in 1925. These groups sought independence for Kenya in opposition to Britain's intent to consolidate East African territories into one country.

From 1930 to 1946 Kenyatta spent most of his time in England studying and meeting other anti-colonial leaders. He returned to East Africa in 1946 to become leader of the new Kenya African Union and to mobilize anti-colonial sentiment. He was imprisoned by the British from 1953 to 1961. After his release he went to London to negotiate Kenya's independence. His party won the pre-independence elections in May 1963, and he became prime minister in December. He became president of Kenya in 1964 and held office until his death at Mombasa on Aug. 22, 1978.

KEPLER, Johannes (1571–1630). The Renaissance astronomer and astrologer Johannes Kepler is best known for his discovery that the orbits in which the Earth and the other planets of the solar system travel around the sun are elliptical, or oval, in shape. He was also the first to explain correctly how human beings see and to demonstrate what happens to light when it enters a telescope. In addition, he designed an instrument that serves as the basis of the modern refractive telescope.

Kepler was born on Dec. 27, 1571, at Weil der Stadt in the duchy of Württemberg, now in southern West Germany. He was a sickly child but had a brilliant mind. At the University of Tübingen he was greatly influenced by the theories of the astronomer Copernicus. He later taught astronomy and mathematics at the university in Graz, Austria. While there he corresponded with two other great astronomers of the time—Galileo and Tycho Brahe. In 1600 he became Brahe's assistant in Prague. When Brahe died Kepler succeeded him as astrologer and astronomer to Rudolph II of Bohemia. His task of doing horoscopes at births and other important events in the royal family was of first importance; astronomy was secondary. Kepler, however, gave all the time he could to the outstanding astronomical problem of the day.

By Kepler's time, many astronomers had accepted that the sun was the center of the solar system and that the Earth turned on its axis, but they still believed that the planets moved in circular orbits. Because of this, they could not explain the motions of the planets as seen from the Earth.

Kepler decided to try explaining these motions by finding another shape for the planetary orbits. Because Mars offered the most typical problem and he had Brahe's accurate observations of this planet, Kepler began with it. He tried every possible combination of circular motions in attempts to account for Mars's positions. These all failed, though once a discrepancy of only eight minutes of arc remained unaccounted for. "Out of these eight minutes," he said, "we will construct a new theory that will explain the motions of all the planets!"

After six years, hampered by poor eyesight and the clumsy mathematical methods of the day, he found the answer. Mars follows an elliptical orbit at a speed that varies according to the planet's distance from the sun. In 1609 he published a book on the results of his work, boldly titling it 'The New Astronomy'.

He then turned to the other planets and found that their motions corresponded to those of Mars. He also discovered that their periods of revolution—time required to go around the sun—bore a precise relation to their distances from the sun.

Kepler's great work on planetary motion is summed up in three principles, which have become known as "Kepler's laws": (1) The path of every planet in its motion about the sun forms an ellipse, with the sun at one focus. (2) The speed of a planet in its orbit varies so that a line joining it with the sun sweeps over equal areas in equal times. (3) The squares of the planets' periods of revolution are proportional to the cubes of the planets' mean distances from the sun. These laws removed all doubt that the Earth and planets go around the sun. Later Sir Isaac Newton used Kepler's laws to establish his law of universal gravitation.

Kepler could now proceed with his task of revising the Rudolphine tables, an almanac of the positions of heavenly bodies that, although unsatisfactory, was the best available at the time. Kepler's new laws enabled him to predict positions of the planets by date and hour that have proved to be substantially accurate even to the present day.

Kepler was one of the first to be informed by Galileo about Galileo's invention of the telescope, and afterward he went on to do valuable pioneer work in optics. It was Kepler who invented the present-day form of astronomical telescope (*see* Telescope). His book on optics, 'Dioptrice', published in 1611, was the first of its kind and founded the scientific study of light and lenses. Kepler died on Nov. 15, 1630, at Regensburg in Bavaria.

KEROUAC, Jack (1922–69). The writer who coined the term "beat generation" and became its leading spokesman was Jack Kerouac. The beat movement, a social and literary experiment, originated in the bohemian artists' colonies around San Francisco, Calif., and Greenwich Village in New York City in the late 1950s. Its adherents felt alienated from conventional society and adopted occasionally bizarre life-styles.

Kerouac was born Jean-Louis Kerouac at Lowell, Mass., on March 12, 1922, to French-Canadian parents. He went to school in New York City and afterward served in World War II. After the war he became a wanderer, traveling through the United States and Mexico, unwilling to hold a steady job. His first novel, 'The Town and the City', published in 1950, was fairly well received. Uncomfortable with conventional writing forms, Kerouac developed an unstructured, flowing, and spontaneous style that first made its appearance in 'On the Road' (1957). This book, the bible of the beat movement, deals with the frenetic travels around the country of young people who, though poor, were in love with life, love, sex, drugs, jazz, and mysticism and completely rejected standard values.

The book and Kerouac's life-style drew public attention to the existence of a widespread subculture of artists, musicians, poets, and eccentrics that he had met on his travels. 'On the Road' made him the culture hero of the movement, but there were other writers such as Allen Ginsberg and Lawrence Ferlinghetti who also became prominent, especially as the beat movement was transformed into the counterculture of the 1960s.

Like 'On the Road', all of Kerouac's books, including 'The Subterraneans' (1958), 'Lonesome Traveler' (1960), and 'Desolate Angels' (1965), are autobiographical. Kerouac died in St. Petersburg, Fla., on Oct. 21, 1969.

KEY, Francis Scott (1779–1843). A lawyer who wrote verse as a hobby, Francis Scott Key wrote the words to 'The Star-Spangled Banner' after a battle in the War of 1812. The words were sung to the tune of the English drinking song 'To Anacreon in Heaven'.

Francis Scott Key was born on Terra Rubra, his family's estate in western Maryland, on Aug. 1, 1779.

Until he was 10 he was taught at home. After attending preparatory school at Annapolis, he entered St. John's College and then prepared for a legal career in the office of Judge Jeremiah Chase. He opened a successful law practice in Georgetown (now part of Washington, D.C.) and served as attorney for the District of Columbia from 1833. He died in Baltimore, Md., on Jan. 11, 1843.

After the burning of Washington by the British in the War of 1812, Key was sent to the British fleet anchored in Chesapeake Bay to secure the release of a friend. He was detained aboard ship overnight on Sept. 13, 1814, during the bombardment of Fort McHenry. When he saw the United States flag still flying over the fortress the next morning, he wrote the words to what was later called 'The Star-Spangled Banner' but was first printed under the title 'Defence of Fort M'Henry'. The song quickly became popular and was adopted by the Army and Navy as the national anthem, but not until 1931 did it become officially recognized as such by an act of Congress.

KEY *see* LOCK AND KEY.

KEYNES, John Maynard (1883–1946). An economist, journalist, and financier, John Keynes is best known for his revolutionary economic theory on the causes of prolonged unemployment. His enduring fame rests on a theory that recovery from a recession can best be achieved by a government-sponsored policy of full employment.

John Maynard Keynes was born in Cambridge, England, on June 5, 1883. He was educated at Eton and Cambridge, where he studied under Alfred Marshall, the leading Cambridge economist. Here Keynes's interest in politics and economics grew. After leaving Cambridge he became a civil servant and worked for the government's India Office. His experience there formed the basis of his first major work, which is still the definitive examination of pre-World War I Indian finance. He returned to Cambridge as a lecturer in economics, but the onset of the war brought him back to government employment. His

John Maynard Keynes as painted by Gwen Raverat

experience as an economic adviser at the Versailles Peace Conference led him to write his scathing 'The Economic Consequences of the Peace', published in 1919, in which he argued against excessive reparations requirements of Germany after the war.

Keynes then followed a financial career in London, where he was regarded as a conventional economist until the depression of the 1930s. In 'The General Theory of Employment, Interest and Money' (1936), Keynes departed from his classical theories. He put forth his ideas about government responsibility and commitment to maintaining high employment. He claimed that because consumers were limited in their spending by the size of their incomes, they were not the source of business cycle shifts. The dynamic participants were business investors and governments.

During World War II most Western democracies affirmed their commitment to this philosophy. Keynes played a central role in British war financing and in 1944 was chief British representative at the Bretton Woods Conference that established the International Monetary Fund. His last major public service was his brilliant negotiation in the autumn and early winter of 1945 of a multibillion-dollar loan granted by the United States to Britain. On April 21, 1946, exhausted and overstrained by wartime exertion, Keynes died in Firle, Sussex, England.

KEYS, FLORIDA. The small islands off Florida are called "keys," from the Spanish word *cayo*. It means "rock" or "islet." The name Florida Keys is restricted to the chain of about 60 keys that extends from Miami Beach to Key West.

The eastern end of the chain is a remnant of an old coral reef. Living corals are still building reefs here (*see* Coral). The western keys are of limestone. Mangrove thickets line the shores and cover some of the low islands. The growth that rises on the higher ground is composed of tropical hardwoods and palms. Some small keys are submerged at high tide.

The largest of the keys is Key Largo—about 30 miles (48 kilometers) long and less than 2 miles (3 kilometers) wide. John Pennekamp Coral Reef State Park is located in the Atlantic waters off this key. Its chief attractions are underwater scenery and living coral formations. Settlements have sprung up on some of the larger keys. There is little agriculture because of the thin soil. Fishing resorts entertain sportsmen who come for deep-sea fishing.

The southernmost city in the United States, outside of Hawaii, is Key West. It spreads over a small island, four miles (six kilometers) long and less than two miles (three kilometers) wide. It lies some 100 miles (160 kilometers) southwest of the mainland. The island is the westernmost in the Florida Keys. Its location provides sunny year-round warmth. Its shores are bathed by warm Gulf Stream water and the southeast trade winds bring mild breezes.

Key West's history has been colorful. Spanish adventurers of the 16th century were early inhabitants. Pirate ships hid in the passes and waterways between the keys. The offshore reefs still hold the sunken wrecks of ships lost in sea battles of long ago.

The settlement on Key West was incorporated as a city in 1828. Cuban cigar makers built a prosperous industry after 1869, and sponge fishing flourished. During the 1890s Key West, with 18,000 people, was Florida's largest city. Today the population (1980 census) is 24,382.

In 1912 a railroad was built along the keys, and Key West became an important port for trade with the Caribbean islands. The railway was abandoned after a hurricane in 1935 destroyed many of the bridges and viaducts between the islands. The federal government used much of the roadbed and bridgework to build a road across the keys.

Since 1938 the Overseas Highway has linked Key West to Miami, 155 miles (249 kilometers) away. Many tourists use the "seagoing highway" to the island city. Hotels, motels, and other tourist facilities have been built.

Today the tourist trade, the naval air station, and fishing provide the greatest employment. Shrimp are caught in the Gulf of Mexico. Giant sea crayfish are sold as "Florida lobsters." A cannery turns sea turtles into green turtle soup.

An aqueduct, about 130 miles (209 kilometers) long, was built by the federal government to supply badly needed fresh water to Key West and the other islands. During World Wars I and II naval and air bases were established at Key West to guard the Gulf of Mexico. (*See also* Florida.)

KHAR'KOV, U.S.S.R. It is said that in the Soviet Ukraine all roads lead to Khar'kov. From its early days as a fort in the 17th century down through World War II, Khar'kov has been repeatedly ravaged by war. Each time a new city was erected. Today Khar'kov is one of the Soviet Union's great manufacturing centers and one of the largest cities in the Ukraine (*see* Ukrainian Soviet Socialist Republic).

Khar'kov became important because of its central position in the upper Donets Basin. This is one of Russia's richest districts. The city stands midway between the Dnepr and Don rivers—each about 125 miles (200 kilometers) away. Moscow is 400 miles (640 kilometers) to the north.

Khar'kov is a collecting point for grain from the Ukraine fields, fruit from the Crimea, and oil from the Caucasus. Late in the 19th century the great Donets coal fields and the iron deposits of Krivoy Rog, to the southwest, were developed. Supplied by these mines, Khar'kov developed iron and steel industries and related manufacturing. Railroads and, later, several airlines were established to serve the area's ever-expanding industries. Machinery of many kinds is manufactured—tractors, coal-mining and

A statue of Lenin stands at Dzerzhinski Square in Khar'kov. Also on the square, behind the statue, is A. M. Gorky University, which was founded in 1805.

oil-drilling equipment, diesel motors, ball bearings, machine tools, combines, locomotives, bicycles, generators, and steam turbines. Light industries include the production of foodstuffs. The Dnepr Dam was built in 1932 at Zaporozh'ye, about 150 miles (240 kilometers) southwest. A resulting flood of hydroelectric power created another large industry—the manufacture of electrical equipment.

The city grew from an agricultural trading center into the "Pittsburgh of Russia." Scientific laboratories, technical schools, and libraries were built. The A. M. Gorky University, which was founded in 1805, was enlarged. The city has six theaters and twenty institutions of higher education. These along with an outstanding collection of Ukrainian art made Khar'-kov a cultural center.

Khar'kov began in 1654 as a Cossack outpost to defend Moscow in its wars against the Poles and Tatars. In the 17th century, it developed important trade and handicraft manufacture and became a seat of provincial government in 1732. At times it replaced Kiev as capital of the Ukraine. The Russian civil wars of 1917 to 1920 overran Khar'kov. From 1918 to 1934 it was the capital of the Ukrainian S.S.R. In World War II it was seized by the Germans. Some 100,000 citizens died during the occupation. The battle to free it in 1943 destroyed half its buildings. The government rebuilt the city and added new factories. Population (1982 estimate), 1,503,000.

KHARTOUM, Sudan. The capital city of The Sudan, the largest African nation, is Khartoum, a name which means "elephant's trunk." Khartoum lies just south of the junction of the Blue Nile and the White Nile rivers (*see* Nile River). The city has bridge connections with its sister towns, which are Khartoum North and Omdurman.

As the country's seat of government and higher education and the center of its commerce and industry, Khartoum is firmly established as its greatest metropolis. Most of the people speak Arabic. The city is also Sudan's communications hub. Its rail lines connect with Egypt as well as the cities of Port Sudan on the eastern coast and Al Ubayyid in the central part of Sudan. Khartoum has an international airport and heavy commercial boat traffic plies each of the Nile rivers.

Khartoum's principal buildings include the palace, parliament, the Sudan National Museum, the University of Khartoum, and the Khartoum Branch of the University of Cairo. Most cultural institutions, including the Industrial Research Institute, the Soviet Cultural Center, and various learned societies, are centered there. The Sudan Natural History Museum is affiliated with the University of Khartoum. There are Roman Catholic, Anglican, and Coptic cathedrals as well as Greek and Maronite churches and several mosques.

Textiles, gums, and glass are produced in Khartoum. The city is also a printing and food-processing center. An oil pipeline between Khartoum and Port Sudan was completed in 1977.

Originally an Egyptian army camp set up in 1821, Khartoum grew into a fortified army town. It was destroyed during a siege in 1885, during which the British governor general of Sudan was killed. Reoccupied by the British in 1898, the city was completely rebuilt and served as the seat of the Anglo-Egyptian Sudan government until 1956. When Sudan became an independent nation in 1956, Khartoum was designated the capital. (*See also* Sudan). Population (1983 census), 476,218.

Ayatollah Ruhollah Khomeini

KHOMEINI, Ayatollah Ruhollah (1902–89).

In January 1979 a revolution overthrew Mohammad Reza Shah Pahlavi, the shah, or monarch, of Iran, one of the wealthiest and best-armed nations in the Middle East. The moving force behind the revolution was the Shi'ah sect of Islam, led by Ayatollah Ruhollah Khomeini. The goal of the revolution was to establish an Islamic state based on the teachings of the Koran, Islam's holy book (*see* Koran).

Khomeini was born in Khomeyn, Iran, in 1902. His father, also an ayatollah, was the leader of the local Shi'ite sect. After his father was killed, Ruhollah was brought up by an older brother. His entire education was in Islamic schools. As an adult he published a number of books on Islamic law, philosophy, and ethics. He was eventually recognized as an ayatollah, a religious title of honor meaning "sign of God." In 1962 he made his home in Qom, one of Iran's leading Shi'ite centers.

Khomeini became a strong critic of the shah, opposing his land-reform policies and his goal of making Iran a wealthy and modern nation, patterned after Western societies. He was briefly imprisoned for his criticisms, and in November 1964 he was banished from Iran altogether.

He settled in An Najaf, Iraq, until 1978 when he was asked to leave because of the problems he was causing within the Muslim community and his antagonism to neighboring Iran. Khomeini then moved to France, where he continued his agitation for the overthrow of the shah. From Paris he received worldwide exposure

through the press. He sent taped messages to Iran that were transmitted by shortwave radio from the nation's mosques. Mounting public opposition forced the shah to leave the country on Jan. 16, 1979. Khomeini arrived on February 1 to take over the government. In December a new constitution created an Islamic republic, with Khomeini named as Iran's political and religious leader for life.

Khomeini wielded considerable power as sweeping changes were made throughout the country. The revolution did not bring peace to Iran. The country was beset with civil strife, economic decline, an eight-year war with Iraq, and opposition from other nations. Khomeini died in Tehran on June 3, 1989, and millions of mourners attended his funeral. A power struggle ensued within the government regarding his successor. (*See also* Iran.)

KHOSROW I and II. During the 6th and 7th centuries there were two eminent rulers of the Sassanid Dynasty of Persia (now Iran) who were named Khosrow. Khosrow I the Just, who ruled from 531 to 579, is known in history and legend as a reformer and patron of culture. After the death of his father, Kavadh I, he won the struggle for the throne and put down a series of social and religious disorders. He established a flat-rate tax system and reorganized the bureaucracy. The frontier defenses of the empire were strengthened, particularly in the west where he carried on intermittent wars against the Byzantine Empire. The army was given a professional standing, making it less necessary to rely on temporary levies of men in times of emergency.

Khosrow I also carried out a large internal improvement program, building roads and bridges. In addition, he encouraged learning. A medical school was founded at Gondeshapur, and, when the Athenian academy was closed in 529 by the Byzantine emperor, Justinian I, Khosrow invited its philosophers to live in Persia (*see* Justinian). After his death, Khosrow was elevated to an almost legendary status for his wisdom and justice.

Khosrow II the Victorious, who ruled from 590 to 628, was the grandson of Khosrow I. Forced to flee Persia by a palace revolt in about 590, he was restored to power only with the help of the Byzantine emperor Maurice. After Maurice was murdered in 602, Khosrow began a series of wars against the Byzantine Empire that lasted for the rest of his reign. For 20 years the Persians were victorious. Mesopotamia, Armenia, Syria, and central Asia Minor were conquered. The tide of conquest was finally turned against Khosrow by the Byzantine emperor Heraclius in a series of campaigns between 622 and 627.

In 628 Khosrow II was condemned and executed by his own people. Under his reign the economy had flagged, taxation had increased, and the professional army had turned into a military aristocracy that weakened the authority of the king. Persia had become sufficiently weakened that the Arabs were able to conquer it easily in 637.

KHRUSHCHEV, Nikita

KHRUSHCHEV, Nikita (1894–1971). Joseph Stalin, dictator of Russia for 29 years, died March 5, 1953. The next day the government radio announced that to "prevent panic" a collective leadership had been formed to rule the Soviet Union. Nikita Khrushchev was not mentioned in the bulletin. Yet within a few years he triumphed over his rivals to become sole dictator of the Soviet Union.

At Stalin's funeral services Khrushchev shared the platform with the Soviet Union's top leaders. He was, however, merely the chairman who introduced the members of the ruling committee. The most important offices went to Georgi M. Malenkov. The other members of the collective leadership were Lavrenti P. Beria, the head of the secret police, and Vyacheslav M. Molotov, who was Stalin's brilliant foreign minister (*see* Molotov).

Nikita Sergeevich Khrushchev was born April 17, 1894, in a peasant's hut in the poverty-stricken village of Kalinovka, in southern Russia. Like his father, he became a coal miner. He joined the Communist party in 1918, during the civil war, and became an untiring organizer. Little is known about his first wife, whom he married in 1920. They had two children, Leonid and Yulia. Leonid was killed in World War II. Khrushchev was reported to have married his second wife, Nina Petrovna, in 1938; but she insisted the marriage took place in 1924. They had one son, Sergei, and two daughters, Yelena and Rada.

Khrushchev entered an industrial school in Moscow in 1929. In the mid-1930s he played a major part in carrying out Stalin's purges. In 1938 Stalin sent him back to the Ukraine to rid the party of anti-Stalinists. After the government had taken almost all the peasants' land, Khrushchev tried to deprive them of the small private plots they still held.

For the last 14 years of Stalin's rule, Khrushchev was party secretary of the Moscow region and a member of the Politburo (later Presidium), the highest organ of the Communist party. By the time Stalin died, many of Khrushchev's supporters had achieved important posts.

Rise to Power

About a week after Stalin's death, Khrushchev wrested control of the party machinery from Malenkov. Then he moved against Beria, head of the secret police. With the help of Marshal Georgi K. Zhukov he had Beria arrested in June 1953. In December Beria and many of his aides were executed. Meanwhile Khrushchev had been named first secretary, the acknowledged head of the Communist party.

In 1955 Khrushchev forced Malenkov to resign as premier, on the ground of "inexperience." The title of premier then was given to Marshal Nikolai Bulganin. At that time Marshal Zhukov replaced Bulganin as minister of defense.

The Plot Against Khrushchev

As first secretary, Khrushchev was not only the most powerful man in the Soviet Union but leader of the world Communist movement. In February 1956 he delivered his famous two-day "secret" speech (later released) before the 20th Communist Party Congress. In this speech Khrushchev denounced Stalin's rule, accusing the dead dictator of infamous crimes. The revelations shocked Communists throughout the world who had blindly followed Stalin's dictates.

Satellite countries were encouraged by the speech to take a more independent line. The Poles rioted, and the Hungarians openly revolted. Stalinists in the Soviet government blamed Khrushchev. Khrushchev put down the revolt in Hungary with Stalinist terroristic methods and eased his stand on Stalinism. (*See also* Hungary; Poland.)

In June 1957 Khrushchev's enemies gained the upper hand in the 11-member Presidium and voted secretly to oust Khrushchev as party secretary. Khrushchev refused to accept the decision and took the fight to the large Central Committee of the party. There, after two days of debate, his leadership was confirmed. Four members of the Presidium—including Molotov and Malenkov—were dropped and forced to confess their "mistakes." In October even Zhukov, who had helped Khrushchev defeat the conspiracy, was dropped from the Presidium. There remained, however, powerful Stalinist dissenters in both the government and the army. In March 1958 the "collective leadership" was ended when Khrushchev took over Bulganin's title as premier.

Personality and Policies

Correspondents from Western nations described Khrushchev as a man of enormous energy and drive, talkative, sociable, earthy, tough, and shrewd. With great self-confidence he took colossal gambles in both foreign and domestic policy. As a dictator he did not have to fear opposition from a parliament or criticism from the press. He could not, however, completely ignore the discontent of the Soviet people. His announced goals were to overtake the United States in productivity and to help spread Communism throughout the world.

At home Khrushchev continued to build up armaments and heavy industry, at the same time promising the people a huge expansion in consumer goods. In foreign affairs he was bold and unpredictable, making quick turnabouts that put other nations at a disadvantage. While talking peace, he made no concessions—except when he was forced to withdraw missiles from Cuba in 1962 and when he agreed to the nuclear test ban treaty of 1963. In the early 1960s Khrushchev's de-Stalinization policy caused a rift with China that split the Communist world into two opposing camps. In 1964 Khrushchev was removed from office. During his remaining years, he lived quietly. He died in a Moscow hospital on Sept. 11, 1971, following a heart attack.

KIANGSI *see* JIANGXI.

KIANGSU *see* JIANGSU.

KIDD, Captain (1645?–1701). Numberless legends about Captain Kidd have made him the most famous of pirates. Oddly enough, acts of piracy were never definitely linked to him, and some authorities now doubt that he was ever a pirate at all.

William Kidd was born about 1645 in Greenock, Renfrew, Scotland. A minister's son, he followed the sea from his youth. In King William's War between the English and the French he became known as the bold captain of a privateer in the West Indies. By the end of the 17th century he had become a successful shipmaster sailing from New York City. British commerce at that time was suffering greatly from marauders. (*See also* Pirates and Piracy.)

At the request of the governor of New York, Kidd was given two commissions from the English king addressed to "our trusty and well-beloved Captain Kidd." One commissioned him to suppress piracy. The other commissioned him to cruise as a privateer against the French.

In 1696 the captain set sail in his ship *Adventure Galley* for Madagascar, Malabar, and the Red Sea region—supposedly the chief haunts of pirates preying on ships of the East India Company. No pirates were found, however. Some time after his arrival off the East African coast Kidd, who still had not seized a prize ship, apparently decided to turn to piracy himself. (A privateer received no pay under his contract unless ships were taken.) In August 1697 he made an unsuccessful attack on ships sailing with mocha coffee from Yemen, but later Kidd's crew took several small ships.

Kidd captured his most valuable prize, the Armenian ship *Quedagh Merchant*, in January 1698 and scuttled the unseaworthy *Adventure Galley*. When he reached the West Indies in April 1699, he learned that he had been denounced as a pirate. He abandoned the *Quedagh Merchant* at the island of Hispaniola and aboard a newly purchased ship, the *Antonio,* sailed to New York City. There he tried to persuade the colonial governor of New York, the Earl of Bellomont, of his innocence. Bellomont, however, sent Kidd to England for trial. In May 1701 he was found guilty of murder of a mutinous sailor and of five counts of piracy. Important evidence concerning two of the piracy cases was suppressed at the trial, and some observers later questioned whether the evidence was sufficient for a guilty verdict.

After Kidd was hanged in London, some of his treasure was recovered from Gardiners Island off Long Island. From time to time people still search fruitlessly along the Hudson River or on the shores of Long Island Sound for the hoard of gold, silver, and precious stones said to have been buried by him.

Captain Kidd's fame was spread abroad by the popular ballad "My name is Captain Kidd, as I sailed, as I sailed." Many romances, such as Robert Louis Stevenson's 'Treasure Island', have been inspired by the legend. A motion picture based on his experiences starred Charles Laughton as the notorious buccaneer.

KIDNAPPING. In March 1932 the 2-year-old son of the Charles A. Lindberghs was abducted from the family home near Hopewell, N.J., and murdered. The kidnapping became one of the most notorious crimes of the century, mostly because Lindbergh was so well known (*see* Lindbergh). But it was not an isolated or unusual crime.

Adults, as well as children, have been kidnapped for many centuries and for a variety of reasons. In wartime it used to be common to abduct men, women, and children for purposes of enslavement. Frequently, a victorious army would carry off males and force them into military service. Sailors in port were often kidnapped, or shanghaied, and forced to serve on ships other than their own. The slaves that were taken to the Americas from Africa had been kidnapped from their tribes and sold to sea captains.

Most modern kidnappings are motivated by extortion or political extremism, or a combination of the two. In a nonpolitical kidnapping, the victim is usually released after the payment of a ransom, though many kidnappers have killed their victims to prevent later identification.

Since the early 1960s a number of political terrorist groups, such as the Baader-Meinhof gang in West Germany and the Red Brigades in Italy, have used kidnapping both to get ransom money and to undermine the stability of the government. Sometimes an abduction is used to assert specific demands. For example, in 1972 an automobile company executive in France was kidnapped to force his company to rehire radical employees who had been fired for demonstrating against their employer.

When terrorists kidnap an individual for ransom, it is usually to get funding for their organizations. In August 1971 Viggo Rasmussen, managing director of the Tuborg brewery in Copenhagen, Denmark, was abducted. He was released after payment of $240,000 to someone who claimed to represent the militant wing of the Palestine Liberation Organization. The kidnapper was soon apprehended. The same year, Theo Albrecht, a wealthy German merchant, was kidnapped and released upon payment of $2.1 million, one of the largest ransoms ever paid.

If terrorists are not motivated by money, their victims are rarely released. Aldo Moro, a former Italian premier, was kidnapped in March 1978 by the Red Brigades and murdered May 9 near Rome. In 1977 members of the Baader-Meinhof gang abducted and killed Hanns-Martin Schleyer, a German industrialist. The American brigadier general James L. Dozier was more fortunate. Kidnapped by members of the Red Brigades in Italy in December 1981, he was rescued after 42 days by an elite Italian commando unit in a raid on an apartment in Padua.

In all countries kidnapping is considered a grave criminal offense punishable by a long prison sentence or death. In the United States, as a result of the Lindbergh kidnapping, a law was passed making the transporting of a kidnap victim across a state line a federal crime punishable by death.

KIDNEYS

KIDNEYS. All active forms of life must get rid of the waste matter left after they have used what they need from the outside environment. They must also keep up a constant internal environment, a sort of inland sea with the right amount of water and dissolved chemicals. In most land animals, including humans, the kidney is the main organ for performing both these tasks. Kidneys filter from the blood excess water and chemicals and dispose of them as waste in the form of urine.

Structure and Function

In the human body the kidneys are a pair of bean-shaped, red-brown organs about 4½ inches (11.4 centimeters) long. They lie one on each side of the backbone, against the back wall of the abdomen and level with the lowest ribs. Each kidney has an outer layer, the cortex, and an inner layer, the medulla. The medulla is arranged in 10 to 15 fan-shaped groups called pyramids. Where the two lobes of the bean shape meet, they form a dent called the hilus. This is the point at which blood vessels enter and leave the kidney, forming the passageway to and from the rest of the body. Blood enters the kidney through the renal (Latin for kidney) artery, which comes directly from the main artery of the body, and leaves through a renal vein. A funnel-shaped structure at the hilus, the renal pelvis, is a urine-collecting chamber for a tube called the ureter, which carries urine down to the urinary bladder, a storage sac in the lower abdomen. From the bladder the urine is expelled from the body through another tube, the urethra.

The entire blood supply of the body runs through the kidneys every few minutes—about a quarter of all the blood is in the kidneys at any one time. The kidneys appear to be very small for such a load, but they are efficiently packaged. Each contains tiny blood vessels called capillaries, which lead to at least a million tiny filtering units that, laid end to end, would stretch for 50 to 75 miles (80 to 120 kilometers).

These filtering units are called nephrons and are in the cortex. Each nephron is composed of a cluster of capillaries known as the glomerulus (Latin for little ball) and a narrow, hairpin-shaped little tube, or tubule. An extension of the tubule forms a capsule partway around the glomerulus. The pressure of blood entering the glomerulus forces about one fifth of the blood's plasma, containing water and small-sized molecules, to filter through the glomerulus and capsule membranes into the tubule. The plasma flow is slowed by the hairpin turn, called the loop of Henle, while a network of capillaries reabsorbs the water and chemicals that the body needs. The selection is controlled by various hormones. The fluid that remains in the tubule on its return to the cortex is the urine. All the tubules end in collecting ducts that merge and ascend to the pyramid floors. There, drop by drop, the urine passes through papillae (Latin for nipples) into the renal pelvis for transport to the bladder, which stores the urine until it can be expelled through the urethra.

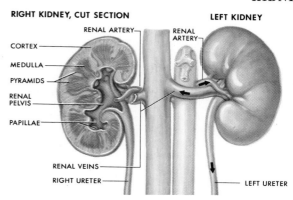

RIGHT KIDNEY, CUT SECTION — CORTEX, MEDULLA, PYRAMIDS, RENAL PELVIS, PAPILLAE, RENAL ARTERY / RENAL ARTERY, RENAL VEINS, RIGHT URETER. LEFT KIDNEY — LEFT URETER.

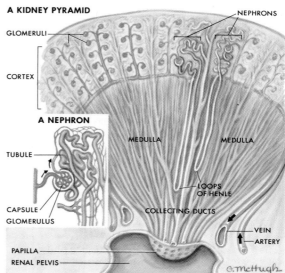

A KIDNEY PYRAMID — GLOMERULI, CORTEX, NEPHRONS, MEDULLA, MEDULLA, LOOPS OF HENLE, COLLECTING DUCTS, VEIN, ARTERY. A NEPHRON — TUBULE, CAPSULE, GLOMERULUS. PAPILLA, RENAL PELVIS. c. mcHugh

Each kidney (top) is about 4½ inches (11.4 centimeters) long and 1¼ inches (3.2 centimeters) thick. The right kidney is a little lower and smaller than the left. The dots in the cortex of the pyramid (above) are balls of capillaries. Each ball (glomerulus), with its tubule, makes up a filtration unit (nephron), which is shown enlarged at the left.

About 99 percent of the body's water is returned to the bloodstream. Only 1 percent, about 1 to 1½ quarts (1 to 1.4 liters) a day, is excreted as urine. If the body needs to conserve water or get more water to dilute excess salt, the kidney returns more water to the capillaries. If the body has more water than it needs, more is excreted in the urine.

Diseases

The kidneys are subject to infection, injury, structural defects, kidney-stone formation, and tumors. The most common disorder is inflammation of the glomeruli (plural of glomerulus), known as nephritis, or glomerulonephritis. It often follows other infections, particularly by bacteria called streptococci. Symptoms vary widely but usually include diminished urine output and edema, or puffiness or swelling from water retention. Most patients recover fully. Urinary tract infections, characterized by frequent and painful urination, may invade the kidney to cause pyelonephritis, which is an acute nephritis with high fever. Obstruction from inflammation or stones can also occur.

Nephrosis, degeneration of kidney tissue, may result from nephritis or from high blood pressure, heart disease, or diabetes, all of which can damage kidney blood vessels. Many chronic kidney diseases are symptom-free until a late-stage failure, when accumulation of harmful wastes presents a crisis.

In the United States kidney failure takes nearly 80,000 lives a year. A technique called dialysis, periodic filtering of the blood by artificial membranes, has kept about 60,000 persons alive. Another 20,000 have received successful kidney transplants.

Recommended reading includes Isaac Asimov's 'The Human Body', published in 1963.

KIERKEGAARD, Søren (1813–55). Neglected in his lifetime, or ridiculed as a dangerous fanatic, the Danish religious philosopher Kierkegaard has come to be regarded in the 20th century as one of the most influential and profound of modern thinkers. Known familiarly to his followers simply as S. K., he was the most brilliant interpreter of Protestant Christianity in the 19th century. He is generally considered the founder of existentialism, a philosophy that in its simplest terms is a complex of views that seeks to explain significance of the freedom of the individual human being within his or her time on Earth.

Søren Aabye Kierkegaard was born in Copenhagen on May 5, 1813. His prosperous father died in 1838, leaving his two sons an inheritance that freed them from the need to work. Søren was able to devote most of his life to study and writing. He studied philosophy and theology at the University of Copenhagen and earned his degree in 1840.

S. K. was a prolific writer of books whose subject matter encompassed three basic areas: the function of the individual human life; vehement opposition to the philosophy of Georg W. F. Hegel, whose thought dominated 19th-century Europe; and a clear delineation of Christianity in opposition to the secularism of the state church of Denmark. His major works on the human predicament are: 'Either/Or', published in 1843, 'Fear and Trembling' (1843), 'The Concept of Dread' (1844), and 'Stages on Life's Way' (1845). His two primary religious-philosophical works, including the attack on Hegel, are: 'Philosophical Fragments' (1844) and 'Concluding Unscientific Postscript' (1846). The works dealing with the nature of Christianity are: 'Edifying Discourses in Divers Spirits' (1847), 'Works of Love' (1847), 'The Sickness unto Death' (1849), and 'Training in Christianity' (1850). His last major work, 'Attack upon "Christendom"' (1855), was a strong, satirical attack on the Lutheran state church of Denmark.

Although the works of Kierkegaard were known in Denmark and Germany in the late 19th century, it was not until after World War II that their influence became widespread in Europe and the United States.

Throughout his career, S. K. led a sort of double life. To his friends, he was a social butterfly: witty, charming, and brilliant in conversation. By himself he was thoroughly melancholy, a man driven to explore the problems of human nature, of philosophy, and of religious discourse. Kierkegaard died on Nov. 11, 1855, in Copenhagen.

KIESINGER, Kurt Georg (1904–88). Although he had been a member of the Nazi party in Germany in the 1930s, Kurt Georg Kiesinger survived politically and was elected chancellor of West Germany in 1966. While in office he unsuccessfully sought improved relations with the Soviet Union, but he did succeed in strengthening West Germany's alliance with the West, especially the United States.

Kurt Georg Kiesinger was born in Ebingen, Germany, on April 6, 1904. After his education at universities in Berlin and Tübingen, he chose a law career. After Adolf Hitler came to power in 1933, Kiesinger joined the Nazi party but was largely inactive. During World War II he served in the radio department of the foreign ministry, and after the war he was briefly interned with other party members.

Kiesinger was elected to the Bundestag (lower legislative house) in 1949 as a member of Konrad Adenauer's Christian Democratic Union (see Adenauer). As a legislator he faithfully followed Adenauer's conservative economic policies, designed to rebuild postwar Germany. He left the Bundestag in 1958 in order to become minister-president of the state of Baden-Württemberg. While in this office, until 1966, he also served in 1962 and 1963 in the Bundesrat (the upper legislative house).

In 1965 and 1966 the administration of Chancellor Ludwig Erhard ran into difficulties over a temporary economic decline, and Erhard resigned on Nov. 30, 1966 (see Erhard). Kiesinger forged an alliance between his party and the Social Democrats and was elected chancellor the next day. He remained in office until Oct. 20, 1969, when he was replaced by Willy Brandt (see Brandt).

KIEV, U.S.S.R. Ancient Kiev, known as the "mother of Russian cities," is now the capital of the Ukrainian Soviet Socialist Republic. Situated on the banks of the Dnepr River just below its confluence with the Desna River, Kiev is a major port  and one of the largest and most important cities of the Soviet Union. With an abundance of parks in and around the city, it is often called the "green city."

Kiev has a moderately continental climate. During winter days temperatures above freezing are common. January temperatures average 22° F (−6° C). Snow covers the ground usually from mid-November to the end of March. Summers are warm and July temperatures average 67° F (18° C).

Most of Kiev's surviving historical monuments are near Bogdan Khmelnitsky Square in the Upper Town. In the foreground is the Cathedral of Saint Sophia. Founded in the 11th century, it is now a museum.

The city's favorable location has made it a major junction of railroads, highways, and air routes. Kiev, as capital of the Ukraine, has major administrative functions, with considerable employment in the offices of ministries responsible for the republic's economy. It is also an important industrial center with a diverse economy. The principal industries are machine building and metalworking. Manufactures include complex and precision machines and machine tools, at the Gor'kiy plant; railroad-car repair, at the Darnitsa plant; and equipment for chemical industries, at the Bolshevik plant. Other engineering products are aircraft, hydraulic elevators, electrical instruments, and computers. The chemical industries produce fibers, fertilizers, household chemicals, varnishes, and paints. The manufacture of wool and silk, knitted goods, clothing, and shoes and boots has developed in recent years. Food-processing industries include a meat-packing plant at Darnitsa, a confectionary factory, wineries, and a tobacco factory. Kiev is also a major printing center.

Power is supplied to the entire industrial sector by the Kiev hydroelectric power plant at Vyshgorod and Tripolye thermal electric station. Rapid economic growth has also been associated with the housing industry; nearly 80 percent of the housing facilities were built between 1946 and 1971.

The surviving historical and architectural monuments are most prominent in the ancient Upper Town. The Cathedral of Saint Sophia, completed in 1037 and reconstructed in the 17th century, is decorated with frescoes and mosaics in its interior. Much of the monastery Pechorskaya Lavra, built during the 11th century, was destroyed during World War II. It is now a museum. Adjacent to the old city are theaters, the central department store, and the main thoroughfare Kreshchatik.

Kiev is the seat of the Ukrainian S.S.R. Academy of Sciences, which includes institutes of cybernetics, microbiology and virology, and physical chemistry. Among the many higher educational institutions are the Kiev T. G. Shevchenko State University, the Kiev Polytechnic Institute, the Kiev Civil Engineering Institute, the Kiev P. I. Tchaikovsky Conservatory, and several medical institutes.

In 1920 the capital of the Ukraine was moved to Khar'kov. During World War II the Germans held Kiev from 1941 to 1943. When the Russians reentered the city, they found the population had dwindled from 846,000 to about 305,000. About 85 percent of the center of the city was demolished. In 1946 a major rebuilding program was begun. (*See also* Ukrainian Soviet Socialist Republic.) Population (1982 estimate), 2,297,000.

KILIMANJARO, MOUNT. A spectacular and imposing mountain in Tanzania, near the Kenya border, Mount Kilimanjaro extends for 50 miles (80 kilometers) and is comprised of three major volcanos. Its central cone, the snow-clad Kibo, is the youngest of the volcanos. It rises to 19,340 feet (5,895 meters), making it the highest point in Africa. The other peaks are called Mawensi, 17,564 feet (5,354 meters), and Shira, 12,395 feet (3,778 meters).

Kilimanjaro has various vegetation zones, which differ according to their altitude. These include, starting at the mountain's base, the semiarid scrub of the plateau; the cultivated and watered southern slopes; dense forest; open moors; alpine desert; and moss and lichen zones. Cattle graze on the slopes. The mountain is also a game reserve.

People live only on the lower slopes. Many of them grow bananas and millet to eat, and coffee is an important cash crop. On the southern and eastern slopes, the Chagga people have long used an effective system of irrigation using the natural ridge and valley structure of the mountains.

The Kilimanjaro formations became known to Europeans in 1848 when they were discovered by German missionaries. The Kibo summit was first reached in 1889 and Mawensi was first climbed in 1912. The chief trading center, located at the southern foot, is Moshi, which is also the departure point for mountain climbers. (*See also* Africa.)

KILLY, Jean-Claude (born 1943). The dominant skier in men's international Alpine competitions from 1965 through 1968 was Jean-Claude Killy. He was a popular sports figure with a magnetic personality.

Jean-Claude Killy was born on Aug. 30, 1943, in Saint-Cloud, a suburb of Paris. He was raised at Val-d'Isère, a ski resort in the French Alps, where he first put on skis at the age of 5. When he was 18 he was chosen to participate in the world championships, but a broken ankle kept him out of the event.

Killy's career was interrupted by illness during his military service in Algeria. By 1964, however, he emerged as the leading French male skier, winning national championships in all three divisions of Alpine skiing—downhill, slalom, and giant slalom—for three years. He was awarded the Golden Skier trophy as best skier of the year in 1965. At Portillo, Chile, in 1966 he won the world combined championship.

During the 1967 season Killy won every downhill race he entered and achieved the maximum possible score of 225 points, a second Golden Skier, and the first World Cup for men. The World Cup is presented for the best overall score in a series of international competitions. In that season and the next, Killy led the French skiers to the world team championship. In 1968 he again won the World Cup and became the second skier in Olympic history to sweep the Alpine racing events. In the Winter Games in Grenoble, France, he won gold medals for the downhill, slalom, and giant slalom races for men.

Killy retired from competitive skiing in 1968. However, he returned to skiing as a professional in 1972 and won the Lange Cup in 1973. He also drove in Grand Prix races during the late 1960s and acted in the films 'Schuss' (1971) and 'Snow Job' (1972).

KIM HONG-DO (born 1745?). A popular painter, Kim Hong-do, also known by the name Tanwon, was one of the first Korean artists to depict the common people in his work. His scenes of 18th-century life were painted with great realism.

Kim was born into a family of officials. He was appointed early to official rank himself and was made a member of the royal art academy. However, he was a spendthrift and was in disfavor with other officials because of his radical ideas.

As a painter he was a master of many styles. Although in most of his paintings of the life of the lower classes, he used the ancient linear style, in one of his most famous works, called 'Immortals', he used an unusual heroic style that made the figures full and robust. He seems also to have been the first Korean painter to try to depict human muscles.

Kim excelled in landscapes. Following a trend that had developed in Korea in the previous century, he moved outside to depict the real world of nature. He went further in this trend than most other artists and developed an interest in the life of the people who lived in these natural settings. His paintings of commoners often suggest the critical view he held of the upper classes. This attitude is best demonstrated in his harvest scenes, which show hardworking farmers in contrast to a landowner lying down on a mattress to smoke in the shade.

KIM IL SUNG (born 1912). Ever since a separate North Korean government was established in 1948, Kim Il Sung has been the head of the dominant Korean Workers' (Communist) party. The first premier of North Korea, he retained the post for about five years after he became president under a new constitution in December 1972.

Kim Song Ju was born on April 15, 1912, near Pyongyang, Korea. He joined the Korean Communist party in 1931. During the 1930s he led armed resistance to the Japanese occupation of Korea and took the name Kim Il Sung from an earlier anti-Japanese guerrilla fighter. After leading a Korean troop in the Soviet Army in World War II, he returned to establish a Communist government under Soviet auspices in northern Korea in 1945.

In 1950 Kim Il Sung made an unsuccessful attempt to extend his rule to the south. With Chinese aid, he then repelled a subsequent invasion of North Korea by forces of the United Nations. While maintaining a claim that he was representing all of the Korean people, Kim Il Sung concentrated on building a socialist state in the north. (*See also* Korea; Korean War.)

As president, Kim Il Sung repeatedly proposed reunification of the two Koreas. The terms of his proposal in 1980 included the withdrawal of American troops stationed in South Korea.

'Immortals', an ink-on-paper drawing by Kim Hong-do, illustrates the artist's departure from the linear style of drawing and painting.

At a kindergarten in China children perform a dance exercise for their classmates.

KINDERGARTEN AND NURSERY SCHOOL.

In the years before children reach school age, it becomes more and more difficult to keep them happily occupied at home. They are able to run, to climb well out of reach, to pedal a tricycle a considerable distance. They are tremendously curious, not only about electrical and mechanical appliances in the home, but also about the steam shovel three blocks down the street. They want to know about the man who brings the mail, the bus driver, the old lady who walks with a cane, and about other children—the little girl with the doll carriage and the twins next door.

To provide a place where the great range of a child's curiosity may be satisfied and organized learning begun, most countries have some form of preschool education. The term preschool is used because the ages of the children involved range from 1 to 5 years, the period of life before they enter elementary school in first grade. Preschools include infant care centers, nursery schools, and kindergartens; though in many countries the kindergartens are part of the public school system. In Communist nations such as the Soviet Union and China, all preschools are operated by the state, but in the United States they are—apart from kindergartens—free of state control.

Preschool education differs from day-care and play centers in that the latter are primarily places where parents can place their children during working hours. The goal of preschool education is to prepare children for the schooling they will get in later years and to foster their social, physical, and emotional development.

The terminology used and the institutional arrangements made for preschool education vary around the world. The terms used for centers of infant care, care during the period of childhood from about 3 months to 3 years, are infant school, nursery school, day nursery, and crèche (a French word meaning "cradle"). The word crèche is used not only in French-speaking places, but in Scandinavia, the United Kingdom, Israel, the Soviet Union, Czechoslovakia, and Poland. The age range for children in nursery schools also varies from country to country. In Sweden, for instance, all children from the age of 3 months until they enter kindergarten at age 5 are ad-

mitted. In English-speaking countries, nursery schools include all children up to kindergarten age.

In countries where the crèches accept children only up to age 3, another institution—the maternal school—cares for the children until they reach kindergarten age. In Italy, children go from the maternal school into first grade instead of kindergarten. Some countries also provide schools for special education problems among very young children. Germany has the *Schulkindergarten,* or school kindergarten, for children who are considered less mature than others of their age. It serves as a preparatory school for first grade. In the Soviet Union there are sanatorium kindergartens for children who are physically handicapped or recuperating from illnesses. The United States has government-supported kindergartens for children who are physically or mentally handicapped.

Reasons for Preschool Education

Although the objectives and methods of preschool education vary from country to country, there is general agreement that nursery schools and kindergartens are very useful steps in the education of children.

In socialist countries the emphasis in most preschool education is on making the child a participating member of society, while in nations where individualism predominates, such as the United States, individual potential is usually emphasized in a competitive atmosphere.

Regardless of the motivation, however, it has been demonstrated that even very young children are capable of schooling beyond the general learning obtained from satisfying their endless curiosity. The Institutes for the Achievement of Human Potential, located in Philadelphia, Pa., have proved that even brain-damaged children can learn to read and do arithmetic before they are one year old. This fact, coupled with other studies in the psychology of children, shows the usefulness of starting the educational process as early as possible.

The Nursery School Program

In the United States, this type of school is for children who are from 2 to 5 years old. It is a counterpart of the European maternal school and of the more inclusive crèche schools. The nursery school provides organized programs of play activities and simple instruction for children who are too young to enter public school kindergarten or first grade classes. Religious institutions, research centers, child welfare groups, and some school systems have organized and conducted these schools.

The school program usually involves at least a daily 2½-hour session, though many of the newer schools operate a full day schedule for the benefit of working parents. The size of classes varies, but they are usually organized in groups of eight to ten children. Sometimes as many as 20 to 25 children are in a class, with more than one adult supervising them. The nursery school teachers generally have special training in early childhood education and childhood development.

Because the importance of nursery school education has become widely recognized, the federal government and local communities lend financial assistance to the schools when needed. In 1965 Project Head Start, a nationally sponsored program for 4- and 5-year-olds was inaugurated. The significance of early training for later success in school was one of Head Start's major concerns.

How Kindergartens Work with Children

What is it like in a good kindergarten? First of all, children can be themselves. Their ideas are respected, while they learn gradually to respect the ideas of others. Their teacher knows that no two children start with the same abilities or grow in quite the same way. Six youngsters who have lived near each other and played together a good deal will carry on with some of the play ideas they have been using in their own backyards. Other children have had an older brother or sister who has fought at least some of their battles for them. Now they need some protection from children their own age. Some children will seize new experiences. They will try everything in the room and chatter about it all when they get home. Others will look, listen, and really enjoy themselves, but say little. Knowing all this, the teacher plans at the start activities for small groups, to let the children become acquainted with one another.

What kind of learning takes place in kindergarten? Social learning—getting along with other people—is important. The setting, however, must provide for other kinds of learning as well. The paint, clay, building blocks, and housekeeping toys found in kindergartens are not solely for enjoyment.

A child stands with brush in hand, chooses a favorite color, sweeps it over a big piece of white paper, and then dots the paper with blobs of black. The child may comment to the teacher, "That's the way the sun is. All red. And the buildings are black." The teacher does not check the child's accuracy, knowing that, as the youngster paints what is seen and felt, the ability to observe is being developed. In growing older the child will become more self-critical and may want to make the sun and buildings look "right."

Three boys are working on a large block construction. One says, "It does so have a second story. And there is an elevator." The teacher asks a question, finds they have enough blocks to make a second story, discusses with them how they could raise things from the first to the second floor, sends one child for the suggested pulleys, helps the others select wood for the elevator. The teacher does not discuss the physical forces of gravity and friction, but obviously the children are learning to deal with them.

There are no arithmetic lessons, but the children learn a great deal about numbers. Sally collects a pile of pie plates in the sandbox. Jane protests, "She has them all. A whole bunch." The teacher helps them count how many there are and plan how they can be shared. "There are six: two for Sally, two for Jane, and two for Rita." Arnold tells his willing helper that four more blocks will be needed to complete their building. When cookies are served, halves and quarters are carefully measured.

Over in one corner, Mary and Jordan are washing doll clothes. "I like to do this," says Mary, "but my mother doesn't. The laundryman takes our clothes every Tuesday and brings them back on Friday." Jordan considers this as he carefully dumps his pile of washed and rewashed clothes back into the soapy water for another rub. "We have a washing machine," he murmurs. How people live, different ways of doing things—these are part of important learning in kindergarten.

In dramatic play children live over many of the things that have happened to them and act out events as they see them. One girl scolds her dolls; another drives a big truck. Both telephone the neighbors. These dramatic creations usually spring from children's own life experiences. They mean more than the stories and poems that are read to them. Fairies, elves, and dragons may enter into dramatic play. Most 5-year-olds, however, are absorbed with the problems of understanding what goes on immediately around them. Too-fanciful material confuses them. Teachers accept whatever fantasy the children introduce, but they do not offer it unless the children are clearly ready for it.

Children and teacher take a lunch break at a toddler house on a kibbutz in Israel.

Richard Nowitz—Black Star

Music's Important Role

Music is always associated with the kindergarten. Children have both listening and creating experiences. An alert teacher picks up the music the children make as they play. The teacher notes the rat-tat-tat of Jerry's hammer as he fastens a railing of nails to his boat, and the chant that Michael sings as he sets the table for lunch. Sometimes the whole group joins in making up a song. This is in addition to all the favorites they have learned together.

Music is not just to be sung. It is something children have in their muscles, too. They love to run, to skip, and to turn somersaults. The teacher's drum is accompaniment enough, but it is fun to have a piano sometimes. Recorded music brings added richness.

Preparing Children for Reading

Children in kindergarten learn to appreciate in many ways what it means to be able to read. They learn to identify their own names and sometimes those of their friends on their various belongings. They know that a sign saying "Do not disturb" left on a half-finished block building is something to be respected. Sometimes they ask questions that can be answered only by consulting books. Children watch their teacher and listen carefully to what is read. They observe that the teacher frequently writes notes so that important items will not be forgotten.

Children's vocabularies expand in kindergarten. The children talk to each other, to the teacher, and to visitors. They delight in knowing the correct term for everything they see. In this environment, in which they can question freely, their vocabularies will probably increase rapidly.

While they are having all these experiences, some children become interested in reading. They ask questions about words they see in books and magazines or on signs and packages. They may indicate that they know some of the letters. Their teacher recognizes these signals of developing reading ability but does not sit the children down with a beginner's reading book. Nor is the teacher concerned about children who show less interest. Those black symbols on the white page are extremely complicated for the young child. It takes a long, long period of seeing other people read and write, of noting how those strange black figures stand for things one knows, before any child is ready to concentrate on learning to read.

Measures to Promote Health

Kindergartens emphasize the health of children. Good programs provide for thorough physical examinations before entering school and continuous health supervision. An effort is made to balance vigorous physical activity, quiet activity, and rest, according to the needs of each child.

History of Preschool Education

The earliest institutions for educating very young children were charitable enterprises that were found-

© Leonard Freed—Magnum

During an exercise period at a kindergarten in New York City, the teacher shows the children some calisthenics.

ed to care for the children of the rural and urban poor while their parents worked. In 1767, in what is now the Alsatian region of France, Johann Friedrich Oberlin organized an infant school called the *salle d'asile* ("hall of refuge") for the care and schooling of small children while their parents worked in the fields. The idea soon caught on, and within a few years similar schools had been founded in a number of French and German cities. In 1833 the French government made these infant schools part of the national educational system.

In 1816 the noted Scottish social reformer Robert Owen founded an "Institute for the Formation of Character" as part of his model community at New Lanark, Scotland. It took care of children of workers at the cotton mills, from about 18 months to 10 years of age; and there were separate infant classes for 2- to 5-year-olds. The New Lanark experiment led to the opening of England's first infant school in London in 1818 by James Buchanan, the man who had directed Owen's institute. (*See also* Owen, Robert.)

In Italy, a Roman Catholic priest named Ferrante Aporti started an infant school at Cremona in 1829. He had been dissatisfied with the progress made by children in elementary schools. Therefore, in order to prepare them for later schooling, he devised an educational plan that combined intellectual, physical, and moral training for preschool children.

The chief drawback of these early maternal schools was that they were largely copies of schools for older children. Young children were required to sit in rows in large classrooms, recite lessons, and spend hours doing reading, writing, and arithmetic.

The change in direction of schooling for the very young came with Friedrich Froebel, the German founder of the kindergarten (*see* Froebel). He believed that childhood was a special phase in life, during which the individual learned largely through play. He felt that young children should not be subjected to formal instruction, as were older children, but should learn through "self-activity" in play and imitation. They should also be allowed to rest during the day and not be forced into rigid classroom patterns of schooling. Froebel opened his first kindergarten at Bad Blankenburg in 1837. Within 25 years after his death in 1852, his educational theories had spread to

241

Art instruction (left) and the ability to distinguish the order of objects are useful exercises in nursery schools.

the extent that kindergartens had been started in Austria, Belgium, Germany, Canada, Great Britain, Hungary, Japan, The Netherlands, Switzerland, and the United States.

Probably the most famous name in the history of preschool education is Maria Montessori, a graduate in medicine and a researcher in educational theory. She began her studies of educational problems while working with culturally deprived and mentally deficient children at the Orthophrenic School in Rome, Italy, in 1899. To put her theories to work on normal children, she opened her *Casa dei Bambini* (Children's House) in 1907. Within a few years her methods had become world famous, and Montessori schools were started in many countries.

The basis of the Montessori theory was that children go through a series of phases during which they are particularly able to learn certain skills such as reading and arithmetic. If these early periods are missed in the schooling process, later difficulties in learning may result. Therefore, she believed, all children should be given a measure of freedom to work at their own pace, without the tension that results from being in competition with others. The amount of freedom allowed was not absolute, however, for she believed that all freedom must be combined with self-discipline and a respect for authority. The individual initiative and self-direction allowed children in her school were combined with group exercises and learning social manners. The children learned to read, write, count, and express themselves artistically. (*See also* Montessori, Maria.)

Group training of children below kindergarten age gained impetus in England shortly before World War I, under the guidance of Margaret and Rachel McMillan. They established nursery schools in the slum districts of London to help improve the physical and mental condition of children living in these poorer areas. The aim of the nursery schools was to make up for any neglect of the children at home and to provide early schooling and care.

The 20th century has also been a time of experiments in "collective upbringing" in several societies. Early in the century, when Jewish settlers were arriving in Palestine, they established communes called *kibbutzim*. Within each kibbutz are separate homes for children to free their mothers for work. All chil-

dren in a kibbutz from birth to 1 year live in an infant house and are cared for by a woman in charge of several babies. Later, they reside in a toddler house until they are 4 years old. Then they move on to kindergarten and elementary school.

In the Soviet Union a program of collective preschool education was started in 1919. Today, parents may voluntarily place their children in crèches from 2 months until 3 years of age. The crèches are operated by the Ministry of Health. Kindergartens, run by the Ministry of Education, accept children from 3 to 7 years of age. The aims of the Soviet system are to instill respect for authority and teach subordination of the individual's needs to those of the collective.

Kindergartens were introduced into the United States by German immigrants. The first kindergarten was opened in Watertown, Wis., in 1856 by Margarethe Schurz, wife of the German-born reformer and politician, Carl Schurz. The first distinctly American kindergarten was started in Boston by Elizabeth Peabody in 1860. In 1873 St. Louis, Mo., became the first city to make kindergartens part of the public school system.

Nursery schools did not make their appearance in the United States until the early 1920s, when several universities, colleges, and research centers established them as experimental schools for training very young children. During the Great Depression of the 1930s nursery schools were subsidized by the federal government to provide work for teachers. Now frequently called day schools, they are operated in all major cities and most smaller communities by churches and other institutions independently of local school systems.

BIBLIOGRAPHY FOR KINDERGARTEN AND NURSERY SCHOOL

Broman, Betty. The Early Years in Childhood Education (Houghton, 1978).

Curry, L. J. and Rood, L. A. Head Start Parent Handbook (Gryphon House, 1978).

Denenberg, V. H. Education of the Infant and Young Child (Academic Press, 1970).

Mialaret, Gaston. World Survey of Pre-School Education (Unipub, 1976).

Ross, Elizabeth. The Kindergarten Crusade (Ohio Univ. Press, 1976).

Suzuki, Shinichi. Ability Development from Age Zero (Accura, 1981).

Whitbread, Nanette. Evolution of the Nursery-Infant School (Routledge, 1972).

Billie Jean King is noted for playing aggressive serve-and-volley tennis, a style once associated only with male players.

Focus on Sports, Inc.

KING, Billie Jean (born 1943). The first woman professional athlete to be paid more than 100,000 dollars in a single year was Billie Jean King, in 1971. The greatest woman doubles player in tennis history, she was also an activist for women's rights. She helped to organize the Women's Tennis Association and to establish a women's pro tour in the early 1970s.

Billie Jean Moffitt was born in Long Beach, Calif., on Nov. 22, 1943. At 11 she began playing tennis in the city's public parks. She married Larry King in 1965. In the 1970s the couple pioneered team tennis.

King holds the record for British titles with a total of 20 championships. She won the women's doubles at Wimbledon in 1961, 1962, and 1965 before achieving her first major singles triumph there in 1966. She also won the Wimbledon singles in 1967, 1968, 1972, 1973, and 1975; women's doubles in 1967, 1968, 1970, 1971, 1972, 1973, and 1979; and mixed doubles in 1967, 1971, 1973, and 1974. King won the United States women's singles in 1967, 1971, 1972, and 1974; women's doubles in 1964, 1967, 1974, 1978, and 1980; and mixed doubles in 1967, 1971, 1973, and 1976. She was the only woman to win United States singles titles on four surfaces—grass, indoor, clay, and hard court.

In a match billed as the Battle of the Sexes at the Houston Astrodome on Sept. 20, 1973, she defeated Bobby Riggs. Riggs, who had many years before been a Wimbledon and United States champion, had criticized the quality of women's tennis. The match set two records: the audience of more than 30,000 was the largest to witness a tennis event, and the 100,000-dollar purse was the largest won by a player. Knee injuries forced King, called the Old Lady, to retire in 1976, but she made a comeback in her late 30s.

KING, Mackenzie (1874–1950). Between 1921 and his retirement in 1948, Mackenzie King was prime minister of Canada for a total of more than 21 years. No other statesman in the British parliamentary system had headed a government for so many years.

William Lyon Mackenzie King was born on Dec. 17, 1874, in Berlin (now Kitchener), Ont. His mother was the daughter of William Lyon Mackenzie, leader of the Rebellion of 1837 (*see* Mackenzie, William Lyon).

King was educated at the universities of Toronto and Chicago and at Harvard University. In Chicago he lived at Jane Addams' Hull House (a neighborhood settlement house), where he first studied the social and labor problems that were his greatest interest for many years. As a traveling fellow at Harvard, he studied labor conditions in Europe.

During a summer vacation King wrote newspaper articles exposing sweatshop conditions in the federal post office of Canada and then conducted a government investigation that helped end the abuses. In 1900 he was asked to organize a bureau of labor in Canada and to become its deputy minister.

Wilfrid Laurier, the Liberal prime minister, was impressed by King's ability (*see* Laurier). At his urging, King ran for and won a seat in the House of Commons in 1908. In 1909 Laurier named him Canada's first Cabinet minister of labor. Upon Laurier's death in 1919, Mackenzie King was chosen to lead the Liberal party. On Dec. 29, 1921, he became prime minister and helped lead Canada from the status of a British dominion to full sovereignty. In 1926 King lost his post briefly after a customs scandal but skillfully forced a new election that overturned the rule of the Conservative Arthur Meighen (*see* Meighen). In 1930, during the depression, his party was again defeated.

Returned to office in 1935, he soon faced the task of leading his nation through World War II. Acting as foreign minister, King negotiated defense and economic pacts with the United States. At home he used his great gift for compromise to maintain unity between French- and English-speaking Canadians. King took an active part in the formation of the United Nations in 1945 and in postwar conferences on atomic power and defense. King died on July 22, 1950, at Kingsmere, his country home near Ottawa.

KING, Martin Luther, Jr. (1929–68). Inspired by the belief that love and peaceful protest could eliminate social injustice, Martin Luther King, Jr., became one of the outstanding black leaders in the United States. He aroused whites and blacks alike to protest racial discrimination, poverty, and war. A champion of nonviolent resistance to oppression, he was awarded the Nobel peace prize in 1964.

Martin Luther King, Jr., was born in Atlanta, Ga., on Jan. 15, 1929. His father, Martin, Sr., was the pastor of the Ebenezer Baptist Church, a black congregation. His mother, Alberta Williams King, was a schoolteacher. Martin had an older sister, Christine, and a younger brother, Alfred Daniel.

Martin encountered racism at an early age. When he was 6, his friendship with two white playmates was cut short by their parents. When he was 11 a white woman struck him and called him a "nigger."

A bright student, he was admitted to Morehouse College at 15, without completing high school. He decided to become a minister and at 18 was ordained in his father's church. After graduating from Morehouse in 1948, he entered Crozer Theological Seminary in Chester, Pa. He was the valedictorian of his class

On Dec. 21, 1956, King rode the first desegregated bus in Montgomery, Ala. His leadership of a black boycott drew national attention to the city's segregated facilities.

in 1951 and won a graduate fellowship. At Boston University he received a Ph.D. in theology in 1955.

In Boston King met Coretta Scott. They were married in 1953 and had two sons, Martin Luther III and Dexter Scott, and two daughters, Yolanda Denise and Bernice Albertine.

Civil-Rights Efforts

King had been impressed by the teachings of Henry David Thoreau and Mahatma Gandhi on nonviolent resistance. King wrote, "I came to feel that this was the only morally and practically sound method open to oppressed people in their struggle for freedom." He became pastor of the Dexter Avenue Baptist Church in Montgomery, Ala., in 1954.

In December 1955 King was chosen to head the Montgomery Improvement Association, formed by the black community to lead a boycott of the segregated city buses. During the tense months of the boycott King's home was bombed, but he persuaded his followers to remain nonviolent despite threats to their lives and property. Late in 1956 the United States Supreme Court forced desegregation of the buses. King believed that the boycott proved that "there is a new Negro in the South, with a new sense of dignity and destiny." In 1957 King became the youngest recipient of the Spingarn Medal, an award presented annually to an outstanding black person by the National Association for the Advancement of Colored People.

In 1958 King became president of a group later known as the Southern Christian Leadership Conference (SCLC). This organization was formed to carry on civil-rights activities in the South. King inspired blacks throughout the South to hold peaceful sit-ins and freedom rides to protest segregated shopping, eating, and transportation facilities.

A visit to India in 1959 gave King a long-awaited opportunity to study Gandhi's techniques of nonviolent protest. In 1960 King became copastor of his father's church in Atlanta. The next year he led a "nonviolent army" to protest discrimination in Albany, Ga. King was jailed in 1963 during a successful campaign to achieve the desegregation of many public facilities in Birmingham, Ala. In a moving appeal, known as the "Letter from Birmingham Jail," he replied to several white clergymen who felt that his efforts were ill timed. King argued that Asian and African nations were fast achieving political independence while "we still creep at a horse-and-buggy pace toward gaining a cup of coffee at a lunch counter."

In 1964 King became the youngest recipient of the Nobel peace prize. He regarded it not only as a personal honor but also as an international tribute to the nonviolent civil-rights movement.

In 1965 King led a drive to register black voters in Selma, Ala. The drive met with violent resistance. In protest of this treatment, thousands of black and white demonstrators conducted a five-day march from Selma to the State Capitol in Montgomery.

King was disappointed that the progress of civil rights in the South had not been matched by improvements in the lives of Northern blacks. In response to the riots in poverty-stricken black urban neighborhoods in 1965, he was determined to focus the nation's attention on the living conditions of blacks in Northern cities. In 1966 he established a headquarters in a Chicago, Ill., slum apartment. From this base he organized protests against the city's discrimination in housing and employment.

King combined his civil-rights campaigns with a strong stand against the Vietnam War. He believed that the money and effort spent on war could be used to combat poverty and discrimination. He felt that he would be a hypocrite if he protested racial violence without also condemning the violence of war. Militant black leaders began to attack his appeals for nonviolence. They accused him of being influenced too much by whites. Government officials criticized his stand on Vietnam. Some black leaders felt that King's statements against war diverted public attention from civil rights.

On Aug. 28, 1963, King was the principal speaker at a giant civil rights march on Washington. His eloquent "I Have a Dream" address was the high point of the demonstration.

Despite criticism, King continued to attack discrimination, violence, and war. He inspired and planned the Poor People's Campaign, a march on Washington, D.C., in 1968 to dramatize the relationship of poverty to urban violence. But he did not live to take part in it. Early in 1968 he traveled to Memphis, Tenn., to support a strike of poorly paid sanitation workers. There, on April 4, he was assassinated by a sniper. King's death shocked the nation and precipitated rioting by blacks in many cities. He was buried in Atlanta under a monument inscribed with the final words of his famous "I Have a Dream" address. Taken from an old slave song, the inscription read: "Free at Last,/ Free at Last,/ Thank God Almighty,/ I'm Free at Last."

King's brief career greatly advanced the cause of civil rights in the United States. His efforts spurred the passage of the Civil Rights Act of 1964 and the Voting Rights Act of 1965. His energetic personality and persuasive oratory helped unite many blacks in a search for peaceful solutions to racial oppression. Although King's views were challenged by blacks who had lost faith in nonviolence, his belief in the power of nonviolent protest remained strong. His writings include 'Stride Toward Freedom' (1958), the story of the Montgomery bus boycott; 'Strength to Love' (1963); 'Why We Can't Wait' (1964); and 'Where Do We Go from Here: Chaos or Community?' (1967).

In 1977, after his death, King was awarded the Presidential Medal of Freedom for his battle against prejudice. Although several black leaders rose to prominence, none could unify and inspire people as effectively as he had. (*See also* Black Americans.)

BIBLIOGRAPHY FOR MARTIN LUTHER KING, JR.

Behrens, June. Martin Luther King, Jr. (Children's, 1979).
Faber, Doris and Harold. The Assassination of Martin Luther King, Jr. (Watts, 1978).
Faber, Doris and Harold. Martin Luther King, Jr. (Messner, 1986).
Garrow, D.J. Bearing the Cross: Martin Luther King, Jr., and the Southern Christian Leadership Conference (Random, 1988).
Garrow, D.J. The FBI and Martin Luther King, Jr. (Penguin, 1983).
Haskins, James. The Life and Death of Martin Luther King, Jr. (Lothrop, 1977).
Oates, S.B. Let the Trumpet Sound: the Life of Martin Luther King, Jr. (New American, 1987).

KING, Stephen (born 1947). With the publication of 'Carrie' in 1974, Stephen King began to establish his reputation as a master of horror literature. The novel was about a young girl who used her power to move objects by telekinesis in order to wreak revenge on her tormentors. This book was quickly followed by 'Salem's Lot' (1975), 'The Shining' (1977), 'The Dead Zone' (1979), 'Firestarter' (1980), 'Christine' and 'Pet Sematary' (1983), and other stories. Most of them, including 'Carrie', were made into highly successful motion pictures.

King was born in Portland, Me., on Sept. 21, 1947. His father abandoned the family about two years later. King's childhood was therefore rather lonely, and to pass time he invented stories and characters for his own amusement. His imagination was spurred by listening to tales of horror on the radio, watching them in the movies, or reading them in paperbacks. After graduation in 1970 with an English major from the University of Maine he taught for three years at Hampden Academy, in Hampden, Me.

Meanwhile King was trying to sell short stories to magazines, but most were rejected. Only with 'Carrie' and the movie based on it did King begin to make a living by writing. Other books included 'Cujo' (1981) and 'The Tommyknockers' and 'Misery' (both 1987). His 'Danse Macabre' (1981) was an autobiographical survey of horror fiction.

The common belted kingfisher (*Megaceryle alcyon*) is the most familiar species in North America.

Annan Photo Features

KINGFISHER. The kingfisher family includes some 80 species, distributed over the greater part of the globe. They are known for their swift dives. From its perch the kingfisher can swoop like an arrow to seize a fish underwater or an insect on land.

The most common species of kingfisher in North America is the belted kingfisher. It nests east of the Rocky Mountains from northern Canada to the Gulf coast and winters in the central and southern parts of the United States. The bird is 11 to 14 inches (28 to 35 centimeters) long and has a shaggy, black crest. Its feathers are bluish gray on the upper parts and white on the underparts. The male has a gray belt of feathers running across the breast. The female has a chestnut belt. The belted kingfisher nests in holes that it digs in banks beside lakes and streams. The eggs are laid in groups of five to eight on a bed of fish bones. The kingfisher call is a loud rattle.

The kingfisher family is most numerous in the East Indies, where there are many vividly colored species. The common kingfisher of Europe is also brightly colored, with iridescent blue-green upper parts and a chestnut breast.

The ancient name of the kingfisher was halcyon. The scientific name of the kingfisher family is Alcedinidae; of the belted kingfisher, *Megaceryle alcyon*; and of the green kingfisher, *Chloroceryle americana*.

KING GEORGE'S WAR. Although it took place in the American colonies, King George's War was part of an 18th-century conflict in Europe. The war was named for King George II because it was fought during his reign over England.

In the European phase of the war Prussia, France, and Spain were allied against Austria and England in the War of the Austrian Succession, fought from 1740 to 1748 (*see* Austria-Hungary). The colonial war was fought from Canada to the Caribbean Sea, with the English against both the French and the Spanish. English expeditions against Cartagena, a great Spanish stronghold on the Caribbean coast of South America, and St. Augustine, on the Atlantic coast of Florida, were unsuccessful.

The chief event of the war was the capture in 1745 of the French fortress of Louisbourg on Cape Breton Island by an English fleet and an army of New England colonials. This fort was built to protect the southern entrance to the Gulf of St. Lawrence. From it the French had hoped to recapture Acadia, which they had lost in Queen Anne's War (*see* Queen Anne's War). In the Peace of Aix-la-Chapelle that ended the war in 1748, Louisbourg was restored to the French. This, however, was a mere truce before the final struggle in which the French lost New France, which eventually became Canada, to the English in the French and Indian War (*see* French and Indian War).

KINGLET AND GNATCATCHER. In the bird world, only the hummingbirds are smaller than the kinglets and gnatcatchers. Although they are not shy, it is difficult to observe these tiny birds because they are always on the move.

Kinglets are only 3½ to 4½ inches (9 to 11 centimeters) long. They have olive-green backs and yellowish underparts. The golden-crowned kinglet, whose scientific name is *Regulus satrapa,* has a golden yellow crown patch, bordered with black, that is always visible. The ruby-crowned kinglet (*R. calendula*) has a ruby red patch that it can display or conceal at will. It is also distinguished by pale wing bars and a white eye ring. It has a beautiful song. Both kinglets nest in spruce forests of the northern United States and Canada during the warmer seasons. They winter from the central states southward.

The blue-gray gnatcatcher (*Polioptila caerulea*) is 4½ to 5 inches (11 to 13 centimeters) long. It is blue-gray above and white below, with a long tail that is black in the center and white on the sides. It nests in woodlands throughout the continental United States (except Alaska) and winters from the Southern states through Mexico. The western black-tailed gnatcatcher (*P. melanura*) has a black cap and not as much white in the tail. Kinglets and gnatcatchers belong to the family Sylviidae, to which the Old World warblers also belong.

KING PHILIP'S WAR. One of the most tragic of all the conflicts between the American colonists and the Indians was King Philip's War. In 1662 Metacomet, or Philip, younger son of the Pilgrims' friend Massasoit, succeeded his father as chief of the Wampanoags. He tried for some years to keep peace and to meet the demands of the white settlers, but the settlers continued to increase in numbers and advanced more and

more on the Indians' lands. The English suspected Philip of secretly plotting against them and forced the Wampanoags to surrender some of their arms in 1671. Whether or not their suspicions were justified is not known. At any rate, an Indian who was acting as informer to the colonists was murdered in 1675, and three Wampanoags were executed for the crime.

This act triggered a bloody war that involved the Nipmucs and Narragansets, as well as the Wampanoags. Up and down the Connecticut River valley in Massachusetts and in the Plymouth and Rhode Island colonies the war raged. The Indians raided and burned settlements and killed men, women, and children. The colonists resorted to similar measures and gradually cleared the region of Indians. Philip was hunted down in a swamp in Rhode Island and killed on Aug. 12, 1676. At his death the war in southern New England was over. In New Hampshire and Maine the Saco Indians continued to raid settlements for another year and a half.

Charles Edward
Kingsford-Smith

Courtesy of the Australian
Overseas Information
Service

KINGSFORD-SMITH, Charles Edward (1897–1935). One of the pioneers in the early history of long-distance airplane flight was the Australian aviator Charles Edward Kingsford-Smith. In 1927, the year that Charles A. Lindbergh crossed the Atlantic, Kingsford-Smith and his friend Charles Ulm flew around the Australian continent in ten days. In May–June 1928 he made the first transpacific flight—from Oakland, Calif., to Brisbane, Australia—in ten days (83 hours and 19 minutes total flying time), with Ulm as copilot, and with a navigator and a radio operator. On June 24–25, again with a three-man crew, he crossed the Atlantic from Portmarnock, Ireland, to Harbour Grace, Newf.

Kingsford-Smith was born in Brisbane, Queensland, on Feb. 9, 1897. He attended Sydney Cathedral School and Sydney Technical College. During World War I he enlisted in the engineers branch of the Australian forces. Transferred to the Royal Flying Corps, he was wounded in 1917 and spent the rest of the war as an instructor for England's Royal Air Force. Kingsford-Smith left the service in 1919 and began his civilian flying career. In 1922 he went to work as chief pilot for West Australian Airways. He later started his own airline, Interstate Services.

One of his most daring ventures was a record solo flight from England to Australia in 1933. In 1934 he crossed the Pacific from Brisbane to San Francisco. In 1935, on his last flight, he was accompanied by another Australian. They were attempting to fly from London to Australia. The airplane was reported missing somewhere off the coast of Burma on November 8. The two men presumably died at sea. Kingsford-Smith Airport in Sydney was named for him.

KINGSLEY, Charles (1819–75). In his own lifetime the clergyman Charles Kingsley was known chiefly as a social reformer. Today he is beloved by children for his delightful fairy story 'The Water-Babies'.

Charles Kingsley was born on June 12, 1819, in Devonshire, England. His father was a clergyman. Charles attended King's College in London. Later he entered Cambridge University. In 1842 he went as curate to the parish of Eversley, in Hampshire, and soon was appointed rector. He held the position for the rest of his life, except for brief intervals.

Kingsley risked his position in the church with his speeches and writings in behalf of the working class. He originated the term sweatshop system to describe abusive working conditions in the manufacturing industries. He associated himself with the Christian Socialists, a group that proposed radical solutions for England's industrial problems. His 'Alton Locke', published in 1850, is a novel dealing with social problems. Kingsley died on Jan. 23, 1875, and was buried in his own churchyard at Eversley.

He is chiefly remembered for his historical novels. 'Hypatia' (1853) deals with the former glories of Alexandria, in Egypt. 'Westward Ho!' (1855) tells the story of a knight in the days of Elizabeth I.

For his children Kingsley wrote delightful stories, such as 'The Heroes', a retelling of the old Greek myths. 'The Water-Babies' (1863) is a fairy tale and nature story combined. Its hero, a little chimney sweep, is changed by the fairies into a water baby and learns about the habits of the water creatures.

KINGSTON, Jamaica. The capital and chief port of Jamaica, Kingston sprawls along the island's southeastern coast. The city is backed by the Blue Mountains and is famous for its fine natural harbor. The harbor is protected by a narrow peninsula that has been widely developed as a resort.

On the city's main streets, modern buildings contrast sharply with the decaying architectural relics of former centuries. The chief industries are food processing, clothing production, and petroleum refining. Kingston is also a tourist center. The Institute of Jamaica maintains a public library, museum, and art gallery specializing in the local culture.

Kingston was founded in 1692. In 1703 it became the commercial capital of Jamaica and in 1872, the political capital. Kingston suffered a violent earthquake in January 1907, after which it was rebuilt. (See also Jamaica.) Population (1982 estimate), city, 104,000; metropolitan area, 524,600.

KING WILLIAM'S WAR. From 1689 until the battle of Waterloo in 1815 the French and the British fought a series of wars in a struggle for power on the European continent. Several of these wars were fought in North America as well, for the French and English were rivals on that continent also.

The first of these European wars began after William of Orange, the chief enemy of Louis XIV of France, was given the English throne. The war was fought chiefly to check the attempt of Louis XIV to push his boundaries east to the Rhine River (see William, Kings of England).

The American phase of the struggle is called King William's War. Both the French and the English were helped by their Indian allies. Neither the British nor French colonists were given much help from the mother countries, both of which were fully occupied on the continent of Europe. In North America the French used Indian methods of warfare, making raids along the frontiers of New York and New Hampshire and against the settlements of Maine. The English planned expeditions against Montreal and Quebec. A British fleet commanded by William Phips captured Port Royal (now Annapolis Royal, N.S.), but Phips's sea expedition against Quebec was defeated by Louis de Pierre Frontenac, the French governor. Pierre Iberville, while in command of French ships, took Newfoundland and Hudson's Bay. (See also Frontenac; Iberville.)

The Peace of Ryswick, signed in 1697, restored to their former owners all territories gained in the colonies. Peace was of short duration, however, for five years later Queen Anne's War, fought from 1702 to 1713, broke out as part of the War of the Spanish Succession in Europe. (See also Queen Anne's War.)

KINO, Eusebio (1645–1711). One of the early explorers of the American Southwest was a Jesuit missionary named Eusebio Kino. Through his exploration in about 1701, he proved that Lower California was a peninsula, the Baja Peninsula—not an island as had previously been thought.

Eusebio Kino was born in Segno, in the Val di Non, a valley in Tirol (now in Italy), on Aug. 10, 1645. He studied mathematics and astronomy in Germany and taught mathematics for a time at the University of Ingolstadt. He became a member of the Society of Jesus, or Jesuits, in 1665. His work as a missionary began in 1678, and he was assigned to Spain's colony in Mexico.

Kino arrived in Mexico City in the spring of 1681. Most of the remainder of his life was spent in the region called Pimería Alta, a district comprising present-day southern Arizona and the northern portion of Sonora State in Mexico. In 1687 he established his first mission among the Indians of Sonora. It became the headquarters for his explorations as well as for the founding of other missions. Among the most famous of these was San Xavier del Bac, founded in 1700 near the present site of Tucson, Ariz. Kino died at Mission Magdalena in Sonora on March 15, 1711.

KINSEY, Alfred C. (1894–1956). Zoologist Alfred Charles Kinsey was one of the most noted students and interpreters of human sexual behavior in the 20th century. In some measure he helped lay the foundations for the sexual revolution that began in the United States in the 1960s.

Kinsey was born in Hoboken, N.J., on June 23, 1894. He was educated at Bowdoin College and earned his doctorate in science at Harvard University in 1920. That same year Indiana University hired him as an assistant professor in zoology, and he became a full professor in 1929. In the late 1930s he turned his attention to the subject of human sexuality. He began his program of studies in 1941, and in 1947 he established the Institute for Sex Research at Indiana University. Through the aid of foundation grants, the institute was able to conduct extensive surveys and interviews among American men and women concerning their sexual behavior and attitudes. Over several years Kinsey and his associates carefully and scientifically interviewed more than 10,000 individuals, always making sure that the identities of these people were safeguarded.

The first results of these inquiries appeared in Kinsey's book 'Sexual Behavior in the Human Male' in 1948. Although basically a scientific compilation, this volume became one of the publishing sensations of the decade. Widely hailed as a landmark in its field, it was also greatly criticized by many people because it shattered many of the myths prevalent in American society about sexual practices and preferences.

Kinsey was amazed at the response to his work—especially at the criticisms and condemnations that came so frequently from people who had not bothered to read the book. The Institute continued its work, however, and in 1953 the companion volume, 'Sexual Behavior in the Human Female', was published.

What made the so-called Kinsey Reports so popular were two basic factors. First, they seemed to be a uniquely American phenomenon—few other societies seemed so curious about the nature of their own sexual behavior. Second, there were at the time virtually no other scientific guides to thinking about sex. Kinsey planned further studies dealing with other nations, with prison inmates, and with animals; but he died on Aug. 25, 1956, in Bloomington, Ind., before they could be realized.

KINSHASA, Zaire. The capital of Zaire is Kinshasa, one of the largest cities in Africa south of the Sahara. The city, formerly called Léopoldville, is in the western part of the country. It sprawls along the south bank of the Congo (Zaire) River for about 8 miles (13 kilometers), downstream of the expansion of the river known as Malebo (formerly Stanley) Pool. Across the river is Brazzaville, capital of the People's Republic of the Congo.

Kinshasa is connected with the Atlantic port city of Matadi by a railroad that parallels an unnavigable stretch of the Congo. Oil pipelines and a motor road also facilitate commerce between the two cities. The city is a vital inland port, collecting and processing goods for export from Matadi and distributing imported goods upstream to the interior.

The city of Kinshasa grew out of two nearby villages, Kinshasa and Kintambo. It was named Léopoldville in honor of Belgium's King Leopold II. In the 1920s Léopoldville became the capital of the Belgian Congo. Its increasing importance attracted immigrant African laborers, who were encouraged by its housing facilities and other social advantages. In 1960, when the new Republic of the Congo (later the Democratic Republic of the Congo) was established, Léopoldville remained the capital. The city was renamed Kinshasa in 1966, five years before the country's name was changed to Zaire.

Kinshasa is a modern city with many tall buildings and broad boulevards lined with palm trees and flowers. The climate is hot and humid. The western part of the city houses administrative buildings and an industrial sector. The commercial section is in the east, near the port facilities. Of two satellite cities, N'djili contains about 20 percent of the metropolitan population, and Kimpoko is being developed as a port facility. N'djili airport provides local and international service. Many ministerial buildings and official residences are in the riverside suburb of Kalina.

Kinshasa serves as the headquarters of major public corporations and of industrial and commercial companies. Kinshasa, the country's leading financial center, contains the central bank, numerous commercial banks, and financial institutions. The city houses the central government offices. Its urban administration, under a governor nominated by the central government, provides such essential services as water supply and sanitation. A special service is the spraying of the area by helicopter to eradicate mosquitoes.

Kinshasa is a center for education. The National University of Zaire, formerly the Lovanium University of Kinshasa, was founded in 1954. In addition to its numerous faculties, the university has an archaeological museum and an experimental nuclear reactor. Kinshasa has an institute of arts, where painting, sculpture, and ceramics are taught, and in or near the city are a zoological garden and a national museum.

Two daily papers and three weekly newspapers are published in French. Kinshasa's radio station, one of the most powerful in all Africa, provides 24-hour service. A government-commercial station, called Tele-Star, offers television.

An important industrial center, Kinshasa's main industries are textiles, food processing, woodworking, and the manufacture of paper, packing cases, tobacco, chemicals, and construction materials. Because of the extensive use of the Congo for transportation, Kinshasa has developed an important shipbuilding and ship-repairing industry. Population (1980 estimate), 3,000,000. (*See also* Zaire.)

Rudyard Kipling

KIPLING, Rudyard (1865–1936). Millions of children have spent happy hours with Rudyard Kipling's 'The Jungle Books' and 'Just So Stories' about the land and people of India long ago. Kipling was a master storyteller. His songs, which are written in a strong marching rhythm, have the same popular style as his other writing.

Rudyard Kipling knew India well. He was born in Bombay on Dec. 30, 1865, when India was part of the British Empire. Beyond the cities and highways of British India, where the English lived, lay strange primitive country. Rudyard and his younger sister, Alice, had an Indian nurse who told them wonderful tales about the jungle animals. These stories remained in the boy's memory.

When Rudyard was about 6, he and his sister were sent to England to be educated. They were left in the unhappy home of a retired naval officer at Southsea, where the boy was often punished by being forbidden to read. Rudyard almost ruined his eyes by reading in secret every book he could lay his hands on. In the story "Baa, Baa, Black Sheep," Kipling later described the six miserable years the two children spent in this "house of desolation."

In 1877 his mother came home from India and remade his world. He and his sister were taken to Devonshire to spend the summer with her. The next year his father came home on leave and took Rudyard to see the great Paris Exhibition, the beginning of Kipling's lifelong love for France. At the end of this holiday the boy was sent to the United Service College at Westward Ho in Devonshire to be educated for the army. Rudyard read constantly—French literature, the English Bible, English poets, and storytellers such as Defoe. In this school also he developed a passionate faith in England and the English people. His years at Devonshire are recorded in 'Stalky & Co.', one of the best stories about schoolboys.

Kipling's father was now principal of the Mayo School of Art at Lahore, in northwest India. When Rudyard was almost 17, he joined his family there.

He became a reporter on the one daily newspaper in the Punjab, the *Civil and Military Gazette*. To get material for his newspaper articles he traveled around India for about seven years and came to know the country as few other Englishmen did.

Now Kipling began to write the poems and short stories about the British soldier in India that established his reputation as a writer. Such books as 'Plain Tales from the Hills', published in 1888, 'Soldiers Three' (1888), and 'Barrack-Room Ballads' (1892) emerged. The slim volume of 'Departmental Ditties' (1886) he edited, printed, published, and sold himself.

In 1890 his book 'The Light That Failed' told of his efforts to make a living as a writer. When his reputation was firmly established, he married an American, Caroline Balestier, and started off with her on a trip around the world. They settled in Vermont, where their first child was born, and where Kipling wrote the tales that were to make up his 'Jungle Books' (1894, 1895). Kipling's father visited them and made the famous drawings that were published first, with the stories, in *St. Nicholas*.

Their family physician had once served with the Gloucester fishing fleet, and he persuaded Kipling to go to Gloucester for the annual memorial service for the men who had been lost or drowned during the year. From this experience came the inspiration for 'Captains Courageous' (1897).

After four years in America, the Kiplings decided that their real home was in England. They rented a house in a Sussex village, where in 1897 their only son, John, was born.

The story that is known as 'Kim' had been in Kipling's mind for years. Now, stimulated by his father's keen interest, he began to write it. The book was first published in 1901.

Long visits to South Africa, where the Kiplings formed a friendship with Cecil Rhodes, and another trip through North America varied the Sussex life. Early in 1902 they bought a house near the Sussex Downs. All around it was land that had been cultivated since before the Norman Conquest. Thus, stories about Roman times, 'Puck of Pook's Hill' (1906) and 'Rewards and Fairies' (1910), were begun. Volumes of history cannot give the vital impression that these stories give of England's past. Together they form a chain of "scents and sights and sounds" that reaches to the very heart of England and its history.

In 1907 Kipling was awarded the Nobel prize for literature. World War I brought personal tragedy when his son was killed fighting in France with the Irish Guards. More and more he withdrew from the active scene, spending the greater part of the year in his Sussex farmhouse. When he was nearly 70 years old, he began to write his autobiography, 'Something of Myself'. This curiously revealing book was published a year after his death.

Kipling died on Jan. 18, 1936, in the same month that brought the death of England's king, George V. The writer was buried in Westminster Abbey among England's honored sons.

KIRGIZ SOVIET SOCIALIST REPUBLIC.

The Kirgiz are a pastoral people whose mountainous territory, also known as Kirgizia, has been occupied by the Russians since the 19th century. Now they form less than half of the population of their land, which has been officially named the Kirgiz Soviet Socialist Republic. Russians, Uzbeks, Ukrainians, and Germans make up most of the remaining population.

Land and People

The republic is bounded on the north by the Kazakh Soviet Socialist Republic, on the east by China, on the southwest by the Tadzhik republic, and on the west by the Uzbek republic. The area of Kirgizia is 76,600 square miles (198,500 square kilometers). The capital is Frunze (formerly Pishpek), with a population of 646,000. The republic contains the second highest peak in the Soviet Union, Pobeda (24,406 feet; 7,439 meters). The major mountain ranges belong to the Tien Shan (Tian Shan) system. The valleys of the Chu and Naryn rivers form the main areas of settlement and farming, along with the fringes of the Fergana region in the southwest. The Issyk-Kul' is a lake situated at about 5,000 feet (1,500 meters) above sea level. Its water is warm due to local volcanic activity, and it does not freeze. The climate of Kirgizia at lower altitudes is hot in summer and below freezing in winter, while at higher altitudes snow falls throughout the year.

The Kirgiz are a Turkic-speaking Muslim people whose traditional way of life consisted of herding livestock between the summer pastures in the mountains and the winter pastures in the valleys. Although this type of herding still exists, many Kirgiz now work in farming or industry.

Because of their pastoral life, the Kirgiz had little traditional written literature or art. Modern Kirgiz writers have been influenced by Soviet ideology.

Economy and Transportation

In addition to herding cattle, sheep, and goats for the production of meat and wool, farmers grow hay, grain, cotton, tobacco, sugar beets, and opium poppies. Coal is mined, and some petroleum and natural gas are extracted. The republic is a source of antimony and mercury. Plants in Frunze and Tokmak produce farm machinery, machine tools, and other engineering products. Textiles are manufactured at Frunze and Osh.

Because of the mountainous terrain, the transport system of Kirgizia is not well developed. The only railroad lines are in the north and in the Fergana region. The mountains are crossed by two highways, one of which leads to China. Frunze is connected by air with several other Soviet cities.

Government and History

The Kirgiz Soviet Socialist Republic has its own government and Communist party, though it has little authority and is controlled by the central government in Moscow. The early Kirgiz lived a nomadic life in tribal groups. By the 19th century they had come under control of the Central Asian state of Kokand. Later in the century Russians invaded the region and began a large-scale settlement. In 1916 the Kirgiz revolted against the Russians, and the 1917 Revolution brought further opposition to Soviet rule. Defeated by the Red Army, Kirgizia became an autonomous soviet socialist republic in 1926 and, ten years later, one of the constituent republics of the Soviet Union. Population (1988 estimate), 4,238,000.

KIRIBATI.

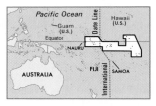

Formerly a British crown colony, Kiribati became an independent republic and member of the Commonwealth in 1979. The country consists of 33 coral atolls and islands that spread over more than 2,000,000 square miles (5,000,000 square kilometers) of the Central Pacific Ocean and straddle both the equator and the International Date Line. It includes the Gilbert Islands, Banaba (formerly Ocean Island), the Line Islands, and the Phoenix Islands. More than 90 percent of the population live in the Gilbert Islands, a group of 16 coral atolls located about 2,800 miles (4,500 kilometers) northeast of Australia.

With a total land area of only 328 square miles (850 square kilometers), Kiribati extends from Washington Island to Flint Island, a north-south distance of about 1,300 miles (2,100 kilometers), and from Christmas Atoll to Banaba, an east-west distance of about 2,250 miles (3,600 kilometers). The capital of Kiribati is Bairiki, which is located on Tarawa Atoll in the Gilbert Islands.

The low-lying islands of the atolls are surrounded by coral reefs and include lagoons. The soil is of poor quality, but the islands are well-covered by coconut palms that provide copra, the only agricultural export. The climate of Kiribati is tropical marine with normal daytime temperatures varying between 80° F (27° C). and 90° F (32° C). A rainy season usually lasts from October to March.

The people of Kiribati are mostly of Micronesian origin. They live in villages of huts built with coconut and pandanus (a type of pine) timbers thatched with pandanus leaves. Most families fish and grow bananas, breadfruit, pawpaws, and pandani for food.

Various explorers visited the islands from 1537 until 1870. Britain declared a protectorate over the Gilbert and Ellice islands in 1892. The formation of the colony began in 1915 and was completed with the inclusion of the Phoenix Islands in 1937. The colony became self-governing in 1971. In July 1979 the name was changed to Kiribati; in a ceremony attended by Princess Anne, representing Britain's Queen Elizabeth II, the islands at that time became an independent republic. Each atoll has a free, government-maintained medical dispensary and a primary school. Population (1980 estimate), 58,500.

KIRIN *see* JILIN.

KISH. The once majestic city of Kish is today only ruins. It lies between the Tigris and Euphrates rivers, about 100 miles (160 kilometers) south of Baghdad, Iraq. Inscriptions in the ruins state that it was "the first city founded after the Flood." As the traditional first capital of the Sumerians, Kish was an early center of civilization (*see* Babylonia and Assyria).

In ancient times, the area was fertile. The Sumerians settled along a bend of the Euphrates river. They built a fortified city, more than five miles (eight kilometers) long and almost two miles (three kilometers) wide. Until as late as the time of Sargon (about 2750 BC), Kish dominated the Near East. Then it declined because the Euphrates changed its course. Finally it was abandoned and desert sand covered its ruins.

Archaeologists from the Field Museum of Natural History in Chicago and England's Oxford University excavated the ruins between 1923 and 1933. Digging to virgin soil, 60 feet (18.3 meters) below the top of the mound, the expedition found remains of several cultures, from Neolithic times to the Christian Era. A band of alluvial soil, about 40 feet (12 meters) below the surface, indicated that Kish had been flooded about 3200 BC. Many take this to be evidence of the great Biblical flood. Astounding also was the discovery, below the flood stratum, of a four-wheeled chariot, the earliest known wheeled vehicle. Other discoveries showing the highly developed Sumerian civilization were thick-walled temple towers, canals, and a library with some of the earliest writing known to have existed in the world.

KISSINGER, Henry (born 1923). The most influential foreign policy figure in the administrations of Presidents Nixon and Ford was Henry Kissinger. It was he who initiated the concept of shuttle diplomacy, making frequent overseas trips to solve complex international problems.

Henry Alfred Kissinger was born in Fürth, Germany, on May 27, 1923. He came with his parents to the United States in 1938 to escape the Nazi persecution of Jews. After receiving his doctorate at Harvard University in 1954, he taught at the school and became professor of government in 1962. His great expertise in matters of national security and strategic planning led to his appointment as national security adviser by President Nixon in 1969. He was secretary of state from 1973 to Jan. 20, 1977.

Among his achievements in foreign policy were the initiation of strategic arms limitation talks in 1969, the policy of detente with the Soviet Union, the initiation of relations with the People's Republic of Chi-

na, the resumption of diplomatic relations with Egypt, and negotiations to withdraw American forces from Vietnam. For his Vietnam negotiations he shared the Nobel peace prize in 1973 with North Vietnam's diplomat, Le Duc Tho.

Herbert Kitchener
BBC Hulton Picture Library

KITCHENER, Herbert (1850–1916). "Your country needs you." With this poster appeal in World War I, Herbert Kitchener, British field marshal and secretary of state for war, assembled and organized one of the mightiest armies in his country's history.

Horatio Herbert Kitchener was born to English parents in County Kerry, Ireland, on June 24, 1850. He was educated at the Royal Military Academy at Woolwich, England, and in 1871 was commissioned in the Royal Engineers.

After serving in various civil service and military posts, he became commander in chief of the Anglo-Egyptian army in 1892. With this army he began a campaign to conquer the Sudan in 1896. At the battle of Omdurman in 1898, he crushed the Arab Mahdists and captured Khartoum, avenging the death there of General Charles George Gordon (*see* Gordon; Sudan). For this feat he was made a baron.

Kitchener was governing the Sudan when the Boer War began. In 1899 he was sent to South Africa as chief of staff. In 1900 he was named commander in chief. He overcame the Boer resistance, ending the war in 1902 (*see* Boer War). Honors were heaped upon him, and he became a viscount. From 1902 to 1909 Kitchener served in India as commander in chief. In 1911 he was named consul general of Egypt. For his work in that country, including his economic reforms, he was made an earl.

When World War I broke out in 1914, Kitchener entered the British Cabinet as field marshal and secretary of state for war. By the end of 1915 he had expanded Britain's expeditionary force from 160,000 to more than 2,250,000 men. Until mid-1915 he was also charged with mobilizing Britain's industries for the war effort—a task for which he was unsuited. Worshiped by the people, he could not get along with his colleagues. He died en route to Russia in 1916, when his ship struck a German mine off the Orkneys.

KITE *see* BIRDS OF PREY.

Kite flying is an ancient sport in Japan. Some kites are so large that it takes several men to launch and fly them.

KITE FLYING

KITE FLYING. Flying kites is a popular pastime all over the world. A kite is a device that soars through the air at the end of a line. It may be large or small, light or heavy, simple or ornate. Kites are flown in competitive sports, for military or scientific purposes, and as a relaxing hobby or pastime. Kites are named after the kite bird, a graceful hawk.

Types of Kites

There are many kinds of kites. Most of them are simple, lightweight wooden frames covered with paper or cloth and attached to a long line held in the hand. Among the best-known types are plane surface kites—such as the Malay and three-sticker (hexagonal)—and box kites. Those with only one flat surface must have tails hanging from the trailing edge to maintain balance. Tails are effective because of their resistance to air. Many light crosspieces of material inserted into knots in a line do well for a tail.

The simplest form of plane surface kite is the common two-sticker (*see* illustration, p. 254). The Malay is a tailless two-sticker with a modified diamond shape. Its two sticks are of equal length. They are crossed and tied with the center of one at a spot one seventh the distance from the top of the other. The bridle, or part to which the flier's line is tied, has two strings, one from the top of the diamond and the other from the lowest point. The strings meet a little below the crossing of the sticks. A string pulled tight across the back of the cross stick bows, or bends, the surface and makes the kite self-balancing. The Eddy, or bow, kite, developed in the 1890s by William A. Eddy, an American, is similar to the Malay kite.

In the three-sticker, or hexagonal, kite all sticks are of the same length, crossed and tied in the middle, and spread symmetrically—with string around the border and the whole covered with light material. This makes a flat surface and requires a tail hung from the center of a short loop attached to the two trailing points of the kite. In the three-sticker the bridle is composed of three cords, each of a length equal to half the width of the kite. One cord leads from the center and two from the two highest points of the kite to the kite's center. They are joined in a knot or by a ring to which the flier's line is tied.

The box kite was invented in the 1890s by Lawrence Hargrave, an Australian. Box kites are popular though more difficult to make than plane surface kites. Box kites are named for their rectangular shape, the frame being twice as long as its width; the ends are left uncovered, with one third of the length covered around each end. The bridle consists of two lines, one to each end. The kite needs no tail. It flies on one edge; that is, with one of its edges facing down. The shape can be other than square in cross section; it may be oblong and fly on a wide side with a four-leg bridle, or it may be triangular, round (barrel kite), or even five- or six-sided. In 1902 the American Silas Conyne added side wings to a triangular box kite, the first of many winged box kites. It is known as the Conyne, or French military, kite.

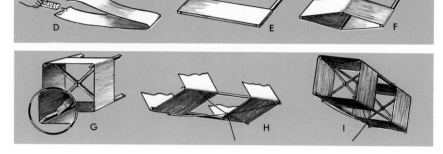

The construction of a box kite begins with assembling the materials (A, B, and C). The ends of the cover sheets are glued together (D) and to the corner sticks (E and F). The notched cross braces are tied with string to prevent splitting, pushed into position, and tied together where they cross (G). A bridle of crossed strings is fastened to one side and the kite line attached where they cross (H). The kite is ready to fly (I).

How Kites Fly

The principle that makes a kite fly is the same as that which keeps an airplane aloft. An airplane creates its own wind by its speed through the air. On a calm day running with a kite in an open space produces the same effect. The kite rises because currents of air, moving parallel to the ground, strike the face of the kite and force it backward. The best wind for kite flying is a steady breeze with a speed of about 8 to 20 miles (13 to 32 kilometers) per hour. Less wind makes it difficult to get the kite up. Stronger winds may drive the kite to the ground before it has a chance to rise to a safe height. The line, or string, holds the kite steady, with the face of the kite tipped forward, and the wind pushes up on the tipped face to lift the kite, much as a wedge pushed under an object lifts it. If the kite were not held by the kite string, the kite would be whirled away and would fall to the ground. The kite rises also because of a reduction in pressure on the upper surface known as the Bernoulli effect (*see* Airplane, illustration in section "Aerodynamics").

A kite should not be flown on rainy days, since a wet kite string is a good conductor of electricity. Wire should never be used for a kite string, and the kite should never be flown where there are electric power lines because of the danger of electrocution.

Kite Flying as a Sport

In East Asia kite flying is an ancient custom. Some Asian kites are musical. When the wind whistles through the reeds or bamboo tubes of the kites, the sound is thought to frighten away evil spirits.

In Korea people fly kites during the first days of the New Year. In China the ninth day of the ninth month—Kites' Day, or the Festival for Climbing Heights—is a holiday honoring kites. Chinese and Japanese kites are brightly colored and elaborately decorated. They may have the shapes of birds, insects, butterflies, or various geometric forms. A favorite Chinese fancy kite is the dragon, a ferocious-looking head kite with many smaller flat body kites strung behind on parallel tie lines.

Kite flying is especially popular in Thailand, where the air is filled with a great variety of kites during the spring months. Here kite fighting is a major league sport. The all-Thailand championships are held in Bangkok every spring. In the Thai variety of kite fighting, each of the two contending teams seeks to bring the other team's kite to earth. The diamond-shaped *pakpao* is flown by one team, the star-shaped *chula* by the other. The superior speed and maneuverability of the smaller *pakpao*s often enable them to defeat the larger *chula*s.

Kite fighting is also popular in India. There the object is to cut the string of the opponent's kite; so the kite string is coated with ground glass. In South American kite fights, the kite frames may be armed with razor blades.

Kite competitions are held in many parts of the United States. Prizes may be given for the best kite of each type as well as to the winning participants in different age groups. Awards may also be presented for the kite with the strongest pull, the highest flight, or the most interesting design. Originality and quality of artisanship may also be classified as prizewinning categories.

A comparatively recent pastime in the United States is ski kiting. In this sport water-skiers cling to large, nonsinkable kites and are pulled behind speeding motorboats to heights ranging from 50 to 75 feet

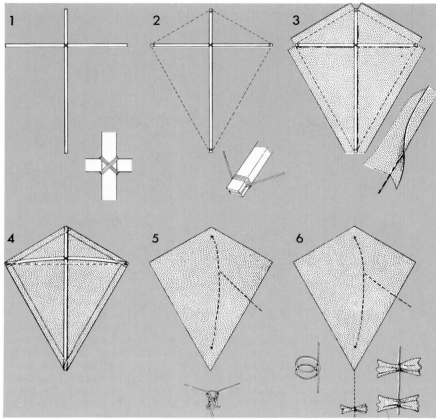

A common plane surface kite begins with two crossed sticks (the longer about 30 inches, or .76 meter, long) tied together (1). The ends of the sticks are notched and tied to prevent splitting (2). A string is stretched through the notches to form a frame, and tissue paper or light treated cloth is cut to fit, leaving wide flaps (3). The flaps are folded over the frame and glued or stapled, and the shorter stick is drawn by string to form a bow (4). A string bridle is fastened to the longer stick and the kite line attached with a special knot (5). A tail is made of strips of cloth tied to a string (6).

(15 to 23 meters). The skier maneuvers the kite by shifting body weight.

Other Uses

Throughout history kites have had many practical uses. In ancient times kites were employed to carry lines across streams or gorges as the first step in building bridges. Tradition states that a Korean general once suspended a lantern from a kite as an inspiring signal to his troops. In 1752 Benjamin Franklin drew electricity from a storm cloud with a kite and a key, demonstrating the electrical nature of lightning. (This is a dangerous experiment, however, not to be repeated without special precautions.) Aerial photography by kite was achieved during the 1880s and was employed extensively in the Spanish-American War. In the early 1900s the United States Weather Bureau measured wind velocity, temperature, and humidity with instrument-carrying kites.

During World War II the United States used kites that could be made to move like enemy airplanes as targets for antiaircraft gunnery practice. Life rafts on United States ships carried kites that served as radio transmission aerials, greatly simplifying searches for lost persons. The Germans launched human-carrying kites from submarines for observation purposes. The hang glider is a specialized kite that carries a person (*see* Aerial Sports).

KIWI *see* BIRDS, FLIGHTLESS.

KLEE, Paul (1879–1940). One of the most inventive and admired painters to emerge from the 20th-century rebellion against representational, or realistic, art was Paul Klee. Fantasy and striking use of color characterize his work.

Paul Klee was born on Dec. 18, 1879, near Bern, Switzerland. His parents were musicians, and he became an accomplished violinist. After attending school in Bern, he went to Munich, Germany, where he studied art from 1898 to 1901. He returned to Bern but was soon off for a trip to Italy, the first of numerous visits there. The Renaissance masters were of particular interest to him, as were the impressionists on his journeys to Paris in 1905 and 1912.

Klee taught at the Weimar Bauhaus from 1921 to 1924 and at the Dessau Bauhaus from 1926 to 1931. When the Nazis came to power in 1933, they condemned his work. Klee then returned to Switzerland. He died at Muralto, near Locarno, on June 29, 1940.

Klee was one of the Blaue Reiter (Blue Rider) artists, who led Germany's experiments in nonobjective art before World War I. His early works were chiefly drawings and etchings. After a trip in 1914 to Tunisia, where he was deeply impressed by the colors he saw, he turned to painting. Later Klee contributed to the art theory of the Bauhaus school, which influ-

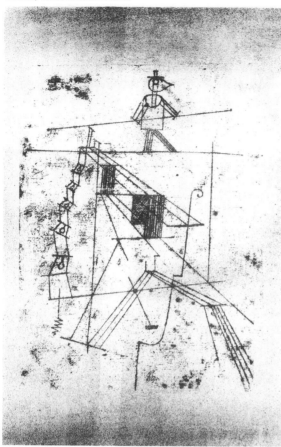

The lithograph entitled 'Seiltanzer' by Paul Klee dates from the year 1923.

enced industrial design, architecture, and painting. He developed pictorial themes in the way a composer develops musical themes. His output ranges from highly realistic portraiture to the abstractionism of such paintings as 'Villa R' and 'Fugue in Red'. Later works—'Fear' and 'Death and Fire', for example—reflect his concern with the approach of his death and of war. (*See also* Drawing; Painting.)

KLEMPERER, Otto (1885–1973). The last surviving member of the 19th-century Austro-German school of conducting was Otto Klemperer. He was also one of the few to promote 20th-century music.

Klemperer was born on May 14, 1885, in Breslau, Germany (now Wroclaw, Poland). He studied music in Frankfurt and Berlin and met Gustav Mahler, who recommended him in 1907 as conductor of German opera at Prague (now in Czechoslovakia). From 1910 Klemperer conducted opera at Hamburg, Strasbourg, Cologne, and Wiesbaden, becoming director of the Kroll Opera in Berlin in 1927. He was forced by the Nazi government to leave Germany, and from 1933 to 1939 he conducted the Los Angeles Philharmonic Orchestra in the United States.

In the latter year he suffered from a massive brain tumor and became incapacitated for some time. But he made a remarkable recovery and, despite injuries and further health problems, resumed his career at the Budapest Opera from 1947 to 1950. From 1951 he conducted the Philharmonia Orchestra in London, with which he made numerous recordings, becoming its principal conductor in 1959.

Although he had introduced works by Leos Janácek, Arnold Schönberg, Paul Hindemith, Igor Stravinsky, and Ernst Krenek while in Berlin, he now became the recognized authority for the Austro-German school from Haydn to Mahler. He died in Zurich, Switzerland, on July 6, 1973.

KLONDIKE *see* YUKON TERRITORY.

KNIFE, FORK, AND SPOON. There was a time when people of the Western world dined without that useful set of tools, the knife, fork, and spoon. Families did not have matching implements to set at the place of each person at the dining table as families normally do in the 20th century. A knife with one sharp edge and a comfortable handle designed just for cutting meat and vegetables or spreading butter and jam was unknown to them. They did not have a fork with four pointed prongs curved conveniently to spear food and carry it to the mouth. Nor did they have spoons of different sizes for soup, dessert, tea, and coffee.

Until late in the 1600s, when Benjamin Franklin's father was a young man, Americans and Europeans nearly always used their fingers at meals as people in the Near East still do. The steel daggers they carried for defense (*see* Sword) cut their meat, and round-bowled spoons with a pencil-like handle helped them eat stews and soup. This hard-to-hold spoon was called a table spoon to distinguish it from the long spoons that stirred things in the kitchen. Few people had small forks with which to eat. Most people thought that forks belonged in the kitchen or at the serving table to hold meat when it was being cut. They called these short-handled forks with their two, long, sharp tines, or prongs, flesh forks.

Knives and spoons were among mankind's earliest inventions. In prehistoric times knives of flintstone, shells, and bones helped men kill and cut up animals for food and scrape their hides to make coverings that kept out the cold and rain. Spoons, made first of shells and later of wood and bone, helped scoop up liquids and soft food. In the Iron Age, when men discovered how to refine the ores they dug from the ground, they made knives and spoons of iron. Before 1350 BC the Hittites in the land that is now Turkey made iron spoons with shallow bowls and straight handles. About 1200 BC the Egyptians made similar

This article was contributed by Louise Conway Belden, Assistant Curator, Winterthur Museum, Winterthur, Del., and author of 'The Festive Tradition: Table Decoration and Dessert in America, 1650–1900' (Norton, 1983).

The silver knife, spoon, and fork (left) are attributed to Antonio Gentili and were probably made in late 16th-century Rome. The stainless steel cutlery in the Blue Shark pattern (above) was designed by Svend Siune and produced in 1965 in Denmark.

Photos (left) The Metropolitan Museum of Art, Rogers Fund, 1947; (above) Georg Jensen Silversmithy of Denmark

spoons of ivory, slate, and wood. They made spoons also of animal horns that they softened in water and molded into shape. The ancient Greeks and Romans made knives and spoons of bronze. Some of these bronze implements had handles shaped like banisters. Others had plain handles with ends like the hoof of a deer. In the Middle Ages, Europeans made spoons of wood, tin, or silver with handles ending in a knob and later, in the 16th century, with handles ending in figures of saints or other religious figures.

The idea of using forks to aid in eating was introduced from Byzantium into Greece about AD 1100 and traveled northward into Italy and France for the next four centuries. England did not adopt the custom until the 15th century and then only for women when they ate certain foods such as preserved fruits. But in the late 1500s, when Queen Elizabeth I was reigning in England, a few well-to-do people began to carry a case fitted with a small pointed metal knife, a round straight-handled spoon, and a small fork with two long metal tines to use wherever they ate a meal. A century and a half later, wealthy Englishmen and American merchants and planters began to use forks along with spoons and knives at the table. Finally, in about 1750 middle-class Americans did, too.

It was about 1700 that dagger-like table knife blades gave way to those rounded at the end. The pencil-like handles of table spoons were abandoned for those flat and widened at the end. The long tines of forks were shortened to 1½ inches (3.8 centimeters) in length and sometimes, particularly in Europe, came in threes and fours instead of in twos. Handles of knives and forks were made with bone or horn instead of metal. Ordinary spoons were made of wood, horn, pewter, copper, brass, wood, or latten, an inexpensive metal somewhat like brass. The best were of silver or even of gold.

About 1730 spoon bowls became egg shaped, and the style of their handle ends changed from flat and broad to spatula-like. The spatulate ends turned upward. Handles had a long rib on the front, a new style known in the 20th century as midrib, or Hanoverian, after the English kings who came from Hanover in Germany. Just before the American Revolution, spoon handle ends changed again. This time they became rounded, oval, or pointed and downturned in a style that in the 20th century is called Old English. Craftsmen engraved delicate designs and the owner's initials on the front and stamped their own name or initials on the back. Knives and forks left their straight handles behind for new ones that were curved like pistol handles.

After the Revolutionary War silversmiths made knives, forks, and spoons to match each other and sold them in sets of six or twelve. Several new kinds then came to the table. Among them were butter servers and fish servers; mustard spoons and salt spoons; large gravy spoons for serving the juices of large roasts of meat; large and small ladles for use in punch bowls and gravy and sauce boats; tea and coffee spoons for the drinks that had been brought from the Orient and the Near East in the 1600s; dessert knives, forks, and spoons; and carving knives and forks to be used at the dinner table.

At the beginning of the 19th century spoon handles looked a bit like violins, or fiddles, in a style that the French had begun 50 years earlier. Pewter and silver forks also had fiddle-like handles. Knife handles, usually of bone, horn, ivory, or porcelain, once again were straight. By 1820 or so, with the Industrial Revolution well under way, power-driven machinery brought a new era. Machines could stamp a piece of silver or pewter, or even of a hard pewter known as britannia, into the fiddle shape and with the same blow raise a shell, thread border, or other decoration onto the front and back. Machine stamping was far easier and quicker than hand hammering. Consequently much more flatware was produced. Designers patented their ideas for handle decoration in the United States patent office and from 1850 on turned out dozens of flatware patterns.

The buyers of the new silver admired its machine regularity and wanted a separate implement for every table purpose. Following the Civil War in America, manufacturers pleased them by making such new forms as luncheon knives and forks; cake and pie knives; salad, pickle, olive, and sardine forks; and soup, egg, sugar, ice cream, jam, and children's spoons. Silver was the favorite material. It was expensive, but, when manufacturers used an inexpensive white metal and coated it with silver, nearly everyone could afford flatware that looked like silver. Objects made of the new electroplated nickel silver were stamped ERNS to distinguish them from objects made of sterling silver, that is, of silver that is 92.5 percent pure.

By the end of the century the designs that decorated the new forms—like the designs of furniture, fabrics, and wallpapers of this late Victorian period—were copied from Roman sculpture, the Italian Renaissance, the scrolls and shells of the rococo 18th century, and Gothic churches. The designs also copied the flowers and leaves of nature.

In the latter half of the 20th century, when people no longer crowd their tables with food as they did earlier, manufacturers make fewer pieces of flatware. A standard five-piece place setting and a few serving pieces are the rule. Stainless steel is more popular than silver or plated silver. Designs derive from 18th-century classical, 19th-century fiddle, and 20th-century art nouveau, art deco, and Scandinavian.

KNIGHTHOOD.

KNIGHTHOOD. The most significant military figure of the feudal system of the European Middle Ages was the knight. He was a mounted warrior dressed in a suit of armor. The word knight is derived from the Old English word *cniht,* the equivalent of the Latin word *caballarius,* meaning "horseman." (*See also* Armor; Feudalism.)

A knight in armor would present a very strange appearance on a modern battlefield. His prancing steed and metal coat of mail, the heavy iron helmet that covered his head, the shield that he carried on his left arm, his lance and shining sword—all of these belong to bygone days and have little place among the swift airplanes, the rapid-shooting automatic weapons, and the scorching flamethrowers of modern warfare.

Knighthood flourished before the time of guns and gunpowder when battles still were won by hand-to-hand conflicts of heavy-armored knights. Even in peacetime knights looked for conflicts in which to engage. Fighting was almost an everyday occurrence, and the common people generally could not protect themselves against an invading foe. In times of danger they fled to the castles or strongholds owned by the nobles. To obtain protection the poorer folk became the serfs or villeins of their powerful neighbors, and those in turn were the vassals of those still more powerful. The institution of knighthood was part of this feudal system.

Training of a Knight

The education of a knight began at the age of seven, when he was taken from his home and sent to the castle of some famous nobleman, perhaps his father's lord. Here he served the lord and lady as a page until he was 14 years old. It was his duty, and he considered it a privilege, to accompany them at all times. He waited on them at the dinner table and went with them to various affairs. He received religious instruction from the chaplain and training in arms from the squires. He was taught by his mistress and her ladies to honor and protect all women. He also learned to sing and to play the lute, to hunt and to hawk. But above all else he learned to ride a horse.

At the age of 14, he became a squire. He now learned to handle sword and lance and to bear the weight of the heavy armor. In addition to his other duties, he had now to carve at the dinner table and to accompany his knight to war. He assisted him in putting on his armor. He saw to it that the knightly sword as well as other arms were polished until they shone. He stood by to give aid in conflict should his lord be overmatched and to lend his horse should the master lose his own. It was the squire who raised his knight when he fell and who bore his body away if he were wounded or killed in battle.

In the Prologue to Geoffrey Chaucer's 'Canterbury Tales' there is this description of a squire: "His clothes were embroidered red and white, as it were a meadow of fresh flowers. All the day he was singing or playing upon a lute, he was as fresh as the Month of May. His coat was short, with long wide sleeves.

Well could he sit a horse and ride, make songs, joust and dance, draw and write. He loved so ardently that at nighttime he slept no more than a nightingale. He was courteous, modest, and helpful, and carved before his master at table."

The Knighting Ceremony

At the age of 21, if he had acquitted himself well as page and squire, the young man was made a knight. This was an occasion of elaborate ceremony and solemn vows. After a purification bath, the candidate for knighthood knelt or stood all night in prayer before the altar on which lay the precious armor he would don on the morrow. In the morning there was a religious ritual, with perhaps a sermon on the knight's duty to protect the weak, to right wrongs, and to honor women. Then in the courtyard in the presence of the assembled knights

In a few days this young squire will be "knighted" with elaborate ceremonies. Here he is seen trying on the honored armor of a knight while his family watches him proudly. The armorer is fitting the metal "garments" with the aid of hammer and pincers.

and fair ladies, a knight's armor was buckled on, piece by piece, a sword was girded about his waist, and spurs were attached to the candidate's feet. He then knelt to receive the accolade. This was a blow upon the neck or shoulder, given by the officiating lord or knight with his fist or with the flat of a sword. As he gave it he said, "In the name of God and St. Michael and St. George, I dub thee knight; be brave and loyal." The ceremony was followed by exhibitions of the young knight's skill in arms.

Sometimes on the occasion of a knighting, the lord at whose castle the ceremony took place gave a tournament. This was often a very gorgeous and extravagant entertainment. Knights for miles around were invited to come and take part, while many persons of distinction came to see the events. Sometimes the visitors came in such numbers that the lodgings of the castle were filled and tents were put up to accommodate the later arrivals. Each knight's shield with its coat of arms served as a sort of doorplate to the passersby, who when they saw a familiar device displayed would say, "Sir Percival is within this tent."

In the morning, after attending mass, the knights would go to the tourney field, or lists. Here the combats or jousts between the knights were fought. Sometimes two knights fought alone, sometimes whole companies met in combat. When all were

assembled, the heralds announced the names of the contestants, and the new knight looked upon the most brilliant scene that the times had to offer. Along the sides of the field were handsome pavilions filled with beautiful ladies, lighthearted young pages, and jewel-bedecked nobles. The knights were resplendent in shining armor, with swords and golden spurs giving back the sunlight. Banners fluttered, and here and there gleamed gorgeous cloth of gold.

The combats which took place in this gay setting were not gentle ones. The points of the weapons, to be sure, were usually encased in blocks of wood to make the encounter less dangerous, but the sport was so rough and the knights jousted in such earnest that many were wounded and some were killed. About each knight's helmet was tied the favor his lady had given him, and he fought to do her honor quite as much as to do himself credit. The joust was attended by much excitement, with the blowing of trumpets, the clash of steel, the shouts of heralds, and the applause of the spectators. It continued until one or the other of the knights was overcome. The defeated knight then yielded his horse and armor to his adversary and was assisted from the field by the squires.

Sometimes a tournament lasted for several days, feasting, dancing, and hawking filling the hours not given to fighting. Hawking was a sport indulged in by the ladies and the squires as well as by the knights.

Almost every lady had her own hawk or falcon which when unhooded was trained to rise into the air and attack game birds.

Often during the festivities of a tournament a large pie was baked and live birds concealed inside. Then in the great hall the pie was opened, the birds flew about, and the falcons were loosed at them. This was considered great sport and has been immortalized in the nursery rhyme—

> Sing a song of sixpence, pocket full of rye,
> Four and twenty blackbirds baked in a pie;
> When the pie was opened, the birds began to sing;
> Wasn't that a dainty dish to set before a king?

Into the Great World of Adventure

After the festivities attending the conferring of knighthood, the young knight was free to go where he pleased. Usually he rode forth in quest of adventure, armor on his back, his spurs on his heels, and with sword, shield, and lance ready to hand. As a knight-errant he sought a fair maiden in need of a champion or a strange knight with whom to joust. Sometimes he stationed himself at a bridge or crossroad to challenge to combat any knight who happened by. He was usually sure of hospitality at any castle to which he came. After a time he might return to his father's castle or join the following of some great lord or become one of the multitude of crusaders who journeyed to rescue the Holy Sepulcher. Whenever or however he went he took with him the three watchwords of a knight: Religion, Honor, Courtesy. The ideal knight is thus described by the poet Chaucer: "And though he was valorous, he was prudent and as meek as a maid of his bearing. In all his life he never yet spake discourteously but was truly a perfect gentle knight."

With the rise of the longbow and the crossbow carrying wounds or death from a distance, and the invention of gunpowder and cannon rendering useless the feudal castle, the knight in armor passed out of existence. Knighthood then came to be merely a title of honor for persons who served the king or country.

During the Middle Ages, several orders of knighthood were founded. The first of these orders arose while the Crusades against the Muslims were in progress. Among these orders were the Knights of the Hospital of St. John of Jerusalem, now called the Knights of Malta; the Poor Knights of Christ and of the Temple of Solomon, known generally as the Knights Templars; the Hospitallers of St. Lazarus of Jerusalem; and the Teutonic Knights. Many of these orders became strong political powers in the late Middle Ages. (*See also* Crusading Orders.)

The orders that were formed during the Crusades had a religious origin. There were also a number of purely secular orders of knights founded by various monarchs in Europe. Some of these orders have persisted into the 20th century; membership is bestowed upon citizens who have made outstanding contributions to society in the arts, sciences, politics, and the military. Perhaps the best-known order is that of the Garter, established by Edward III of England about 1348. Other orders of the British Empire are that of the Bath, founded by George I in 1725; the Order of St. Michael and St. George, founded by prince regent, subsequently King George IV, in 1818; the ancient Scottish Order of the Thistle, thought to have founded about 787 and revived by James II in 1687; the Royal Victorian Order, founded by Queen Victoria in 1896; and the Order of the British Empire, founded by George V in 1917. The Irish Order of St. Patrick was founded by George III in 1783.

Other countries had organizations of knights as well. In France the Order of the Golden Fleece was founded in 1430. It later became the principal knightly order of both Austria and Spain. Portugal had the Order of St. Benedict of Avis. In Germany there were the orders of the Black Eagle and of the Red Eagle. Russia had three orders: St. Andrew, St. George, and St. Nicholas. The Danish Order of the Elephant was founded in the 15th century and revived in 1693. The Norwegian Order of St. Olav was not founded until 1847. In the Far East, Japan had two orders: the Chrysanthemum and the Rising Sun. In countries that are no longer monarchies, the best-known modern order is the French Legion of Honor which was established by Napoleon in 1802. Other republics have similar orders of merit to award civilian and military honors.

KNIGHTS OF COLUMBUS *see* FRATERNAL SOCIETIES.

Jousting knights were the featured event at medieval tournaments. The joust continued until one of the knights was overcome. The defeated knight would then yield his horse and armor to his victorious opponent.

London Electrotype Agency

KNITTING. The production of fabric by interlocking loops of yarn is called knitting. Knitted fabrics usually stretch more than woven ones and are lightweight, wrinkle resistant, and often need no ironing. The two basic types are weft knits and warp knits.

Weft knits are usually made from one continuous yarn. The basic weft stitches are the knit stitch, a loop passed through the front of the preceding loop, and the purl stitch, which is drawn through the back. Weft knits include single knits such as jersey, velour, terry, fleeces, and high pile, or fake fur; double knits; and ribbed fabrics. Because weft knitting produces a very elastic fabric, it is used for stockings, sweaters, and other garments. A run can occur, however, when one loop breaks and releases other loops in the same row. Although double knits are weft knits, they are produced by machine with two yarns and two sets of needles. Double knits are heavy and firm and rarely run. Rib knits have pronounced lengthwise ribs formed by wales, or vertical columns of loops, alternating on both sides of the fabric. They are heavy, elastic, and more durable than plain knits.

Warp knits are usually run resistant and are less elastic than weft knits. Many yarns are used in warp knitting: as many as the number of loops in the width of the fabric. These yarns zigzag so that the loops directly above one another are formed by different yarns. Warp knits include tricot and raschel. Tricot has a fine texture and is often used for lingerie and loungewear. Raschel knits are made with a heavy-textured yarn held in place by a much finer yarn, but they can be either coarse or fine. Raschel is usually less elastic than tricot.

Weft knits are usually tubular; warp knits are often flat. Tubular (circular) knits can be shaped by tightening or stretching stitches. Flat weft knits can be shaped by a process called fashioning.

Knitting Industry

The knitting industry is divided into three parts: fabrics, hosiery, and outerwear. About 40 percent of clothing fabrics manufactured in the United States are knitted. Knitted fabric production has increased from approximately 325 million pounds (147 million kilograms) in the 1960s to more than 1.7 billion pounds (770 million kilograms) in the 1980s. This growth was based on the introduction of modern double-knit fabrics, with many textile companies entering the knitting business.

The introduction of panty hose in the early 1960s caused a revolution in the hosiery industry. Panty hose supplanted traditional women's hosiery and other undergarments. Sweaters comprise a large part of the outerwear segment of the knitting industry, but foreign imports have led to a decline in United States sweater production.

Modern industrial knitting machines are large, fast, and complex. They use sophisticated electronic technology and are computer controlled. Tubular fabrics and seamless stockings are made on circular machines. Flat fabrics and flat-shaped pieces such as those used to make sweaters, gloves, and full-fashioned hosiery are produced on flatbed machines.

The needle is the basic element of all knitting machines, whether circular or flatbed. The needles are moved up and down by cams or similar devices. Their hooklike heads close as they pull newly forming loops through other loops that are being slipped off to form the body of the fabric.

Knitting in the Home

Because the knitting industry has become highly automated, hand knitting is now done mainly at home as a hobby. An experienced hand knitter can make such items as scarves, socks, afghans, sweaters, shawls, and mittens.

Hand knitting is done with a single yarn looped on two or more needles. Knitting needles vary in shape and size and are usually made from wood, plastic, or metal. The knitter catches the yarn with a needle to form loops and then transfers rows of loops from one needle to another.

Although most home knitting is done by hand, small high-quality home knitting machines are also in use. Home knitting machines are faster than hand knitting and allow the user to produce more complex patterns. Home knitting machines can be programmed with punched pattern cards. Some home knitters now use personal computers to assist them when they design knitting patterns.

History

People have known how to knit since ancient times. Early tribes knitted fishnets. Knitted socks have been found in an Egyptian tomb that dates from before the Christian Era. During the Middle Ages knitters formed guilds, or craft groups. By the 15th century knitted clothing was common throughout Western Europe.

All knitting was done by hand until 1589. In that year a young English clergyman, William Lee, invented the first knitting machine. Because the machine knit stockings flat, they had to be hand sewn up the back. Lee presented a pair of wool stockings to Queen Elizabeth I and asked for a patent on his machine. She asked him to try to make silk stockings, perhaps because she was afraid that the new machine would take work from her many subjects who made a living by hand knitting woolen clothing. In 1598 Lee produced a pair of silk stockings for the queen on a machine with 20 needles to the inch. Although pleased, the queen still refused to grant him a patent. Lee then started manufacturing operations in France at the invitation of King Henry IV. By the 18th century knitting machines were in widespread use in Europe. In 1816 another English inventor, Sir Marc Brunel, built the first circular knitting machine.

In America knitting was an important craft for colonial families. Many pioneer and farm families depended upon women in the household for knitted clothing. As cities and trade grew, machine-knitted goods became more widespread.

By courtesy of American Textile Manufacturers Institute, Inc.

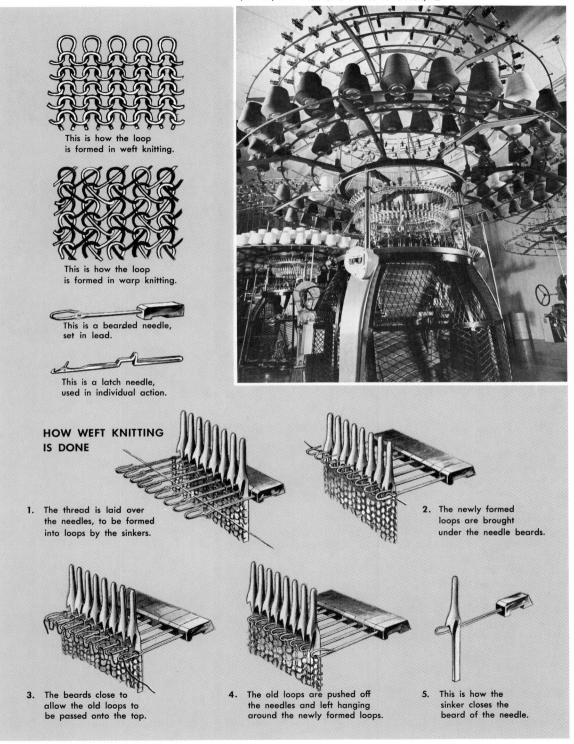

This is how the loop is formed in weft knitting.

This is how the loop is formed in warp knitting.

This is a bearded needle, set in lead.

This is a latch needle, used in individual action.

HOW WEFT KNITTING IS DONE

1. The thread is laid over the needles, to be formed into loops by the sinkers.

2. The newly formed loops are brought under the needle beards.

3. The beards close to allow the old loops to be passed onto the top.

4. The old loops are pushed off the needles and left hanging around the newly formed loops.

5. This is how the sinker closes the beard of the needle.

The photograph (upper right) shows a circular machine knitting tubular fabric. The drawings at the left show plain weft knitting (top), warp knitting, and two kinds of needles. The drawings below show weft knitting. After the thread, or yarn, has been laid over the needles (1) the sinkers dip down to form loops in the thread. With the same movement these loops are pushed under the needle beards as shown (2) and the beards are closed. As the sinkers rise again (3) the old loops are ready to slide over the new ones (4) and complete the row. No. 5 shows detail of operation.

261

KNOT, HITCH, AND SPLICE. The ability to tie knots is a skill that can prove valuable to everyone. Children learn at an early age that it is necessary to tie a good knot in their shoelaces in order to keep shoes firmly on their feet. They also soon discover that if such a knot is made properly, it can be untied with only a little effort.

A *knot*, correctly made, remains secure but may be easily untied. A *hitch* is a knot that is less secure and is usually looped around a stationary object. A *splice* is a permanent knot formed by interweaving the strands of a single rope or of two ropes.

The professions and trades in which knots are used are many and varied. The surgeon must be able to tie knots deep within an incision. The rancher, fisherman, and seaman must all know many good knots and how to apply them to best advantage.

Many types of knots have been employed for decorative purposes. Some have served as badges in heraldry. The carrick bend—a knot now used for tying two ropes together—was the heraldic badge of Hereward Wake, a Saxon leader of the 11th century.

Knot-making was a highly developed skill long before the Christian era. Stone Age men made fishnets by knotting together strands of fiber. The sailors of ancient Egypt were proficient knot makers. Pottery and sculpture reveal that the ancient Greeks were familiar with the square knot.

KNOTS

Some knots are especially valuable because of the speed with which they can be made. The best, however, are those that hold firmly without slipping, yet do not bind so tightly that they are difficult to untie. The long portion of a rope, about which the loose end is woven, is called the *standing part*. A loop of rope is termed a *bight*.

Overhand Knot. The simplest of all knots is the *overhand*, or *thumb*, *knot*. Although usually a part of other, more complex, knots, it may also be employed by itself, to provide a handhold on a rope, to prevent a rope from raveling, and to keep a rope end from running through a pulley or a sewing thread from pulling through cloth. The overhand knot is made by holding the standing part in one hand, forming a closed loop with the free end, and drawing the end around and through the loop.

OVERHAND KNOT

SQUARE KNOT

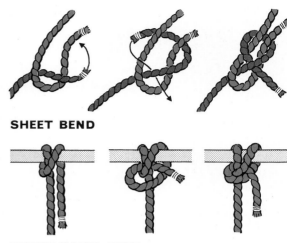

SHEET BEND

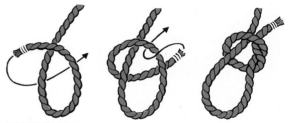

FISHERMAN'S BEND

SLIPKNOT

Square Knot. The knot that is most commonly used for fastening ropes or strings together is the *square knot*, also known as the *sailor's*, or *reef*, *knot*. Shoelaces, for example, are customarily tied by means of the square knot. The square knot is always used by sailors in *reefing* a sail, that is, shortening a sail by tying back a portion. Made with ropes of the same thickness, the square knot is extremely reliable and easy to untie. It is less reliable if it is made with ropes of different thicknesses. Even if the ropes are stiff and wet, they can be loosened without difficulty by pushing the free ends back against the knot, then completely untied by pulling out the loops—as one does when untying shoelaces.

To tie a square knot the loose ends of two ropes are passed around each other once and then again in such a way that the standing part and the end of each rope come out on the same side of the loop.

If the standing parts and the ends of the ropes are brought out on opposite sides of the loop, the result is a *granny*, or *lubber's*, *knot*. The granny knot is unreliable, for it slips easily and gives way under strain.

Sheet Bend. The term *bend* is generally applied to knots that connect two ropes or that connect one rope with a solid object. The *sheet bend*, or *weaver's knot*, is one of the most useful of these. Weavers tie ends of thread together with this knot because it passes smoothly through the needle. The sheet bend is begun like the square knot, but one of the ends is then turned back under itself.

Fisherman's Bend. The *fisherman's*, or *anchor*, *bend* is commonly used by sailors to fasten a rope to a buoy or an anchor ring. The rope is looped twice around the securing object, the second loop passing over the first. The end is looped again, this time passing through the first two loops. The knot is frequently made secure by binding the end with string against the standing part.

Slipknot. One of the easiest knots to tie is the *slipknot*, or *running knot*. It is made by first forming a bight, then making an overhand knot around the standing part. The slipknot is not strong and will give under strain. It frequently serves a temporary purpose.

Bowline. One of the most useful of all knots, the *bowline* is sometimes called the "king of knots." It is quickly and easily tied and will never slip. The bowline is tied by forming a loop in the standing part and passing the end through this loop, around the standing part above it, then back through the loop. The *bowline on a bight* is formed with a length of rope that has been doubled back upon itself. It is begun in the same way as the bowline; but after being passed through the loop, the bight is spread open and the parts of the knot already formed are pulled through it. The bowline on a bight is used to support a person working along the side of a ship or along other steep worksites.

HITCHES

Usually a hitch is formed around a solid object, such as a spar, post, or ring. Some types of hitches work loose by themselves if the standing part is not subjected to a constant strain.

Clove Hitch. Perhaps the most widely used of the hitches is the *clove*, or *ratline*, *hitch*. It is especially

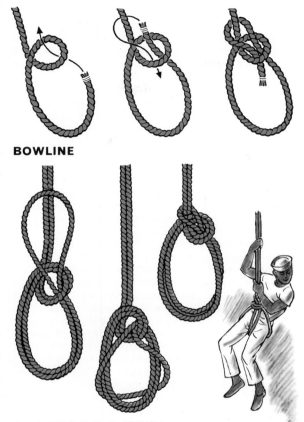

BOWLINE

BOWLINE ON A BIGHT

practical for making a rope fast to a pole or similar object. The end is passed over the object twice, the second loop crossing back over the standing part; it is then pulled through the inside of the loop so that it lies along the standing part.

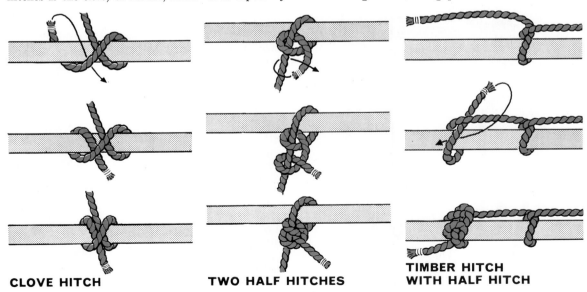

CLOVE HITCH   **TWO HALF HITCHES**   **TIMBER HITCH WITH HALF HITCH**

Half Hitch. A basic segment of many knots is the *half hitch*. This is a simple loop around a pole or other stationary object, with the end and the standing part in tension against each other. Two half hitches—providing considerably more security than a single half hitch—are commonly used for such purposes as tying up a boat to a dock post.

Timber Hitch. The *timber hitch* is often used in towing logs or other cylindrical objects. These can be towed lengthwise by adding one or more half hitches to the timber hitch. The timber hitch is formed by making a half hitch and then winding the end around the loop.

Sheepshank. The *sheepshank* is the most practical knot for shortening a rope without cutting it. The rope is first folded back and forth along its length. A clove hitch is then made at each end to secure the folds.

Figure Eight Halter Hitch. Among the most valuable of the hitches are the *halter hitches*, which are customarily employed to fasten the halters of horses and cows to posts and hitching rings. The *figure eight halter hitch* has a special advantage—it can be untied quickly. To tie a figure eight halter hitch, the end is passed through a hitching ring or a similar secure object, then turned against itself to form a closed loop; the remaining part of the end is passed around the standing part and doubled to form a bight; the bight is then drawn through the first loop, and the hitch is tightened by pulling on the standing part. It is easily untied by pulling on the end of the rope. However, an animal that has been restrained by means of this hitch cannot free itself, no matter how hard it struggles.

SHEEPSHANK

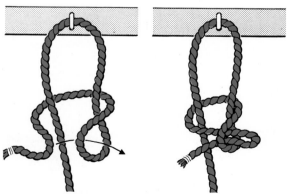

FIGURE EIGHT HALTER HITCH

264

SHORT SPLICE

SPLICES

A splice is used to connect the ends of two ropes or to form a loop at the end of a rope. Splices are considerably stronger than knots, but they do not have the advantage of being easily undone. Wire rope is always repaired by splicing, since it is too stiff for the satisfactory formation of knots.

Short Splice. The simplest type of splice is the *short splice*, in which the strands of two ropes are *unlaid*, or untwisted, to a convenient length and then interwoven to form one rope. When the strands have been untwisted, the ropes are placed end to end with the strands spread out. The ropes may be temporarily tied into this position with a string. Each strand of one rope is then laced under one strand and over a second strand of the other. This process is repeated until the unlaid portions of both ropes have been completely interwoven. The resulting splice is somewhat bulkier than the rest of the rope, since it contains twice as many strands.

Eye Splice. The *eye splice* is made in the same way as the short splice. In the eye splice, however, the end of a single rope is woven back into itself, to form a loop, or eye.

In splicing Manila rope, the openings between strands are made with a pointed wooden *fid*. For wire rope, a metal or metal-tipped *marlinespike* is used. The art of working with fiber and wire rope is known as *marlinespike seamanship*. (*See also* Rope and Twine; Fishing.)

EYE SPLICE

KNOX, John (1514–72). The leader of the Protestant Reformation in Scotland was John Knox. For years he lived in exile or was hunted as an outlaw at home. Courageous and dogmatic, he finally established Presbyterianism as Scotland's national church.

Little is known of Knox's early life. Probably he was born at Giffordgate in Haddington. He may have entered Glasgow University but was never graduated. He studied toward becoming a priest in the Roman Catholic church, then turned to tutoring.

Knox was a tutor when he became involved in church reform in 1546. At the time, Scotland was a Catholic nation, but many were angry at church abuses. Knox was a follower of George Wishart, a Lutheran reformer. When Cardinal Beaton had Wishart burned as a heretic, a mob killed the cardinal and occupied his castle. Knox joined the castle garrison and began teaching the gospel. Soon the leaders of the revolutionaries asked him to act as their preacher, and he accepted.

In July 1547 the Catholics regained the castle with French help, and the defenders were made French galley slaves. In February 1549 Knox was released. For a time he preached in England and Germany. Later he was pastor of an English congregation in Geneva, Switzerland. There he became a student of the Protestant leader John Calvin.

By 1559 Scotland was ready for the new doctrine. Knox returned home and his preaching soon roused the people to wreck churches and monasteries. In 1560 the Scottish Parliament established Presbyterianism as the national faith. Thereafter Knox devoted himself to strengthening the new church. One of his chief targets was Mary Stuart, Catholic ruler of Scotland. In 1567 she was deposed. Knox then knew his church was safe. (*See also* Mary, Queen of Scots.)

Knox married when he was about 48 and had two sons. Following the death of his first wife he remarried at 59 and had three daughters. Knox died in Edinburgh, Scotland, on Nov. 24, 1572.

KNOXVILLE, Tenn. The industrial city of Knoxville prospers because of the nearness of raw materials and because it is the center for a vast recreational area.

Burley tobaccos and livestock are raised in the fertile Tennessee Valley. Marble is quarried and coal mined nearby. About 20 miles (30 kilometers) west is Oak Ridge National Laboratory, an energy research center. Great Smoky Mountains National Park begins 35 miles (56 kilometers) southeast. Close by are beautiful lakes, formed by the dams of the Tennessee Valley Authority.

Knoxville is located in east-central Tennessee, just four miles (six kilometers) below the point where the Holston and French Broad rivers join to form the Tennessee River. The city is a trade center and the headquarters for the Tennessee Valley Authority (*see* Tennessee Valley Authority). The city's industries produce textiles and clothing; machinery and other metal goods; processed foods; stone, glass, and clay products; chemicals; plastics; and wooden articles. Knoxville is host to many conventions. The Tennessee Valley Agricultural and Industrial Fair is held annually in September. The University of Tennessee and Knoxville College are there. The Lawson McGhee Library houses the notable McClung Historical Collection.

Knoxville's first settler, James White, built a log fort on the site in 1786. The town was named for General Henry Knox, President Washington's secretary of war. From 1792 to 1796 it was the capital of Territory South of the River Ohio and then of the state until 1812. Knoxville's first rail line, from Chattanooga, reached the town in 1855. Knoxville gained population steadily after the American Civil War and rapidly in the 1900s. Its downtown section became a model of redevelopment. The city gained many improvements in 1982 as a result of its hosting a world's

The 1982 World's Fair was held at Knoxville.

fair. City plans called for the 70-acre fairgrounds highlighted by the 25-story Sunsphere to become a permanent recreational facility.

The city has a mayor-council form of government. (*See also* Tennessee.) Population (1980 census), 175,030; metropolitan area, 476,517.

KOBE, Japan. One of Japan's chief domestic and international ports is Kobe, the capital of Hyogo Prefecture. The city is part of the huge Osaka-Kobe Metropolitan Area. This region is the second largest urban and industrial cluster in Japan after the Tokyo region. Usually it is defined to include the ancient city of Kyoto as well as many satellite industrial and residential cities. Total population of this metropolitan area in 1981 was estimated at 16,224,000. Urbanization extends 25 miles (40 kilometers) east of Osaka to Nara, and 25 miles northwest to Kyoto. A dense network of railways winds throughout the metropolitan area.

Kobe is located on the northwestern shore of Osaka Bay. The city is backed by the granite peak of Mount Rokko, which rises 3,057 feet (932 meters) and which has forced the city to spread along the seacoast. Main streets run east and west, crossed by short north-south streets and occasional longer, winding roads that extend up into the hills to hotels and expensive homes. The central shopping street, Motomachi, runs between two railroad stations. The central business district is near the harbor. Elevated expressways extend through the central parts of Kobe and out to Osaka International Airport. Other highways span the entire region.

The major industrial activities in Kobe are shipbuilding and steel production. Other industries produce sake, machinery, books, and textiles. Together with Osaka, Kobe is the leading port for foreign trade. Although sewage facilities are inadequate, electricity is available everywhere and natural gas is available throughout most of the area.

The cultural and educational aspects of Kobe life combine with those of Osaka. There are several universities, numerous science and art museums, art galleries, and libraries. Traditional and modern Japanese drama and music are performed at theaters and halls in the metropolitan area, as are Western music, operas, and plays. The area has four professional baseball teams. At the top of Mount Rokko, which can be reached by road or by cable car, are a golf course and ponds for swimming.

The name Kobe was originally applied to a small fishing village separated by the Minato River from the town of Hyogo, the area's chief port. During the Tokugawa period in Japanese history (from 1603 to 1868), Hyogo served as the outer port of Osaka until Japan was reopened to foreign trade in the mid-1800s. Soon Hyogo was outstripped and absorbed by Kobe, which has a deeper harbor. The combined ports have been called Kobe since the establishment of the Kobe customhouse in 1872. Hyogo and Kobe were incorporated as the city of Kobe in 1889. The port continued to grow and to absorb adjacent communities through the 1950s, although much of the city was destroyed during World War II. The city and its harbor facilities were quickly rebuilt after the war. (*See also* Japan.) Population (1980 census), 1,367,390; (1982 estimate), 1,375,006.

KOBO DAISHI, or KUKAI (774–835). One of the best known and most beloved figures in the history of Japanese Buddhism was Kobo Daishi, also known as Kukai. He was the founder of the Shingon ("True Word") sect of Buddhism, as well as being a philosopher, poet, educational reformer, painter, and calligrapher.

Kobo Daishi was born on June 15, 774, to a wealthy family in Zentsuiji. He was well schooled in the classics of Confucianism (*see* Confucius). But at age 17, in his first major work, 'Essentials of the Three Treatises', he proclaimed the superiority of Buddhism over Confucianism and Taoism, two other major beliefs. In the years 804 to 806 Kobo Daishi was in China, studying Buddhism under one of its great masters, Hui-kuo. Afterwards, he returned to Japan to make his form of Buddhism known.

The doctrine of Shingon is a kind of mysticism, teaching that the truth of the supreme wisdom of Buddha is within all living beings and can be realized through certain rituals. The goal is to attain perfect communion between Buddha and the individual. (*See also* Buddhism.) Kobo Daishi died on March 21, 835, at the monastery, which he had founded in 816, on Mount Koya.

KOCH, Robert (1843–1910). A German country doctor helped raise the study of microbes to the modern science of bacteriology. By painstaking laboratory research, Robert Koch at last demonstrated how specific microbes cause specific diseases.

Koch was born on Dec. 11, 1843, in Clausthal, Germany (now in West Germany), a mining town in the Harz Mountains. He studied geology; made collections of minerals, plants, and small animals; and dreamed of being a great explorer. In 1862 he entered the University of Göttingen, in Germany, and began the study of medicine. He hoped to explore as an expedition doctor. After graduation, Koch interned at a hospital for the insane in Hamburg. In Hamburg he met and married Emmy Fraatz. Emmy wanted a safe, settled life, so Koch set aside his dreams and became a country doctor.

Koch began studying bits of matter through a magnifying glass. He wanted a microscope, and by much scrimping, his wife managed to buy one for his 28th birthday. Koch began his study of anthrax, a deadly disease of warm-blooded animals. He identified and raised cultures of anthrax microbes. With these cultures he gave the disease to well animals. His work took four years. When he brought the results of the work before scientists of the University of Breslau, in Poland, his proofs—the first of their kind—were undeniable.

In 1882 Koch isolated the bacterium tubercle bacillus. The next year he became head of a commission to study cholera in Egypt and India. He announced the discovery of the cholera microbe in 1883. Germany acclaimed him. He was given $25,000 and made director of a great institute to pursue his researches. In 1890 he announced the discovery of tuberculin. This substance, at first wrongly thought to be a cure for tuberculosis, is now widely used to detect the presence of the disease. Koch went on to study tropical diseases in East and West Africa. In 1905 he was awarded the Nobel prize in medicine. Koch died of a heart attack on May 28, 1910, in Baden-Baden, now in West Germany.

KOKO NOR, or **QINGHAI HU.** The largest drainless mountain lake of Central Asia is the azure-blue Koko Nor. It is situated at an altitude of 10,515 feet (3,205 meters) in a depression in the Qilian Shan mountain system of China. Twenty-three rivers and streams empty into it.

The length of Koko Nor is approximately 65 miles (105 kilometers), the width 40 miles (64 kilometers). The surface area varies according to the water level. In years when the level is high, the surface is approximately 2,300 square miles (6,000 square kilometers). When the water level is low, the area is about 1,600 square miles (4,200 square kilometers). The greatest known depth is 123 feet (37 meters). Numerous sandy islands dot the lake.

The mountain-ringed depression in which Koko Nor is set is a plain more than 10,500 feet (3,200 meters) high. The plain is covered mainly with red and gray sandstone and light-gray limestone.

Carp is the main kind of fish found in the lake. There are a few large mammals in the neighboring area, including the wolf, the Przhevalski's horse—the last wild horse to survive into the 20th century—and blue sheep in the mountains. The waterfront and the adjacent slopes are inhabited by a large variety of birds.

Mongolians occupy the northern shores and Tibetans the southern. Most of these people raise cattle and tend sheep, horses, and camels.

KOLMOGOROV, A. N. (1903–87). The most influential Soviet mathematician of the 20th century was A. N. Kolmogorov. His original contributions to the fields of probability theory and topology have had a significant impact on modern physics, chemistry, biology, and cybernetics. He also played a major role in the restructuring of the mathematics curriculum in the school system of the Soviet Union.

Andrei Nikolayevich Kolmogorov was born in Tambov, Russia, on April 25, 1903. He was graduated from Moscow State University in 1925 and was elected professor there in 1931. In 1933 he became director of the university's Institute of Mathematics. His first major publication in mathematics was a paper entitled "General Theory of Measure and Probability Theory," published in 1929. In the 1930s he published two papers on geometry: "On Topological Group Formulation of Geometry" and "On Formulation of Projective Geometry," as well as "Foundations of the Theory of Probability." Later in his career he became interested in information theory and its related fields (*see* Information Theory).

KONOPNICKA, Marja (1842–1910). An author of short stories, Marja Konopnicka was also one of the important poets of the Positivist period in Polish literature. This was a period marked by a mood of practical thinking and action, in contrast to the earlier Romantic style.

The writer was born Marja Wasilowska on May 12, 1842, in Suwalki, Poland. She spent much of her life in exile from Russian-dominated Poland and developed strong patriotic convictions toward her homeland. These convictions are reflected in her poems and short stories.

One of her most ambitious works, written between 1892 and 1909, is "Mr. Balcer in Brazil." It describes a Polish peasant emigrant's disillusionment with the New World. The poem cycle 'Italy', written in 1901, contains some of Konopnicka's most beautiful verses. Her short stories, considered to be among the best in Polish literature, include "The German Children" and "Our Old Mare." Konopnicka died in Lwow, Poland, on Oct. 8, 1910.

Thousands of birds of many varieties frequent the shore of Koko Nor.

China Photo Service/Eastfoto

KORAN. "We have revealed the Koran in the Arabic tongue that you may grasp its meaning. It is a transcript of Our eternal book, sublime, and full of wisdom." The speaker was Allah (God), and the one who received the message was Muhammad, Allah's chosen prophet to the Arab peoples. The message is contained in the holy book of Islam, the Koran. The word "Koran" means "recitation"; and the followers of Islam, Muslims, believe that God revealed the contents of the Koran to Muhammad through the angel Gabriel in order that the Prophet could recite it to the Arabs (see Islam).

The Koran was revealed to Muhammad in Arabic so he could provide the Arabs with a holy book in their own language, comparable to the Scriptures of Judaism and Christianity (see Bible). For Muslims, the Koran is the revealed, eternal, and infallible word of God. It is an ultimate authority in all religious, social, and legal issues. It is also considered the finest example of classical Arabic prose.

Throughout the Koran, the speaker is Allah, except in scattered passages in which the Prophet or the angel Gabriel speaks. The message of the book is straightforward: There is no God but Allah, and He has given His message to Muhammad to be relayed to the Arabs as both a warning and a promise. The warning is to all who refuse to believe in the one God, and the promise is of eternal rewards to those who believe in Allah and do His will: "We have revealed to you (Muhammad) the Koran in your own tongue that you may thereby proclaim good tidings to the upright and give warning to a contentious nation."

Form of the book. The Koran is comparable in length to the Christian New Testament and is divided into 114 chapters of unequal length. With the exception of the first chapter, which is a short prayer, the remaining 113 are arranged generally according to length, with chapter 2 being the longest and the last few the shortest. The chapters are not presented in chronological order.

Each chapter has a title from some significant word in the chapter, such as "The Moon," "The Believers," and "The Greeks." These titles do not indicate the full contents of a chapter, and the word may only be mentioned in passing. After the title occurs the formula: "In the name of Allah, the merciful, the compassionate." In the standard Arabic version, there is an indication whether the chapter was revealed to Muhammad at Mecca or Medina and of the number of verses.

The general tone throughout is poetic. This is more evident in the earlier chapters. These chapters are characterized by short sentences in which the rhyming is more apparent. Later chapters have much longer sentences and verses, and it is often difficult to determine whether a rhyme is intended to indicate the end of a verse.

Origins and content. That the Koran relies heavily on both Jewish and Christian traditions is evident throughout the book. It was Muhammad's contention that Judaism and Christianity had departed from belief in God's message as revealed in their Scriptures. God had sent many prophets, among them Abraham, who is considered the founder of the faith for Islam, as he is also for Judaism and Christianity (see Abraham). The Koran, using sources in the older Scriptures and later traditions, relates the stories of Abraham, Joseph, Moses and Aaron, David, Solomon, Jesus, and others, all of whom are declared to have been true prophets whose messages were largely ignored: "We sent forth Noah and Abraham, and bestowed on their offspring prophethood and the Scriptures.... After them we sent other apostles, and after those, Jesus the son of Mary." The lack of success these prophets had was reflected in Muhammad's own experience, as he preached the oneness of God to the Arabs in Mecca. The implication was that he was the last in the series of prophets, the last revealer of divine truth.

Islamic tradition states that Muhammad, beginning in the year 610, had a series of visions and revelations from God, spreading over 20 years. In the first of these, he had a vision of the angel Gabriel telling him: "You are the messenger of God." The revelations were kept in memory by Muhammad and his followers, and sometimes they were written down.

After Muhammad's death in AD 632, it was feared that the content of the revelations might be lost, as those who had originally memorized it died. It was therefore decided to collect all the revelations, from whatever source, and make a compilation. Even at this early date, variations in the Koranic revelations were becoming common in different parts of the new Islamic empire. So that there would be a definitive version, the Caliph 'Uthman (the caliphs were successors of Muhammad) commissioned one of the Prophet's followers, Zayd ibn Thabit, and others to sort through and pull together all the material and compare it with the remembrances of those who had learned it by heart. In this manner, an authorized version was created.

The arrangement of putting the longer chapters first and the shorter ones last violates the chronological order of the revelations as they came to Muhammad. But a fairly accurate chronology can be worked out on the basis of knowledge about his life: He began his work in Mecca, spent a long period in Medina, and returned again to Mecca. The chapters indicate in which place the many revelations came to him.

The main emphasis of the book is on the oneness of Allah, in contrast to the multiplicity of gods worshiped by the Arabs. These gods are denounced as powerless idols who will be unable to help unbelievers on the day of judgment. Other doctrines, common to Israel's later history and early Christianity, were incorporated into the Koran, as well. There is a strong assertion of belief in the resurrection from the dead, in angels and devils, and in heaven and hell.

All of humanity is regarded as subject to the will and power of Allah. It is He who has created and will one day judge mankind. The faithful are called upon to believe in Allah and to listen to His Prophet.

A link with Korea's past, the ancient South Gate of Seoul stands in the new city that has risen from the ruins of war.

KOREA

KOREA. On a mountainous peninsula jutting southward from the eastern Asian mainland is Korea, the historic land bridge and buffer between China and Japan. Today Korea is a land divided into a Communist north and a non-Communist south. It is torn by rival political and economic systems and by bitterness stemming from the Korean War. However, the people of both North Korea and South Korea are still united by a common cultural heritage and continue to regard themselves as a single nation.

The two halves of Korea have been rebuilt from the devastation of the Korean War. But they still suffer from huge military expenditures, dependence on foreign aid, and economies unbalanced by the partition of Korea after World War II. In addition new difficulties are being created by the growing conflicts between their traditional and modern ways of life.

Most of Korea lies on the Korean peninsula, between the Sea of Japan on the east and the Yellow Sea on the west. South Korea occupies the southern

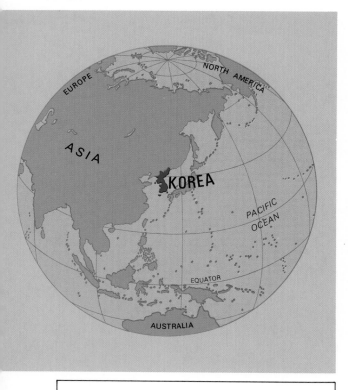

part of the peninsula, while North Korea spreads north and northeast beyond the peninsula's base. Between them is the demilitarized zone, set up by the truce ending the Korean War in 1953. It runs from about 40 miles north of the 38th parallel on the east to about 20 miles south on the west. Korea extends more than 600 miles from northeast to southwest. The Korean peninsula is about 150 miles wide.

South Korea's only land border, on the north, is with North Korea. North Korea is bounded by South Korea on the south and by China on the northwest. It touches the Soviet Union in the extreme northeast. The main islands of Japan lie 120 miles southeast of the South Korean coast across the Korea Strait.

Korea is about the size of Utah. Its total area is 85,288 square miles—47,077 in the north, 38,211 in the south. Korea's total population is more than 57 million—about 39 million in the south, more than 18 million in the north. South Korea is one of the world's most densely populated countries. Its capital, Seoul, is the largest city in Korea. Pyongyang is the largest city and the capital of North Korea.

Facts About Korea

Official Name: South Korea—Republic of Korea (*Taehan Minguk*); North Korea—Democratic People's Republic of Korea (*Choson Minjujuui Inmin Konghwaguk*).

Capital and Largest City: South Korea—Seoul; North Korea—Pyongyang.

Population (1981 estimate): South Korea—38,720,000; North Korea—18,320,000.

Area (in square miles; square kilometers): Korea—85,288; 220,895 (South Korea—38,211; 98,966. North Korea—47,077; 121,929).

Population Density (1981): Korea—669 persons per square mile; 258 per square kilometer (South Korea—1,013 per square mile; 391 per square kilometer. North Korea—389 per square mile; 150 per square kilometer).

Form of Government: South Korea—Republic; North Korea—People's Republic.

Flag: *See* Flags of the World.

Extent: Northeast to southwest—635 miles (1,024 kilometers).

Highest Elevation: Mount Paektu, 9,003 feet (2,744 meters).

Climate: Warm, moist summers; cool to cold winters.

National Anthem: South Korea—'Aegug-ga'.

Monetary Unit: South Korea—1 won = 100 chon; North Korea—1 won = 100 jon.

Major Language: Korean.

Major Religions: Buddhism, Christianity.

Included in the article are the following special features: "A Tour of Korea," 279; "Korea—North vs. South," 286; "Notable Events in Korea's History," 288.

At the end of the sections "People," "Government," "Economy," "Culture," "Natural Features," and "History" are two study aids—"Words to Remember" and "Questions to Think About."

The following contributors and consultants assisted in the preparation of this article: Byong-uk Chung, Professor of Korean Literature, Seoul National University; Earle Ernst, Senior Professor and Chairman, Department of Drama and Theatre, University of Hawaii; John D. Eyre, Professor of Geography, University of North Carolina; Pyong-choon Hahm, Professor of Law, Yonsei University; William E. Henthorn, Professor, Department of Oriental Studies, Princeton University; Jun-yop Kim, Professor of History, Korea University; Kyung-sung Kim, Professor of Geography, Seoul National University; Kwang-rin Lee, Professor of History, Sogang University; John Roderick, Foreign Correspondent; Jack Sewell, Curator of Oriental Art, The Art Institute of Chicago; Suk-kee Yoh, Professor of English Literature, Korea University.

KOREA —People

The Koreans are a culturally and racially homogeneous people. They have a common language and, like the Chinese and the Japanese, they are of Mongoloid stock.

Korea's population from the 17th to the late 19th centuries has been estimated at between 7 and 10 million. The first modern census, taken in 1925, recorded 19,020,000 inhabitants. By the 1975 census, South Korea alone had a population of 34,678,972, and the 1981 population estimate totaled 38,720,000. The 1981 population estimate for North Korea was 18,320,000.

Both South Korea and North Korea have high annual birthrates—about 28 per 1,000 population. Their death rates are about seven per 1,000. The rate of population growth in Korea is about 2 percent per year. Medical advances have raised the average life expectancy of Koreans to about 65 years. But the population of Korea is young. About half its people are under 20.

Korea's population is heavily concentrated on the coastal plains, particularly along the west coast of South Korea. South Korea is one of the most densely populated nations in the world, averaging more than 1,000 persons per square mile. North Korea's population density averages more than 380 persons per square mile.

Until recently the Koreans were a mainly rural people. In 1925, less than 5 percent of the population lived in cities. By 1975, however, more than half of all South Koreans and probably almost as high a proportion of North Koreans were city dwellers. Seoul, Korea's largest city and South Korea's capital, has about 8,400,000 inhabitants; Pusan, also in South Korea, is second, with about 3,200,000; and Pyongyang, the largest city and the capital of North Korea, is third, with about 2,100,000.

EVERYDAY LIFE

Under the impact of the West, the everyday life of the Korean people has been gradually changing. The Japanese occupation, the post-World War II partition, and the Korean War—all of these helped to spur this change and to deepen the differences between the old rural traditions and a newly developing urban way of life.

The Family

Historically, Korean families were formed into clans that shared the same family name. As a result, only a few hundred major surnames are used today. Kim, the most common, is the surname of about one fifth of all Korean families. In Korea, family names are customarily placed first and women do not change their names when they marry.

The Korean family has been traditionally domi-

nated by the husband. The wife has had only a secondary influence in family affairs, though her status improved after she bore one or more sons.

A first son is especially welcomed because his arrival ensures the continuity of the family line. On his first birthday, a baby usually has a big party at which he is formally introduced to his family and their friends. As a child grows up, he is taught to behave properly and to respect and obey his elders.

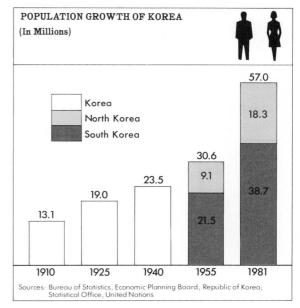

POPULATION GROWTH OF KOREA (In Millions)

Sources: Bureau of Statistics, Economic Planning Board, Republic of Korea; Statistical Office, United Nations

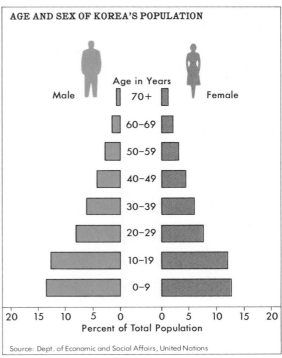

AGE AND SEX OF KOREA'S POPULATION

Source: Dept. of Economic and Social Affairs, United Nations

271

WHERE THE KOREAN PEOPLE LIVE

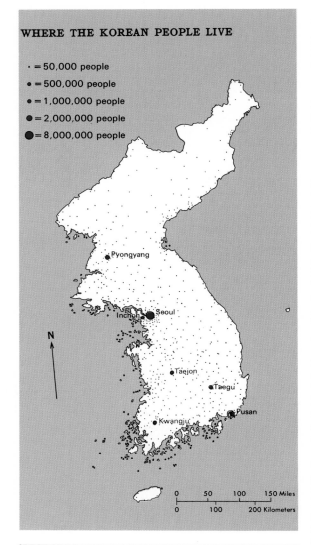

- · = 50,000 people
- ● = 500,000 people
- ● = 1,000,000 people
- ● = 2,000,000 people
- ● = 8,000,000 people

N

Pyongyang

Inchon · Seoul

Taejon

Taegu

Kwangju

Pusan

| 0 | 50 | 100 | 150 Miles |
| 0 | 100 | | 200 Kilometers |

Everyday Expressions in Korean

Yes. *Nye.*
No. *Anio.*
Good-bye. *Annyong i kasio.*
How are you? *Annyonghasipnika?*
What is your name? *Irum ul muorago hasimnika?*
My name is Jones. *Jones io.*
I am very glad to see you. *Tcham pankap so.*
What time is it? *Myossi-yo?*
What is this? *Igosi muosio?*
What is that? *Chogosun muosio?*
What are these? *Ikosi muosio?*
I know. *Ao.*
I don't know. *Moruo.*
Thank you. *Komapsupnida.*
Please. *Sipsiyo.*
Excuse me. *Yongso hasipsiyo.*

In the past, marriages were arranged by parents or by go-betweens called *chungmae.* Today, however, young people—particularly those living in cities—more often choose their own mates. Men usually marry at about the age of 21; women, at about 18. City dwellers tend to marry at a somewhat later age.

One of the most important milestones in a Korean man's life is his *hangab* (60th birthday). This date symbolizes the completion of a full life cycle and is marked by a big anniversary party.

Housing, Food, and Clothing

Traditional rural houses in Korea were one-story structures, with mud-plastered wood walls and a thatched roof of rice straw. There were usually three rooms—a kitchen with a dirt floor, a bedroom, and a living room—arranged in an L or U shape. Flues under the floor carried hot smoke from a wood or coal stove in the kitchen to a chimney at the opposite end of the house. This provided a system of radiant heating called *ondol.* The living room usually had a board floor. Koreans removed their shoes before entering it from the kitchen or the outdoors. They sat on mats and slept on quilts spread out on the floor. Traditional city houses were similar, although slate or tile was used for roofs.

Houses today are commonly built of concrete, but radiant heating is still often used. City houses generally have modern conveniences such as electricity. The construction of large housing projects—including Western-style apartment buildings—has helped ease the housing shortage caused by the destruction of the Korean War and by the rapid growth of the urban population.

Rice, the staple food of the Korean diet, is eaten at most meals. Millet, wheat, barley, corn, and sorghum are also eaten, especially in the north. The vegetables Koreans eat include potatoes, Chinese cabbage, turnips, and onions. Garlic and red peppers are used as seasoners. *Kimchi* (pickled vegetables) is a favorite dish. Fish and other seafoods are the usual sources of proteins. Eggs have also become popular. Milk is now drunk by youths, especially in the cities, a practice unheard of a generation ago. *Ttog,* or rice cake, is a popular confection.

Traditional clothing, made of cotton or synthetic materials, is worn only by some people in the rural areas and by others on special occasions. Loose-fitting, long-sleeved jackets and oversized trousers that are tied at the waist and bound or left loose at the ankles are traditional garments for men. Nearly all men in the cities and most of the farmers have adopted Western-style shirts, trousers, and suits. Western-style shoes have largely replaced the traditional sandals, which were made of various materials.

The traditional dress of Korean women includes the *chima,* a long, high-waisted, pleated skirt worn over a slip or loose trousers called *paji.* The *chogori,* a short, flared blouse, is worn open in front over a tight-fitting undergarment. In the cities today, nearly all Korean women wear Western-style clothing.

Education, Recreation, and Welfare

In South Korea, elementary education is compulsory for children 6 to 11 years of age. Secondary education is provided in middle schools for 12- to 14-year-olds and in academic and vocational high schools for 15- to 18-year-olds.

Higher education is offered in two- and four-year colleges and universities. Seoul National University is South Korea's largest institution of higher education. Among its better-known private universities are Yonsei University, Ewha Women's University, and Korea University, all in Seoul.

In North Korea, 4- and 5-year-olds attend preschools, while 5- and 6-year-olds attend kindergartens. Education in primary schools is compulsory for 7- to 10-year-olds, and 11- to 15-year-olds are required to attend middle schools that provide general and technical courses. Graduates may go on to a vocational school, a higher technical school, or a college-preparatory high school. There are 11-year postkindergarten programs for specialization in music, ballet, drama, the arts, or foreign languages. Kim Il Sung University, in Pyongyang, is the principal institution of higher education.

For recreation and relaxation, Koreans enjoy weddings, family gatherings, picnics, and sight-seeing. The Lunar New Year, in late January or early February, and the Harvest Moon Festival, in late September, are widely celebrated traditional holidays. Folk dancing and zither playing are very popular. Movies are well attended. Hiking, swimming, and Western sports—soccer, baseball, basketball, track, and boxing, for example—have large followings.

Among the social services provided by the South Korean government are day nurseries and old-age, maternity, and children's homes. The number of public health services, hospitals, and clinics staffed by trained medical personnel has been increasing. In some rural areas, however, midwives and herb doctors still provide the only available medical assistance. North Korea is a welfare state. Government and industrial workers are entitled to free medical care, and factories have kindergartens and nurseries for the children of working mothers.

Religion

Most Koreans do not belong to an organized religion. The Confucian ethical system, however, has greatly influenced Korean culture. Buddhism, introduced from China in the 4th century, has a following of about 13 million persons in South Korea. Confucianists number about 4.7 million. There are about 6 million Christians, mostly Protestants. Chondogyo, a native Korean religion known originally as *Tonghak* (Eastern Learning), had about 815,000 adherents in the late 1970's. It was founded in the mid-19th century in opposition to foreign cultural influences. Shamanism, the superstitious worship of spirits, is widespread in rural areas. Religion is discouraged by the North Korean government.

In lowland South Korea, farmers usually live in compact villages near a stream, surrounded by their fields. They plant, cultivate, and harvest their crops cooperatively.

Modern South Korean schools stress science and technology to train students for industrial careers. Many South Koreans feel that an academic education offers greater prestige.

K. M. Lee

Words to Remember

chungmae—a go-between in Korean marriages.
hangab—a Korean man's 60th birthday.
ondol—the radiant heating system in Korean homes.
kimchi—pickled vegetables.
chima and *chogori*—a Korean woman's traditional skirt and blouse.
Chondogyo—a Korean religion founded in the mid-19th century to combat foreign cultural influences.

Questions to Think About

1. Give possible reasons why the population of Korea has been predominantly rural.
2. How might the regimes of North Korea and South Korea differ in their impact on the traditional Korean way of life?
3. What social problems are South Korea and North Korea likely to face in the future?

273

KOREA—Government

'Aegug-ga'

Moderato

Dong-hae-mul-gwa Baeg-du-san-i   ma-reu-go dal-   to-rog
Un - til the East Sea goes dry and Paek-tu Moun- tain falls,

Ha - neu-nim - i bou - ha - sa u - ri - na-ra-man - se.
May our glor-ious na-tion last,   and God pre-serve its walls.

Mu - gung - hwa sam - cheon-li hwa-ryeo-gang -   san.
Rose of Sha-ron, fair-est blos-som, flow-er of our   land!

hwa ryeo gang san.
flower of our land!

Dae - han-sa-ram Dae-hane-u - ro gi - ri-bo-jeon-ha-se.
God pre-serve this folk as one,   the peo-ple of Dae-han.

Source: Ministry of Culture and Information

South Korea

The Republic of Korea, or South Korea, was established in 1948 as a democratic republic. Its constitution of 1987 provides for three separate and independent branches of government—the executive, the legislative, and the judicial—and an elaborate system of checks and balances.

The executive branch of the government is headed by the president of the republic, who is head of state, chief administrator, and commander in chief of the armed forces. The president also has the powers to handle national emergencies. He is elected by direct popular vote for one five-year term. There is no vice-president.

The State Council, which serves as a presidential cabinet, is composed of the president, the prime minister, the deputy prime minister, and the heads of the ministries. The prime minister is appointed by the president and directs the State Council. The president appoints the heads of the ministries upon recommendation of the prime minister.

The one-house National Assembly is responsible for lawmaking, approving the national budget, and ratifying treaties. Two thirds of the seats are filled by popular vote, and the remaining are apportioned among the political parties according to their share of the popular vote. Assembly members hold office for four-year terms.

The Supreme Court has a maximum of 13 justices, including the chief justice, who is appointed for a single six-year term by the president. The other justices are appointed by the president on the chief justice's recommendation and serve renewable six-year terms. All justices must be approved by the National Assembly. The Supreme Court is the court of last resort and determines constitutionality of administrative decrees. Constitutionality of laws enacted by the National Assembly is determined by the Constitution Court, a state agency.

The government administrative agencies of the Republic of Korea are housed in the Capitol in Seoul.

Frederick Olson—Black Star

The lower courts of the Republic of Korea consist of the district courts, family courts, and appellate courts. The district courts have primary jurisdiction over civil and criminal cases. The family courts also try cases for the first time, but they deal only with such matters as domestic relations and juvenile delinquency. The appellate courts hear appeals from the district and family courts. Military courts try members of the armed forces and may also try civilians accused of such military crimes as espionage.

The major political parties in South Korea in the 1980s were the Democratic Justice party (DJP) and the opposition, the Party for Peace and Democracy and the Reunification Democratic party. Since 1963, the year of its organization, the DJP (until 1981 the Democratic Republicans) has controlled the government. It was headed by President Park Chung Hee until his assassination in 1979.

The electoral system in South Korea is based on direct, equal, and secret suffrage. All citizens over the age of 20 have the right to vote. Participation in the elections of South Korea has been high, with about 80 percent of the registered voters casting ballots in presidential elections. In addition to the ballot, South Koreans often use other forms of political expression, such as organized protest demonstrations. The press is also an important voice of South Korean political opinion.

North Korea

North Korea, or the Democratic People's Republic of Korea, has a Communist government. According to the North Korean constitution, the country's highest legislative body is the Supreme People's Assembly. It is made up of representatives who are supposed to be elected every four years. A permanent presidium is empowered to act on behalf of the assembly when it is not in session.

The Administration Council, or cabinet, which is legally accountable to the assembly, acts as the government's executive branch. It includes the premier and several vice-premiers. Since 1972 the secretary-general of the Workers' (Communist) party has been the president of North Korea and its head of state. There are three vice-presidents.

North Korea's judicial structure functions on three levels, with the Central Court at the top, the provincial courts at the intermediate level, and people's courts in the cities, counties, and districts at the base. Closely linked to the courts is the Procuracy, or law-enforcement agency. The Procuracy is headed by a procurator-general with broad powers. He participates in sessions of the Central Court and has the authority to issue directives on judicial procedure to the lower courts.

The Workers' party has almost complete control over the government of North Korea. As a result, the government functions differently from what the nation's constitution prescribes. Elections to the Supreme People's Assembly are held irregularly, and the cabinet has assumed absolute power.

**GOVERNMENT ORGANIZATION OF
THE REPUBLIC OF KOREA (EXECUTIVE BRANCH)**

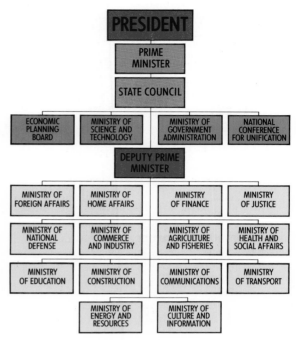

Source: Foreign Area Studies of the American University

There are no opposition parties of any influence in North Korea. All of the country's major political decisions are made within the Korean Workers' party.

In recent years the Korean Workers' party has begun to educate a new corps of industrial managers and technicians and to incorporate them into the party structure. As a result of these efforts more North Koreans have been participating in the affairs of the Korean Workers' party, and North Korea's one-party government has to that extent become somewhat more representative. However, most of the North Korean people still have little voice in the policies and operation of their government.

Words to Remember

Republic of Korea—the official name of South Korea.

Democratic Republican party—the ruling political party in South Korea.

Democratic People's Republic of Korea—the official name of North Korea.

Korean Workers' party—the ruling political party in North Korea.

Questions to Think About

1. Compare the role of political parties in the governments of North and South Korea.
2. Which of the two Korean governments is best suited to maintain social order? Explain.

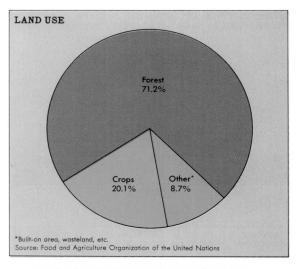

LAND USE

Forest
71.2%

Crops
20.1%

Other*
8.7%

*Built-on area, wasteland, etc.
Source: Food and Agriculture Organization of the United Nations

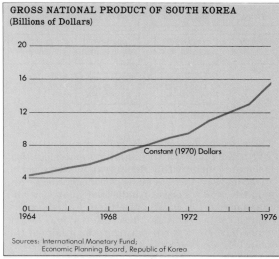

GROSS NATIONAL PRODUCT OF SOUTH KOREA
(Billions of Dollars)

20

16

12

8

4

0
1964   1968   1972   1976

Constant (1970) Dollars

Sources: International Monetary Fund;
Economic Planning Board, Republic of Korea

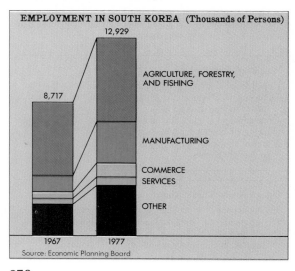

EMPLOYMENT IN SOUTH KOREA (Thousands of Persons)

12,929

8,717

AGRICULTURE, FORESTRY,
AND FISHING

MANUFACTURING

COMMERCE

SERVICES

OTHER

1967   1977
Source: Economic Planning Board

KOREA—Economy

Korea's traditional economy was agricultural. Not until the late 1800's did industry begin to develop. Under Japanese rule, Korea became a source of Japan's raw materials and a market for its products. Modern transportation, communications, and electric power facilities were built, but on the whole Japanese rule stunted Korea's economic development. The partition of Korea after World War II dislocated its economy. Most of the factories and electric power plants, the bulk of the mineral deposits, and the largest forests were in North Korea. The best ports, most of the railway mileage, most of the good farmland, and over two thirds of the people were in South Korea.

South Korea and North Korea have taken different paths of economic development since the partition. The South Korean government provides central guidelines for economic development and some financing for industry. But it encourages private enterprise and capital investment by foreign companies. South Korea's economy has been financed in part by aid and loans from the United States. The Communist regime of North Korea controls all the means of production and has a highly centralized economy. It stresses the development of heavy industry. North Korea has received economic aid from the Soviet Union, China, and other Communist nations.

The Economy of South Korea

Agriculture is the economic mainstay of South Korea. About two fifths of the people work in agriculture, forestry, and fishing. The average farm household has less than 2½ acres of land, usually on several scattered plots. Some farming is now done with modern machines. The generally low yields have been rising with the increased use of fertilizer. The mild winters permit double-cropping on most lowland fields. In irrigated areas, rice is generally grown in the summer; other grains, in the winter.

Rice is by far the major crop—in tonnage, acreage, and value. Other leading crops include sweet potatoes, barley, soybeans, wheat, corn, millet, cotton, mulberry leaves, fruits, and vegetables. Pigs and chickens are the principal livestock.

The government has sought to raise agricultural output by increasing fertilizer production and reclaiming farmland from west coast tidal flats. A program to increase the number of farm owners has made progress.

The fishing industry is an important source of food for South Korea. The catch is sufficient to meet domestic demand and to allow some exports. Pusan is the largest fishing port.

South Korea's forests were badly overcut during and after World War II. There has been some reforestation, but the fast-rising demand for lumber must be met through imports. Because of the government's forest preservation policies, coal has mostly replaced wood as the fuel used in homes.

Most of South Korea's electric power is generated by coal- and oil-fired thermal plants in the coastal cities. Some comes from hydroelectric plants in the northeastern mountains. South Korea's petroleum refineries use imported crude oil. The nation's first major refinery was built at Ulsan in 1964. The chief mineral product of South Korea is anthracite coal. The nation is a leading producer of tungsten and graphite. Other commercially important minerals are iron ore, limestone, fluorite, gold, silver, and kaolin.

Before partition, South Korea had little manufacturing industry. Its few plants produced textiles, machinery, and foodstuffs. Since partition, emphasis has been placed on the development of heavy industry. The new stress on heavy industry has greatly boosted the output of cement, fertilizer, petrochemicals, ships, and automobiles. However, the textile industry is still one of the largest. It now uses not only cotton but also nylon, rayon, and other synthetic fibers. In addition to textiles, South Korea's light industries produce foodstuffs, plastics, plywood, plate glass, porcelain, cutlery, tires, wigs, cosmetics, sewing machines, toys, and leather goods. Artisans in small shops still engage in traditional handicrafts. South Korea's industry is heavily concentrated in the Seoul-Inchon area and at Pusan and Ulsan. An integrated steel mill has been built at Pohang.

A modern transportation network is being built in South Korea. Main railroad lines have been electrified; new lines have been built to the northeast; and old rolling stock has been replaced. Modern expressways, beginning with one between Seoul and Inchon (1968) and one between Seoul and Pusan (1970), have been built. Trucks carry more than one half of the country's domestic freight traffic. South Korea's principal seaports are at Pusan, Ulsan, and Inchon. Modern air service links the major cities with each other and with the rest of the world. The nation has modern telephone, telegraph, and postal services as well as many newspapers and radio and television stations.

South Korea's foreign trade grew substantially in the 1970's. Manufactured goods, especially clothing and textiles, make up two thirds of the value of its exports. Other leading exports are wood veneers, foods, and raw materials. The chief imports are machinery, transportation equipment, petroleum, textiles, foods, chemicals, and wood. The United States and Japan are South Korea's main trading partners.

The South Korean government owns and operates the major transportation services, communications facilities, and electric power plants. Private companies dominate most other sectors of the economy.

The Economy of North Korea

Agriculture is one of the weakest segments of North Korea's economy. Since the winters are long and cold, most of the farmland supports only a summer crop. Yields are low. Rice is well over a half of the total

SOUTH KOREAN SPENDING PATTERNS

CLOTHING	FOOD AND BEVERAGES	FUEL AND LIGHT	HOUSING	OTHER
9.3%	42.1%	5.1%	20.3%	23.2%

Source: Economic Planning Board

Principal Products of Korea

CROPS	NORTH KOREA Acres (In Thousands)	NORTH KOREA Tons (In Thousands)	SOUTH KOREA Acres (In Thousands)	SOUTH KOREA Tons (In Thousands)
Rice	1,927	5,082	3,039	9,193
Barley	457	375	1,275	897
Corn	1,013	2,006	124	99
Potatoes*	383	1,940	356	1,647
Soybeans	988	342	692	375
Wheat	346	342	99	99
Millet	1,161	461	67	29

MINERALS	Tons (In Thousands)	Tons (In Thousands)
Coal	44,092	19,009
Iron ore	10,361	871
Tungsten	2,370	5
Graphite	83	72
Limestone	†	25,059
Magnesite	1,874	†

ELECTRIC POWER	Kilowatt-Hours (In Millions)	
	16,500	23,117

MANUFACTURES (South Korea)	Value Added (Millions of Dollars)
Food, beverages, tobacco	630
Textiles, wearing apparel, leather	756
Chemicals, petroleum, coal, rubber, plastic products	693
Basic metal industries	262
Fabricated metal products, machinery and equipment	561
Paper and paper products, printing and publishing	153
Other	415
Total	3,470

*Includes Sweet Potatoes.
†Data not available.

Sources: Food and Agriculture Organization of the United Nations; Economic Planning Board, Republic of Korea; The Mining Journal

The sea is an important source of food for South Koreans. Here a day's catch is being cleaned.

John Launois—Black Star

In North Korea, emphasis has been placed on the expansion of steelmaking and other heavy industries. Less stress has been given to increasing the production of consumer goods.

FOREIGN TRADE OF KOREA

South Korea Leading Areas

Exports to

Other · Japan · United States · Other Asian Countries · Europe

Imports from

Japan · Other · Other Asian Countries · United States · Europe

Leading Commodities

Exported

Clothing · Other · Textiles and Textile Fibers · Food · Iron and Steel · Wood Veneer

Imported

Machinery and Transportation Equipment · Other · Textiles and Textile Fibers · Food · Petroleum and Petroleum Products · Chemicals · Wood

North Korea Leading Areas

Exports to

Soviet Union · Other · People's Republic of China · Japan

Imports from

Soviet Union · People's Republic of China · Other · Japan

Sources: Economic Planning Board, Republic of Korea;
Foreign Area Studies of the American University

grain harvest. Other leading crops are corn, potatoes, millet, barley, soybeans, and wheat. More than 90 percent of the cultivated land is in state-controlled collective farms; the remainder in state-operated farms. Farm machinery is in only limited use. Crop production falls short of the nation's needs and is supplemented by imports, mainly wheat.

Fish are an important part of North Korea's food supply. Cod, herring, sardines, salmon, swordfish, and crabs are leading marine products. The major fishing ports are Kimchaek (Songjin), Chongjin, and Nampo.

Although North Korea's forests were depleted under Japanese rule, enough stands remain to support logging operations. Spruce, fir, larch, pine, and oak are the main commercial species. Sinuiju, Hoeryong, and Pyongyang are the major centers of the lumber, woodworking, and pulp industries.

North Korea is rich in mineral deposits. It is a leading producer of tungsten, graphite, and magnesite. Other principal mineral products are coal, iron ore, limestone, nickel, zinc, copper, lead, titanium, fluorite, mica, and gold. Power is provided by hydroelectric plants on the Yalu River and its tributaries and by thermal plants.

Manufacturing dominates North Korea's economy. Although the nation's industries were largely destroyed during the Korean War, they have since been rebuilt and expanded. Important products include iron and steel, nonferrous metals, machinery, machine tools, chemicals, cement, tractors, automobiles, railway rolling stock, and small ships. Consumer goods include textiles, foodstuffs, medicines, and plastics. Pyongyang is the leading manufacturing center.

Railways serve the main industrial areas of North Korea, but until the early 1970's the Pyongyang-Wonsan line was the only transpeninsular link. Other lines connect with Chinese and Soviet railways. There are domestic air links and flights from Peking and Moscow. The principal ports are Unggi, Najin, Wonsan, and Nampo. North Korea's foreign trade is mainly with the Soviet Union and China. Japan is its principal non-Communist trading partner. Major imports are machinery, oil, coking coal, rubber, and wheat. Iron ore and processed metals are the major exports.

Words to Remember

double-cropping—raising two crops a year on the same plot of soil.

collective farm—a form of state-controlled cooperative farm in North Korea.

Questions to Think About

1. What might be advantages and disadvantages of living under the economic system of North Korea? Of South Korea?
2. Would consolidating the small farms in South Korea help its economy? Why or why not?

A Tour of Korea

3

4

1

5

2

1. KYONGBOK PALACE and its grounds in Seoul are now a public park. This old Buddhist pagoda stands in the park.

2. POPJU TEMPLE is at the foot of Mount Songni. Its huge Buddha—nearly 95 feet high—is the tallest statue in Korea.

3. BULGUKSA TEMPLE, at Kyongju, was built about A.D. 540. It houses many historic treasures of the Silla Dynasty.

4. CHOMSONGDAE, an early astronomical observatory, is in Kyongju. It was erected in the mid-7th century A.D.

5. CHONJEYON WATERFALL is one of the many scenic attractions on rugged Cheju Island.

KOREA —Culture

The Korean Language

Korean is not closely related to any other modern language. Despite the longtime cultural influence of China upon Korea and the use of Chinese as the official written language of Korea until the late 19th century, Korean and Chinese belong to entirely different linguistic families. However, some experts believe that Korean may belong to the Ural-Altaic family—along with Japanese, Mongolian, and Turkish.

Spoken Korean is soft and lilting. There are no heavy nasal tones and no strong accents to emphasize words in sentences. Although half a dozen dialects are spoken in Korea, the differences among them are not very great. People from various sections of the nation can understand one another easily.

Formal manuscripts did not appear in Korea until the 4th century A.D., when educated Koreans wrote in

Chinese. Later, systems were developed by which Korean words could be written in Chinese ideograms. The mastery of Chinese ideography was very difficult, however, and only scholars could read and write.

Hangul, an alphabet suited to the Korean language, was developed at the direction of King Sejong and introduced in 1446. It was used by the common people, but educated Koreans continued to write in Chinese. Hangul did not come into general use until the end of the 19th century, when it became the official alphabet for all laws and decrees.

After the Japanese assumed complete control of Korea in 1910, they discouraged and then abolished the use and teaching of Korean. With the liberation of Korea at the end of World War II, hangul was revived. Today Korean texts and parts of Korean newspapers are printed in hangul. Chinese ideography is still taught, but most writers use hangul.

Korean Literature

The first Korean literature is thought to have been primitive poetry which, accompanied by music and dance, was used in prehistoric religious rites. The evolution of Korean poetry as an independent art form is believed to have begun in the 1st century A.D. The brief *Sijo* probably developed late in the Koryo period and is still popular today. It was used as a vehicle for romantic and naturalistic themes.

Under the Yi Dynasty, the novel gradually replaced poetry as the most popular literary form. The early Korean novelists sought primarily to edify their readers. The works of later novelists mocked the *yangban* (aristocracy).

The late 17th and early 18th centuries are known as "the golden age of the classic novel" in Korea. The most popular novel of this era, 'Chunhyangjon' (The Story of Spring Fragrance), is about the love of an aristocrat's son for a lower-class girl. Many of the classic Korean novels had romantic themes.

Growing Western influence in the last half of the 19th century inspired the "new novel." The "new novels" promoted such ideas as political democracy and social equality. The best known of these novels was 'The Tears of Blood' by Yi Injik.

New writers in many branches of literature emerged. Such authors as Yi Kwangsu, Ch'oe Namson, Kim Tongin, and Kim Sowol assimilated Western literary trends and contributed to the development of modern Korean literary forms.

During World War II, the progress of Korean literature was blocked by a Japanese ban on native culture. After the Korean War, however, new writers emerged who drew their inspiration from contemporary trends in world literature, and there was a surge of activity. (*See also* Korean Literature.)

The Fine Arts

Korea's artists have been strongly influenced by the cultures of neighboring nations. Nevertheless, they have always produced sculptures, paintings, and pottery that are peculiarly their own.

KOREAN ALPHABET (HANGUL)

Vowels

ㅏ	ㅑ	ㅓ	ㅕ	ㅗ	ㅛ	ㅜ	ㅠ	ㅡ	ㅣ
A	YA	AW	YAW	O	YO	OO	YOO	EU or U	I or EE

Consonants

ㄱ	ㄴ	ㄷ	ㄹ	ㅁ	ㅂ	ㅅ	ㅇ	ㅈ	ㅊ	ㅋ	ㅌ	ㅍ	ㅎ
K or G	N	D or T	R or L	M	B or P	S	NG	J	CH	K	T	P	H

Mi Kook = America

ㅁ M + ㅣ I = 미 = Mi   ㄱ K + ㅜ OO + ㄱ K = 국 = Kook

Source: Ministry of Culture and Information

Ceramics is regarded as Korea's most notable fine art. This Yi Dynasty porcelain jar has designs in underglaze iron.

Consulate General, Republic of Korea

Little early Korean sculpture has survived, though a few fine stone figures and relief carvings remain. The golden age of Korean sculpture reached its height in the late 7th century during the reign of the Silla Dynasty. Most of the sculpture of this period is of bronze, small in scale, and dedicated to Buddhist deities.

Except for some tomb frescoes dating from the 4th through the 7th centuries, few examples of early Korean painting have survived. Painters of the last Yi Dynasty (1392–1910), however, left a rich legacy. Their paintings were executed on silk or paper scrolls and album leaves. They depicted towering landscapes, important personages, and scenes of daily life.

The ceramics of Korea almost certainly represent the country's most significant artistic contribution. Functional as well as decorative, Korean ceramics have an unmistakable character. The utilitarian vessels of the Silla period are of sturdy dark-gray earthenware with modest, usually incised, decoration. The rich-green celadons of the Koryo period are adorned with brilliant brushed or inlaid designs that are admirably adapted to their forms. The heavier wares of the Yi Dynasty bear designs, usually on a white porcelaneous base, which seem swiftly executed, almost offhand, yet masterly.

Early Korean architecture is exemplified by the tombs of Koguryo and the remains of great, walled fortresses. From the late 7th century into the Koryo Dynasty many Buddhist temple complexes—actually small villages—were built. Although their general features were Chinese, they were adapted to local materials and landscape by their Korean builders.

Under the Yi Dynasty the increasing popularity of Confucianism was mirrored in the construction of Confucian shrines. There was also an upsurge of non-religious architecture, including imposing palaces, town gates, and watchtowers.

The Performing Arts

Korea's performing arts were greatly influenced by those of China, whose dance, music, and instruments the Koreans adopted. Korea, in turn, played a major role in transmitting music and dance to Japan.

Among the earliest extended performances in Korea were the danced mask plays that originated around the 9th century. Their purpose was magical—to make crops grow, to ward off evil spirits and disease, to placate the spirits of the dead. Toward the end of the 14th century, various elements of these plays were combined in the "typical" mask play, the *Sandae*. Accompanied by drums, flutes, and the Korean harp, or *kayageum*, the Sandae satirized the nobility and corrupt priests.

Korea's puppet plays may have originated at about the same time as the mask plays. The puppet plays were performed on a two-story stage. The puppets— one to three feet tall—were in the upper story; their manipulators were hidden below.

A kind of musical drama was created by combining a narrative with folk tunes. The first permanent Korean theater for performances of this type was built in Seoul in 1902. This genre survives partially in the popular *Pan-Sori* (folk opera).

Unlike other Asian countries, Korea failed to develop a classical theater from its popular theatrical forms. Folk dances and mask plays, once established, remained unchanged over the centuries.

During the 20th century the Korean performing arts were greatly influenced by the West, at first by way of Japan, where a type of play called *shimpa* developed about 1890. The shimpa plays were patterned on realistic Western drama. In later decades adaptations of shimpa plays became very popular in Korea. The Earth-Moon Society, formed by men who had studied theater in Tokyo, began presenting plays by Anton Chekhov, Henrik Ibsen, and George Bernard Shaw in 1923. Familiarity with the work of contemporary Western playwrights led, increasingly, to the writing of Korean plays that dealt with existing social conditions.

Since 1945 much has been done to encourage the performing arts of Korea. A government-sponsored National Theater opened in April 1950. The Seoul Cultural Center for the performing arts and a new National Theater, also located in Seoul, were opened during the 1970's.

Words to Remember

hangul—the Korean alphabet.
Sijo—a brief poetic form developed in the Koryo period.
kayageum—a 12-stringed Korean harp.
Pan-Sori—a form of Korean folk opera.
shimpa—a play based on Western realistic drama.

Questions to Think About

1. How did the lack of a written Korean language affect Korea's development?
2. How did Korea develop a distinctive culture despite the influence of its neighbors?

The Kang Gang Su Wol Lae is one of Korea's many traditional folk dances. The circling women chant rhythmically to the beat of the accompanying music.

KOREA — Natural Features

Land

The Korean peninsula is dominated by mountains. From the northern interior, where several peaks reach over 8,000 feet, a mountainous backbone—the Taeback Mountains—extends southward along the east coast. The range has many spurs to the west and south. The longest spur—the Sobaek Mountains—extends to the southwestern corner of the peninsula.

There are no active volcanoes in Korea today, nor are there any earthquakes. But volcanic activity in past geologic times helped shape the rugged Korean landscape. Korea's highest point is Mount Paektu (9,003 feet), an extinct volcano on the North Korean-Chinese border. The highest point in South Korea is Mount Halla (6,398 feet), on Cheju (Quelpart Island).

Many short, swift, and shallow rivers flow from the mountains to the coast. Most of them drain to the south and west, into the Yellow Sea and the Korea Strait. Korea's two longest rivers—the Yalu and the Tumen—are along the boundary with China and the Soviet Union. The Yalu flows west for 491 miles into the Yellow Sea. The Tumen flows east for 324 miles into the Sea of Japan. Other important rivers are the Taedong, which flows through the North Korean capital of Pyongyang; the Han, which flows through the South Korean capital of Seoul; and the Naktong, in southeastern Korea. The lower courses of the larger rivers are navigable by small boats. Some rivers have been dammed to generate hydroelectric power. Korea has no large lakes.

Most of Korea's plains are small and nestled among mountains or between mountains and the sea. Except for the plain around Wonsan, the plains along the east coast are especially narrow. Most of the plains in the southeast are clustered around the Naktong River and its tributaries. The most extensive lowlands are along the west coast, but even these are broken into pockets by hills and mountains. The southeastern and western lowlands comprise most of Korea's productive cropland and its major urban centers and support the bulk of the Korean population. Many of the significant historical developments in Korea have taken place on these plains.

The Korean peninsula has a long, varied coastline. The east coast is relatively straight and rocky, with a tidal range of only one or two feet. The west coast is low and deeply indented and has long stretches of mud flats. It has a tidal range of more than 17 feet. Major ports are Pusan and Masan on the south coast; Inchon and Nampo, on the west coast; and Ulsan, Unggi, and Wonsan on the east coast.

The south and west coasts are fringed with more than 3,300 islands, of which about 200 are inhabited. The largest islands of Korea are Cheju, Koje, Kanghwa, Chin, and Namhae, off the south and west coasts, and Ullung, in the Sea of Japan.

Climate

Most of Korea has a humid, continental climate marked by sharp seasonal changes. In winter, cold, dry air from the Asian interior—warmed somewhat as it crosses the Yellow Sea—moves across Korea. In summer, air flows across Korea from the opposite direction. Regional variation in climate is greatest during the winter and slight during the summer. In general, however, the south is warmer than the north and the coasts are warmer than the mountainous interior. The Korean peninsula juts far enough south to reach the warm waters of the Kuroshio, or Japan Current. Korea's southern coast has a humid, subtropical climate. The length of the frost-free period ranges from about 130 days in the northern interior to 220 days in the extreme south.

Cool weather begins in October and November, when winds start to come from the north and northwest. A long winter follows. Winter in the northern interior is bitterly cold. From November to April, the average monthly temperature there is below 32° F. and sub-zero readings are common. Temperatures in the south for the same period are considerably higher. The cold weather is relieved by numerous warm spells. January is Korea's coldest month.

Spring arrives in April and is noted for its pleasant, sunny weather. Summer comes in June. By July, it is hot and humid everywhere in Korea except the higher mountains and the northeast coast. Daytime temperatures commonly reach the high 80's and low

TOPOGRAPHY OF KOREA

MT. PAEKTU
(9,003 FT.)

Tumen R.

Yalu R.

Taedong R.

Yellow Sea

N

Han R.

TAEBACK MTS.

Naktong R.

Sea of Japan

0   100   200
Miles

CHEJU

MT. HALLA
(6,398 FT.)

East China Sea

| Sea Level | 100 m. 328 ft. | 200 m. 656 ft. | 500 m. 1,640 ft. | 1,000 m. 3,281 ft. | 2,000 m. 6,562 ft. | 5,000 m. 16,404 ft. |

© C. S. HAMMOND & Co., N.Y.

90's. In September, humidity decreases and clear, cloudless days become more frequent. The first cold spells come at night in October, but the October days remain sunny, dry, and warm. October and May are Korea's pleasantest months.

Precipitation is moderate in Korea, ranging from less than 25 inches to more than 55 inches annually. Most falls as rain, which is heaviest in the period from April to September. The remainder of the year is relatively dry. Summer downpours often cause flooding. In late summer and early autumn, torrential rains accompany the typhoons that strike the peninsula from the south and east. Winter snows accumulate to a depth of several feet in the northern mountains, but snow that falls in the south soon melts.

The heaviest precipitation, more than 55 inches annually, is along the south and east coasts and on Cheju. Parts of the mountainous north receive less than 25 inches annually.

Plant and Animal Life

Korea's plants and animals are transitional between those of Manchuria and Siberia and those of the Japanese islands. The original vegetation of the Korean peninsula was notable for its many varieties of trees, shrubs, and flowering plants. But the rich forests that once covered most of Korea have been largely removed from the plains and adjacent mountain slopes. Some species were merely thinned out, but broad areas were cut too often to allow new trees to mature, and artificial plantings favored a few fast-growing species. Both North Korea and South Korea have undertaken reforestation. Fir, spruce, larch, and pine forests prevail in the northern mountains. Central and southern Korea have mixed forests of oak, pine, elm, beech, and poplar. The natural vegetation of the south coast is broadleaf evergreen forest and bamboo.

Early in the 20th century, Korea still had a rich variety of wild animals, including sables, marten, foxes, beaver, otter, deer, antelope, goats, tigers, and leopards. Most of these wild animal species have either disappeared completely or are found only in small numbers in remote northern mountain areas. They were killed for their fur or their forest habitat was destroyed. Pheasants and rabbits are now the most common wildlife. There are also many smaller mammals and birds, as well as reptiles and fish.

Words to Remember

Mount Paektu—Korea's highest peak.
Yalu—Korea's longest river.
Kuroshio—the warm Pacific current that washes the southern shores of Korea.

Questions to Think About

1. How has Korea's topography and peninsular location affected its history and economy?
2. How does Korea's climate compare with that of the New England section of the United States?

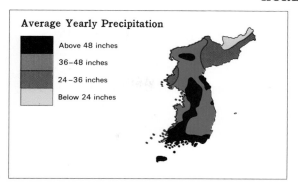

Average Yearly Precipitation

Above 48 inches
36–48 inches
24–36 inches
Below 24 inches

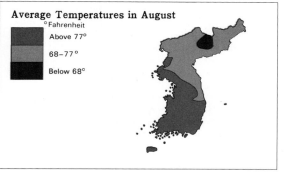

Average Temperatures in August
°Fahrenheit

Above 77°
68–77°
Below 68°

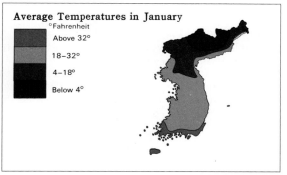

Average Temperatures in January
°Fahrenheit

Above 32°
18–32°
4–18°
Below 4°

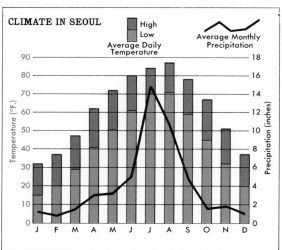

CLIMATE IN SEOUL

High
Low
Average Daily Temperature

Average Monthly Precipitation

KOREA —History

Early History and the Three Kingdoms

Archaeological evidence indicates that men lived in southwestern Korea well before 10,000 B.C. Later, Korea was inhabited by at least two distinct groups of people who migrated from the north. One group consisted of fishermen and shellfish gatherers, who settled along the rivers and the seacoast about the third millennium B.C. They produced an earthenware which is known as "comb ceramic" from the linear decoration on its surface. The second group entered the Korean peninsula around the 7th century B.C. It was made up of hunters and gatherers who produced *mumun* (undecorated pottery). They developed a primitive agriculture and may have built the great stone-slab tombs, or dolmens, found throughout Korea. Wet-field rice agriculture and the use of metal appear to have been introduced from China by 300 B.C.

By the 2d century B.C. the state of Choson had developed in northwestern Korea, with its capital at the present city of Pyongyang. In 108 B.C., Choson and the northern part of the peninsula fell to the armies of the Chinese Han Dynasty. Four Chinese commanderies were established; the great walled city of Lo-lang was built; and the advanced civilization of China began to penetrate the Korean peninsula. Native resistance soon compelled the Chinese to abandon three of the commanderies.

Confederations of the many Korean tribes led to the rise in the 1st century B.C. of the Three Kingdoms—Koguryo, in the Yalu River basin in the north; Paekche, in the Han River basin in the west; and Silla, in the southeast. In the following centuries Buddhism was introduced into the Korean peninsula from China. It was adopted by Koguryo in 372, by Paekche in 384, and by Silla in 528. Buddhism was accompanied by T'ang Dynasty art and the study of Chinese characters, which remained the basic written language of Korea until the 20th century.

The Korean states battled for primacy. After centuries of warfare, the combined forces of Silla and T'ang China defeated Paekche in 660 and Koguryo in 668. The greater part of Korea was now unified under Silla, and a period of peace and strong Chinese influence followed. A great cultural and technical flowering centered at the capital of Silla (the present Kyongju). Astronomy, medicine, metal casting, sculpture, and textile manufacture reached especially high levels. Hundreds of Buddhist temples were built. A brisk maritime trade was conducted with China.

The Koryo and Yi Dynasties

In the 9th century, the ruling clans of Silla lost control over warlords in the outlying provinces. After a century of fighting, the peninsula was reunified under the state of Koryo (935–1392), from which

the modern Western name of Korea is derived. During the Koryo period, hundreds of Buddhist monasteries were built in the mountains around the Koryo capital of Kaesong. Maritime trade with Sung Dynasty China fostered a new flowering of culture. The Korean authorities modeled their methods of government on the example of China, including a system of civil service examinations.

In the 11th century, Korea was invaded by the Ch'itan people of Manchuria. During the 12th century, it was ruled by military overlords. The Mongols launched the first of a series of invasions against Korea in 1231. To gain divine assistance in removing the invaders, the Koreans carved over 81,000 wood blocks for the printing of the entire Buddhist canon, the Tripitaka. The enterprise took 16 years. In 1270 Korea made peace with the Mongols and became a partner in Mongol campaigns of conquest, including two disastrous attempts to invade Japan in 1274 and 1281. By 1368 the Koreans had ousted the Mongols, who had suffered defeats in China that drove them back to their homeland. In 1392 a Korean general, Yi Songgye, seized the throne as the ruler of the new Yi Dynasty.

Under the Yi Dynasty, landowners formed a ruling elite called the *yangban*. They were firmly anti-Buddhist, and the withdrawal of their patronage from the Buddhist establishment led to the decline of Buddhism in Korea. The social attitudes of the yangban were expressed in Confucian terms. In their view relationships of superiority and inferiority existed between ruler and subject, father and son, husband and wife, elder and younger brother, and among friends. The Yi class system was rigidly hierarchical and hereditary, from the royal caste down to the peasants and slaves. There was little social mobility.

Comparative peace and increasing international trade fostered a period of intellectual achievement. Under the direction of King Sejong, the fourth ruler of the Yi Dynasty, an alphabet called *hangul*, or "script of the Korean people," was completed in 1446. Although hundreds of years passed before it was widely used, the alphabet made it possible for any Korean to read his language. Literacy and knowledge were no longer the monopoly of the yangban.

From 1592 to 1598 Korea was devastated by two invasions under the Japanese military ruler Hideyoshi Toyotomi. Aided by the armies of Ming Dynasty China and the brilliant tactics of a native naval genius, Yi Sunsin, the Koreans drove the Japanese out. Yi Sunsin invented the ironclad Korean "turtle ship" early in 1592. From 1627 to 1637 Korea was invaded by the Manchus, who founded the Ch'ing Empire in China. Korea remained tributary to this empire until the late 19th century. The strict political, social, and economic controls imposed by the Yi authorities were thoroughly disrupted by the wars. The destruction of land, tax, and slave registers enabled many Koreans to escape the bonds of caste and class.

In the first half of the 17th century a number of Dutchmen visited Korea. Several of them fought with the Koreans against the Manchu invaders. They were among the first Westerners in Korea, though knowledge of Europe had been brought back earlier by Korean embassies to Peking.

In the first half of the 19th century, Jesuit priests entered Korea from China and Western ships began to appear off the Korean coast. A few of the ships requested trading privileges for their nations, which the Koreans refused to grant. Korean shore batteries at times exchanged fire with ships entering Korean bays or rivers. In 1876, negotiations resulting from a Korean attack on a Japanese naval vessel led to the signing of the Treaty of Kanghwa, which opened three Korean ports to Japan. Acting on advice from the Chinese, the Korean authorities attempted to dilute Japanese influence by also signing treaties with Western nations. The first of these was a treaty of friendship with the United States, signed in 1882.

Japanese Occupation

The period from 1876 to 1910 was marked by power struggles between the pro-Chinese conservative ruling Min family and rival factions which wanted to modernize Korea along Japanese or Russian lines. Meanwhile, the antiforeign *Tonghak* movement, which advocated "Eastern Learning" as opposed to *Sohak*, or "Western Learning," was developing in the countryside. In 1894, antiforeign sentiment, coupled with peasant demands for political and social reforms, culminated in the Tonghak Rebellion. Both Japan and China sent armies to help quell the rebellion. Their rival interests led to the Sino-Japanese War of 1894–95. The victory of Japan ended China's influence over Korea. Japanese-backed administrations unsuccessfully attempted to institute reforms in 1894.

John Holstein

Admiral Yi Sunsin's statue towers over Seoul's Sejong Avenue. The admiral's "turtle ships," believed to have been the world's first ironclads, routed Japanese invaders in the 1590's.

Rivalry between imperial Japan and czarist Russia over dominance in the Korean peninsula led to the Russo-Japanese War of 1904–5. The victorious Japanese declared Korea to be a protectorate of Japan. In 1910 they formally annexed Korea as a Japanese colony, bringing the end of the Yi Dynasty.

The Japanese helped modernize the Korean economy, but during their occupation many Korean government workers, farmers, and businessmen lost their positions to Japanese immigrants. The Japanese

Japan and China clashed over Korea in the Sino-Japanese War of 1894–95. The defeat of China was followed by a long period of Japanese domination in Korea.

The Bettmann Archive

Continued on page 287

285

Korea—North vs. South

by John Roderick

Relations between South Korea and North Korea have been strained by a clash of ideologies, memories of their bitter military conflict, and differences over how to reunify the divided country.

In 1945 the people of Korea hailed Japan's defeat in World War II. It marked the end of 35 years of Japanese colonial rule. But the joy of the Koreans was short-lived. They were denied independence and unity by the two great antagonists of the cold war—the Soviet Union and the United States.

Through an agreement made in 1945, Soviet troops occupied the portion of Korea north of the 38th parallel and United States forces occupied the portion south of the 38th parallel. From this agreement stemmed much of the tragedy of postwar Korea.

Initially, the Soviets cooperated in a move to establish a provisional, united Korean government. In 1947, however, the Soviet Union resisted a United Nations General Assembly resolution that elections be held throughout Korea. The following year, because of Soviet obstruction, no elections were held north of the partition line. Meanwhile, Soviet advisers had been creating a strong military machine.

Korea has always been a strategic factor in the Asian policies of Russia's rulers. This continued to be the case after World War II, when Soviet Premier Joseph Stalin viewed Korea as vital to the existence of the Far Eastern sphere of influence the Russians had gained by invading Manchuria after entering the war against Japan in August 1945. By 1949, the newly established Communist Chinese People's Republic of Mao Tse-tung was also coveting Korea, a historic route of China-bound invasion armies.

With the encouragement of the Soviet Union and Communist China, North Korea's premier, Kim Il Sung, undertook to destroy the Republic of Korea. On June 25, 1950, North Korean troops invaded

Improved North Korean-South Korean relations were encouraged by talks on reuniting families that had been separated by the division of Korea. Official meetings were held in 1972–73.

Korean Overseas Information Service

South Korea. The move was influenced by a United States decision to exclude Korea from the area in the western Pacific that it was prepared to defend.

Reacting quickly to the invasion, United States President Harry S. Truman reversed his country's position and brought the United States and other members of the United Nations into the conflict. The initial successes of the North Koreans, the intervention of Communist China, and widespread destruction in the south hardened South Korea's opposition to Communism. When the war ended, Korea remained a divided country. (*See also* Korean War.)

Having failed to unify Korea militarily, Kim Il Sung launched a campaign of infiltration and subversion. With North Korea's population less than half that of South Korea and with no assurance that aid from the quarreling Soviets and Chinese would be forthcoming, Kim realized that North Korea could not enforce its will on South Korea through a new war.

Since the early 1960's Kim Il Sung has asserted that the question of unification must be settled by the Koreans themselves. He proposed the withdrawal of all United Nations forces from the south, the reduction of the armed forces of each of the country's two sections to a maximum of 100,000 men, and the beginning of economic and cultural relations between North Korea and South Korea. These moves would be followed by a confederation permitting the continuation of independent activities by the two Korean governments. Kim's overtures were rejected both by the Republic of Korea and the United Nations General Assembly, which maintained the position that unification could be achieved only through general elections supervised by the United Nations. South Korean officials also said that, if United Nations forces left, another North Korean attack might succeed.

His political overtures rebuffed, in 1966 Kim spelled out a detailed blueprint for the overthrow of President Park Chung Hee's South Korean government. He called for the creation of a South Korean Marxist-Leninist workers' and peasants' party. He increased infiltration into the south by propaganda-terrorist teams. On Jan. 21, 1968, a group of North Korean guerrillas on a mission to assassinate President Park were stopped less than a mile from the presidential mansion in Seoul. On January 23, the United States intelligence ship *Pueblo* was seized by North Korea off Wonsan. These acts inflamed public opinion in South Korea and the United States.

As the decade of the 1970's opened, shooting incidents were common in the demilitarized zone between North Korea and South Korea, and the two nations continued to strengthen their military forces. In 1971, however, the rival regimes opened discussions to reunite millions of Korean families that had been separated by the division of their country after World War II. A South-North Coordinating Committee was established in 1972, but in mid-1973 the north began boycotting its sessions. As the decade ended, the south sought further reunification talks; joint political meetings were short-lived, however.

Shinto religion was taught in Korean schools, while the Korean language was forbidden.

In 1919 the Koreans staged a passive resistance campaign known as the *Samil* (March First) Independence Movement. Thousands of people were killed or imprisoned by the Japanese authorities. A Korean provisional government-in-exile was formed in Shanghai, China, with Syngman Rhee as president.

Recent Times

Korea was liberated in 1945 after Japan's defeat in World War II. Under a wartime agreement concerned solely with the surrender of the Japanese forces, Soviet troops occupied the area north of the 38th parallel and United States troops occupied the area south of the 38th parallel. For the next three years there were fruitless negotiations on how to reunify Korea. The United Nations proposed nationwide elections. Although the north refused, elections were held in the south. As a result, the Republic of Korea was established in the south in August 1948 and Syngman Rhee was elected president by its new National Assembly. In September the Democratic People's Republic of Korea was established in the north, with Kim Il Sung, a Communist, as its premier. Kim had gained prominence in the 1930s as a leader of a group of anti-Japanese Korean guerrillas that was based in Manchuria. (*See also* Rhee.)

By 1950 all United States and Soviet troops had been withdrawn from Korea. But in June the Soviet-equipped North Korean army invaded South Korea, beginning the Korean War. The United Nations voted to aid South Korea, but most of the troops sent to fight the North Koreans were furnished by the United States. At the end of 1950 Communist China entered the war in support of North Korea. In 1953 a truce was signed, with the truce line at approximately the prewar border. (*See also* Korean War.)

The war crippled industrial and agricultural production. In the north a recovery program was begun in 1953, with aid from the Soviet Union and Communist China. In the south the government was left weak and unstable. In 1960 Rhee was ousted.

A military junta seized control of South Korea in 1961. General Park Chung Hee, a junta leader, was elected president in 1963. The country's rapid economic growth led to Park's re-election in 1967 and again in 1971. In 1972 he declared martial law, banned all political activity, and dissolved the National Assembly. The Yushin Constitution, giving Park almost unlimited powers, was adopted; he was re-elected in 1972 and 1978. North Korea also revised its constitution in 1972. Premier Kim was named to the new post of president. (*See also* Park Chung Hee.)

On Oct. 26, 1979, Park was assassinated. The caretaker president, Choi Kyu Hah, restored the civil rights of dissidents, but a return to democratic rule depended on constitutional reform. In 1980 Chun Doo Hwan, a former lieutenant general, was elected president. A new constitution, reducing presidential powers, was approved by voters in 1981. During 1986–87 tens of thousands of people in several cities held violent protests against the constitution and its electoral-college system of selecting a president. An amended constitution, approved in a national referendum on Oct. 27, 1987, provided for direct popular election of the president. On December 16 Roh Tae Woo won an election that was marked by violence and charges of vote fraud. In 1988, for the first time, the ruling Democratic Justice party lost its majority in the National Assembly. (*See also* Roh Tae Woo.)

A Soviet fighter plane shot down a South Korean commercial airliner that strayed off course and into Soviet airspace over Sakhalin Island in September 1983. All 269 passengers were killed. An investigation was undertaken by the United Nations.

Reunification meetings, which began in 1972 between North and South Korea, remained largely deadlocked into the 1980s, mostly because of hostile reactions by each to the other's policies. North Korea was blamed by South Korea for a 1983 bomb explosion in Rangoon, Burma, that killed 21 people, including four South Korean cabinet ministers. In 1988 a long-standing ban on discussion of reunification was lifted. Roh called for political dialogue, trade relations, and cultural and humanitarian exchanges between the North and South.

South Korea hosted the summer Olympic Games in the fall of 1988. In December Roh shuffled his cabinet in order to remove any figures remaining from the abusive regime of Chun Doo Hwan.

BIBLIOGRAPHY FOR KOREA

Ashby, Gwynneth. A Family in South Korea (Lerner, 1987).
Covell, J.C. Korea's Cultural Roots (Hollym International, 1986).
Farley, Carol. Korea: a Land Divided (Dillon, 1983).
Kim, R.E. Lost Names: Scenes from a Boyhood in Japanese-Occupied Korea (Universe, 1988).
Lee, Ki-waik. A New History of Korea (Harvard Univ. Press, 1984).
Lye, Keith. Take a Trip to South Korea (Watts, 1985).
McNair, Sylvia. Korea (Children's, 1986).
Moffett, Eileen. Korean Ways (Tuttle, 1986).

Words to Remember

mumun—undecorated ancient Korean pottery.
yangban—the Yi Dynasty's landowning elite.
hangul—the Korean alphabet.
Tonghak (Eastern Learning)—an antiforeign Korean movement of the late 19th century.
Samil (March First)—a 1919 resistance movement against Japan's occupation of Korea.

Questions to Think About

1. How has Korea's history been affected by its location between China and Japan?
2. Give possible reasons why some 19th-century Koreans preferred *Sohak,* or "Western Learning," while others advocated *Tonghak,* or "Eastern Learning."
3. Could the political division of Korea after World War II have been prevented? Explain.

Notable Events in Korea's History

1592–98—Korea's Adm. Yi Sunsin uses ironclad vessels—the so-called "turtle ships"—to battle Japanese invaders. Ming Dynasty China helps Korea repel Japanese land forces.

Hakwon-Sa Co., Ltd.

1950–53—Korean War, an attempt by North Korea to forcefully reunify Korea, ends in stalemate; truce signed between North Korea and United Nations, 1953.

Wide World

| 1600 | 1900 | 1950 | 2000 |

UPI Compix

1919—Mass arrests and executions put down Samil Independence Movement against Japan's occupation of Korea. Syngman Rhee heads Korean government-in-exile based in China.

Wide World

1963—Park Chung Hee is elected president of South Korea; served until assassination, 1979; Park's administrations distinguished by political stabilization and economic advances.

THE KOREAN PEOPLE BUILD THEIR NATION

2d century B.C.—Choson state established.

108 B.C.—Northern Korea conquered by Han China.

1st century B.C.—Rise of the Three Kingdoms.

4th century A.D.—Buddhism introduced into Korea.

660–68—Paekche and Koguryo kingdoms conquered by T'ang China and Silla kingdom.

935—Koryo kingdom gains control of Korea.

1392—Yi Dynasty established.

1592–98—Japanese invade Korea.

1627–37—Manchus invade Korea; Korea becomes vassal of Ch'ing China.

1876—Korea signs Treaty of Kanghwa with Japan; signs treaties with Western powers, 1882–86.

1894–95—Antiforeign Tonghak Rebellion quelled. Sino-Japanese War ends China's influence over Korea.

1905—Japan establishes protectorate over Korea after victory in Russo-Japanese War, 1904–5.

1910—Japan annexes Korea; Samil Independence Movement against Japanese occupation crushed, 1919.

1945—United States and Soviet troops occupy Korea after Japan's defeat in World War II.

1948—Separate North Korean and South Korean governments set up.

1950—North Korea's invasion of South Korea triggers Korean War; truce signed, 1953.

1960—April Revolution in South Korea forces Syngman Rhee's resignation; military coup ousts successor, 1961.

1963—Constitutional rule restored in south. Park elected president; reelected, 1967, 1971, 1972, 1978.

1972—North Korea and South Korea revise constitutions. South-North Coordinating Committee established; reunification sessions disbanded, 1973; attempts to reopen joint talks resumed, 1979, 1980.

1979—Park assassinated.

KOREA – Fact Summary

HOW KOREA COMPARES . . .
. . . IN AREA AND POPULATION

. . . IN ECONOMIC ACTIVITY

Total Area—About the Size of Utah (South Korea about the size of Indiana; North Korea about the size of Mississippi)

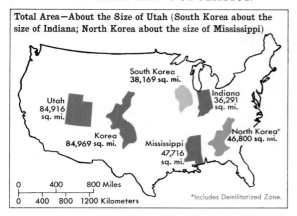

South Korea
38,169 sq. mi.

Utah
84,916
sq. mi.

Indiana
36,291
sq. mi.

Korea
84,969 sq. mi.

Mississippi
47,716
sq. mi.

North Korea*
46,800 sq. mi.

0   400   800 Miles
0   400   800   1200 Kilometers

*Includes Demilitarized Zone.

Population—About as Large as the States of Massachusetts, Michigan, Ohio, Illinois, Texas, and Minnesota (1978 Population Estimates in Millions)

Mass. 5.8	Michigan 9.2	Ohio 10.7	Illinois 11.2	36.9

South Korea	37.0

Texas 13.0	Minn. 4.0	17.0

North Korea	17.1

Sources: Bureau of the Census, U.S. Dept. of Commerce;
Statistical Office, United Nations

—South Korea Near the Top in Population Density*

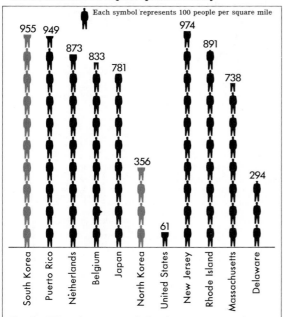

Each symbol represents 100 people per square mile

South Korea 955
Puerto Rico 949
Netherlands 873
Belgium 833
Japan 781
North Korea 356
United States 61
New Jersey 974
Rhode Island 891
Massachusetts 738
Delaware 294

*Based on 1978 population estimates of selected countries, regions, and states.
Sources: Bureau of the Census, U.S. Dept. of Commerce;
Statistical Office, United Nations

Slow Increase in Gross National Product (GNP)*

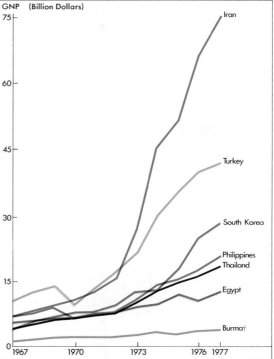

GNP (Billion Dollars)

Iran
Turkey
South Korea
Philippines
Thailand
Egypt
Burma†

1967   1970   1973   1976 1977

* The populations of the countries shown were between 36 and 45 million in mid-1977.
†Gross Domestic Product.
Sources: International Monetary Fund; World Bank

Korea Ranks High in the Output of Several Products

Product	SOUTH KOREA World Rank	SOUTH KOREA Share of World Output	NORTH KOREA World Rank	NORTH KOREA Share of World Output
Graphite	5	10.7%	2	17.5%
Magnesite	*	*	2	17.0%
Tungsten	6	6.2%	8	5.0%
Cabbages	4	4.8%	15	1.3%
Soybeans	10	0.4%	11	0.4%
Rice	10	2.3%	12	1.3%
Sweet potatoes	3	1.3%	18	0.3%
Salted and dried herring, anchovies, and sardines	8	1.6%	*	*

*Data not available.

Sources: Food and Agriculture Organization of the United Nations;
The Mining Journal

289

KOREA

After the start of the Yi Dynasty in 1392, mask plays became a popular amusement for the lower classes. They were used to make fun of the upper classes.

Korea National Tourism Corp.

KOREAN LITERATURE. There is an ancient Korean legend about Tangun, the son of a sky god and a she-bear, whose reign over the land that became Korea began in 2333 BC. The story was told and retold through the centuries, but it was not written down until the 13th century AD, and then it was written in Chinese characters.

The legend is characteristic of the rich heritage of folktale, myth, history, and lyric poetry that is blended into Korean literature. It demonstrates, too, the Chinese influence that pervaded Korean culture for thousands of years.

Early Literature

Traditional Korean literature was mainly poetic, accompanied by music and folk dancing. Ancient Korean songs dealt with religious ceremonies, praise of nature, and peasant life.

After 57 BC there were three warring kingdoms in Korea—Koguryo, Paekche, and Silla. Then, in 668, Silla conquered the other two kingdoms and absorbed their arts. With the creation of a peaceful, unified nation, Korean culture flourished.

The government sent students to China to study and welcomed Buddhist priests into the country to train young people to be soldiers, statesmen, and poets. The Korean love for poetry and music impressed the Chinese, and both the Buddhist monks and the native poets created lyric poetry that was delicate and mystical, with an enduring sensory appeal. Unlike Western poetry, Korean poetry was meant to be sung, not read. Of the 25 *hyangga* that survive from the Silla Kingdom, the most famous lyric poems were composed by two 8th-century Buddhist priests. They are the 'Requiem for a Dead Sister', by Wolmyong, who flourished from 742 to 765, and 'Song in Praise of Knight Kip'a', by Ch'ungdam.

Korea had no written language system at this time, so its scholars invented a syllable system based on Chinese characters and adapted to Korean language sounds. This writing system was called *idu*, and the *hyangga* were transcribed in it.

While some Korean poets were writing in the new system, others wrote in classical Chinese. Perhaps the most renowned of these poets was Ch'oe Ch'i-won (857–?), the first individual author of a collection of poetry surviving from that era. His poems 'In Autumn Rain' and 'At the Ugang Station' reveal his love for nature and a lyrical melancholy.

In the late 8th century political unrest over succession to power began to seethe under the Silla reign. Frequent rebellions occurred, and finally, in 935, a new unified kingdom was formed on the Korean peninsula, the Koryo Dynasty. It was during this period that a distinctive cultural style began to emerge.

Koryo Literature

Although Silla had fallen, the Silla aristocrats were part of the ruling class of Koryo. The *hyangga* were passed from Silla to Koryo, but gradually these became so stylized that the writers lost interest in them. A new poetry form became the dominant literary genre in Koryo. Called *pyolgok*, meaning a "special song," or *changga*, the poems were characterized by a repeated refrain. Like other Korean poetry, they were designed for singing, not reading. Often the poems were presented on huge stages for special feast days and entertainments.

The *pyolgok*, or *changga*, speak powerfully of love and grief and betrayal and of the inexorable victory of time over all human aspirations. Many of the anonymous poets were women who left moving testimonials to the place that their sex held in the literary culture of the Koryo Dynasty.

The new dynasty was troubled by social and political crises and by the savage raids of Mongol armies. As a result, the *pyolgok* writers became more and more introspective and lost favor with the intellectual class. Although a new form of poetry, called *sijo*, was created, it did not become popular until the next dynasty took power.

During the Koryo period, epic literature also developed. The epics included myths, legends, folklore, and the history of Buddhism. While these tales were often traditional, the scribes who wrote them changed them to their individual liking. In one popular type of epic, the hero was a personified inanimate object, as in 'The Tale of Pure Malt' and 'The Tale of the Square-Holed Coin'. One of the masterpieces of epic literature was 'King Tongmyong' by Yi Kyu-bo (1168–1241), who also wrote charming prose essays and poetry in classical Chinese.

Early Yi Literature

In 1392, after the Koryo Dynasty fell, the Yi Dynasty established a reign that lasted until the Japanese annexed Korea in 1910. The literature of this long era is usually divided into two periods, separated by the end of the Japanese invasion in 1598.

With the beginning of the Yi Dynasty, great changes came to Korea. Buddhism, which had been the national religion for about 800 years, was replaced by Confucianism as the official political and moral philosophy. During the reign of Sejong (1397–1450), a humanist, learning and research in many fields were encouraged. But the king's greatest gift to the Korean people was his introduction of the Korean alphabet in about 1446. For the first time, Koreans had a set of 28 (now 24) phonetic letters with which ideas and speech could be expressed in writing. This alphabet, called *hangul*, helped the educated Korean writers to free themselves from their dependence on Chinese culture and the Chinese language.

The first literary work to use *hangul* was 'The Songs of Flying Dragons', a cycle in praise of the founding of the Yi Dynasty by the king's grandfather. Traditionally, the song cycle blended myth, folklore, and history to paint the portrait of a legendary hero who personified the ideal ruler, the best of Confucian humanism, and an example for other rulers to follow.

In the Yi Dynasty two important forms of Korean poetry arose—the *sijo* and the *kasa*. Both forms were ideally suited to the Confucian philosophy.

Sijo had originated in the Koryo Dynasty, but it flowered in the Yi Dynasty and has never lost its popularity with Korean writers. With the *sijo*, writers could express joy and sorrow, praise and satire, a lyrical appreciation of love and nature, and the puzzle of time.

A *sijo* consists of three stanzas in three or four lines, made up of about 45 syllables. Each line has four rhythmic groups with a minor pause at the end of the second group and a major pause at the end of the fourth. With great skill and ingenuity, *sijo* poets try to give a twist to phrasing or meaning in the third line. But the blending of meaning, sound, and rhythm is the keynote of the *sijo*.

The *kasa*, on the other hand, is a narrative poem that has no stanza divisions or fixed length. The *kasa* form gave poets the opportunity to write at length about Confucian thought and philosophy and to describe realistically, for example, the life of the common people, as in 'The Farmer's Works and Days'.

Among the major *sijo* poets of the early Yi period were Yi Hwang (1501–70), with his evocative query to nature in 'The Green Hills', and Hwang Chini (1522?–65?), often regarded as Korea's greatest woman poet. The depth of feeling, the rich symbolism, and the rhythmic lyricism of her love poems, such as 'Taking Leave of Minister So Se-Yang', make them unforgettable.

Considered the master of sung literature, Chong Ch'ol (1536–93) wrote both *sijo* and *kasa* and is credited with helping to perfect the *kasa* form. His versatile poems varied from the brilliant descriptions in 'The Wanderings' to the courtier praise of 'Little Odes on Mount Star'.

Another master of the *kasa* was Ho Nansorhon (1563–89). She was a distinguished writer in both Korean and Chinese, and her dramatic narrative 'A Woman's Sorrow' strikes a universal and timeless chord in its cry of unrequited love.

There were also notable prose writers in the first part of the Yi Dynasty. Kim Si-sup (1435–93), one of the first Korean short-story writers, led the way. The five stories in his collection 'New Stories from Golden Turtle Mountain' are marked by rich imagination,

The oldest known Korean printed text is believed to be a Buddhist scroll (below) found at the Kyongju temple (bottom).

Wide World

fantasy, and the use of the supernatural. His "dream tales," as they were called, set a model that Korean writers followed through the 17th century.

Yi Literature After 1598

After the defeat of the Japanese invasion, prose became the major literary genre of the Yi Dynasty. As Confucianism gave way to practical idealism, writers were free to explore a new form—the novel.

Ho Kyun (1569–1618) was one of the pioneers in prose. His novel 'The Tale of Hong Kiltong' is the story of an illegitimate youth who became a bandit in his rebellion against class discrimination. It was one of the first novels to deal with social problems and to show the life of the people, not the court.

Kim Manjung (1637–92) demonstrated the climate of the period in another way in his novel 'Dream of Nine Clouds'. Half romance, half allegory, the story depicts a man torn between Buddhism and Confucianism in his search for ultimate bliss.

Court ladies were also contributing to literature. Lady Hong (1735–1815), the princess of Hyegyong Palace, recreated the tragedy of her life in her diary 'Random Record in the Midst of Leisure'. Under the pen name Uiyudang, Lady Kim wrote an impressionistic account of her travels in 'Diary of a Sightseeing Tour of Kwanbuk'.

Dramatic *p'ansori*—or stories in song, mask plays, and puppet shows—also were popular in the later part of the Yi Dynasty. They were often used by the people to express their approval or disapproval of social and political events.

Korean Literature in the 20th Century

By the close of the 19th century, the power of the Yi Dynasty was dwindling. In the beginning of the 20th century, Korea became a protectorate and then a colony of Japan. Korea opened contact with the Western world, and Western ideas, culture, and literature opened new dimensions for Korean writers. This period is often called the Era of Enlightenment. It was also a time when many of the writers of Korea were trying to build a bridge from their traditional literary heritage to a new literature that was influenced by the Japanese political novel.

Among the foremost writers of the so-called "new novel" was Yi Injik (1862–1916), who had lived as a refugee in Japan. His novels 'A Demon's Voice', 'The Tears of Blood', and 'Silver World' broke tradition by using contemporary language to tell their stories, the first time this had been done in centuries. With 'Plum Blossom in the Snow', he also launched the "new drama" movement.

Yi Haejo (1869–1927) was the most versatile and entertaining of these pioneer writers. In his best novels, 'Snow on the Temples' and 'Bleeding Flowers', he called for rapid change in the social structure, especially in freedom for women. He also dramatized old Korean romances; 'The Imprisoned Flower', for example, was based on the 'Story of Spring Fragrance' by an unknown 18th-century actor.

The lady at the left teaches her companion to read during a literacy campaign in Korea after World War II.

Many critics consider Yi Kwangsu (1892–1950?) the most important Korean writer of the century. He was a leader in introducing Western literature to his country, and his short stories fostered social progress. In his novel 'The Heartless', he urged a fight for independence from Japan and attacked social barriers.

Another fighter for Korean nationalism was Ch'oe Namson (1890–1957), considered one of the fathers of modern Korean poetry. In 'From the Sea to Children', he made the first attempt to break away from the traditional verse forms and experiment with new and free rhythms and structures.

The novelist and essayist Kim Tongin (1900–51) was also an outstanding short-story writer. He contributed to the use of colloquial prose as a recognized literary device in his story 'The Potato'.

The early stories of Yi Sang (1910–37), who experimented with symbolism and adapted psychoanalysis to creative writing, were often considered too surrealistic. Such works as 'Wings' and 'The Last Chapter of My Life' stimulated Korean intellectuals, and his influence on writers lasted until the 1950s.

Another writer whose influence on Korean literature has endured was Yom Sangsop (1897–1963). His most famous story, 'The Green Frog in the Specimen Room', had little plot, but its brilliant and realistic description had the power to carry the reader into another world. The formless, or stream-of-consciousness, story was to remain one of the characteristic genres in modern Korean literature.

In poetry one of the trailblazers was Chong Chiyong (born 1903), who showed the full potential of the Korean language. In his collection 'White Deer Lake', the poems sing with sensuous delight, rhythmic cadence, fresh imagery, and an emotional depth.

During World War II Japan outlawed the Korean language, the voice of the country's major writers. In 1950, when a national literature had begun to thrive again, the Korean War broke out.

Considering the political obstacles that Korean writers have had to surmount, the amazing resilience of postwar Korean literature is a tribute to their courage and creativity. (*See also* Korea, "Culture.")

KOREAN WAR. Early in the morning of June 25, 1950, the armed forces of Communist North Korea smashed across the 38th parallel of latitude in an invasion of the Republic of Korea (South Korea) that achieved complete surprise. Although attacks came all along the border, the major North Korean thrust was in the west of the Korean peninsula, toward Seoul, the capital of South Korea.

South Korea's army, smaller and not as well trained and equipped as that of North Korea, was unable to stem the onslaught. By June 28, Seoul had fallen, and across the peninsula, everywhere south of the Han River, the shattered remnants of South Korea's army were in full retreat.

The World Reacts

Within hours after the invasion of South Korea began, the United Nations Security Council called for an immediate cease-fire and the withdrawal of North Korean forces from South Korea. North Korea ignored the resolution. Two days later the Security Council urged United Nations members to assist South Korea in repelling its invaders. Both resolutions passed because Russia was boycotting Security Council meetings. Had the Soviet delegate been present, he surely would have vetoed the measures.

In response, 16 nations sent troops to the aid of South Korea. The United States sent an army; Great Britain, a division; and other nations, lesser units. The heaviest burden of the war, however, was borne by South Korea itself. Its army reached a peak

Delivering fire support to United Nations ground forces in Korea, the battleship USS *Wisconsin* looses a salvo of one-ton, 16-inch projectiles at a Communist position.

strength of some 400,000 men, maintained that strength only by a steady flow of hastily trained replacements, and sustained an estimated 850,000 combat casualties. The United States Army in Korea ultimately numbered some 300,000 men, supported by about 50,000 Marine, Air Force, and Navy combatants.

The United States reacted even more quickly than did the United Nations. Upon hearing of the North Korean attack, President Harry S. Truman directed General of the Army Douglas MacArthur, commander of the United States occupation forces in Japan, to insure the safe evacuation of United States civilians and to supply weapons and ammunition to South Korea.

On June 26, United States air and naval forces were directed to support South Korean ground units. The commitment of United States ground forces was authorized after General MacArthur inspected the battlefront. The ground forces available to General MacArthur in Japan were four understrength Army divisions composed largely of inexperienced, undertrained men and lacking in heavy weapons.

Early in July the United Nations asked the United States to appoint a commander for all United Nations forces in Korea. President Truman named General MacArthur. Soon thereafter, South Korea placed its forces under the United Nations command.

After the fall of Seoul, North Korea's forces paused briefly to regroup, then resumed their southward drive. South Korea's army resisted bravely

David Douglas Duncan, *Life* © Time Inc.

Members of the first Marine brigade to reach Korea advance during the defense of the Pusan perimeter. The Marines, though few in number, were instrumental in thwarting the initial Communist offensive that nearly overran South Korea.

but was pushed back steadily. Three United States divisions sent to its aid were committed in small units. They too were driven into retreat. By late July the remnants of South Korea's army and the United States units had been pressed into a small, roughly rectangular area surrounding the port of Pusan at the southeastern tip of Korea. Here, defending a perimeter roughly 150 miles long, the United Nations forces finally were able to hold as reinforcements poured in.

The Origins of a War

The roots of the Korean War are deeply embedded in history. While few regions are less suited to warfare than is the mountainous, river-slashed Korean peninsula, few have known more conflict. For centuries, Korea's three powerful neighbors—China, Japan, and the Soviet Union—vied for its control. By 1910, Japan had established a supremacy that it was to maintain until its defeat in World War II.

Seven days before the Japanese surrender that ended World War II, the Soviet Union declared war on Japan. Soviet troops entered Korea. By agreement, the Soviet Union accepted the surrender of all Japanese forces in Korea north of the 38th parallel of latitude, while the United States accepted the surrender of Japanese units south of the 38th parallel.

The Soviet Union quickly sealed off the 38th-parallel border. It soon set up an interim civil government for the 9 million Koreans of the north, which contained most of Korea's industry. The government was run by Soviet-trained Communist officials.

The United States maintained a military government in the south. The 21 million Koreans of the largely agricultural region were not satisfied with it.

A United States–Soviet commission that was established to make plans for the reunification of Korea under a free government made no progress. In 1947 the United States took the problem before the United Nations, which voted that free elections—under its supervision—should be held throughout Korea in 1948 to choose a single government. The Soviet Union refused to permit the United Nations election commission to enter the north. Elections were thus held only in the south, where a National Assembly and a president—Syngman Rhee—were chosen. The new democracy was named the Republic of Korea.

In the north, the Soviet Union proclaimed a Communist dictatorship called the Democratic People's Republic of Korea (North Korea). Pyongyang was named its capital. Late in 1948, Soviet forces began to withdraw from North Korea, leaving behind an entrenched Communist regime and a well-trained, well-equipped North Korean army. United States occupation forces left South Korea in 1949. They left behind a government still "feeling its way" and an army ill-trained compared with that of the north. This army also lacked air power, tanks, and artillery.

South Korea, however, successfully resisted North Korean attempts at subversion, Communist-supported guerrilla activities, and border raids by North Korean forces. Frustrated, North Korea early in 1950 decided upon war to achieve its goal of Korean unification under Communist rule.

In June 1950 North Korea's army totaled some 135,000 men. North Korea's infantry was supported by some 150 Soviet-made medium tanks, ample artillery, and a small air force. South Korea's ground

THE HUMAN COST OF THE KOREAN WAR			
UNITED NATIONS	*Dead*	*Wounded and Missing*	*Total*
Republic of Korea	591,285	1,293,592	1,884,877
United States	33,629	103,308	136,937
Turkey	725	2,234	2,959
United Kingdom	493	1,680	2,173
Canada	320	1,211	1,531
France	219	815	1,034
Australia	180	748	928
Thailand	114	799	913
Greece	187	615	802
Netherlands	120	648	768
Colombia	140	517	657
Ethiopia	120	536	656
Belgium	101	354	455
Philippines	81	233	314
New Zealand	37	80	117
South Africa	22	12	34
Totals	627,773	1,407,382	2,035,155
COMMUNIST			
North Korea			926,000
People's Republic of China			900,000
Total			1,826,000

Marines of the first assault wave scramble over the seawall at the port of Inchon in September 1950. The daring amphibious attack led to the recapture of Seoul and the complete destruction of North Korea's army as an effective fighting force.

forces included a 45,000-man national police force and an army of 98,000 men. South Korea was armed largely with light infantry weapons supplied by the United States. It had no tanks or combat aircraft, and its artillery was inferior to that of North Korea. Its officers and men had generally less training and experience than did those of North Korea.

Masterstroke Reverses Course of War

While North Korea continued to hurl furious but ineffective attacks at the Pusan perimeter, General MacArthur readied the counterstroke that was to reverse the course of the war—an amphibious assault in his enemy's rear at the port city of Inchon, southwest of Seoul. On September 15, a Marine division swarmed ashore after preparatory bombardment by aircraft and naval guns. An Army division followed. Simultaneously, the Eighth Army—by now a well-equipped and cohesive force—broke out of the Pusan perimeter. Although bloody fighting was required, Seoul was recaptured within a few days. Thereafter the North Korean army—its supply line severed and its principal withdrawal route blocked by the capture of Seoul—rapidly collapsed. By October 1, utterly destroyed as a fighting force, its remnants had retreated above the 38th parallel.

North Korea had also met disaster in the air. Late in June, United States jet fighters had streaked westward from Japan after a North Korean fighter fired on an American transport. Within two weeks the North Korean air force had ceased to exist, and the United Nations had established an air superiority that it generally was to maintain throughout the war. Even when, later in the war, the Communist forces were supplied with Russian-built jet fighters equal or superior to the United States aircraft flown by the United Nations, their Chinese—and sometimes Russian—pilots proved no match for those of the United Nations. In the course of the war, 14 Communist aircraft were shot down for every United Nations plane lost in aerial combat. At sea, under

the guns of United States and British warships, North Korea's minuscule navy—a few patrol boats—suffered a fate similar to that of its air force.

North to Disaster

In the United Nations, Communist delegates indicated that North Korea would now be willing to accept restoration of the 38th parallel as the border between the two Koreas. The United States and South Korea, however, decided to forcibly reunite North and South Korea under the government of South Korea. They disbelieved the threat of Communist China that it would intervene if United Nations forces entered North Korea.

United Nations forces began in early October 1950 to press northward. They met only light resistance and by late November had captured virtually all of North Korea. At two points, units reached the Yalu River, the border between North Korea and Red China.

Shortly after the United Nations advance into North Korea began, however, Communist China had secretly begun to infiltrate troops into North Korea. United Nations air patrols detected no sign of them.

United Nations forces had advanced northward in two columns, the Eighth Army in the west and the X

This map shows how the conflict surged back and forth. The truce line added 850 square miles to North Korea below the 38th parallel, 2,350 square miles to South Korea above it.

Corps in the east, separated by up to 50 miles by the central mountain chain of North Korea. Units of both columns were also dispersed and open to attack.

Contacts with Communist Chinese units—some in strength—began in late October and continued into early November. Chinese aircraft—Russian-built MiG-15 jet fighters—first appeared early in November. However, the United Nations command underestimated the strength of the Chinese forces and misread China's intentions. The command planned a final offensive that would bring all of North Korea under United Nations control, confident that United Nations air power could prevent the Chinese from crossing the Yalu River in sufficient strength to stop the offensive. By this time, however, Chinese Communist troops in North Korea numbered 300,000.

Soldiers of the North Korean army advance toward the front. Severed telephone lines offer mute evidence that United Nations air forces had previously patrolled the road.

Late in November, across the snow that heralded a harsh North Korean winter, the Chinese struck. Attacking largely at night, the Chinese—though they suffered tremendous casualties—rapidly dislodged the Eighth Army and X Corps.

In the east, X Corps units were withdrawn by sea from the ports of Hungnam and Wonsan. Surrounded far inland, the 1st Marine Division reached Hungnam in one of the great fighting retreats of history. In the west, by land and sea, the Eighth Army also fell back. By the end of December the United Nations forces had been pushed back to a line just south of the 38th parallel. In the face of a renewed Chinese offensive, they withdrew from Seoul and the Han River line early in January 1951.

In the more open terrain of South Korea, the United Nations forces were able to form a fairly continuous line of resistance. They continued to withdraw slowly, exacting a terrible toll of the advancing Chinese, until in mid-January the front stabilized

along an undulating line running from the 37th parallel in the west to a point midway between the 37th and 38th parallels in the east.

Reunification Abandoned

The entry of Red China into the war had a heavy impact upon the United States. Draft calls were increased, and more reservists were called to active duty. President Truman declared a state of national emergency, and economic controls were imposed.

Fearing that the wider war with China that would be necessary to reunify Korea would cost too many American lives and raise the risk of nuclear war with Russia, the United States abandoned the idea of forcibly reuniting the two Koreas. Instead, it decided to accept a rough restoration of the situation that had existed before the war. Although the United Nations declared Communist China an aggressor, it agreed with the new United States policy. United Nations forces would repel China from South Korea but would not seek to retake the north.

By late January 1951 the Eighth Army—reformed and strengthened and incorporating the X Corps—was ready to advance against the now-weakened Chinese and North Korean armies. Thrusts of infantry and armor were supported by the vastly superior United Nations artillery and air power. Where the Communist forces chose to stand, they were slaughtered. In one action alone, 6,000 Chinese men were killed, 25,000 wounded. Seoul was reoccupied by the United Nations in mid-March. By March 31 the battle line stood roughly along the 38th parallel.

Enraged at China's intervention, General MacArthur had dissented vigorously from the new United Nations policy. He wished to press an expanded war against Communist China, including forbidden attacks upon "sanctuaries" above the Yalu River. He made his views public. Believing the general's actions to be both insubordinate and dangerous, President Truman relieved him of his commands in April (see MacArthur; Truman). General MacArthur was replaced by Lieut. Gen. Matthew B. Ridgway, who had commanded the Eighth Army in the field since the death of Lieut. Gen. Walton H. Walker in a jeep accident in December 1950. Command of the Eighth Army was passed to Lieut. Gen. James A. Van Fleet.

Truce Talks Begin

Above the 38th parallel, the Chinese and North Korean forces once again regrouped. In April and in May, their commanders hurled them against the United Nations lines. In response, General Van Fleet's forces slowly withdrew, scourging their attackers with superior firepower. When their adversaries were exhausted by massive casualties and supply shortages, the United Nations forces counterattacked. By mid-June, save for a small sector north of Seoul in the west, the United Nations line stood well above the 38th parallel.

Late in June, the Soviet Union indicated that the Communists might be prepared to seek a truce. On

CHRONOLOGY OF THE KOREAN WAR*

1950

June
25. North Korean (Red) armored forces invade South Korea, or Republic of Korea (ROK), Sunday morning at dawn (Saturday afternoon, June 24, Eastern Standard Time), starting the conflict.
25. At 5:45 P.M. EST (Sunday), the United Nations (UN) issues cease-fire order. Reds ignore it.
26. President Harry S. Truman orders the United States air and naval forces in Far East to give armed aid to South Korean forces.
27. The UN empowers its members to send armed forces to aid South Korean forces.
28. Seoul abandoned.
30. Truman orders U. S. ground troops into action.

July
1. First U.S. troops arrive from Japan.
5. U. S. troops in first battle.
7. The UN asks U. S. to create a unified command.
8. Truman names Gen. Douglas MacArthur commander of UN forces in Korea.
10. First Red atrocities reported.
12. U. S. troops and ROK forces retreat toward Taejon.
13. Lieut. Gen. W. H. Walker takes command of U. S. forces.
20. Reds take Taejon.
31. First reinforcements land direct from U. S.

August
5. U.S. and ROK troops pushed back to Naktong River line in a small defense perimeter based on Pusan; Reds within 40 miles of Pusan.
7. U. S. troops counterattack.

September
1. Reds within 30 miles of Pusan.
15. Amphibious landing at Inchon.
16. UN forces launch counterattack.
24–28. UN forces regain Seoul.

October
1. ROK pushes across 38th parallel; Reds ignore MacArthur's demand to surrender.
7–11. U. S., British, Australian forces join ROK beyond 38th parallel.
15. Truman, MacArthur confer.
19. UN forces take Pyongyang, North Korean capital.
26. ROK reaches Yalu River at Chosan; UN forces capture first Chinese Communist troops.

November
1. Peiping (Peking) radio announces Red China "will let volunteers fight in defense of Yalu area"; UN pilots engage first Russian-built MiG-15 jet fighters. U. S. forces hard hit by Red Chinese at Unsan.
24. UN forces launch "end of war" offensive.
26. Red counterattack smashes UN drive; UN forces begin long retreat.
27. U. S. forces cut off in Chosen Reservoir area.

December
5. Pyongyang abandoned to Reds.
23. Lieut. Gen. W. H. Walker killed. Lieut. Gen. Matthew B. Ridgway takes command of UN forces.
24. End evacuation, by ship, of 105,000 U. S. troops from Hungnam.

1951

January
1. Reds launch general offensive.
4. UN forces again abandon Seoul.
17. Reds reject UN cease-fire request.
25. UN forces launch offensive for "war of maneuver."

February
1. UN denounces Red China as "aggressor."
12. ROK drives across 38th parallel.

March
7. MacArthur asserts conflict will stalemate if UN forces are not permitted to attack Red bases in Manchuria.
14. UN forces retake Seoul.
24. MacArthur invites retreating Communist leaders to confer with him in the field to end the war "without further bloodshed." Refused. UN forces resume northward drive.

April
11. General MacArthur relieved of all his commands by Truman. General Ridgway made Supreme Commander of Allied Powers. Lieut. Gen. James A. Van Fleet takes command in Korea.
22. Reds launch counteroffensive with some 600,000 troops.
29. Red offensive halts on outskirts of Seoul in west and 40 miles below 38th parallel in central Korea.

May
3. UN forces launch limited counterattack.
16. Reds advance in offensive drive.
19–21. UN forces stem drive and counterattack.

June
23. Russia's delegate to the UN suggests possibility of a cease-fire.
30. General Ridgway proposes meeting to discuss armistice.

July
10. First meeting of UN and Red representatives, at Kaesong.

August
23. Reds suspend armistice talks.

September
13. UN launches attack on "Heartbreak Ridge."

October
25. Armistice talks resume, after move to Panmunjom.

December
18. UN and Red commands exchange prisoner of war lists. Reds list 11,559 names; UN has 132,474 Red POWs.

1952

January
24. Armistice talks stalemated.
27. Talks resumed.

February
6. Chinese Reds drop their title of "volunteer troops" and list themselves as equal partners with North Korea in "opposing the UN in Korea."
18. Red prisoners riot in UN camp on Koje Island off Pusan.
22. Reds broadcast charges that UN wages "germ warfare" in Korea.
24. U. S. Navy starts second year of shelling Wonsan.

March
4. Syngman Rhee protests armistice talks; insists on unified Korea and withdrawal of Chinese Reds.

April
12–15. Battle lines seesaw in intensified fighting.

May
7. Red prisoners on Koje Island seize Brig. Gen. F. T. Dodd, compound commander; hold for 3 days.
12. Gen. Mark W. Clark succeeds General Ridgway.

June
21–22. U. S.-Philippine troops hold hills against savage Red attacks.
23. UN bombers blast hydroelectric plants on the Yalu.

July
3. Russia vetoes U. S. request in UN to have International Red Cross investigate North Korean charges that UN forces engage in germ warfare.
10. Armistice talks enter second year.
11–12. UN land and carrier-based planes bomb Pyongyang.

August
1. U. S. troops win "Old Baldy."
6–7. ROK takes "Capitol Hill."
12. U. S. Marines take "Siberia Hill" and "Bunker Hill."

September
17. U. S. Navy uses guided missiles on North Korean plants.
28–30. Reds seize three hill positions.

October
6. Reds attack 35 UN positions.
8. Truce teams take indefinite recess in armistice talks.

November
1–30. Hill positions change hands repeatedly in hard fighting.

December
2–5. Dwight D. Eisenhower, U. S. president-elect, tours combat zone.

1953

January
25. UN launches heavy attack.

February
11. Lieut. Gen. Maxwell D. Taylor takes over command from General Van Fleet, retiring from Army.
22. General Clark proposes exchange of sick and wounded prisoners.

March
17. UN throws back heavy attack on "Little Gibraltar."
26. Reds capture "Old Baldy."

April
11. Reach agreement on wounded prisoner exchange: 605 UN troops for 6,030 Reds.
20. Exchange starts.

May
1–31. Ground and air fighting sharpen.

June
9. South Korean assembly votes against truce terms.
12–15. Reds step up attack.
18. President Syngman Rhee defies UN and releases 27,000 anti-Red North Korean prisoners.
20. Truce talks stall.

July
8. Reds agree to renew truce talks.
27. Armistice signed at Panmunjom at 10:01 A.M., after 3 years and 32 days of conflict; hostilities ended 12 hours later.

*All dates of action in Korea are Korean time, which is 14 hours ahead of Eastern Standard Time.

UPI Compix

Helicopters were used to transport troops into combat for the first time in the Korean War. The versatile aircraft were also used extensively in the evacuation of the wounded.

June 30, General Ridgway offered to open truce negotiations. North Korea and China accepted.

Truce talks opened on July 10 at Kaesong, some 35 miles northwest of Seoul. It quickly became apparent that the opposing sides had different goals at the truce table. The United Nations sought only an honorable end to the war. North Korea and Red China, however, undertook to win in conference what they had been unable to attain on the battlefield. The Communists made every effort to embarrass and humiliate United Nations delegates, to force concessions through intransigence and delay, and to use the conference as a propaganda forum.

Although it was agreed that hostilities were to continue during the truce talks, no more major offensives were conducted during the war. A lull in the fighting developed as the talks opened; both sides used it to strengthen their forces. The Communist buildup was hampered—though not halted—by United Nations naval and air forces.

Late in August, the Communists broke off the truce talks. General Van Fleet promptly launched a limited offensive to straighten and improve the United Nations lines. By mid-October, defeated again, the Communists offered to reopen the truce talks.

The meeting site was moved to Panmunjom, some five miles east of Kaesong. Here the armistice talks were to drag on, with intermittent recesses, for another year and a half, stalling repeatedly over such issues as the establishment of a truce line and the repatriation of prisoners. Along the front, meanwhile, the fighting settled into a modernized version of the grinding trench warfare of World War I.

A Long and Uneasy Truce

In order to maintain the military pressure that seemed essential to serious negotiations, the United Nations insisted that the truce line be the line of contact between the opposing armies at the time the truce was signed. Finally, a line was agreed upon. Finally, too, the Communists agreed that prisoners who did not wish to return to their homelands did not have to. At first, they had insisted that the United Nations return, by force if necessary, all the Communist prisoners it held. Nearly half of all the prisoners held by the United Nations—and three quarters of the Chinese—did not wish to return to Communist rule. The truce agreement was finally signed July 27, 1953, and that day, at 10:00 P.M., Korean time, the guns fell silent along the blood-soaked main line of resistance.

The conclusion of the cease-fire had probably been hastened by events outside of Korea. First, General of the Army Dwight D. Eisenhower, who succeeded Truman as president of the United States in January 1953, had hinted broadly that military pressure might be sharply increased if the fighting did not end soon. Second, the death in March 1953 of Soviet dictator Joseph Stalin caused a general turning inward of the Communist world.

After the cease-fire, the opposing forces each withdrew two kilometers from the truce line. The armistice agreement had provided for a conference to seek a permanent peace, but—in the face of Communist intransigence—it was delayed for many years. Today, United States troops remain in South Korea, and heavily armed North Korean and South Korean forces still face each other across a narrow demilitarized zone. Truce violations are common.

In the 1980s, there was no lessening of tensions, but also no serious move toward armed confrontation. North Korean President Kim Il Sung offered a unification plan that was rejected by South Korea. Kim also berated the United States for a plan to install medium range nuclear missiles in the South. But he renewed his call for a peace treaty with the Americans, probably desiring to decrease his dependence on the Soviet Union and China. (*See also* Kim Il Sung.)

A lonely sentinel watches a sector of the demilitarized zone between the two Koreas. To his left, the South Korean defense line stretches westward across the rugged peninsula.
UPI Compix

KORZYBSKI, Alfred (1879–1950). The Polish-born scientist and philosopher Alfred Korzybski originated general semantics, a discipline that rests upon the belief that the structure of language intimately affects the way people think. Central to his theory was the belief that human beings are unique among living creatures in their ability to transmit ideas and information from generation to generation. Korzybski called such ability man's "time-binding capacity," and he tried to expand it through the study and refinement of ways of using and reacting to language.

Alfred Habdank Skarbek Korzybski was born in Warsaw, Poland, on July 3, 1879. He was educated at the Warsaw Polytechnic Institute. During World War I he served in the intelligence department of the Russian army's general staff. In 1915 he was sent on a military mission to the United States and Canada. He later became a United States citizen.

His best-known book is 'Science and Sanity: an Introduction to Non-Aristotelian Systems and General Semantics', which was published in 1933. He intended it as a manual for training people in their semantic reactions to situations. Korzybski held that retraining in sane linguistic usage is ultimately beneficial to passing on ideas and information to subsequent generations of "time-binders." Korzybski died in Sharon, Conn., on March 1, 1950. The Institute of General Semantics in Lakeville, Conn., where he taught his system, continues his work.

KOSCIUSKO, Thaddeus (1746–1817). The Polish general Thaddeus Kosciusko fought for freedom on two continents. In 1776 he came to America from Warsaw to serve in the Revolutionary War. He became an engineer and a colonel of artillery in the Continental army and built the first fortifications at West Point. Later he defended his native land.

Kosciusko was born on Feb. 4, 1746, in Mereczowszczyzna in the Kingdom of Poland (now in the Belorussian Soviet Socialist Republic). He was educated at the Piarist college in Lubieszów and the military academy in Warsaw, where he later served as an instructor.

After the Revolutionary War Kosciusko was rewarded with the rank of brigadier general, a grant from the public lands, and an annual pension. Poland meanwhile was suffering from external aggression and internal anarchy. Kosciusko returned to fight valiantly but unsuccessfully at Dubienka and elsewhere in 1792 against the Russian invasion.

In 1794 Kosciusko became dictator and commander in chief and successfully defended Warsaw against siege by the Russian and Prussian armies. On Oct. 10, 1794, his army of 7,000 Poles was defeated by 16,000 Russians at Maciejowice, where he was wounded.

Kosciusko was released from a Russian prison in 1796. He revisited America, living for a time in Philadelphia, Pa. Unlike many Polish patriots, he refused to serve under Napoleon Bonaparte. He died in Switzerland on Oct. 15, 1817. A statue honoring him stands in Washington, D.C. (*See also* Poland.)

KOSINSKI, Jerzy (born 1933). The haunting novels of Jerzy Kosinski reflect the haunted life of a man whose career was marred by the eccentricities and myths that he had cultivated. In a literary controversy as bizarre as any of his books, some critics attacked him as a fraud whose works were taken from other authors or written largely by editors he had hired, while others defended him as the victim of longtime efforts to discredit both his life and his art.

Jerzy Nikodem Kosinski was born in Łódź, Poland, on June 14, 1933. He was an only child who, sent away by his parents during World War II in order to escape Nazi brutality, wandered through villages throughout the war. Many of his physical and spiritual traumas provided material for his books.

Reunited with his parents after the war, Kosinski returned to school and received degrees in history and political science from the University of Łódź in the mid-1950s. After studying in the Soviet Union he went to the United States in 1957.

Kosinski writes only in English. He taught himself by memorizing words from a Russian-English dictionary, repeatedly viewing movies, and memorizing poems by Shakespeare and Edgar Allen Poe.

Under the pseudonym Joseph Novak, Kosinski had two nonfiction books published in 1960. He catapulted to fame in 1965 with 'The Painted Bird', a mythic story about a hideous childhood in Nazi-occupied Eastern Europe. 'Steps', which deals with cultural manipulation of human beings, was published in 1968 and won the National Book Award. Two other well-known novels are 'Being There' (1971) and 'The Devil Tree' (1973).

KOSSUTH, Lajos (1802–94). A brilliant lawyer, speaker, and journalist, Lajos Kossuth was a revolutionary who led the revolt of Hungarians for independence from Austria in 1848.

Kossuth was born in Monok, Hungary, on Sept. 19, 1802, to one of the country's poorest noble families. For years he sought greater freedom for Hungary, which Austria then regarded as little more than an eastern province of its empire. His liberal publications, many written as letters to avoid censorship, angered the Austrian Hapsburg monarchy. In 1837 the royal government arrested Kossuth. He was charged with treason and imprisoned.

Widespread protest led to his release in 1840. He became the leader of the Liberals and a member of the Hungarian diet, or legislature. His savage attacks on the feudal rights of nobles led to the abolition of serfdom in Hungary (*see* Hungary).

In March 1848, inspired by the revolution in France, Kossuth demanded parliamentary government for Hungary. When it seemed that Austria would try to end the freedom movement by force, he rallied the Hungarians to rise in self-defense. He became the virtual dictator of Hungary, declaring it independent of Austria on April 19, 1849, but his rashness and egotism alienated other leaders. His forces were defeated, and he fled to Turkey.

He visited the United States, where he spoke eloquently for Hungarian independence. In 1852 he went to England, where he stayed for about 17 years. He died on March 20, 1894, in Turin, Italy.

KOSYGIN, Aleksei (1904–80). A longtime Communist statesman, Aleksei Kosygin became the Soviet Union's premier in 1964. He promoted a policy of peaceful coexistence with the West.

Aleksei Nikolaevich Kosygin was born on Feb. 20, 1904, in Saint Petersburg (now Leningrad), then the capital of Russia. When he was 15 years old he joined the Red army to fight in his country's civil war. In 1921 Kosygin entered the Leningrad Cooperative Technical School. Later he worked in cooperatives in Siberia. From 1929 to 1935 he attended the Leningrad Kirov Textile Institute, and at the same time began to rise in the Communist party, which he had joined in 1927. In 1939 he was elected to the party's Central Committee and worked for the national government as commissar of the textile industry.

In 1940 Kosygin was elected a deputy premier of the Soviet Union. Under the regime of Joseph Stalin, he advanced to the head of the finance and light-industry ministries and was appointed to the Politburo, the party's decision-making body.

After Nikita S. Khrushchev succeeded Stalin in 1953, Kosygin became chairman of the State Planning Commission. He was made a first deputy premier in 1960 and by 1964 ranked second to Khrushchev. On Oct. 14, 1964, when Khrushchev was deposed, Kosygin was elected premier. In failing health, Kosygin resigned on Oct. 23, 1980. He died in Moscow on Dec. 18, 1980.

KOUSSEVITZKY, Serge (1874–1951). The first major Russian conductor, Serge Koussevitzky began as a virtuoso player of the double bass, for which he composed a concerto and some small pieces. He advanced the performance of 20th-century music.

Koussevitzky was born on July 26, 1874, in Vyshniy Volochek, Russia. His father and three brothers were all amateur musicians. He played the trumpet and at the age of 14 went to Moscow. He was given a fellowship to the institute associated with the Moscow Philharmonic and studied the double bass, joining the orchestra of the Bolshoi Opera Theater in 1894. In 1901 he succeeded his teacher in the first-chair position and began to play recitals.

Soon after his marriage in 1905 Koussevitzky moved to Germany. He hired the Berlin Philharmonic Orchestra for his conducting debut in 1908. The next year he founded his own orchestra in Moscow and also a publishing house that printed the works of Sergei Rachmaninoff, Sergei Prokofiev, Igor Stravinsky, and Alexander Scriabin.

After the Russian Revolution in 1917 Koussevitzky was appointed to the State Symphony, conducted in Paris from 1921, and finally led the Boston Symphony Orchestra from 1924 to 1949. He took over the Berkshire Festival at Tanglewood, Mass., in 1936

and added a school in 1940. The Koussevitzky Foundation was established in 1942 to commission and provide performances of new works. He died in Boston on June 4, 1951.

KOVALEVSKY, Sonya (1850–91). A Russian mathematician who was also a novelist, Sonya Kovalevsky made valuable contributions to the mathematical theory of differential equations. In 1888 she was awarded the Prix Borodin of the French Academy of Sciences for a physics paper considered so remarkable that the value of the prize was doubled.

Sonya Korvina-Krukovsky was born on Jan. 15, 1850, in Moscow. The daughter of an artillery general, she married a young paleontologist (a scientist who studies fossils), Vladimir Kovalevsky, in 1868. They went to Germany to continue their studies, and Sonya worked with a German physicist at the University of Heidelberg during the year 1869. Since public lectures were not open to women, she next studied privately with a German mathematician at Berlin between the years 1871 and 1874. The University of Göttingen granted her a degree in 1874 for her doctoral thesis on partial differential equations, which was so outstanding that no oral examination was required. In 1884 Kovalevsky became a lecturer at the University of Stockholm. Five years later she was appointed professor of higher mathematics.

The mathematician also gained a considerable reputation as a writer of autobiographical sketches. One of her best-known works is the novel 'Vera Vorontzoff', published two years after her death, which depicted her life in Russia. Sonya Kovalevsky died on Feb. 10, 1891, in Stockholm.

KRAKATOA, or KRAKATAU. The volcano Krakatoa is located on Rakata, an island in the Sunda Strait between Java and Sumatra, Indonesia. Its eruption in 1883 was one of the most catastrophic ever witnessed in recorded history. Its only known previous eruption was a moderate one in 1680.

On the afternoon of Aug. 26, 1883, the first of a series of increasingly violent explosions occurred. A black cloud of ash rose 17 miles (27 kilometers) above Krakatoa. On the morning of the next day, tremendous explosions were heard 2,200 miles (3,540 kilometers) away in Australia. Ash was propelled to a height of 50 miles (80 kilometers), blocking the sun and plunging the surrounding region into darkness for two and a half days. The drifting dust caused spectacular red sunsets throughout the following year. Pressure waves in the atmosphere were recorded around the Earth, and tsunamis, or tidal waves, reached as far away as Hawaii and South America. The greatest wave reached a height of 120 feet (36 meters) and took 36,000 lives in the coastal towns of nearby Java and Sumatra. Near the volcano masses of floating pumice produced from lava cooled in the sea were thick enough to halt traveling ships.

Everything on the nearby islands was buried under a thick layer of sterile ash. Plant and animal life did not begin to reestablish itself to any degree for five years. The volcano was quiet until 1927, when sporadic weaker eruptions began. These tremors have continued into the 1980s.

KRAKÓW, or CRACOW, Poland.

During the Middle Ages the ancient city of Kraków was the capital of Poland and a well-known center of learning. After Poland lost its independence in the 18th century Kraków's great Jagiellonian University continued to be the center of Polish learning. The third largest city in Poland, Kraków is also known for its grand historical architecture.

Kraków is situated on both sides of the Vistula River about 155 miles (250 kilometers) southwest of Warsaw. The river is navigable downstream from the city, and several rail lines intersect there. The country around it is low and flat, but a few miles to the south the great chain of the Carpathian Mountains rises along the border of Czechoslovakia.

The city serves a rich farming and mining area. About 8 miles (13 kilometers) to the southeast are the famous Wieliczka salt mines. Zinc, lead, coal, and other minerals are also obtained in the vicinity. Kraków's chief manufactures are machinery, agricultural implements, and chemicals.

The Medieval City

The core of the city is the ancient town. Seven suburbs now surround it, and the walls that once enclosed it have been leveled to form a wide parkway, with walks, gardens, and chestnut trees. The principal square is Rynek ("marketplace"). On it stand a Gothic church, St. Mary's, and the Cloth Hall, both built in the 13th century. The main building of the university, which was founded in 1364, is a 19th-century Gothic structure. The library, built around a beautiful court, is a jewel of medieval architecture. In the court stands a statue of the astronomer Copernicus, who studied there. Southwest of the old town on a rock hill (Wawel) stands the huge royal castle, once the residence of Polish kings. Near it is a 14th-century Gothic cathedral in which Poland's kings were crowned and buried. Other famous Poles, among them Kosciusko, are also buried there. Modern cultural attractions include more than 20 museums, several theaters, and an opera house.

A legendary Slavic chieftain, Krak, or Krakus, is supposed to have founded Kraków around the year 700. The city became the capital of Poland in the 14th century. Throughout the 14th century Kraków served as Poland's economic and political center and as a major trading point between England and Hungary. Its university achieved fame throughout Europe in the 15th and 16th centuries. In 1609 the court moved to Warsaw.

At various times Kraków was ruled by Prussia and Russia before it passed to Austria in the third partition of Poland (1795). In 1815 the great powers made the small Kraków district an independent buffer state and called it the Republic of Kraków. The city passed again to Austria in 1846 and was joined to Galicia, a crownland of Austria-Hungary, from 1849 to 1918, when Poland became independent.

During World War II the German occupation forces made the city the seat of their government. The Soviet army entered it in January 1945. It suffered almost no war damage. (*See also* Poland.) Population (1980 estimate), 706,100.

KREISKY, Bruno

(born 1911). Although Austria is not a major world power, its chancellor, Bruno Kreisky, has played a significant role in international affairs. He has attempted to mediate between the parties in the Middle East crisis and, through his policy of active neutrality, to help resolve problems between Eastern- and Western-bloc countries in Europe. He has also presided over a period of great prosperity and social harmony in Austria.

Bruno Kreisky was born in Vienna on Jan. 22, 1911. He studied jurisprudence at the University of Vienna and earned a degree as doctor of law. When Germany annexed Austria in 1938, he was imprisoned for his socialist political views, but he escaped to Sweden, where he remained until 1951. After his return to Vienna he served as a secretary of state in the foreign ministry from 1953 to 1956. He was elected to Parliament in 1956 and held the post of foreign minister from 1959 to 1966. In 1967 he took over the leadership of Austria's Socialist party and, after its election victory in 1970, became chancellor.

One of Kreisky's most controversial moves in diplomacy was inviting Yasir Arafat, leader of the Palestine Liberation Organization, to Vienna in 1979 (*see* Arafat). Kreisky was convinced that Western recognition of Arafat's organization was necessary in order to reach a meaningful Middle East peace settlement. Kreisky has also allowed Austria to serve as a gateway to the West for refugees coming from the Soviet Union and other Eastern-bloc countries.

KREISLER, Fritz

(1875–1962). One of the most widely acclaimed violinists of his day, Fritz Kreisler also composed many short violin pieces. His playing was known for its intense vibrato, or rapid variations in pitch, and an economy of bowing, or short strokes with the violin bow.

Kreisler was born on Feb. 2, 1875, in Vienna, Austria. He entered the Vienna Conservatory at age 7 and then the Paris Conservatoire, where he won the Grand Prix de Rome at age 12. After a successful concert tour of the United States in 1888 and 1889 he returned to Vienna to study medicine. He later studied art in Paris and Rome and was an Austrian Army officer. He resumed his musical career in 1899.

Sir Edward Elgar's 'Violin Concerto' was composed for Kreisler, who played the first performance in 1910. Kreisler published arrangements of pieces supposedly composed by Antonio Vivaldi, François Couperin, Johann Stamitz, Padre Martini, and others. In 1935 he admitted the pieces were his own works. He died in New York City on Jan. 29, 1962.

KREMLIN. A kremlin was a medieval Russian fortress, usually built at a strategic point along a river and separated from the surrounding parts of its adjoining city by a wooden—later stone or brick— wall with a moat, ramparts, towers, and battlements. A number of capitals of principalities—such as Moscow, Pskov, Novgorod, Smolensk, Rostov, Suzdal, Yaroslavl, Vladimir, and Nizhniy Novgorod—were built around old kremlins, which usually contained cathedrals, palaces for princes and bishops, governmental offices, and munitions stores.

The best known kremlin, the Moscow Kremlin, dates to 1156 but lost its importance as a fortress in the 1620s. It served, however, as the center of Russian government until 1712 and again after 1918. Originally constructed of wood, it was rebuilt in brick in the 14th century. Frequently repaired and altered, its architecture reflects its long history, encompassing Byzantine, Russian Baroque, and Classical styles. It is triangular in shape; its east side faces Red Square; and it has four gateways and a postern, or back gate, that conceals a secret passage to the banks of the Moscow River.

The Kremlin's present crenellated (notched, or having battlements) red brick walls and 19 towers were built at the end of the 15th century. Of the most important towers, the Spasskaya (Saviour's) Gate Tower leading to Red Square was built in 1491 by Pietro Solario, who designed most of the main towers. Its belfry was added in 1624 and 1625 by an Englishman, Christopher Galloway. The chimes of its clock, dating from 1852, are broadcast by radio as a time signal to the whole Soviet Union. Also on the Red Square front is the Nikolskaya Tower, built originally in 1491 and rebuilt in 1780. The two other principal gate towers, those of the Troitskaya (Trinity) Gate and the Borovitskaya Gate, lie on the western wall.

Cathedral Square. Within the walls is one of the most striking and beautiful architectural ensembles in the world. Around the central Cathedral Square are grouped three cathedrals, superb examples of Russian church architecture at its height in the late 15th and early 16th centuries. The white stone Cathedral of the Assumption (Uspensky Sobor) is the oldest, built from 1475 to 1479 by the Italian Aristotele Fioravanti in the Italianate-Byzantine style and modeled on the Cathedral of the Assumption in Vladimir. Its pure, simple, and beautifully proportioned lines and elegant arches are crowned by five golden domes. The interior frescoes and paintings of the iconostasis, or altar screen, date from the 17th century. The Russian Orthodox Church's metropolitans and patriarchs of the 14th to 18th century are buried here. Across the square is the Cathedral of the Annunciation (Blagoveshchensky Sobor), built from 1484 to 1489 by craftsmen from Pskov. Although burned in 1547, it was rebuilt from 1562 to 1564. Its cluster of chapels is topped by golden roofs and domes. Inside are a number of early 15th-century icons, or painted religious images, attributed to Theophanes the Greek and to Andrey Rublyov, the

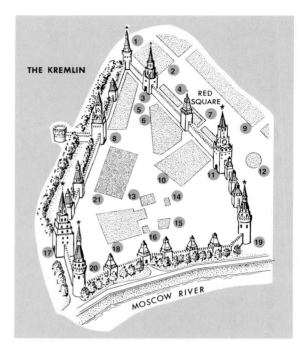

THE KREMLIN

RED SQUARE

MOSCOW RIVER

1. Arsenal Tower
2. State Historical Museum
3. Nikolskaya Tower
4. Reviewing Stand
5. Arsenal Building
6. Council of Ministers Building
7. Lenin Mausoleum
8. Troitskaya Tower
9. State Department Store (GUM)
10. Presidium of the Supreme Soviet of the U.S.S.R.
11. Spasskaya Tower
12. Cathedral of St. Basil the Blessed
13. Cathedral of the Assumption
14. Bell Tower of Ivan III the Great
15. Archangel Cathedral
16. Cathedral of the Annunciation
17. Borovitskaya Tower
18. Great Kremlin Palace
19. Beklemishevskaya Tower
20. Water Tower
21. Palace of Congresses

greatest of all Russian icon painters. The third cathedral, the Archangel (Arkhangelsky), was rebuilt by Alevisio Novyi from 1505 to 1509. In it are buried the czars of Russia up to the founding of St. Petersburg.

Just off the square stands the splendid, soaring, white bell tower of Ivan III the Great. Built in the 16th century and destroyed in 1812, it was rebuilt a few years later. At its foot is the world's largest bell, the Czar Kolokol (see Bell). Nearby is the Czar Pushka, a cannon cast in 1586 but never fired for fear of explosion. Intended to project one-ton cannonballs, it has a caliber of 35 inches (89 centimeters) and weighs 40 tons (36 metric tons). Beside the gun is the Cathedral of the 12 Apostles (Dvenadtsati Apostolov), built from 1653 to 1656, and the adjoining Patriarch Palace.

Palaces. On the west of Cathedral Square is a group of palaces of various periods. The Palace of Facets (Granovitaya Palata)—so called from the exterior finish of faceted, white stone squares—was built from 1487 to 1491. Beside it is the Terem Palace, built in 1635 and 1636, which incorporates the Church of the Nativity of Our Lady, dating from 1393. Both abut on the Great Kremlin Palace, built from 1838 to 1849 as a royal residence by Konstantin

Thon and today used for sessions of the Supreme Soviet of the U.S.S.R. Its long, yellow-washed façade dominates the riverfront. It is connected to the Armory (Oruzheynaya) Palace, built by the same architect from 1844 to 1851, and now houses a spectacular collection of treasures of the czars. Along the northeast wall of the Kremlin is another group of buildings, including the Arsenal (1702–36) and the former Senate building (1776–88), designed by M. F. Kazakov and now housing meetings of the Council of Ministers. The one modern building within the Kremlin is the Palace of Congresses (1960–61) with a vast auditorium, which seats 6,000 and is used for Communist party congresses and as a theater.

Red Square. Along the east wall of the Kremlin lies Red Square, the ceremonial center of the capital and scene of the May Day and October Revolution parades. Beneath the walls stands the bulky Lenin Mausoleum. At the southern end of Red Square is the Intercession (Pokrovsky) Cathedral, or Cathedral of Saint Basil the Blessed. Built by the architects Barma and Posnik Yakovlev from 1554 to 1560 to commemorate the defeat of the Tatars (Mongols) of Kazan and Astrakhan by Ivan IV the Terrible, it is a unique and magnificent architectural fantasy, each of its 10 domes differing in design and color. Along Red Square facing the Kremlin is the State Department Store, GUM, which is in the revivalist imitation Old Russian style. In the same style is the slightly earlier State Historical Museum, built from 1875 to 1883, which closes the northern end of the square. (*See also* Moscow.)

The east wall of the Kremlin is along Red Square (below), with the State Historical Museum on the left, the Cathedral of St. Basil the Blessed in the distance, and the Arsenal Tower and Building on the right. The Archangel Cathedral (below right) contains a dazzling iconostasis (right). The Spasskaya Tower (far right) is also on the east wall.

(Right) Novosti Press Agency; (others) EB Inc.

Peter Kropotkin
Brown Brothers

KROPOTKIN, Peter (1842–1921). Although he could have had a distinguished career as a geographer and zoologist, Peter Kropotkin turned away from other work to pursue the life of a revolutionary. For more than 40 years he was the leading theorist of the anarchist movement in Europe. His notion of "anarchist communism" proposed that private property and unequal distribution of wealth should give way to the free distribution of goods and services. Society should become a cooperative endeavor in which all people should do both manual and mental labor (*see* Anarchism; Communism).

Kropotkin was born in Moscow, Russia, on Dec. 9, 1842, to an aristocratic family. He was educated in Saint Petersburg (now Leningrad) and served for a time as an aide to Czar Alexander II. From 1862 to 1867 he was an army officer in Siberia, where he began to study the area's animal life and geography. This work opened the door to a scientific career, but in 1871 he rejected an offer to become secretary of the Russian Geographical Society. He dedicated himself to working for social justice and promoting the philosophy of anarchism.

In 1874 Kropotkin was imprisoned for his revolutionary activities. Two years later he escaped and fled to Western Europe. He was expelled from Switzerland in 1881 and jailed for three years in France. In 1886 he moved to England and remained there until the Russian Revolution of 1917 gave him a reason to return home. During his exile, he wrote his major political works: 'Words of a Rebel', published in 1885, 'In Russian and French Prisons' (1887), 'Fields, Factories and Workshops' (1899), 'Memoirs of a Revolutionist' (1899), and 'Mutual Aid' (1902).

Kropotkin returned to St. Petersburg (then known as Petrograd) in June 1917 with high hopes for the revolution. The Bolshevist seizure of power dashed his hopes however. "This buries the revolution," he commented. He nevertheless remained in Russia and died near Moscow on Feb. 8, 1921.

KRUGER, Paul (1825–1904). As one of the great patriots and statesmen in the history of South Africa, Paul Kruger is best remembered as a staunch defender of the Transvaal, or South African Republic, at the time when British imperialism in the region was at its height. He is credited with being one of the builders of the Afrikaner (Dutch colonial) nation in South Africa. Although his dream of independence from Britain did not come to fruition in his lifetime, it was finally attained in 1961 when South Africa became an independent republic (*see* South Africa, section on History).

Stephanus Johannes Paulus Kruger was born in the Cradock district of Britain's Cape Colony in Africa on Oct. 10, 1825. Although he had little formal education, he was well instructed by his parents in the strict beliefs of their Dutch Calvinism. At age 10 he and his family joined in a general migration of frontier farmers who wanted to escape British rule and to establish an independent Dutch society in the area north of the Vaal River, the Transvaal. Two of the major influences in his youth were the struggles against hostile African tribes and the opposition of the British to Transvaal's independence.

The Transvaal was annexed by Britain in 1877, and Kruger soon became a leader and negotiator in the struggle to regain independence. This goal was achieved in 1883, and he was elected president of the restored republic—a post he held until 1902, when the region was again taken by the British as a result of the Boer War (*see* Boer War).

Kruger's main antagonist on the Transvaal issue was Cecil Rhodes, Britain's prime minister in the Cape Colony and a man determined to pursue British interests in all of South Africa. The discovery of gold in 1886 in the Witwatersrand area of the Transvaal compounded Kruger's problems, because many "outlanders"—mostly of British background—flocked to the gold strike and threatened the separate national identity of the Afrikaners. The result of the conflict was the Boer War, fought from 1899 to 1902. Early in the war, Kruger went to Europe to live. He died at Clarens, Switzerland, on July 14, 1904. (*See also* Rhodes, Cecil.)

KRUPP FAMILY. From 1587 to 1968, members of the Krupp dynasty, the world's largest manufacturers of armament and ammunition, dominated the German city of Essen. When the drums of German conquest rolled in 1870, 1914, and 1939, it was Krupp factories that provided first Prussia and then the German Empire with field guns, shells, tanks, battleship armor, and flotillas of submarines—always at immense profit to the House of Krupp.

Arndt Krupp (died 1624), the first member of the family to settle in Essen (now in West Germany), arrived before a plague epidemic and bought large tracts of land from fleeing natives. Although Arndt and the four generations of Krupps who succeeded him grew wealthy, the family's rise to international significance did not begin until Friedrich Krupp

(1787–1826) founded the dynasty's cast-steel factory in 1811. Friedrich's son, Alfred, was born on April 26, 1812, in Essen. Although he was eccentric, had difficulty sleeping, and was suspicious of everyone, he succeeded brilliantly in the art of casting steel and was the Krupp responsible for the beginning of the munitions business. Known variously as Alfred the Great and the Cannon King, Alfred perfected his technique by manufacturing rails and seamless-steel railroad wheels. Then he turned to guns. In 1851 his cast-steel cannon was the sensation of London's Crystal Palace Exhibition. In the Franco-Prussian War of 1870 to 1871, the Prussians largely owed their triumph to Krupp's field guns, whose accuracy and range easily outperformed Napoleon III's bronze artillery. Almost overnight Krupp guns became a status symbol for 19th-century nations.

In many ways Alfred Krupp was the founder of modern warfare. But he was also the first industrialist to introduce sick pay, a free hospital for his workmen and their families, pensions, and homes for retired workers. By the time of his death on July 14, 1887, he had armed 46 nations. As much as any other single individual, he had set the stage for World War I.

Alfred's son, Friedrich Alfred Krupp, was born in 1854. He shared his father's uncanny business sense and remarkable gift for management and tripled his own fortunes in a seven-year span. Public outrage over events in his private life plagued him, however, and he committed suicide in 1902, leaving his teenage daughter, Bertha (1886–1957), an heiress. Because it was unthinkable for Germany's most martial industry to be run by a woman, the emperor himself found Bertha a husband, Gustav von Bohlen und Halbach (1870–1950), a Prussian diplomat. The emperor gave the bride away, and, as a surprise for the newlyweds, he had the groom's name changed to Gustav Krupp von Bohlen und Halbach. The couple was thus granted the privilege of passing on not only the family fortune but also the Krupp name to their eldest son.

In World War I Gustav Krupp provided many memorable contributions to Germany's arsenal. One, named in honor of his wife, was the 98-ton Big Bertha howitzer that shelled Liège and Verdun. Because the Germans lost, the war was, on the whole, bad business for Krupp. But with money earned from a prewar agreement with a British manufacturer of artillery shells (which placed him in the awkward position of having profited from Germany's war dead) and with subsidies from the German government, he began secretly rearming Germany. He then helped finance the Nazis' so-called ''terror election'' of 1933, which tightened Hitler's grip on the reins of government. As president of Germany's equivalent of the United States Chamber of Commerce, Krupp expelled all Jewish industrialists and became one of the country's most ardent Nazis.

Meanwhile, the Krupps' oldest son, Alfried (born on Aug. 13, 1907, in Essen), had been a member of the Nazi elite since 1931. He devoted his time to improving an antiaircraft, antitank, antipersonnel 88-millimeter gun, a weapon that was first used in the Spanish Civil War and, a decade later, became the most famous artillery piece of World War II.

Even before 1939, the extent of the family's wealth had been staggering. Now Alfried augmented this empire by seizing property in every country conquered by Germany. When Robert Rothschild refused to sign over his French holdings to Alfried, Rothschild was sent to the Auschwitz concentration camp and murdered. It was incidents of this kind, together with his exploitation of slave labor, that put Alfried in the prisoners' dock at the Nuremberg war-crimes trials after the war. The Nuremberg tribunal sentenced him to 12 years in prison and ordered him to forfeit all his property. However, in 1950 Krupp was granted amnesty by the United States high commissioner in American-occupied Germany and all of his holdings were restored. He rebuilt the family firm and by the early 1960s was worth more than a billion dollars.

Then the family suffered two blows from which it would not recover. Short-term notes for money borrowed from Eastern European firms came due during West Germany's recession of 1966–67. The only way Krupp could meet these commitments was to give up sole control of his firm, opening it to investment and selling stock. At the same time Alfried's only son, Arndt, named after the family's founder, decided he did not wish to take over the family business and renounced his succession rights. Alfried died on July 30, 1967; the firm became a corporation in January 1968. The dynasty that had ruled for almost four centuries had come to an end.

KRYPTON *see* CHEMICAL ELEMENTS; PERIODIC TABLE.

KUALA LUMPUR, Malaysia. Long one of the fastest-growing cities in Southeast Asia, Kuala Lumpur is the national capital and largest city of  Malaysia. Kuala Lumpur is an administrative center of Selangor, one of the country's 13 states.

Kuala Lumpur is in the south-central part of the Malay Peninsula, near the west coast. It lies at the junction of the Gombak and the Kelang rivers. The Kelang provides a waterway westward to the Strait of Malacca, 25 miles (40 kilometers) away. Across the strait is the Indonesian island of Sumatra. The city is built on hilly land near equatorial rain forests.

Chinese and Malays comprise most of the population of Kuala Lumpur. There are also many people of Indian and European origin. The varied backgrounds of Kuala Lumpur's inhabitants are reflected in the city's architectural mix of Chinese shops, Muslim minarets, and modern skyscrapers. Among the landmarks are the National Museum, the gigantic National Mosque, two sports stadiums, and the 20-story Parliament House, which is part of a complex of government buildings. These are surrounded by a zone of Chinese two-story wooden shop houses and mixed

Picturepoin

The National Mosque in Kuala Lumpur is the pride of Malaysia. Muslims come from across the country to praise the Prophet Muhammad.

residential areas of Malay *kampongs* (villages), modern bungalows, and middle-income brick homes. The exclusive Kenney Hill sector is a showcase for domestic architecture. The city's educational facilities include two universities, a Federal Technical College, and a Language Institute.

Kuala Lumpur is a commercial, cultural, and transportation center in an area rich in tin and rubber. It has access to deepwater shipping facilities at Port Kelang, at the mouth of the Kelang. Light industry abounds in Kuala Lumpur proper as well as in Petaling Jaya, a satellite industrial area. The industrial sector of Sungai Besi (Iron River) has iron foundries and engineering works and processes food, soap, and margarine. The Sentil and Ipoh Road area is the site of railway and engineering workshops and sawmills. Cement is manufactured at Rawang to the north, and small-scale tin and rubber smelting is also common in the area.

Immigrant Chinese tin miners founded Kuala Lumpur in the mid-1800s. Since 1895 it has been the capital, successively, of the Federated Malay States, the Federation of Malaya, and Malaysia. Most of its expansion has taken place since 1950. In 1972 Kuala Lumpur was designated a municipality and in 1974 an area of 94 square miles (243 square kilometers), including the municipality, was designated the Federal Territory of Kuala Lumpur. (*See also* Malaysia.) Population (1980 census), 937,900.

KUBLAI KHAN (1215–94). The founder of China's Yüan (Mongol) dynasty was a brilliant general and statesman named Kublai Khan. He was the grandson of the great Mongol conqueror, Genghis Khan (*see* Genghis Khan; Mongols). The achievements of Kublai Khan were first brought to the attention of Western society in the writings of Marco Polo, the

Venetian traveler who lived at the Chinese court for nearly 20 years (*see* Polo, Marco).

Kublai Khan was born in 1215. He began to play a major role in the consolidation of Mongol power in 1251, when his brother, the emperor Möngke, resolved to complete the conquest of China. After Möngke's death in 1259, Kublai had himself proclaimed khan. During the next 20 years he completed the unification of China. He made his capital at what is now Peking (Beijing). Kublai's major achievement was to reconcile China to rule by a foreign and culturally inferior people, the Mongols, who had shown little ability at governing. His failures were a series of costly wars, including two disastrous attempts to invade Japan; they brought little benefit to China. Kublai's extravagant administration slowly impoverished China, and in the 14th century the ineptitude of his successors provoked rebellions that eventually destroyed the Mongol dynasty.

KUDU *see* ANTELOPE.

KUIBYSHEV, or KUYBYSHEV, U.S.S.R. One of the largest industrial cities of the Soviet Union is Kuibyshev, located 530 miles (850 kilometers) from Moscow on the west bank of the Volga River where it meets the Samara River. Kuibyshev is the administrative center of the Kuibyshev *oblast* (region), and a group of industrial and residential suburbs and satellite towns surround the city.

Since Kuibyshev is the center of a network of pipelines, oil refining and petrochemicals are major industries, especially in the satellite town of Novokuybyshevsk. Kuibyshev has huge engineering factories that produce petroleum equipment, machinery, ball bearings, cables, and precision machine tools. There are also many building-materials and consumer-goods industries. Much of Kuibyshev's power comes from a hydroelectric plant completed in 1957 at Zhigulevsk, a few miles upstream. The Soviet Union's largest chocolate factory is located in Kuibyshev.

The city has several theaters and museums, research establishments, and institutions of higher education. It is also an important transportation center with the Volga capable of handling seagoing ships; and railways westward to Syzran, where lines radiate out to all parts of European Russia, and eastward to Ufa, Orenburg, Siberia, and Central Asia.

The site of Kuibyshev was Samara, a fortress founded in 1586 to protect the Volga trade route. It soon became a major focus of trade and later a provincial seat. It was renamed Kuibyshev in 1935. The growth of the city was stimulated during World War II by its position far behind the war zone and by the evacuation there of many government functions when Moscow was threatened by German attack. The postwar development of the Volga-Urals oil field has also been an important growth factor in this region. Population (1982 estimate), 1,243,000.

KŪKAI *see* KOBO DAISHI.

KU KLUX KLAN. A secret terrorist organization, the Ku Klux Klan was the leading underground resistance group that fought the political power of the newly freed slaves during Reconstruction after the American Civil War. Its goal was to reestablish the dominance of the prewar plantation aristocracy. It was revived in an altered form in the 20th century.

Organized in 1866 by Confederate veterans as a social club in Pulaski, Tenn., the Ku Klux Klan was restructured along political and racial lines a year later in Nashville, Tenn. Sometimes called the Invisible Empire of the South, the KKK, or the Klan, it was presided over by a grand wizard and a descending hierarchy of grand dragons, grand titans, and grand cyclopses. They took their name from the Greek word *kyklos,* meaning "circle," and the English word clan. Dressed in robes and hoods designed to frighten superstitious victims and to prevent identification by Federal troops, Klansmen whipped and killed innocent freedmen in nighttime raids. With intimidation and threats, they drove blacks and white sympathizers out of their communities, destroying their crops and burning their houses and barns.

Because of an increase in the number of kidnappings and murders, the grand wizard of the Klan ordered it disbanded in 1869, but local groups remained active. The rest of the country reacted strongly to the increased violence in the South, and Congress passed the Force Act in 1870 and the Ku Klux Klan Act in 1871, authorizing the president to suspend the writ

A Klansman stands in front of a burning cross, a symbol of the Ku Klux Klan's belief that it is one of the few defenders of white Christian America.

UPI/Bettmann Newsphotos

of habeas corpus, suppress disturbances by force, and impose heavy penalties on terrorist organizations. Resulting federal prosecution of Klan members, however, created widespread Southern sympathy in their behalf. As Southern political power gradually reverted to traditional white Democratic control during the 1870s, the need for anti-Republican, antiblack organizations to remain secret decreased.

The Klan was reorganized in 1915 near Atlanta, Ga., and peaked in the 1920s when its membership exceeded 4 million nationally, with strong organizations in the Midwest as well as in the South. To the old Klan's hostility toward blacks, the new Klan added bias against Roman Catholics, Jews, foreigners, Communists, and organized labor. Stressing white Protestant supremacy, the Klan enjoyed a last spurt of growth in 1928 when Roman Catholic Alfred E. Smith received the Democratic presidential nomination. During the Great Depression of the 1930s, the Klan's membership dropped drastically, but in the mid-1960s, as civil-rights workers attempted to spur compliance with the Civil Rights Act of 1964, it revived once again. The Klan faded rapidly after President Lyndon Johnson denounced the organization in 1965, only to revive with renewed vigor in the late 1970s. The Klan fragmented into several separate and competing groups, some of which allied with neo-Nazi and other right-wing extremist groups. By the late 1980s it was estimated to have fewer than 10,000 members active in 24 states but with many thousands more sufficiently interested to give personal and financial support.

KUNLUN MOUNTAINS. Connecting dozens of separate mountain ranges, the Kunlun Mountains are the longest mountain system in Asia. From the Pamir Mountains on the Sino-Soviet border they extend eastward for about 1,675 miles (2,696 kilometers) in China. The Kunlun Mountains form the northern wing of the Plateau of Tibet, which is part of the highest region in the world.

The highest groups of peaks in the western Kunluns include the 25,325-foot (7,719-meter) Kongur Shan, the 24,757-foot (7,546-meter) Muztagata, and the 23,891-foot (7,282-meter) Muztag. In the eastern Kunluns are found the highest peaks of the entire system. These include, in the Przhevalsky Range, the 25,340-foot (7,723-meter) Ulu Muztag and the 25,328-foot (7,720-meter) Tekiliktag, which are also known as the Great Snow Range.

There are few automobile roads through the Kunluns, because the mountains are virtually impassable. Evidence of mineral resources exists, but their exploitation has been hindered by the harsh natural environment. (*See also* China; Tibet.)

Most of the Kunluns are unpopulated. Only the large river valleys, up to an altitude of about 10,000 feet (3,000 meters), contain any inhabitants. The Uigurs, the most numerous people, live mainly in large settlements in the foothills bordering the Tarim Basin to the north. Tajiks live in the western mountains and Mogols in the eastern ranges. Farming and small-scale breeding of sheep, goats, and yaks are the basic occupations of these people. Their main crops are wheat and barley.

"The Times," London/Pictorial Parade

A typical Kurdish village

KURDS. Most Kurds live in a mountainous region of the Iranian Plateau called Kurdistan, an area where Turkey meets Iran, Syria, and Iraq. Kurds also live in the Caucasus region of the Soviet Union. The total Kurdish population is estimated at 10 million. Kurds are predominantly Sunnite Muslims. Although their language is Iranian, the Kurds' ethnic origins are uncertain. Most Kurds were converted to Islam in the 7th century (see Islam).

The Kurds traditionally herded sheep and goats in the mountains that they have occupied since prehistoric times. Today many Kurds are nomads, taking their livestock to mountain pastures in summer and returning to valley villages in winter. Most Kurds are settled farmers, however. While nomadic groups retain the traditional tribal organization under chiefs, some settled Kurds have become urbanized and assimilated into their respective nations.

The Kurds have repeatedly tried to become independent. They have fought the Sumerians, Assyrians, Persians, Mongols, crusaders, and Turks. One of their great leaders was Saladin (see Saladin). Since World War I, Turkey, Iran, and Iraq have put down many major Kurdish uprisings. After Kurds in northern Iraq revolted in 1961 a 1970 agreement finally granted them several concessions, including autonomous local government. A Kurdish group led by Mustafa al-Barzani opposed the final implementation of the agreement in 1974, and fighting broke out again. Although the rebellion collapsed within a year, occasional hostilities continued (see Iraq). Following the 1979 revolution in Iran there was severe fighting between government forces and Kurds demanding political and cultural autonomy (see Iran).

KUWAIT. Of all the oil-producing Arab countries of the Middle East, Kuwait was the first to benefit nationwide from its vast petroleum reserves. Kuwait lies at the northeastern tip of the Arabian Peninsula, on the shore of the Persian Gulf. It is bordered by Iraq on the north and northwest, and by Saudi Arabia on the south and southwest. Kuwait shares much of the same Muslim-Arab cultural heritage with both those nations.

Kuwait is a good example of a traditional society that advanced rapidly into the 20th century because of its oil wealth. For example, in the early 1950s the nation's capital, also named Kuwait, was a fortified town surrounded by a mud wall for protection against raiding tribes. Today, the city has high-rise buildings, a busy port, stores that sell the latest products, and an extensive petrochemical industry.

Land and Climate

The state of Kuwait covers only 6,880 square miles (17,818 square kilometers). The country is largely desert, but it has 120 miles (195 kilometers) of coastline. A number of small offshore islands, including Faylakah, Bubiyan, and Warbah, belong to Kuwait.

Most of the people live in the city of Kuwait and in such suburbs as Al Jahra and Hawalli because of the harsh desert climate farther inland. Maximum temperatures in the desert region usually range between 108° F (42° C) and 115° F (46° C) during the day in summer and drop close to freezing at night in winter. There are occasional dust storms, some accompanied by thunder and light rain. Along the Persian Gulf, the humidity is high, making the summer months very unpleasant. Kuwait's average annual rainfall of less than 6 inches (150 millimeters) occurs almost entirely between November and May.

The People

Although traditionally a tribal society, composed of groups from the Arabian Peninsula, Kuwait is today largely urban. Many Kuwaitis can trace their origins to such tribes as the Aneza, Ajman, Utaibah, Awazim, and Dawasir, though a majority of the labor force is non-Kuwaiti.

The population of Kuwait is made up of about 42 percent Kuwaitis, 41 percent other Arabs, and 17 percent South Asians, Iranians, and other nationalities. Kuwait's people receive government-subsidized housing, education, and health services. To obtain this assistance, however, they must prove that their families have lived in Kuwait for at least two generations. The continual influx of tribespeople from Saudi Arabia has made such proof difficult to provide, and the government is still working to distribute social services equitably.

The nomadic Bedouins of Kuwait have virtually disappeared since the early 1960s because of housing built by the government for the rural population. Many of these modern structures include not only fuel and electricity, but also special enclosed courtyards for livestock. Kuwait no longer officially has a

Bedouin population, but rather a growing suburban populace composed largely of former nomads.

Kuwait is a Muslim nation, with a court system based on a combination of civil and Islamic law. Islam is the state religion, and the official language is Arabic. English, the second language, is taught in public schools. The influence of Western dress, education, and technology has been combined with traditional customs to produce a society with elements of both cultures. In Kuwait, men often wear a *disdasha*, or traditional white robe; a *guttra*, or head cloth; and open-toed leather sandals. Kuwaiti women in the cities do not wear veils but can be seen with scarves and long-sleeved dresses. There has been a resurgence of traditional Islamic ways of life among many young Kuwaiti women. This trend is often reflected in their dress, unlike the early 1970s, when Western styles were more common.

About 60 percent of Kuwait's people can read and write, a high rate for a Middle Eastern country. Since the 1950s, education has been patterned on Western systems. Women as well as men receive a free education from kindergarden through the university level, but only Kuwait University offers coeducational instruction through a college for women.

The Economy

Kuwait's economy is based on oil and petrochemicals. The Kuwait Oil Company was established in 1934 by British and American firms. However, extensive production did not begin until after World War II, when oil was discovered in the Neutral Zone, which Kuwait shares with Saudi Arabia, and, a few years later, in northern Kuwait. In the early 1960s, a Japanese oil company discovered commercial quantities of off-shore oil in Kuwaiti waters. Natural gas, a by-product of the oil industry, is utilized by the Kuwait National Petroleum Company's refinery at Ash Shu'aybah. Petroleum accounts for about 90 percent of Kuwait's exports. Less then 1 percent of the economy is based on agriculture, especially because about 75 percent of the nation's water must be distilled from seawater or imported.

Until the manufacture of cultured pearls by Japan in the early 1930s, Kuwait's coral reefs accounted for a major portion of the world market in pearls. The Kuwaitis used *dhows*, or small sailing vessels, for commerce along the eastern coast of the Arabian Peninsula and as far away as India. Fishing was also an important part of the economy prior to World War

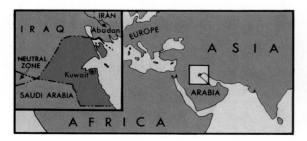

Kuwait Airways Corporation

The Telecommunications Center, right, and the water towers in the background are landmarks in Kuwait City.

II, and there has been renewed interest in revitalizing fishery products for export.

Government and History

Kuwait is a constitutional monarchy based on the rule of the Al Sabah family. The ruler, called the amir, appoints the prime minister. A constitution went into effect in 1963 providing for a 50-man National Assembly elected by adult males born in the country or naturalized after 20 years of residence. There are no legal political parties.

Kuwait was a British protectorate from 1899 until 1961, when it became independent. The country joined the United Nations in 1963.

Kuwait and Saudi Arabia have had close ties since Abdul Aziz Ibn Saud, the founder of Saudi Arabia, took refuge in Kuwait before reconquering Riyadh in 1906. The two nations also share a common tribal and cultural heritage that does not seem to have been disturbed by Western technology and vast oil wealth.

The Kuwaiti government officially took over the British and American interests in the Kuwait Oil Company in 1975. Today the state has full control of the country's oil industry. In 1976 the government resigned after charging that the National Assembly had blocked significant legislation. At the same time the amir dissolved the assembly and suspended parts of the constitution. Constitutional government was not restored until after elections in 1981. Population (1983 estimate), 1,668,400.

311

KYOTO, Japan. A city important in the history of Japan, Kyoto lies on a fertile plain in south-central Honshu, between Lake Biwa and the Inland Sea. Fifth among Japan's cities in population, it is the capital of Kyoto Prefecture in Kinki District. It was the capital of Japan for more than 1,000 years and was the birthplace of the nation's culture. Its Shinto shrines, Buddhist temples, and palaces with elaborate gardens have made it one of Japan's most visited cities.

Kyoto is also a major industrial center. Traditional industries include silk weaving, dyeing, embroidery, and the making of porcelain, lacquerware, and decorative enamelware called cloisonné. Modern industries include the making of heavy machinery, copper products, and chemicals. It is noted for the production of foodstuffs and as a center of the sake, or rice wine, industry.

Kyoto has a mild, moist climate. Mean temperatures range from an average of about 80° F (27° C) in July, the hottest month, to an average of about 38° F (3° C) in January, the coldest month. Average annual precipitation is about 70 inches (1,780 millimeters).

In Kyoto's early days it was known as Heian-kyo, or "capital of peace and tranquillity." The city grew around the court of Emperor Kwammu in the late 8th century. It later became known as Kyoto, or "capital city." Kyoto was originally laid out according to Chinese concepts, with long streets intersected by broad avenues. The city was surrounded by a low earthen wall with 18 gates.

Kyoto was the scene of several conflicts during Japan's medieval era. After 1336 it was continually ravaged by feuding warlords. It was not rebuilt to any extent until the second half of the 16th century, when Hideyoshi restored its temples and laid out the streets once more.

Kyoto was the only major Japanese city that escaped bombing raids during World War II. The Allies spared the city because it held so many of Japan's cultural treasures. Among Kyoto's historic landmarks are the Kyoto Imperial Palace, Nijo Castle (now a museum), Higashi Honganji Temple, Sanjusangendo (a 13th-century hall), Yasaka Shrine, Daitokuji Temple, Koryuji Temple, and Toji Temple. Modern edifices include the Kyoto International Conference Hall, which is representative of present-day Japanese architecture, and—in front of Kyoto Station—the Kyoto Tower, which is 430 feet (131 meters) high. Exhibits of Japan's traditional and industrial arts are housed in Kyoto National Museum, Nishijin Textile Museum, and Gion Corner.

Kyoto is the principal center of education for western Japan. In 1875 Joseph Niijima and Yamamoto Kakuma, in cooperation with the American Board of Foreign Missions, established the Christian Doshisha University of Kyoto. Kyoto University, which incorporates a school of agriculture, was founded in 1897. Other institutions of higher education include Kyoto Prefectural University and the Kyoto Municipal College of Fine Arts. (*See also* Japan.) Population (1980 census), 1,473,065.

The Katsura Imperial Villa, located on a vast tract of land in the southwest section of Kyoto, is one of the city's most popular tourist attractions.

Camera Tokyo

312

The letter J

The history of the letter J is linked with the history of I. The Romans and their European successors used I both for the vocalic "i" and for the consonantal "y" (as in the English word "yet"). The English letter J did not come into existence until the end of medieval times, when scribes began to use a tailed form of "i," with or without the dot, next to the short form of "i" (1).

When printing was invented, the tailed form of "i" (2) was often used for an initial "i," which is usually consonantal. Not until the 17th century, however, was the distinction between J or j as a consonant and I or i as a vowel fully established.

i   j

1

ȷ   ʄ

2

Jab, in boxing B-388, *picture* B-389

Jabalpur, India. *see in index* Jubbulpore

Jabbok (modern Nahr ez Zerka), river in Jordan, flows 50 mi (80 km) w. to Jordan River n. of Dead Sea.

Jabir ibn Hayyan, Abu Musa (721?–813?), Arabic scientist; held sound views on chemical research; suggested geologic formation of metals
  scientific breakthroughs, *list* S-114

Jacana, small raillike bird with extremely long toes and claws that enable it to walk on the floating leaves of water plants, and with strong spurs at the bend of each wing; plumage black with usually bright chestnut back and parts of wings; two species in tropical America; one, the Mexican jacana, ranges n. to Texas.

Jacaranda, genus of tropical shrubs and trees (*Jacaranda*) of bignonia family; one species, green-ebony, grows 30 ft to 60 ft (9 m to 18 m); leaves fernlike; flowers blue, in loose clusters.

'J'Accuse', work by Zola Z-456
  Dreyfus case D-272
  France F-341

Jachymov (in German, Sankt Joachimsthal), Czechoslovakia, town in n.w. near Germany; silver mine discovered 1516; word dollar derived from Joachimsthaler, a coin minted in 1519; pop. 6,806.

Jacinth (or hyacinth), gemstone J-115

Jacinth, perennial plant of the lily family; three species are common garden flowers: Japanese jacinth (*Scilla japonica*); Peruvian jacinth (*Scilla peruviana*), also called Cuban lily; Spanish jacinth (*Scilla hispanica*), called bell-flowered squill.

Jack, donkey. *see in index* Ass

Jack, a small flag flown from the prow of a ship, *list* F-149

Jack (or jak, or jaca, or jackfruit tree), East Indian tree of same genus as breadfruit; wood is hard, yellow, and used for almost every purpose; fruit weighs 5 to 50 lbs (2 to 23 kg).

Jack, part of a harpsichord M-688

Jackal, carnivore of the genus *Canis* of the family Canidae, *table* F-464

'Jack and Jill', nursery rhyme N-444

'Jack and the Beanstalk', fairy tale F-261

Jackass, donkey. *see in index* Ass

Jackdaw, bird of crow family B-258
  crow C-784, *picture* C-785

Jackfish. *see in index* Northern pike

Jackfruit, tree. *see in index* Jack

Jackhammer (or paving breaker), tool
  mining M-428
  pneumatic device P-476

Jack-in-the-pulpit (or India turnip), American perennial herb of family Araceae F-240, *picture* F-233

Jackleg, an air cylinder M-428

Jackling, Daniel Cowan (1869–1956), U.S. mining engineer and metallurgist, born near Appleton City, Mo.; began Utah's copper industry by utilizing low-grade ore.

Jack London Square, waterfront area in Oakland, Calif. O-453

Jack mackerel, food fish caught in Pacific Ocean off California; iridescent green above and silvery on sides and belly; belongs to jack family Corangidae and has scientific name *Trachurus symmetricus*, *table* F-136

Jack-o'-lantern, Halloween pumpkin H-17

Jack-o'-lantern, mushroom (*Clitocybe illudens*) M-665
  poisonous plants P-443

Jack pine, first large tree (*Pinus banksiana*) to grow after a forest fire or lumbering; shelters trees that follow; grows in Canada and Great Lakes states; pulpwood, packing cases, posts. *see also in index* Lodgepole pine

Jack plane, a tool T-218

Jackrabbit R-30
  speed record, *picture* A-425

Jacks, Lawrence Pearsall (1860–1955), British philosopher; entered ministry as assistant to Stopford Brooke; professor of philosophy and principal, Manchester College, Oxford University, 1915–31; editor of *Hibbert Journal*, a Unitarian review ('Among the Idol-makers'; 'The Challenge of Life').

Jackson, Alexander Young (1882–1974), Canadian impressionist painter, born in Montreal; noted for rugged landscapes of Canada.

Jackson, Andrew (1767–1845), 7th president of the United States J-2
  Bank of the United States B-72, B-73
  Calhoun C-31
  Clay C-487
  folklore F-268
  Hall of Fame, *table* H-16
  Houston H-307
  Indian policy I-149
  journalists N-236
  postal service P-558
  public relations P-645
  Statuary Hall, *table* S-609
  Tennessee T-88, *picture* T-93
  United States U-161, 163
  Van Buren V-273
  War of 1812 W-32

Jackson, Charles Reginald (1903–68), U.S. novelist, born in Summit, N.J.; novels about psychologically abnormal individuals ('The Lost Weekend'—motion-picture version won Academy award 1945; 'The Fall of Valor'; 'The Outer Edges').

Jackson, Charles Thomas (1805–80), U.S. chemist and geologist, born in Plymouth, Mass.; discovered anesthetic property of ether independently of W.T.G. Morton.

Jackson, Chevalier (1865–1958), U.S. laryngologist, born in Pittsburgh, Pa.; perfected methods for oral removal of foreign bodies from lungs and throat; established the techniques of modern laryngeal surgery.

Jackson, Claiborne Fox (1807–62), U.S. political leader, born in Fleming County, Ky.; governor Missouri 1860–61; brigadier general in army of Confederate States of America Missouri M-494

Jackson, Helen Hunt (also called H.H.) (1830–85), U.S. poet and novelist, born in Amherst, Mass.; her lyric 'Verses by H.H.' won praise from Emerson; her most famous novel, 'Ramona', was a plea for justice for American Indians.

Jackson, Henry. *see in index* Armstrong, Henry

Jackson, Henry Rootes (1820–98), U.S. diplomat and soldier, born in Athens, Ga.; U.S. minister to Austria 1854–58, to Mexico 1885–86; major general commanding all Georgia state troops at beginning of Civil War; later Confederate brigadier general.

Jackson, James Caleb (1811–95), U.S. physician and abolitionist, born in Manlius, N.Y.; operated spa in Danville, N.Y., 1858–79; author of 'How to Treat the Sick Without Medicine' B-432

Jackson, Jesse (born 1941), U.S. clergyman, political and civil rights leader J-9
  black Americans B-302
  Cuban prisoners S-804

Jackson, Joseph Harrison, U.S. religious leader, born in Rudyard, Miss.; pastor of Olivet Baptist Church in Chicago, Ill.; president National Baptist Convention U.S.A.; vice-president Baptist World Alliance; observer at Second Ecumenical Council of the Vatican.

Jackson, Mahalia (1911–72), celebrated U.S. gospel singer, born in New Orleans, La.; concerts, radio, and television
  popular music M-678

Jackson, Michael (born 1958), U.S. pop entertainer, born in Gary, Ind.; lead singer with brothers in band, The Jackson 5 (1969–75), known later as The Jacksons; in 1972 began solo career that exploded with 1979 album, *Off The Wall*; winner of unprecedented eight Grammy awards for solo album *Thriller* 1983; top music videos included 'Thriller', 'Beat It', 'Billy Jean', and 'Bad'; his trademarks, a single sequined glove and the "moon walk," caused great sensation
  mime M-423
  popular music M-681

Jackson, Reggie (born 1946), U.S. baseball player, born in Wyncote, Pa.; played for Kansas City Royals 1967, Oakland Athletics 1968–75, 1987, Baltimore Orioles 1976, New York Yankees 1977–81, California Angels 1982–86; voted most valuable player in American League and World Series 1973; among all-time leaders in home runs, runs batted in, strikeouts.

Jackson, Robert Houghwout (1892–1954), U.S. judge, born in Spring Creek, Pa.; assistant attorney general of U.S. 1936–38; solicitor general 1938–39; attorney general 1940–41; appointed associate justice U.S. Supreme Court 1941; in 1945 appointed chief prosecutor, war crimes trials, Nuremberg, Germany; author of 'The Nürnberg Case' and 'The Supreme Court in the American System of Government'.

Jackson, Sheldon (1834–1909), U.S. Presbyterian missionary, born in Minaville, N.Y.; established many churches; Alaska's first superintendent of public instruction 1885–1909; imported reindeer to replace Eskimos' dwindling food supply.

Jackson, Shirley (1919–65), U.S. writer, born in San Francisco, Calif.; noted for macabre tales ('The Lottery'; 'The Haunting of Hill House'; 'We Have Always Lived in the Castle').

Jackson, Stonewall (1824–63), general, army of Confederate States of America J-9
  Civil War C-474, 480, 643
  Lee L-116
  Stuart S-678
  Hall of Fame, *table* H-16
  Stone Mountain, *picture* G-88
  warfare W-21

Jackson, William Henry (1843–1942), U.S. photographer, best known for his Western landscapes and American Indian portraiture P-351, *list* P-348

Jackson, Mich., manufacturing and railroad city on Grand River 70 mi (110 km) w. of Detroit; automobile and airplane parts, tires, metal products; state prison; pop. 39,739
  Michigan, *map* M-372

Jackson, Miss., capital and largest city of state; on Pearl River; pop. 202,895 J-10

Mississippi M-469, *maps* M-468, 482, *pictures* M-475, 477
North America, *map* N-350
state capitals, *list* S-595

Jackson, N.J., 8 mi (13 km) n.w. of Lakewood; farming and fruit growing; pop. of township 25,644
  New Jersey, *map* N-210

Jackson, Tenn., city about 75 mi (120 km) n.e. of Memphis; railroad center; textile products, wood products, aluminum foil, batteries, food products; Union University, Lambuth College, Lane College; Federal base in Civil War; pop. 49,131 T-85, *map* T-98

Jackson, Wyo., town on branch of Snake River, about 5 mi (8 km) s. of Grand Teton National Park; annual rodeo; pop. 4,511
  Wyoming, *map* W-400

Jackson College, in Medford, Mass.; for women; chartered 1910; liberal arts. *see also in index* Tufts University

Jackson Five, U.S. music group; featured Michael Jackson
  popular music M-681

Jackson Hole, region in Snake River valley, n.w. Wyo.; about 400 sq mi (1,040 sq km); named in 1829 for David E. Jackson, partner of William Sublette, the fur trader; became retreat of cattle thieves; now a hunting and fishing ground, *picture* N-49
  Wyoming, *map* W-400, *picture* W-394

Jackson Lake, Wyo., near w. boundary; 8 mi (13 km) long; in Grand Teton National Park; its outlet feeds Snake River; waters irrigate Idaho
  United States, *map* U-193
  Wyoming, *map* W-400

Jackson Military Road, road in s. U.S. M-470

Jackson's chameleon, lizard, *picture* L-273

Jackson State University (until 1974 Jackson State College), in Jackson, Miss.; established 1877 as Natchez Seminary, became state college 1956; liberal studies, education and technical studies; graduate program; quarter system.

Jacksonville, Ark., city 15 mi (25 km) n.e. of Little Rock; transportation center; metal products, lumber, shipbuilding, chemicals; Little Rock Air Force Base nearby; pop. 27,589
  Arkansas, *map* A-624

Jacksonville, Fla., inland port, railway center, tourist resort; pop. 540,898 J-10
  Florida F-196, *maps* F-195, 210
  North America, *map* N-350

Jacksonville, Ill., city 30 mi (50 km) w. of Springfield; vegetable products, clothing, bookbinding, polyethylene film

Jacksonville / James

and bags, ferris wheels; Illinois College, MacMurray College; state institutions for blind, deaf, and mentally ill; pop. 20,284, *map* I-52

Jacksonville, N.C., city on New River 46 mi (74 km) n.e. of Wilmington; wood products; Camp Lejeune (U.S. Marine Corps) nearby; pop. 17,056
  North Carolina, *map* N-370

Jacksonville State University, in Jacksonville, Ala.; established in 1883; formerly a teachers college; arts and sciences, and teacher education; graduate division A-226

Jacksonville University, in Jacksonville, Fla.; private control; founded 1934; arts and sciences, music and fine arts, teacher education; graduate studies; trimester system.

'Jack Sprat', nursery rhyme N-442

'Jack Tales, The', work by Chase S-660

Jack the Dripper. *see in index* Pollock, Paul Jackson

'Jack the Giant Killer', fairy tale F-262

Jack the Ripper, unidentified murderer who killed at least seven women in London in 1888 J-11

Jack-up ship, petroleum drilling P-257

Jacob, Hebrew patriarch, 2nd son of Isaac, supplanter of his brother Esau; husband of Leah and Rachel and progenitor of Israelites (Bible, Gen. xxv, 1). *see also in index* Israel
  Abraham A-12

Jacob, François (born 1920), French biologist, born in Nancy; with Pasteur Institute 1950–, Collège de France 1964–
  genetics G-54

Jacobean lily. *see in index* Sprekelia

Jacobi, Abraham (1830–1919), U.S. physician, born in Hartum-in-Minden, Westphalia, Germany; called founder of American pediatrics; started clinics for children in New York City.

Jacobi, Frederick (1891–1952), U.S. composer, born in San Francisco, Calif.; assistant conductor, Metropolitan Opera Company, New York City, 1913–17; teacher of composition, Juilliard Graduate School; used Indian melodies; wrote music for Jewish religious service.

Jacobi, Karl Gustav Jakob (1804–51), German mathematician, brother of Moritz H. Jacobi; professor at Königsberg and lecturer at Berlin; contributed to higher mathematics
  Abel A-8
  mathematics M-216, *table* M-218

Jacobi, Moritz Hermann (1801–74), German physicist and architect, brother of Karl Gustav Jacobi; said to have constructed first electrically propelled boat.

Jacobin Club (formerly Breton Club, or Friends of the Constitution), French political club
  Jacobins J-11

Jacobins, in French history J-11
  French Revolution F-403
  Lafayette L-20
  Napoleon N-13

Jacobites, adherents of James II or the direct Stuart line after English Revolution of 1688; famous uprisings in 1715 and 1745 to restore Stuart pretenders P-585

Jacobs, Amos. *see in index* Thomas, Danny

Jacobs, Joseph (1854–1916), British Judaic scholar and folklorist, born in Sydney, Australia; in U.S. after 1900 ('English Fairy Tales'; 'Celtic Fairy Tales')
  storytelling S-654, 658

Jacobs, William Wymark (1863–1943), British humorist, born in London, England; wrote sea stories and horror tales ('Snug Harbour'; 'Collected Stories').

Jacobsen, Jens Peter (1847–85), Danish novelist and poet J-11

Jacob's fan shell (or St. James's scallop shell) S-225

Jacobs house, Usonian house in Madison, Wis. W-367

Jacobson's organ, a chemically sensitive organ R-170
  snake S-331

Jacob's staff. *see in index* Ocotillo

Jacobus Jonker (or Jonker), diamond D-131, *picture* D-129

Jacoby, Oswald (1902–84), U.S. bridge expert, born in Brooklyn, N.Y.; bridge player of the year 1959 and 1961–63; elected to Bridge Hall of Fame 1965; wrote syndicated column on bridge and numerous books on card games.

Jacquard, Joseph-Marie (1752–1834), French inventor J-12
  Industrial Revolution I-179
  lace machine L-13
  rug and carpetmaking R-344
  spinning and weaving S-543

Jacquard, in textiles
  rug and carpet R-341, *diagram* R-341
  weaving S-543

Jacquard loom, in weaving S-543

Jacquard weave, in weaving S-543

Jacque, Charles Émile (1813–94), French etcher and genre painter of the Barbizon School; favored rural scenes and subjects ('Flock of Sheep', in the Louvre).

Jacques-Cartier, Mount, peak of e. Quebec, on Gaspé Peninsula; highest point 4,160 ft (1,270 m) in Quebec Q-11, *map* Q-20

Jade, semiprecious stone ranging in color from white to nearly black, most valuable when emerald-green shade; old jade dug from tombs has often turned blue, yellow, red, or brown
  carving, *picture* A-685
  jewelry and gems J-112

Jadeite (also called Chinese jade), a variety of jade, most treasured in emerald-green shade; occurs both in Burma and in Tibet; chemical formula $NaAl(SiO_3)_2$ M-436

Jade plant, houseplant H-289

Jaeger, seabird, belonging with the skuas to the family Stercorariidae; dark, falconlike birds that chase gulls and terns, forcing them to drop their catch of fish; flash of white across base of primary feathers, and long central tail feathers distinguish them; nest in Arctic regions, migrating across U.S. and Europe to winter in Southern Hemisphere; three species: pomarine jaeger *(Stercorarius pomarinus)*, parasitic *(S. parasiticus)*, long-tailed *(S. longicaudus)*.

Jael, Hebrew woman exalted in the 'Song of Deborah' as "blessed among women" because she killed Sisera, leader of the Canaanites (Bible, Judges iv).

Jaffa, Israel. *see in index* Tel Aviv-Yafo

Jagannath, India. *see in index* Puri

Jagannath (or Juggernaut), title of Hindu god Vishnu; temple at Puri, India; at annual festival idol is drawn on enormous car under which some devotees have cast themselves.

Jagger, Mick (born 1944), U.S. rock musician
  popular music M-680, *picture* M-680
  Rolling Stones R-261

Jaggery, brown sugar obtained chiefly from the sap of East Indian jaggery palms; similar in appearance to cane sugar.

Jagiellon Dynasty, royal family J-12
  Casimir IV C-196
  Poland P-494

Jagiellonian University, in Kraków, Poland K-303

Jaguar, member of the cat family J-12
  fur, *table* F-464
  leopard L-135

Jaguarundi, wild cat *(Felis yagouaroundi)*, *picture* C-216

Jahan. *see in index* Shah Jahan

Jahangir (1569–1627), Mughal emperor of India.

Jahiz, al- (776–868), Muslim writer I-366

Jahn, Friedrich Ludwig (1778–1852), German educator; strove for the awakening of German national feeling by organizing youth of all classes into groups called Turnvereine (gymnastic societies).

Jai alai, game J-13

Jail (or gaol), a type of prison P-600

Jaimes Freyre, Ricardo (1870–1933), Bolivian writer L-69, 72

Jainism, religion J-14
  Hinduism H-157
  India I-68
  Mahavira M-48
  monks and monasticism M-539

Jaipur, former princely Rajputana state of India, now part of Rajasthan state; chiefly agricultural; some marble, copper, and cobalt.

Jaipur, capital of Rajasthan state, in n.w. India, 150 mi (240 km) s.w. of Delhi; famous for jewelry and other handicrafts; site of the pink palace and the Hall of the Winds; pop. 613,144, *map* I-83, *picture* I-71

Jaisalmer, city in n.w. India; pop. 20,355, *map* I-84, *pictures* I-64, 69

Jajce, Yugoslavia, town 65 mi (105 km) n.w. of Sarajevo; chief outpost of eastern Christendom from 1463 until it was captured by the Turks in 1528.

Jajmans, caste families I-70

Jakarta, Indonesia, capital and largest city; pop. 6,556,000 J-15
  Asia, *map* A-697
  Indonesia I-160, *map* I-166

Jalal Ud-Din Rumi (1207–73), Persian poet J-17
  Iqbal I-304
  Islamic literature I-367

Jalan Thamrin, boulevard in Jakarta, Indonesia, *picture* J-15

Jalap, herbaceous climbing plant *(Ipomoea purga)* with alternate heart-shaped leaves and large purplish-pink flowers; grows in Mexico near the town of Xalapa, whence its name; large root tubers contain a resin used in cathartics.

Jalisco, Mexico, state on central w. coast; 30,941 sq mi (80,137 sq km); cap. Guadalajara; corn, wheat, cotton, tobacco; cattle; iron, silver, gold, lead, copper, zinc; one of wealthiest states; pop. 4,157,357, *map* M-341

J. Allen Hynek Center for UFO Studies, Chicago, Ill. U-9

Jaluit, atoll of Marshall Islands, in Pacific; measures 38 by 23 mi (61 by 37 km); chief island Jaluit; naval base; occupied by U.S. forces in 1945; pop. 925.

Jamahiriya, form of socialism L-190

Jamaica, island nation of the West Indies; 4,244 sq mi (10,992 sq km); cap. Kingston; pop. 2,407,000 J-17
  Caribbean literature C-167
  cities. *see in index* city listed below and other cities by name
  Kingston K-247
  colonial history A-337
  Commonwealth membership C-602
  flag, *picture* F-166
  North America, *map* N-350, *table* N-346
  reggae music M-680
  United Nations, *table* U-84
  West Indies W-155, *map* W-159, *picture* W-158
  world, *map* W-297
  World War II W-325

Jamaican fruit bat, *picture* B-104

Jamaica pepper. *see in index* Allspice

Jamaica sorrel. *see in index* Roselle

James, Saint, called in Bible's New Testament the "brother of Jesus"; often identified with James the Less; traditional author of Epistle of James.

James I (1566–1625), king of England and Scotland J-19
  Acadia A-14
  England E-245
  Fawkes F-49
  Ireland I-322
  Mary, Queen of Scots M-164
  Nova Scotia N-398, 403
  Puritans P-667
  Raleigh R-99
  Scotland S-129
  Stuart line S-677
  United Kingdom U-68

James II (1633–1701), king of England J-19
  Anne A-467
  England E-247, P-585
  Glorious Revolution G-168
  Gwyn G-322
  Ireland I-322
  Marlborough M-147
  New York N-260
  religious controversies A-418
  William III W-207

James I (1394–1437), king of Scotland, poet and constitutional reformer; succeeded 1406 while captive in England; released 1424; murdered by rebel nobles.

James IV (1473–1513), king of Scotland; succeeded 1488; disputes with Henry VIII led to invasion of England; killed at Flodden S-128

James V (1512–42), king of Scotland; succeeded 1513; refused to become involved in policies of his uncle, Henry VIII of England, and failed to rout Henry's invading army at Solway Moss (1542) because of lack of support of Scottish nobles; died as result of this humiliation; succeeded by infant daughter, Mary, queen of Scots; appears in Sir Walter Scott's 'Lady of the Lake' S-128

James VI (1566–1625), king of Scotland. *see in index* James I, king of England

James, Daniel, Jr. (Chappie) (1920–78), U.S. Air Force officer, born in Pensacola, Fla.; flew combat missions in Korean and Vietnam wars; became second black general in Air Force history 1970; assistant secretary of defense for public affairs 1970–73; principal deputy assistant secretary of defense for public affairs 1973–74 B-298

James, Edmund Janes (1855–1925), U.S. educator, born in Jacksonville, Ill.; president Northwestern University 1902–4; University of Illinois 1904–20; active also in civic affairs.

James, Edwin, U.S. geographer
  quotation U-123

James, Frank (1843–1915), U.S. outlaw O-619

James, Harry (1916–83), U.S. composer, trumpeter, and bandleader; born in Albany, Ga.; at 15 won state championship as trumpeter; organized own orchestra 1939
  popular music M-682
  Sinatra S-300

James, Henry (1843–1916), U.S. novelist and essayist J-20
  American literature A-351
  creative writing W-377
  psychological novels N-410

James, Jesse (1847–82), notorious U.S. outlaw J-20
  folklore F-268
  Missouri M-494
  outlaws O-619
  Younger brothers Y-425

James, Marquis (1891–1955), U.S. writer, born in Springfield, Mo.; began career as a news reporter in Enid, Okla., at age of 14 ('The Raven: a Biography of Sam Houston', Pulitzer prize 1930; 'Andrew Jackson', 2-vol. biography, Pulitzer prize 1938; 'The Cherokee Strip', story of Marquis James's boyhood).

James, Phyllis Dorothy (born 1920), detective story writer D-119

James, Thomas (1782–1847), U.S. trader and trapper; with Missouri Fur Company's first expedition (1809) and later with Andrew Henry in Wyoming; made trading expedition to Santa Fe (1821) with John McKnight by way of Mississippi and Arkansas rivers; another expedition (1822) to perilous Comanche territory, now Oklahoma; member of Illinois legislature (1825–27).

James, William (1842–1910), U.S. philosopher and psychologist J-21
  parapsychology P-630
  philosophy P-318
  psychology P-638

James, William Roderick (1892–1942), U.S. writer and artist, born near Great Falls, Mont.; left an orphan and adopted by fur trader; ranch life and horses his specialty; illustrated his own books; awarded Newbery Medal for 'Smoky, the Cowhorse' 1927 ('Sand'; 'Cowboys North and South'; 'Horses I've Known';

Jedediah / Jersey

were a cause of intervention by Napoleon III.

Jedediah Smith, state park in California N-57

Jeejeebhoy, Jamsetjee (1783–1859), Indian merchant and philanthropist, born in Bombay of Parsee parents; famed for philanthropy among all sects and nationalities in India; given knighthood and baronetcy by England.

Jeep, U.S. Army, a midget ¼-ton combat motor vehicle carrying 3 to 6 people, antitank guns, mortars, and machine guns up to 800 pounds (360 kilograms); its mobility and high speed have made it valuable in attack and reconnaissance work; name derived from g.p. (general purpose); also trade name for small civilian vehicle of similar type.

Jefferies, Richard (1848–87), English naturalist and writer, born near Swindon, England; remembered for portrayal of English countryside ('The Gamekeeper at Home: Sketches of Natural History and Rural Life'; 'The Story of My Heart'; autobiography).

Jeffers, Robinson (1887–1962), U.S. poet, born in Pittsburgh, Pa.; work shows rugged strength, tragic, often violent intensity of passion ('Selected Poetry'; 'Be Angry at the Sun'; 'The Double Axe & Other Poems'; 'Hungerfield, and Other Poems').

Jefferson, Joseph (1829–1905), U.S. actor, born in Philadelphia, Pa.; most famous role as title character in the popular play 'Rip Van Winkle' A-27

Jefferson, Thomas (1743–1826), 3rd president of the U.S. J-89
- archaeological excavation A-535
- architecture A-572
- Bill of Rights B-196
- bioethics B-214
- constitutional law views C-685
- Declaration of Independence D-53
- 1800 presidential election U-198, U-215
- Enlightenment E-289
- federal government U-208
- freedom of the press N-235
- friends and associates
  - Adams A-34
  - Burr B-513
  - Hamilton H-22
  - Jackson J-8
  - Madison M-26
  - Washington W-42
- Hall of Fame, *table* H-16
- human rights H-320
- Louisiana Purchase L-324
  - Lewis and Clark Expedition L-143
  - Missouri River M-510
  - New Orleans N-233
- Missouri Compromise M-507
- Mount Rushmore, *picture* S-137
- pasta P-149
- social class S-345
- Thomas Jefferson Memorial N-59
- United States U-159
- Virginia V-364
- War of 1812 W-29
- Washington, D.C. W-71
- writings A-344

Jefferson, Mount, peak in the Cascades of Oregon, in w. Jefferson County; 10,495 ft (3,200 m), *map* O-597

Jefferson Airplane, U.S. rock band
- popular music M-679

Jefferson City, Mo., state capital, on s. bank of Missouri River in center of state; pop. 33,619 J-96
- Missouri M-491, 500, *maps* M-489, 505, *picture* M-497
- North America, *map* N-350
- state capitals, *list* S-595

Jefferson Heights, La., unincorporated community just w. of New Orleans; pop. 16,489.

Jefferson Memorial. *see in index* Thomas Jefferson Memorial

Jefferson National Expansion Memorial National Historic Site, memorial in Missouri N-51, *map* M-506

Jefferson River, headstream of Missouri River in s.w. Montana; flows n.e. 140 mi (225 km)
- Montana, *map* M-565

Jeffersonville, Ind., port city on Ohio River opposite Louisville, Ky.; toiletries, chemicals, cement, boats, metal products; pop. 20,008, *map* I-102

Jeffreys, George Jeffreys, first **Baron** (1648–89), English judge, chief justice, and later lord chancellor under James II; notorious for brutality in bloody assizes.

Jeffreys, Harold (1891–1989), British astronomer; theory of origin of solar system.

Jeffries, James J. (1875–1953), U.S. boxer, born in Carroll, Ohio B-391
- Johnson J-128

Jehlam River. *see in index* Jhelum River

Jehoash, king of Israel. *see in index* Joash

Jehol, China. *see in index* Chengteh

Jehoshaphat (9th century BC), son of Asa and king of Judah; first king of Judah to maintain peace with kingdom of Israel.

Jehovah (or Yahweh), the Hebrew name for the God of Israel; means the self-existent or unchangeable One; in English generally rendered the Lord
- Tabernacle T-2

Jehovah's Witnesses, Christian society founded in 1872 by Charles Taze Russell J-96
- Russell R-347

Jehu, king of Israel; killed Jezebel and massacred house of Ahab (Bible, II Kings ix–x), enemy of Baal worshipers; furious driver, hence, nickname of coachman.

Jejunum, middle part of small intestine; lies between duodenum and ileum; attached to posterior wall of abdomen.

Jekyll, Dr., the kindly, reputable physician in Robert Louis Stevenson's 'The Strange Case of Dr. Jekyll and Mr. Hyde' who discovers a drug by which he can transform himself into criminal Mr. Hyde.

Jellicoe, John Rushworth Jellicoe, first **Earl** (1859–1935), British admiral, entered navy 1872; command of Grand Fleet in World War I, notable services at battle of Jutland; first sea lord, and chief of naval staff; admiral of the fleet, 1919; served as governor general of New Zealand, 1920–24 W-306

Jelliffe, Smith Ely (1866–1945), U.S. neurologist, born in New York City; managing editor of *Journal of Nervous and Mental Diseases* 1902–45 and *Psychoanalytic Review* 1913–45; pioneer in psychoanalysis in U.S.

Jellyfish, primitive coelenterate animal of the class Scyphozoa, *diagram* J-97
- deep-sea forms D-60
- invertebrate group I-282
- oceanography O-485
- phylogenetic tree, *diagram* Z-468
- prehistoric life A-459

Jelutong (or pontianak), name of a Malayan tree, also of its rubberlike juice.

Jemappes, Belgium, village 3 mi (5 km) w. of Mons; decisive defeat of Austrians by French Revolutionary army 1792; pop. 13,092.

Jemez, pueblo about 45 mi (70 km) w. of Santa Fe, N.M.; on the Jemez River; Jemez Indians belong to the Tanoan language group of Pueblo Indians; pop. 1,197
- New Mexico, *map* N-229

Jemison, Mae C. (born 1956), U.S. astronaut, born in Decatur, Ala.; B.S., B.A., Stanford University 1977; M.D., Cornell University 1981; general practitioner, Glendale, Calif.; selected by NASA as mission specialist for space shuttle program 1987, thus becoming first black woman astronaut.

'Jemmy Green', work by Rashleigh A-799

Jena, East Germany, city on Saale River 45 mi (70 km) s.w. of Leipzig; optical instruments; university (founded 1558); pop. 82,113, *map* G-131

Jena, battle of (1806) G-122
- Prussia P-628

Jenghiz Khan. *see in index* Genghis Khan

Jenifer, Daniel of St. Thomas (1723–90), U.S. statesman, born in Charles County, Maryland; member of Continental Congress 1778–82; favored permanent union of states and congressional power of taxation; delegate to Constitutional Convention 1787; signed United States Constitution.

Jenkins, Charles Francis (1867–1934), U.S. inventor, born near Dayton, Ohio; took out more than 400 patents, chiefly in the field of motion pictures and radio
- motion pictures M-617

Jenkins, Charles Jones (1805–83), U.S. jurist, born in Beaufort district, S.C.; justice Georgia Supreme Court 1860–65; governor of Georgia 1865–68, removed by General Meade for opposing reconstruction acts.

Jenkins, Tom, U.S. wrestler W-366

Jenkins' Ear, War of (1739–43), in English history, grew out of trade and colonial rivalry A-829
- England E-248

Jenks, Jeremiah Whipple (1856–1929), U.S. economist and educator, born in St. Clair, Mich.; professor of political economy, Cornell University, 1891–1912; served U.S. and other governments in administrative and advisory positions ('The Trust Problem'; 'Principles of Politics'; 'The Immigration Problem').

Jenner, Edward (1749–1823), English physician J-98
- medicine M-283, *list* S-115
- microbiology M-376
- vaccine V-264

Jenner, William (1815–98), British physician, born in Chatham, Kent; in 1847 began a study that established separate identities of typhoid fever and typhus; professor at University College, London, 1849–72; physician in ordinary to Queen Victoria 1862–90.

Jennet, name of small Spanish horse, also of female ass A-702

Jenney, William LeBaron (1832–1907), U.S. architect, born in Fairhaven, Mass.; engineer in Union Army in Civil War; noted for innovations in structure of office buildings
- architecture A-566, *picture* A-563
- building construction B-496
- Home Insurance Building A-668, *picture* A-668, U-170

'Jennie Gerhardt', novel by Dreiser D-259

Jennings, Henry (fl. 1714), Welsh pirate P-393

Jennings, Herbert Spencer (1868–1947), U.S. naturalist, born in Tonica, Ill.; with Johns Hopkins University 1906–38; noted for research in animal behavior, physiology of microorganisms, and genetics ('The Universe and Life').

Jennings, Hugh Ambrose (Ee-yah) (1870–1928), U.S. baseball shortstop, born in Pittston, Pa.; played chiefly for Baltimore, N.L., 1893–99; won 3 pennants as manager Detroit, A.L., 1907–20.

Jennings, Sarah. *see in index* Marlborough, Sarah Jennings Churchill, duchess of

Jennings, Thomas L. (1791–1859), U.S. inventor, the first black person known to patent an invention; in 1821 in New York City he received letters of patent for a dry-cleaning process.

Jennings, La., city in s.w., about 34 mi (55 km) e. of Lake Charles; trade center for agricultural area; flower growing; oil, fishing, timber; pop. 12,401, *map* L-322

Jennings, Mo., city 8 mi (13 km) n.w. of St. Louis; residential suburb; settled 1870; incorporated 1946; pop. 17,026
- Missouri, *map* M-505

Jenny, spinning. *see in index* Spinning jenny

Jensen, Alfred (1903–81), U.S. painter, *picture* M-212

Jensen, J. Hans D. (1907–73), West German physicist, born in Hamburg; professor of physics University of Heidelberg after 1949; lectured in U.S. 1951–53, 1961
- nuclear physics N-432

Jensen, Johannes Vilhelm (1873–1950), Danish novelist and poet, born in North Jutland; noted for trilogy 'The Long Journey', consisting of 'Fire and Ice', 'The Cimbrians', and 'Christopher Columbus' S-89

Jenson, Nicolas (1420–80), Italian printer, born in France; probably learned printing at Mainz from Gutenberg; printed at Venice ten years; his roman type used as model by Morris, Cobden-Sanderson, and Rogers
- typeface, *picture* B-349

Jephthah, judge of Israel; in fulfillment of a rash vow, sacrificed to the Lord the first creature that met him on return from victory, his only daughter (Bible, Judges xi).

Jerba. *see in index* Djerba

Jeremiah (650?–570? BC), one of the major Hebrew prophets J-98
- painting P-37

'Jeremiah Symphony', work by Bernstein B-176

Jerez de la Frontera (or Jerez, or Xeres), Spain, city in s.w., 14 mi (22 km) n.e. of Cadiz; famous for sherry wine, to which it gave the name; pop. 96,209, *map* E-360
- vineyard, *picture* S-491
- wine W-236

Jericho (or Eriha), Jordan, town 7 mi (11 km) n. of Dead Sea; important city of ancient Palestine; captured and destroyed by Joshua (Bible, Joshua vi, 20–4); later rebuilt and destroyed a number of times; pop. 5,312
- archaeology, *picture* A-529
- fort and fortifications F-319

Jericho, N.Y., community 23 mi (37 km) n.e. of New York City; residential suburb; agricultural region; pop. 14,010
- New York, *map* N-268

Jericho, rose of. *see in index* Rose of Jericho

Jeritza, Maria (stage name of Marie Jedlitzka) (1887–1982), Austrian operatic singer, born in Brünn, Austria, now Brno, Czechoslovakia; with Metropolitan Opera Company 1921–32; popular on concert stage.

Jermaq, Jebel, in upper Galilean mountains; highest point in Palestine proper; 3,934 ft (1,199 m).

Jernigan, Fla. *see in index* Orlando

Jeroboam I (died 912? BC), leader of revolting 10 tribes and first king of Israel (10th century BC) after separation from Judah (Bible, I Kings xii, 20).

Jeroboam II (died 744? BC), king of Israel, son of Joash, regained much territory previously lost (Bible, II Kings xiv, 23–9); Amos and Hosea preached during his reign.

Jerome, Saint (or Eusebius Hieronymus) (340?–420), most learned of early Fathers of Latin church; born in Strido, Dalmatia, of wealthy family; festival September 30
- Bible translations B-184
- Fathers of the Church F-45
- Latin literature L-78
- Middle Ages M-385
- women's rights W-271

Jerome, Jerome Klapka (1859–1927), British humorist and dramatist ('Idle Thoughts of an Idle Fellow'; 'The Passing of the Third Floor Back'; 'Three Men in a Boat').

Jerome, Ariz., town near Verde River, 25 mi (40 km) n.e. of Prescott; formerly important copper camp; pop. 420.

Jerome brothers, North American fur traders, *picture* F-468

Jerome of Prague (died 1416), learned and eloquent Bohemian religious reformer; studied in England; friend of Huss; condemned as heretic.

Jerrold, Douglas William (1803–57), British dramatist and humorist; contributed to *Punch* ('Black-Eyed Susan', 'Heart of Gold', plays; 'Chronicles of Clovernook', novel).

Jersey, breed of cattle C-226, *picture* C-227

Jersey, largest of Channel Islands, 20 mi (30 km) from Normandy coast of France; 45 sq mi (116 sq km); chief city

Joachim / Johnson, Ben

Joachim, Joseph (1831–1907), Hungarian violinist and composer; first public appearance at the age of 7; concert master under Liszt ('Hungarian Concerto')
Brahms B-395

Joachimsthal, Czechoslovakia. *see in index* Jachymov

Joad, Cyril Edwin Mitchinson (1891–1953), British philosopher, born in London, England; professor, University of London, 1930–53 ('Meaning of Life'; 'Guide to the Philosophy of Morals and Politics'; 'God and Evil').

Joan, mythical woman pope J-118

Joan (also called Joanna, or Joan the Mad) (1479–1555), queen of Castile, daughter of Ferdinand and Isabella, and mother of Emperor Charles V and Emperor Ferdinand I; did not actually rule because of mental deficiency
Austria-Hungary A-828
Ferdinand and Isabella F-54
Philip I P-282

Joannes, island, n.e. Brazil. *see in index* Marajó

Joan of Arc (1412–31) J-119
Charles VII C-277
France F-361
Henry V H-130
Hundred Years' War H-325
Orléans O-607
Rouen R-331

João Pessoa, Brazil, capital of state of Paraíba on Paraíba River; cement, footwear; trade in sugar, cotton, manioc; pop. 203,935, *map* B-425
South America, *map* S-418

Joash (or Jehoash), king of Israel, about 798–790 BC; expelled Syrians; captured Amaziah, king of Judah; plundered temple at Jerusalem (Bible, II Kings xiii–xiv).

Joash (or Jehoash), king of Judah, about 837–797 BC; slain by conspiracy of his servants (Bible, II Kings xi, xii; II Chronicles xxii–xxiv).

Job, long-suffering hero in the Book of Job in the Old Testament.

Jobs. *see in index* Vocation

Jobs, Steven (born 1955), U.S. electronics engineer C-47

Job's Coffin, constellation. *see in index* Delphinus

Job's-tears, a tall grass *(Coix lacryma-jobi)* named from hard, white oval seedcases, used in making beads; cultivated for food in some countries and for its supposed medicinal properties in China.

Jocasta, in Greek mythology; mother of Oedipus O-493

Jochum, Eugen (1902–87), Bavarian conductor, *list* O-579

Jockey, in horse racing H-276, *picture* H-275

Jockey Hollow, site in New Jersey where the Army encamped in 1779–80 N-54

Jodhpur, India, city in Rajasthan State; was capital of princely state Jodhpur (Marwar); gave name to riding breeches; pop. 317,612, *map* I-83

Jodl, Alfred (1890–1946), German general, born in Würzburg, Bavaria; signed World War II surrender May 7, 1945; executed as war criminal at Nuremberg 1946 W-336

Jodoshinsu (True Pure Sect), largest Buddhist sect in Japan B-483

Joel (5th century BC), Hebrew minor prophet, author of the Book of Joel, the 29th book of the Old Testament; he prophesied the judgments that were to come to Israel, and urged the people to repent.

Joel, Billy (born 1949), U.S. pop pianist and song composer, born on Long Island, N.Y.; albums include *Piano Man* (1973), *The Stranger* (1977), *52nd Street* (1978), *Glass Houses* (1980), *Innocent Man* (1983); won Grammy awards for best record, best song, best male vocals.

Joe-Pye weed, American perennial herb *Eupatorium purpureum* and *E. maculatum* with whorled leaves and end clusters of white, pink, or rose-purple flowers; often grows 12 ft (3½ m) high.

Joey, baby kangaroo K-172
Australia A-779

Joey, type of clown, also nickname for all clowns C-436

Joffre, Joseph-Jacques-Césaire (1852–1931), French general and marshal of France J-120

Joffrey, Robert (originally Abdullah Jaffa Bey Khan) (1930–88); choreographer and ballet dancer, born in Seattle; founded Joffrey Ballet D-24

Jogging, exercise J-121
weight control, *picture* W-136

Jogues, Saint Isaac (1607–46), French Jesuit missionary, born in Orléans; captured by Mohawks, first time mutilated, 2nd time killed, at Ossernenon (a Mohawk village now a part of Auriesville, N.Y.), today a place of Roman Catholic pilgrimage; feast day March 16.

Johanan ben Zakkai (died AD 80?), Jewish scholar, pupil of Hillel; after destruction of Jerusalem by Romans founded school outside Jerusalem that preserved Jewish law and learning.

Johannesburg, South Africa, in s. Transvaal, largest city in southern Africa; center of goldfields; pop. 1,536,400 J-122
Africa, *maps* A-115
South Africa S-395

Johanson, Donald C. (born 1943), U.S. anthropologist A-487, *picture* A-485

Johansson, Ingemar (born 1932), Swedish boxer, born in Göteborg B-392

John, saint, one of the Twelve Apostles, called the Evangelist; festival, Roman Catholicism, December 27, Anglican, May 6 A-506

John VIII, legendary pope J-118

John XXIII (1881–1963), pope J-123
College of Cardinals C-165
Paul VI P-156
Vatican II R-266, V-283

John XXIII (or Baldassare Cossa) (1370?–1419), antipope 1410–15; called Council of Constance by which he was deposed; imprisoned in Germany
Hus H-334

John V Palaeologus (1332–91), Byzantine emperor
Byzantine Empire B-536

John VI Cantacuzenus (1292–1383), statesman, Byzantine emperor, and historian B-536
Byzantine Empire B-536

John VIII Palaeologus (1392–1448), Byzantine emperor; responsible for Council of Ferrara-Florence 1438, which effected reunion of Eastern and Western Church; repudiation of union soon after hastened downfall of Byzantine Empire.

John, king of England. *see in index* John of England

John (1319–64), king of France, called the Good; enthroned 1350 at Poitiers; English prisoner after defeat at Poitiers (1356); died in England, unable to obtain ransom
Hundred Years' War H-325

John I Albert (1459–1501), king of Poland; reigned 1492–1501 J-12

John III, king of Poland. *see in index* Sobieski, John

John I (1357–1433), king of Portugal, called the Great and father of his country, chosen king 1385; father of Henry the Navigator.

John II (1455–95), king of Portugal, called the Perfect; known as able political leader and patron of Renaissance art and learning; refused help to Columbus C-591
Diaz D-133

John VI (1769–1826), king of Portugal; came to throne 1816 (regent from 1799); accepted Portugal's constitution after insurrection (1821) and recognized independence of Brazil (1825)
South America S-413

John, Augustus Edwin (1878–1961), British painter, born in Wales; powerful draftsmanship; portraits of David Lloyd George and George Bernard Shaw; elected member of Royal Academy of Arts 1928.

John, Elton (born 1947), British musician, born in Middlesex, England; worked mainly with lyricist Bernie Taupin; first Western rock singer to perform in U.S.S.R.; received Gold Discs for 'Elton John', 'Goodbye Yellow Brick Road', 'Captain Fantastic and the Brown Dirt Cowboy'.

John, Epistles of, 23rd, 24th, and 25th books of Bible's New Testament, attributed to Apostle John; first book, exhortations to Christian faith; second and third are short notes; authorship disputed B-183

John, Gospel of, 4th book of Bible's New Testament, attributed to Apostle John; authorship disputed; purpose to present life and works of Jesus so as to arouse faith in readers B-183
Apostles A-507

John Birch Society, U.S. organization; anti-Communist, politically right-wing; founded 1958 by Robert H.W. Welch; named for Capt. John Birch, U.S. Army officer, killed 1945 by Chinese Communists; known for extremism.

'John Brown's Body', U.S. Civil War song by Benét B-161
American literature A-356
poetry P-485
popular music M-681

John Brown University, in Siloam Springs, Ark; private control; established in 1919; arts and sciences, teacher education.

John Carroll University, in University Heights, near Cleveland, Ohio; Roman Catholic; established in 1886; arts and sciences, business, and education; graduate school C-495

John Crerar Library, in Chicago, Ill.; scientific library established 1894 by John Crerar, Chicago railroad magnate; famous collections include works on medicine, international law, and aeronautics.

John Day Fossil Beds National Monument, in Oregon N-52, *map* N-40

John Doe, fictitious name of plaintiff in action in which real plaintiff's name is withheld; a John Doe proceeding is a process to fix liability for a known wrong committed by an as yet unknown wrongdoer.

John Dory, gold or silvery food fish *(Zeus faber)* about 1 ft (30 cm) long, living in warm seas about Europe; legend says it is fish from which St. Peter took tribute money, dark spot on each side represents imprint of his thumb and finger.

John D. Rockefeller, Jr., Memorial Parkway, scenic corridor in Wyoming N-52

John Fitzgerald Kennedy National Historic Site, in Brookline, Mass. N-52

John F. Kennedy Center for the Performing Arts, cultural center in Washington, D.C. W-69

John F. Kennedy International Airport, New York, N.Y. N-257, 261
artistic symbolism A-669
Saarinen S-2

John F. Kennedy Plaza, in Philadelphia, Pa. P-278

John F. Kennedy Space Center. *see in index* Canaveral, Cape

John F. Slater Fund, established in 1882 by donation of $1,000,000 by John Fox Slater; for the education of Southern freedmen. *see also in index* Southern Education Foundation, Inc.

John Henry, legendary black hero of prodigious strength; worked himself to death trying to beat a machine, usually a rock drill, or, according to another version, a cotton-rolling machine; legend has been traced to drilling of Big Bend tunnel in Summers County, West Virginia, 1870–72
folklore F-266

'John Henry and His Hammer', work by Felton S-661

John Howard Association, prison reform H-312

John Mohegan. *see in index* Chingachgook

John Muir National Historic Site, in w.-central California N-52

John Newbery Medal. *see in index* Newbery Medal

Johnny and the Moondogs. *see in index* Beatles, the

'Johnny I Hardly Knew You', work by O'Brien I-328

Johnny-jump-up. *see in index* Wild pansy

John of Austria (or Don Juan) (1545–78), son of the Emperor Charles V and half brother of Philip II of Spain; victor over Turks (1571) in famous naval battle of Lepanto.

John of England (1167–1216), king of England J-124
democracy D-93
Eleanor of Aquitaine E-144
England E-241
habeas corpus H-2
Henry II H-129
Magna Carta M-41
Richard I R-218

John of Gaunt (1340–99), duke of Lancaster; 4th son of Edward III of England, ancestor of House of Lancaster and, through his daughters, of Tudor, Stuart, and Hanover-Windsor sovereigns of England
Henry IV H-129

John of Leiden (1509?–36), Dutch religious (Anabaptist) fanatic and revolutionary; ruled Kingdom of Zion in Münster; executed after capture of city; central figure in Meyerbeer's opera, 'The Prophet', produced 1849.

John of Pisa. *see in index* Pisano, Giovanni

John Paul I (1912–78), pope J-124

John Paul II (born 1920), pope J-124
assassination attempt E-355, I-398
liberation theology C-409
outdoor Mass, *picture* P-108

John Pennekamp Coral Reef State Park, in Florida K-230

Johns, Jasper (born 1930), U.S. painter, born in Augusta, Ga.; moved to South Carolina in youth; exhibits in U.S. and Europe
sculpture S-151

John's Hill, hill in Budapest, Hungary B-479

Johns Hopkins Glacier, active glacier in Alaska, *picture* I-6

Johns Hopkins University, in Baltimore, Md.; private control; opened 1876; arts and sciences, education, hygiene and public health, medicine; graduate schools; advanced international studies at Washington, D.C.; research activities at Baltimore, Md., Washington, D.C., Silver Spring, Md.; technical publications B-49, *map* B-48

John Sigismund (1572–1620), elector of Brandenburg
Prussia P-628

John Simon Guggenheim Memorial Foundation, founded in 1925 by Mr. and Mrs. Simon Guggenheim, in memory of their son, John Simon (died 1922) L-241

Johnson, Andrew (1808–75), 17th president of U.S. J-125
amnesty and pardon A-373
Grant G-218
impeachment I-58, U-210
Reconstruction period R-120
Stanton S-579
Tennessee T-88
United States U-167
veto power V-331

Johnson, Ban (1864–1931), U.S. baseball league organizer B-96

Johnson, Ben (born 1961), world's fastest man on record despite Olympic disgrace for drug abuse, born in Falmouth, Jamaica; to Canada 1976; performed indifferently in track until 1977–78 spurt in height and weight; took up weight lifting to develop supermuscular upper torso; unusual strength and unorthodox stance of starting races with elbows bent were considered keys to his ability to break out of the block with extraordinary acceleration; by 1985 developed strong finish as well and began winning races (his rocket starts sometimes protested, but judged legal); on Aug. 30, 1987, ran 100 meters in 9.83 seconds; broke his own world record with 9.79-second race in 1988 Olympic Games, but stripped of gold medal after testing positive for steroids;

Johnson, Byron / Johnstown

two-year ban from world competition (lifetime ban by Canada) as well as loss of big advertising contracts; in 1989 drug probe admitted to regular injections of illegal drugs through 1980s.

Johnson, Byron Bancroft (1864–1931), U.S. baseball organizer and first president (1901–27) of American League, born in Norwalk, Ohio B-96

Johnson, Charles Spurgeon (1893–1956), U.S. sociologist, born in Bristol, Va.; made head of Fisk University October 1946; wrote of black Americans' problems ('Ebony and Topaz'; 'Negro in American Civilization'; 'Black Man's Burden').

Johnson, Daniel (1915–68), Canadian political leader, born in Danville, Que.; leader Union Nationale party 1961–68; premier province of Quebec 1966–68.

Johnson, Earvin, (Magic) (born 1959), U.S. basketball player, born in Lansing, Mich.; attended Michigan State University 1977–79; played on NCAA championship team 1979; played for Los Angeles Lakers 1979– ; on NBA all-star team 1980, 1982–84; named league's most valuable player 1987, 1989.

Johnson, Edward (1881–1959), U.S. tenor, born in Guelph, Ont.; sang five seasons at La Scala in Milan, Italy; member Chicago and Metropolitan Opera companies; general manager Metropolitan Opera Assn., Inc., New York City, 1935–50.

Johnson, Emily Pauline (1861–1913), Canadian poet, born near Brantford, Ont.; daughter of Mohawk Indian chief and English mother ('Flint and Feather', collected poems; 'Legends of Vancouver', Indian tales) C-121

Johnson, Esther (Stella) (1681–1728), friend of Jonathan Swift S-732

Johnson, Eyvind (1900–76), Swedish author, born in Svarbjörnsbyn; wrote more than 40 novels and short-story collections, including 'Olof' cycle of autobiographical novels; a fellow of the Swedish Academy
- Scandinavian literature S-88

Johnson, Garret (or Gerard Johnson, or Garratt Johnson, or Geraert Janssen) (fl. 1616), Dutch sculptor and tomb maker who lived in London.

Johnson, Guy, U.S. superintendent of Indian affairs
- portrait by West P-50, *picture* P-49

Johnson, Harold Keith (1912–83), U.S. Army officer, born in Bowesmont, N.D.; commandant Command and General Staff College 1960–63; Army deputy chief of staff for operations 1963–64; chief of staff 1964–68.

Johnson, Hiram Warren (1866–1945), U.S. lawyer and political leader, born in Sacramento, Calif.; as prosecuting attorney convicted Ruef, chief of San Francisco boodlers; governor of California 1911–17; elected to U.S. Senate 1917.

Johnson, Hugh Samuel (1882–1942), U.S. soldier, lawyer, born in Ft. Scott, Kan.; in charge of U.S. draft 1917–18; NRA administrator 1933–34; editorial commentator for newspaper and radio after 1934
- National Recovery Administration R-302

Johnson, Jack (1878–1946), U.S. boxer J-128
- heavyweight champion B-391

Johnson, James P. (1891?–1955), U.S. jazz pianist, born in New Brunswick, N.J.; also songwriter J-87

Johnson, James Weldon (1871–1938), U.S. writer, educator, diplomat, born in Jacksonville, Fla.; professor Fisk University 1930–38; edited 'Book of Negro Spirituals'; wrote 'God's Trombones', poems; 'Along This Way', autobiography; won 1925 Spingarn medal for literature B-294, 302, *list* B-299

Johnson, John (1742–1830), Loyalist, born near Johnstown, N.Y.; son of Sir William Johnson; kept the Six Nations on British side during Revolutionary War.

Johnson, John H. (born 1918), U.S. editor and publisher, born in Arkansas City, Ark.; president Johnson Publishing Company, publishers of *Ebony* 1945–, *Jet* 1951–, *Hue* 1953–59; won 1966 Spingarn medal.

Johnson, John Mercer (1818–68), Canadian politician and lawyer; born in Liverpool, England C-118, *picture* C-116

Johnson, Josephine Winslow (born 1910), U.S. novelist and poet, born in Kirkwood, Mo.; 1934 Pulitzer prize for first novel 'Now in November'; mature and subtle in portrayal of emotion; poetic and sensitive in style ('Winter Orchard'; 'Jordanstown'; 'Year's End'; 'The Dark Traveler').

Johnson, Lady Bird (originally Claudia Alta Taylor) (born 1912), wife of President Lyndon B. Johnson J-130, *pictures* J-133, U-183

Johnson, Louis Arthur (1891–1966), U.S. lawyer and government official, born in Roanoke, Va.; asst. secretary of war 1937–40; secretary of defense March 1949–Sept. 1950.

Johnson, Lyndon B. (1908–73), 36th president of U.S. J-129
- human resource policies C-678
- Lyndon B. Johnson N.H.P. N-53
- Kennedy's assassination K-203, 205, T-123, *pictures* K-201, 205
- Ku Klux Klan K-309
- Texas ranch, *picture* T-130
- United States U-181, *picture* U-183
- Vietnam War V-348

Johnson, Martin Elmer (1884–1937), U.S. explorer and author, born in Rockford, Ill.; with his wife, Osa Johnson, made motion-picture records of expeditions to South Seas, Borneo, Australia, Africa; killed in plane accident; wrote, with his wife, 'Cannibal Land', 'Camera Trails in Africa', 'Safari', 'Lion'.

Johnson, Mordecai Wyatt (1890–1976), U.S. educator, born near Paris, Tenn.; became first black American to hold presidency of Howard University, president 1926–60; won 1929 Spingarn medal (education).

Johnson, Osa Helen (1894–1953), U.S. explorer, writer, and motion-picture producer; born in Chanute, Kan.; in 'Over African Jungles', 'I Married Adventure', she told of experiences with her husband, Martin Johnson.

Johnson, Owen McMahon (1878–1952), U.S. author, born in New York City; son of Robert Underwood Johnson; won popularity for his school and college stories ('The Varmint'; 'The Tennessee Shad'; 'Stover at Yale'); novels of contemporary social life ('The Salamander'; 'Sacrifice'); plays ('The Comet'; 'A Comedy for Wives').

Johnson, Philip Cortelyou (born 1906), U.S. architect, born in Cleveland, Ohio; director department of architecture and design Museum of Modern Art 1946–54; co-architect Seagram Building, New York City; architect glass house, New Canaan, Conn.; Rappite shrine, New Harmony, Ind.; New York State Theater, Lincoln Center, New York City A-566, 569
- interior design, *pictures* I-251
- 190 S. LaSalle Building, *picture* A-669

Johnson, Rafer Lewis (born 1935), U.S. track athlete, born in Hillsboro, Tex.; set world and Olympics records in decathlon 1960; won Sullivan Trophy 1960.

Johnson, Reverdy (1796–1876), U.S. political leader and jurist, born in Annapolis, Md.; U.S. senator; attorney general; minister to England; treaty he negotiated for adjustment of *Alabama* Claims rejected.

Johnson, Richard (fl. 18th century), Australian chaplain A-792

Johnson, Richard Mentor (1780–1850), U.S. statesman and soldier, born near Louisville, Ky.; 9th vice-president of U.S.; only vice-president ever elected by the Senate.

Johnson, Robert, (1912-38), U.S. blues singer
- popular music M-678

Johnson, Robert Underwood (1853–1937), U.S. editor, diplomat, and poet; born in Washington, D.C.; editor *Century* 1909–13; ambassador to Italy 1920–21 ('The Winter Hour'; 'Italian Rhapsody'; 'Remembered Yesterdays').

Johnson, Samuel (1709–84), British writer J-136
- art of conversation C-695, *picture* C-694
- Boswell B-376
- cat, *list* C-202
- Garrick G-36
- literary contribution E-272
  - biography standards B-222
  - dictionaries R-132
  - magazines M-32
  - novel N-408
- Milton M-419
- Newbery N-151
- spelling S-526

Johnson, Tom Loftin (1854–1911), U.S. municipal reformer and iron manufacturer, born in Georgetown, Ky.; mayor of Cleveland 1901–09; strenuous advocate of single tax, public ownership of utilities; called father of 3-cent streetcar fare C-495

Johnson, Uwe (1934–84), German novelist G-108

Johnson, Walter Perry (Barney) (1887–1946), U.S. baseball pitcher, born in Humboldt, Kan.; with Washington, A.L., 1907–27; called the greatest fastball pitcher in baseball history; won 414 games (2nd highest total) for team that often finished in 2nd division; set many strike-out and shutout records B-92

Johnson, William (1715–74), British colonial landowner and soldier; father of Sir John Johnson; superintendent of Indian affairs in North America; influence with Indians of Six Nations kept them neutral in French and Indian War.

Johnson, William (1899–1989), U.S. baseball player, born in Snow Hill, Md.; third baseman, Negro leagues 1918–38.

Johnson, William Samuel (1727–1819), U.S. statesman, born in Stratford, Conn.; colonial agent in London for Connecticut (1767–71); his conservative attitude toward Revolutionary War cause changed to able work in Constitutional Convention; signed United States Constitution; president of Columbia College (now Columbia University) (1787–1800).

Johnson City, N.Y., industrial village 2 mi (3 km) w. of Binghamton; shoes, ordnance, reproduction machines, felt; pop. 17,126
- New York, *map* N-268

Johnson City, Tenn., city in resort area 92 mi (148 km) n.e. of Knoxville; textile products, hardwood flooring, furniture, tobacco, food products, brick; East Tennessee State University; Veterans Administration hospital; pop. 39,753 T-85, *map* T-98

Johnson City, Tex., town 44 mi (71 km) w. of Austin; early home of Lyndon B. Johnson; pop. 872
- Texas, *map* T-136

Johnson County War, in Wyoming
- cowboy C-753
- frontier F-423

Johnson C. Smith University, in Charlotte, N.C.; Presbyterian; founded 1867 as Biddle Memorial Institute; arts and sciences, education, theology.

Johnson of Boone, Benj. F. *see in index* Riley, James Whitcomb

Johnson-Sea-Link, submersible O-463

Johnson Shut-ins State Park, in Missouri, *picture* M-498

Johnson Space Center, in Houston, Tex. H-311, *picture* H-310

Johnson State College, in Johnson, Vt.; established in 1867; formerly a teachers' college; liberal arts, teacher education; graduate studies.

Johnston, Albert Sidney (1803–62), U.S. soldier, born in Mason County, Ky.; one of ablest Confederate generals; leader in struggle for Texas' independence
- Shiloh C-480

Johnston, Alexander (1849–89), U.S. historian, born in Brooklyn, N.Y.; admitted to bar 1876; professor of jurisprudence and political economy at Princeton University after 1883 ('History of American Politics'; 'American Political History, 1763–1876'; 'History of Connecticut').

Johnston, Alvanley (1875–1951), U.S. labor leader, born in Seeley's Bay, near Kingston, Ont.; headed Brotherhood of Locomotive Engineers 1925–51.

Johnston, Edward (1872–1944) British teacher of calligraphy who had great influence on 20th century typography and calligraphy; called father of modern revival of lettering C-59

Johnston, Eric Allen (1896–1963), U.S. industrialist, born in Washington, D.C.; organizer and president, electric companies, Spokane, Wash.; president of U.S. Chamber of Commerce 1942–46, of Motion Picture Producers and Distributors of America 1945–63, took leave of absence to serve as administrator of Economic Stabilization Agency 1951; special representative of Presidents F.D. Roosevelt, Truman, and Eisenhower.

Johnston, Harriet Lane (1833–1903), niece and hostess of President Buchanan B-475

Johnston, Harry Hamilton (1858–1927), British administrator, African explorer, zoologist, and author; originator of plan for British Cape-to-Cairo route; author of books on Africa as well as several novels; in 'The Gay-Dombeys' and 'The Veneerings' he follows the careers of supposed descendants of characters in novels by Charles Dickens.

Johnston, Joseph Eggleston (1807–91), U.S. soldier, born near Farmville, Va.; served in Black Hawk, Seminole, and Mexican wars with distinguished gallantry; became Confederate general 1861; commanded early operations against McClellan in Peninsular Campaign; Fabian tactics against Sherman in Georgia campaign won his opponent's praise as "the equal in all the elements of generalship to Lee"; elected to U.S. Congress 1876
- Civil War C-473
- First Bull Run C-480
- Sherman N-360, S-238

Johnston, Mary (1870–1936), U.S. novelist, born in Buchanan, Va.; author of popular historical romances ('Prisoners of Hope'; 'To Have and to Hold'; 'Sir Mortimer').

Johnston, R.I., 5 mi (8 km) w. of Providence; granite quarries; once part of Providence, separate town 1759; pop. of township 24,907, *map* R-210

Johnston Atoll, U.S. naval base in the Pacific about 700 mi (1,150 km) s.w. of Honolulu; area less than ½ sq mi (1.3 sq km); taken over by U.S. in 1918; U.S. atomic-testing site 1958 and 1962; pop. 1,007.

Johnstown, N.Y., manufacturing city of historic interest, 40 mi (65 km) n.w. of Albany; leather, gloves, knit goods, gelatin, metal products; courthouse built in 1762 named national monument; city named for Sir William Johnson whose mansion, built in 1762, still stands; pop. 9,360
- New York, *map* N-268

Johnstown, Pa., city 58 mi (93 km) s.e. of Pittsburgh, on Conemaugh River, in soft-coal district; iron and steel mills; machine tools, textile products, food processing; Johnstown Center, branch of University of Pittsburgh; flood of 1889 took about 2,200 lives; pop. 35,496 P-188, *map* P-205
- United States, *picture* U-106

Jordan / Jude

Jordan River, river of Syria, Israel, and Jordan; 200 mi (320 km) long J-143
  Dead Sea D-45
  Israel I-369
  Jordan J-141
  Palestine P-84
  Sea of Galilee G-5
Jordan River, river in Utah, flows from n. end of Utah Lake into Great Salt Lake
  Great Salt Lake G-250
  Utah, *map* U-259
Jörmungand, evil serpent in Norse mythology M-703
Joseffy, Rafael (1852–1915), U.S. pianist and composer, born in Hungary; after 1880 lived in New York and was famous as teacher and concert virtuoso; author of 'School of Advanced Piano Playing'.
Joseph, saint, husband of Mary the mother of Jesus; patron of the workingman; festival March 19 J-103
Joseph I (1678–1711), Holy Roman emperor, succeeded to throne 1705; vigorously prosecuted wars against France and Hungary, and forced pope to acknowledge his brother Charles as king of Spain.
Joseph II (1741–90), Holy Roman emperor, son of Maria Theresa; benevolent despot; upset old customs and provoked discontent and revolt; died disillusioned and unhappy A-830
  Mozart M-643
  Potemkin P-563
Joseph, Hebrew patriarch, son of Jacob and Rachel; father of Ephraim and Manasseh (Bible, Gen. xxxvii) F-259
Joseph, Chief (1840?–1904), chief of Nez Percé J-143
  Montana M-551
'Joseph and His Brothers', novel by Mann M-109
'Joseph Andrews', novel by Fielding F-79
  English literature E-272
'Joseph and the Amazing Technicolor Dreamcoat', a Broadway production, *picture* F-259
Josephine (1763–1814), empress of France J-144
  Napoleon N-15
Joseph of Arimathea, rich Israelite who entombed the body of Jesus in his own sepulcher; commemorated as saint March 17.
Joseph's-coat, an annual plant *(Amaranthus tricolor)* of the amaranth family, native to tropical regions; leaves thin, oval, pointed; each leaf has several colors in it, giving a patched appearance.
Josephson, Brian D. (born 1940), British physicist, born in Cardiff, Wales; research in superconductivity and electron tunneling in solids; discovered Josephson effect used in measuring magnetic fields; professor of physics Cambridge University 1974–.
Josephson, Matthew (1899–1978), U.S. author, born in Brooklyn, N.Y. (biographies: 'Victor Hugo', 'Stendhal', 'Sidney Hillman', 'Edison'; U.S. economic and political studies: 'The Robber Barons' and 'The President Makers'; memoirs: 'Life Among the Surrealists', 'Infidel in the Temple').
Josephson junction, electronic device to provide superconductivity E-176
Josephus, Flavius (AD 37?–100), Jewish historian ('The Jewish War', 170 BC–AD 70; 'The Jewish Antiquities', from earliest time to reign of Nero) H-172
  educational views E-78
  Herod H-141
Joshua, sixth book of Bible's Old Testament, named for Joshua, successor to Moses; account of Israelites' settlement in Canaan
  espionage E-305
Joshua tree (also called Joshua yucca, or yucca palm, or tree yucca), a species of yucca *(Yucca brevifolia)* native to w. and s.w. U.S.; clusters of stiff spikelike leaves N-52
Joshua Tree National Monument, in s. California N-52, *map* N-40
Josiah (645?–608 BC), king of Judah; abolished idolatry and reestablished worship of Jehovah (Bible, II Kings xxii–xxiii)
  Jeremiah J-98
Joslin, Elliott Proctor (1869–1962), U.S. physician, born in Oxford, Mass.; joined faculty of Harvard Medical School 1898, clinical professor 1922–37; authority on diabetes.
Joslyn Art Museum, cultural center in Omaha, Neb. O-543
Josquin (1440?–1521), Flemish composer J-144
  vocal music V-388
Joss, Adrian (1880–1911), U.S. baseball player, born in Juneau, Wis.; pitcher for Cleveland A.L. 1902–10; 45 shutouts in 160 career victories.
Joss flower (or Chinese sacred lily), type of narcissus N-18
Jostedalsbreen, glacier in Norway N-389
Jota, Spanish dance of exaggerated pattern and movement performed, usually by a couple, with castanets.
Jot Travis Dining Commons, building on University of Nevada at Reno campus, Reno, Nev., *picture* N-140
Jotunheim, in Norse mythology, land of frost giants M-703
Jotunheimen, mountain range in Norway N-389
Joubert, Joseph (1754–1824), French philosopher and writer, born in Montignac, near Périgueux, France; famed for brilliance of his conversation and correspondence.
Joubert, Petrus Jacobus (1834–1900), Boer general, commandant general in 1st and 2nd Boer wars; repelled Jameson Raid.
Jouffroy d'Abbans, Claude François Dorothée, marquis de (1751–1832), French inventor; pioneer in steam navigation; forerunner of Fulton.
Jouhaux, Léon (1879–1954), French labor leader, born in Paris; delegate to Versailles Peace Conference 1919 and League of Nations 1925–28; became head of General Confederation of Labor 1909, withdrew 1947 to found Workers' Force, anti-Communist labor union.
Joule, James Prescott (1818–89), British physicist, born in Salford, Lancashire; a large inheritance enabled him to devote his life to research; important work in subjects of heat, thermodynamics, electricity H-106
  scientific breakthroughs, *list* S-115
Joule, unit of energy equal to 10 million ergs; named for James Prescott Joule.
Journal M-31. *see also in index* Magazine
'Journal', work by Thoreau P-480
Journalism
  newspaper. *see in index* Newspaper
  public relations P-646
'Journal of a Tour to the Hebrides', work by Boswell
  Boswell B-376
'Journal to Stella', diary by Swift S-733
'Journey from Saint Petersburg to Moscow, A', book by Radishchev U-33
Journeyman, in medieval guild G-313
  apprenticeship A-511
  labor L-2
  labor movements L-6
'Journey to the Seven Streams, A', work by Kiely I-328
Joust (or just), knighthood combat K-258, *picture* K-259
  Middle Ages, *picture* M-389
Jouvenel, Henry de (1876–1935), French political leader and writer; editor *Le Matin* 1905–24; delegate League of Nations 1922 and 1924; minister public instruction 1924; high commissioner Syria 1925; wrote 'The Stormy Life of Mirabeau'; first wife was Mme. Colette, the French novelist.
Jovanovic, Jovan (1833–1904), Serbian poet and journalist; pen name Zmaj (the dragon) from one of two humorous periodicals he founded; educated in law and medicine; best known for his lyrics and humorous poems ('Saran', a play; 'Faded Roses', verse).
Jove, in Roman mythology. *see in index* Jupiter
Jovian (Flavius Jovianus) (331–364), Roman emperor, *list* R-275
Jovian planets S-375
Jowett, Benjamin (1817–93), British scholar, theologian, and teacher; master of Balliol College, Oxford University; great influence on English life through eminent pupils; translated works of Plato, Aristotle, and Thucydides.
Joyce, James (1882–1941), Irish writer J-144
  artistic style A-667
  literature L-243
    'A Portrait of the Artist as a Young Man' N-411
  English E-281
  Irish I-328, *picture* I-327
  short story S-276
  Svevo I-377
  Woolf W-292
Joyner-Kersee, Jackie (born 1962), U.S. athlete
  athletics A-741
  track and field T-245
Joystick, computer device C-630
Juan, Don. *see in index* Don Juan legend
Juan Carlos I (born 1938), king of Spain J-145
  House of Bourbon B-384
  Spain S-499
Juan de Fuca, Strait of, strait in the Pacific Ocean between Vancouver Island in Canada and Washington in the U.S. W-48, *maps* C-109, W-49, 65
  North America, *map* N-350
  United States, *map* U-193
Juan Fernández, group of three small islands in South Pacific; Más a Tierra (Isla Róbinson Crusoe), which ranks as largest, Más Afuera (Isla Alejandro Selkirk), and Santa Clara; explored by Juan Fernández in 1574; owned by Chile; name formerly applied only to Más a Tierra; pop. 540
  national park status N-27
  South America, *map* S-418
Juárez, Benito Pablo (1806–72), Mexican statesman J-145
  Mexico M-336
Juárez, Mexico. *see in index* Ciudad Juárez
Jubal, son of Lamech and Adah; called father of musicians (Bible, Gen. iv, 21); traditional inventor of musical instruments (harp and organ).
Juba River, river in Africa, rises in Ethiopia and flows s.e. to Indian Ocean
  Somalia S-386
Jubbulpore (or Jabalpur), India, manufacturing and trading city in Madhya Pradesh state; makes cotton goods, wire netting, statuary; once home of Thugs, society of religious assassins; pop. 426,224, *map* I-83
Jubilee, diamond, *picture* D-129
Jubilee, in Jewish history, every 50th year from entrance of Hebrews into Canaan to be set aside for rejoicing, Israelite slaves to be freed, alienated ancestral possessions to be restored, no sowing or reaping of land; term now applied to 50th anniversary of any event, or to a season of rejoicing.
Júcar River, river in e. Spain; about 310 mi (500 km) to the Mediterranean S-489
Juchi, son of Genghis Khan M-534
Judah, Hebrew patriarch, 4th son of Jacob and Leah, traditional ancestor of tribe of Judah, one of the 12 tribes of Israel.
Judah, s. kingdom of Palestine; remained faithful to house of David after break in kingdom of the Jews; cap. Jerusalem. *see also in index* Judea
  Jeremiah J-98
Judah Halevy (1085–1141?), Spanish poet, rabbi, and philosopher; born in Toledo; famed Hebrew writer; religious and secular poetry; prose work 'Sefer ha-Kuzari' declared superiority of faith over logic.
Judah ha-Nasi (AD 135?–220?), scholar and rabbi who collected Jewish Oral Law into the Mishna, the code of religious and civil laws governing society T-18
Judaism, religion J-146
  beliefs
    bioethical issues B-214
    creation W-296
    ethics and morality E-310
    God G-173
    mythology M-698
  calendar C-29
  church and state C-409
  comparative religions
    Asian religions A-683
    Christianity C-397
    Islam I-359, K-268
  discrimination
    martyrdom M-161
    migration M-402
    minority group M-461
    refugees R-147
    segregation S-168
  education E-78
    religious education R-156
      Bar mitzvah. *see in index* Bar mitzvah
      Bas mitzvah. *see in index* Bas mitzvah
  history
    Abraham A-12
    Amsterdam A-381
    ancient Egypt B-318
    Arab-Israeli conflicts H-6
    Australia H-179
    Babylon B-3
    Baeck B-17
    Denmark C-463
    England E-106, E-233
    Europe E-337
    France F-349
    Germany G-123
      concentration camps C-638
      genocide G-60
      Hitler H-175
      Holocaust H-205
    India I-69
    Jesus Christ J-103
    Moses M-595
    New York City N-272, 275
    Paul P-155
    Persia P-229
    Philo P-457
    Sa'adia ben Joseph S-2
    United Nations U-83
    Warsaw W-34
  holy days F-67
    citron used C-447
    Hanukka. *see in index* Hanukka
    Passover P-148
    Rosh Hashana N-243
    Yom Kippur. *see in index* Yom Kippur
  Israel I-369, 373, M-395, *map* I-371, *pictures* I-370, 372
  language. *see in index* Hebrew language; Yiddish
  literature. *see also in index* Hebrew literature
    American fiction A-362
    Bible B-181, 184
    Dead Sea scrolls D-47
    folklore F-263
    Josephus H-172
    storytelling S-646, 657
    Talmud T-18
    Torah T-227
    Yiddish literature Y-416
  religious movements
    revivalism R-180
    Zionism Z-455
      Herzl H-145
  rites and practices
    ancestor veneration A-204
    birth control B-283
    circumcision C-422
    fasting F-44
    marriage M-151
    meat consumption M-247, M-253
    monks and monasticism M-539, 542
    names N-7
    pilgrimage P-383
    vegetarianism V-289
Judas, Saint (also called Saint Jude, or Saint Thaddeus), one of the Twelve Apostles; said to have been martyred; festival October 28 A-506
Judas Iscariot, disciple who betrayed Jesus for 30 pieces of silver (Bible, Matthew xxvi, 14–16, 25, 47–50) A-506
  Jesus Christ J-104
Judas Maccabaeus. *see in index* Maccabees
Judas tree. *see in index* Redbud
Judd, Charles Hubbard (1873–1946), U.S. psychologist, born in Bareilly, India; professor at Yale University and University of Chicago; made many surveys of schools.
Jude, Saint. *see in index* Judas, Saint
'Jude, Der', journal edited by Buber B-473
Jude, Epistle of, twenty-sixth book of Bible's New Testament; doubtful authorship, often attributed to Judas Thaddeus (St. Jude); contains exhortation to constancy in Christian faith B-183

Judea / Jupiter

Judea (or Judaea, or Judah), a Greek and Roman name for s. Palestine; in time of Jesus part of province of Syria and also kingdom of the Herods; in Roman times southernmost division of Palestine.

Judeo-Spanish language (or Sephardic language), in Spain R-267

'Jude the Obscure', work by Hardy N-413

Judge, in law
courts of justice C-746
criminal law C-776
jury system J-159
law L-94
Supreme Court S-712, U-201

Judge advocate general, U.S. Air Force, Army, and Navy; has charge of legal matters arising in his or her respective department A-646

Judges, Book of, seventh book of the Bible's Old Testament; describes history of Israelites under the rule of the Judges.

Judgment, in law, *table* L-93

Judicial review
administrative law A-46
bureaucratic limitation B-505
constitutional law C-685, 686
supreme courts S-712, 713, U-200

Judicial sale, acquisition of property S-615

Judiciary. *see in index* Courts of justice

Judiciary Act (1789), United States court decision
constitutional law C-686
Supreme Court S-711, U-220

Judiciary Act of 1925, U.S. law S-711

Judith, Jewish heroine, captivated Assyrian general Holofernes and killed him while he slept, thereby delivering the besieged Israelites; story told in book of Judith in the Apocrypha.

'Judith of Bethulia' (1913), early silent film spectacle by Griffith M-618

Judo W-366
Japan J-57

Judson, Adoniram (1788–1850), missionary to India J-151
Baptists B-76

Judson, Clara Ingram (1879–1960), U.S. writer of children's books, born in Logansport, Ind. ('Mary Jane' series of stories; biographies: 'Soldier Doctor; the Story of William Gorgas', 'Abraham Lincoln, Friend of the People', 'George Washington, Leader of the People', 'Thomas Jefferson, Champion of the People', 'Benjamin Franklin'; Sault Sainte Marie Canal history: 'Mighty Soo'; 'St. Lawrence Seaway'); Laura Ingalls Wilder Award, 1960.

Judson, Edward Zane Carroll (pen name Ned Buntline) (1823–86), U.S. author and adventurer; originator of the dime or pulp novel W-151

Judson, Harry Pratt (1849–1927), U.S. educator, born in Jamestown, N.Y.; educated Williams College; teacher and principal high school, Troy, N.Y.; professor history University of Minnesota; at University of Chicago after 1892, first as professor political science; as president 1907–23; writer on political science and history.

Judson, Wilfred (born 1902), Canadian jurist, born in Todmorden, England; to Canada 1923; admitted to Ontario bar 1932; justice of Supreme Court of Ontario 1951–58, Supreme Court of Canada 1958–77.

Judson College, in Elgin, Ill.; Baptist; founded 1963; liberal arts, education.

Judson College, in Marion, Ala.; affiliated with Southern Baptist Convention; founded 1838; opened 1839; arts and sciences, teacher education.

Judy. *see in index* Punch-and-Judy show

Jug (also called geophone), device used in petroleum exploration P-255

Juggernaut. *see in index* Jagannath

Jug hustler, profession in the petroleum field P-265

Juglandaceae. *see in index* Walnut family

Jugoslavia. *see in index* Yugoslavia

Jugular vein, a large vein in the neck, *pictures* A-395–8

Jugurtha (died 104 BC), usurping king of Numidia; defied Roman power for several years, defeating and bribing opposing generals; captured by Marius
Rome R-274

Juhl, Finn (born 1912), Danish furniture designer and architect F-462

Juilliard, Augustus D. (1836–1919), U.S. businessman, born in Canton, Ohio; head of dry-goods commission house, New York; prominent in banking and insurance.

Juilliard School, The, in New York City; private control; founded 1905; located at Lincoln Center after 1969; music, dance, drama; concurrent studies in humanities or liberal arts; graduate study N-254, 273
string quartet, *picture* S-672

Juiz de Fora, Brazil, manufacturing city on Paraibuna River about 90 mi (145 km) n. of Rio de Janeiro; knitted goods; lumber, coffee, sugar, cotton; pop. 224,275, *map* B-425
South America, *map* S-418

Jujitsu (or jujutsu) W-366
Japan J-57

Jujube, a genus *(Zizyphus)* of shrubs and trees grown for foliage and small, brown, fleshy, oval fruits; used in candy or as preserved fruit; believed to have originated in Syria, carried by Romans to Europe, now found in all tropical regions; common, or Chinese, jujube grows to 40 ft (12 m); leaves oval, with 2 spines at base; flowers small, green or white, in clusters.

Jukes, fictitious name of a family in New York State investigated by R.L. Dugdale and known for large percentage of pauperism and criminality; records of 709 of 1,200 members show 280 paupers, 140 criminals, and large proportion of moral and physical deviates. *see also in index* Kallikak

Juku (or cram school), school in Japan T-208

Julia Augusta. *see in index* Livia Drusilla

Julian (Flavius Claudius Julianus) (331–363), Roman emperor, called the Apostate; nephew of Constantine the Great; brought up as Christian, became philosophic pagan; proclaimed emperor by army 361; able ruler and last pagan emperor, *list* R-275

Julian, Percy Lavon (1899–1975), U.S. chemist, born in Montgomery, Ala.; known for fundamental organic research and for research made with soybeans; synthesized chemicals to combat glaucoma and arthritis; achieved first successful method for commercial isolation of soya sterols and bulk preparation of the hormones progesterone and testosterone from these sterols; won 1947 Spingarn medal for chemistry; studied and taught at DePauw University in Greencastle, Ind. B-260, 302

Juliana (born 1909), queen of The Netherlands 1948–80
Beatrix B-119

Julian Alps, mountains in n.w. Yugoslavia, *maps* B-25, I-404

Julian calendar (or Old Style calendar, or O.S. calendar) C-28
Caesar C-15

Julius II (1443–1513), pope J-151

Julius Caesar. *see in index* Caesar, Gaius Julius

'Julius Caesar', tragedy by Shakespeare, written about 1599; relates story of death of Caesar, portraying characters of Brutus and Mark Antony; ends with Brutus' death.

Julius Nepos. *see in index* Nepos, Julius

Julius Rosenwald Fund, founded 1917 in Chicago, Ill., for (1) improving rural education, especially in the South; (2) developing leadership among black and white Southerners through fellowships; (3) facilitating advanced education and health among blacks F-333. *see also in index* Rosenwald, Julius

July, 7th month of the Gregorian calendar
birthdays of famous persons. *see in index* Birthdays, *table*
calendar C-30

July Fourteenth (or Bastille Day), national independence festival of France, celebrating the fall of the Bastille F-66

July Revolution, in Paris, France. *see in index* Revolution of 1830

Jumbo, Barnum circus elephant B-81

Jumbo, mine device M-428

Jumeau bisque, extremely fine type of porcelain made famous by the French Jumeau family; used in bisque dolls D-221

Jumna River. *see in index* Yamuna River

Jump band, small swing band M-677

Jump cutting, movie editing technique M-613

Jumper, military uniform U-16

Jumping, in equestrian sports E-295

Jumping bean (also called Mexican jumping bean, or bronco bean), triangular seeds of any of several Latin American swamp trees of the spurge family, containing the full-grown larva of a small gray moth; when a seedpod falls to ground the larva jumps and rolls, taking the bean with it.

Jumping event, in track and field T-244

Jumping mouse, North American mouse with very long hind legs; able to leap 9–15 ft (3–5 m) M-640

Jumping spider, arachnid of the family Salticidae S-536, 539

Jump River, river in n.-central Wisconsin, rises in Price County and flows 70 mi (115 km) s.w. to Holcombe Flowage at Chippewa River
Wisconsin, *map* W-265

Junco, bird of the family Fringillidae, *picture* B-260

Junction City, Kan., city about 61 mi (98 km) w. of Topeka, at junction of Smoky Hill and Republican rivers; trade center for agricultural and livestock area, mobile homes, clothing; Fort Riley nearby; pop. 19,305
Kansas, *map* K-186

June, 6th month of the Gregorian calendar
birthdays of famous persons. *see in index* Birthdays, *table*
calendar C-30

Juneau, Solomon Laurent (1793–1856), U.S. pioneer, born near Montreal, Que.; first mayor of Milwaukee, Wis. (1846) M-422

Juneau, Alaska, state capital, on inlet of Pacific 100 mi (160 km) n. of Sitka; pop. 19,528 J-152
Alaska A-242, *maps* A-240, 254, *picture* A-249
North America, *map* N-350
state capitals, *list* S-595
United States U-144

'Juneau', U.S. naval ship W-345

Juneautown, Wisconsin, town founded in 1835 by Solomon Juneau M-422

Juneberry. *see in index* Shadbush

June bug (or May beetle)
larva, *picture* L-51

Jung, Carl (1875–1961), Swiss analytical psychologist J-152
psychiatry P-631
psychoanalysis P-634
Switzerland S-740

Jünger, Ernst (born 1895), German novelist, born in Heidelberg; realistic novels influenced by his experiences in World Wars I and II G-109

Jungfrau (maiden), Alpine peak 13,667 ft (4,166 m) in Switzerland; scientific station for study of cosmos, human body at high altitudes, other phenomena S-738, *picture* S-741

Jungle J-153
forest types F-309

'Jungle, The', novel of social criticism by Sinclair (1906); on Chicago Stockyards S-301
food and drug laws F-274
public relations P-646
Roosevelt R-318
social criticism N-412

'Jungle Books, The', two collections of animal stories by Kipling; 'The Jungle Book' and 'The Second Jungle Book'
Kipling K-249

Jungle cat (or swamp cat), wild cat *(Felis chaus)*, *picture* C-214

'Jungle Peace', work by Beebe B-130

Juniata College, in Huntingdon, Pa.; private control; established in 1876; arts and sciences, teacher education.

Junior, Democritus. *see in index* Burton, Robert

Junior Achievement, Inc., U.S. organization founded 1919 in Springfield, Mass.; provides young people of high-school age with practical business experience by helping them to organize, finance, and operate miniature companies of their own under guidance of business-executive volunteers; offers scholarships, awards, trips for outstanding achievement; operates in United States and Canada; headquarters Stamford, Conn. Y-431

Junior Classical League, second largest youth organization in U.S.; membership open to junior high school and high school students studying Latin, Greek, or other classical subjects; promotes interest in culture of ancient Greece and Rome and its influence; founded 1936.

Junior college (or community college), in education U-223

Junior Engineering Technical Society (JETS), a national high school organization that aims to stimulate interest in engineering and science; headquarters East Lansing, Mich., where first club was formed at Michigan State University in 1950; money, materials, and experts contributed by industries.

Junior Grange. *see in index* Grange, National

Junior high school. *see in index* Secondary school

Junior Leagues, The Association of, an organization to promote social welfare; made up (since 1921) of individual Junior Leagues, the first of which had been founded in 1900; branches in communities of U.S., Canada, Mexico, and London, England, with main office in New York City W-270

Juniper, J-157
liquor production L-235

Junípero Serra, Miguel José. *see in index* Serra, Junípero

Junípero Serra Museum, San Diego, Calif. S-41

Junius, pen name of author of a famous series of scorching English political letters attacking George III and his ministers 1769–72; real authorship never proved, attributed to more than 40 persons, but generally conceded to Sir Philip Francis; recent research names Laughlin Macleane, British army surgeon.

Junk, Chinese boat C-367, *pictures* C-373, T-263
harbors and ports, *picture* H-34

Junk bonds S-627

Junkers, Prussian social class A-641

Junk food, *picture* H-83

Juno, in Roman mythology, goddess identified with Greek Hera, sometimes called Moneta M-701. *see also in index* Hera

Junonia shell, mollusk shell, *picture* S-226

Junta (from Spanish word meaning joined), a group with political or administrative purposes; usually in control of government, often as a result of a seizure of power; frequently military; term generally used in Spanish and Latin American countries.

Junto Club, debating society formed by Benjamin Franklin in Philadelphia, Pa., in 1727; later developed into American Philosophical Society A-51

Jupiter, in Roman mythology M-701. *see also in index* Zeus

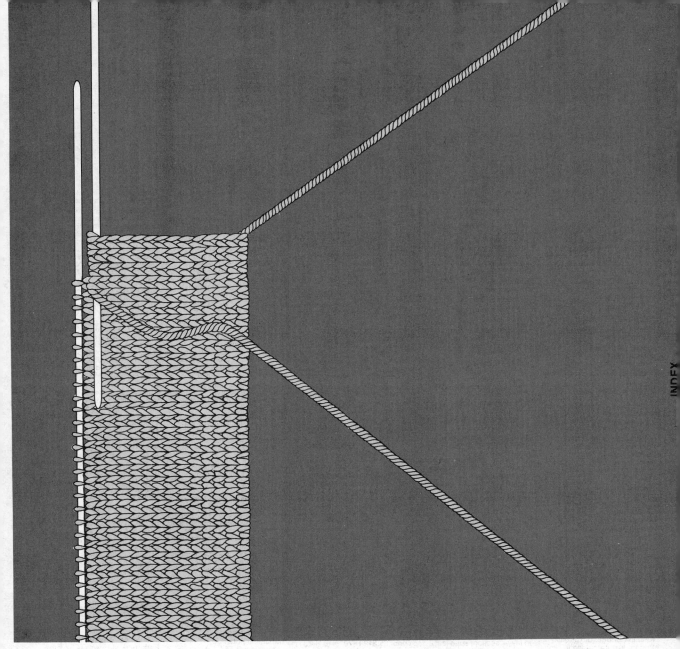

The letter K

may have started as a picture sign of the palm of the hand, as in Egyptian hieroglyphic writing (1) and in a very early Semitic writing used about 1500 B.C. on the Sinai Peninsula (2). About 1000 B.C., in Byblos and other Phoenician and Canaanite centers, the sign was given a linear form (3), the source of all later forms. In the Semitic languages the sign was called *kaph*, meaning "palm."

The Greeks changed the Semitic name to *kappa*. They also turned the letter around to suit the left-to-right direction of their writing (4).

The Romans took the sign over into Latin, but they used it sparingly. From Latin the capital letter K came into English unchanged.

The English small handwritten "k" is simply a capital K with small, straight strokes, which were gradually rounded. The printed "k" is similar to the handwritten form.

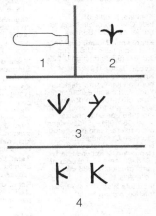

K, chemical element. *see in index* Potassium

K2 (or Mount Godwin Austen), peak in Karakoram Range, n. Kashmir; altitude 28,250 ft (8,610 m); 2nd highest mountain in world K-166
 Asia, *map* A-697
 height, comparative. *see in index* Mountain, *table*
 Karakoram Range K-192

Kaaba (or Caaba, or Kaabeh), Muslim shrine at Mecca
 Abraham A-12
 Islamic pilgrimage I-360
 Mecca M-254
 pilgrimage P-384

Kabah, Mayan pilgrimage center M-237

Kabak, Abraham (1883–1944), Israeli writer
 Hebrew literature H-113

Kabinda. *see in index* Cabinda

Kabir (1440–1518), Indian mystic and poet who tried to bridge or unite Hindu and Islamic thought and preached the essential unity of all religions and the equality of all people H-158

Kabotie, Fred (born 1900), American Indian artist and author, born in Shungopavy, Ariz.; author of 'Designs from the Ancient Mimbrenos', *picture* I-130

Kabuki, Japanese dance drama
 Japanese culture J-49
 masks M-187

Kabuki Theater, theater in Tokyo, Japan T-207, *picture* T-210

Kabul, Afghanistan, capital, in province of Kabul; pop. 891,750 K-166
 Afghanistan A-89
 Asia, *map* A-697

Kabul University, university in Kabul, Afghanistan A-90

Kachina, spirit of an ancestor, also a portrayal of the spirit
 American Indians I-117
 doll D-215

Kachina Bridge (or Caroline Bridge), natural bridge in Utah N-55

Kachins, people of Indo-Chinese origin living along border of upper Burma.

Kachkanar, Mount, peak in Ural Mountains, U.S.S.R.; 3,000 ft (9,000 m) high U-229

Kádár, János (1912–89), Hungarian political leader, born in Fiume, now Rijeka, Yugoslavia; active Communist from 1931; rode to power when Soviet troops put down the 1956 uprising; premier 1956–58, 1961–65; developed more tolerant and prosperous "goulash Communism" in Hungary; general secretary Hungarian Communist party 1956–88; ceremonial post of party president 1988–89
 Hungary H-330

'Kaddo's Wall', West African folktale, *picture* S-650

Kadiak Island. *see in index* Kodiak Island

Kaesong, North Korea, city 5 mi (8 km) n.w. of Panmunjom; commercial center; ginseng grown in area; fine porcelain ware; capital of Korea 915–1392; first city occupied by North Koreans in 1950 invasion; pop. 139,900 K-300, *chart* K-299, *map* K-290

Kaffir Wars (1779–1879), African history; sometimes called Cape Frontier Wars K-166
 frontier wars F-425

Kafir (or kafir corn), variety of sorghum introduced to U.S. from South Africa; grown in s.w. U.S.; grain used for livestock feed.

Kafka, Franz (1883–1924), Czech writer K-167
 expressionism N-414
 German literature G-107
 short story S-277

Kagame, Abbe, Rwandan priest A-121

Kaganovich, Lazar Moiseevich (1893–1963?), Soviet government official, born in the Ukraine; joined Central Committee of Communist party 1924, Politburo 1926; as secretary of Ukrainian Central Committee 1925–28 built Dnieper Dam; as Communist party boss of Moscow 1930–35 reconstructed city and began subway; member of Presidium 1952–57; a first deputy premier 1953–57; expelled from Communist party in 1960s.

Kagawa Toyohiko (1888–1960), Japanese preacher and social reformer, born in Kobe, Japan; converted to Christianity in his teens; author of poetry, essays, religious studies, stories for children, and novels.

Kagera River, river in e.-central Africa, flows into Lake Victoria; about 450 mi (725 km) long; courses through marshlands and lake regions; navigable in lower section; supplies hydroelectric power
 Lake Victoria V-334

Kagoshima, Japan, one of chief cities of Kyushu Island; home of crackled Satsuma ware; space-industries center; pop. 1,729,150, *map* J-75

'Kaha Bird: Tales from the Steppes of Central Asia, The', work by Ginsburg S-656

Kahanamoku, Duke (1890–1968), U.S. swimming champion, born in Honolulu, Hawaii; won 100-meter free-style race in 1912 and 1920 Olympics; revolutionized swimming by introducing flutter kick; called "greatest swimmer of his time."

Kahn, Louis (1902–74), U.S. architect A-566, 569
 museum design M-663

Kahn, Otto Hermann (1867–1934), U.S. banker and patron of music and art, born in Mannheim, Germany; came to U.S. 1893; member firm Kuhn, Loeb & Co., New York City, after 1897 ('Of Many Things').

Kahoolawe, island of Hawaii; 45 sq mi (115 sq km) H-59, *map* H-58
 United States U-145, *map* U-193

Kahului, Hawaii, port town set in Iao Valley on n. coast of Maui; sugar, pineapples; Hawaii's first telephone line installed 1876 between Kahului and Wailuku; pop. 8,280, *map* H-73

Kaibab National Forest, forest in Arizona, adjoining Grand Canyon National Park; 1,780,475 acres (691,395 hectares); forest headquarters Williams, Ariz.
 ecological problem E-58

Kaieteur Falls, falls in central Guyana W-98, *picture* W-97

Kaifeng, China, city in Honan Province; flour, oilseed processing; pop. 318,000.

Kaifu, Toshiki (born 1932), Japanese prime minister, born in Nagoya; in 1960 became youngest member ever elected to Diet, re-elected nine times; minister of education 1976–77, 1985–86; despite lack of experience in foreign policy or economic affairs, became prime minister, third chosen in 1989 (predecessors resigned in face of voter resentment over scandal-tainted leadership and tax increases); named president of Liberal-Democratic party after it lost control of upper house in July 1989 elections; vowed support for "intimate" ties to U.S.

Kailasa Temple, temple in Ellora, India I-71

Kailua, Hawaii, residential center on Kailua Bay on s.e. coast of Oahu; in livestock-raising region about 11 mi (18 km) n.e. of Honolulu; pop. 35,812 H-70, *map* H-73

Kailua-Kona, Hawaii, resort area on the w.-central coast of Hawaii Island; Captain James Cook landed at Kailua in 1779; Kona district is center of the state's coffee industry
 Mokuaikaua church, *picture* H-69

Kailyard school, term applied to group of Scottish novelists who wrote of life of common people with copious use of dialect; best represented by Ian MacLaren and Sir James M. Barrie.

Kainite, mineral M-435

Kairouan (or Kairwan), Tunisia, sacred city of Muslims; Ukbah mosque, rebuilt in 827; pop. 46,200 T-309

Kaisaria. *see in index* Kayseri

Kaiser, Georg (1878–1945), German dramatist and critic, born in Magdeburg; a leader of expressionist school; his plays focus on various social problems G-107

Kaiser, Henry John (1882–1967), U.S. industrialist, born near Canajoharie, N.Y.; constructed piers for San Francisco-Oakland Bay Bridge; built Hoover, Bonneville, and Grand Coulee dams; shipbuilder, World War II; industries include cement, sand and gravel, aluminum, steel, chemicals, automobiles, electronics, aircraft components, real-estate development I-195

Kaiser, official title of German and Holy Roman emperors. *see also in index* Holy Roman Emperors, *table*
 Germany G-122. *see also in index* William I, first German emperor; William II, German emperor

Kaiser-Permanente plan, health-care system
 private and group practice M-279

Kaiserslautern, West Germany, industrial city 35 mi (55 km) w. of Mannheim; Frederick Barbarossa built castle here about 1152; pop. 99,617, *map* G-131

Kaiser Wilhelm Memorial Church, church in West Berlin B-168, *map* B-170, *picture* B-169

Kajima Peace Award, gold medal and engraved certificate presented annually by Kajima Institute of International Peace, in Tokyo, "to the person or persons who have contributed toward peace in various fields of endeavor"; institute founded by Dr. Morinosuke Kajima, Japanese industrialist.

Kakapo (also called owl parrot), bird P-147

Kakemono, Japanese scroll painting J-50

Kakia, mythological figure; represents pleasure H-138

Kakiemon (1596–1666), Japanese potter
 porcelain P-567

Kakiemon ware, pottery P-567, *picture* P-566

Kakinomoto Hitomaro (died 710), Japanese poet J-79

Kala azar, a fatal malarialike fever common in certain parts of India, transmitted by the bite of a sand fly.

Kalachi-Jo-goth. *see in index* Karachi

Kalahari Desert, desert in s. Africa, lying chiefly in Botswana; about 240,000 sq mi (620,000 sq km)
 Africa, *map* A-115, *picture* A-97
 Botswana B-382

Kalakaua, David (1836–91), king of Hawaii 1874–91; because of his extravagant and disorderly rule was forced to grant a new constitution (1887) that restricted royal power H-62

Kalakshetra, classical dance institute in Madras, India M-29

Kalamazoo, Mich., industrial city in s.w. on Kalamazoo River, about 40 mi (65 km) e. of Lake Michigan; celery and fruits; paper, pharmaceuticals, chemicals, metal products; Western Michigan University, Kalamazoo College, Nazareth College; pop. 79,722 M-359, *map* M-372

Kalamazoo Case, The, in history of education; citizens of Kalamazoo, Mich., challenged (1872) collection of taxes for support of a public high school; the Michigan Supreme Court decided (1874) state had right to levy taxes for support of complete system of public education, including high schools and universities; case set a precedent for other states.

Kalamazoo College, college in Kalamazoo, Mich.; Baptist; chartered 1833 as Michigan and Huron Institute, as college 1855; arts and sciences, education; quarter system; programs in France, Spain, and West Germany.

Kalamazoo River, river in Michigan M-355, *maps* M-356, 373

Kalanianaole, Prince Jonah Kuhio. *see in index* Kuhio, Prince

Kalantiaw, Code of, ancient Filipino legal code written by Lakan (Prince) Kalantiaw; admired by juridical scholars for its simple language, common sense, and clarity; consists of 18 orders.

Kalat (or Khelat), division of Baluchistan Province in Pakistan; formerly a princely state of India; joined Pakistan 1948.

Kalatozov, Mikhail (born 1903), Soviet film director, born in Tiflis, now Tbilisi, U.S.S.R. M-623

Kalaupapa National Historical Park, park in Hawaii N-52, *map* N-40

Kale, vegetable C-2, *picture* C-3

Kaleidoscope, scientific toy invented by Sir David Brewster; tube that encloses angled mirrors and colored bits of glass between two flat plates.

'Kalevala', ancient Finnish epic
 Finland F-89
 folklore F-259
 Lönnrot L-297
 storytelling S-646

KAL flight 007. *see in index* Korean Air Lines flight 007

Kalgan, China, city at gate in Great Wall, in Hopei Province, 100 mi (160 km) n.w. of Peking; historic trade and transportation center; pop. 1,000,000.

Kalgoorlie, mining town, Australia A-788, *map* A-822

Kali. *see in index* Devi

Kali / Kansas

Kali, martial arts. *see in index* Arnis

Kalidasa (5th century? AD), great dramatic and lyric poet of India K-167

Kalimantan. *see in index* Borneo

Kalina, Zaire K-248

Kaline, Albert William (born 1934), U.S. baseball player, born in Baltimore, Md.; outfielder with Detroit, A.L., 1953–74; career batting average .297.

Kalinin, Mikhail Ivanovich (1875–1946), Soviet statesman, born near Tver, later named Kalinin in his honor; a peasant himself, represented peasants in Soviet government in which he became president of central executive committee 1919, chairman 1923; chairman of Supreme Soviet of U.S.S.R. 1938–46.

Kalinin (formerly Tver), U.S.S.R., city on Volga River, 100 mi (160 km) n.w. of Moscow; capital of independent principality 13th to 15th century; pop. 345,000
- Europe, *map* E-360
- U.S.S.R., *maps* U-59, 63

Kaliningrad (in German, Königsberg), U.S.S.R., fortified seaport, former capital of East Prussia, on Pregel River, 4 mi (6 km) from mouth; included in U.S.S.R. since 1945; university, castle; pop. 297,000
- Europe, *map* E-360
- U.S.S.R., *maps* U-59, 63

Kalispell, Mont., city in Flathead Valley near Glacier National Park; tourist center in farm region; aluminum, lumber products; settled 1883; pop. 10,648 M-552, 560, *map* M-564

Kalix River, river in Sweden, flows s.e. 208 mi (335 km) to Gulf of Bothnia.

Kallikak, fictitious name of a two-branch U.S. family dating from Revolutionary War days, investigated by H.H. Goddard in his studies of heredity; of 480 descendants of a feeble-minded mother and a sound father 282 were mental, moral, or physical defectives; all below normal in intelligence; of 496 descendants of same father and a mother of normal intelligence only 4 were defective; all were of sound mentality. *see also in index* Jukes

Kalm, Peter (Per) (1715–79), Swedish botanist, born in Finland; visited North America to make survey of natural history 1748–51 ('Travels into North America') F-222

Kalmar (or Calmar), Sweden, port and cathedral town 200 mi (320 km) s. of Stockholm; historic castle dating from 12th century; pop. 34,918.

Kalmar Union (1397), in Scandinavian history, *table* T-274
- Scandinavia S-88
- Sweden S-730

Kalmia, genus of plants of heath family, best-known species being mountain laurel *(Kalmia latifolia). see in index* Mountain laurel

Kalmus, Herbert Thomas (1881–1963), U.S. chemical engineer, born in Chelsea, Mass.; director Research Laboratory of Electrochemistry and Metallurgy, Canadian government 1913–15; invented Technicolor in motion pictures with wife, Natalie.

Kaloko-Honokohau National Historical Park, park in Hawaii N-52, *map* N-40

Kalthoeber, Charles, one of best of colony of German bookbinders who lived in London at end of 18th century; influenced by Roger Payne; style recognizable by ornaments in back panels.

Kamakura, Japan, seacoast city on Honshu s. of Yokohama; seat of shogunate 1192 to 1333; pop. 165,552, *map* J-75
- shogunate S-266

Kamakura shogunate, family of political warlords, *list* S-266

'Kamalampal Carittiram', work by Aiyar I-108

Kama River, river in e. European Russia, largest tributary of Volga River; over 1,000 mi (1,600 km) long; timber trade, *map* E-360
- U.S.S.R., *map* U-63

Kambalda, Western Australia A-814, *map* A-822

Kamchatka, mountain range in n.e. Siberia U-23

Kamchatka, peninsula of e. Siberia; 105,000 sq mi (270,000 sq km); pop. 280,000
- U.S.S.R. U-23, *map* U-59
- world, *map* W-297

Kame, a hill of stratified drift G-151

Kamehameha I (1758?–1819), king of Hawaii (1795–1819) K-167
- Hawaii H-63, *picture* H-67
- Statuary Hall, *table* S-608
- United States U-145

Kamehameha III (1814–54), king of Hawaii (1825–54)
- Hawaii H-61, 64

Kamehameha Day, holiday, *list* F-63

Kamel, George Joseph (1661–1706), Moravian botanist, Jesuit missionary to Philippines; made study of plant and animal life and minerals on islands.

Kamerlingh Onnes, Heike (1853–1926), Dutch physicist, born in Groningen, The Netherlands; discovered method of liquefying helium; professor of physics, Leiden University in The Netherlands. *see also in index* Nobel Prizewinners, *table*

Kamerun. *see in index* Cameroons

Kami, in Shinto religion S-238

Kamik, type of boot, *picture* S-262

Kamikaze, Japanese for divine wind; applied to typhoon that swept away Kublai Khan's fleet during attempt to invade Japan 1281.

Kamikaze planes, term used for suicidal Japanese air force units in World War II A-159, W-336

Kamimura, Hikonojo, Baron (1850–1916), Japanese admiral; notable victory over Russian cruiser squadron off coast of Korea in Russo-Japanese War.

Kaminsky Theater, Jewish theater in Warsaw, Poland Y-420

Kamishak Bay, bay in Alaska, *picture* U-143

Kamloops, B.C., city at junction of North and South Thompson rivers 155 mi (250 km) n.e. of Vancouver; railway divisional point; oil refinery; lumber, cattle, fruit, vegetables; pop. 64,048, *maps* C-109, N-350

Kammerspiele (chamber play), in drama R-150

Kamo Chomei (1155–1216), Japanese priest and author J-81

'Kampaku', Japanese political office F-445

Kampala, Uganda, capital and chief commercial center; pop. 330,700 K-167
- Africa, *map* A-115
- Uganda U-3

Kampen, The Netherlands, city near mouth of IJssel River; formerly a Hanseatic town; 14th-century town hall, church; pop. 25,464.

Kampong, term applied to slums in s.e. Asia
- Indonesia I-160

Kampuchea (formerly Cambodia), nation in s.w. Indochina on lower Mekong River; area 69,898 sq mi (181,035 sq km); cap. Phnom Penh; pop. 7,688,000 K-168
- Asia, *map* A-697, *table* A-694
  - Indochina I-157
  - Thailand T-147
  - Vietnam V-343, 346
- Communist world, *map* C-619
- flag, *picture* F-166
- genocide G-60, M-461
- Mekong River M-288
- national anthem, *table* N-64
- tea T-45
- United Nations, *table* U-84
- United States U-182
- Vietnam War V-437
  - Ho Chi Minh City H-192
  - Nixon N-326
- world, *map* W-297

Kana, Japanese language J-48, J-79

'Kanadehon Chushingura', play by Izumo Takeda J-56

Kanakas, Polynesians A-785

Kan-ami' Kiyotsugu (1333–84), Japanese dramatist A-27

Kananaskis River, river in Alberta, *picture* R-254

Kananga (formerly Luluabourg), Zaire, city 500 mi (800 km) s.e. of Kinshasa; pop. 601,239 K-171
- Africa, *map* A-115

Kanawha River, river in West Virginia; formed in w.-central part of state by junction of New and Gauley rivers; flows n.w. and joins Ohio River at Point Pleasant; length about 100 mi (160 km); Little Kanawha rises in central West Virginia and flows w. and n.w. about 100 mi (160 km) into Ohio River at Parkersburg
- West Virginia M-165, *map* W-182, *picture* W-173

Kanazawa, Japan, city on w. coast of Honshu Island; bronze and lacquer work, silk; fine public gardens; pop. 395,263, *map* J-75

Kanban system, Japanese inventory control I-192

Kanchenjunga (or Kinchinjunga), 3rd highest mountain in world 28,146 ft (8,579 m); one of the e. Himalayas; on boundary between Nepal and India; first successfully climbed 1955, *map* I-86
- Himalayas H-152

Kandahar (or Qandahar), Afghanistan, trade center in province of Kandahar, 300 mi (480 km) s.w. of Kabul; captured by Genghis Khan, Timur Lenk, and others; prominent in wars between British and Afghans; pop. 160,684.

Kandinsky, Wassily (1866–1944), Soviet painter K-171

Kandy, Sri Lanka, highland city in s.-central part of island on artificial lake; capital of former kingdom of Kandy; Buddhist and Brahman temples; pop. 93,602 S-562

Kane, Elisha Kent (1820–57), U.S. Arctic explorer and scientist, born in Philadelphia, Pa.; accompanied Grinnell expeditions (commanded 2nd) searching for Sir John Franklin; attained Kane Basin (1853) and the then farthest north.

Kane, Harnett Thomas (born 1910), U.S. author, born in New Orleans, La. ('Queen New Orleans'; historical novels: 'Bride of Fortune' on Mrs. Jefferson Davis, 'The Lady of Arlington' on Mrs. Robert E. Lee, 'The Smiling Rebel' on Belle Boyd, Confederate spy; 'Gone Are the Days', pictorial history of the South).

Kane, Paul (1810–71), Canadian painter, born in Mallow, Ireland; large collections in Royal Ontario Museum, Toronto, and Parliament buildings, Ottawa S-64

Kaneohe, Hawaii, residential center on s.e. coast of island of Oahu; noted for coral gardens; Hawaii Loa College; missile-tracking station; pop. 29,919 H-70, *map* K-73

Kangaroo, marsupial animal of family Macropodidae K-171
- Australia A-778
- fur, *table* F-464
- leather L-109
- lifespan, *chart* A-423
- mammal M-81
- marsupials M-154, 157

Kangaroo paw, an Australian plant A-783

Kangaroo rat A-429, *picture* A-428

Kang Gang Su Wol Lae, Korean folk dance, *picture* K-281

K'ang Hsi (1655–1722), Chinese emperor (1661–1722); encouraged arts and literature; consolidated empire C-368

Kangnam, district in Seoul, South Korea S-177

K'ang te. *see in index* Pu-yi

Kania, Stanislaw (born 1927), first secretary of Polish United Worker's Party P-495

Kanji, Chinese characters adopted into Japanese language; each character stands for a word J-48. *see also in index* Kana

Kankakee, Ill., city about 50 mi (80 km) s. of Chicago; agricultural area; furniture and home appliances, farm implements, food processing; mental hospital; Olivet Nazarene College; pop. 30,141, *map* I-52

Kankakee River, river that rises in n.w. Indiana and flows s.w. into Illinois; headstream of Illinois River
- Illinois, *map* I-53
- Indiana, *maps* I-89, 102

Kannada, Dravidian language; spoken in s.w. India; official language of Karnataka state I-106

Kannapolis, N.C., community in Cabarrus and Rowan counties, 23 mi (37 km) n.e. of Charlotte; home of Cannon Mills, Inc., manufacturer of household textiles, including towels and bedsheets; mills established 1877, community founded 1905; pop. 36,293 N-357, *maps* N-355, 370

Kano, Nigeria, industrial center and capital of Kano State, n. Nigeria on Jakara River; prehistoric tools found on site; largest mosque in Nigeria; pop. 487,100
- Great Mosque, *picture* N-311

Kano Masanobu (1453–90), Japanese artist J-51

Kanpur (or Cawnpore), India, industrial city on Ganges River; pop. 1,154,388, *map* I-83

Kansa, a Siouan people formerly living along Kansas River, now in Oklahoma, *map* I-149

Kansan. *see in index* Mindel

Kansas, a central state of U.S.; 82,264 sq mi (213,063 sq km); cap. Topeka; pop. 2,363,208 K-173
- cities. *see also in index* cities by name
  - Kansas City K-188
  - Topeka T-227
  - Wichita W-201
- flag, *picture* F-159
- history
  - Civil War B-476
  - Kansas-Nebraska Act K-189
- national parks N-47
- North America, *map* N-350
- state capitals, *list* S-595
- Statuary Hall, *table* S-608
- taxation, *tables* T-37, 39
- tornado, *picture* S-633
- United States U-123, 165, *table* U-187

Kansas, University of, university in Lawrence, Kan.; state control; founded 1865; liberal arts and sciences, architecture and urban design, business, education, engineering, fine arts, journalism, law, pharmacy, and social work; graduate school; medical school at Kansas City, *picture* K-181

Kansas City, Kan., 2nd city of state, on Kansas River; pop. 161,148 K-188
- Kansas K-176, *maps* K-175, 186
- North America, *map* N-350

Kansas City, Mo., 2nd city of state, at confluence of Kansas and Missouri rivers; pop. 448,159 K-188
- Missouri M-491, *maps* M-489, 505, *picture* M-499
- North America, *map* N-350
- United States, *picture* U-125

Kansas City Chiefs, U.S. football team, *table* F-297

Kansas grayfeather. *see in index* Gayfeather

Kansas-Nebraska Act (1854), United States K-189
- Douglas D-233
- Kansas K-175, 177
- Lincoln L-219
- Michigan M-361
- Missouri M-494
- Nebraska N-101
- Pierce P-376
- slavery territorial issue B-291
- Sumner S-703
- United States U-165

Kansas Newman College. *see in index* Sacred Heart College, Kansas

Kansas River (or Kaw River), river in Kansas, formed by junction of Smoky Hill and Republican rivers, Geary County, Kan.; flows 169 mi (272 km) across state to Missouri River
- Kansas, *maps* K-175, 186
- Missouri River M-509
- North America, *map* N-350
- United States, *map* U-193

Kansas State College at Pittsburg, college in Pittsburg, Kan.; founded 1903; formerly a teachers' college; arts and sciences, education, and technology; graduate studies.

Kansas State Teachers College. *see in index* Emporia Kansas State College

Kansas State University of Agriculture and Applied Science, university in Manhattan, Kan.; founded 1863; arts and sciences,

Kansas / Kasavubu

agriculture, architecture, commerce, education, engineering, home economics, veterinary medicine; graduate school.

Kansas Wesleyan, university in Salina, Kan.; school affiliated with United Methodist church; established in 1886; liberal arts.

Kansk-Achinsk Basin, basin in Siberia S-282

Kansu. *see in index* Gansu

Kant, Immanuel (1724–1804), German philosopher K-189
citizenship C-438
Enlightenment E-289
God G-173
Mendelssohn M-297
philosophy P-313, 317
aesthetics A-662
political theories C-463
psychology P-637

Kantara. *see in index* Qantara, El

'Kantchil's Lime Pit, and Other Stories from Indonesia', work by Courlander S-655

Kanto Plain (or Kwanto Plain), lowland in Japan
Japan J-59
Tokyo T-210

Kantor, MacKinlay (1904–77), U.S. novelist, short-story writer, and poet, born in Webster City, Iowa; awarded 1956 Pulitzer prize for 'Andersonville', Civil War novel ('Turkey in the Straw', 'Glory for Me', poetry; 'Long Remember', 'God and My Country', 'Spirit Lake', novels; 'The Voice of Bugle Ann', 'The Daughter of Bugle Ann', dog stories).

Kantorovich, Leonid (1912–86), Soviet economist, born in Leningrad (then St. Petersburg); head of mathematical economics laboratory at Institute of Economic Management, Moscow. *see also in index* Nobel Prizewinners, *table*

Kantrowitz, Adrian (born 1918), U.S. heart surgeon, born in New York, N.Y.; director of surgery Maimonides Medical Center, Brooklyn, 1964–70; chairman department of surgery Sinai Hospital, Detroit 1970– ; pioneer research in motion pictures inside the heart, pump oxygenators, and mechanical hearts; first permanent partial mechanical heart surgery 1966; first U.S. heart transplant 1967; Max Berg Award 1966.

Kantrowitz, Arthur Robert (born 1913), U.S. physicist, born in New York, N.Y.; collaborated with brother Adrian in heart research projects; professor Cornell University 1946–56; director Avco-Everett Research Laboratories 1955–72, chairman 1972–.

Kaohsiung, Taiwan, seaport of s. Taiwan; pop. 1,242,400 K-190

Kao K'o-kung (fl. 13th century), Chinese painter, one of six great masters of Mongol period; took up painting after retiring from government service under Kublai Khan.

Kaolin (or China clay)
clay C-488
pottery P-564

Kaolinite, mineral M-437

Kaon, atomic particle N-432

Kapa cloth. *see in index* Tapa cloth

Kapidagi. *see in index* Cyzicus

'Kapital, Das' (Capital), work by Marx M-162

Kapitza, Peter Leonidovich (1894–1984), Soviet physicist, born in Kronshtadt, Russia; director Institute for Physical Problems, Moscow, 1935–46, 1955–84; noted for work with intense magnetic fields and low temperatures, also for atomic researches; a key figure in development of Sputniks. *see also in index* Nobel Prizewinners, *table*

Kaplan, Joseph (born 1902), U.S. physicist, born in Hungary; became U.S. citizen 1920; professor University of California at Los Angeles 1940–70; head of U.S. program, I.G.Y., 1957–58.

Kaplan turbine, hydraulics H-340

Kapok, fiber K-190
milkweed M-415
natural fibers F-76

Kaposi's sarcoma, form of cancer
AIDS A-145, *table* S-196

Kapp, Wolfgang von (1858–1922), German monarchist, leader of revolt, March 1920, in which Berlin republican government was seized, but which failed because of a general strike; fled to Sweden; arrested for treason on return to Germany 1922; died before trial.

Kappa Alpha, U.S. fraternity F-388

Kappa Delta Pi, national college honor society in education, founded at University of Illinois, Urbana, 1909, for high-ranking junior, senior, and graduate students.

Kappel, Switzerland, village in canton of Zürich; pop. 648.

Kapteyn, Jacobus (1851–1922), Dutch astronomer; directed work of computing positions of stars on Sir David Gill's photographic plates of s. heavens; pioneered in modern study of Milky Way.

Karachi (formerly Kalachi-Jo-goth), Pakistan, capital of Sind Province; port on Arabian Sea; was also capital of province under Indian Empire; pop. 5,208,132 K-190
Indus River I-168
laundry area, *picture* L-84
Pakistan P-82

Karafuto. *see in index* Sakhalin

Karaganda, U.S.S.R., city in e.-central Kazakh Soviet Socialist Republic; center of Karaganda coal basin; mining machinery, boots, candy, soft drinks; technical institutes, including medicine and mining; pop. 522,000
Kazakh Soviet Socialist Republic K-194
U.S.S.R., *map* U-59

Karageorge (Black George) (1766?–1817), nickname given by Turks to George Petrovitch, or George Czerny, Serbian peasant, leader of first Serbian war of independence (1804–8) and founder of Karageorge dynasty.

Karagiye Depression, lowest point in U.S.S.R; at bottom of Caspian Sea; 433 ft (132 m) below sea level U-19

Karaite, follower of early Judaic sect Karaitism
Sa'adia ben Joseph S-2

Karajan, Herbert von (1908–89), Austrian conductor K-191

Karajich, Vuk Stefanovich (1787–1864), Serbian writer, called father of modern Serbian literature; bent efforts toward adoption of Serbian mother tongue as literary language; wrote grammar and dictionary, published Serbian folk songs.

Karakoram Range, system of mountains in n. Jammu and Kashmir K-192, *map* I-86
Himalayas H-153
K2 K-166
Pakistan P-78

Karakorum, Mongolia, ruined city 200 mi (320 km) s.w. of Ulaanbaatar; capital of Mongol Empire; established by Genghis Khan in early 13th century; capital moved to Peking by Kublai Khan in 1267
Genghis Khan G-58

Karakul (or Caracul), a breed of sheep
furs F-463, *table* F-464
sheep S-222
Turkmen Soviet Socialist Republic T-327

Karakum, a desert in U.S.S.R., e. of Caspian Sea T-326
proposed canal construction C-129
U.S.S.R. U-22, *map* U-59

Karamanlis, Konstantinos (or Constantine Caramanlis) (born 1907), Greek political leader, born near Serrai, Greece; member of Parliament 1935–55; prime minister 1955–63, 1974–80; president 1980–85 G-260

Karami, Rashid (1921–87), Lebanese politician, born in Miriata, Lebanon; served as prime minister on and off for over 30 years from 1955; was assassinated in 1987 L-113

Karamzin, Nikolai Mikhailovich (1765–1826), Russian historian, novelist, and critic; born in Mikhaylovka
Russian literature R-349, 353

Karankawa, American Indian people who formerly lived in Texas, *map* I-136, *table* I-138
Cabeza de Vaca's imprisonment C-4

Kararkiozis, name given by Greek to main character in a puppet show, also to a puppet or to a puppet theater P-664

Kara Sea (also called Karskoe More), arm of Arctic Ocean between Novaya Zemlya and n.w. coast of Siberia
U.S.S.R., *maps* U-59, 63

Karat. *see in index* Carat

Karate, method of weaponless self-defense developed in the Orient in early times; hands, elbows, feet, and knees are used to strike various areas of the body; can maim or kill opponent
Japan J-57
martial arts M-159

Karawanken Tunnel, tunnel that crosses Austria-Yugoslavia border.

Karbala (or Kerbela), Iraq, town 60 mi (95 km) s.w. of Baghdad; sacred city and place of pilgrimage of Shi'ite Muslims; tomb of martyr Husein; pop. 211,214.

Karelian Isthmus, land between Lake Ladoga and Gulf of Finland; in Russian Soviet Federated Socialist Republic F-91
lakes U-23

Karens, people
Burma B-509
Thailand T-147

Kariba, Lake, lake on Zambezi River; 175 mi (282 km) long; formed by the Kariba Dam
Zambia Z-447
Zimbabwe Z-452

Kariba Dam, dam between Zambia and Zimbabwe, on Zambezi River
Africa A-106
Zambezi River Z-447
Zambia Z-448

Karikal, India, former French settlement in s.e. on Coromandel coast; 52 sq mi (135 sq km); became part of India in 1954; town of Karikal (pop. 26,080) in former settlement.

Karl August, duke of Saxe-Weimar. *see in index* Saxe-Weimar

Karlfeldt, Erik Axel (1864–1931), Swedish poet; wrote of life of peasants in Dalecarlia, his native region. *see also in index* Nobel Prizewinners, *table*

Karl Johansgate, street in Oslo, Norway O-610

Karl-Marx-Stadt (formerly Chemnitz), East Germany, city 38 mi (61 km) s.w. of Dresden; textiles, machinery, chemicals, food products; pop. 318,917, *maps* E-360, G-131

Karl Marx University (formerly University of Leipzig), university in Leipzig, East Germany; 3rd in size and 3rd in age of the universities of Germany; established 1409 by 400 teachers and students who seceded from University of Prague as result of Hussite agitations; medicine, law, theology, and liberal arts and sciences; renamed by government of East Germany in 1953 U-225

Karloff, Boris (originally William Henry Pratt) (1887–1969), U.S. stage, motion-picture, and television actor; born in London, England; to U.S. 1909; in 'Frankenstein' (released 1931), began career as "menace" in horror films.

Karlovy Vary (or Karlsbad, or Carlsbad), Czechoslovakia, resort in Bohemia; ceded to Germany 1938, restored to Czechoslovakia 1945; Karlsbad decrees issued here at conference of German states (1819); pop. 43,091.

Karlowitz (or Carlowitz, modern Sremski Karlovici), Yugoslavia, town on Danube River, 40 mi (65 km) n.w. of Belgrade; peace between Turkey, Austria, Poland, Venice, and Russia signed here (1699).

Karlsbad. *see in index* Karlovy Vary

Karlskrona (or Carlscrona), Sweden, port on Baltic Sea, 238 mi (383 km) s.w. of Stockholm; Swedish naval headquarters; exports fish and lumber; pop. 33,010, *map* E-360

Karlsruhe (or Carlsruhe), West Germany, city 39 mi (63 km) n.w. of Stuttgart; mineral springs; pop. 249,528, *maps* E-360, G-131

Karlův Most (Charles Bridge), in Prague, Czechoslovakia P-577

Karma (or Karman), religious belief
Hinduism H-156
India I-68

Karmal, Babrak (born 1929), Afghan politician, born near Kabul A-91

Kármán, Theodore von (1881–1963), U.S. aeronautical scientist K-192
helicopter H-122

Karmaprabhrta, Jainist scripture J-14

Karnak, El, Egypt, town beside Nile River on n. part of site of ancient Thebes E-125, T-162, *picture* E-130

Karnaphuli River, river in Bangladesh
Bangladesh B-61

Karnataka (formerly Mysore), state in s. India; area 74,122 sq mi (191,975 sq km); cap. Bangalore; gold, manganese, iron ore; coffee, tea, rice, cotton; early a Hindu kingdom; in mid-1700s taken by Muslim, Hyder Ali, and maintained as princely state until 1947; pop. 29,299,014 B-58, *map* I-86

Karneval (or Fasching), Roman Catholic pre-Lenten carnival celebrated in German-speaking countries P-13

Kärnten. *see in index* Carinthia

Karok, American Indian people who lived in Klamath River valley in n.w. California; a Quoratean division of Hokan language family
mythology M-697

Károlyi, Mihály, Count (1875–1955), Hungarian statesman, born in Budapest; although from wealthy family was early influenced by Marxian socialism; president of Hungary 1918–19; resigned when Bolshevists seized government, lived in exile ('The Struggle for Peace'; 'Memoirs').

Kárpathos (in Italian, Scarpanto), island of Dodecanese in Aegean Sea; area 111 sq mi (287 sq km).

Karrer, Paul (1889–1971), Swiss chemist, born in Moscow, Russia; research on vitamins A and B_2, carotenids, and flavins. *see also in index* Nobel Prizewinners, *table*

Kars, Turkey, town 110 mi (175 km) n.e. of Erzurum; Muslim holy city, with 11th-century Cathedral of the 12 Apostles; capital of a medieval Armenian principality; pop. 32,141.

Karsavina, Tamara (1885–1978), Soviet dancer; ballerina of the Maryinsky Theater, the Russian Imperial theater, at St. Petersburg (now Leningrad), and of Diaghilev's company B-34, D-24

Karsh, Yousuf (born 1908), Canadian photographer, born in Armenia; to Canada 1924; known for sensitive portraits of the famous ('Faces of Destiny'; 'Portraits of Greatness'; autobiography, 'In Search of Greatness')
Shaw, *picture* S-221

Karskoe More. *see in index* Kara Sea

Karstens, Harry, mountain climber M-21

Karun River, only navigable river in Iran; rises in western mountains and flows into the Shatt-al-'Arab; 400–500 mi (650–800 km) long I-305, *map* I-312

Kas, large cupboard F-459

Kasa, Korean poetry K-293

Kasack, Hermann (1896–1966), German author G-107

Kasai River, river that rises in n.e. Angola and flows n.w. 1,000 mi (1,600 km) to Congo River; important for transportation; diamonds found in Tshikapa area, lower section known as Kwa River, *map* A-115

Kasavubu, Joseph (1910?–69), Congolese political leader, born near Léopoldville; president of Democratic Republic of the Congo (now Zaire) 1960–65
Lumumba L-335
Mobutu M-513
Zaire Z-446

Keane / Kelly

College), college in Union, N.J.; founded 1885; liberal arts and teacher education; graduate study.

Keane, John Joseph (1839–1918), U.S. Roman Catholic archbishop and educator, born in Ireland; founded churches and schools for black Americans in South; rector Catholic University of America 1886–97; archbishop Dubuque, Iowa, 1900–1911.

Kearney, Denis (1847–1907), U.S. labor organizer, born in County Cork, Ireland; in 1868 emigrated to San Francisco, Calif.; helped organize the Workingmen's party of California in 1877.

Kearney, Neb., city on Platte River, 125 mi (200 km) w. of Lincoln; livestock raising, metal products; Kearney State College, city was named for Fort Kearney (sometimes spelled Kearny), built nearby in 1848 to protect emigrants on Oregon Trail but abandoned in 1871; pop. 21,158 N-104, *map* N-108
  Fort Kearney State Historical Park, *picture* N-99

Kearney State College, college in Kearney, Neb.; founded 1905; fine arts and humanities, business and technology, education, and natural and social sciences; graduate school.

Kearns, Utah, community s.w. of Salt Lake City; pop. 17,071, *map* U-258

Kearny, Philip (1814–62), U.S. brigadier general and cavalry leader, born in New York City; served in Mexican War, French cavalry, and Civil War; killed at Chantilly; nephew of Gen. S. W. Kearny
  Statuary Hall, *table* S-609

Kearny, Stephen Watts (1794–1848), U.S. major general K-194
  California C-45
  Carson C-177
  frontier movement F-422
  Mexican War M-320
  New Mexico N-221

Kearny, N.J., town on Passaic River opposite Newark; shipyards, twine, plastics, linoleum, telephones, metal products; named for Gen. Philip Kearny; pop. 35,735, *map* N-210

Keating, Geoffrey (1569–1644), Irish author I-326

Keating, Kenneth B. (1900–75), U.S. public official, born in Lima, N.Y.; Republican congressman from New York 1946–58; senator from New York 1958–65; associate justice New York State Court of Appeals 1965–69; ambassador to India 1969–72.

Keaton, Buster (1895–1966), U.S. actor A-27

Keaton, Diane (originally Diane Hall) (born 1946), U.S. actress, born in Los Angeles ('Looking for Mr. Goodbar'; 'Shoot the Moon'; 'Reds'; 'Annie Hall'), *picture* A-309

Keats, Ezra Jack (born 1916), U.S. author and illustrator, born in Brooklyn, N.Y.; awarded Caldecott Medal 1963 for 'The Snowy Day'; 'Whistle for Willie'; 'John Henry'; 'God Is in the Mountain'.

Keats, John (1795–1821), English poet K-195
  creative writing W-379
  literary contribution E-275
  poetry P-485

Keble, John (1792–1866), English poet and clergyman, born in Fairford, near Swindon; professor of poetry at Oxford University for 10 years; Keble College built as a memorial ('The Christian Year').

Kebnekaise, highest peak in Sweden, in Kjölen Mountains 6,965 ft (2,123 m); in n. 25 mi (40 km) from Norwegian border; glaciers S-726

Kecoughtan. *see in index* Hampton

Kecskemét, Hungary, city 50 mi (80 km) s.e. of Budapest; center of fruit, cattle, grain area; farm implements, chemicals, shoes, fruit preserves, wine, flour; pop. 68,327, *map* E-360

Kedah, state in former Federation of Malaya; 3,660 sq mi (9,480 sq km); rice, rubber, tapioca; tin, tungsten; became part of Malaysia 1963; pop. 955,374. *see also in index* Malay State, Unfederated

Keddah, corral for trapping elephants in s.e. Asia E-185, *picture* E-184

Kedron, Valley of (or Valley of Cedron, or Valley of Kidron), deep depression e. of Jerusalem where brook flowed in Biblical times, *map* J-101

Keefe, Tim (1856–1933), U.S. baseball pitcher, born in Cambridge, Mass.; began career 1880, Troy, N.L., finished Philadelphia, N.L., 1893; won 346 games (19 in row 1888), lost 225.

Keel, in boat, *diagram* B-326
  sailing B-328
  ship S-240, 247

Keel, muscular structure in birds B-276

Keeler, William H. (1872–1923), U.S. baseball outfielder, born in Brooklyn, N.Y.; outfielder with 3 N.L. teams and 1 A.L. team 1892–1910; famed for his batting philosophy "Hit 'em where they ain't!"; hit safely in 44 consecutive games 1897.

Keeley, Leslie E. (1832–1900), U.S. physician, born in Saint Lawrence County, N.Y.; originator of Keeley Cure, treatment for alcoholics and drug addicts; first sanitarium Dwight, Ill., 1879–1966; many branches.

Keeling Islands. *see in index* Cocos Islands

Keelung, Taiwan, seaport and naval base in n. Taiwan, 15 mi (25 km) n.e. of Taipei; shipbuilding; chemicals, food products; pop. 349,600.

Keen, William Williams (1837–1932), U.S. surgeon, born in Philadelphia, Pa.; professor of surgery Jefferson Medical College 1889–1907; pioneer work in delicate operations of brain and nervous system; wrote and edited books on surgery and anatomy.

Keene, Charles Samuel (1823–91), British pen-and-ink artist, born in Hornsey, England; for 40 years a contributor to *Punch;* foremost among English craftsmen in black and white; work unconventional.

Keene, Laura (1826?–73), U.S. actress and manager; her company was playing 'Our American Cousin' at Ford's Theater, Washington, D.C., when Lincoln was shot.

Keene, N.H., city on Ashuelot River, 42 mi (68 km) s.w. of Concord; ball bearings, machinery, textiles, furniture, leather products; Keene State College; pop. 21,449 N-186, *map* N-191

Keene State College, college in Keene, N.H.; part of University of New Hampshire; state control; founded 1909; liberal arts, teacher education, and vocational courses; graduate study N-182

Keep. *see in index* Dungeon

Keeshan, Bob, U.S. actor
  Captain Kangaroo, *picture* T-69

Keeshond, dog, *picture* D-206

Keet Seel, cliff-dwelling ruin in Arizona N-55

Keewatin, District of, district in e. Canada, part of Northwest Territories in Canadian Shield; 228,160 sq mi (590,930 sq km); tundras; pop. 3,403.

Keewatin ice sheet I-7, *map* I-8

Kefar Nahum. *see in index* Capernaum

Kefauver, Estes (1903–63), U.S. political leader, born near Madisonville, Tenn.; five terms in U.S. House of Representatives; U.S. senator 1948–63; chairman Senate Crime Investigating Committee 1950–51 ('Crime in America'); Democratic vice-presidential nominee 1956.

Keighley, England, town in Yorkshire, 55 mi (90 km) n.e. of Liverpool; Leeds-Liverpool Canal connects it with Hull; worsted, tools, machines, paper; pop. 55,400.

Keihin, industrial zone, Japan J-40
  Tokyo T-208
  Yokohama Y-422

Keijo. *see in index* Seoul

Keiser, Reinhard (1674–1739), German opera composer O-561

Keitel, Wilhelm (1882–1946), German army officer, born in Helmscherode, near Brunswick, Germany; made commander in chief of German armed forces 1938; signed World War II surrender 1945; hanged for war crimes 1946 W-336, *picture* W-326

Keith, Arthur (1866–1955), British anthropologist and anatomist, born in Aberdeen, Scotland; a leading authority in study of human race and its antiquity and expert on reconstruction of prehistoric humans from fragments of fossil remains ('The Antiquity of Man'; 'A New Theory of Human Evolution'; 'An Autobiography').

Keith, Harold (born 1903), U.S. children's author, born in Watonga, Okla. ('Boy's Life of Will Rogers'; 'A Pair of Captains'; 'Sports and Games'; 'Rifles for Watie', awarded Newbery Medal 1958).

Keith, James Francis Edward (1696–1758), Scottish soldier, born near Peterhead; Jacobite adherent, field marshal under Frederick the Great in Seven Years' War.

Kejimkujik National Park, park in Nova Scotia N-30

Kékes Peak, peak in the Mátra Hills in Hungary; 3,330 ft (1,015 m) H-326

Kekkonen, Urho (1900–86), president of Finland K-195
  Finland F-91

Kekulé (full name Friedrich August Kekulé von Stradonitz) (1829–96), German chemist, born in Darmstadt; chemistry of explosives, dyestuffs, and coal-tar products based largely upon his researches.

Kelantan, state in former Federation of Malaya; 5,746 sq mi (14,882 sq km); rice, coconuts, rubber; tin, iron ore, gold; pop. 680,626. *see also in index* Malay States, Unfederated

Kelland, Clarence Budington (1881–1964), U.S. writer of novels and short stories, born in Portland, Mich.; created fictional characters Mark Tidd and Scattergood Baines; story 'Opera Hat' basis for movie 'Mr. Deeds Goes to Town'.

Kellar, Harry (1849–1922), U.S. magician M-38

Keller, Friedrich Gottlob (1816–95), German weaver of Saxony, patented a machine to make wood pulp.

Keller, Gottfried (1819–90), German poet and novelist, born in Zurich, Switzerland; combined realism with imagination and sincerity G-106

Keller, Helen Adams (1880–1968), U.S. author who overcame blindness and deafness K-195

Kellermann, Bernhard (1879–1951), German novelist, born in Fürth; early novels subjective ('The Fool'); later work on social problems ('The Ninth November'; 'The Tunnel').

Kellermann, François-Christophe (1735–1820), French Revolutionary general, marshal of France, victor at Valmy (1792); father of François-Étienne Kellermann, one of Napoleon's ablest generals.

Keller milling machine, in industry
  automobile manufacture A-872

Kelley, DeForest, U.S. actor, *picture* S-117

Kelley, Florence (1859–1932), U.S. social worker, born in Philadelphia, Pa.; resident Hull House 1891–99, Henry Street Settlement 1899–1924; secretary National Consumers League 1899.

Kelley, Joseph James (1871–1943), U.S. baseball outfielder, born in Cambridge, Mass.; began career with Boston 1891, finished with Cincinnati 1906.

Kelley, Oliver Hudson (1826–1913), U.S. farmer and agrarian reformer, born in Boston, Mass.; founded National Grange of the Patrons of Husbandry 1867 G-214
  Minnesota M-446

Kellgren, Johan Henrik (1751–95), Swedish poet and critic, born in Floby, near Falköping; cofounder and editor *Stockholmsposten;* librarian and private secretary to Gustavus III.

Kellogg, Frank Billings (1856–1937), U.S. lawyer and diplomat, born in Potsdam, N.Y.; U.S. senator from Minnesota 1917–23; ambassador to United Kingdom 1923–24; secretary of state 1925–29; coauthor of Kellogg-Briand Pact to outlaw war; elected to International Court of Justice 1930, resigned 1935
  Coolidge administration C-704
  World War I W-321

Kellogg, Vernon Lyman (1867–1937), U.S. zoologist, born in Emporia, Kan.; professor entomology, Stanford University, 1894–1920; secretary National Research Council 1919–31; wrote on zoology, entomology, heredity.

Kellogg, Will Keith (1860–1951), U.S. industrialist and philanthropist, born in Battle Creek, Mich.; in 1906 founded giant cereal industry
  breakfast cereals B-433
  industry I-195

Kellogg, Idaho, city 33 mi (53 km) s.e. of Coeur d'Alene; center for mining and smelting district producing lead, zinc, silver, cadmium, antimony; pop. 3,417, *map* I-30
  mine, *picture* I-18

Kellogg-Briand Pact (or Pact of Paris) (1928), *table* T-274
  Coolidge administration C-704
  post World War I W-321
  United States U-173
  war crime definitions W-11

Kells (or Ceanannus Mór), Ireland, market town of County Meath in e.; of ancient origin; pop. 2,274, *map* U-78

'Kells, Book of'. *see in index* 'Book of Kells'

Kelly, Colin Purdie, Jr. (1915–41), U.S. Army aviator ("America's first hero of World War II"), born in Madison, Fla.; in B-17 bomber, Dec. 10, 1941, he attacked Japanese heavy cruiser *Ashigara;* killed when his bomber crashed on Mt. Arayat on Luzon.

Kelly, Ellsworth (born 1923), U.S. artist, born in Newburgh, N.Y.; noted for bright geometrics on large canvas, also ink and pencil drawings, sculpture, and lithographs; numerous awards
  'Blue, Black, Red' P-67

Kelly, Emmett (1898–1979), U.S. clown, born in Sedan, Kan.; famed for his tramp C-437
  mime M-422

Kelly, Eric Philbrook (1884–1960), U.S. writer of children's books and educator, born in Amesbury, Mass.; lectured at University of Krakow (Poland) 1925–26 and wrote 'The Trumpeter of Krakow', awarded 1929 Newbery Medal; professor of journalism at Dartmouth College 1929–54 ('The Land of the Polish People'; 'In Clean Hay').

Kelly, George (1887–1974), U.S. playwright, born in Philadelphia, Pa.; uncle of Grace Kelly; author of penetrating plays tinged with satire ('Craig's Wife', won Pulitzer prize 1926; 'The Showoff').

Kelly, George Lange (High Pockets) (1896–1984), U.S. baseball player, born in San Francisco, Calif.; first baseman with New York, N.L., 1915–17, 1919–26, Pittsburgh, N.L., 1917, Cincinnati, N.L., 1927–30, Chicago, N.L., 1930, Brooklyn, N.L., 1932; batted .331 with Chicago 1930.

Kelly, Grace. *see in index* Grace

Kelly, John (1822–86), U.S. political leader, born in New York City; joined Tammany organization 1853; U.S. congressman 1855–59; sheriff of New York County 1859–61 and 1865–67; opposed Tweed Ring and controlled Tammany 1874–82.

Kelly, Michael Joseph (King) (1857–94), U.S. baseball player, born in Troy, N.Y.; colorful catcher and outfielder with 4 N.L. teams 1878–93;

Kelly / Kent

batted .394 and stole 84 bases for Boston, 1887.
Kelly, Ned (1855–80), Australian criminal K-196
Kelly, Oakley, U.S. aviator A-204
Kelly, Walt (1913–73), U.S. cartoonist, born in Philadelphia, Pa.; animator Walt Disney Studio 1935–41; commercial artist New York, N.Y., 1941–48; political cartoonist *New York Star* 1948–49; creator of satirical comic strip "Pogo", *picture* C-190
Kelly, William (1811–88), U.S. inventor, born in Pittsburgh, Pa.; invented process for making steel now known as Bessemer process; designated (1857) by U.S. Patent Office as originator of the invention I-351
Kelly, petroleum drilling P-256
Kelly Air Force Base, in San Antonio, Tex. S-37
Kelmscott Press T-338
Keloid, scar tissue
  plastic surgery P-455
Kelowna, B.C., city on Okanagan Lake 165 mi (265 km) n.e. of Vancouver; center for growing and processing of fruits, vegetables; lumbering, resort; pop. 59,196, *map* C-109
Kelp, a large coarse seaweed *(Macrocystis pyrifera), picture* S-162
  algae A-283
Kelp crab, crustacean *(Pugettia producta), picture* C-791
Kelpies, water fairies
  fairy tales F-12
Kelsey, Henry (1670?–1724?), English explorer, born in London; with Hudson's Bay Company 1684–1722, led expedition to northern Saskatchewan 1690–92, governor of posts 1718–22 C-95
Kelso, Wash., city on Cowlitz River at Oregon border, 74 mi (119 km) s.e. of Aberdeen; boat building; incorporated 1889; pop. 11,129, *map* W-64
Keltie, John Scott (1840–1927), British geographer, born in Dundee, Scotland; editor *Statesman's Year Book* for 43 years ('History of the Scottish Highlands and Clans'; 'The Partition of Africa').
Kelts. *see in index* Celts
Kelvin, Lord (originally William Thomson) (1824–1907), British scientist and inventor K-196
  analog computer S-112
  heat H-106
  transatlantic communication cables C-10
Kelvin scale, temperature
  cryogenics C-793
  heat H-103
  Kelvin K-196
  sun S-704
  weights and measures, *table* W-141
Kemal, Yashar (born 1922), Turkish novelist and journalist; self-taught ('Memed, My Hawk'; 'The Wind from the Plain'; 'Anatolian Tales').
Kemal Atatürk. *see in index* Atatürk
Kemble, famous family of English actors (18th and 19th centuries); most celebrated members were Mrs. Sarah Siddons, her brothers John Philip and Charles, and her niece Fanny.
Kemble, Fanny (full name Frances Anne Kemble) (1809–93), British actress and author, born in London; daughter of Charles Kemble; married Pierce Butler, an American, and lived in U.S. 1834–48 ('Journals', interesting picture of U.S. life).
Kemble, Gouverneur (1786–1875), U.S. Congressman and manufacturer S-608
Kemerovo, U.S.S.R., city in s. Siberia, on Tom' River; coal mining; fertilizers, paint, plastics, pharmaceuticals, coke by-products, machinery; sawmilling; pop. 385,000
  U.S.S.R., *map* U-59
Kemmel, Mont, isolated rocky hill 6 mi (10 km) s.w. of Ypres, Belgium; overlooks Flanders plain to n.e. and s.e.; taken by Germans in World War I, 1918.
Kemmerer, Edwin Walter (1875–1945), U.S. economist, born in Scranton, Pa.; professor economics and finance, Cornell University, 1909–12, Princeton University 1912–43, professor emeritus after 1943; financial adviser to U.S. Philippine Commission, to Mexico, Guatemala, Colombia, South Africa, Chile, Poland, Ecuador, Bolivia, China; author of works on economics.
Kemp, Jack (born 1935), U.S. politician, born in Los Angeles, Calif.; conservative U.S. representative (Republican) from New York 1971–89; former quarterback with San Diego Chargers and Buffalo Bills professional football teams.
Kemp Coast, district in Antarctica between 56° and about 59°40' E.; discovered 1833 by Peter Kemp, a British sealing captain.
Kempis, Thomas à (1380?–1471), German monk and mystic, born in Kempen, near Krefeld; remembered for one book, 'Imitation of Christ', a classic of devotional literature.
Ken, Thomas (1637–1711), English bishop, born in Great or Little Berkhamstead, near St. Albans; one of seven imprisoned for refusing to read Declaration of Indulgences issued by James II; following the revolution, lost bishopric rather than transfer loyalty from James II to William of Orange; remembered today for his hymns ('Praise God from Whom All Blessings Flow'; 'Awake, My Soul, and with the Sun Arise').
Ken, Japanese unit of measure, *table* W-141
Kenaf, a fiber plant, botanically known as *Hibiscus cannabinus;* original home in India, grown now in Cuba and other Latin American countries, also in Florida; from 8 to 12 ft (2½ to 3½ m) high; fiber, which is in bark, used as substitute for jute.
Kenai birch, tree B-239
Kenai Fjords National Park, park in Alaska N-52, *map* N-40
Kenai Mountains, mountains in Alaska A-242
Kenai Peninsula, s. Alaska; 150 mi (240 km) long; farmlands, coal deposits; includes city Kenai (pop. 4,324), on Cook Inlet, and ice-free seaports Seward and Whittier; severe earthquake 1964, *maps* A-240, 254
Kendall, Amos (1789–1869), U.S. newspaper editor and public official, born in Dunstable, Mass.; auditor in Treasury Department under Jackson 1829–35; postmaster general 1835–40; reorganized Post Office Department and paid off debt; S.F.B. Morse's agent in development of telegraph systems; helped found Columbia Institute for Deaf P-645
Kendall, Edward Calvin (1886–1972), U.S. biochemist, born in South Norwalk, Conn.; isolated thyroxin 1914; professor of physiological chemistry Mayo Foundation for Medical Education and Research, Rochester, Minn., 1914–51. *see also in index* Nobel Prizewinners, *table*
Kendall, Henry Clarence (1841–82), Australian poet, born in New South Wales; son of missionary; held government posts at Sydney; journalist at Melbourne 1869–73 A-797
Kendo, martial art, *picture* M-160
Kendrew, John Cowdery (born 1917), British biochemist, born in Oxford; deputy chairman Medical Research Council Laboratory for Molecular Biology, Cavendish Laboratory, Cambridge 1946–75; director general European Molecular Biology Laboratory. *see also in index* Nobel Prizewinners, *table*
  protein study B-237
Kendrick, John (1745?–1800), U.S. navigator, born in Boston, Mass., died in Hawaii; commanded privateer during Revolution; explored n.w. coast of North America and Pacific islands.
Kendrick, John Benjamin (1857–1933), U.S. cattleman and political leader, born in Cherokee County, Texas; governor of Wyoming 1915–17; U.S. senator (Democrat) 1917–33.
Kenilworth, England, town in Warwickshire; ruins of castle given by Queen Elizabeth I to earl of Leicester; scene of Sir Walter Scott's novel 'Kenilworth'; pop. 21,000, *map* U-75
'Kenilworth', work by Scott S-132
Kenilworth ivy, a creeping perennial plant *(Cymbalaria muralis)* of the figwort family, native to Europe; trailing stems root at nodes (joints); leaves lobed; flowers lilac with yellow throat, tiny.
Kenmore, N.Y., village 5 mi (8 km) n. of Buffalo; chemicals, machinery, silk, electrical appliances: incorporated 1899; pop. 18,474, *map* N-268
Kenna, John Edward (1848–93), U.S. statesman, born in Valcoulan, W. Va. (then Virginia); entered Confederate army at 16; admitted to bar 1870; served in House of Representatives and in U.S. Senate; Democrat
  Statuary Hall, *table* S-609
Kennan, George Frost (born 1904), U.S. diplomat, born in Milwaukee, Wis.; in foreign service 1926–53, ambassador to Soviet Union 1952–53; professor Institute for Advanced Study, Princeton University 1956–61, 1963–74; ambassador to Yugoslavia 1961–63; won two Pulitzer prizes, one in history 1956 for first volume of 'Soviet-American Relations, 1917–1920', the other in biography 1968 for 'Memoirs, 1925–1950'
  Cold War C-545
Kennebec River, 2nd largest river of Maine; rises in Moosehead Lake, flows s. 190 mi (305 km) to Atlantic
  Maine, *maps* M-53, 67
Kennedy, Anthony (born 1936), U.S. jurist, born in Sacramento, Calif.; professor of constitutional law 1963–87; appointed to U.S. Court of Appeals by Gerald Ford 1975; following Ronald Reagan's unsuccessful nominations of Robert Bork and Douglas Ginsburg, Kennedy unanimously confirmed as associate Supreme Court justice to replace retired justice Lewis Powell in 1988
  Reagan R-114
Kennedy, David Matthew (born 1905), U.S. public official, born in Randolph, Utah; president Continental Illinois National Bank and Trust Company of Chicago 1956–59, chairman 1959–69; special assistant to U.S. secretary of the treasury 1953–54, secretary 1969–71; ambassador at large, state department, 1971–72; ambassador to NATO 1972–73
  Nixon N-325
Kennedy, Edward Moore (born 1932), U.S. political leader K-206
  Kennedy, John F. K-201, *pictures* K-200, 203
Kennedy, Jacqueline Bouvier. *see in index* Onassis, Jacqueline Bouvier Kennedy
Kennedy, John E., U.S. advertiser A-59
Kennedy, John Fitzgerald (1917–63), 35th president of the United States K-197
  assassination A-703, D-10, T-125
  church and state issue C-408
  Cuban missile crisis and embargo C-803
  U.S.S.R. U-56
  Eisenhower E-143
  Johnson J-129
  medals M-270
  Nixon N-320
  tariff T-31
  United States U-180
  Vietnam War V-347
Kennedy, John Pendleton (pen name Mark Littleton) (1795–1870), U.S. author and statesman, born in Baltimore, Md.; fought in War of 1812; Whig representative from Maryland 1838, 1840, 1842; secretary of the Navy 1852–53 A-346
Kennedy, Joseph Patrick (1888–1969), U.S. banker, business executive, and statesman K-206
  Kennedy, John F. K-197
Kennedy, Margaret (1896–1967), British novelist, born in London; married David Davies.
Kennedy, Robert Francis (1925–68), U.S. lawyer and government official K-206
  assassination, *list* A-704
  Kennedy administration K-200, 204, *picture* K-203
  United States U-182
Kennedy, Rose Fitzgerald (born 1890), U.S. civic leader K-206
  Kennedy, John F. K-197
Kennedy, Ted. *see in index* Kennedy, Edward Moore
Kennedy, Mount, St. Elias Mountains, Yukon Territory; height about 14,000 ft (4,300 m); named by Canadian government in memory of President John F. Kennedy; Robert Kennedy first to climb.
Kennedy Round, in international trade T-31
Kennedy Space Center. *see in index* Cape Canaveral
Kennelly, Arthur Edwin (1861–1939), U.S. electrical engineer, born in Bombay, India; principal electrical assistant to Thomas Edison 1887–94; professor at Harvard 1902–39.
Kennelly, Brendan (born 1936), Irish poet I-328
Kennelly-Heaviside layer, in upper atmosphere; suggested by Oliver Heaviside and A.E. Kennelly A-749
Kenner, La., city 9 mi (14 km) w. of New Orleans, on Mississippi River; trading and shipping center; sheet metal, concrete and wood products; pop. 66,382, *map* L-322
Kennesaw Mountain National Battlefield Park, park in Georgia, where Confederate troops repulsed Sherman's army inflicting heavy losses June 27, 1864 N-52, *map* G-101
Kenneth I, MacAlpine (died 860?), king of the Scots and conqueror of Picts, called first king of Scotland
  Scotland S-128
Kennett Square, Pa.; pop. 4,876, *table* B-379
  Pennsylvania, *map* P-205
Kennewick, Wash., city in s.e. part of state, on Columbia River opposite Pasco; river port; fruit and vegetable farming; chemicals, metals, cement; pop. 34,397 W-60, *map* W-64
Kenney, George Churchill (1889–1977), U.S. Air Force officer, born in Yarmouth, N.S., to U.S. citizens; commander of Allied air forces in Southwest Pacific during World War II.
Kenny, Sister (1886–1952), Australian nurse who developed method for treating polio K-207
Kenny Institute, in Minneapolis, Minn., medical therapy training school K-207
'Kenny's Window', work by Sendak S-172
Kennywood Park, amusement park in Pittsburgh, Pa. A-386
Kenora, Ont., manufacturing town and summer resort on Lake of the Woods, 195 km (120 mi) e. of Winnipeg, Man.; flour, lumber, pulp and paper mills, boat factories, fisheries; gold, silver, copper, mica nearby; pop. 10,952, *map* C-112
  North America, *map* N-350
Kenosha, Wis., manufacturing city and port on s.w. shore of Lake Michigan, 33 mi (53 km) s. of Milwaukee; automobiles, metal products, industrial tools, wire rope, cranberries; Carthage College, Gateway Technical Institute; pop. 77,685 W-260, *map* W-264
Kensington, P.E.I., town 8 mi (13 km) n.e. of Summerside; near Malpeque Bay; agricultural market and shipping center; butter and cheese; pop. 1,143, *map* P-594
Kensington and Chelsea, borough in w.-central section of Greater London, England; Kensington district has Kensington Palace (birthplace of Queen Victoria) and Gardens; pop. 208,480, *map* U-75
  London L-293, *maps* L-287, 288
Kent, Edward Augustus, duke of (1767–1820), English prince, 4th son of George III; father of Queen Victoria; born in London.

Kent / Ketchikan

Kent, James (1763–1847), U.S. jurist and author K-207
Hall of Fame, *table* H-16
law L-94

Kent, Rockwell (1882–1971), U.S. artist K-207
Moby Dick, *picture* N-413
Paul Bunyan, *picture* F-266

Kent, William (1684–1748), English architect F-459

Kent, ancient kingdom of Anglo-Saxons in England; settled by Jutes; conquered by Egbert, king of Wessex, made part of Wessex.

Kent, county of s.e. England; 1,525 sq mi (3,950 sq km); pop. 1,388,820.

Kent, Ohio, city 11 mi (18 km) n.e. of Akron; electric motors, motor vehicles, machine parts, school blackboards, plastic products; Kent State University; pop. 26,164, *map* O-517

Kent, Wash., city 16 mi (26 km) s. of Seattle; aerospace research and products, fiberglass, telephone equipment; pop. 23,152, *map* W-64

Kente cloth, ritual garments in Africa A-101

Kenten-mon, Japanese gate, *diagram* J-31

Kent Island, largest island in Chesapeake Bay, Maryland, 7 mi (11 km) e. of Annapolis; oyster fisheries, *maps* M-169, 183

Kenton, Simon (1755–1836), U.S. frontiersman; birthplace probably Fauquier County, Virginia; scout for Daniel Boone 1775–78; with George Rogers Clark in capture of Kaskaskia and Vincennes; became brigadier general of militia 1805; in War of 1812.

Kenton, Stan (1912–79), U.S. bandleader, born in Wichita, Kan.; band noted for progressive jazz; introduced new compositions and arrangements after mid-1940s.

Kent State University, Kent, Ohio; founded 1910; arts and sciences, business administration, education, fine and professional arts, library science, and nursing; graduate school; regional campuses at Ashtabula, East Liverpool, New Philadelphia, North Canton, Salem, and Warren C-495

Kentucky, an e.-central state of U.S.; 40,395 sq mi (104,625 sq km); cap. Frankfort; pop. 3,661,433 K-208
cities. *see also in index* cities by name
Frankfort F-378
Lexington-Fayette L-145
Louisville L-324
flag, *picture* F-159
history
Boone B-365
Civil War C-473, C-642
national parks N-41, 43, 53, *map* N-40
North America, *map* N-350
state capitals, *list* S-595
Statuary Hall, *table* S-608
taxation, *tables* T-37, 39
Tennessee Valley Authority T-100, *map* T-101
United States U-109, 112, 159, *table* U-187

Kentucky, University of, Lexington, Ky.; state control; founded 1865; arts and sciences, agriculture, allied health professions, architecture, business and economics, dentistry, education, engineering, home economics, law, library sciences, medicine, nursing, pharmacy, and social professions; graduate school; Lexington Technical Institute; 14 community colleges K-213, *picture* K-217

Kentucky and Virginia Resolutions, in U.S. history
Alien and Sedition Acts A-307
Jefferson J-93
states' rights S-599

Kentucky coffee tree, a medium-sized tree *(Gymnocladus dioicus)* of the pea, or pulse, family; so called because its seeds resemble coffee beans; grows w. of Appalachian Mountains to Great Plains; state tree of Kentucky.

Kentucky Dam, dam in Kentucky, on Tennessee River D-17
Kentucky, *maps* K-210, 222

Kentucky Derby, in horse racing H-275
Kentucky K-214, *picture* K-209
Louisville L-324

Kentucky Fried Chicken, fast-food chain F-43

Kentucky Lake, lake in Kentucky, *maps* K-210, 222, *picture* K-218
United States, *map* U-193

Kentucky Resolutions
Jefferson's contribution J-93

Kentucky rifle S-267

Kentucky River, river in Kentucky, formed by several forks, rising in Cumberland Mts. of s.e.; flows 250 mi (400 km) n.w. to Ohio River, *maps* K-210, 222

Kentucky State University, Frankfort, Ky.; founded as normal school 1886; arts and sciences, applied sciences, and teacher education; graduate studies.

Kentucky Wesleyan College, Owensboro, Ky.; Methodist; founded 1858; opened 1866; arts and sciences, education.

Kentwood, Mich., city 5 mi (8 km) s.e. of Grand Rapids; pop. 30,438; residential; incorporated 1967, *map* M-373

Kenya, African nation on Indian Ocean s. of Ethiopia; area 224,081 sq mi (580,367 sq km); cap. Nairobi; pop. 22,919,000 K-224
Africa A-105, *map* A-115, *table* A-112
Commonwealth membership C-602
flag, *picture* F-166
gross national product, *table* P-576
Kenyatta's leadership K-228
national anthem, *table* N-64
national parks A-95, N-26
population P-538
United Nations, *table* U-84
world, *map* W-297

Kenya, Mount, volcanic peak 17,058 ft (5,199 m) in central Kenya, Africa, near equator; discovered 1849; first ascended 1899 K-224, G-250, *map* A-115

Kenyahs, a people of Borneo; traditionally rice growers; entire village often lives in one huge communal house.

Kenyatta, Jomo (1894?–1978), African political leader K-228
Kenya K-227

Kenyon College, Gambier, Ohio; Protestant Episcopal; founded 1824 (at Worthington, moved 1827 to Gambier); arts and sciences.

Kenzo (born 1939), Japanese dress designer D-271

Keogh, James (born 1916), U.S. journalist and government official, born in Platte County, Nebraska; on staff of *Time* 1951–68, assistant managing editor 1961–68, executive editor 1968; chief writer and researcher for Nixon for President campaign 1968; special presidential assistant 1969–70; director U.S. Information Agency 1973–76 ('This Is Nixon'; 'President Nixon and the Press').

Keogh account, in investment S-82

Keokuk (one who moves alertly) (1780?–1848), member of the Fox clan; became leader of Sauks and Foxes and secured for them the territory of Iowa from the government; buried in Keokuk, Iowa, which was named for him; his son, **Moses Keokuk** (1818?–1903), was a famous orator.

Keokuk, Iowa, city on Mississippi and Des Moines rivers at s.e. corner of state; metal products, corn and cereal products, carbides; pop. 13,536 I-289, *map* I-302

Kephallenia (or Cephalonia), mountainous Greek island w. of mainland; largest of Ionian group; about 290 sq mi (750 sq km); currants and olives; pop. 31,787.

Kepler, Johannes (1571–1630), German astronomer K-228
astronomy A-713, S-106, *list* S-114
Galileo G-6
gravitation G-239
mathematics M-214
planetary orbits P-414
space travel S-458

Kepler's laws of planetary motion A-713, G-239, K-228, S-106

Keppel, Frederick Paul (1875–1943), U.S. educator, born in Staten Island, N.Y.; assistant secretary of war 1918–19; president Carnegie Corporation 1923–41.

Kerala, state in s.w. India; area 14,980 sq mi (38,800 sq km); cap. Trivandrum; formed 1956 from parts of former Travancore-Cochin and Madras states; pop. 21,347,375, *map* I-83

Keratin (or horn), fibrous protein in hoof H-231

Keratocyte cell, a type of epidermal cell S-315

Kerazeh. *see in index* Chorazin

Kerbela, Iraq. *see in index* Karbala

Kerch', U.S.S.R., port of Crimea, on Kerch' Peninsula; steel mills; pop. 128,000, *maps* E-360, U-63

Kérékou, Mathieu, president of Benin B-162

Kerensky, Alexander Feodorovich (1881–1970), Soviet revolutionary statesman, born in Simbirsk (now Ulyanovsk); fled to Paris, France, when Bolsheviks overthrew his government Oct. 1917; moved to U.S. 1940; author of 'Russia and History's Turning Point'
Russian Revolution R-354, U-52
World War I W-309

Keres (or Queres), a linguistic group of North American Indians living in pueblos on the Rio Grande and Rio Jemez and New Mexico.

Kerguélen Island, volcanic island 100 mi (160 km) long in s. Indian Ocean; French possession; whaling, seal-hunting base; discovered 1772 by Yves Joseph de Kerguélen-Trémarec.

Kerguélen-Trémarec, Yves-Joseph de (1734–97), French explorer, born in Quimper; discovered (1772) what he thought was rich continent in Antarctic and named it South France; realizing it was only a barren island, renamed it Isle of Desolation; later called Kerguélen Island
polar exploration P-499

Kérkyra. *see in index* Corfu

Kermadec Islands, group in Pacific about 600 mi (950 km) n.e. of New Zealand, to which it was annexed in 1887; total area, 13 sq mi (34 sq km); Raoul, or Sunday Island, largest; pop. 9.

Kerman (or Kirman, ancient Carmana), Iran, city in s.e.; capital of province of Kerman; Iran's chief rug exporter; 11th-century mosque, now restored; pop. 110,000
Iran and Iraq, *map* I-312
rug, *picture* R-341

Kermanshah, Iran, city in w.; on road between Baghdad and Tehran; trade in grain, rugs; pop. 250,000.

Kermit, Tex., city 40 mi (65 km) w. of Odessa; in area producing oil and natural gas; cattle ranching; incorporated 1938; pop. 8,015
Texas, *map* T-136

Kermit the Frog, muppet P-666, *picture* P-663

Kern, Jerome (1885–1945), U.S. composer, born in New York City; with Oscar Hammerstein II wrote the musical comedy 'Show Boat' (1927) M-685
popular music M-682

Kernel, fruit seed
corn C-722
nuts N-448

Kerner, Otto, U.S. governor of Illinois
United States U-182

Kernite (or rasorite), mineral yielding borax M-435

Kern River, stream rising in mountains of s.e. California; flows s.w. and n. to Lake Tulare
California, *map* C-52

Kerogen, a substance in oil shale
gas G-39

Kerosene (or kerosine, also called coal oil), an oil distilled from petroleum; ending "ine" adopted 1957 by petroleum chemists because "ene" suggests falsely that oil consists of unsaturated compounds
asphalt distilled A-702
fuel F-441
jet fuel A-74
petroleum P-261, 264
lighting and lamps L-205

Kerouac, Jack (1922–69), U.S. author; spokesman for the beat generation K-229
Ginsberg G-145

Kerpestein, LeRoy. *see in index* Loring, Eugene

Kerr, Jean Collins (born 1924), U.S. writer, born in Scranton, Pa.; married Walter F. Kerr 1943 ('Please Don't Eat the Daisies', 'The Snake Has All the Lines', humorous pieces; 'Mary, Mary', play and movie).

Kerr, Robert Samuel (1896–1963), U.S. lawyer, oil producer, and political leader; born in Ada, Okla.; governor of Oklahoma 1943–47; U.S. senator (Democrat) 1949–63.

Kerr, Walter Francis (born 1913), U.S. drama critic and playwright, born in Evanston, Ill.; on faculty Catholic University of America (drama department) 1938–49; drama critic *New York Herald Tribune* (1951–66), *The New York Times;* husband of Jean Kerr (play: 'Sing Out, Sweet Land'; criticism: 'How Not to Write a Play', 'The Theater in Spite of Itself', 'Tragedy and Comedy').

Kerrey, Bob, U.S. senator from Nebraska, former governor of Nebraska
Nebraska N-101

Kerrville, Tex., city 55 mi (90 km) n.w. of San Antonio, at mouth of Guadalupe River; wool processing, ranching, incorporated 1942; pop. 15,276, *map* T-136

Kerry, county of s.w. Ireland in province of Munster; 1,815 sq mi (4,700 sq km); beautiful mountain scenery; lakes of Killarney; pop. 112,785.

Kerry, Mountains of, in Ireland I-317

Kerry blue terrier, dog, *picture* D-204

Kersey, a thick, coarse woolen cloth used to make clothing; woven first in medieval England.

Kerst, Donald William (born 1911), U.S. physicist, born in Galena, Ill.; joined faculty of University of Illinois 1938, professor of physics 1943–57; invented betatron there.

Kerulen River, 780 mi (1,255 km) long, rises in n.e. Mongolian People's Republic, flows into Hulun Nor (lake) in China, *map* A-697

Kerwin, Joseph P. (born 1932), U.S. astronaut, physician, born in Oak Park, Ill.; flight surgeon with U.S. Marine Corps 1956–58, with U.S. Navy 1958–; scientist-astronaut 1965–; member Skylab crew 1973 S-478

Kerwin, Patrick (1889–1963), Canadian jurist, born in Sarnia, Ont.; created king's counsel 1928; appointed judge of the Supreme Court of Canada 1935, chief justice 1954–63.

Kesselring, Albert (1885–1960), German army officer; born in Marktstedt, Bavaria; led air attacks on Poland 1939, on The Netherlands, Belgium, Britain 1940, on U.S.S.R. 1941–42; became commander in Italy 1943, in West 1945; death sentence for war crimes in Italy commuted to life imprisonment, later to 21 years; freed by British 1952; wrote 'Kesselring: a Soldier's Record'.

Kestrel (also called windhover), a bird of prey, one of smallest of true falcons *(Falco tinnunculus)* found throughout Old World; resembles common sparrow hawk of Americas, to which it is related; strong flier, hovers for minute or two in one spot.

Keswick Dam, dam in California C-38

Keta salmon. *see in index* Chum salmon

Ketch, sailing ship, *pictures* B-327, S-242

Ketchel, Stanley (originally Stanislaus Kiecal) (1887–1910), U.S. middleweight boxer, born in Grand Rapids, Mich.; scored 46 knockouts, 14 in succession; was shot to death.

Ketchikan, Alaska, city and port of entry in s.e. Alaska 235 mi (380 km) s.e. of Juneau; pulp mill; salmon canning, halibut processing, lumbering; totem pole collection; Ketchikan King Salmon Derby; pop. 7,198

Ki Tsurayuki / Knight

husband of sculptor **Theo Ruggles Kitson** (1871–1932); his many monuments to national and historic figures include 'The Pilgrim Maiden' at Plymouth, Mass., *picture* M-194

Ki Tsurayuki (or Tsurayuki Ki-no) (884?–946), Japanese poet and government official at the old capital of Heian (now Kyoto); his literary criticism influenced court poetry for centuries
- Japan J-49
- literature J-79

Kittatinny Mountain, a ridge of the Appalachians, mainly in n.w. New Jersey along Delaware River; extends from Shawangunk Mountains in s.e. New York to Blue Mountain in e. Pennsylvania
- New Jersey N-194, *maps* N-194, 211, *picture* N-195

Kittery, Me., community across bay from Portsmouth, N.H.; site of Portsmouth Navy Yard; incorporated 1647; pop. of township 11,028, *map* M-66, *picture* N-179

Kittim. *see in index* Citium

Kittinger, Joseph William, Jr. (born 1928), U.S. Air Force officer, born in Tampa, Fla.; broke many records as high altitude test parachutist
- ballooning B-44

Kittiwake, a gull *(Rissa tridactyla)* that breeds in the Arctic regions and winters as far south as the Atlantic and Pacific coasts of the United States; about 18 in. (46 cm) long and has white plumage with a pale bluish-gray mantle; hind toe is entirely absent or rudimentary G-317

Kittl, Ema. *see in index* Destinn, Emmy

Kitt Peak National Observatory, 45 mi (72 km) s.w. of Tucson, Ariz., on Papago Indian reservation; dedicated 1960; maintained by National Science Foundation, coordinated with NASA astronomy in space program; world's largest solar telescope; 84 in. (213 cm) reflecting telescope O-457

Kittredge, George Lyman (1860–1941), U.S. educator and philologist, born in Boston, Mass.; professor of English at Harvard University 1894–1936; author of standard works on English grammar and philology; authority on Shakespeare.

Kittson, Norman Wolfred (1814–88), Canadian fur trader; born in Chambly, Lower Canada; joined American Fur Company 1830; ran trading post at Pembina on Red River and helped break Hudson Bay Company monopoly 1844–54.

Kitty Hawk, N.C., village in n.e. on strip of land between Albemarle Sound and Atlantic Ocean; Wright Brothers National Memorial nearby; pop. 600
- first airplane flight A-202, *table* A-206
- North Carolina N-353, *map* N-370, *picture* N-364
- Wright W-368

Kiushu. *see in index* Kyushu

Kiva, North American Indian architecture I-128

Kivu, Lake, e.-central Africa on e. border of Zaire; 60 mi (95 km) long, 30 mi (50 km) wide; tourist center, *map* A-115

Kiwanis clubs, organizations of business, professional, and agricultural men for the rendering of civic and social service to their communities; the first Kiwanis club was formed in Detroit in 1915, and Kiwanis International was organized in 1917; clubs have two members of each business or profession in the community; motto, "We build" F-387

Kiwi (or apteryx), a flightless bird native to New Zealand; about size of domestic fowl; nocturnal B-277
- New Zealand N-288

Ki-Wives International, women's organization affiliated with the Kiwanis clubs W-270

Kizilirmak (ancient Halys), river in Turkey, rises near border of Armenia; flows n. and w. into Black Sea; 600 mi (950 km) long T-318

Kjelgaard, James Arthur (1910–59), U.S. author of children's books, born in New York City; American history and the outdoors ('Big Red'; 'Snow Dog'; 'Explorations of Père Marquette'; 'Haunt Fox'; 'Desert Dog'; 'Rescue Dog of the High Pass'; 'The Black Faun'; 'Boomerang Hunter').

Kjölen Mountains, between Sweden and Norway E-329
- Europe, *map* E-360

Klabund (pen name of Alfred Henschke) (1890–1928), German author of lyrics, novels, and dramas; born in Crossen on the Oder; in his short life made important contribution to German literature; among his plays are 'Kirchblütenfest' with Japanese setting and Chinese play 'Kreidekreis'; novels, mainly historical, include 'Mohammed', 'Pjotr', and 'Borgia'.

Klagenfurt, Austria, city in s., capital of province of Carinthia; in manufacturing area; tourist center; pop. 69,218.

Klaipeda. *see in index* Memel

Klamath, a people of s. Oregon O-583. *see also in index* Modoc

Klamath Falls, Ore., city at s. tip of Upper Klamath Lake, about 15 mi (25 km) n. of California line; railroad and tourist center in lumbering, farming (barley, potatoes), and livestock-raising area; farm machinery; Kingsley Field; annual rodeo; pop. 16,661, *map* N-350
- Oregon O-585, *maps* O-582, 596

Klamath Mountains, mountains that are a part of the Pacific Coast Ranges
- California C-36, *map* C-34
- Oregon O-583, *map* O-582

Klamath River, 180 mi (290 km) long rising in Upper Klamath Lake in s. Oregon and flowing through n. California into Pacific
- California, *map* C-53
- Oregon, *map* O-597
- United States, *map* U-193

Klaproth, Martin Heinrich (1743–1817), German chemist and mineralogist, born in Wernigerode, Prussia; his research led to discovery of uranium and zirconium
- titanium T-193
- uranium U-230

Klar River, short stream in s. of Scandinavian peninsula; flows into Lake Vänern.

Klassen, Elmer Theodore (born 1908), U.S. public official, born in Hillsboro, Kan.; with American Can Company 1925–68, president 1965–68; deputy postmaster general 1969–71, postmaster general 1972–75.

Klassen, Jan, name given by Dutch to main character in a puppet show, also to a puppet or to a puppet theater P-665

Klaus, Karl Karlovich (1796–1864), Russian chemist and biologist, known as the discoverer of ruthenium; also investigated flora and fauna of Volga steppes.

Klausenburg. *see in index* Cluj

Kléber, Jean-Baptiste (1753–1800), French Revolutionary general, one of greatest of epoch; born in Strasbourg; assassinated while subjugating Egypt.

Klebs, Edwin (1834–1913), German pathologist, born in Königsberg; professor at Bern, Würzburg, Prague, Zürich, and Rush Medical College, Chicago; known for work in pathology of infectious diseases; with Friedrich Löffler discovered diphtheria bacillus.

Klebsiella pneumoniae, bacterium, *picture* D-170

Klee, Paul (1879–1940), Swiss surrealist painter K-254
- 'Intention' P-27
- 'Old Man Figuring' D-255
- Switzerland S-740

Kleiber, Erich (1890–1956), Austrian opera conductor, born in Vienna; general director Berlin Staatsoper 1923–35; guest conductor New York Philharmonic Orchestra.

Klein, Abraham Moses (1909–72), Canadian poet, born in Montreal, Que. C-124

Klein, Anne (1923–74), U.S. dress designer D-271

Klein, Charles Herbert (1904–58), U.S. baseball player, born in Indianapolis, Ind.; N.L. outfielder for Philadelphia 1928–33, Chicago 1934–36, Philadelphia 1936–39, Pittsburgh 1939, Philadelphia 1940–44; career batting average .320.

Klein, Herbert George (born 1918), U.S. newspaper editor, born in Los Angeles, Calif.; editor *The San Diego Union* 1959–68; manager of communications for Richard M. Nixon's presidential campaign 1968; U.S. director of communications for the executive branch 1969–73.

Kleindienst, Richard Gordon (born 1923), U.S. public official and lawyer, born in Winslow, Ariz.; attorney general 1972–73
- Nixon N-326

Kleist, E.G. von (1700–1748), German administrator and cleric; discovered Leyden jar E-161

Kleist, Heinrich von (1777–1811), German romantic dramatist and poet, born in Frankfurt-an-der-Oder ('Penthesilea', tragedy; 'The Broken Pitcher', comedy) G-109

Klem, William J. (1874–1951), U.S. baseball umpire, born in Rochester, N.Y.; N.L. umpire 1905–40, chief of N.L. umpires 1941–51; worked in 18 world series for all-time record for umpires.

Klemperer, Otto (1885–1973), German conductor K-255
- orchestra, *list* O-579

Kleppe, Thomas S. (born 1919), U.S. public official, born in Kintyre, N.D.; member U.S. Congress (Republican) 1967–70; administrator Small Business Administration 1971–75; secretary U.S. Department of Interior 1975–77.

Kleptomania, neurotic impulse to steal, especially when there is no economic need; articles often useless but symbolic.

Klerk, Michel de (1884–1923), Dutch architect, identified with modern movement in The Netherlands; obtained decorative effects with brick and tile; especially noted for municipal buildings and a housing project in Amsterdam.

Kleve (or Cleves), West Germany, town in n.w. near frontier of The Netherlands; formerly capital of duchy; castle associated with the legend 'Knights of the Swan', in Wagner's 'Lohengrin'; pop. 22,100, *map* G-131

Klima, ancient Greek climate zones C-499

Kline, Franz (1910–1962), U.S. artist
- 'Painting No. 7', *picture* A-665

Klinefelter's syndrome, genetic disorder G-48

Klinger, Friedrich Maximilian von (1752–1831), German dramatist, born in Frankfurt; leading figure of the Storm and Stress (in German, Sturm und Drang) period of German romanticism named after his drama of that title; other works: 'Die Zwillinge' (The Twins) and 'Fausts Leben, Taten und Höllenfahrt' (Faust's Life, Deeds, and Journey to Hell).

Klinger, Max (1857–1920), German painter, sculptor, and etcher, born in Leipzig; his works are highly personal, subjective, morbidly imaginative; sculptures 'Salome' and 'Cassandra' are typical; renowned is a statue of Beethoven, in marble, ivory, fine metals, and bronze.

Klinokinesis, animal behavior A-441

Klint, Kaare (1888–1954), Danish furniture designer F-462

Klismos, Greek chair F-455

KLM. *see in index* Royal Dutch Airlines

Klondike, a gold-mining region in Yukon Territory Y-440
- Alaska A-246
- gold rush G-184
- Northwest Territories N-388
- Seattle S-162
- Yukon River Y-439

Klondike, type of card game C-164, *picture* C-163

Klondike Gold Rush National Historical Park, park in Alaska and Washington N-52, *map* N-40

Klondike National Historical Site, historical site in Dawson, Y.T. N-30

Klopstock, Friedrich Gottlieb (1724–1803), German epic, lyric, and dramatic poet, born in Quedlinburg, Prussian Saxony; deeply religious and patriotic; sought to restore ancient German spirit G-106

Kluane National Park, park in Yukon Territory N-30

Kluck, Alexander von (1846–1934), Prussian general and field marshal of World War I, born in Münster, Germany; forced to retire 1916 because of wounds suffered in 1915.

Klutznick, Philip M. (born 1907), U.S. executive and public official, born in Kansas City, Mo.; U.S. representative to UN Economic and Social Council 1961–63; founder and former head Urban Investment and Development Co.; president World Jewish Congress 1977–79; secretary of commerce 1979–81.

Klystron, type of electronic tube
- electronics E-177

Klyuchevskaya (or Kluchev), active volcano in Kamchatka, Siberia
- U.S.S.R., *map* U-59

KMT. *see in index* Kuomintang

Knapweed (also called hardheads), a perennial plant *(Centaurea nigra)* of composite family, native to Europe but now common to North America; the plant grows to 2 ft (0.6 m); leaves lance-shaped, to 6 in. (15 cm) long; small flowers rose-purple.

Knee, in anatomy
- joint J-137
- skeleton S-310

Knee jerk, a simple reflex R-138
- nervous system, *diagram* N-121

'Kneeling Cupid, The', sculpture by Michelangelo, *picture* M-352

'Kneeling Woman', work by Lehmbruck
- sculpture S-149

Kneisel, Franz (1865–1926), violinist and musical conductor, born in Bucharest, Romania, of German parents; founder and first violinist of Kneisel Quartet.

Kneller, Sir Godfrey (1646–1723), court painter to Charles II and succeeding English sovereigns to time of George I; born in Germany.

Knickerbocker, Diedrich, pretended author of Washington Irving's burlesque history of New York City; the Knickerbockers were an old Dutch family; name now applied to descendants of the original Dutch settlers of New York, more widely to any New Yorker A-345

Knickerbocker Baseball Club of New York City B-95

Knife, utensil or weapon K-255. *see also in index* Fork; Spoon
- etiquette E-319, *pictures* E-320, 321
- industrial design, *picture* I-171
- weapon, *picture* W-111

Knight, Charles Robert (1874–1953), U.S. painter, illustrator, sculptor, and muralist; born in Brooklyn, N.Y.; favorite subjects animals and birds, prehistoric people and animals.

Knight, Eric Mowbray (1897–1943), U.S. author, born in Yorkshire, England; to U.S. 1912; in British Army in World War I; major, U.S. Army, World War II; killed in airplane crash ('Lassie Come Home', 'This Above All').

Knight, Frank Hyneman (1885–1972), U.S. economist and author, born in McLean County, Ill.; professor of economics University of Chicago 1928–52.

Knight, Gladys (born 1944), U.S. singer
- popular music M-679

Knight, John Shively (1894–1981), U.S. journalist and publisher, born in Bluefield, W. Va.; publisher of many daily newspapers including *Miami Herald, Detroit Free Press, Akron Beacon Journal, Philadelphia Inquirer,* and *Philadelphia Daily News;* owner-editor-publisher of *Chicago Daily News* 1944–59; won Pulitzer prize for editorial writing 1968, many other awards.

Koritsa / Kristofferson

Koritsa (in Albanian, Korçë), Albania, town in s.e.; pop. 39,386.

Kornberg, Arthur (born 1918), U.S. biochemist, born in Brooklyn, N.Y.; professor, Washington University 1953–59, Stanford University from 1959; won Max Berg Award 1968. *see also in index* Nobel Prizewinners, *table*

Körner, Karl Theodor (1791–1813), German poet and patriot, born in Dresden; wrote patriotic songs; died fighting against Napoleon.

Korngold, Erich Wolfgang (1897–1957), U.S. composer, born in Brünn, in Moravia; was child prodigy; at age of 11 composed pantomime, 'The Snowman', produced in Vienna; to U.S. 1934, became citizen 1943; won Academy award for motion-picture scores of 'Anthony Adverse' 1936 and 'The Adventures of Robin Hood' 1938 (opera, 'The Dead City').

Kornilov, Lavr Georgievich (1870–1918), Russian general, commanded in Galician campaign during World War I; his unsuccessful mutiny against Kerensky's provisional government (1917) prepared way for later Bolshevik victory; killed in battle against Red army while leading Volunteer army in the Kuban region R-354

Korolenko, Vladimir (1853–1921), Russian fiction writer and publicist; born in Zhitomir, Russia, of Russian-Polish family; opposed czarism and Communism ('Makar's Dream and Other Stories'; 'The Blind Musician'; 'The Day of Atonement'; autobiography, 'The History of My Contemporary').

'Korolu, the Singing Bandit', work by Walker S-656

Korsakoff's syndrome, memory disorder M-295

Kortrijk. *see in index* Courtrai

Koryak, mountain range in n.e. Siberia U-23, *map* A-697

Koryo period, in Korean history K-284
  Korean literature K-292

Korzeniowski, Teodor Josef Konrad. *see in index* Conrad, Joseph

Korzybski, Alfred (1879–1950), U.S. scientist K-301

Kos (in Italian, Coo), island of Dodecanese in Aegean Sea; area 111 sq mi (288 sq km).

Kosciusko, Thaddeus (1746–1817), Polish general K-301
  Polish history P-494
  Thaddeus Kosciuszko N. Mem. N-59

Kosciusko, Mount, in Australian Alps, New South Wales, highest peak in Australia 7,310 ft (2,230 m) A-769, *map* A-819
  height, comparative. *see in index* Mountain, *table*
  New South Wales N-234
  Snowy Mountains S-339

Koshare, Pueblo priest who acts as holy clown at public religious ceremonies.

Kosher, Judaic term meaning fit or proper; applies especially to food made ceremonially clean according to Mosaic law
  meat industry M-253

'Koshoku gonin onna' (Five Women Who Loved Love), novel by Saikaku Ihara J-81

'Koshoku ichidai otoko', novel by Saikaku Ihara J-81

Košice, Czechoslovakia, city in e. part; held by Hungary 1938–45; wool center; 14th-century Gothic cathedral; pop. 222,200 C-813, *maps* C-814, E-360

Kosinski, Jerzy (born 1933), Polish-born author K-301

Koslov, Peter Kuzmich (1863–1935), Russian archaeologist; made major discoveries in Mongolia; including Genghis Khan's capital Karakorum (1899).

'Kosmos', work by Humboldt H-321

Kosmos 112, Soviet military observation satellite A-163

Kossel, Albrecht (1853–1927), German physiologist, born in Rostock; conducted research on chemistry of the cell and proteins. *see also in index* Nobel Prizewinners, *table*

Kossuth, Lajos (1802–94), Hungarian patriot K-301
  Hungary H-329

Kostelanetz, André (1901–80), U.S. orchestra conductor, born in Russia; to U.S. 1922; married singer Lily Pons 1938, divorced 1958; won popularity on radio.

Koster, Laurens Janszoon. *see in index* Coster, Laurens Janszoon

Kosygin, Aleksei (1904–80), Soviet government official K-302
  Johnson J-135
  Nixon, *picture* N-328

Koto, a Japanese harp consisting of a long box over which are stretched 13 strings, each with a bridge; played with both hands and tuned by shifting the bridges.

Kotor (or Cattaro), Yugoslavia, fortified town on Gulf of Kotor, inlet of Adriatic; excellent harbor; pop. 8,572.

Kotte, ancient capital of the Sinalese kings S-561

Kotzebue, August Friedrich von (1761–1819), German playwright, born in Weimar; prolific; popular all over Europe; best-known play 'The Stranger'.

Kotzebue Sound, inlet of Chukchi Sea in Alaska, 40 to 65 mi (64 to 105 km) long, *map* A-254

Kouchibouguac National Park, park in New Brunswick N-31, *map* N-29

Koufax, Sandy (born 1935), U.S. left-handed baseball pitcher, born in Brooklyn, N.Y.; with Brooklyn Dodgers 1955–57, Los Angeles Dodgers 1958–66; set many pitching records; TV sportscaster 1967–73, *list* B-95

Kountché, Seyni (1931–87), president of Niger N-309

Koussevitzky, Serge (1874–1951), Russian conductor K-302

Kovalevsky, Sonya (1850–91), Soviet mathematician K-302

Kovno. *see in index* Kaunas

Kowloon, peninsula and port city of Hong Kong colony, on Chinese mainland opposite island of Hong Kong; pop. 716,272 H-228

Koxinga (or Cheng Ch'eng-kung) (1623–63), Chinese pirate and patriot
  Taiwan T-14

Kozhikode (formerly Calicut), India, city and port on s.w. coast, in Kerala state; exports copra, coffee, ginger, tea, rubber; pop. 333,979, *map* I-83

Kozlov, Frol Romanovich (1908–65), Soviet government official, born near Kasimov; member of Communist party 1926–65, of Presidium 1957–65; a first deputy premier 1958–60; member of Central Committee secretariat 1960–64.

Kozyrev, Nikolai A. (born 1908), Russian astronomer, born St. Petersburg; first to discover volcaniclike activity on the moon M-580

KQX, radio station in San Jose, Calif. R-51

Kr. *see in index* Krypton

Kraepelin, Emil (1856–1926), German psychiatrist, born in Neustrelitz; professor at University of Munich; revised classification of mental diseases; analyzed fatigue process and studied effect of alcohol on the mind
  mental illness M-302

Krafft, Adam (1455?–1509), principal German sculptor of late Gothic period; birthplace probably Nuremberg, Germany; executed tabernacles, tombs, reliefs, and religious figures.

Kraft process
  forest products F-316
  paper products P-111

Krait, reptile of the family Elapidae S-337

Krak (or Krakus), legendary Slavic chieftain K-303

Krakatoa (or Krakatau), volcanic island in Indonesia between Java and Sumatra K-302
  flood F-182
  Indonesia, *map* I-166
  volcano V-402
  world W-296

Kraków, Poland; pop. 706,100 K-303
  Europe, *map* E-360
  Poland, *picture* P-490

Krakowskie Przedmieście Street, a main thoroughfare in Warsaw, Poland W-33

Kramer, Jack (full name John Albert Kramer) (born 1921), U.S. tennis player, born in Las Vegas, Nev.; won U.S. singles 1946–47; Wimbledon champion 1947; turned professional 1947; promoter 1952–62; first executive director Association of Tennis Professionals T-107

Kranach, Lucas. *see in index* Cranach, Lucas

Krasnodar (formerly Ekaterinodar), U.S.S.R., city of n. Caucasia on Kuban' River in farm area e. of Black Sea; food products, machinery; petroleum refining; pop. 465,000, *map* E-360
  U.S.S.R., *maps* U-59, 63

Krasnov, Peter (1882–1947), Soviet author R-353

Krasnoyarsk, U.S.S.R., Siberian city on Yenisey River and Trans-Siberian Railroad; machinery; lumber, paper, and cement industries; flour milling; world's largest hydroelectric plant nearby; pop. 748,000
  U.S.S.R., *map* U-59

Krasnozem, kind of soil found in U.S.S.R. U-28

Kratzer, Nicholas (1487–1550?), astronomer to Henry VIII of England, born in Munich, Germany.

Kraus-Weber, minimum muscular fitness test H-94

Kravis, Henry R. (born 1944), U.S. investment banker and king of the leveraged buyout, born in Tulsa, Okla.; founding partner Kohlberg, Kravis, Roberts and Company 1976; senior partner 1987– ; instrumental figure in shaping practice of the leveraged buyout; led a group in purchase of RJR Nabisco for a record buyout price of $25 billion 1988.

'Krazy Kat', comic strip C-189, *picture* C-188

Krebs, Hans Adolf (1900–81), British scientist, born in Hildesheim, Germany; professor of biochemistry Oxford University 1954–67. *see also in index* Nobel Prizewinners, *table*
  Krebs cycle B-202, *diagram* B-200

Krebs cycle, in biochemistry
  cellular activity B-202, *diagram* B-200
  metabolism M-306

Kredel, Fritz (1900–73), U.S. artist and illustrator, born in Michelstadt, Germany; taught art in Germany; to U.S. 1938; illustrated for children: Andersen's 'Fairy Tales'; Grimm's 'Fairy Tales'; 'Pinocchio', by Carlo Lorenzini.

Krefeld, West Germany, manufacturing town 30 mi (50 km) n.w. of Cologne; famous textile institute; pop. 216,871.

Krehbiel, Henry Edward (dean of American critics) (1854–1923), U.S. music critic and writer, born in Ann Arbor, Mich.; music critic *Cincinnati Gazette*, 1874–80, *New York Tribune*, 1880–1923 ('How to Listen to Music'; 'Chapters of Opera').

Kreisky, Bruno (born 1911), Austrian chancellor K-303

Kreisler, Fritz (1875–1962), U.S. violinist and composer K-303

Kremer, Gerhard. *see in index* Mercator Gerhardus

Kremlin, in Soviet architecture K-304
  Moscow M-591, U-47, *picture* U-18

Krenek, Ernst (born 1900), U.S. composer, born in Vienna, Austria; to U.S. 1938, became citizen 1945; extreme modernist in style; won first widespread fame with 'Jonny spielt auf', jazz opera; other operas include 'The Life of Orestes'.

Kreps, Juanita M. (born 1921), U.S. educator and public official, born in Lynch, Ky.; member faculty Duke University 1955–77, professor 1968–77, vice-president 1973–77; U.S. secretary of commerce 1977–79.

Kresge, Sebastian Spering (1867–1966), U.S. merchant and philanthropist, born in Bald Mount, Pa.; partner Kresge and Wilson, Detroit, 1907, incorporated as S.S. Kresge Company 1912.

Kress, Samuel Henry (1863–1955), U.S. merchant and art patron, born in Cherryville, Northampton County, Pa.; founded S.H. Kress & Co. (chain of 5-, 10-, and 25-cent stores) at Memphis, Tenn., 1896; established Samuel H. Kress Foundation 1929; donated many art treasures to National Gallery of Art and other leading museums.

Krete. *see in index* Crete

Kretschmer, Ernst (1888–1964), German psychiatrist who tried to correlate body build and physical constitution with personality characteristics and mental illness P-234

Kreuger, Ivar (1880–1932), Swedish "match king" and financial wizard, born in Kalmar; built a huge international match trust; committed suicide when faced with bankruptcy.

Kreutzer, Konradin (1780–1849), German pianist, conductor, and composer of operas, church music, and chamber music; born near Konstanz; among best-known works is light opera, 'Nachtlager von Granada'.

Kreutzer, Rodolphe (1766–1831), French violinist of German extraction, born in Versailles; wrote many operas and instrumental works; Beethoven dedicated to him the sonata for violin and piano known as the Kreutzer Sonata in A Major.

Krieghoff, Cornelius (1812–72), Canadian painter, born in Düsseldorf, Germany; with U.S. Army in Seminole Wars 1837–40; known for landscapes, portraits, and portrayals of early French-Canadian life.

Kriegsakademie, in Berlin, Germany; founded in 1810
  military education M-411

Kriemhild, wife of the hero Siegfried in the Nibelungenlied
  'Song of the Nieblungs' N-303

Krill, animal
  Antarctic food chain A-473

Krim. *see in index* Crimea

Krio, language
  Sierra Leone S-285

Kris, type of sword S-745, *picture* S-744

Krishna, a Hindu god H-157
  pearl P-166

'Krishna Holding Mount Govardhan', Indian painting P-73

Krishna Menon, Vengalil Krishnan (1897–1974), Indian diplomat, born in Calicut, now Kozhikode; worked for Indian independence; delegate to UN 1946–47, 1952–62; high commissioner of India in London 1947–52; minister for defense 1957–62.

Krishna River. *see in index* Kistna River

Kriss Kringle. *see in index* Santa Claus

Kristallnacht (or Night of Broken Glass), Nov. 9–10, 1938, Germany
  Holocaust H-205

Kristensen, Leonard, Norwegian whaling captain; member of small party of first persons to land on Antarctic Continent (1895)
  polar exploration P-501, *list* P-502

Kristiansand, Norway, seaport on s. coast; exports wood pulp, lumber, nickel, fish; has 17th-century Gothic cathedral; founded 1641; pop. 50,217, *map* E-360

Kristofferson, Kris (born 1936), erratic singer-songwriter-actor, born in Brownsville, Tex.; won Rhodes Scholarship to Oxford 1958; failed novelist, but prizewinning short-story writer; success with haunting ballads began when Roger Miller and Janis Joplin each recorded 'Me and Bobby McGee'; 'Sunday Morning Coming Down' (Johnny Cash), 'Help Me Make It Through the Night' (Sammi Smith), 'Nobody Wins' (Frank Sinatra); film success with straight-acting roles, 'Rollover', 'Semi-Tough', 'Heaven's Gate', 'Trouble in Mind'.

Kríti / Kunin

Kríti. *see in index* Crete
Krivoy Rog (or Krivoi Rog), U.S.S.R., city in s. Ukrainian Soviet Socialist Republic; pop. 573,000, *map* E-360
U.S.S.R., *maps* U-59, 63
KRM. *see in index* Kurzweil Reading Machine
Kroeber, Alfred Louis (1876–1960), U.S. anthropologist, born in Hoboken, N.J.; taught anthropology at University of California 1901–46; expert on North American Indians and archaeology of Mexico and Peru; wrote textbook, 'Anthropology'.
anthropology A-487
Kroger, Bernard Henry (1860–1938), U.S. grocer, born in Cincinnati, Ohio; founded Kroger Grocery and Baking Co. (1882) which became a grocery chain.
Krogh, Schack August Steenberg (1874–1949), Danish physiologist, born in Grenaa; noted for experiments in respiration and for researches in capillaries and the blood. *see also in index* Nobel Prizewinners, *table*
Krohg, Christian (1852–1925), Norwegian painter and author, born in Oslo; depicted sea and seamen with realism and strength; wrote novels and books on art
painting, *picture* A-328
Krol, John Joseph, Cardinal (born 1910), U.S. Roman Catholic prelate, born in Cleveland, Ohio; auxiliary bishop of Cleveland 1953–61; archbishop of Philadelphia 1961– ; created cardinal 1967; president National Conference of Catholic Bishops 1972–74.
Kroll, Leon (1884–1974), U.S. painter, born in New York City; simple, strong, and highly individual in landscape, still life, and figure work.
Kroll Process, titanium production T-193
Kronborg Castle, castle in Denmark, *picture* D-99
Kronshtadt (or Kronstadt), U.S.S.R., port and naval base on island of Kotlin in Gulf of Finland 20 mi (30 km) w. of Leningrad; founded 1710 by Peter the Great, *map* U-63
Kronshtadt Rebellion (1921), in Russian history R-356
Kroo. *see in index* Kru
Kropotkin, Peter (1842–1921), Russian geographer and anarchist K-306
anarchism A-388, R-282
Kru (or Kroo, or Croo), a people of Liberia and adjacent parts of w. Africa; famous as canoe men and sailors; tribal mark (black or blue line) tattooed on forehead.
Krueger, Karl (1894–1979), U.S. orchestral conductor, born in Atchison, Kan.; studied at Heidelberg, Germany, and Vienna, Austria; conductor Seattle Symphony Orchestra, Kansas City Philharmonic; Conductor Detroit Symphony Orchestra 1943–49.
Krueger, Walter (1881–1967), U.S. general, born in Flatow, Germany; participated in Spanish-American War; commanded Sixth Army in World War II W-346
Krug, Julius Albert (1907–70), U.S. public power expert and government official, born in Madison, Wis.; with Tennessee Valley Authority 1938–40, War Production Board 1942–45, chairman after Sept. 1944; U.S. secretary of the interior 1946–49.
Kruger, Paul (1825–1904), Boer patriot K-306
Krugerrand, gold coin C-540
Kruglov, Sergei Nikiforovich (born 1900?), Soviet government official; deputy commissar for internal affairs during World War II; minister of internal affairs 1946–56.
Krumgold, Joseph (1908–80), U.S. author and motion-picture producer, born in Jersey City, N.J.; writer and producer for major motion-picture companies 1931–41, for Office of War Information during World War II, operated own company in Israel 1946–50 ('. . . and now Miguel', awarded 1954 Newbery Medal; 'Onion John', awarded 1960 Newbery Medal).
Krummholz (or elfinwood), stunned forest characteristic of mountainous regions M-636
Krung Thep. *see in index* Bangkok
Krupa, Gene (1909–73), U.S. jazz drummer and bandleader, born in Chicago, Ill.; associated with Chicago style before becoming first drummer to win large public acclaim, *picture* P-214
Krupp, Alfred (Alfred the Great, or Cannon King) (1812–87), German cannon maker K-307
artillery A-660
Krupp, Arndt (died 1624) K-306
Krupp, Friedrich (1787–1826), German ironmaster K-306
Krupp, Friedrich Alfred (1854–1902), German industrialist K-307
Krupp von Bohlen und Halbach, Alfried (1907–67), German industrialist K-307
Krupp von Bohlen und Halbach, Bertha (1886–1957), eldest daughter of Friedrich Alfred Krupp; brought up to manage Krupp works at Essen, which she inherited at 16; married **Baron Gustav von Bohlen und Halbach** (1870–1950), who added Krupp to his name and became chief director of works K-307
Krutch, Joseph Wood (1893–1970), U.S. critic and essayist, born in Knoxville, Tenn.; drama critic and associate editor *The Nation* 1924–32, literary editor 1933–37; professor of English 1937–43, of dramatic literature 1943–52, Columbia University ('Samuel Johnson'; 'The Twelve Seasons'; 'The Desert Year'; 'The Best of Two Worlds'; 'The Measure of Man'; 'The Great Chain of Life'; 'Human Nature and the Human Condition'; 'The Forgotten Peninsula'; 'If You Don't Mind My Saying So'; 'More Lives Than One', autobiography).
Krylov, Ivan Andreevich (1768–1844), Russian fabulist, born in Moscow; wrote fables largely in language of peasants, satirizing life of his time, often borrowed themes from Aesop and La Fontaine
Russian literature R-348, 353
Krynica Run, luge run in Poland S-322
Krypton (Kr), colorless, odorless gas
air composition, *picture* A-146
noble gases N-330
periodic table P-224, *list* P-226, *table* P-225
Kshatriya, Hindu of the soldier caste
India I-68
Kt. *see in index* Carat
KT (kiloton), unit of measure for the explosive force of a nuclear weapon
nuclear explosion effects N-434
Kuala Lumpur, Malaysia, capital, on Malay Peninsula near w. coast; pop. 937,900 K-307
Asia, *map* A-697
Islam, *picture* I-361
Malaysia M-70
Kuang-hsü (1871–1908), Chinese emperor during whose reign the empress dowager Tz'u-hsi dominated the government C-370
Kuang Wu Ti (ruled AD 25–57), emperor in China's Han Dynasty C-362
Kuan Han-ch'ing (1241?–1320?), Chinese playwright C-389
Kuan-t'ing Reservoir, in Peking, China P-173
Kuban' River, in n. Caucasus, rises on slopes of Mt. El'brus; flows about 585 mi (940 km) to Sea of Azov; rushing mountain river becomes sluggish stream lower C-232
U.S.S.R., *map* U-63
Kubasov, Valery N. (born 1935), Soviet cosmonaut, born in Vyazniki, n.e. of Moscow; flight engineer in Soyuz 6.
Kubelík, Jan (1880–1940), Bohemian violinist; father of Rafael Kubelík; popular and brilliant concert virtuoso.
Kubelík, Rafael (born 1914), Czechoslovak conductor and composer, born near Prague; made tour as conductor and piano accompanist for father, Jan Kubelík, 1934–35; chief conductor Czech Philharmonic Orchestra, Prague, 1942–48; musical director Chicago Symphony Orchestra 1950–53, Covent Garden Opera Company, London, 1955–58; chief conductor Bavarian Radio, Munich, 1961– ; music director Metropolitan Opera, New York City 1972–74
orchestra, *list* O-579
Kubelka, Peter, Austrian-born filmmaker M-626
Kubelsky, Benjamin. *see in index* Benny, Jack
Kubik, Gail (born 1914), U.S. composer, born in South Coffeyville, Okla.; studied under Piston and Sowerby; chamber music, choral and orchestral works, film scores; won Pulitzer prize 1952.
Kubitschek, Juscelino de Oliveira (1902–76), Brazilian statesman, born in Diamantina in state of Minas Gerais; president of Brazil 1956–60 B-408
Kublai Khan (1215–94), Mongol ruler, grandson of Genghis Khan K-308
China C-367
Marco Polo P-530
Mongol Empire M-535
zoo history Z-466
Kuching, seaport, capital of Sarawak, Malaysia, on Borneo; Sarawak Museum, set in gardens; pop. 37,949.
Kuder General Interest Survey, guidance and vocational testing, *diagrams* G-304
Kudu (or koodoo), one of the largest of African antelopes; white stripe down the back and 8 or 10 vertical stripes descending from it down the sides A-478
Kudzu (or kudzu vine), a perennial climber *(Pueraria thunbergiana)* of the pea family, native to China and Japan; leaves in 3 parts, flowers in purple clusters; in Japan, roots used as starch source and inner bark in cloth; in s. United States, plant used as forage crop, to enrich worn-out land, and to protect against erosion
legume L-118
Kufra Oasis, group of oases in Sahara in s.e. Libya; camels; dates, barley, grapes, olives; caravan trade; pop. 9,530
Oasis O-454
Kuhio, Prince (full name Jonah Kuhio Kalanianaole) (1871–1922), Hawaiian statesman, born in Koloa on Kauai; descendant of last independent king of that island; Congressional delegate to U.S. 1903–22; obtained legislation for Hawaiian back-to-the-land movement.
Kuhlmann, Richard von (1873–1948), German diplomat, born in Constantinople; secretary of state for foreign affairs 1917–18, negotiating treaties with U.S.S.R. and Romania; opposition of army high command and Chancellor Hertling caused him to resign.
Kuhn, Bowie (born 1926), U.S. lawyer, born in Takoma Park, Md.; admitted to bar 1951; commissioner of baseball 1969–84.
Kuhn, Richard (1900–1967), Austrian chemist, born in Vienna; awarded 1938 Nobel prize in chemistry for work on carotenoids and vitamins, but declined because of a Nazi decree; received diploma and gold medal after World War II. *see also in index* Nobel Prizewinners, *table*
Kuhn, Walt (1877–1949), U.S. modernist painter, born in New York City; simple, positive design; brilliant often raw color; paintings of women of stage and circus, also of flowers.
Kuibyshev (or Kuybyshev), U.S.S.R., port city on Volga and Samara rivers 525 mi (845 km) s.e. of Moscow; capital of the Soviet Union in World War II; pop. 1,243,000 K-308
Europe, *map* E-360
U.S.S.R., *maps* U-59, 63
Kuiper, Gerard Peter (1905–73), U.S. astronomer, born in the Netherlands; to U.S. 1933, became citizen 1937; with University of Chicago at Yerkes Observatory 1936–60, professor 1943–60, director of Yerkes and McDonald observatories 1947–49 and 1957–60; head Lunar and Planetary Laboratory, University of Arizona, 1960–73; author of books on astronomy.
Kukai. *see in index* Kobo Daishi
Ku K'ai-chih (350?–412), Chinese painter; remarkable expression with minimum detail; sure, rhythmic line; best known for a series of paintings on silk in British Museum, illustrating an essay 'The Admonition of the Instructress in the Palace'.
Kukla, hand puppet on Kukla, Fran, and Ollie Show P-666
Ku Klux Klan, (or The Invisible Empire of the South), U.S. secret terrorist organization K-309
black Americans B-294
Reconstruction period R-122
Tennessee T-88
United States U-110, 173
Ku Klux Klan Act (1871), United States
Klan violence K-309
Kukri, type of sword S-745, *picture* S-744
Kukui (also called candle nut, or candleberry, or lumbang, or varnish tree), tropical tree *(Aleurites molluccana)*, native to Malay region, found throughout tropics; state tree of Hawaii; fruit contains large seeds (candlenuts) useful in making candles, oil, dyes, paint, gum, food, and medicine
Hawaii state tree, *picture* H-66
nuts N-449
Külek Bogazi. *see in index* Cilician Gates
Kulikovo, battle of (1380), Russian history, *picture* U-50
Kumamoto, Japan, city on w. coast of Kyushu Island; textiles, tile; Kumamoto Medical University, school of pharmacy; pop. 488,166, *map* J-75
Kumar, Jainendra (born 1905), Hindu author I-108
Kumara Gupta (died 455? AD), ruler of India G-318
Kuma River, in n. Caucasus, U.S.S.R.; flows e. until lost in swamps; reaches Caspian Sea in flood time only; about 360 mi (580 km) long
U.S.S.R., *maps* U-59, 63
Kumasi (formerly Coomassie), Ghana, city in w. Africa; pop. 260,286, *map* A-115
Kumina, Jamaican cult J-17
Kumkum, forehead decoration worn by Indian girls and women, except orthodox Hindu widows.
Kun, Béla (1886–1938?), Hungarian leader; captured by Russia in World War I, he became follower of Lenin; organized revolution in Hungary and set up a Soviet rule; overthrown; became member of executive committee, Communist International.
Kunersdorf, Poland, former Prussian village 4 mi (6 km) e. of Frankfurt-an-der-Oder; Prussians defeated by Russians and Austrians 1759 (Seven Years' War); included in Poland since 1945.
Kung, Hsiang-hsi (H.H. Kung) (1881–1967), Chinese leader, born in Shansi; governor, Central Bank of China, 1933–45; vice-president of executive department of national government 1933 and 1939; minister of finance 1933–44. *see also in index* Soong
!Kung, African language of the Khoisan language family A-119
Kung fu, martial art M-160
K'ung-fu-tzu. *see in index* Confucius
Kungsör, town in e.-central Sweden, 80 mi (129 km) w. of Stockholm; pop. 3,170, *picture* S-730
Kunin, Madeleine (born 1933), third Democrat and first woman to become governor of Vermont, born in Zürich, Switzerland; refugee from Holocaust, immigrated to U.S. with mother at age 6; to Vermont as reporter for Burlington Free Press; moved by Swiss homeland struggle for women's voting rights, entered politics; aldermanic race loss 1972 followed by three terms in state House of Representatives; won lieutenant governor campaign 1978, re-elected 1980, serving with Republican governor; won